INTERSECTING MODERNITIES

LATIN AMERICAN ART *from* THE BRILLEMBOURG CAPRILES COLLECTION

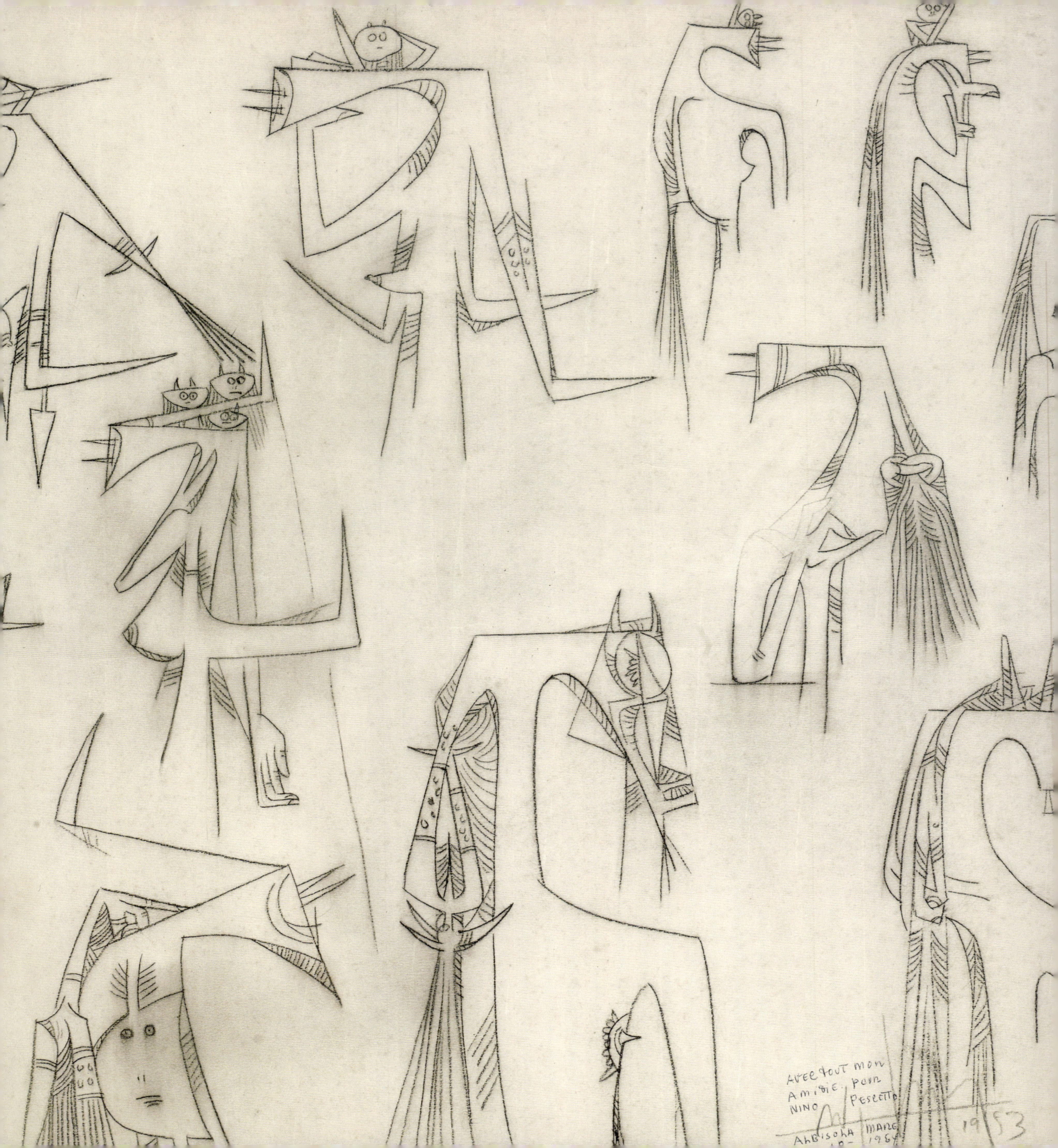
Avec tout mon
Amitié pour
NINO Pesetto
Albisola Marg
1964
1953

INTERSECTING MODERNITIES

LATIN AMERICAN ART *from* THE BRILLEMBOURG CAPRILES COLLECTION

EDITED BY
Mari Carmen Ramírez

WITH CONTRIBUTIONS BY Cecilia Fajardo-Hill, María C. Gaztambide, Marcela Guerrero, Abigail McEwen, Rachel Mohl, James Oles, Mari Carmen Ramírez, AND Michael Wellen

THE MUSEUM OF FINE ARTS, HOUSTON
THE INTERNATIONAL CENTER FOR THE ARTS OF THE AMERICAS
DISTRIBUTED BY YALE UNIVERSITY PRESS
NEW HAVEN AND LONDON

This book was published to accompany the exhibition of the same title that was presented at the Museum of Fine Arts, Houston, from June 23 to September 2, 2013.

THE EXHIBITION WAS ORGANIZED BY THE MUSEUM OF FINE ARTS, HOUSTON.

Generous funding was provided by:
LUTHER KING CAPITAL MANAGEMENT
LESLIE AND BRAD BUCHER

PRODUCED BY the Publications Department of the Museum of Fine Arts, Houston
ICAA PUBLICATIONS AND TRANSLATIONS EDITOR: Héctor Olea
SENIOR EDITOR: Melina Kervandjian
EDITOR: Michelle Dugan
TRANSLATIONS (from Spanish to English): Tony Beckwith
TRANSCRIPTIONS (in Spanish): Estella van Zoest
INDEX: Kay Banning
COVER AND BOOK DESIGN: Henk van Assen, HvADesign, New York, with Loide Marwanga and Sarah Eidelson.
TYPESET IN: DTL Documenta and Thesis Sans
PRINTED BY Everbest Printing, Nansha, China

Distributed by Yale University Press
New Haven and London
www.yalebooks.com/art

LIBRARY OF CONGRESS CATALOGING-IN-PUBLICATION DATA

Intersecting modernities : Latin American art from the Brillembourg Capriles collection/edited by Mari Carmen Ramírez; contributions by Cecilia Fajardo-Hill, María C. Gaztambide, Marcela Guerrero, Abigail McEwen, Rachel Mohl, James Oles, Mari Carmen Ramírez, and Michael Wellen.
pages cm
Includes bibliographical references and index.
Summary: "Tanya Capriles de Brillembourg has assembled a superb private collection of Latin American modern masterworks by towering figures such as Wifredo Lam, Matta, and Joaquín Torres-García. The collector has a particular point of view that public collections rarely attain"—Provided by publisher.

ISBN 978-0-300-19645-0 (hardcover)

1. Art, Latin American—20th century—Exhibitions. 2. Art, Latin American—20th century—Exhibitions. 3. Brillembourg, Tanya C.—Art collections—Exhibitions. 4. Art—Private collections—United States—Exhibitions. I. Ramírez, Mari Carmen, 1955– editor of compilation. II. Museum of Fine Arts, Houston.

N6502.5.I59 2013
709.8'0747641411—DC23 2013005167

COVER, FRONT
Diego Rivera
Naturaleza muerta con limones
[Still Life with Lemons] (detail), 1916
(see p. 45)

COVER, BACK
Wifredo Lam
Femme violette [Woman in Violet]
(detail), 1938 (see p. 105)

FRONTISPIECE
Wifredo Lam
Femmes-Cheval [Horse-Headed Women]
(detail), 1953 (see p. 125)

PAGE 8
Armando Reverón
Figura bajo un uvero [Figure under a Sea-Grape Tree] (detail), 1920
(see p. 61)

PAGE 14
Antonio Seguí
Una ciudad, una historia, un tormento
[A City, A History, A Torment] (detail), 1990
(see p. 184)

FOUNDERS OF THE LATIN AMERICAN ART COLLECTION AND THE INTERNATIONAL CENTER FOR THE ARTS OF THE AMERICAS AT THE MUSEUM OF FINE ARTS, HOUSTON | *p. 6*

ACKNOWLEDGMENTS | *p. 7*

FOREWORD
Gary Tinterow | *p. 9*

COLLECTOR'S STATEMENT
Tanya Capriles de Brillembourg | *p. 11*

A PHILANTHROPIC PATH OF HER OWN: A CONVERSATION WITH TANYA CAPRILES DE BRILLEMBOURG
Mari Carmen Ramírez | *p. 15*

THE FUNDAMENTAL FORCES OF LIGHT AND SPACE IN **EMILIO PETTORUTI**'s EARLY WORKS • Rachel Mohl | *p. 38*

DIEGO RIVERA: PARIS TO NEW YORK TO TEHUANTEPEC • James Oles | *p. 44*

DAVID ALFARO SIQUEIROS: MIDCENTURY CHALLENGES • James Oles | *p. 56*

BEYOND BOREDOM: **ARMANDO REVERÓN**'s PORTRAITS OF WOMEN • Michael Wellen | *p. 60*

MOVING *TO* AND *FROM* ABSTRACTION: **JOAQUÍN TORRES-GARCIA**'s UNCODIFIED ECLECTICISM • Mari Carmen Ramírez | *p. 70*

FRANCISCO MATTO's MAGICAL MODERNISM • Rachel Mohl | *p. 84*

THE IMAGE IS NOT A THING: FORM AND DYNAMIC PERCEPTION IN **MATTA** • María C. Gaztambide | *p. 88*

WIFREDO LAM CIRCA 1942: METAMORPHOSIS AND THE FEMALE FORM • Michael Wellen | *p. 104*

THE ELUSIVE MYSTICISM OF **RENÉ PORTOCARRERO** • María C. Gaztambide | *p. 130*

RUFINO TAMAYO: ESCAPE AND ECSTASY • James Oles | *p. 136*

THE PAINTER AS CRAFTSMAN: **ARMANDO MORALES**'s INNOVATION THROUGH TRADITION • Rachel Mohl | *p. 148*

FRANCISCO TOLEDO: FEAR AT THE CIRCUS • James Oles | *p. 162*

THE SKINNY ON **FERNANDO BOTERO** • Marcela Guerrero | *p. 166*

ANTONIO SEGUÍ: THE CHORUS OF *ACTIVE* FOOTSTEPS • Marcela Guerrero | *p. 182*

THE DIALECTIC OF **JACOBO BORGES**: RECONCILING AESTHETICS AND POLITICS IN THE EARLY 1970s • María C. Gaztambide | *p. 192*

LOLÓ SOLDEVILLA, CUBAN *CONCRETA* • Abigail McEwen | *p. 198*

CUBA'S MADISTA: **SANDÚ DARIÉ** IN THE 1950s • Abigail McEwen | *p. 214*

CARLOS ROJAS's SUBJECTIVE LANDSCAPES • Rachel Mohl | *p. 220*

ELIAS CRESPIN: THE INTERPLAY BETWEEN THE MATERIAL AND THE IMMATERIAL • Cecilia Fajardo-Hill | *p. 230*

Checklist of the Exhibition | *p. 238*
Biographies of the Artists | *p. 248*
Contributors | *p. 253*
Index | *p. 254*
Copyright and Photographic Credits | *p. 256*

FOUNDERS *of* THE LATIN AMERICAN ART COLLECTION *and* THE INTERNATIONAL CENTER FOR THE ARTS OF THE AMERICAS *at* THE MUSEUM OF FINE ARTS, HOUSTON

PLATINUM FOUNDERS

AT&T Inc.
Cruz-Diez Foundation, Houston
The Bruce T. Halle Family Foundation
Caroline Wiess Law Foundation
The Wortham Foundation, Inc./Mr. and Mrs. R. W. Wortham III

GOLD FOUNDERS

Leslie and Brad Bucher
Fundación Gego
Petrobras America, Inc.

SILVER FOUNDERS

Dr. Luis and Cecilia Campos
The J. Paul Getty Trust

BRONZE FOUNDERS

Sofia Adrogué and Sten L. Gustafson
Bernard Chappard
Mary and Roy Cullen
Fulbright & Jaworski LLP
Linnet F. Deily
Ada Atuña de Matto
Cecilia de Torres
The Ford Foundation
Alfred C. Glassell, III
Eduardo Carlos Grüneisen and
Maria Eugenia Salimei de Grüneisen
Marion and Jorge Helft
Celina Hellmund
Olive McCollum Jenney
Linda and George Kelly
The Henry Luce Foundation
The Latin Maecenas
Mr. and Mrs. William V. Morgan
Frank Ribelin
Miguel Angel Ríos
The Rockefeller Foundation
Emilio Sanchez Foundation
César Segnini
Andy Warhol Foundation

SUSTAINING FOUNDERS

Anonymous
Mr. and Mrs. Louis K. Adler
Mary and Bernardino Arocha
Antonio Asis
Dr. and Mrs. Donald E. Baxter
Mr. and Mrs. Benbow Bullock
Ms. Patricia Phelps de Cisneros
Fundacíon Pan Klub - Xul Solar, Ciudad Buenos Aires
The Favrot Fund
Samuel F. Gorman
Ms. Karol Kreymer and Dr. Robert Card
Mrs. Karen Benbow McRae
Anne and Jack Moriniere
Ms. Rebecca Leach
Mr. and Mrs. Meredith J. Long
Mr. and Mrs. Ernesto Poma
Kristi and John Schiller
Sotheby's
Judy and Charles Tate
Juan Carlos Uriarte
Carolina and Sergio Weitzman

FOUNDERS

Patricia and José Luis Barragán
Suzette and Darrell Betts
Mr. Luis Benshimol
Ms. Tanya Brillembourg
Deutsche Bank
Jean-Marie and Araceli Diederichs
Susan and Mac Dunwoody
Claudia Alemán Gallegos
Mr. Glen Gonzales
Maria and Pablo Henning
Ms. Cecily E. Horton
Lee and Joe Jamail
Adolpho Leirner
Stephanie and Paul Madan
Daniel Joseph Martinez
Oscar Muñoz
Dr. Michele Sartori
Maria Inés Sicardi, Allison and David Ayers and Carlos Bacino
Gabriel Werthein

ACKNOWLEDGMENTS

THE MUSEUM OF FINE ARTS, HOUSTON, WISHES TO THANK THE FOLLOWING INDIVIDUALS FOR THEIR EXPERT ASSISTANCE IN THE REALIZATION OF THIS PROJECT.

Nicolás Acquavella • GALERIA ACQUAVELLA, CARACAS
Francisco Arévalo • ARÉVALO GALLERY, MIAMI
Andrea di Bagno • HOUSTON
Mariana Benítez-Morales • MIAMI
Inés and José Antonio Berni • MADRID
Jacobo Borges and Diana Carvallo • CARACAS
Fernando Botero • PARIS, MONTE CARLO, PIETRASANTA, AND NEW YORK
Todd Brandow • ESTATE OF MATTA
Virginie Canal • ARCHIVES ANTONIO SEGUÍ, PARIS
Ramón Cernuda • CERNUDA ARTE, MIAMI
Roberto Cobas Amate • MUSEO NACIONAL DE BELLAS ARTES, HAVANA
Emily Codik • CERNUDA ARTE, MIAMI
Maxine Cohen • SAN ANTONIO
Elias Crespin • PARIS
Arden Decker • NEW YORK
Dorota Dolega • SDO WIFREDO LAM, PARIS
Maitena de Elguezabel • PROYECTO ARMANDO REVERÓN, CARACAS
Fundación Alberto Vollmer • CARACAS
Alexandra Gauthier • IDEOBOX ARTSPACE, MIAMI
Laura Jiménez Galvis • BOGOTÁ
Marianna Gelussi • ATELIER ELIAS CRESPIN, PARIS
Amy Giarmo • HIRSHHORN MUSEUM AND SCULPTURE GARDEN, WASHINGTON, DC
Beatriz González • BOGOTÁ
Antonio de la Guardia • TRESART GALLERY, MIAMI
Geaninne Guimaraes • MUSEUM OF MODERN ART, NEW YORK
Nohra Haime • NOHRA HAIME GALLERY, NEW YORK
Carmen María Jaramillo • UNIVERSIDAD DE BOGOTÁ JORGE TADEO LOZANO
Eskil Lam • SDO WIFREDO LAM, PARIS
Pablo Lazo • CERNUDA ARTE, MIAMI
Herman Leyba • IDEOBOX ARTSPACE, MIAMI
Luisa Lignarolo • CERNUDA ARTE, MIAMI
Victor Losito • ARTENS, INC., MIAMI
Mary-Anne Martin • MARY-ANNE MARTIN FINE ART, NEW YORK
France Mazin Fernández • PARIS
Marta Minujín • BUENOS AIRES
Molly Moog • ST. LOUIS
Alejandra Morales • LONDON
Gary Nader • GARY NADER FINE ART, MIAMI
Patricia Newcomer • ATELIER ANTONIO SEGUÍ, PARIS
Guadalupe Ramírez Oliberos • MUSEO DE ARTE MODERNO DE BUENOS AIRES
Juan Ignacio Parra • PROYECTO ARMANDO REVERÓN, CARACAS
Juan Carlos Pereda • MUSEO TAMAYO ARTE CONTEMPORÁNEO, MEXICO CITY
Mariana Pérez Amor • GALERÍA DE ARTE MEXICANO, MEXICO CITY
Luis Pérez-Oramas • THE MUSEUM OF MODERN ART, NEW YORK
Sagrario Pérez Soto • NEW YORK
Wynne Phelan • HOUSTON
Dan Pollock • CECILIA DE TORRES, LTD, NEW YORK
Gabriela Rangel • THE AMERICAS SOCIETY, NEW YORK
Ana María Reyes • HIGHLAND PARK, ILLINOIS
Heriberto Rodríguez • MUSEO NACIONAL DE BELLAS ARTES, HAVANA
Lynn Rogerson • ART SERVICES INTERNATIONAL
Rosse Mary Rojas González • BOGOTÁ
Rafael Romero • PROYECTO ARMANDO REVERÓN, CARACAS
Ada Romero C. • FUNDACIÓN ALBERTO VOLLMER, CARACAS
Antonio Seguí • PARIS
Lowery Stokes Sims • MUSEUM OF ARTS AND DESIGN, NEW YORK
Siulnas (Oscar Vázquez Lucio) • BUENOS AIRES
Edward Sullivan • NEW YORK UNIVERSITY
Clelia Taricco • PARIS
Laureana Toledo • MEXICO CITY
Cecilia de Torres • CECILIA DE TORRES, LTD, NEW YORK
Sofía Vollmer de Madero • FUNDACIÓN ALBERTO VOLLMER, CARACAS
Alejandra Yturbe • GALERÍA DE ARTE MEXICANO, MEXICO CITY
Eric M. Wolf • THE MENIL COLLECTION, HOUSTON

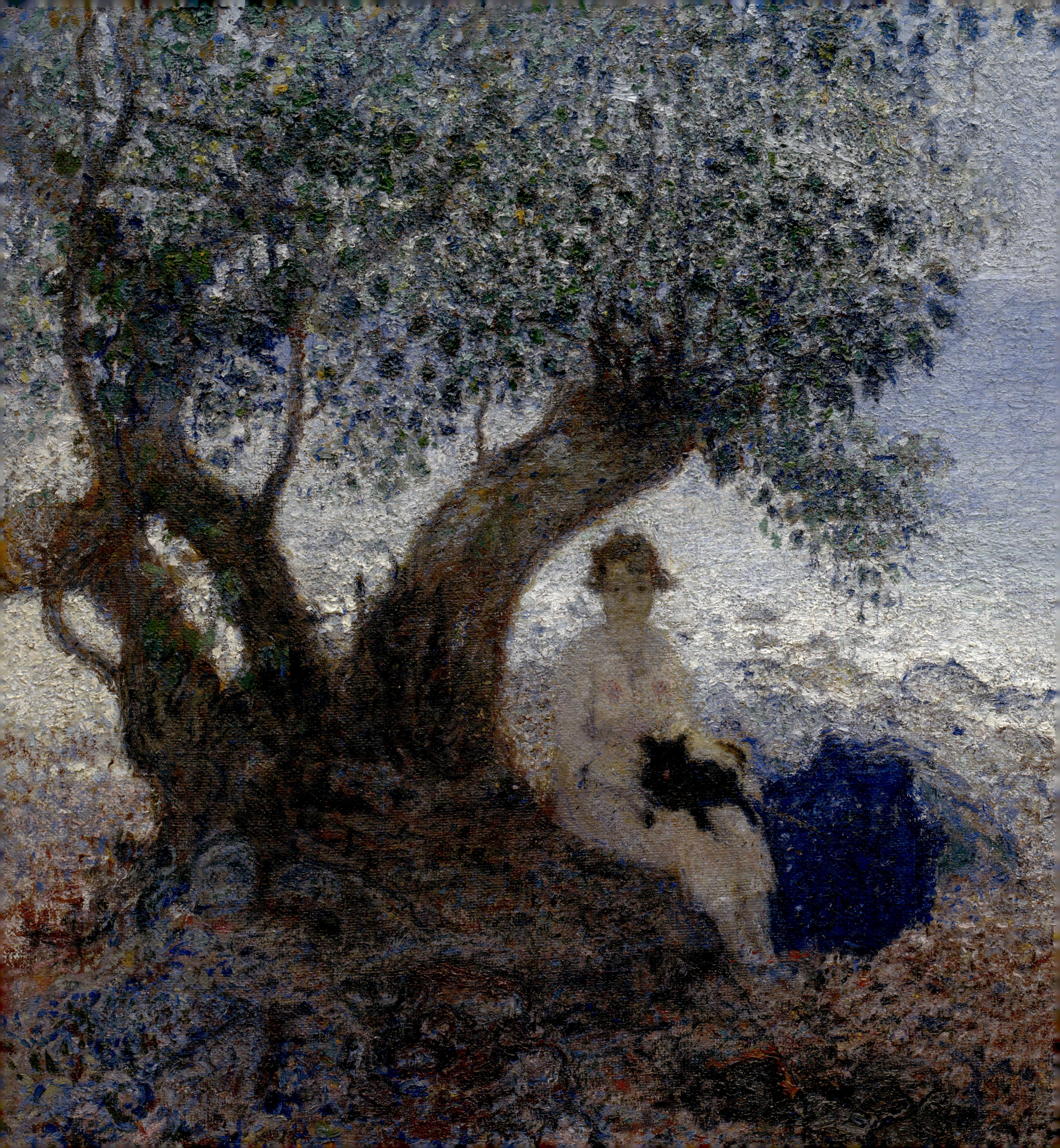

FOREWORD

Gary Tinterow

DIRECTOR, THE MUSEUM OF FINE ARTS, HOUSTON

THIS EXHIBITION IS THE FIRST TO BE ORGANIZED of the extraordinary collection assembled over the last thirty years by philanthropist Tanya Capriles de Brillembourg. Ms. Capriles de Brillembourg is an honorary trustee of the Museum who has placed her collection here on long-term loan. Both the exhibition and its accompanying catalogue are the result of an ongoing partnership between this distinguished collector and the Museum. The goals of this extremely productive association are to promote Latin American art in Houston and beyond as well as to support new research in this rapidly emerging field of study and collecting. This innovative partnership has provided the Museum with access to over one hundred works by Latin American masters of the first half of the twentieth century. These works serve to both enhance and complement the Museum's holdings of post-1945 Latin American art, thereby allowing us to tell the story of Modernism and Post-Modernism in Latin America with greater depth and variety.

Born in Venezuela to a prominent family associated with the country's leading media corporation, Ms. Capriles de Brillembourg developed a strong interest in journalism and social work. Since the 1980s, she has been a pioneer in developing programs for children suffering from cancer as well as physical and mental disabilities. First through Fundación Amigos del Niño con Cáncer [Friends of the Child with Cancer Foundation] (Caracas, 1984) and, more recently, as founder and president of SaludArte (2003)—a nonprofit foundation based in Madrid and Miami—she has sought to bridge the gap between art, music, and these special constituencies. In the 1970s, she began collecting modern Venezuelan art; however, by the 1980s her interests had expanded to collecting modern art from Latin America and Europe. Eventually she was joined in this endeavor by her husband, the real-estate developer and politician David Brillembourg. Working closely with the art historian and dealer Clara Diament Sujo, the Brillembourgs developed a collection that corresponded with their broad tastes and one that shows the diversity of twentieth-century Latin American art. David lost his battle with cancer in 1993, when he was only 56. Tanya has continued to build the collection over the last decade by acquiring outstanding examples of Latin American Constructivism as well as contemporary art.

Intersecting Modernities provides our audiences with an introduction to many of the most influential artists of the Latin American avant-garde through a display of beautiful and daring works produced by these creators at the heights of their respective careers. These include Diego Rivera, David Alfaro Siqueiros,

Joaquín Torres-García, Armando Reverón, Wifredo Lam, Matta, Fernando Botero, Antonio Seguí, Jacobo Borges, Armando Morales, René Portocarrero, and Francisco Toledo. The exhibition also includes a cluster of Cuban Constructive works as well as the more contemporary production of Paris-based Venezuelan artist Elias Crespin. These works, which the public has rarely seen before, offer insights into each artist's formal skill and conceptual innovation. Arranged in loose clusters, *Intersecting Modernities* showcases the divergent paths taken by the modern artists of Latin America, as well as shared affinities and silent resonances across their artistic production.

I encountered Ms. Capriles de Brillembourg soon after my arrival at the Museum a year and a half ago, and I was immediately impressed by her passion, determination, and boundless generosity in both the fields of philanthropy and art. The Museum of Fine Arts, Houston, is privileged to have her as a friend and patron, and we are delighted to share her collection with audiences in Houston and elsewhere. My profound appreciation goes to Tanya, her family, and her devoted staff for allowing the Museum to study this collection and to share with the world the fascinating insights and discoveries of our curatorial team, led by Mari Carmen Ramírez.

COLLECTOR'S STATEMENT

Tanya Capriles de Brillembourg

IS COLLECTING AN ART OR IS IT THE ART ITSELF THAT MAKES ONE COLLECT? Collecting is the result of a vocation, an inner calling, an irrepressible impulse that can only be compared to a passion. But an art collection is also the result of a series of choices; choices that arise from decisions made when confronted with discoveries, with fortunate encounters with each of the pieces in the collection.

I have been able to see, in the works of Latin American art that I have assembled during the past thirty years, a reflection of our roots, our reality, our conflicts, and our own unique sensitivity. Collecting is the result of a creative act that involves a particular vision of the world, a personal attitude about art, thought, and culture.

When I first started collecting, three people stood by me and played decisive roles in this fascinating adventure: my husband David Brillembourg, who unhesitatingly supported my venture; my sister Mayra Capriles, whose shrewd instinct and vision helped me to find many of the works of art that are now in the collection; and my very dear friend Clara Diament Sujo, who not only advised me on the acquisition of many of the works, but who also introduced me to Mari Carmen Ramírez and Peter C. Marzio at the Museum of Fine Arts, Houston.

More than five years ago, when Clara Sujo mentioned the idea of loaning my collection to the Museum of Fine Arts, Houston, I met with Mari Carmen and immediately understood the ambitious scope of her vision, the transcendent motivation for her project: to promote an international reevaluation of Latin American art by systematically exhibiting it, researching it, studying it, and disseminating it, by giving it pride of place on a level with European and North American art beyond the confines of our regional borders. Later, when I met Peter Marzio and sensed his enthusiasm, I felt committed and obligated to contribute to the consolidation of the dream proposed by these two dedicated professionals—and this exhibition is the result.

My involvement in the preparation of this exhibition has allowed me to rediscover my own collection. These works have been studied, researched, documented, restored, refurbished, and reframed by the extraordinary team of experts at the Museum of Fine Arts, Houston, with all the love, mystique, and professional skill at their disposal. In the process, many old, unknown, revealing stories about the origins of these works and their meaning have resurfaced. Through this exhibition, it is my great pleasure to share these stories with audiences in Houston and elsewhere.

I hereby extend my personal thanks to Gary Tinterow, director of the Museum of Fine Arts, Houston; to Richard W. Wortham III and the Latin American Art Subcommittee at the Museum; and to Mari Carmen Ramírez, Wortham Curator of Latin American Art and director of the International Center for the Arts of the Americas, and the entire team that has been with us on this long journey.

I dedicate this exhibition to my grandchildren and great-grandchildren.

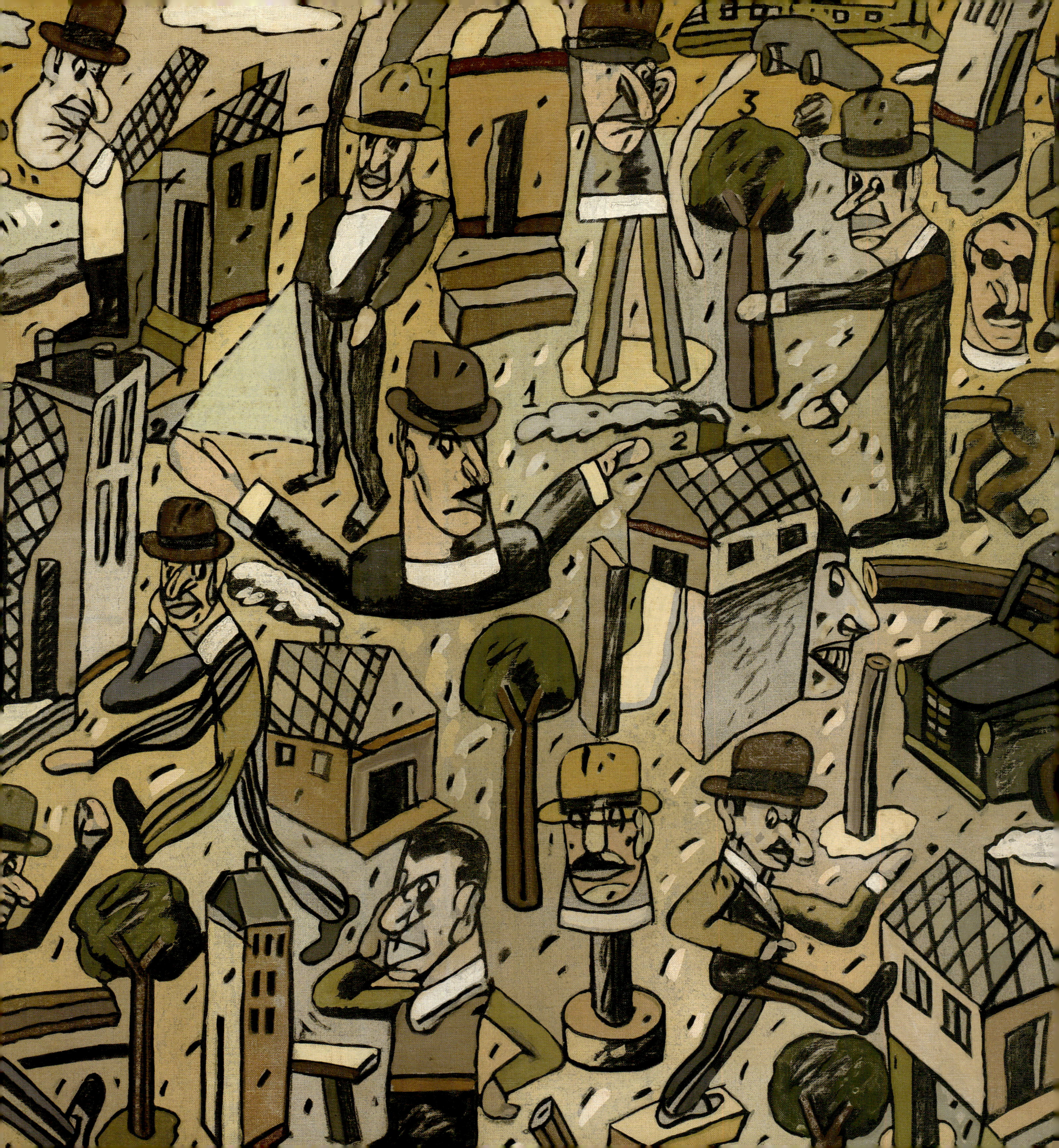
3
1
2
2

A PHILANTHROPIC PATH OF HER OWN

A CONVERSATION WITH TANYA CAPRILES DE BRILLEMBOURG

Mari Carmen Ramírez

PART ONE

THE BRILLEMBOURG CAPRILES COLLECTION: IN THE BEGINNING

MARI CARMEN RAMÍREZ Let us begin, as does everything, at the beginning. What experiences stimulated your passion for art? Did your parents collect art? Did they take you to art exhibitions? When you were a little girl, did you take any drawing or painting classes? How, and at what age, did you start to take an interest in art?

TANYA CAPRILES DE BRILLEMBOURG I always say that there was nothing particularly glamorous about my development as a collector, and I often wonder if collecting is an art or if it is the art itself that inspires one to collect. I started buying art by chance in Venezuela in the 1960s. I had a large house in Caracas that I wanted to fill with art objects, to make it cozier and to enhance the spiritual experience of our daily life. My husband, David, and I later built a very large house in Miami, and I felt the same need, but by then I was more knowledgeable about buying works of art. When I began, of course, I bought works by Venezuelan artists but later, in the 1980s, I broadened my scope and started looking at art from other Latin American countries as well. Why does this kind of art interest me? I have always been attracted to the color and to the passion that resonates in this art, and I have sympathized with its implicit criticism of social injustice in our countries.

MCR But what was it that attracted you specifically to art? You could have bought furniture, or silver, or porcelain, or any expression of the "decorative arts." So, what was there in your education, in your family—even among your circle of friends—that prompted that interest?

TCB Neither my father, Don Miguel Ángel Capriles, nor my mother, Perla, influenced my feelings for art. My father began to collect art late in his life, in the 1980s, also by chance. He had suffered a heart attack and his doctor advised him to find a hobby, an activity that would give him something to do, since all he had ever done was to work full time. That was how he started his art collection; not as a result of a lifelong passion but as a form of therapy. After that, we occasionally ran into each other at auction at Sotheby's or Christie's. Sometimes we even fought over a piece of art. I would never bid at auction because I have never liked drawing attention to myself. It is just not in my nature to do so. If I saw that he was interested in a work that I also liked, I would yield to him.

With that said, my older sister, Mayra, did influence me to collect in the visual arts. During the late 1970s, she became interested in Joan Miró, Jean Dubuffet, and Pablo Picasso, to name just a few of the more important artists she liked. She took me to see their work in Geneva, Paris, and New York. Mayra introduced me to Latin American maestros such as Joaquín Torres-García, some of whose works had recently been lost in a fire at the Museu de Arte Moderna in Rio de Janeiro, Brazil (1978). If she only could have found the discipline to be a collector, I doubt there would be a more important collection in the world than Mayra's.

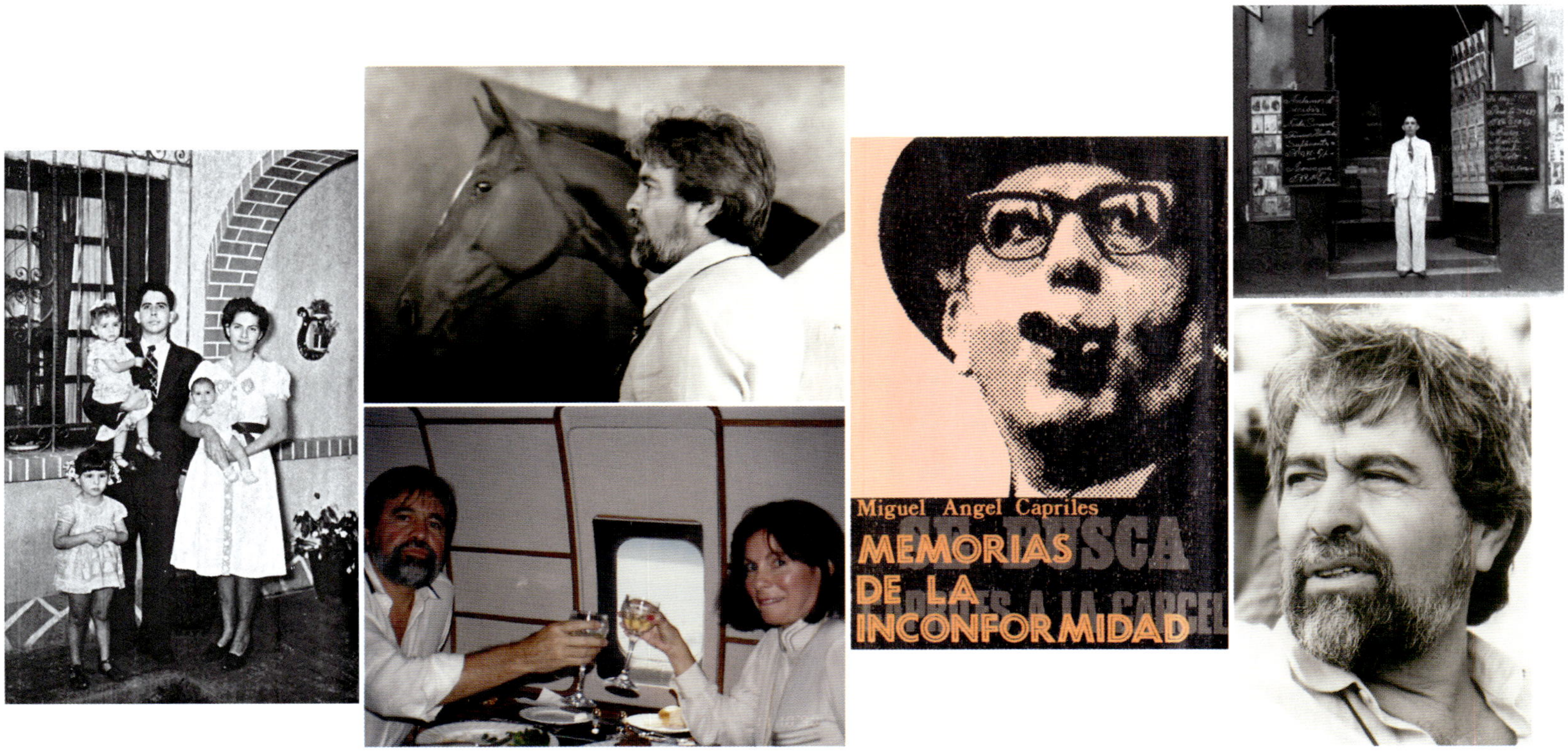

CLOCKWISE FROM LEFT

Tanya Capriles, held by her father Miguel Ángel Capriles, and surrounded by her mother and two sisters, Caracas, Venezuela, 1944; David Brillembourg with one of his thoroughbred horses, Alydavid, at his ranch "David's Farm," Georgetown, Kentucky, 1989; Cover of *Memorias de la inconformidad*, written in 1973 by Tanya Capriles de Brillembourg's father while he was exiled in Puerto Rico; From *Memorias de la inconformidad*: Miguel Angel Capriles wrote, "On the doorsteps of my little bookstore in Valencia in 1935. In December, I would announce to the people of Valencia—on the same blackboards where I would typically write the titles of the magazines received—the death of General (Juan Vicente) Gómez; David Brillembourg at "David's Farm," Georgetown, Kentucky, c. 1990; David and Tanya Brillembourg on their private plane, a Challenger, c. 1989.

MCR What was your sister's original field of interest?

TCB Mayra studied law, but she always loved art and she passed that love on to me. More than anyone else, I owe my involvement with the art world to her.

MCR Let's return to discussing your father, whom I have heard you talk about on a number of occasions. I have always had the impression that he was a key figure in your life.

TCB He was unquestionably a key figure for me and my six siblings. My father was a very strong man, a powerful man, a self-made man. But, on a personal level, he never had much time for his children because his passion was working, working, working, working....

MCR What did he do for a living?

TCB He was one of the major newspaper publishers in Venezuela, a wealthy man with a great deal of political influence. His publishing group is the Cadena Capriles, which distributes many publications, including a mainstream newspaper, *Últimas Noticias*, which has the largest circulation in Venezuela and is the third largest in Latin America. My father launched the evening newspaper *El Mundo* on the day that the Pérez Jiménez dictatorship was overthrown in 1958; it is now a financial newspaper, more in tune with our current times. The group also publishes sports and show-business newspapers and has modernized its content-delivery systems, adapting to the demands of readers who rely on their digital devices.

My brother, Miguel Ángel Capriles López, now runs the media conglomerate and has invested in new printing presses and the most modern facilities in Latin America, an extraordinary step considering Venezuela's current political and economic instability. In this respect he is very much like my father, who believed in Venezuela and made his fortune there; my brother is following in his footsteps.

I must admit that my father was a powerful influence on me and my siblings. He was a great intellectual and a very good writer; whenever I picture him, he is reading in his library at home. He wrote his memoirs while living in Puerto Rico for a few years, exiled by one of the many governments he opposed. *Memorias de la Inconformidad* [Memoirs of a Nonconformist] tells the story of his early life, before the fall of the Venezuelan dictatorship. It describes in vivid detail how he was orphaned at age 21 and had to take care of his fourteen younger siblings. His book also describes the poverty in the country before the oil boom. My mother, on the other hand, was a simple, rather submissive woman, who was always involved in our lives without ever taking a dominant role. She was always just there, quietly, never judging us or criticizing what we did. They were two very different people.

MCR How did you get along with your sisters and brother?

TCB There were seven of us: six girls and a boy, who was the youngest. There was a gap in ages between the three oldest and the others. As the second oldest, I am what some call a "sandwich child." The first- and third-born were very strong women. Unlike them, I was always more of an introvert and kept very much to myself. I like silence and introspection, and would find places to hide where I could write, which is what led me to study journalism when I was a 30-year-old mother with four children.

My father instilled in us a passion for social work. He had an amusing way of explaining it: We—whom he called the Princesses of the Printed Paper—should earn what we had and who we were. In his view, having it all (money, family, beauty) was unhealthy. Therefore, as his daughters, we had to earn people's respect on our own merits. In the mid-1950s, when I was about 12 years old, my father made us wait tables in the newsboys' dining room at the corporate offices, serving the kids who sold newspapers on the streets of Caracas.

MCR So, you absorbed a work ethic and learned about social responsibility in your childhood. But, where did that sense of humility come from?

TCB Although my father was a very wealthy man, he was also extremely frugal.

MCR Was he a self-made man?

TCB As I said earlier, he was orphaned and, as the oldest child, had to take care of his siblings, the youngest of whom was only a year old. Interestingly, my husband was the total opposite. They were, however, similar in that they were both self-made men, and David, as the third son, also took charge of his family. In his case, though, he went to school in Canada, Venezuela, and the United States, and he experienced a very different Venezuela from the one my father knew. David worked with him for many years and helped him to make a fortune outside the media. My father had never borrowed money to start any of his businesses, and David taught him how to do it. He started the real-estate business and got into politics, creating the first parliamentary group outside a political party, with twelve delegates and one senator, my father. He established a mortgage bank that was later expropriated by the same government he had helped get elected in 1968, which then exiled him to Puerto Rico.

IDEAS AND IDEALS: ESTATE, COUNTRY, AND FATHER

TCB My father got into all kinds of trouble because he always stood up for his ideas and his ideals; as a result, he was imprisoned hundreds of times by the government. He argued with the people then in power and challenged them when they didn't make sense. His newspapers were always open to any political group seeking to express its ideas. That was frowned on by our governments, which, though called "democratic," always tend to be authoritarian and *caudillista* [rallied around one strong leader]. He was inclined to protect the weaker ones or those he considered most disadvantaged. His newspaper editorials expressed his concept of justice and cost him his freedom.

My father's ideals also cost him a lot of money. Rather than take advantage of the various governments, we had to make a profit, as most of the Latin American aristocracy does. He remained true to his ideals, constantly risking the fortune he had worked so hard to build. I certainly inherited that trait from him, and am proud of having done the same with my family inheritance. My mother did so too, when she left the peace and financial stability provided by her family and went to Spain forty-six years ago.

MCR Your father was an honorable man. And *patrimonio*—the Spanish word for "estate," in this context—derives from both *patria* [country] and *padre* [father]. Evidently, your vocation as a journalist was influenced by a family environment of ideas and ideals, and was driven by strong filial love.

TCB I do not deny it. It is entirely possible. In those days, however, my father was roundly hated by the media schools because—according to them—he was a "right- wing" publisher, although in fact he was anything but that. When I enrolled at the Escuela de Comunicación Social [Media School] at the Universidad Central de Venezuela in 1972, it was a hotbed of leftist politics, and people didn't appreciate having a publisher's daughter on campus. They said terrible things about my father, and I just had to put up with it if I wanted to stay there.

My father was always in danger. I learned so much from this extraordinary man, who also shone brightly as a great conversationalist. Our after-dinner family conversations were an ongoing education in politics and philosophy.

POWERFUL ROLE MODELS

MCR Your father was obviously a role model. But he was not the only powerful influence in your life.

TCB David was pivotal because, among other things, he let me do whatever I wanted to do, including buy as much art I wanted. I was 19 when I married, which means that I spent my entire adult life with him.

MCR What did your husband do for a living?

TCB David was an economist, a banker, a developer, and a politician. He was, among other things, one of the youngest representatives to be elected to the Venezuelan Congress in 1968. He was also the first to sell a 40-story building in Venezuela, the "Torre de David" [Tower of David]. There had never been a transaction of this magnitude in Venezuela. David was an extraordinarily gifted businessman; he was called "King Midas" because everything he touched turned to gold. He was an extremely positive, generous man. Today, twenty years later, he is remembered for doing business in such a way that the other party was never on the losing end of the deal.

MCR Was David interested in art? Was he knowledgeable about art history?

TCB His passion was thoroughbred race horses, never art. We were fortunate to have had a horse in the Kentucky Derby in 1991. We came in eighth but, you know, some people spend their whole lives in this business and never get to race. Our farm there, "David's Farm," won the University of Kentucky's architecture prize. David didn't get involved with art until the end of his life, which was relatively short, only 56 years. Partly as a result of watching me assemble my collection, he became interested in art about four or five years before he died from cancer. We had just bought an apartment in Paris at the time, and we also had one in New York, in spite of the fact that I had been very busy buying works of art.

There is an amusing story about a conversation between my father and David. When David became sick, in 1992, my father visited him at our house in Boca Raton [Florida], where I had hung many of the works in my substantial collection of Latin American art. My father walked around looking at the art, and he stopped to admire *Tótem* [Totem] by Wifredo Lam. He asked David where he had bought it and what had impressed him about the work. My husband said, "Oh, I didn't buy that one. Your daughter bought it." To which my father replied, "What? Tanya? But, Tanya is never anywhere to be seen; she is always hiding somewhere, always writing. I can't believe it!" That was when my father finally saw that I was just as strong as my older sisters. He was just a little late in his realization, don't you think?

MCR Tell me about your education. What did you study in college?

TCB I trained in the humanities. I studied journalism and social work. Ever since I was a child I've been interested in journalism, perhaps because—as some say—it is in my blood. I have also always loved writing and have written since I was very young. It wasn't until I had my first child, at age 20, that I started studying for my degree. Later, after my fourth child, I began my career in journalism.

THE DOUBLE-EDGED SWORD OF JOURNALISM

MCR I would like to talk now about your professional career.

TCB My two older sisters and I were groomed to be married. We were, therefore, seriously restricted, but we all had enquiring minds and went to school when we were "old ladies"—each of us more than 30 years old. I never was formally employed, but when my husband was in politics, he bought a 50 percent share in the newspaper *Diario de Caracas*, where I worked for a while. We later bought stock in *Televén*, a Venezuelan TV company, where I was more of a director than a journalist.

MCR Journalism is a double-edged sword, standing between vested interests and the unvarnished truth.

TCB Yes, even though there is no longer any "cold, hard" truth in journalism, what with vested interests and everyone seeing "their truth" in very subjective ways. Sometimes the publisher's views prevail, and, of course, journalism is also subject to deeply ingrained human traits. Although I worked as a journalist, I was not hired in a professional capacity. I wish I had because I know I could have "changed the world" as I tried to do through the Friends of Children with Cancer Foundation that I started in 1984 with a group of doctors and parents of children with cancer, and as I am still trying to do with the SaludArte Foundation.

WHY LATIN AMERICAN ART?

MCR Your collection is well endowed with Latin American maestros and contemporary regional artists. Why Latin American art? Other than being born in Venezuela, what stimulated your interest in the art produced in this region? What sort of connections did you have with Latin America at that time, and how much had you traveled in the different countries?

TCB I became interested in Latin America when I was very young. My father traveled a great deal in Latin America; he had many connections with media groups and magazine distributors there. He took us with him on several occasions, which is odd when you think that he practically never took us to Europe. But, when we were kids, he took us to Mexico, Chile, Uruguay, Argentina, Brazil, and so on. Since then I have been interested in anything to do with our continent, but especially Latin American politics, literature, and art. I discovered Latin American literature when I was studying journalism at college. I became even more interested some years later when I met the Cuban writer Alejo Carpentier; he came to Venezuela in 1973 and I had the great fortune to take literature classes from him in my own home.

MCR Do you have especially close ties to, or more personal relationships with, any Latin American countries?

TCB The closest relationship is with Mexico, where I went countless times with my father to visit his many colleagues and friends. I have always loved Mexico for its people, its culture, its towns, its food, and above all, its art. Mexico is an extremely surreal country. Many years later, when David died in 1993, I spent a wonderful year in Mexico. I took an introductory course in music while there, which eventually led to what I do with the SaludArte Foundation. Then, there are Brazil and Argentina.

MCR Did you live there, too? What do you like about Brazil?

TCB I have never lived in Brazil, but I love everything about the country. The music is wonderful and so are the people, and the food. I'm sure you agree that Brazilian art is amazing.

MCR Now, after all these years collecting Latin American art, do you think it is different from the art produced in the rest of the world? I mean, is there a particular quality that identifies something as "Latin American?"

TCB I do not think that art, by and large, is regional or national. Art is and will always be universal. From that perspective, globalization has always existed; it began with culture and art. For example, if Jackson Pollock had not been influenced by Diego Rivera or David Alfaro Siqueiros, he might never have evolved into the great experimental artist he actually became. Clara Diament Sujo and I talked about this a great deal. She sold me two Diego Rivera watercolors and two Pollock drawings that reveal that influence, and the influence of the famous New York Experimental Workshop (1936).

MCR For more than a century, art critics in Latin America have been bogged down by the notion of "identity." In the wake of the two volumes on the subject published by the International Center for the Arts of the Americas (ICAA) at the Museum of Fine Arts, Houston—one on "Latin-ness" and the other on "Nationalism" —I can say that the problem of identity both exists and does not exist, just like witches, which both exist and do not exist. Also, in any work with essentially artistic content, this problem is no longer an issue.

TCB That is why I do not like to tag art as something from one place: from Europe or North America or Latin America. Perhaps, for that reason, I believe that Latin American art is just as important as European art or North American art. I have great confidence in Latin American art, now more than ever. Whereas I used to buy works by European and North American artists, I am now far more invested in Latin American artists' production and contribution. On the other hand, I do not feel bound by geographic restrictions if I come across something that interests me.

MCR What makes you now appreciate Latin American art to this extent?

TCB What I'm saying is that Latin American art should be considered as an equal, as long as the artistic expression is of a certain quality. Latin American art has a more personal appeal for me, perhaps because I can see—can feel—such development everywhere and especially in art. We are constantly reinventing ourselves. In addition to its financial woes, Europe appears to be tired or exhausted, and this is reflected in its cultural and artistic production, which is predictable, with obvious exceptions.

MCR I totally agree.

TCB On the other hand, as the reflection of an emerging region, Latin American art projects a sense of strength, a magnetism that is very appealing. Artists are expressing their particular time—according to their political, social, or economic perspective—so Latin American art has much more to say. And, therefore, much more ground to gain, don't you think?

MCR Absolutely. These days, populations in European countries (especially Spain and Italy) are in a state of negative growth, and this is apparent in their cultural production, which has *aged* because there are fewer young people. In that sense, emerging regions like Latin America have so much more to contribute: a glimpse of the future, an innovative view of art. That may sound like a cliché, but it is nonetheless true today.

TCB Exactly. That is precisely what I love about contemporary Latin American art. The younger generation express themselves through art and music with far more passion than they do in Europe or the United States. In this case, passion means innovation, being unafraid to go beyond the accepted canon. We can't ignore the fact that, in the United States, children are being born to Latin American immigrants, who will one day be the largest minority, both in Europe and in North America.

LATIN AMERICAN ART IS UNDERVALUED

MCR Yet, it has not been possible to value Latin American art within those parameters.

TCB On the whole, I believe that Latin American art has been and continues to be undervalued.

MCR Yes, I agree.

TCB I am not an expert who can say that a type of art, say Latin American, should, in the future, be considered equally important to European art or on a par with North American art. Yet, I am constantly amazed to see that Latin American art is still dismissed by curators and art experts who specialize in modern art. I am outraged that it has not been taken as seriously as it deserves, or granted its fair due, no more, no less.

MCR That is precisely the goal we have always pursued at the Department of Latin American Art, which I direct at the Museum.

TCB You have waged an impressive campaign, and there are others who have also championed this cause. Mary-Anne Martin and Clara Diament Sujo [coming from a different, New York perspective] have fought hard to place Latin American art on the same level as European or North American art. It is nonetheless denied an equal value—and I'm talking about value based on numbers, not on quality.

MCR You are touching a nerve.

TCB When you think about it, [our artists face] far greater challenges than artists do in Europe or the United States. There is a huge difference in terms of political realities.

MCR And in terms of how they do things. This is what amazes European and North American scholars. An artist like Piet Mondrian, for example, took just one great step to evolve from representative art to absolute abstraction, and then he stopped. It was a consistent development: he went from one thing to another and did not backtrack. Torres-García, on the other hand, produced a still life, then a landscape or a mask, then a sculpture fashioned out of rough wood.

TCB Yes, he went back and forth.

MCR While he was producing Constructive art, he was also developing theories about primitive art. Critics interpreted that pursuit as a sign of inconsistency and labeled him an uneven artist; in a word, he was considered "eclectic." At a particular point in time that was deemed—and I believe is still deemed by the official, canonical history of Western art—to be something "negative," of lesser value.

TCB Yes, we must "re-value" him.

MCR But, for unknown reasons, he was tagged with a *negative label*. And, since cosmopolitan critics couldn't read what he was writing, they denied him his place in history. That attitude underscores the importance of the ICAA's project (the digital archive of primary-source material). The archive makes critical materials available to the public, from any computer anywhere in the world. People didn't understand Torres-García—his ideas or where he was really coming from or what he was proposing. This lack of understanding has prevented many artists like him from being fairly acknowledged for their considerable contributions. That is why we, in Houston, believe that all that information should be made available to the public, over and above what is provided in catalogues, books, symposia, and research into Latin American art and the region as a whole. After all, this is what will really put Latin American artists on a larger map. Under no circumstances should these matters be based solely on market values. There must be a far broader approach that includes research and serious communication via all platforms currently available.

TCB Do you think the ICAA will accomplish that "mission" and succeed in its ambitious goal of using your department's vast research to promote a broader awareness of Latin American art?

MCR I am convinced of it, as are the other members of the team. Especially since this is a very long-term project. The response so far shows that people (in Latin America and beyond) want this kind of unbiased information, undistorted by myth. Again, a "re-valuing" of what is already obvious.

Attitudes toward Latin American art have changed dramatically in the market and at the institutional level. These days, Latin American art is ascendant; many people want to buy it, exhibit it, and promote it. Things are very different now compared to what (curators like me) had to contend with when we "took off" thirty years ago. Things are changing, but only up to a point. When you look at popular magazines like *Art in America* or *Art Forum*, you can see that Latin American art gets very minimal coverage. Postmodernism generated a sort of triumphal euphoria, a rather simplistic, naive reaction that prompted the gullible to say, "We've arrived!" But that isn't entirely accurate. "Otherwise," as Roberto Schwarz put it, "we would be witnessing the 'Latin Americanization' of the First World." It will be a long time before that happens.

TCB Yes, you are right.

MCR There is still a great deal to do. But we (Héctor Olea, the series editor, and I) believe that the *ICAA Documents Project* will inspire some radical changes in the United States in the near future, especially when "Latino" minorities attain majority status over the course of the next four decades. Their electoral clout is already undeniable, and the deeper their understanding of Latin American artistic creation and contribution, as explained in these documents, the more this "revalued" cultural knowledge has the power to change their point of view. They will, therefore, be far better informed about artistic developments and will be in a qualified position to challenge "Official History."

TCB Yes, it is essential to study the intellectual underpinnings of Latin American art in order to understand why this art is important and, in many cases groundbreaking.

THE BRILLEMBOURG CAPRILES COLLECTION OF LATIN AMERICAN ART: EARLY ACQUISITIONS

MCR I'd like to return to the question of your knowledge of art, without which, in my opinion, you would never have assembled your magnificent collection. In the 1970s and 1980s, when you first became interested in art, did you take any courses?

TCB I never took any art courses, not even in college. I enjoyed looking for works and finding them, and then trying to understand them. It was like a personal adventure. As I became more involved, I spent more time trying to learn (about works of art and about artists), but I never went about it in a formal way. There were, of course, certain people—like Clara Diament Sujo—whose influence was crucial to my development as a collector.

MCR Do you remember some of the first pieces you bought?

TCB One of the first was a *Physichromie* by Carlos Cruz-Diez.

MCR Really? What attracted you to that piece?

TCB What I liked most about Carlos's work at that time—I didn't know him personally—was the visual color effect created by walking in front of it. I hung it where there was plenty of light, and I loved how it was always different; it all depended on the light and where one was standing. I have a great deal of affection for this piece because it holds so many memories and evokes so many feelings.

MCR When you first saw the *Physichromie*, were you surprised that it was not a painting? Were you aware of the innovative nature of the work?

TCB Actually, no. That is, it was obviously not a traditional painting. But that wasn't what most attracted me. What seduced me was the piece itself, because of its effect on the viewer. I felt a powerful emotional reaction when I looked at it.

STRATEGIES FOR BUILDING ART COLLECTIONS

MCR What did you buy next?

TCB At first, I bought exclusively Venezuelan art. Other than Carlos Cruz-Diez, I bought several works by Alejandro Otero, including some marvelous drawings such as *Don Quijote* (1977), and *Orbital Sculpture for the Interior of a Building* (1970). I also acquired *Banda plata* (1968) by Jesús Rafael Soto. In those early years, unfortunately, I was not yet looking at Latin American art as such. That came much later.

MCR There is also an international section within your collection. When did you start buying that kind of art?

TCB Actually, both collections were assembled at the same time.

MCR What international artists did you buy in the early years?

TCB Jackson Pollock, two drawings from the 1940s, each titled *Psychoanalytic*. Henry Moore, *Head Working Model*, sculpted in 1984. I later bought several sculptures by the Englishman Anthony Caro; they range from figurative to geometric works from various periods. Also Arman, Lynn Chadwick, Alexander Archipenko, Lucio Fontana, and Manolo Valdés, among others.

MCR Does this mean that your international collection was focused on sculpture? What sparked your interest in three-dimensional works?

TCB Yes, the international collection is mainly sculpture. I love sculpture. I have always had houses with large gardens, so I have been able to collect large three-dimensional works and enjoy them in ways that I can't enjoy paintings, which are much smaller, more intimate. The large sculptures I acquired are all designed for the outdoors.

MCR In terms of strategy, to what extent were you trying to create a dialogue between the international and the Latin American artists? Or were you building two parallel collections without having a specific intent in mind?

TCB I have never had a strategy for collecting. I've never done it that way. Nowadays I am probably a little more aware of the need for a more systematic approach, but I still have trouble with it. I have always gone about it intuitively: I'm offered a work of art, I like it, I buy it. I might have a sculpture by Agustín Cárdenas in my garden standing next to one by Joan Miró, for example. For me, the implicit dialogue, the conversation between those two pieces was totally natural. But I was not consciously trying to prompt that dialogue.

MCR These days many collectors specialize in a school or movement. The Patricia Cisneros collection, for example (and the Ella Fontanals de Cisneros collection, too), is well endowed with works by Constructive and/or Geometric artists. In your case, were you trying to represent a trend or movement within the collection?

TCB When I began collecting, I had no deliberate or specific strategy. Now, however, my collection is more focused. It is also very large, and I can allow myself the luxury of concentrating on a period such as Geometric art. In recent years I have focused on types of art that I had never really looked at very closely. So I am now more rational in my approach to collecting. I am more interested in buying works with some history and trying to understand the context in which the work was created and the artist's motivation for creating it.

MCR Do you mean that when you began you were not interested in the fundamental history of the work of art?

TCB That is true! I began to take a more thoughtful approach to collecting when I decided to loan my collection to the Museum of Fine Arts, Houston. You will remember that about seven years ago, when Clara Diament Sujo introduced us—and we spoke for the first time—I had no plans to extend or expand my collection, which, at the time, was almost entirely in storage. After coming to an agreement with the Museum, I realized that this decision provided an unexpected opportunity for a new beginning. Having bare walls to fill meant I could start collecting again, a different type of art this time and, this time, to do so in a more rational, organized way.

INFLUENTIAL ADVICE ON COLLECTING ART

MCR So, when you started buying art in the 1970s, you followed your intuition and you did it because you enjoyed it, but you did not develop a plan to guide you.

TCB Exactly. I think that sort of planned approach comes with time and with the maturity one gains as a collector. These days I am enjoying it much more, I am more passionate about collecting.

MCR As with other collectors we know, your relationship with art has deepened considerably over time.

TCB Yes, I think it has. In a sense it is a natural process, like everything in life.

MCR No doubt about it. How much was your husband involved in that enormous undertaking, even in the final years of his life?

TCB David did not get very involved in decisions about what to buy until the end of his life. He loved to listen to my stories about artists and the people I was meeting. He also loved seeing how people reacted when they came to our house and enjoyed the works of art; he thought that was marvelous because it was a world he knew nothing about. Little by little he began to realize that those works had a value beyond their financial worth. I have to admit that, like me, he was a compulsive buyer. We had an apartment in the Museum Tower, in New York, and living in New York also helped to raise his awareness of art. He used to go to CDS Gallery (Clara Sujo's gallery) and buy everything she suggested. For example, on the day he bought Henry Moore's *Head Working Model*, he also bought *Still Life with Lemons* (1916), a work from Diego Rivera's Cubist period. There was no plan there: an English sculptor's work standing next to a Latin American Cubist painting.

MCR And not just that. In my opinion, one work practically negates the other!

TCB Exactly! David also bought *El Reto* [The Challenge (1954)] by David Alfaro Siqueiros and kept it with him from the time he learned that he had cancer until the day he died. He even took it with him to Kentucky. For him, *El Reto* was a metaphor for getting well, a challenge he was ultimately unable to overcome. It was also an important painting in Siqueiros's career; the Mexican government has borrowed it on a number of occasions.

MCR Some titles are necessary, some are redundant. Others are forced or misleading. This one exceeds the content of the work.

TCB I cannot begin to tell you what David would have bought if he were still alive, because he liked to buy in volume. If Clara told him she had ten important works of the kind he liked, he would take all ten.

MCR You have mentioned Clara Diament Sujo and the guidance that she, as a gallery owner, provided on your acquisitions. How did you meet her? How did you develop a relationship with this woman who was so influential in critical and cultural circles in Venezuela?

TCB I met Clara in Caracas when she had the Estudio Actual. I bought several works from her there, including *Los pájaros liberados* [Released Birds (1956)] by Rufino Tamayo. By the way, my son David—when he was about ten years old—chose that painting for our collection. I don't know why he loved it so much, but I wanted to treat him to his first work of art.

Clara and I developed a deeper relationship a few years later when she settled in New York and founded CDS Gallery, and I started going to auctions at Sotheby's and Christie's. But, as I mentioned earlier, I never liked being out in public, least of all at an auction. So I would look at the catalogue and choose the works that I found interesting; Clara would then go and look at them and tell me what she thought. She would then represent me at auction.

MCR Apparently, Sotheby's and Christie's auctions played an important part in the development of your collection.

TCB No question about it. In the 1980s and 1990s, I bought many works of art at auction. Among them, for example, were the magnificent *La voce* [The Voice (1919)] by Emilio Pettoruti and *Figura bajo un uvero* [Figure under a Sea-Grape Tree (1920)] from Armando Reverón's "Blue Period" (1919–25). There is an amusing story about how I came to buy this important work of art. I was in Kentucky at a horse sale one day when my sister Mayra called to tell me that a very important work by Maestro Reverón was coming up for auction at Sotheby's. I immediately called Clara, who confirmed that the painting was indeed very important and very good, and was in perfect condition. We made our plans. I spoke to David, who had been called back to Caracas on business. To my surprise he said no; he said that buying that painting was out of the question because at the time he had no money. I think what he was working on in Caracas left him little time to consider buying a painting. At first I didn't know what to do. David had never balked at an important purchase before. In the end I was so sure of the importance of the work that I authorized Clara to buy it. And that is how that marvelous painting by Reverón became part of my collection. Of course, when David saw it he could only laugh at how "out of it" he had been to refuse buying one of the most widely discussed and published paintings from Reverón's "Blue Period."

MCR Incredible! It is also a landmark work that is of great importance in understanding Reverón's entire career.

TCB Yes, it is a work of art with a long history. I should clarify that I did not buy most of the important works at auction; I bought them through CDS and other well-known galleries. As you know, Clara has impeccable judgment and an eye for undiscovered or little-known masterpieces. I bought Diego Rivera's *La mujer de Tehuantepec* [Woman from Tehuantepec (1950)] from her, a spectacular piece that has almost never been shown. When I bought it, I don't think many people outside Mexico were aware of it. Sometime later I was invited to show it at the *Image of Mexico* exhibition at the Dallas Museum of Art.

MCR It is a monumental portrait by Rivera that is very seldom seen. It is, however, listed in the *catalogue raisonné* of his work. As Jay Oles observes in this catalogue, although formally conservative, *Woman of Tehuantepec* emblematizes the idealized Mexican imagery that became so popular after the Revolution and has been actively sought by collectors and museums since then.

TCB It is a wonderful piece, of which very few people are aware.

MCR Please tell me a little more about your relationship with Clara. Did she draw up a list of possible acquisitions that you both approved? Or did she advise you to buy certain artists and periods that she thought you might find interesting? Obviously, with an important gallery like CDS Gallery in New York, she would have had a long list of preferred artists.

TCB Clara never tried to convince David and me one way or another, or forced us to buy artists that did not interest us. She called us when she had something important that she thought would help to complete our collection. That's what happened with Torres-García. One day she called to say that she had received some significant works that she would hold for me if I was interested. I went to see her immediately and chose all six: *Constructivo con dibujo inciso* [Constructive Composition with Incised Drawing (1932)]; *Pez AAC* [AAC Fish (1939)]; *Composición constructiva de estructura coloreada* [Constructive Composition with Colored Structure (1943)], all of which were exhibited at *Crosscurrents of Modernism: Four Latin American Pioneers* at the Hirshhorn Museum and Sculpture Garden in Washington, D.C., from June to September 1992. Also *Constructivo* (1945), *Muchedumbre* [Crowd] (1940), and *Pez* [Fish] (1932). I found them all interesting and they are now in the collection! Clara has an extraordinary eye, not to mention a vast knowledge of art history; it was almost impossible to refuse anything she recommended for purchase.

INTUITIVE, VISCERAL COLLECTING

MCR Let's talk about your style of collecting. There are, of course, different types of collectors. Some collect art because they see it as a good investment; others do it for social prestige; still others can't help themselves, they are compulsive about it, as you said you used to be when you began. And then there is a small group—smaller all the time—of people who are genuinely passionate about art. They search, they study, they educate themselves, and then they buy works of art. Where do you think you fit within that spectrum?

TCB I don't fit in either of those first two categories. When I first started collecting, it never occurred to me to sell a painting to make a profit. Obviously, I have sold works that I no longer wanted in my collection, but there have been just a few, very few. It's more about continuing to refine the collection. The social prestige you mention does not interest me in the least; I never hold an open house so that people can see what I have bought. My collection is for my close friends and family, and for me to enjoy every day. I collect for my own pleasure.

MCR Well, selectively selling works is normal and perfectly justified as a means of purging and improving the collection. Almost all the serious collectors I know sell or exchange works that no longer fit comfortably in the mature version of their collections.

TCB Now, I certainly am compulsive in my approach to collecting! When I see a work of art that I like, I find it very hard to say "no." I can't stop thinking about it, wondering "how would it look in such and such a spot? How would it converse with this or that piece?" In the end, the desire becomes a nightmare.

MCR So, would you agree that your relationship with art is more emotional and intuitive than rational?

TCB Yes, totally emotional. Art moves me very deeply. When I see a work of art that I like, it inevitably sparks an emotional response. That encourages me to learn more about the artist and to look at his or her work more closely. I don't know whether my approach is a good one or a bad one, but I've never been guided by a set plan in looking for art. I've also had fantastic works brought to my house, but after living with them for a month or two, I realize that they say nothing to me, they don't work for me.

MCR So you relate to a work of art at a really visceral level.

TCB Yes, completely visceral. Though perhaps less so as time goes by. I have begun to adopt a more rational approach to buying art, but am always guided by what I love.

MCR And you don't care what a critic or a curator might think about a piece. What's important is the dialogue between you and the artwork.

TCB I do *not* want a critic telling me what is going on in the work or trying to influence me in any way. I may seek professional advice on the historical value of a work and where it fits in the artist's career, and so on. But I decide whether or not to buy it based on my emotional reaction. In many cases the work is not necessarily from the artist's most important period, but that is of no importance to me. The question is whether it "moves me."

MCR So, what really counts is how you converse with a work.

TCB Exactly. I sometimes say there is no *glamour* there. Unlike many collectors who produce lengthy statements to explain why they bought a work based on the subject matter, the period, or the artist's career, treating it like a well-thought-out, well-articulated package. One with a certain cachet, as well. But that is not my style, which explains why my decisions lack the glamour that is usually associated with the world of collecting. I'm not criticizing, since everyone does it differently and perhaps there are more rational and intelligent approaches than mine. A work must "touch" me; I will live with it, and then I invite opinions. If they are negative, I couldn't care less. But if they are positive, they confirm that I am not mistaken. I would say that 95 percent of the time I have been right, as demonstrated by the exhibition that you have organized in Houston.

MCR I detect an authentic quality in how you look for art and in your reaction when you find it. As though it were a genuine find, your "encounter" negates mistakes. Do you see what I mean?

TCB Yes, which is why I don't think I have been mistaken. My intuition has undoubtedly helped me to be honest with myself. Perhaps even to the point of being a little naive.

MCR That naïveté should actually be an essential component of every form of collecting, unless you are an expert or a scholar. It is what facilitates an "uninhibited" inspection of the work that, in turn, triggers the desire to own it, and so on.

TCB Yes, that is how I see it. I have read a lot about how other collectors—Eduardo Costantini and Adolpho Leirner, for example—built their collections, and I see that none of them began with a plan that set specific goals, like starting a museum. Nobody buys art thinking they will exhibit their collection; in the early days, it is a fairly personal process. All the rest takes time.

MCR In Eduardo Costantini's case, I agree. He didn't start out thinking about his collection's potential as a community project. He didn't create a public collection until after he got the project going.

TCB That is certainly not what happened in my case. I never start things with a vision of what they will become: I just start. For me, things happen naturally.

MCR Life taught you how to take full advantage of your own sense of identity.

TCB Maybe I don't take full advantage. People tell me that I miss many opportunities because I always seem to be "one step behind." I prefer to be backstage. I enjoy doing things, but I like to approach them indirectly.

MCR Well, it is very important to understand the dialectic that motivates you. On one hand, you are visceral and compulsive; on the other hand, you shy away from exposure. A total balance. You seem to be able to skillfully express both your compulsion (externally) and the most intimate side of your introspective shyness (internally). Your vision of art is part of that dynamic.

THE PERSONAL REWARDS OF SHARING THE COLLECTION

TCB I don't think art is exclusively for hanging in people's homes. Art should be where people can see it, contemplate it, and identify with it. To have art in my home just so that people can come and say that I have good taste? That is not my style. Never! I have a large family but I move in a very small, close circle. Every day I enjoy the art that is hanging in my home. When I come up the stairs and turn on the lights, I am thrilled with the paintings I see. Every time I look at them, it feels as though I am seeing them for the first time. This is the kind of intimate relationship I have with art. On the other hand, as I mentioned earlier, art was born to be shown, to be shared.

MCR As José Ortega y Gasset suggested in 1925: "Exhibiting exposes us." And we are exposed to all kinds of values.

TCB "Values," did you say? What started to worry me a little while ago, probably about six years ago, was the thought that the personal project one had worked on for so many years could be threatened by other people, perhaps even one's own children, and that the collection that had taken so much passion and so many years to build might disappear. I started worrying about seeing it slip away bit by bit, and that was when I remembered the first time you and I spoke about the possibility of placing the collection on long-term loan with the Museum of Fine Arts, Houston. I was very impressed with "your passion" for Latin American art and with all that you have accomplished at the Museum. I realized that I had not followed up with you after our first meeting, so I called Clara right away and she arranged another meeting with you and with the then-director of the MFAH, Peter Marzio. I went to Houston and met Peter, and I must admit that I fell in love with him. With his distinct, precise words! I remember that he lifted up his hands and said, "This is like a marriage." Do you remember that?

MCR It is indelibly etched in my memory.

TCB I remember so clearly that Peter discussed how, like in a marriage, we must have rules and parameters, but that we also must get on very well together. That was when I made my decision. I said to myself: "This collection must go to an institution where it can be exhibited so that people can see it and enjoy it." Looking back, I must admit that it has been a marvelous experience. More than thirty years ago, when I bought my first work of art, I never thought it would end up on a museum wall. That thought never occurred to me then. It all still seems rather unreal.

Yet, I am convinced. I don't think I could have agreed to this loan anywhere else. There are many important institutions in New York, for example, such as the Metropolitan Museum of Art or the Museum of Modern Art, but, in my opinion the Museum of Fine Arts, Houston, is doing more than any other museum to promote Latin American art. You are like a large family, one where I have seen far fewer egos than one normally finds in large institutions. I do not like to be flattered, and I like to form my own opinions and/or make my own decisions. I like new projects that require a lot of hard work with others who feel the same passion that I do, projects that one must believe in to make them happen. The ICAA project is exactly the sort of thing I'm referring to, the sort of thing I have tried to work on throughout the course of my life.

MCR Your low profile is, in my opinion, what makes you great. It ennobles you.

TCB I found no snobbish attitudes or paraphernalia in Houston. On the contrary, the MFAH is like a large family with one common interest—the well-being and the future of the Museum. There are no egos. Everyone wants the Museum to have the best of everything—the best exhibitions and the best collections—and to be well known around the world. This is what excited me so much about my experience in Houston. I was also impressed with the Museum's trustees, the very professional staff, the Latin Maecenas who help to support your efforts with gifts of art and fund-raising, and all your colleagues at the museum.

THE WELFARE OF PUBLIC MUSEUMS

MCR How much contact do you have with artists?

TCB During my early years of collecting, I did not have much contact with living artists. But in this second phase of building the collection, I am far more involved with them. I travel and try to see artists and visit them in their studios, and I listen to them talk about what led them to produce a work of art. Works can often be hard to understand until you have listened to the artist explain what prompted the piece, what experiences led up to its creation, and the process. I have a great deal of respect for what the artist does and says. Of course, I never go to the studios only to buy. In fact, I do not like to deal directly with the artist about purchasing a work, least of all on the first visit.

MCR Did it ever occur to you, at any time in your trajectory as a collector, that you were building an important collection that deserved to be housed in a private museum named after you?

TCB No! That never occurred to me. I am delighted that there are private museums like MALBA, founded by Eduardo Costantini, here in Buenos Aires. But that sort of project does not appeal to me. More than thirty years ago I decided to support existing institutions rather than create new ones. That policy has guided my decisions concerning the collection and those involving the SaludArte Foundation that I created and chair.

For example, many years ago I was approached with a proposal to build a hospital for children with cancer. David loved the idea and wanted us to do it, but I flatly refused. How were we going to create a hospital? It is one thing to construct a building; it is an entirely different matter to provide the infrastructure required for doctors, nurses, patients; that is crazy! To do all that just so that it could be named for

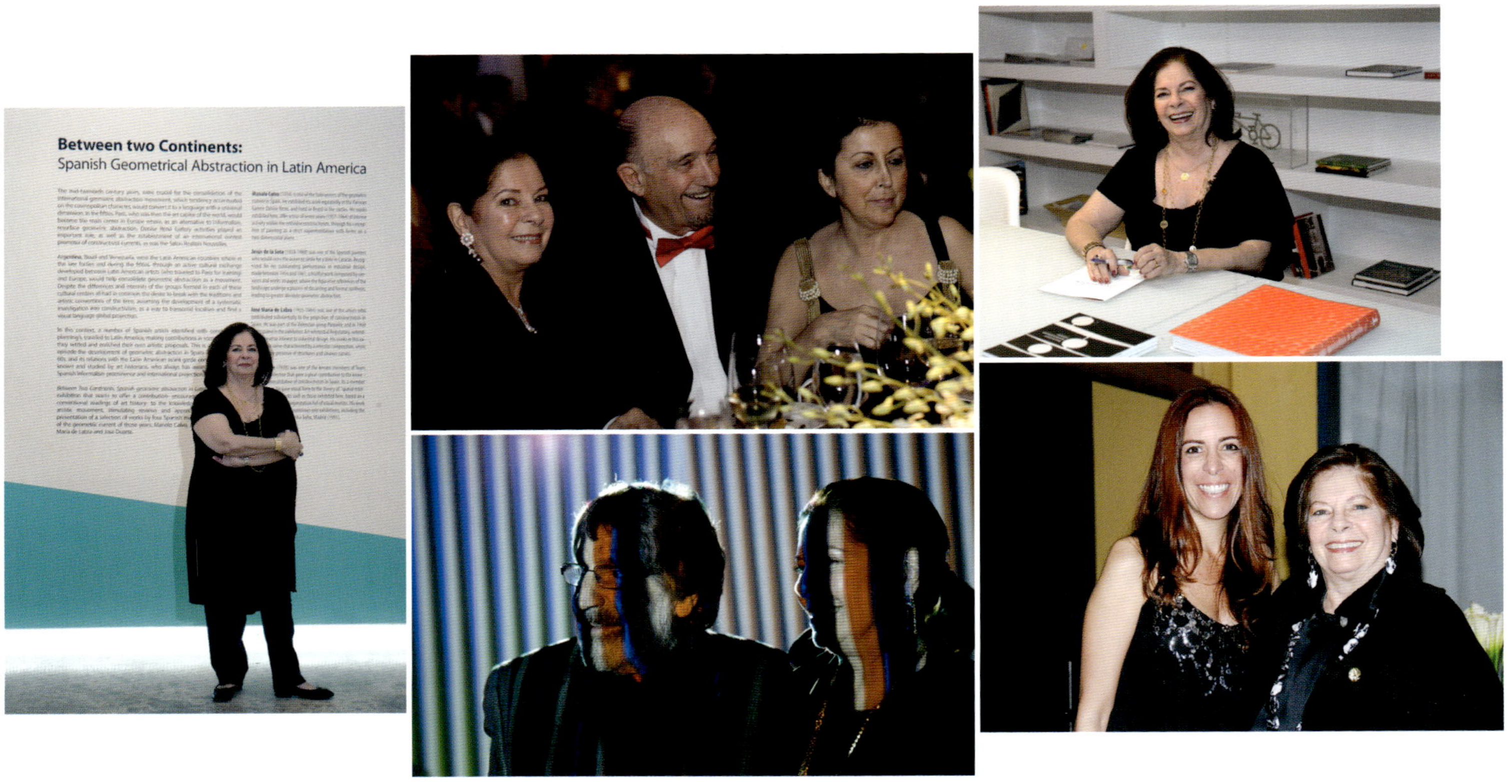

CLOCKWISE FROM LEFT
Tanya Capriles de Brillembourg at SaludArte Foundation, 2013; Tanya Capriles de Brillembourg (left) and guests at the Latin American Experience Gala at the Museum of Fine Arts, Houston, February 5, 2011; Tanya Capriles de Brillembourg at Ideobox ArtSpace, 2012; Tanya Brillembourg Capriles (left) and her mother, Tanya Capriles de Brillembourg, Machu Picchu, Peru, 2010; Franco-Venezuelan artist Carlos Cruz-Diez and Tanya Capriles de Brillembourg at the opening gala for the retrospective *Carlos Cruz-Diez: Color in Space and Time* at the Museum of Fine Arts, Houston, 2011.

its founder is very egocentric. No, that's not who I am! The important thing is to support existing institutions and fight for their survival. Why duplicate efforts?

MCR Yes, that is true.

TCB As I say, I have never wanted, and never would want, to create a private museum named after me. Now, I will admit that when I first went to Peggy Guggenheim's museum-home in Venice—which moved me deeply—I did consider the possible merit of buying a large house and doing something like that. But then I came to my senses and said, "No, that is madness."

MCR The fact is that many collectors do not realize the immense responsibility involved in a museum. Once they have assembled their collection, they think that all they have to do is to find or build a place in which to show it. But the real problem is structural: How will the museum support itself financially in the short and long term? What will happen to the institution in ten, fifteen, or twenty years? Who will be responsible for the legacy? Who will take care of preserving and promoting the collection?

TCB You are absolutely right. Collections often end up being lost, either due to a lack of resources or because of fights between heirs and other interests that cannot see eye to eye. The future of private museums is undoubtedly a very complicated matter.

MCR Once you have built a significant collection, it is very easy to create and fill your own private museum. I'm not saying that it doesn't take work. But then what? One must remember that the fundamental reason for a museum is, essentially, to keep things for posterity. Regardless of how cutting edge it may seem, the museum's purpose is "preservation."

TCB The fact is that "professional" museums attract far larger audiences than private museums do, in most cases at least. Professional museums have more resources and staff to attract the public.

MCR Museum management is not a job for individuals. It is something only the state or nonprofit foundations should undertake. The "North American model" is very successful because it involves a group of individuals—the trustees—who take responsibility for the institution, with joint legal authority and shared decisions. I think that is a far more balanced and rational approach than the so-called French model implemented in most Latin American museums. Private museums rely for their subsistence on other mechanisms that do not depend on centralized decisions or periodic shifts of political administrations.

TCB Yes, there are no political, bureaucratic, or personal interests that affect the future of the institution. As I said earlier, in museums like the MFAH, everyone is focused 100 percent on the welfare and future of the museum. In the long term, this is the source of an institution's strength; it is what allows it to survive.

What the MFAH is doing in the United States—your commitment to research, exhibition, and promotion of Latin American art—is priceless and will only be fully appreciated over the course of time.

THE STARS OF THE BRILLEMBOURG CAPRILES COLLECTION

MCR The more than one hundred highlights from your collection that we are showing at the Museum focus on Latin American masters of the first half of the twentieth century, artists of the stature of Lam, Matta, Siqueiros, Rivera, Pettoruti, and Torres-García. Do you feel that this collection is closed? Is it complete?

TCB I am very aware that my collection lacks certain key figures [from the Río de la Plata region], such as Xul Solar and Pedro Figari. I would like to be able to complete the collection, but not by buying fifty works by one artist or another. I would prefer to focus on the artists that are missing, and to try to acquire top-level works.

MCR Well, you are now obviously in another phase. I get the impression that, after you closed or *partly closed* this chapter, you started collecting the Constructive avant-garde. I see that you have recently bought many Geometric and Constructive pieces; not counting works by contemporary artists, of course. So, how would you define this second phase of your collecting career?

TCB As I said when we started this conversation, I am trying to take a more rational approach to assembling the collection. I am trying to be more systematic about the artists and the works involved. But I have been unable to control my compulsive collecting completely, as you can see by the presence of works by Loló Soldevilla and Sandú Darié, two Cuban artists. So, yes, I have decided to assemble a collection of Geometric art of a historical nature that will be as complete as possible, but this does not mean that I will abstain from collecting certain contemporary artists when I discover them and like their work.

MCR When you talk about a collection of Geometric art of a historical nature, what are you referring to, exactly?

TCB I am referring to the key landmark groups in the history of international Constructive art, like the Grupo MADI, Arte Concreto–Invención [Concrete Art Invention] (both from Argentina), or the Venezuelans Soto, Cruz-Diez, Otero, Gego, and so on.

MCR That means that, in this second phase you have developed a strategy, correct?

TCB Yes, my goal now is to seek out the art that was created as a form of protest in earlier periods by the various movements in the 1940s and 1950s in Venezuela, Argentina, and Brazil. Why was it abandoned? Why have those abstract forms—created to break with tradition, with the prevailing figurative art—been forgotten? My choices will now be driven by chance encounters with works of art, yet always guided by the intuition and the instinct that, as a collector, I have always had.

MCR As we were saying earlier, a defining quality of your career is the depth with which you collected certain important artists. Let me clarify: many collectors will buy one or two works each from a large number of different artists. That is why their collections never fully represent the various periods of artists who, as we know, often veer in different directions and produce works that reflect a variety of styles or movements. In your case the opposite is true: you have collected certain artists in great depth. Is that something you consciously decided to do from the beginning, or did it simply happen without any planning on your part?

TCB It happened with no planning on my part. When an artist's work appealed to me, I bought everything I liked of what he or she produced, regardless of his or her standing in the art world. I never set out to buy exclusively "canonical" works that have been acknowledged in art history. Nor have I tried to include in the collection whatever is considered to be the artist's "best" period. I repeat: the work must move me very powerfully. That is, and will always be, what is most important to me. Having said that, I have often come across atypical works whose appeal was derived precisely from the fact that they were unlike the artist's usual production. One such example is *Muchedumbre* [Crowd] (1940) by Joaquín Torres-García (plate 17), which we might describe as a figurative painting, quite the opposite of the Constructive Universalism that he introduced and for which he was known in the international art world. Even Clara Sujo—from whom I bought that painting—was amazed that I bought it because it did not represent any of the artist's known phases [at that point]. But I liked it enormously.

MCR That painting is from Torres-García's final period, when he returned to what he called "the recovery of the object." It is a very important but, unfortunately sparsely researched period of his work.

TCB I loved it. I bought it at the same time I bought a very important work of his, *Pez* [The Fish] (1932) (plate 16), which has been shown countless times.

PART TWO

PHILANTHROPIC ACTIVITIES

MCR Now, let's talk about the social and philanthropic work you have been doing more or less simultaneously with your collecting. I am referring to your relentless efforts on behalf of social projects involving health, culture, and music. In the mid-1980s you reached out to several institutions and, of course, established your own organizations. What are these foundations?

TCB My philanthropic activities began when I was very young and became inspired by my father's philosophy of giving back to our community. In 1984, a group of doctors invited me to chair the first foundation in Venezuela to care for children with cancer. This initiative was spearheaded by the parents of children afflicted with this disease who were being treated at the J.M. de los Ríos Children's Hospital in Caracas.

We created the country's first Pediatric Hematology/Oncology unit at that hospital, and then organized affiliates in other parts of the country, like Puerto La Cruz, Barquisimeto, and Maracaibo. Those facilities still exist today, so that children do not have to travel far from their homes, leaving their siblings behind. We organized the First Pediatric Oncology Conference in Caracas, attended by doctors from around the world. The First Meeting of Parents of Children with Cancer was organized in Valencia, Spain; this was a groundbreaking step that gave parents a voice at international pediatric oncology conferences.

MCR What exactly did the foundation do?

TCB The first thing was to provide adequate treatment. At the time, there were hardly any specialists or doctors in Venezuela who treated infantile cancer. There was only one pediatric oncologist-hematologist, who created and started the foundation. He had studied medicine in the United States and, finding inadequate conditions upon his arrival in Venezuela, joined forces with other pediatric doctors, psychologists, surgeons, and the parents of the children. The other issue was providing adequate accommodation for children and their mothers or their family during the full course of treatment.

As you well know, Venezuelan, Puerto Rican, or Colombian mothers have many children, making it difficult to take one of them to Caracas. In the first place, they lack the financial means; in the second place, children with cancer have immunological issues that require care, and if you put them in a hospital where other children have contagious diseases, they could catch something and die. In fact, that is what motivated doctors to start the Friends of Children with Cancer Foundation, in 1984.

MCR How did you deal with that situation? What resources did you use to confront such a complex problem?

TCB David was a member of the Venezuelan Congress, and I used his connections as both a developer and a politician to launch a five-year campaign to open the Pediatric Hematology/Oncology unit at the hospital. I had to fight to get them to let me have a two-story building next to the hospital that had been abandoned and was infested with rats. This all caused quite a stir; I was summoned to appear before a doctors' commission, and the Commissioner of the Venezuelan president's office called me to discuss the matter, implying that I was trying to privatize medicine in Venezuela. Nothing could have been further from the truth, and I argued that it was actually up to the government to care for those children. It was not a job for individuals, and the state should provide the space required to care for those patients.

MCR Yes, health and public assistance issues can often provoke territorial and political reactions.

TCB Anyhow, they got their way because they denied me the use of the building. But, to shut me up they gave us a basement filled with all the junk the hospital threw away. Not even the doctors or the health-care staff wanted the basement. But I convinced them, and we transformed the space into an incredible unit with four isolation beds and twenty beds for hospital patients. The governor at the time presented me with the keys as guarantor of the first Pediatric Hematology/Oncology unit in the country.

Meanwhile, David was in the process of buying a city block in the area where the Banco Mercantil is today. I convinced him to let me have a four-story building right in front of the hospital. That building became the only place in Venezuela to provide accommodation for mothers from the interior of the country who brought their children to Caracas for cancer treatment. This facility, *Mi Casita*, is still the only place where they can stay. It has two floors with rooms for families, another with recreational facilities for the children and, most important, a kitchen where mothers can feed their children regardless of when they finish their treatment. At that time, people believed that cancer was contagious, which made it very difficult to find accommodation for patients and their families.

MCR Has that original plan been taken to other parts of the country?

TCB The foundation now has affiliates in Maracaibo, Puerto La Cruz, and Barquisimeto, in addition to the one in Caracas. A hospital for children with cancer has just opened in Maracaibo, fully equipped with all the latest in cancer technology.

SALUDARTE: ART SERVING A PURPOSE

MCR How did "SaludArte" come about?

TCB I created SaludArte and started the foundation in Miami in 2003, because I believe that art should serve a purpose beyond satisfying one's personal passion. I decided to combine health with art, hence the name. I wanted to use art, especially the visual arts, as a means of raising funds and helping children in Latin America and the Caribbean.

SaludArte's main mission is to introduce art to children and youngsters regardless of their degree of exclusion, sickness, or disability: to bring art to everyone. Keep in mind that when children with cerebral palsy or mental disability or from a marginalized background attempt to explore music, dance, or the visual arts, they are faced with many kinds of architectural and educational barriers. The arts are our best tool for facilitating our mission.

MCR SaludArte also does a lot of work with musicians. What prompted that interest in music?

TCB We use music as a means to achieve our objectives, so we organize our fund-raising activities around a series of concerts in

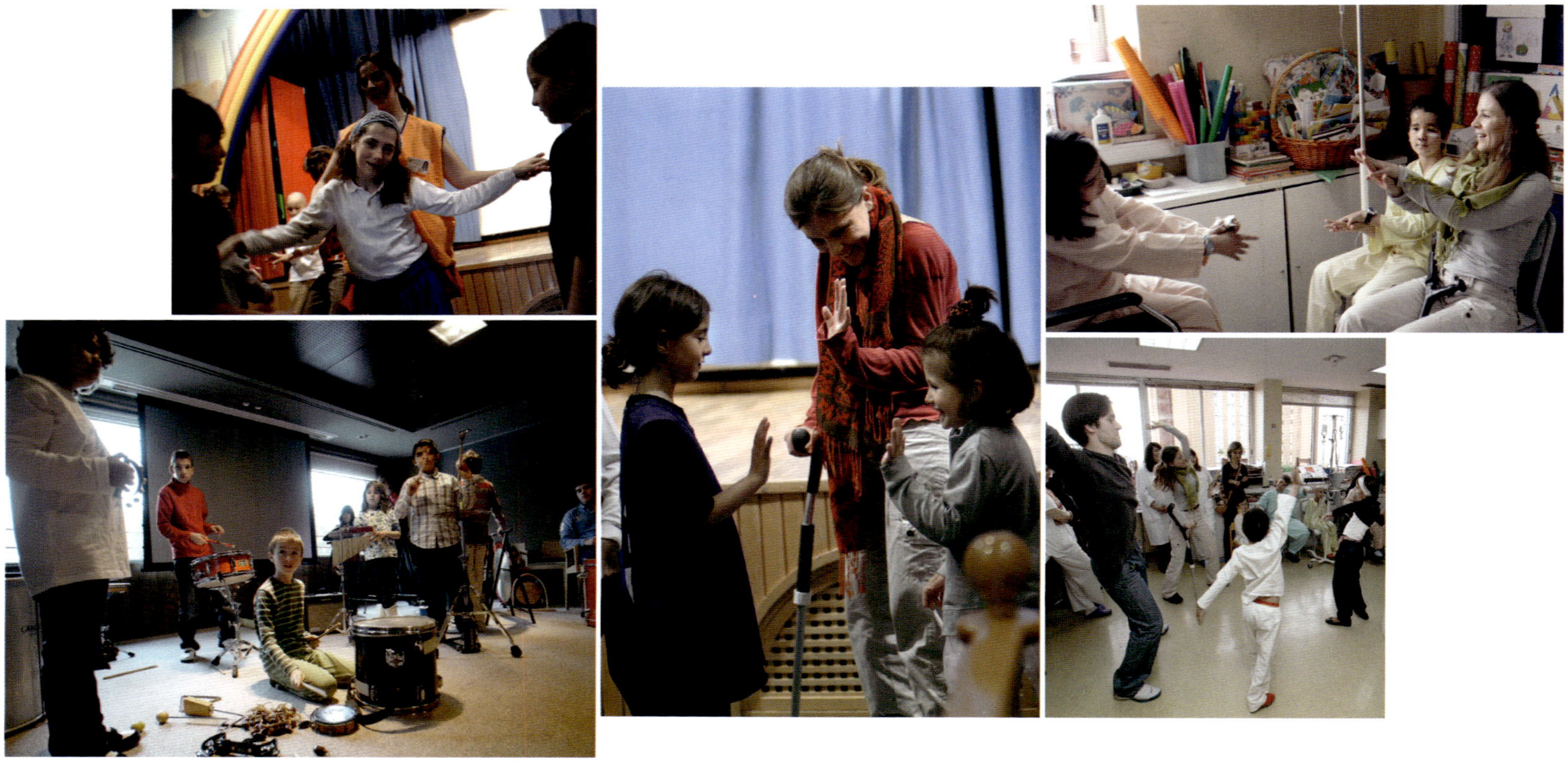

ABOVE
At the SaludArte Foundation, dance workshops are offered to children with cancer, motor disabilities, and cerebral palsy. Also offered are music workshops that bring together groups of children both with and without intellectual disabilities.

Miami. We also hold art auctions, exhibitions, and other events with the same goal. I have met many instrumental people who have helped me to achieve my objectives for SaludArte. Pablo Mielgo is a Spanish classical-orchestra conductor who took over as artistic director of the foundation and incorporated more music into what we do. Vicente Galaso, a psychologist, has worked with people with disabilities for many years and is interested in art and creativity and its application in the field of social work.

MCR And how is the foundation structured?

TCB We work in three areas: health, education, and social inclusion. We bring art into the hospital environment to improve the patient's quality of life and to provide non-pharmacological therapy (the CURARTE program). We focus on the importance of art and creativity in the educational system (EDUCARTE). And we provide art training for people with disabilities and from marginalized backgrounds (INTEGRARTE).

As the name implies, the SaludArte Foundation was created to use the arts as a means of improving the health of those living in marginalized communities. We are not the only ones who do this; on the contrary, you would be amazed by the number of foundations and people devoted to this kind of work around the world. We get emails from people in Argentina, Chile, Peru, and Colombia asking for advice on working together or creating a SaludArte in their country.

One of our initiatives aims to work with other institutions that provide assistance to people with a variety of disabilities, to try to integrate them into a more humane world. We are mainly interested in the creative process. Many unexpected things can happen during this process, things that could not have been foreseen during the planning of an art workshop.

MCR I think that the kind of healing your foundation fosters and provides is a creative act, whatever form it may take.

EDUCARTE: ART AND CREATIVITY AT SCHOOLS

TCB Our EDUCARTE Project supports educational initiatives that emphasize the importance of creativity at school. Six years ago, we started a program in Spain, with the Teatro Real in Madrid, which enables 6- to 12-year-olds to produce an original opera that they themselves create—script, costumes, set, music, everything. They work on it as part of the curriculum during school hours. A classroom becomes an opera company, and the project is based on "Creating Original Opera" at the Metropolitan Opera Guild in New York.

During the first year of the project we shot a documentary. One of the operas created by the children was called "Escucha mi voz" [Listen to My Voice], in which 6-year-olds expressed the frustration they felt when their parents did not listen to them. We loved the title and used it for the documentary. After six years, dozens of opera companies have presented their work in a number of schools.

MCR In Spain?

TCB Yes, throughout Spain. The project has evolved and we are now working with a special education school and a prison for adults. It is very interesting to see how people react when given the chance to use art to express what's going on.

Now we would like to take it to Miami, since the project originally came from the United States. That is our next goal, although we know that the educational system is resistant to this kind of pedagogical innovation.

MCR Why?

TCB Unlike Spain, innovative programs in the United States have to be submitted to and approved by the school board in each city, which means a huge amount of work that takes a great deal of time. We strongly believe that the educational system should stress the importance of art in education. We and cultural institutions, foundations, and educational centers should all be working together toward this goal.

MCR Is it an extracurricular, experimental sort of program?

TCB No, it is part of the curriculum. The kids work on it during school hours throughout the nine months of the school year.

MCR So, the children produce and present the opera?

TCB Yes, they do everything. The lesson we've learned so far is that, when you give children a chance to express themselves, they do so surprisingly well.

MCR Do they also sing?

TCB Yes. At the beginning of the course the kids choose what they would like to do in the project. The actors must learn to sing and act; the musicians must learn to compose and play an instrument.

MUSIC AND PHILANTHROPY: THE SOCIAL ASPECT OF ART

MCR In our conversation so far, we have been discussing your role as a collector and your involvement with art. But, it seems that you also have strong feelings for music. How did you develop an interest in music?

TCB To me, music—more than any other form of art—has an evocative power that can take us out of ourselves. It can change our mood from negative to positive. Music can distract children living in marginalized circumstances from their social exclusion. But, ultimately, for me, it is all about the social aspect of art.

MCR How do you define that kind of philanthropy? Do you see it as a form of charity to others, of the sort that Catholicism teaches? Or as something more closely related to one's social responsibility to one's community?

TCB I do not believe in the kind of charity taught by the Catholic Church. Anyone who has interacted with people with disabilities or with those who live in a state of social exclusion will tell you that they have received much more than they have given. For example, a few months ago we brought one of the top violinists from the London

Symphony to Miami to give a workshop for children and youngsters with Down Syndrome. One of the young boys asked the violinist to play "Romeo and Juliet." When the violin began to play, the boy walked over to a young girl with Down Syndrome, knelt in front of her, and declared his love for her. There is no charity involved in something like that; it is more a question of being in tune on a human level.

BUILDING CREATIVE BRIDGES

MCR So many different stories, all taking place simultaneously as facets of your personal experience. Fantastic!

TCB They are things we have mentioned in our conversation.

MCR But they are very important because they reveal the richness of your life. You are so involved in SaludArte and in your collecting; how do you manage to balance the two? Does it all seem natural to you? Art and music side by side, and then your collection, and the many examples you set with your generosity to the community.

TCB There is no sense of division in how I spend my time because, to me, both activities are interrelated. When I am organizing an exhibition, for example, I ask the artist to give a workshop about his or her work to groups of people with disabilities.

MCR A full-time job. As I see it, Tanya, one of your greatest gifts is your ability to connect things that do not appear to have any connection to each other; your ability to "bridge the gap," as they say in English; to establish creative bridges. I truly admire what you have achieved. Look where art has taken you, or rather, your social reading of what art can do. It would seem that your goal—over and above collecting as such—has morphed into a continuum that honors art and health in which foundations and funds combine to achieve one goal: to serve the community.

TCB Yes, that is definitely the ultimate goal.

ART ENRICHES THE SOUL

MCR Is there anything about art or your related activity that you are more aware of now, something you couldn't even have imagined when you started? Have you had any revelations during the course of your experiences?

TCB These days I get more involved with the artist when I know him or her, when I am fully aware of his or her reasons for making a piece. I admire and respect artists who continuously explore, who keep working within a style, but who still keep searching, evolving. I identify with their ability to use their creative work to criticize their social environment via their artistic expression. I am amazed by artists who use new techniques, not just to paint and draw, but to create installations and use previously unknown media and materials. I think this understanding of the artistic process is new, compared to how I assembled and chose art in the early stages of the collection.

MCR You mean that your personal contact with artists has changed you at an emotional level, a human level?

TCB I find it more satisfying, more enjoyable now. Yes, and it is not only about human feelings and being involved with the artists; it is also about being able to help them and work with them. I feel exactly the same human and social responsibility that I feel from having lent my collection to the Museum of Fine Arts, Houston. Why? Because my collection is a part of them, period.

MCR It would be hard to add anything to that.

TCB All I could add would be that the effort to involve art with social projects has been worth it. What more could we ask for?

ESSAYS *on* THE BRILLEMBOURG CAPRILES COLLECTION

Rachel Mohl

THE FUNDAMENTAL FORCES OF LIGHT AND SPACE IN EMILIO PETTORUTI'S EARLY WORKS

THE MONTH BEFORE EMILIO PETTORUTI opened his first exhibition in Buenos Aires on October 10, 1924, his friend and fellow artist Xul Solar published an article in the Argentine art journal *Martín Fierro* praising Pettoruti's artistic achievements. Xul declared that his friend's "new, broad perspectives. . .contribute to a relief and a liberation."[1] Pettoruti's new sensibility, which would change the face of Argentine art, developed during his eleven-year stay in Europe, from 1913 to 1924. Pettoruti's period in Europe began in Florence, where he enrolled in his only official academic course, taught by Augusto Giacometti, at the Accademia Internazionale.[2] Pettoruti was not a full-time art student; rather, he strove to understand, through personal experience, the various artistic currents of both the contemporary avant-garde circles and the Old Masters. By combining an array of principles drawn from Futurism and Cubism, and Quattrocento masters, Pettoruti created a unique artistic vocabulary in which light and space appear as tangible forces in his early works.

By his third month in Florence, Pettoruti had viewed numerous Renaissance masterpieces, as well as *L'esposizione futurista di "Lacerba"* [The Futurist Exhibition "Lacerba"], the 1914 exhibition that introduced him to the movement.[3] He began associating with the leader of Florentine Futurism, Ardengo Soffici, who was also an ardent promoter of French Cubism. Through Soffici's writings, including *Il cubismo e oltre* [Cubism and Beyond] (1913), Pettoruti learned about the practice of Cubism in France.[4] At the same time, he apprenticed in mosaic and fresco workshops, honing his artistic techniques.

Pettoruti's collage *La Voce* [The Voice] (1914) (plate 1) in the Brillembourg Capriles Collection of Latin American Art presents an excellent early example of how the artist intertwined and translated the diverse languages of modern and classical art. Pettoruti masterfully assembled a number of different types of paper, including a strip from the Futurist periodical *La Voce*, on the pictorial plane, creating an interior space as seen from multiple perspectives. Although the work resembles other collages from the period, such as Juan Gris's *La botella de anís* [The Bottle of Anise] (1914) (fig. 1), Cubist artists tended to dissect and present objects from differing viewpoints on a flat, pictorial surface. In comparison, Pettoruti's collage breaks, distorts, and examines space, rather than a tangible object, from multiple perspectives. Thus, space becomes an actual, moving entity. The clearly placed objects, such as the three-dimensional cup drawn in red crayon and the canister made from an amalgamation of paper, serve as contrasts to the other abstract shapes. In the upper-right-hand corner, Pettoruti mimicked the one-point perspective, producing a recessed corner that leads to a door. The illusionistic depth is distinguished from the flat, white shape onto which he placed the cup, the canister, and a bottle. The constant push-pull sensation between three and two dimensions, which does not exist in Gris's Cubist collage, creates the sensation of movement. Space becomes an active force, which fluidly guides the viewer's gaze through the entire composition.

Pettoruti presented light in a similar manner to space—as an independent element in his work. In Soffici's *Il cubismo e oltre*, the Futurist artist and writer stated that Cubism "considers light as something

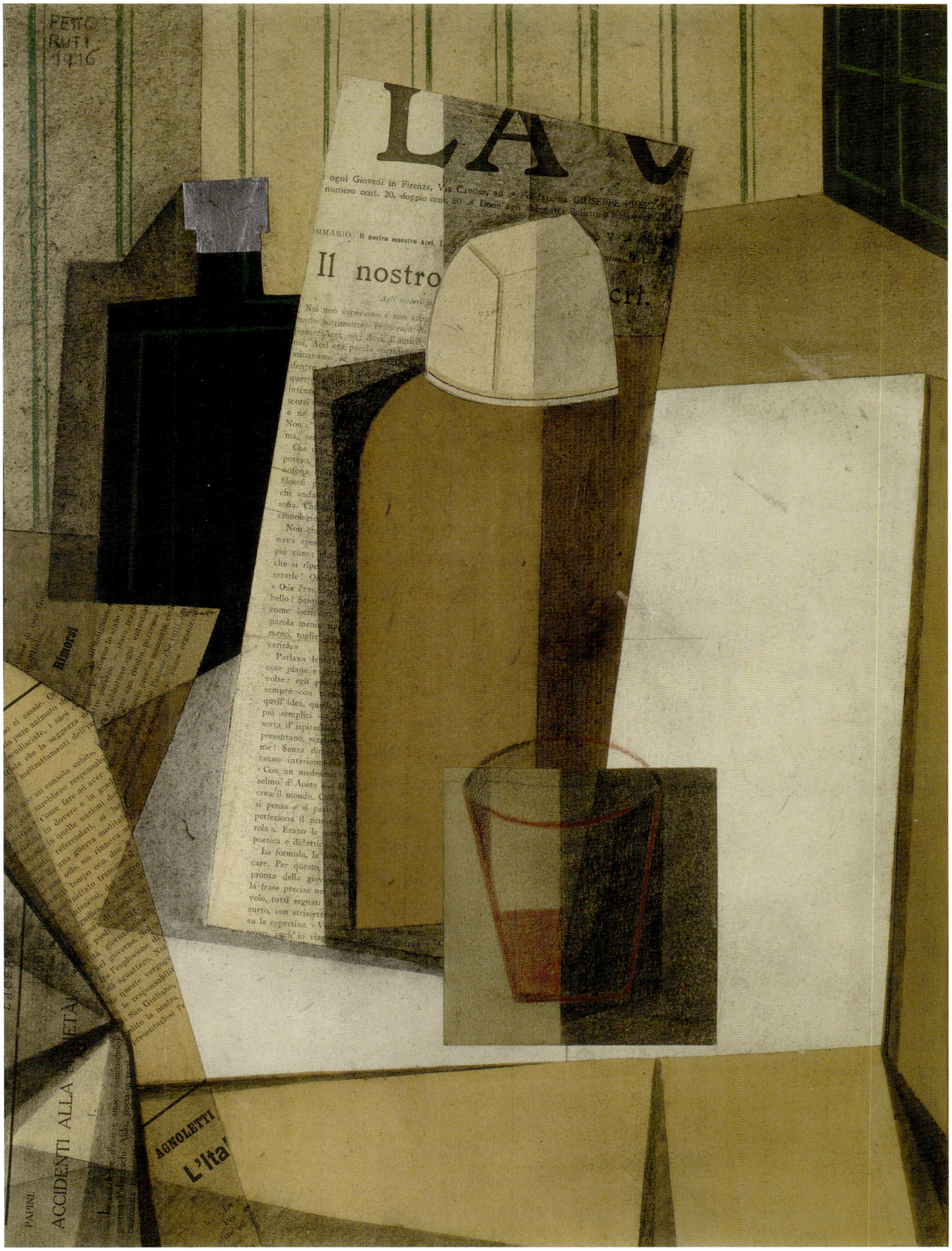

PLATE 1

Emilio Pettoruti • *La Voce* [The Voice], 1916

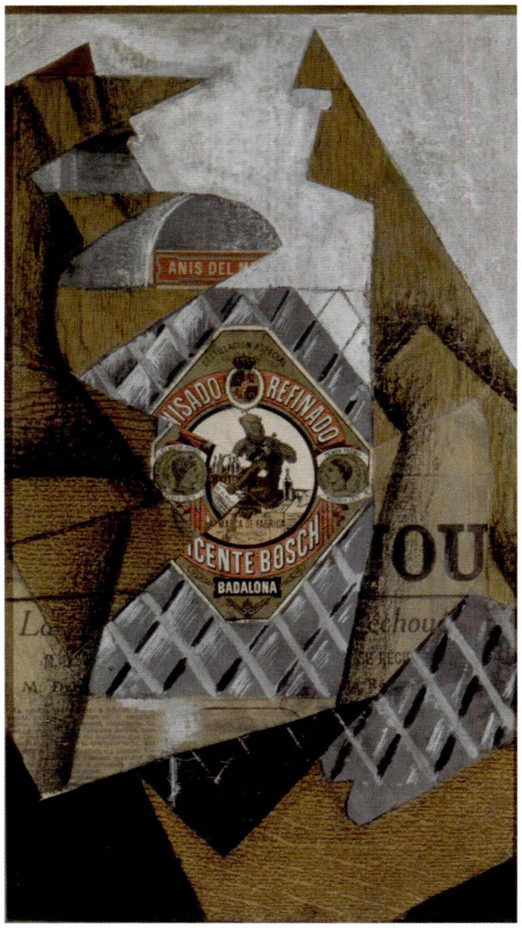

FIG. 1

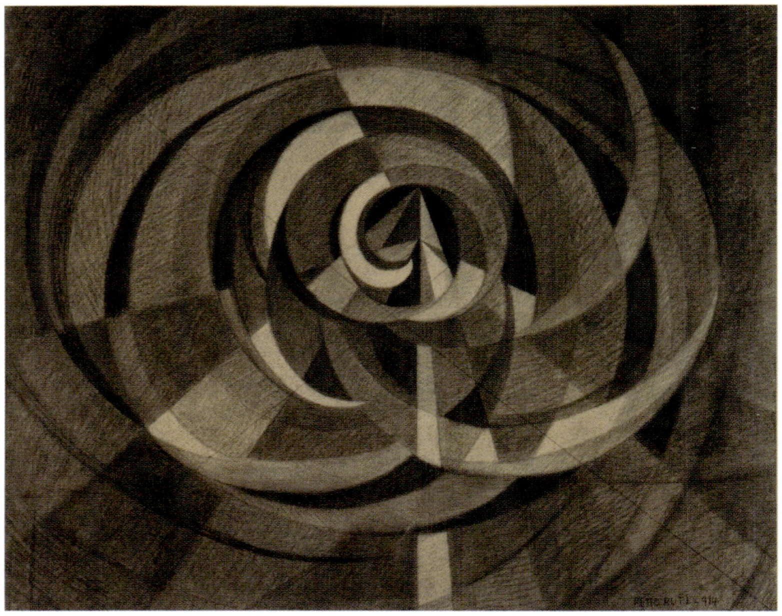

FIG. 2

measurable and... as something that can be transformed into objects."[5] Pettoruti took this idea a step further, needing "to find an autonomous light for an autonomous entity: the light of an invented picture."[6] For Pettoruti, light became more than an object, and was, instead, an autonomous force in his works—a principle that, as he notes, distinguished him from other artists.[7] Indeed, the shadows in Pettoruti's *La Voce* do not adhere to a single or particular light source. The artist juxtaposed the shaded areas of the work with lighter patches of color, creating a unique rhythm. For instance, Pettoruti outlined the shadow of the canister at the center of the composition with a lighter grey, which gives a rippling effect that emanates from the object. Light acts as a separate entity, producing harmonious shapes that balance the composition. The energy of light seems to converge at one point in the bottom-right-hand corner of the work, and then explodes into an array of shades of gray. This resembles other Pettoruti works from 1914, such as *Armonia-movimiento-spazio (disegno astratto)* [Harmony-Movement-Space (Abstract Design)] (fig. 2), in which he further investigated the idea of space and movement as unseen, though active, forces.

The artist's interest in invisible, physical energy directly related to the cultural milieu in Europe at the time. Discoveries at the turn of the century, such as the X-ray and non-Euclidean geometry, encouraged the recognition of the limited nature of visual reality and the relativity of human perception. Intellectual circles speculated about alternative kinds of space. This, in turn, caused artists to question traditional modes of representation and to strive to propose different ideas for articulating invisible energies.[8]

For the Italian Futurists, these currents manifested themselves as an interest in dynamic space and simultaneous movement, observed in Umberto Boccioni's *States of Mind I: The Farewell* (1911) (fig. 3), which Pettoruti saw in the 1914 "*Lacerba*" exhibition. Despite his interest in the work of his European counterparts, Pettoruti carved his own path. His artistic practice departed in several significant ways from that of his contemporaries. The Futurist exploration of movement, for example, typically required an object to displace space, like the train in Boccioni's *States of Mind I*. In contrast, Pettoruti's works isolate light, space, and movement as abstract forces, often without a connection to the physical word. Futhermore, while Boccioni took the investigation of invisible forces to a spiritual level,[9] Pettoruti grounded his ideas of space and light in the logic and equilibrium of his own works.

While Pettoruti absorbed the European avant-garde, he also looked to the past for inspiration, specifically in the way he balanced the elements in his works to achieve proportion. He admired the many Quattrocento masters he had studied in Florence for their ability to "reduce the elements of their painting to clear and legible expressions."[10] Pettoruti noted "the many deformations that appear in the entirety of the composition and in its details: which actually are not deformations because they obey a certain rhythm, the general rhythm of the work."[11] *La Voce* is a testament to Pettoruti's ability to exquisitely render a harmonious composition through the strategic placement of form and the juxtaposition of light and space.

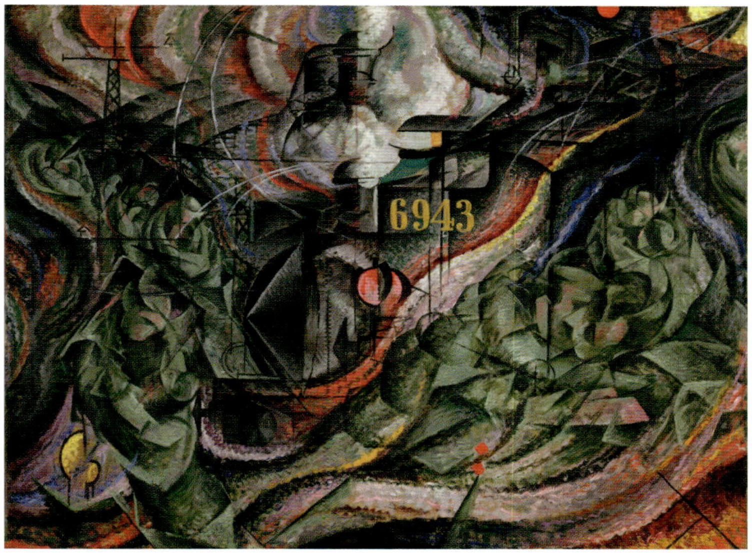

FIG. 3

In 1917, Pettoruti traveled to Milan and began associating with the intellectual group that would eventually establish the Novecento movement. Artists in this circle, such as Achille Funi, Pietro Marussig, Aldo Carpi, and Mario Sironi, promoted the traditional principles of classical Italian art—an idea that, naturally, appealed to Pettoruti.[12] His involvement with these artists explains the return to realism seen in his *Still Life* (1918). Yet Pettoruti established a more nuanced relationship with realism, rendering the objects on the table in three-dimensional terms while maintaining a dynamic sense of light and space. He created a rhythm in this work by painting large patches of brushstrokes that seem to flow in a certain, determined direction. The fluidity of Pettoruti's space makes the creases in the tablecloth and the wrinkles in the crumpled piece of paper appear to vibrate. Thus, the artist combined the traditional with the Futurists' dynamism to convey a distinctive sense of space.

Pettoruti also used light as a driving force to balance this painting. The folds of the tablecloth, which the artist masterfully rendered with light and shadow, recall the Quattrocento interest in drapery, epitomized by Masaccio's *Tribute Money* (1427), one of the many masterpieces Pettoruti saw in Florence. In his autobiography *Un pintor ante el espejo* [A Painter before the Mirror], he wrote of his admiration of the Renaissance masters' treatment of light,[13] an appreciation evident in his *Still Life*, in which he developed light as an autonomous entity moving within the painting, evidenced by his manipulation of color and transparency in the glass cup on the table. On one hand, Pettoruti provided a realistic sense of the glass in the way he allowed viewers to see through it. On the other hand, his use of various tones and fervent patches of brushstroke bestowed light with an active power, which reflects in incongruous directions off of the cup.

The two small drawings by Pettoruti in the Brillembourg Capriles Collection are important examples of his experimentation with space. With its clean, crisp lines and perfected proportions, the *Untitled* charcoal sketch (1917) presents a better and more thoughtful execution than the undated illustration in red crayon, whose sketchy lines only loosely intimate a flat, Italian coffee pot. Indeed, the 1917 drawing displays Pettoruti's ability to precisely place shapes in a harmonious, albeit asymmetrical, composition—a skill that he probably began to develop while creating mosaics during his earlier years in Italy. The artist's cross-hatched lines double as both a surface pattern and shadowing. Thus, the same element in the work that pushes the

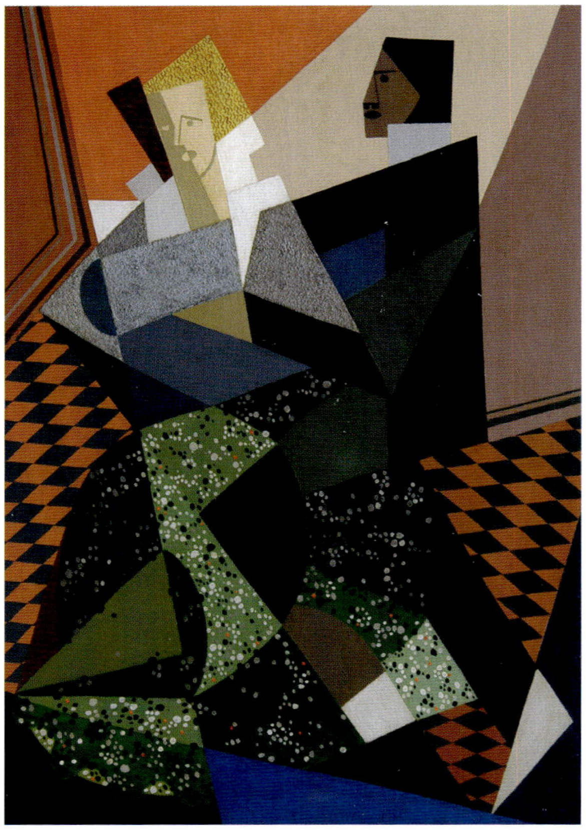

FIG. 4

viewer's gaze back toward an illusionistic depth also causes the eye to focus on the surface. Pettoruti extended this understanding of formal relationships and patterns in his finished paintings from the period, including *Bailarines* (1918) (fig.4). In this work, he incorporated the same technique of elegantly overlapping various shapes, which gives the dancers rhythm and motion. The patterns in this painting, particularly the alternating blue and orange rhombi, exist on the surface and simultaneously recede into the depths of the dance hall depicted. While he may have been influenced by the Cubist geometric planes and the Futurist dynamism, no other artist was using superficial, yet depth-inducing, patterning quite like Pettoruti.

Once Pettoruti returned to Argentina, in 1924, he joined a group of like-minded intellectuals, the Martin Fierristas, who revolted against what they saw as their country's old-fashioned preoccupation with Realism and Impressionism. When Pettoruti exhibited the works from his formative European period at the Witcomb Gallery in Buenos Aires, the exhibition not only caused a scandal: it also marked a watershed moment in Argentina. Pettoruti is deservedly credited with helping to thrust Argentine art into the twentieth century.

ILLUSTRATIONS IN TEXT

FIGURE 1
Juan Gris
The Bottle of Anís del Mono, 1914
Oil, collage, and graphite on canvas
16 1/2 x 9 3/8 inches (41 x 24 cm)
Museo Nacional Centro de Arte
Reina Sofia, Madrid, Spain

FIGURE 2
Emilio Pettoruti
Armonía-movimiento-spazio
(disegno astratto)
[Harmony-Movement-Space
(Abstract Drawing)], 1914
Charcoal and pencil on paper
17 5/8 x 22 13/16 inches (44.8 x 57.9 cm)
Colección Eduardo F. Costantini,
Buenos Aires

FIGURE 3
Umberto Boccioni
States of Mind I: The Farewells, 1911
Oil on canvas
27 3/4 x 37 3/8 inches (70.5 x 96.2 cm)
The Museum of Modern Art, New York,
Gift of Nelson A. Rockefeller

FIGURE 4
Emilio Pettoruti
Bailarines [Dancers], 1918
Oil on canvas
30 3/4 x 21 5/8 inches (77 x 55 cm)
Colección Museo Provincial
de Bellas Artes Emilio A. Caraffa
Córdoba, Argentina

NOTES

1
Xul Solar, "Pettoruti," *Martin Fierro: Periódico quincenal de arte y crítica libre* 1, no. 10–11 (1924): 7–8.

2
Miguel Ángel Muñoz, "Emilio Pettoruti," *Art Nexus* 34 (1999–2000): 79.

3
Emilio Pettoruti, *Un pintor ante el espejo* (Buenos Aires: Ediciones Solar), 35–47.

4
Muñoz, "Emilio Pettoruti," 79–80.

5
In Ardengo Soffici's "Il cubismo e oltre," *Lacerba*, from January 15, 1913 (quoted in Muñoz, "Emilio Pettoruti," 79).

6
Pettoruti, *Un pintor*, 52.

7
Ibid., 52.

8
Linda Dalrymple Henderson, "Vibratory Modernisms: Boccioni, Kupka, and the Ether of Space," in *From Energy to Information: Representation in Science and Technology, Art and Literature*, eds. Bruce Clarke and Linda Dalrymple Henderson (Stanford: Stanford University Press, 2002), 126–35.

9
Ibid., 133–36.

10
Pettoruti, *Un pintor*, 51.

11
Ibid.

12
Edward Sullivan, "Emilio Pettoruti: an International Perspective," in *Pettoruti*, ed. Edward Sullivan (Buenos Aires: Fundación Pettoruti, 2004): 73.

13
Pettoruti, *Un pintor*, 32.

James Oles

DIEGO RIVERA

PARIS TO NEW YORK TO TEHUANTEPEC

THE VARIED WORKS BY DIEGO RIVERA in the Brillembourg Capriles Collection of Latin American Art allow an overview of several of his major concerns as an artist over a wide-ranging and prolific career, as well as insight into the history of collector interest in his work, already well-established in the early twentieth century, when, as the leading student in Mexico City's Academy of San Carlos, he won a privately-funded fellowship to study in Europe, departing for Madrid in 1907. This essay focuses on several works that, while visually disparate in terms of iconography, and created in diverse locales, reveal Rivera's interest in controlled and disciplined line—a concept reinforced in the rather conservative Academy—as well as in the underlying structure of the composition.

Imagining Space in a Paris Café

Although famous today mainly as a muralist and painter of Mexico's traditional culture, Diego Rivera spent the 1910s moving rapidly through a series of styles, from Symbolism to Cubism to Cézannisme. Of these, however, his engagement with Cubism had the greatest ramifications for his subsequent work. Around 1916, along with an international circle that included painters Juan Gris, André Lhôte, Jean Metzinger, and Gino Severini, and sculptor Jacques Lipchitz, Rivera emerged as a major practitioner of a theoretical and rationalist branch of Synthetic Cubism, based on highly intellectualized doctrines and scientific research rather than personal intuition, the approach favored by Picasso and Braque. French critic Maurice Raynal called this branch "Classical" or "Crystal" Cubism, terms that highlighted its order, elegance, and severity, where forms have become reduced to a minimum and resemble faceted crystals.

Obsessed by the concept of the fourth dimension, in 1917 Rivera invented a secret viewing device (now lost, and known only as *la chose*, or "the thing") that apparently allowed him to reconsider traditional rules of perspective, and ultimately, transform objects observed in "real" space and time into the equally "real," but now two-dimensional and permanent, space of the canvas. His theories, which even his colleagues did not always understand—compounded by French xenophobia—led to a bitter fight that March with critic Pierre Reverdy at Lhôte's studio: as artists and dealers took sides, Rivera was eventually ostracized, and, by the end of 1917, he abandoned Cubism altogether.[1]

Rivera's *Still Life with Lemons* (1916) (plate 2) was painted in Paris in March 1916, at the height of the artist's achievements as an abstract painter. Here, as part of an ongoing investigation into the representation of space, Rivera—like his Modernist colleagues—used familiar objects that appear in other works, like the constants and controls of mathematical or scientific proofs, in order to make his formal discoveries more evident. The painting shows a variety of these objects arranged on a table top against a deep blue background. Rendered in a clockwise spiral are a coffee grinder, with the metal handle swinging out; a narrow bottle with a lozenge-shaped label, perhaps of anise-flavored liquor; a tapered glass vessel that might hold wine; a knife resting on something (perhaps bread); a distinctive glass *porrón* (a

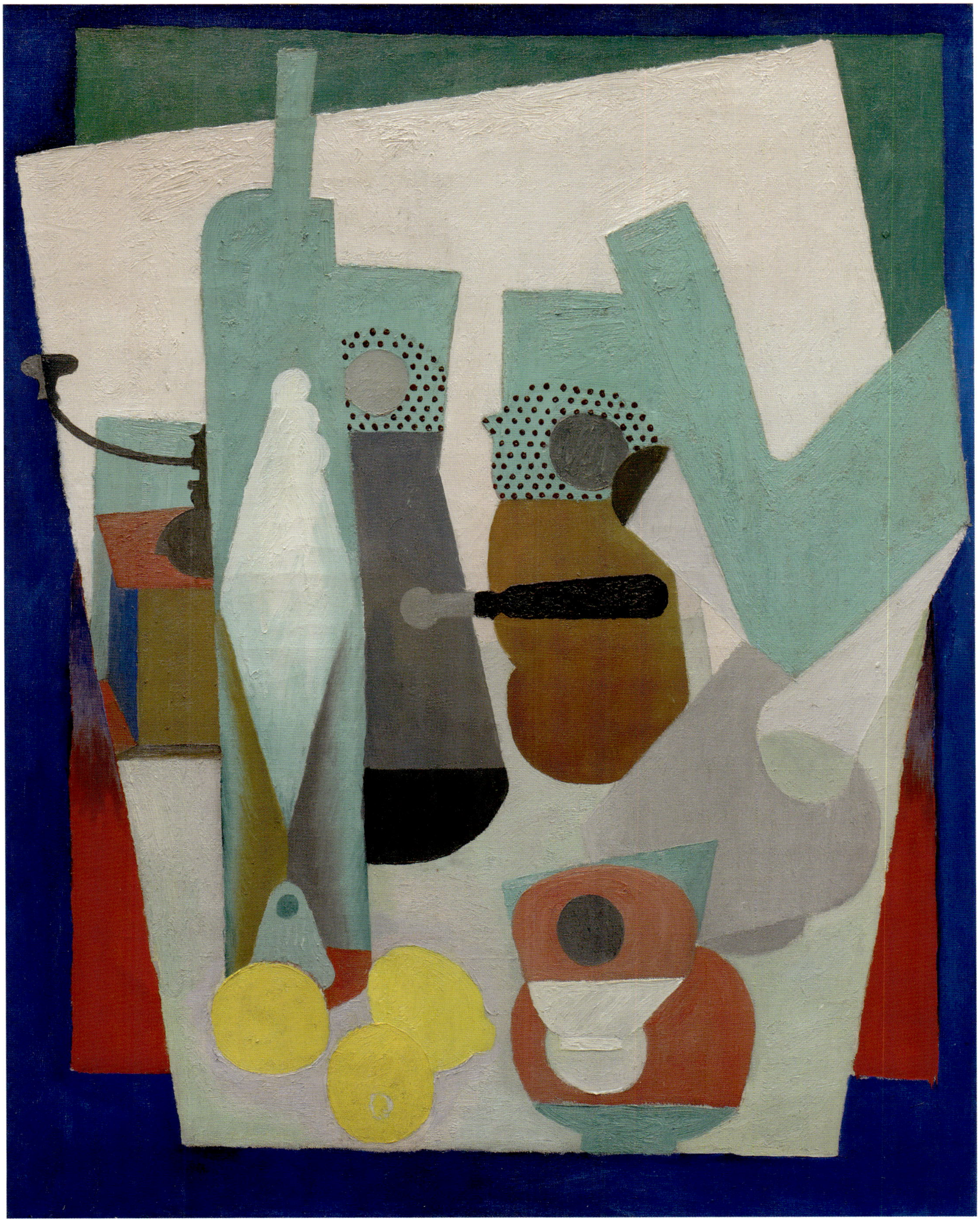

PLATE 2

Diego Rivera • *Naturaleza muerta con limones* [Still Life with Lemons], 1916

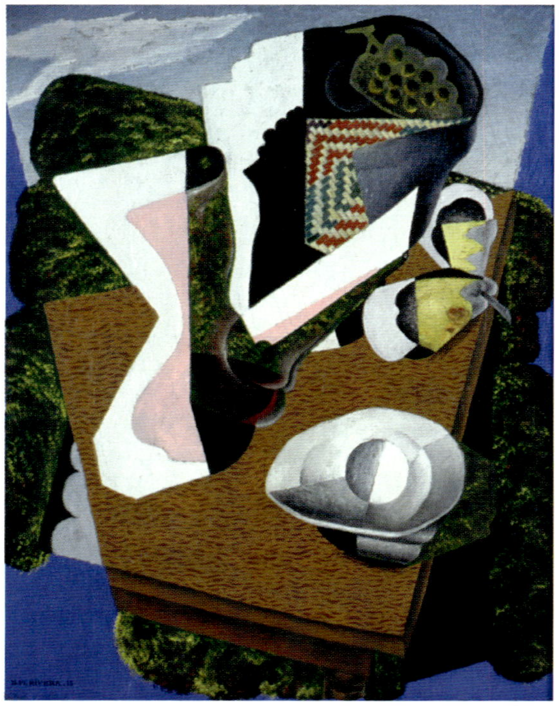

FIG. 1

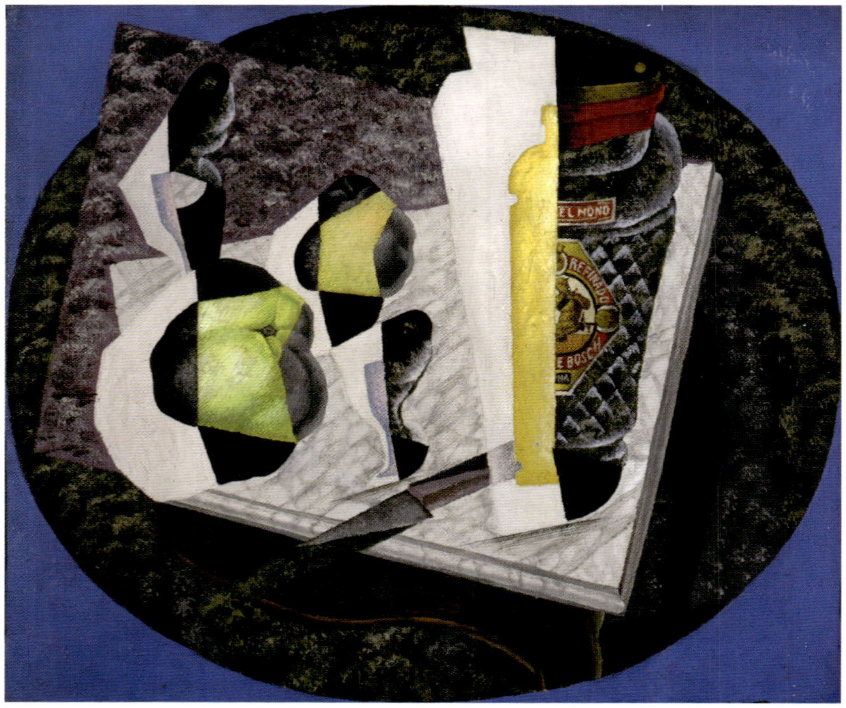

FIG. 2

Spanish wine pitcher); an indistinct orange-colored form, perhaps a coffee cup and saucer; and three lemons. Areas of blue-gray, like the V-shaped form above the porrón, are apparently shadows, while two speckled forms—one of which clearly has the outline of another lemon—are like traces of objects moved during the creation of the picture. Rivera has rendered these objects from a variety of perspectives, showing them as solid, transparent, three-dimensional, or simply silhouetted: in fact, the liquor bottle, which anchors the left side of the picture, is all of these at once. Rivera distilled these complex objects down to their indispensible features (yellow for lemons, the prominent label), and if today some are a bit hard to decipher, it may be because we are far less familiar with the offerings of an early-twentieth-century French café.

Although primarily concerned with formal explorations, *Still Life with Lemons* speaks to an intellectual life lived in the cafés of Montparnasse and stimulated by drinks, alcoholic or not; yet it also seems to reference Spanish more than French culture. The clearest example of this nod to regional identity is the porrón, which also appears in Rivera's *Still Life with Gray Bowl* (1915) (fig. 1) and Picasso's earlier *Still Life with Bottle of Rum* (1911), but the lemons—featured in so many still lifes by Rivera, Matisse, and others, and here related to mixing drinks—may also have symbolized contact with Spain. The bottle is more ambiguous: although the proportions are elongated, it might contain Anis del Mono, produced near Barcelona (it is more explicitly identified in two other Rivera paintings, *Bottle of Anis* and *Still Life with Bread Knife* [fig. 2], both of 1915, as well as in works by Braque and Picasso). Perhaps the painting in the Brillembourg Capriles Collection is a nostalgic nod to days spent in Madrid and Mallorca, far from the deprivations of wartime Paris.

Still Life with Lemons formed part of one of the first important collections of Rivera's work, assembled by a former Mexican cultural attaché in Paris, Enrique Freyman (d. 1956), an elusive character partly lost to history, and his wife, Amélie Hermann.[2] Freyman was born in Tepic, Nayarit: Octavio Paz, who knew him later in life, said he was "the son of a German Jew and a Huichol mother."[3] Freyman may have studied at the Academy of San Carlos, for in April 1909 he was on his way to Paris on an artist's fellowship. He established contact with Rivera soon after arriving, joining a group that included fellow painters Angelina Beloff, María Blanchard, Marie Vassilieff, and Angel Zárraga.[4]

Over the next decades, Freyman was associated with many Mexican artists and intellectuals passing through Europe; a reporter called him the "most interesting Mexican in Paris."[5] Whether independently wealthy or relying on his wife's fortune, Freyman collected paintings, prints, books, and Pre-Columbian ceramics, including twenty-seven works by Rivera dated between 1909 and 1917.[6] All were acquired directly from the artist, though the circumstances are unclear: according to dealer Inés Amor, the works had been left in Freyman's care by Rivera, and never reclaimed.[7] In fact, Freyman may have also been an informal dealer.

Of the paintings from Freyman's estate sold at auction in New York in 1959, just two years after Rivera's own death, ten were Cubist still lifes. There were several prominent buyers competing for these works, including Rivera ally and politico Marte R. Gómez, retailer Stanley Marcus, film director Otto Preminger (who acquired *Still Life with Lemons*), actor Edward G. Robinson, and, most important, Mexican businesswoman Dolores Olmedo, a major patron of Rivera. Prompted by Rivera around 1950 to search out his best works, Olmedo had been on the trail of Freyman before his death, and acquired eleven works at the sale, forming the core of her renowned collection.

Workers and Steel in New York City

After 1918, Rivera never created works as abstract as *Still Life with Lemons*, but we can detect a continuing fascination with underlying structure in his murals and paintings, including a group of watercolors depicting the construction of Rockefeller Center in New York. Accompanied by his wife, Frida Kahlo, Rivera disembarked from the SS *Morro Castle* in New York City on November 13, 1931: he was then perhaps *the* most famous artist in the Americas, though not because of his adventures in Montparnasse. In his retrospective at the Museum of Modern Art, the event that had brought him to the city, only seven of over 140 works—including mural sketches and portable fresco panels—provided evidence of his Cubist experiments. Instead, visitors flocked to the show to see his images of Mexico's folk culture and revolutionary struggles from the 1920s, featured in easel paintings, of course, but more famously in his murals.

At the time, the United States was suffering through the worst months of the Great Depression, but somewhat ironically, New York was enjoying a construction boom that would result in some of Manhattan's greatest landmarks, including the Empire State Building (1931) and Rockefeller Center (1932–33). Rivera, ever fascinated by technology and labor, would have been drawn immediately to the excavation sites, especially those bounded by Fifth and Sixth avenues, from 48th to 51st streets, twenty-two acres that had been demolished to make way for Rockefeller Center, the largest privately-funded building project in history and one of the few places in the city where one could then have observed so many workers actually at work (fig. 3). In fact, as one scholar has noted, "Although seemingly paradoxical, Rivera's interest in Rockefeller Center stemmed from a leftist fantasy that socialized labor would emerge from capitalist endeavors like this."[8]

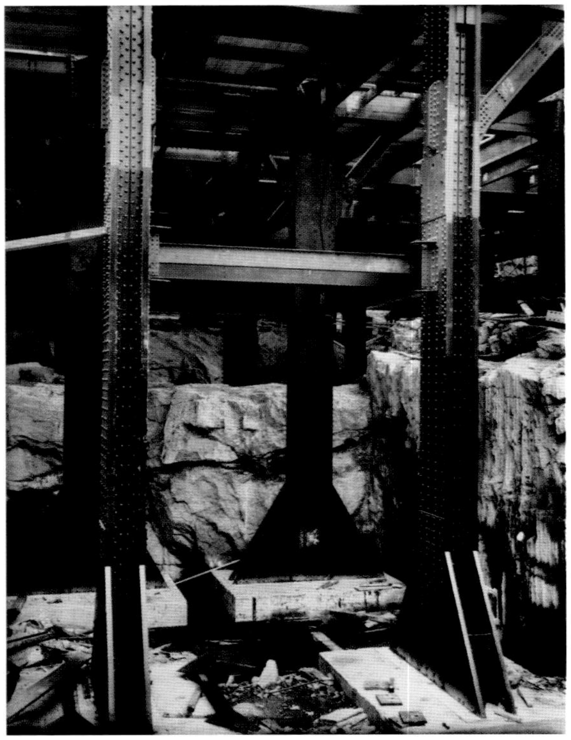

FIG. 3

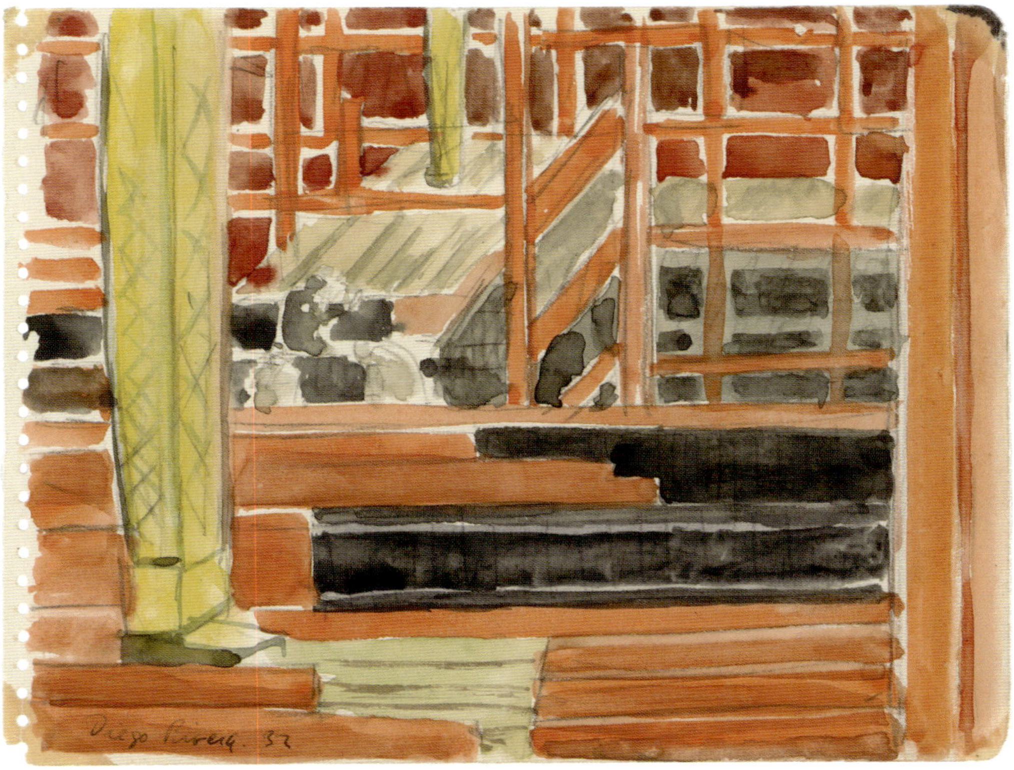

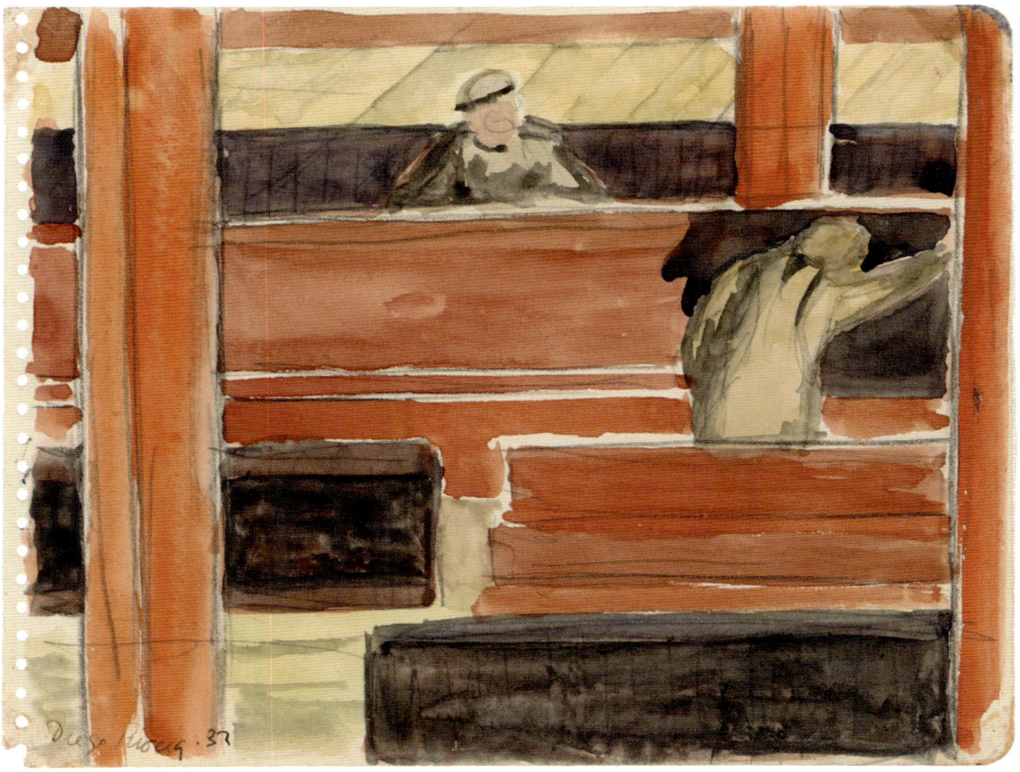

PLATES 3–6

Diego Rivera • *Construction of Rockefeller Center: Four Notebook Sketches,* 1931–32

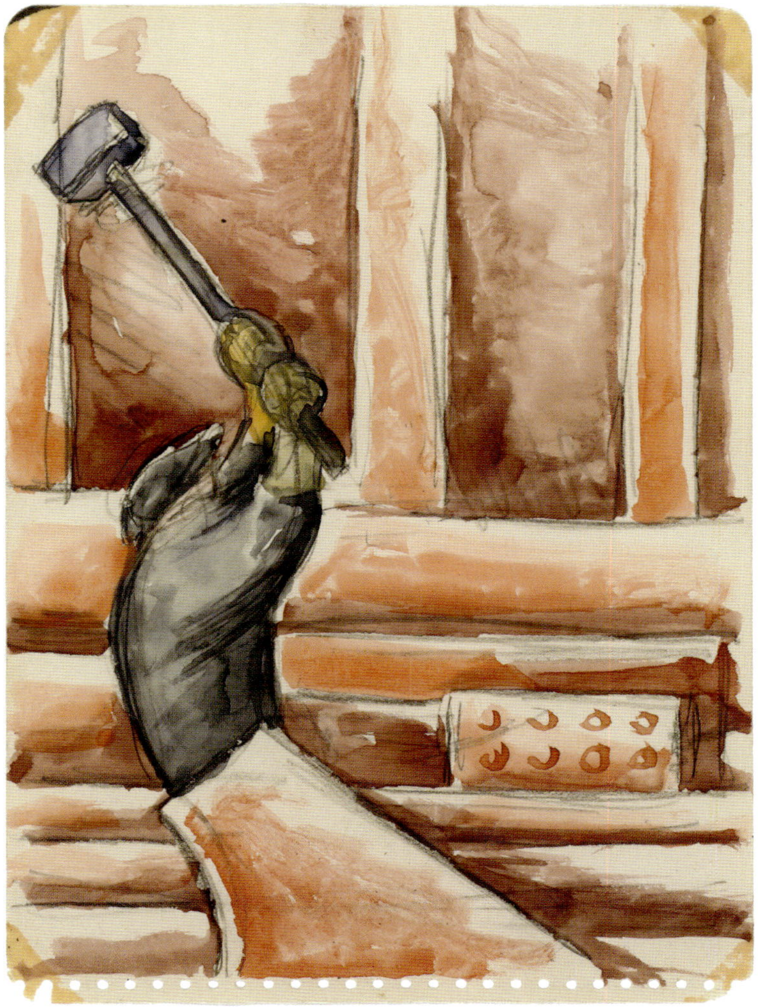

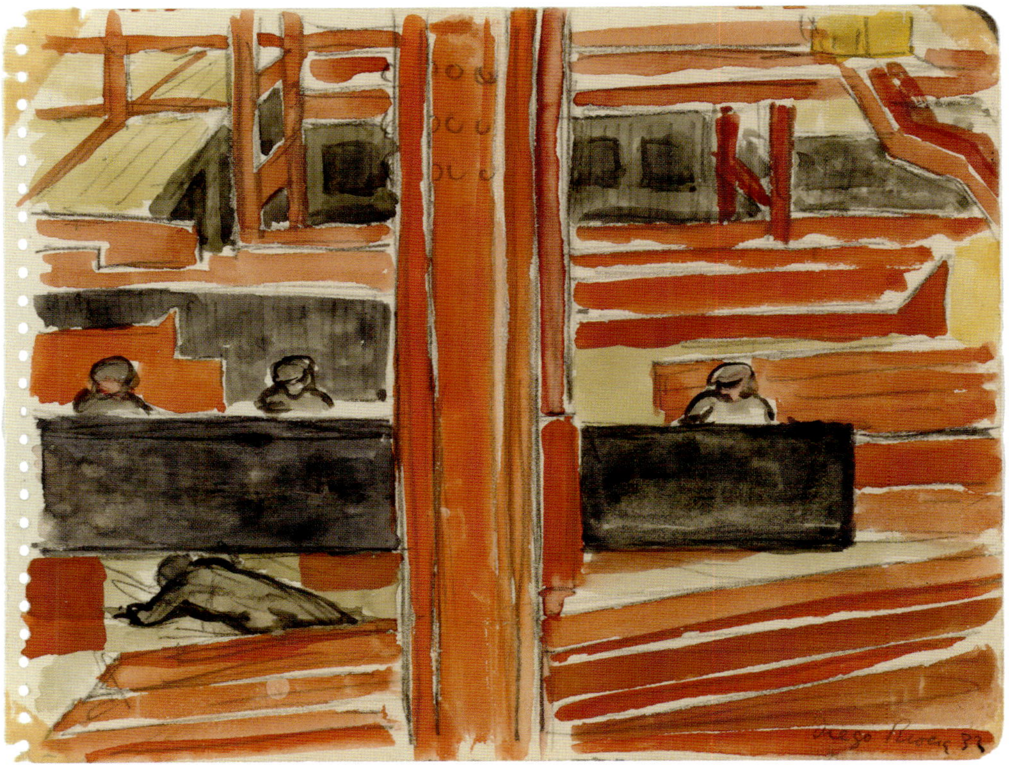

Images of workers among steel girders, covered in bright red primer, probably at Rockefeller Center, are featured in four drawings in the Brillembourg Capriles Collection (1931–32) (plates 3–6). They were all apparently taken from a small sketchbook, measuring around five by seven inches; several other drawings from the same sketchbook are known.[9] The images resonate with those in his more famous Moscow sketchbook of 1927, acquired by Abby Aldrich Rockefeller and later donated to the Museum of Modern Art.[10] This is true partly because of his use of red as a powerful framing device and political referent: banners in Moscow, steel in New York. But they also have the same careful compositions and controlled use of watercolor: in both cases, and despite the candid nature of the scenes, this indicates that they were probably not finished on site.

On most sheets, workers are observed from a distance (perhaps reflecting safety barriers), almost lost amid the girders, wood planks used for scaffolding, dark black beams not yet covered in primer, and the yellow supports of construction cranes. The faceless men wearing overalls and cloth caps generally work alone, painting girders, engaged in a foundry, or swinging sledgehammers. One drawing in the Brillembourg Capriles Collection highlights the elegant backward S-curve of a worker's body, but most of the images are composed of rigid horizontals and verticals, reflecting the building process. In fact, each of these drawings seems to be a meditation on line and structure, apparent in the rigorous formal qualities of each scene as well as in the subject itself. The multiple vantage points seen simultaneously in a Cubist painting like *Still Life with Lemons* are here split apart and analyzed separately. Rivera might not have known how or when he would use the drawings, but he was certainly fascinated by the girder as a metaphor of the modern age, and symbolic of social, economic, and political progress, especially in the Americas.

A Rather Conservative Portrait

If Rivera was skilled at representing anonymous workers—whether in U.S. cities or the Mexican countryside—he was equally a master at creating formal portraits; and here, too, careful attention to outline and compositional balance are evident. Early in his career, Rivera's portraits tended to be of artists and intellectuals who were friends, but with his fame well established by the 1930s, wealthy and sophisticated clients, local and international, increasingly sought his services. Apart from those depicting leading members of Mexico's bourgeoisie, his images form a Who's Who of prominent visitors, from cosmetics magnate Helena Rubinstein to Brazilian poet Adalgisa Nery, wife of the ambassador; all were usually depicted in his studio. Of course, such works, usually paid for by rich patrons, might seem to contradict Rivera's commitment to the working class evident in his public murals. But Rivera—like Kahlo—was no ascetic, and he enjoyed his own fame and the fame of those around him. These portraits also forged bonds of friendship, cultivated relationships with leading collectors, and helped him finance ongoing projects, like the construction of Anahuacalli, a neo-Aztec museum to house his collection of Pre-Hispanic art, begun in the mid-1940s.

An elegant charcoal drawing of 1938 (plate 7) by Rivera in the Brillembourg Capriles Collection—perhaps a preparatory sketch for a never-completed painting—shows the U.S. writer Alice-Leone Moats (1908–1989). Rendered with an economy of line, Moats, wearing a simple dress, rests on an angle and leans with a slight curve against what appears to be a three-legged stool, her hands on her barely formed lap. Not much can be said about the composition except that the sitter appears modern, with none of the local references to Mexico—like Aztec sculptures or the traditional wooden chairs called *equipales*—frequent in his portraits. Rivera seems to have liked the pose, for it appears in four other portraits of the previous year in which each sitter (all are in chairs) is shown on a diagonal with hands on lap.[11]

Moats was a U.S. journalist and author, born in Mexico to wealthy and socially prominent parents; at a time when progressive sitters appeared in Modernist close-ups or wearing nationalist costume, she was photographed by Edward Weston during his residence in

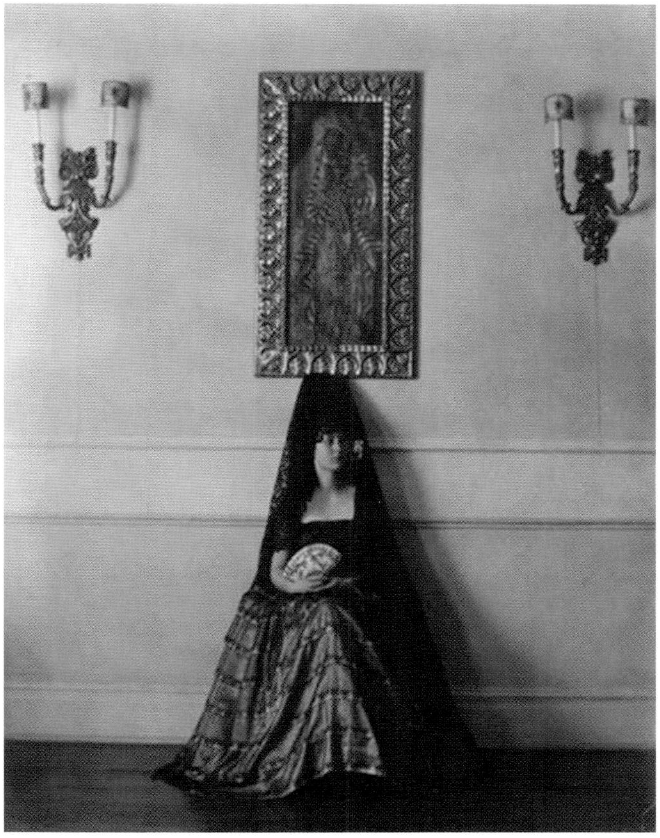

FIG. 4

Mexico City in 1924 in the guise of a Spanish señorita (fig. 4). By the time of Rivera's drawing, she was mainly known for a humorous and bestselling book of etiquette titled *No Nice Girl Swears* (Knopf, 1933); Moats later became a widely-read war correspondent and wrote two books about Mexico.[12] That she and her mother, Leone, whose portrait Rivera had painted in 1929, were both politically conservative seems not to have affected what appears to have been a rather close friendship with the artist, in part commemorated by this drawing.

The Screen-Tested *Tehuana*

Far more spectacular is another portrait by Rivera in the Brillembourg Capriles Collection, an almost life-size depiction of a traditionally dressed woman, dated 1950 (plate 8). Though conservative in formal terms, the work emblematizes the idealized and overtly Mexican imagery frequently seen in exhibitions of Mexican art and sought after by collectors. At first glance, the painting seems to be a simple, naturalistic, and even seductive rendition of an indigenous woman in the countryside, but in every aspect it is an artificial construction, as fictional as the films in which the subject, actress Columba Domínguez, starred at the time. In fact, the alternate titles remind us that the painting should be interpreted both in the context of *tehuana* imagery—a vast and complex field of representation in the history of Mexican art—as well as with regard to Rivera's command of portraiture.

Like a runway model, Domínguez walks barefoot down an earthy slope that seems to suddenly fall away, or perhaps reaches the base of a wall: indeed, the sketchily rendered tropical vegetation resembles the backdrop in a photographer's studio. Her hair is braided with red yarn and tied up in typical indigenous fashion, and she wears the loose red *huipilili* (or "little *huipil*"), richly embroidered in gold, that remains common on the Isthmus of Tehuantepec; the shellfish-dyed purple cotton skirt with soft yellow stripes, however, was rapidly disappearing by the 1940s, and connoisseurs of indigenous costume would have appreciated its rarity when this picture was made.[13]

Domínguez holds a wooden gourd (*guaje*) in the palm of her raised left hand; its elegant rounded forms clearly evoke her own, underscoring themes of sensuality and fertility and reminding us of that ancient topos of woman as vessel. A text inscribed on the leaf at the lower left gives the title and date of the work, a quaint device reminiscent of the scraps of text-bearing papers in portraits of more formally dressed subjects. As a rendition of a tehuana, the painting falls squarely within a visual tradition first set in place by Claudio Linati in his 1828 lithographic album *Costumes civils, militaires et réligieux du Mexique*, where a young and sexualized tehuana stands barefoot in a natural setting. Since then, the tehuana has been invented and reinvented as authentic, tropical, and exotic, her matriarchal qualities exaggerated and her life wrapped in myth by travelers as well as residents of urban Mexico, from Saturnino Herrán to Sergei Eisenstein.[14]

In Rivera's case, though he might have been familiar with previous renditions, specific interest in tehuanas began in December 1922,

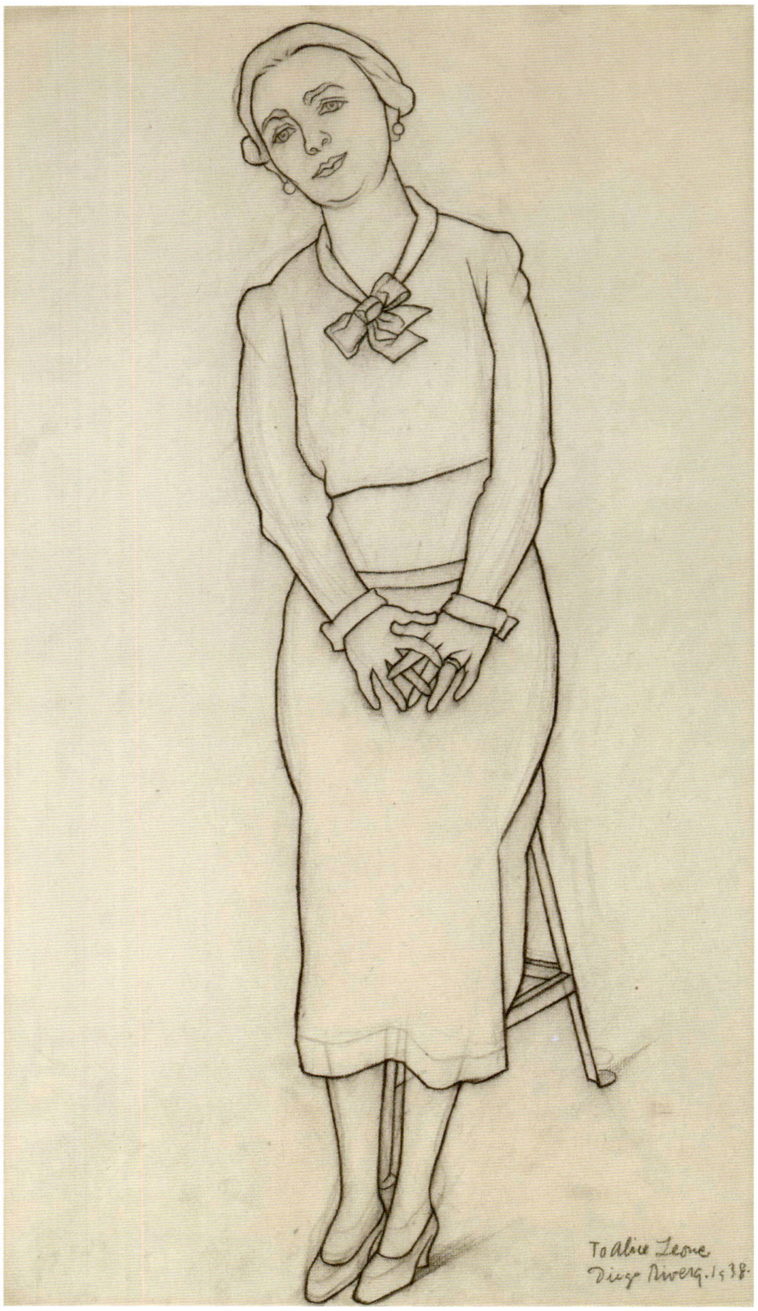

PLATE 7

Diego Rivera • *Retrato de Alice-Leone Moats* [Portrait of Alice-Leone Moats], 1938

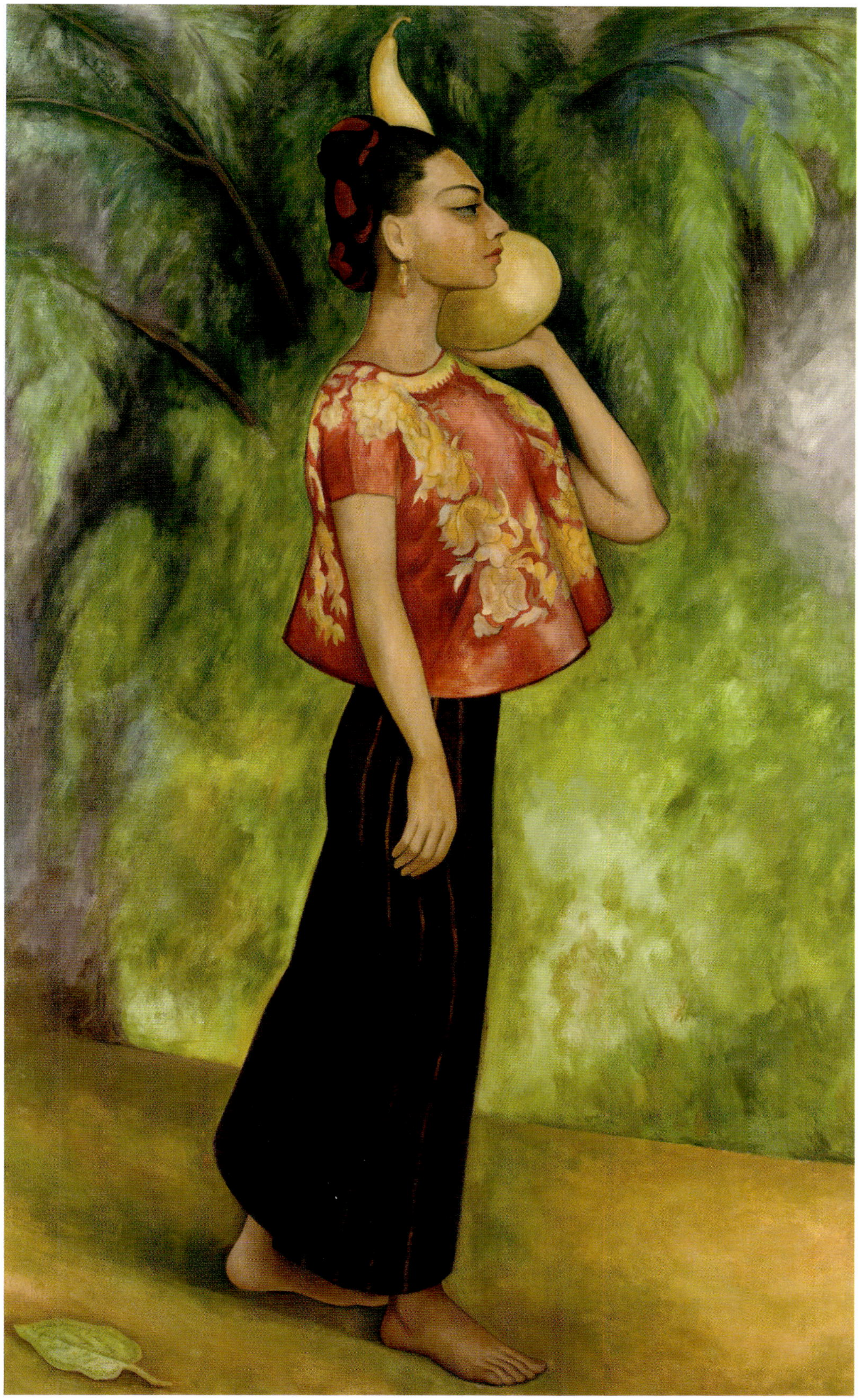

PLATE 8

Diego Rivera • *Retrato de Columba Domínguez* o *Tehuana* [Portrait of Columba Domínguez or Woman from Tehuantepec], 1950 when José Vasconcelos, his patron in the Education Ministry, funded the artist's trip to Tehuantepec, hoping that the Mexican might rediscover (or perhaps invent) his nationalist roots. Rivera's first images of tehuanas, both in murals and easel paintings, date to 1923, and they soon became an iconographic constant in his work, appearing as well in book illustrations and costume designs. Rivera was not the first to pose non-indigenous women in tehuana costumes (Herrán showed his wife wearing a ceremonial huipil in 1915), but he did so by the late 1920s, well before Kahlo adopted the convention. Unlike almost all of these previous works, including Rivera's *Portrait of Cuca Bustamante* (1946) (fig. 5), the 1950 painting shows the tightly wrapped skirt instead of the more common loose flowing ones, surely to exaggerate the model's slender form.

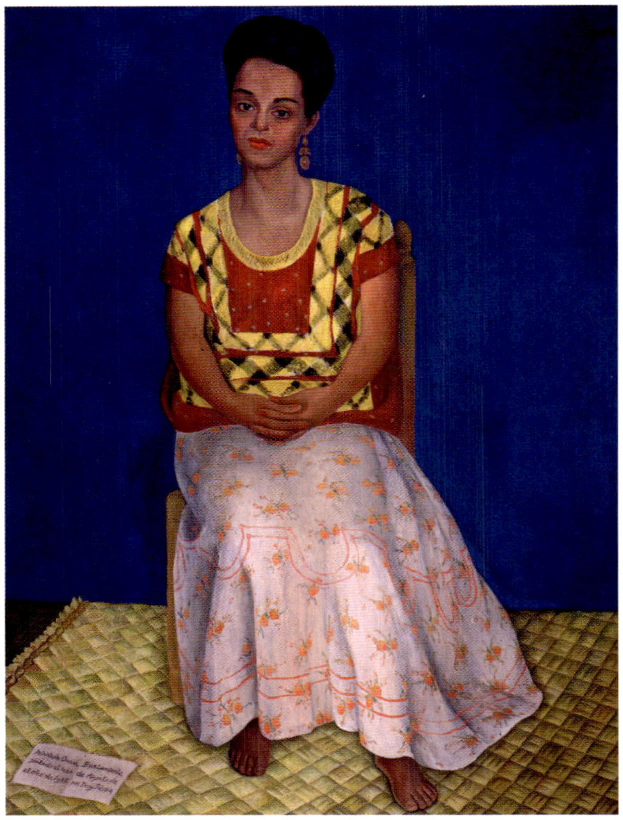

FIG. 5

The portrait is also one of several Rivera painted of sexy actresses in the 1940s, including Paulette Goddard (1940), Linda Christian (1947), María Félix (1948), and Silvia Pinal (1948), although the present image is the least eroticized of the group. Columba Domínguez was born in 1929 in Guaymas, Sonora, and appeared in a rapid-fire succession of films by Emilio "El Indio" Fernández, including "La Perla" (1947), "Río Escondido" (1948), and "Pueblerina" (1949); she married the director in 1949. A studio card for "Pueblerina" includes a portrait of Domínguez draped in a *rebozo* (shawl) painted by the Mexican artist Miguel Covarrubias (fig. 6). None of these films deal with Tehuantepec, however, and it is unclear whether the portrait was a commission or meant for sale.

Like many of Fernández's movies, Rivera's painting is a nostalgic idealization of rural culture at a time of rapid urbanization and post-war industrialization, engineered during the administration of Miguel Alemán (1946–1952). Mexican elites were particularly drawn to such images, which seemed to confirm national glory even as the country was opened to greater foreign investment: it is no coincidence that the same year of this painting, Rivera, Siqueiros, Orozco, and Tamayo represented Mexico at the 1950 Venice Biennale to much critical acclaim, affirming the continuing ascendancy of the post-revolutionary "Mexican School" even as varied forms of Abstract Expressionism and Informalism were triumphing in New York and Paris, even as the first skyscrapers and Modernist housing blocks were rising in Mexico City. More troubling, perhaps, is that this "perfect Indian" was not actually from Tehuantepec: like Kahlo, Dolores Olmedo, and many other sophisticated urban women whose ethnicity was primarily European, Domínguez is here playing a role, performing an essentialized indigenousness cleansed of social and racial injustice: her screen-tested beauty all too neatly obscures the difficult lives faced by actual indigenous citizens across the country.[15]

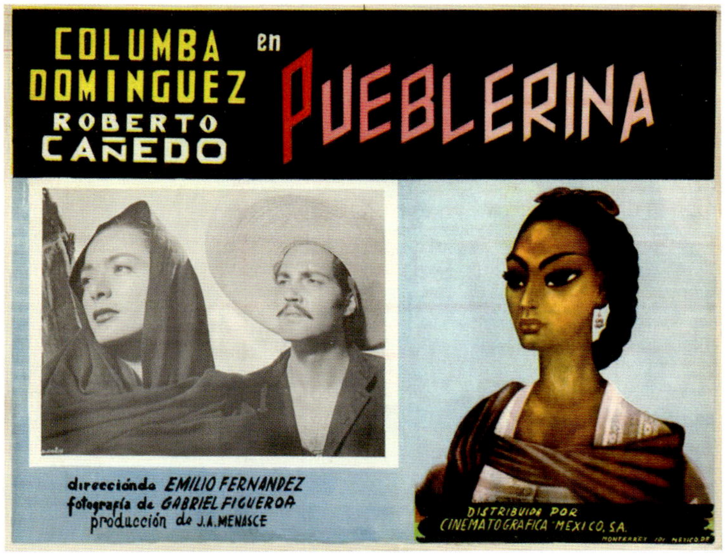

FIG. 6

ILLUSTRATIONS IN TEXT

FIGURE 1
Diego Rivera
Still Life with Gray Bowl, 1916
Oil on canvas
31 1/4 x 25 1/8 inches (79.4 x 63.8 cm)
Lyndon Baines Johnson Presidential Library and Museum, Austin, Texas, Gift from His Excellency Gustavo Díaz Ordaz, President of the United Mexican States

FIGURE 2
Diego Rivera
Still Life with Bread Knife, 1915
Oil on canvas
19 5/8 x 23 1/2 inches (49.9 x 59.7 cm)
Columbus Museum of Art, Ohio, Gift of Ferdinand Howald, 1931.089

FIGURE 3
Berenice Abbott
Rockefeller Center under Construction, c. 1930
Gelatin silver print
13 1/4 x 10 3/8 inches (33.7 x 26.4 cm)
Davis Museum, Wellesley College, Gift of Lucienne and Claude Bloch, M.D. (Lucienne Schupf, Class of 1959) 1997.39.

FIGURE 4
Edward Weston
Alice-Leone Moats, 1924
Platinum print
9 1/2 x 7 1/2 inches (24.1 x 19.1 cm)
Center for Creative Photography, Arizona

FIGURE 5
Diego Rivera
Portrait of Cuca Bustamante, 1946
Oil on canvas
62 1/4 x 48 1/4 inches (158 x 122.5 cm)
Museo de Arte Moderno, Mexico City

FIGURE 6
Studio card for the film "Pueblerina" (1949) with portrait of Columba Domínguez by Miguel Covarrubias (1904–1957)
16 x 12.2 inches (40.8 x 31 cm)
Collection of James Oles

NOTES

1
See Ramón Favela, *Diego Rivera: The Cubist Years* (Phoenix: Phoenix Art Museum, 1984), 121–43. See also Olivier Debroise, *Diego de Montparnasse* (Mexico City: Fondo de Cultura Económica, 1985) and Sylvia Navarrete, et al., *Diego Rivera: The Cubist Portraits, 1913–1917* (Dallas: Meadows Museum, Southern Methodist University, 2009).

2
Amélie was the daughter of Arthur Hermann, founder of the Hermann Publishing House in Paris, which Freyman ran after 1927. See Oswald Goetz, "Preface," in *Diego Rivera: Twenty-Seven Paintings of the Period 1913–1917* (New York: Parke-Bernet Galleries, 1959), n.p.; further information at http://www.editions-hermann.fr/en_presentation.php.

3
"Fábula de la piedra," *Vuelta* (April 1979), 48.

4
Angelina Beloff, *Memorias* (Mexico City: UNAM, 1986), 30–31.

5
Ibid. Ortega (see note 6) implies that he had been "first secretary of the Mexican legation," and Inés Amor (see note 10) calls him "consul," but most sources refer to him as cultural attaché.

6
Information from the sales catalogue (see note 2); [Febronio] Ortega, "Enrique Freyman, el mexicano de 'La Rotonda,'" *El Universal Ilustrado*, no. 552 (December 8, 1927). In January 1960, Parke-Bernet sold Freyman's collection of Pre-Columbian and other art.

7
Jorge Alberto Manrique and Teresa del Conde, *Una mujer en el arte mexicano: Memorias de Inés Amor* (Mexico City: UNAM, 1987), 97–98.

8
Anna Indych-López, notes to *Pneumatic Drilling*, in Leah Dickerman and Anna Indych-López, *Diego Rivera: Murals for the Museum of Modern Art* (New York: The Museum of Modern Art, 2011), 101.

9
Seventeen drawings have been located. Eleven are illustrated in Luis-Martin Lozano and Juan Rafael Coronel Rivera, *Diego Rivera: The Complete Murals* (Cologne: Taschen, 2005), 302–7; 314.

10
Sometimes called the May Day sketchbook, but actually done in November 1927. See Leah Dickerman, "Leftist Circuits," in *Diego Rivera: Murals for the Museum of Modern Art*, n17, 45. This sketchbook includes forty-five drawings, perhaps an indication that there are more images of construction sites yet to be discovered.

11
Illustrated in *Diego Rivera: Catálogo general de obra de caballete* (Mexico City: Conaculta/INBA, 1989), 181.

12
Alice Leone Moats and Leone B. Moats, *Off to Mexico* (New York: Scribner's, 1940), and Alice-Leone Moats, *A Violent Innocence* (New York: Duell, Sloane and Pearce, 1951).

13
Donald and Dorothy Cordry, *Mexican Indian Costumes* (Austin: The University of Texas Press, 1968), 101, 273–75.

14
This vast subject was first surveyed in *Del istmo y sus mujeres: Tehuanas en el arte mexicano* (Mexico City: Museo Nacional de Arte, 1992).

15
For a rich discussion of these issues, see Adriana Zavala, *Becoming Modern, Becoming Tradition: Women, Gender, and Representation in Mexican Art* (University Park: Penn State University Press, 2010), especially chapter six.

James Oles

DAVID ALFARO SIQUEIROS

MIDCENTURY CHALLENGES

IN DAVID ALFARO SIQUEIROS'S *The Challenge* (plate 9), a young man, clearly identified as a *campesino* by his broad straw sombrero and shirt made from *manta*, a cheap white cloth, is braced by a woman wearing bright red who stands directly behind him. Perhaps his mother, she anxiously presses her hands onto his shoulders. Several other women, some wearing *rebozos* and two carrying babies, occupy the background: all look to some unidentified force to the right, perhaps a threat, judging from the title. Along with details of costume and physiognomy, Siqueiros localized the subjects by subtly incorporating the colors of the Mexican flag into the composition. And, as was rather common in Mexican post-Revolutionary painting, references to Christian iconography are also present, most notably in the man's halo-like sombrero, a detail reminiscent of Diego Rivera's *The Embrace of the Peasant and the Worker* (1923), a fresco panel in the headquarters building of the Ministry of Public Education.

The brilliant colors and powerful brushstrokes provide evidence of the artist's masterful use of pyroxilin, a commercial enamel paint that Siqueiros used almost exclusively after the mid-1930s. Like Masonite and plywood, which the artist privileged for supports, pyroxilin was an industrial material Siqueiros theorized as appropriate to the creation of modern proletarian art, not only because it was itself inherently modern, but also because it was manufactured by industrial workers and employed in factory production lines. The subjects here, however, while not anachronistic, are also not members of the urban proletariat; instead, they are timeless representatives of a rural world that was frequently idealized in Rivera's work but was often shown as harsh and troubled by Siqueiros.

The monumentality of the figures and seriousness of the theme more closely resonate with the dark paintings on burlap Siqueiros completed in the remote colonial town of Taxco in the early 1930s, including the rebozo-clad woman featured in *The Yell* (1931; San Antonio Museum of Art), who also looks off to the right. The centralized and balanced pyramidal composition, however, most directly echoes *The Patroness* (1939; private collection, U.S.), a work that similarly emphasizes the noble strength of the rural peasantry (fig. 1).[1] Although serious rather than optimistic in tone, compared to other easel paintings of the 1940s and early 1950s, *The Challenge* is neither brutal nor antagonistic, and may have been intended to appeal to collectors less tolerant of radical pamphleteering than Dr. Alvar Carrillo Gil, Siqueiros's leading patron at the time, and more interested in a quintessentially "Mexican" picture.[2]

If it originated from the artist, the title of the painting is ambiguous: the "challenge" might refer to some particular if unseen political event, despite the fact that the contemporary presidency of Adolfo Ruiz Cortines (1952–1958) was one of relative stability, with few serious confrontations with workers and peasants. Perhaps these traditional figures, whether symbolizing rural workers or Mexicans in general, are instead facing the broader "challenge" of rapid economic and social transformations, as the pro-development policies of the

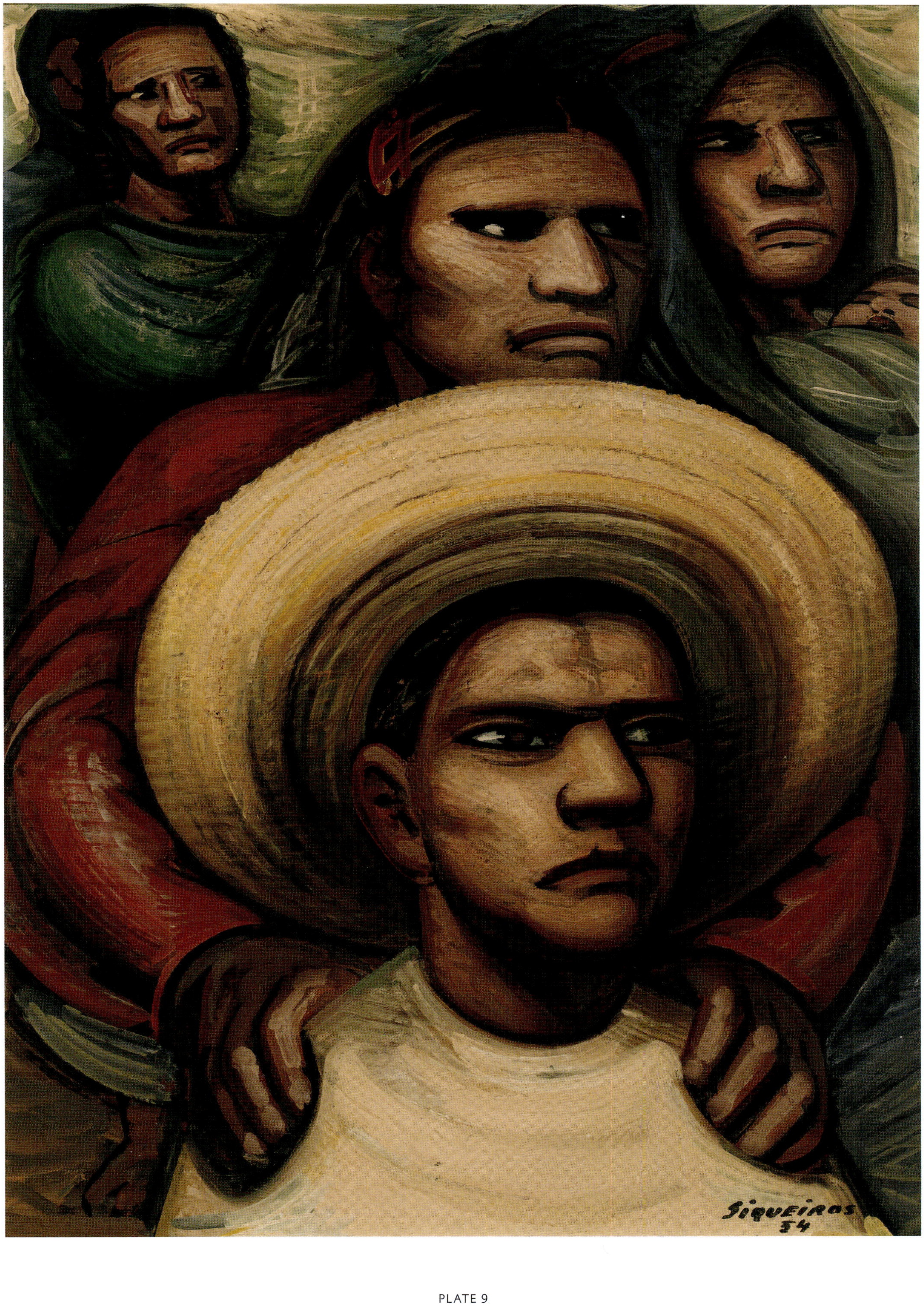

PLATE 9

David Alfaro Siqueiros • *El reto* [The Challenge], 1954

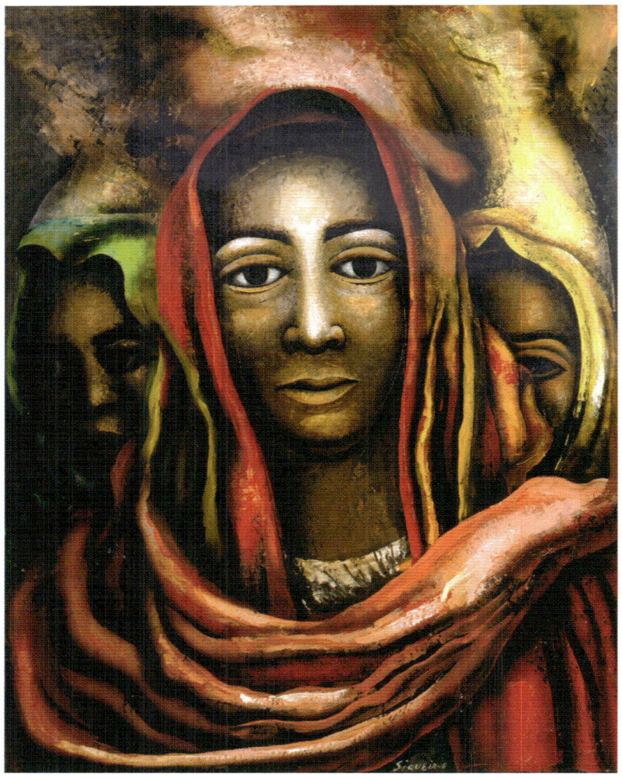

FIG. 1

previous administration continued through the 1950s, encouraging greater industrialization and urbanization.

The Challenge was painted during an especially successful period for the artist. In 1950, Mexico was officially invited to participate in the Venice Biennale for the first time. Although the organizers originally requested works by Rufino Tamayo alone, the invitation was soon extended to include the three famous post-Revolutionary muralists, José Clemente Orozco, Rivera, and Siqueiros. The show, curated by Fernando Gamboa, then sub-director of the Instituto Nacional de Bellas Artes (INBA), included fifteen works by each artist. Soon after the June opening, Siqueiros was notified that he had won the prize for best foreign painter (Henri Matisse won the overall first prize). Olivier Debroise has suggested that the decision of the international jury may have been shaped, in part, by French opposition to the ascendancy of the New York School, but it might also—as Rivera sensed at the time—be due to the content of Siqueiros's pictures, several of which, like *Echo of a Scream* (1937; The Museum of Modern Art) and *The Sob* (1939; The Museum of Modern Art), were anti-war allegories which must have resonated with European audiences in the post-war period.[3]

This award triggered debates in the press between Siqueiros and Tamayo, but, for the moment, it seemed sufficient evidence that social realism—or at least Siqueiros's version of it—remained a viable option for artists even as abstraction gained traction across Europe and the United States.[4] As Rivera put it, this was an "important victory over 'artpurism' in precisely what until now has been the shrine of this tendency."[5] Although Siqueiros dismissed Tamayo for his proximity to the School of Paris, he strategically took the prize in the name of "our pictorial movement," and justified his selection over his two colleagues as the result of Gamboa's poor selection of the latter artists' works.[6] *The Challenge* thus takes up, at least conceptually, the "challenge" of abstraction, visually asserting the continuing vitality of figurative and localized subject matter, what Siqueiros referred to as Neo-Realism or a "new humanist art."[7]

By the time this picture was completed, Siqueiros had surmounted numerous challenges, aesthetic and political, at home as well as abroad, emerging from the shadows of his 1940 assassination attempt on Leon Trotsky as the most dynamic muralist in Mexico—Orozco, of course, had died in 1949, and Rivera had entered a rather decadent phase, even if he was painting in the prestigious venue of the National Palace. Siqueiros was free enough from political controversy—despite fears of arrest after a 1952 May Day rally—to actually dedicate himself to muralism. In just the first half of the decade, he completed murals in the Palacio de Bellas Artes (1951–53); the Instituto Politécnico Nacional (1952); the new Ciudad Universitaria (1952–54); Fábricas Automex (1953); and Hospital No. 1 of the Instituto Mexicano de Seguro Social (1952–54).

In fact, the composition of *The Challenge* seems formally related to the latter two murals. Both also show groups of figures looking toward the future, though in the murals, they surge forward with unbridled optimism. The slightly more anxious stares of the monumental figures in *The Challenge* may reflect the fact that in working on an easel painting rather than a public, state-funded project Siqueiros did not have to take such a positive or conciliatory approach. But it is also a question of the figures' relative identities. The students in *The*

People for the University, The University for the People, on the exterior of the university's rectory, and the mothers and workers in *For the Complete Social Security of All Mexicans,* at the IMSS (fig. 2), are identified not as agricultural workers but rather as modern members of the urban middle class, who by the 1950s were emerging as the principal beneficiaries of state policy.

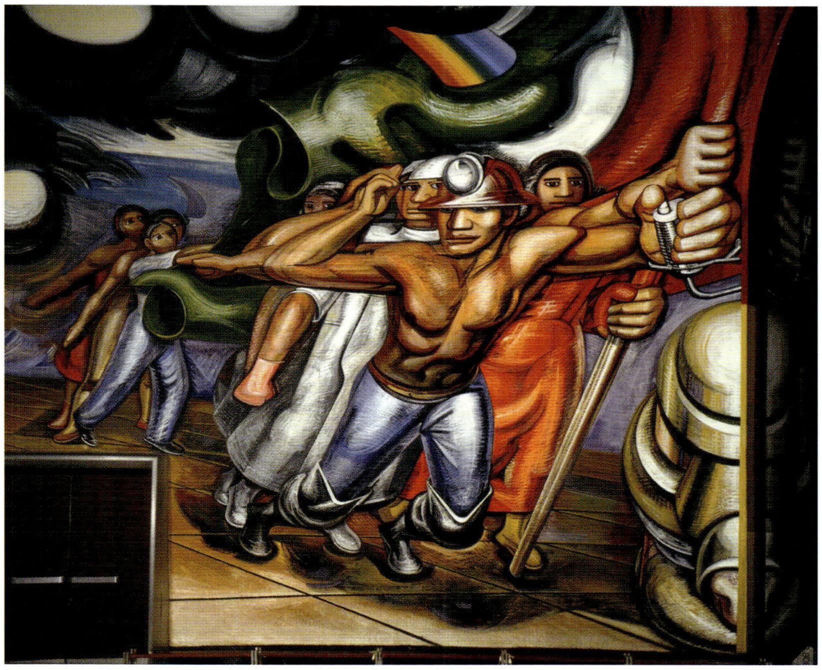

FIG. 2

ILLUSTRATIONS IN TEXT

FIGURE 1
David Alfaro Siqueiros
La patrona [The Patroness], 1939
Pyroxylin on composition board
29 1/2 x 24 inches (74.9 x 60.9 cm)
Private collection

FIGURE 2
David Alfaro Siqueiros
For the Complete Social Security of All Mexicans (detail), 1953–56
Vinylite and pyroxyline
310 square meters
Hospital de La Raza, Mexico City

NOTES

1
For more on these works, see James Oles, "Catalogue," in Olivier Debroise, ed., *Portrait of a Decade: David Alfaro Siqueiros, 1930–1940* (Mexico City: Museo Nacional de Arte, 1994), 97–197.

2
See *Siqueiros en la colección del Museo Carrillo Gil* (Mexico City: Museo de Arte Contemporáneo Alvar y Carmen T. de Carrillo Gil/INBA, 1996). For example, the doctor had no trouble buying paintings that showed the lynching of African Americans (*Cain in the United States*, 1947) or a Communist rally (*May Day Parade*, 1952).

3
Debroise, "Reaching Out to the Audience: Tamayo and the Debate on Modernism," in Diana C. du Pont, ed., *Tamayo: A Modern Icon Revisited* (Santa Barbara: Santa Barbara Museum of Art, 2007), 384; Diego Rivera, editorial in *El Nacional* (June 18, 1950), cited in Philip Stein, *Siqueiros: His Life and Works* (New York: International Publishers, 1994), 187.

4
For more on the debates launched in Mexico, see Víctor Alba, "Tamayo habla a *Hoy* desde Paris!," *Hoy*, no. 723 (December 30, 1950): 24–25 [DIGITAL ARCHIVE 758996]; and Rufino Tamayo, "Gangsterismo en la pintura Mexicana," *Excélsior* (November 14, 1950): 7. [DIGITAL ARCHIVE 758210]

5
Rivera (1950).

6
"México triunfa en Venecia," *Tiempo: Semanario de la vida y la verdad* (Mexico City) 17, no. 426 (June 30, 1950): 24–27. [DIGITAL ARCHIVE 759059]

7
See David Alfaro Siqueiros, "Tesis general del Centro de Arte Realista Moderno, para liquidar la crisis actual del arte en México ... y fuera de México," in *No hay más ruta que la nuestra: Importancia nacional e internacional de la pintura mexicana moderna*, 2d ed. (Mexico City: 1978). The first edition of this text was published in 1945.

Michael Wellen

BEYOND BOREDOM

ARMANDO REVERÓN'S PORTRAITS OF WOMEN

IN 1922, TERESA DE LA PARRA spent several months in the beach town of Macuto writing her first novel, *Iphigenia: The Diary of a Young Lady Who Wrote Because She Was Bored*. The work became a sensation when it was published two years later for boldly describing a modern woman's frustration with conservative life in Venezuela. Armando Reverón was also in Macuto in the 1920s, and his paintings capturing the austere beauty of the coastal landscape would make the small town famous. His home and studio—what Reverón and his partner Juanita Ríos called "El Castillete" (Little Castle) and where the couple received many visitors wishing to see the artist at work and perhaps to have their portraits made—became a landmark by the 1930s. There is no evidence that Parra and Reverón ever met, but their residence in Macuto in the same period suggests that the town attracted and inspired artists and intellectuals. Furthermore, underlying similarities in the work of the writer and the artist confirm that many of those drawn to Macuto in the 1920s were interested in challenging tradition. Parra and Reverón both made work that can be read as being in opposition to societal conventions. Pursuing independent yet parallel paths on the coast of Venezuela, both concentrated on creating complex images of women.[1]

The paintings by Reverón in the Brillembourg Capriles Collection of Latin American Art present three such depictions of women. The earliest, *Figura bajo un uvero* [Figure under a Sea-Grape Tree] (1920) (plate 10), was painted before the artist settled permanently in Macuto in 1921. It is a masterpiece of Reverón's "Blue Period" (1919–25) and attests to the early inspiration he found in the light and landscape of the Caribbean coast.[2] The painting is one of about twenty he made that year. It is believed to be a portrait of the wife of Luis Enrique Yanes, one of the first to collect Reverón's work in that period. Rather than capturing a likeness, the painting shows Reverón's interest in developing a *sui generis* approach to the representation of landscape based on the exploitation of light, shadow, thick surfaces, and textural effects. Thickly applied white paint represents the crashing waves and spume along the beach; the paint projects from the canvas, giving a heightened sense of the water's presence. The other two works, *Retrato de mujer* [Portrait of a Woman] and *Figura reclinada* [Reclining Figure] (alternately titled *Mujer con mantilla acostada* [Reclining Woman with Mantilla], both done on paper around 1934, are part of a group of about fifty he made toward the end of his "White Period" (1925–37). These works on paper have often been ignored by scholars because they appear to lack the subtlety and creative depth of his nearly monochromatic canvas paintings of the period. Painted relatively quickly on cheap paper and presumably for tourists or other visitors to "El Castillete," they lead us to wonder about the identity of the depicted women. They may be locals from Reverón's circle of friends, or they may be worldly travelers like the "bored woman" who serves as protagonist in Parra's novel. Without clear referents, they seem to be muses, unidentifiable figures whose "timeless faces and dramatically stylized bodies," in the words of art historian Juan Calzadilla, look like "no one from [Reverón's] daily world."[3]

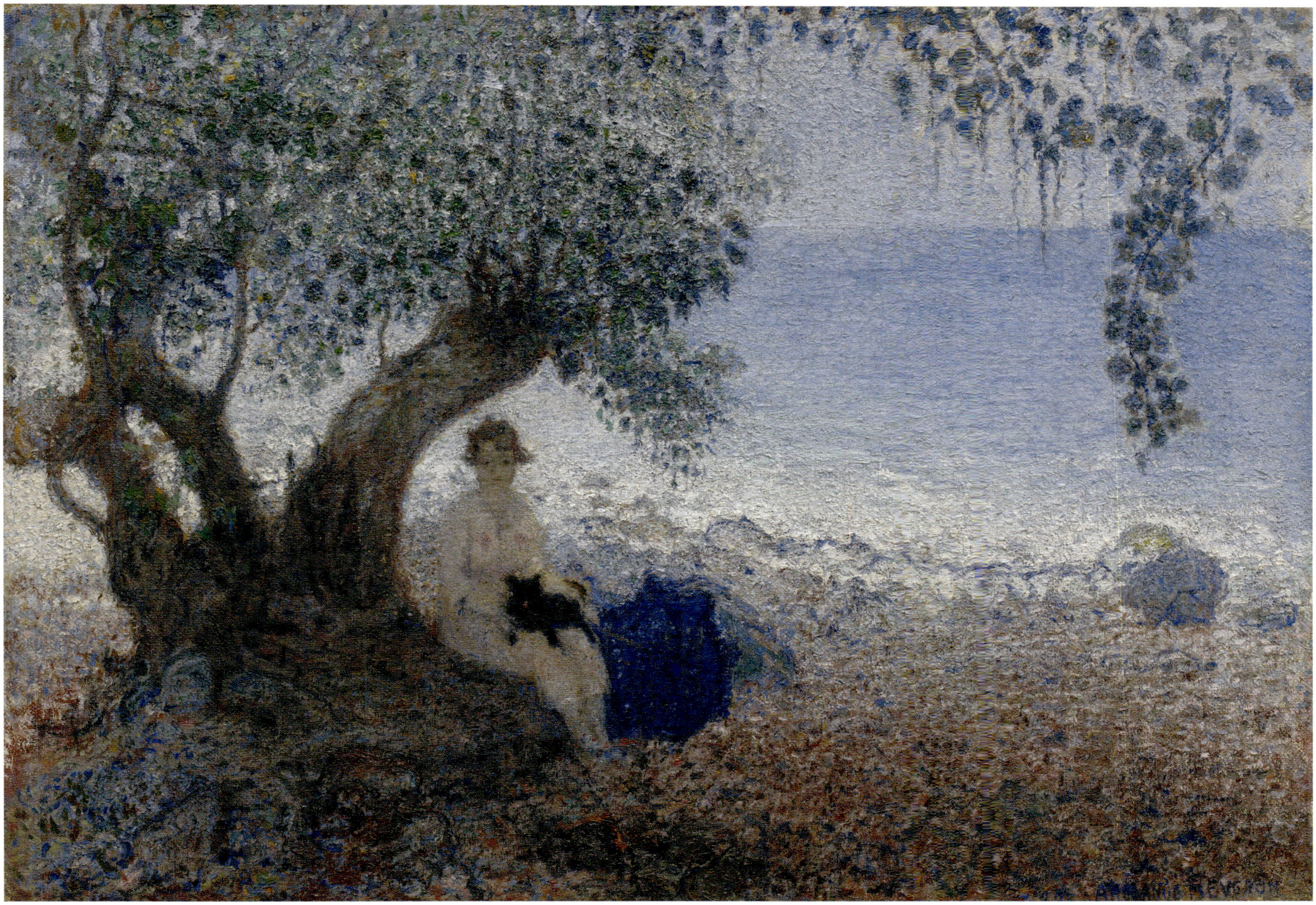

PLATE 10

Armando Reverón • *Figura bajo un uvero* [Figure under a Sea-Grape Tree], 1920

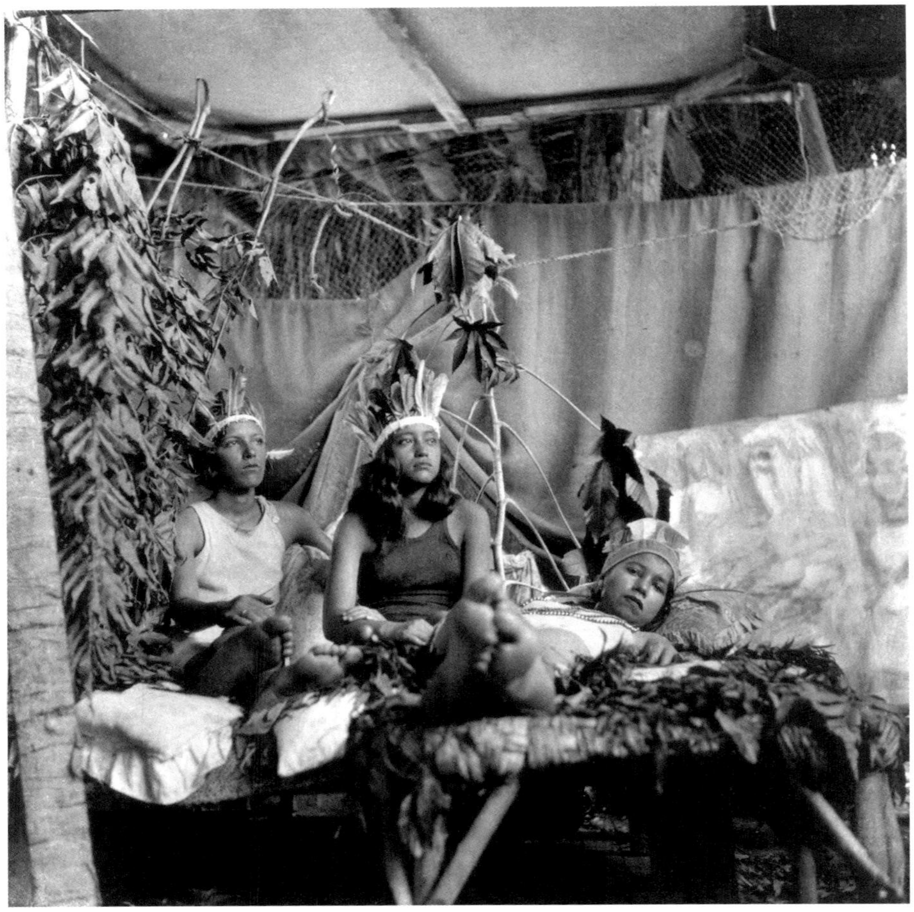

FIG. 1

Yet there is another way of viewing these portraits. If these are in fact upper-class, "bored" women or friends from Reverón's circle, it is possible that in the moment of their making, Reverón's portraits provided a temporary release for his female sitters from prescribed societal roles. This liberating potential might be described in relation to "carnival." Literary scholar Mikhail Bakhtin writes about the notion of carnival, noting that it "celebrated temporary liberation from the prevailing truth and the established order; it marked the suspension of all hierarchical rank, privileges, norms, and prohibitions."[4] Through the protagonist of Parra's novel, María Eugenia Alonso, one sees that expectations of decorum and manners prevented women from participating fully in their own lives. Despite her wishes, Alonso must be chaperoned in public; in conversation she cannot say what she actually believes; she must hold back laughter and anger at the absurd and racist statements of her aunts and uncles; she cannot wear her French-made clothing without being criticized for indecency; and, most detrimental of all, she suddenly finds herself penniless because she holds no rights to inherit and manage her father's estate.

Such restrictions stand in contrast to the circumstances of the carnival and to its costumes and humor, which provide the opportunity to dress and behave differently. For Reverón's sitters, the walls of "El Castillete" demarcated a carnivalesque setting that broke with the expected decorum of daily life. Visitors from the 1930s onward described the minimal clothing worn by Reverón and Ríos, the menagerie of animals that lived on the property, the rustic buildings and furniture made by the artist, and the appearance of marionettes and dolls to whom the artist ascribed names and distinct personalities. Reverón and Ríos—she, it is worth noting, first met him at a carnival celebration in La Guaira in 1918—were known for encouraging their guests to dress in costumes, offering them feathers and loincloths to appear like a lost tribe of natives, or providing black veils like those worn by Spanish *majas* (fig. 1).[5] Visitors also remarked on the artist's unusual painting technique, which involved an elaborate ritual featuring a mysterious set of gestures and quiet utterances during which Reverón seemed entranced.

In 1934, photographer and art critic Alfredo Boulton famously documented one of these sessions when Reverón painted a portrait of Luisa Phelps, Boulton's sister-in-law.[6] The photographs show the encounter between artist and sitter as a dynamic one. Phelps is not simply modeling for the artist; she too is intently involved in watching Reverón as he performs, clowns around, and earnestly engages in a shamanistic mode of painting (fig. 2). Bahktin writes, "in fact, carnival does not know footlights, in the sense that it does not acknowledge any distinction between actors and spectators." Carnival, more than a spectacle, is a participatory event. Posing for Reverón likewise meant a temporary disintegration of the roles of actor and spectator.

These works not only document a carnivalesque interaction between Reverón and his subjects, they retain something of the carnival's suggestiveness, its playful ambiguity, social permissiveness, and subversive attitude. *Figura bajo un uvero* is an unusual portrait that seems more like an allegorical image of a sea nymph or siren seated by the rocky shore. The central figure holds a small dog on her lap and rests a blue umbrella at her side. She wears a rosy and somewhat translucent beach robe, its sleeves covering three quarters of her arms. Yet, through his thick application of paint, Reverón deliberately makes the scene ambiguous. The dark blue of the umbrella can be confused with a rock. And, despite her robe, the woman appears nude; even the pink coloring at her chest—likely an indication of her bathing suit underneath her robe—is suggestive of nipples. Speckles of blue along the branches and ground represent ripe grapes, an allusion to fecundity. Reverón's painting transforms a woman resting after a leisurely stroll on the beach into a fertility goddess born from the ocean spray—a mythological theme popularized by French academic painters such as William-Adolph Bouguereau and Alexandre Cabanal in the late nineteenth century. But whereas the academic painters despised loose and impressionistic brushwork, Reverón exploits those techniques to give the scene its charge and sensuality.

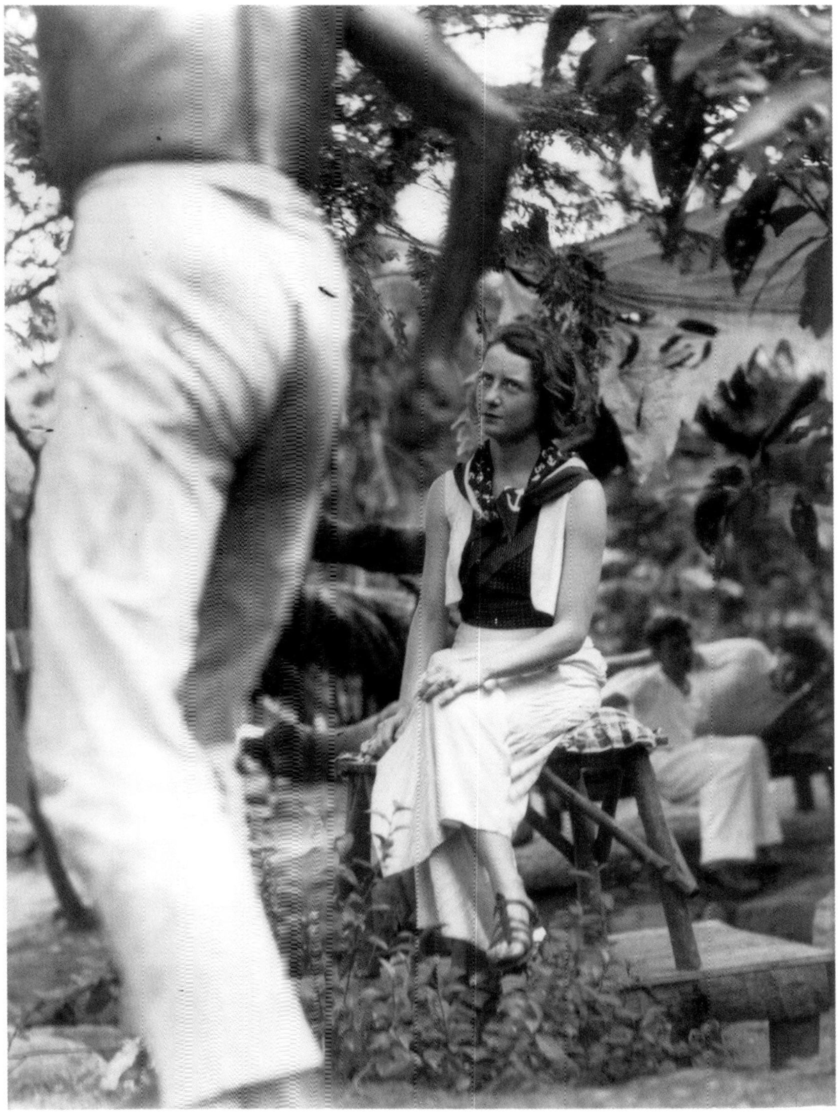

FIG. 2

Retrato de Mujer presents another figure whose appearance vacillates between the ordinary and the mythical (plate 11). Before a thin wall of plant stalks sits a woman in a high-backed chair. She gazes beyond the picture plane. She wears a red blouse with a dark shawl draped over her shoulders. Above her head are two patches of color—one red, one blue—that give the impression of feathers. Reverón often portrayed women with feathers in their hair or with radiant lines around their heads, suggesting halos or inner radiance. In this case, the red and blue patches are painted over in white, suggesting that the artist may have had a change of heart, but the result is a more mysterious scene. Reverón's composition presents a stately woman whose grace mingles with and transcends the more mundane aspects of her appearance.

The carnival marks a moment of release and social permissiveness, but the celebrations correspond to religious practices that Reverón also drew from and willfully recast. Reverón painted various religious festivals throughout his career. *Procesión de la Virgen en el Valle* [Procession of the Virgin in the Valley] (1920), *Fiesta en Caraballeda*

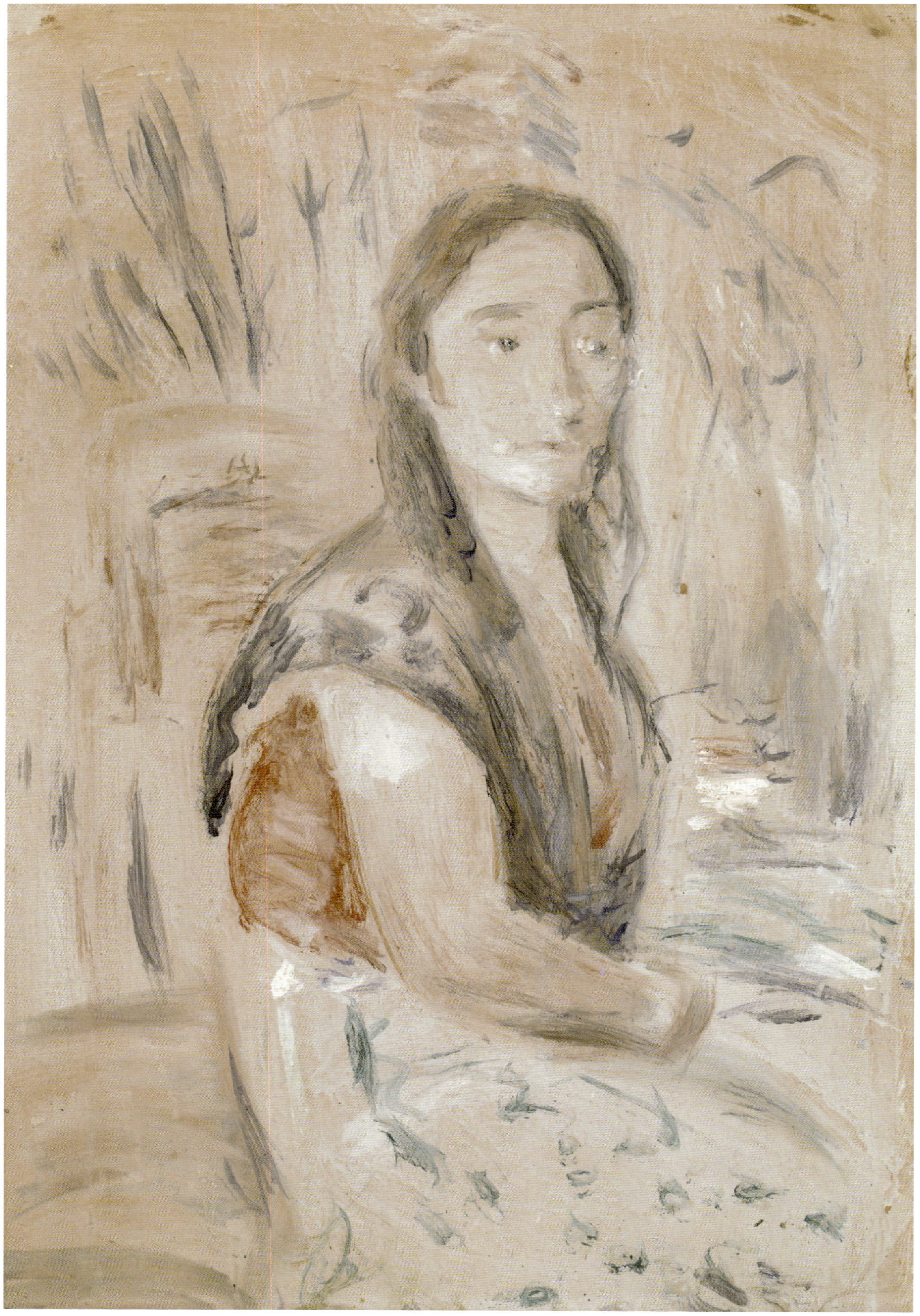

PLATE 11
Armando Reverón • *Retrato de Mujer* [Portrait of a Woman], c. 1934

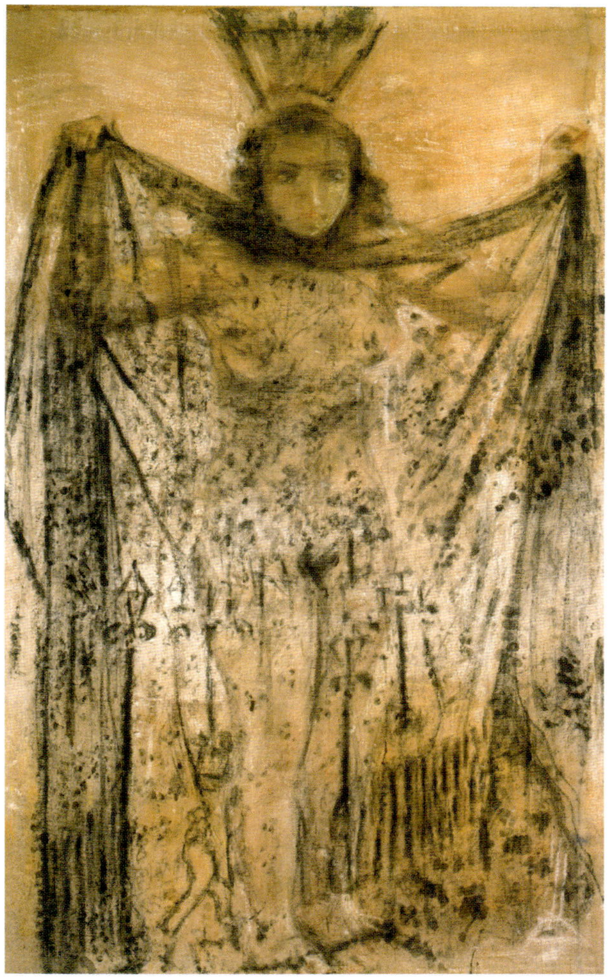

FIG. 3

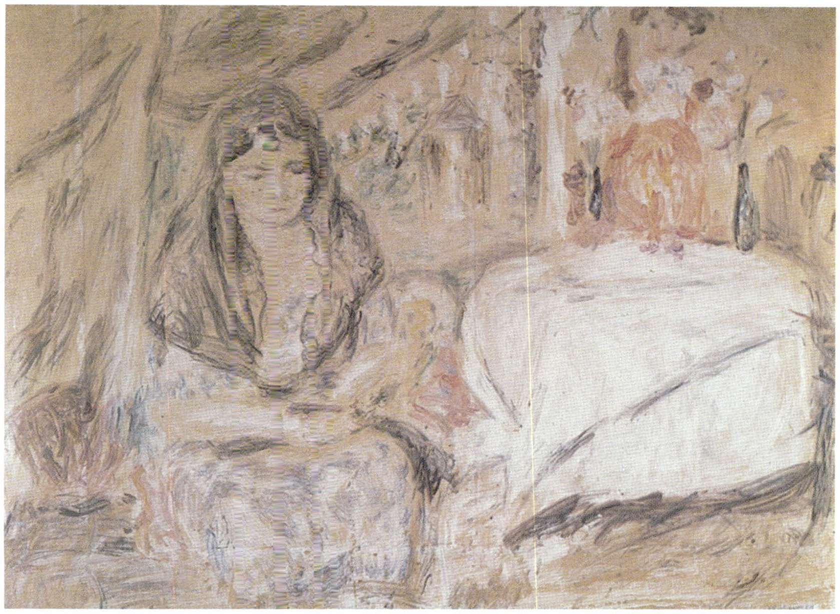

FIG. 4

[Festival in Caraballeda] (1928), and his *Cruz de Mayo* [May Cross] paintings of the 1930s suggest the artist's continual interest in local religious celebrations. Yet his portraits of women, particularly those of the 1930s and 1940s, show Reverón defying religious conventions. In works such as *Desnudo detrás de la mantilla* [Woman behind the Mantilla] (1946), he uses props like the mantilla, an article symbolizing piety and typically worn to Sunday mass, as a sensual adornment and means of representing transparency (fig. 3). In *Figura reclinada* (plate 12), the central figure wears the mantilla in a more traditional fashion. However, instead of kneeling before an altar (visible in the right portion of the painting), she reclines in a position with implicit sexual undertones. The painting is one in a series Reverón made showing women in mantillas seated or lying before altars for the *Cruz de Mayo*, or *Fiesta de las cruces* [Festival of the Crosses], a Catholic celebration popular in Spain and Venezuela celebrating the month dedicated to the Virgin Mary. The holiday involves adorning altars with brightly colored flowers and making offerings to mourn Christ's crucifixion. These altars are paraded through the streets and installed in homes and in churches.[7] In *Mujer con mantilla* (1933) and *Cruz de Mayo* (1935), Reverón legibly depicts altars with different offerings (red flowers, red and white candles, a bottle of wine, and a black pyramidal-roofed lantern) (figs. 4 and 5). The central figures are seated with their hands in their laps. One casts her eyes downward, as if deep in thought or prayer; the other woman, leaning slightly to one side, appears more restless, as she looks outward and is more confrontational. In contrast, the woman in *Figura reclinada* appears at ease. Like a heroine in one of Parra's novels, she is rebellious. In front of an altar, she takes a pose that suggests her seductiveness and that is meant to shock conventional morality. Reverón was interested in the erotic undertones in traditional Catholic imagery, a theme exploited by Romantic poets, writers and painters of Europe in the nineteenth century.[8] The artist combines sensual imagery with religious symbols, creating iconoclastic images that draw together the sacred and the seductive. They present scenes of a carnivalesque world turned upside-down where figures seem to teeter between religious faith and defiance.

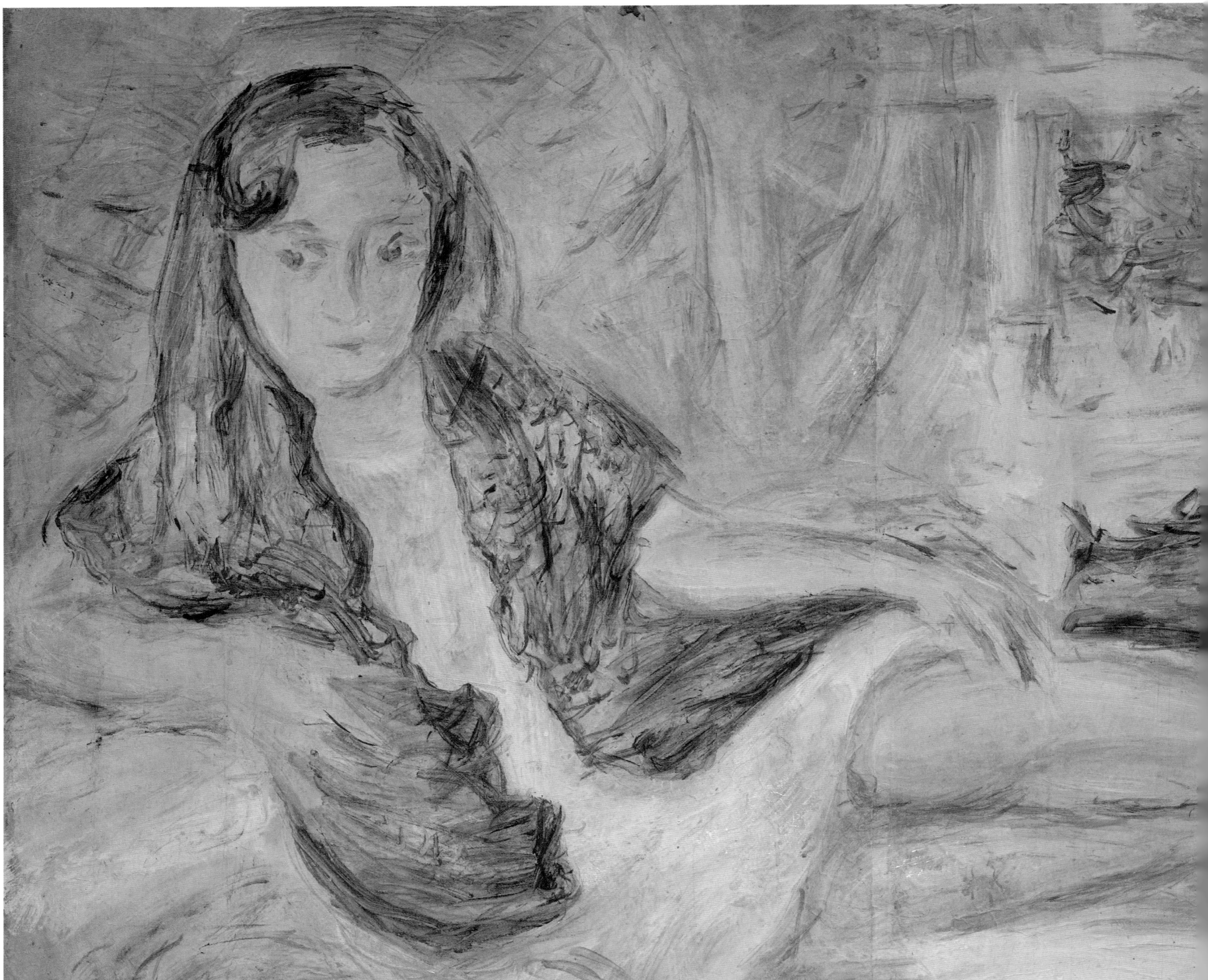

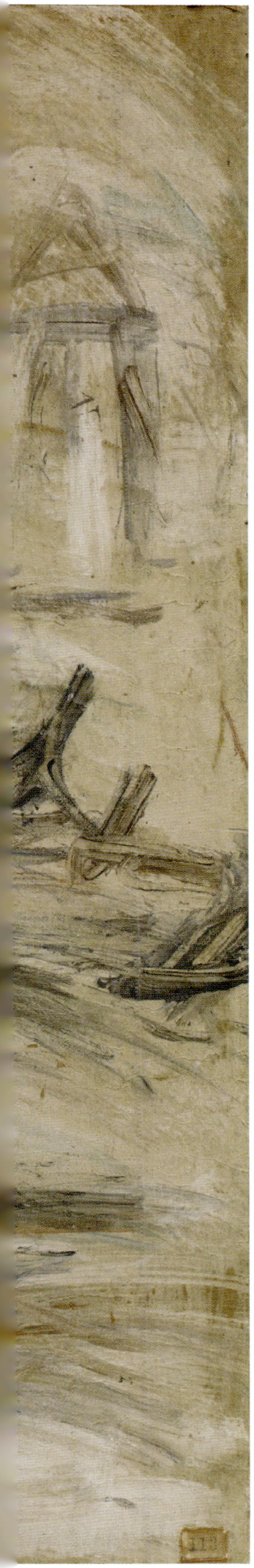

PLATE 12

Armando Reverón • *Figura reclinada* o *Mujer con mantilla acostada* [Reclining Figure or Reclining Woman with Mantilla], c. 1934

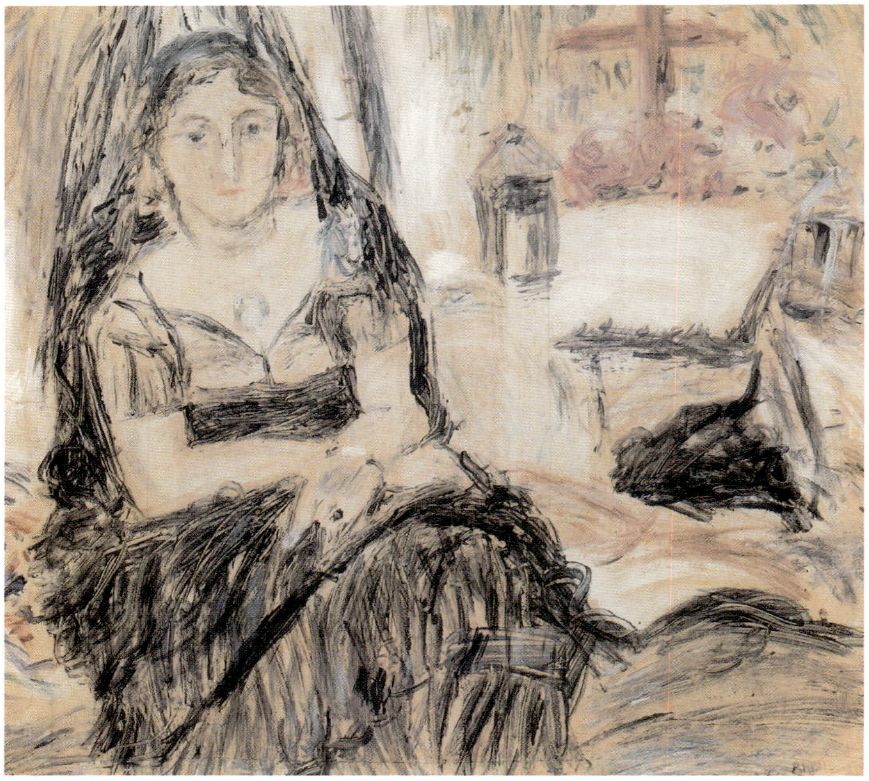

FIG. 5

In the closing passages of Parra's *Iphigenia*, the protagonist describes her life as a long battle with a "Sacred Monster with seven heads that are called society, family, honor, religion, morality, duty, conventions and principles."[9] In her book, Parra voices her conflict with the conventions prescribed for women in this era. In Macuto, Reverón established a lifestyle and an art that challenged certain conventions, but he did not grapple with those societal monsters to the same degree as Parra and the women of her time. Reverón benefited from a tradition whereby the eccentricities and bohemian lifestyles of male artists were generally accepted as indications of their genius and exceptionalism. Moreover, most of Reverón's artistic concerns were quite different from Parra's, and his eroticization of women ran at cross purposes with Parra's aspirations for self-representation and the empowerment of women. These differences in circumstance and in approach, however, do not diminish the carnivalesque elements of Reverón's work. The carnival, by definition, is a momentary escape—one that in briefly overturning societal conventions, also reinforces them. The paintings in the Brillembourg Capriles Collection offer a glimpse of an extraordinary world occupied by Reverón and the women who modeled for him—a space, albeit a temporary one, for self-expression and for play.

ILLUSTRATIONS IN TEXT

FIGURE 1
Young women posing as Indians at "El Castillete," photographed by Alfredo Boulton, 1934

FIGURE 2
Reverón painting Luisa Phelps, photographed by Alfredo Boulton, 1934

FIGURE 3
Armando Reverón
Desnudo detrás de la mantilla
[Nude behind the Mantilla], c. 1946
Tempera, chalk, and charcoal on sacking
67 ⅞ x 42 ¼ inches (170.5 x 107.cm)
Colección Pérez Simón, Mexico

FIGURE 4
Armando Reverón
Mujer con mantilla
[Woman with Mantilla], 1933
Tempera on paper on board
40 ⅜ x 56 ⅛ inches (102.5 x 142.4 cm)
Private collection

FIGURE 5
Armando Reverón
Cruz de Mayo o *Dama con mantilla*
[May Cross or Lady with Mantilla], 1935
Tempera on paper on masonite
35 ½ x 39 ¾ inches (90 x 101 cm)
Private collection

NOTES

1
During her lifetime, Parra was considered an independent and worldly woman, rebellious like the "bored woman" of her novel. Reverón's rebellion was of a different kind: he was a European-trained artist who rejected the trappings of middle- and upper-class life and instead sought out a bohemian existence. Writers often described him as a hermit, who turned his back on the modern world either by choice (like Gauguin) or because he suffered from madness (like Van Gogh). For a discussion of public perceptions of Parra, see RoseAnna Mueller, *Teresa de la Parra: A Literary Life* (Newcastle upon Tyne, UK: Cambridge Scholars Press, 2012). For perceptions of Reverón, see Juan Calzadilla, ed., *Reverón: 18 testimonios* (Caracas: Galería de Arte Nacional, 1979).

2
Art critic Alfredo Boulton first defined these periods—Blue, White, and Sepia—in his introduction to the catalogue for *Exposición retrospectiva de Armando Reverón* (Caracas: Museo de Bellas Artes, 1955), 7–14. Scholars continue to examine, modify, and contend with these classifications. Juan Calzadilla offered a revision to these periods in his essay "Reverón: su universo como idioma" (1979), excerpts of which are published as "Reverón: His Universe as Language," translated by Inés Huiz de Campbell, in *Armando Reverón: Luz y cálida sombra del Caribe* (Caracas: Fundación Museo Armando Reverón, 1996), 121–28. More recently, John Elderfield noted that Boulton likely modeled his periodization on the categories that define Picasso's early work. See John Elderfield, Luis Pérez-Oramas, and Nora Lawerence, *Armando Reverón* (New York: The Museum of Modern Art, 2007), 26.

3
Juan Calzadilla, "Reverón: His Universe as Language," 123.

4
Mikhail Bakhtin, *Rabelais and His World*, trans. Hélène Iswolsky (Bloomington and Indianapolis: Indiana University Press, 1984), 10.

5
Mention of their meeting appears in Marta Traba, "Reverón descansa en Juanita," in *Reverón: 18 testimonios*, 65.

6
For images and excerpts of Boulton's account, see Boulton, "Una sesión de trabajo, Reverón en 1934," in Armando Reverón (1880–1954). Exposición antológica (Caracas: Fundación Galería de Arte Nacional, 1992) 15–29.

7
The Festival of the Crosses also involves a number of traditional folk songs and sung rosaries. Several of Reverón's paintings from the period depict women playing guitar in celebration of the holiday. For more on the holiday, see Malena Kuss, ed., *Music in Latin America and the Caribbean: An Encyclopedic History. Vol II: Performing the Caribbean Experience* (Austin: The University of Texas Press, 2008), 163–64. For an example of Reverón's female guitar players, see Juan Calzadilla, *Armando Reverón* (Caracas: Ernesto Armitano Editor, 1979), 133.

8
For a discussion of nineteenth-century fusions of aesthetics, the erotic, and the Catholic Church, see Ellis Hanson, *Decadence and Catholicism* (Cambridge, MA: Harvard University Press, 1997).

9
Teresa de la Parra, *Iphigenia: The Diary of a Young Lady Who Wrote Because She Was Bored*, trans. Bertie Acker (Austin: The University of Texas Press, 1993), 353.

Mari Carmen Ramírez

MOVING *TO* AND *FROM* ABSTRACTION

JOAQUÍN TORRES-GARCÍA'S UNCODIFIED ECLECTICISM

An Unprecedented Proposal

THE URUGUAYAN MASTER Joaquín Torres-García has become well known in accounts of the Latin American avant-garde for his pioneering and sui generis pursuit of a form of pictographic, grid-based abstraction that he labeled Constructive Universalism. Such a system—a combination of schematically rendered visual and linguistic signs placed inside a flat compartmentalized structure—represented the consolidation of a lifelong, indefatigable journey begun as early as 1913 that, according to him, was aimed at bringing an "abstract logic to the world."[1] For Torres-García, attaining that goal required a metaphysical exercise to turn deeds and things from real life into abstract ideas that—by means of an artistic operation—would become the "real thing."[2] The key milestones of that journey have been documented thoroughly in the increasing literature about his variegated production.[3] Lesser known, however, are the steps he took toward the end of his long life and career to retrace his arduous path toward abstraction by *recovering* the object/subject of his artistic proposal. This phase is exemplified by a series of paintings made during his last decade that depict, among others, urban characters (1939–40), portraits of remarkable men (1939–46), as well as Constructive-universal compositions (1943–48) based on scenes of everyday life that, in their tendency to "humanize" the symbols, represent a departure from the rigorous (and by now classic) version of the language he created in the previous decade. The lines that follow mainly address that latter phase.

To understand the complex dialectics at the core of Torres-García's proposal, however, it is important to bear in mind that Constructive Universalism—as is generally assumed—did not represent the end of his ongoing back-and-forth between figuration and abstraction that characterized the Uruguayan master's work almost from inception. Instead, his response was a rather fragile and unstable synthesis whose function was "to disguise" the quite persistent tensions between irreconcilable opposites: idea/nature, concrete/real, abstract/figurative. Such antinomies remained productive tensions throughout the entire span of Torres-García's career, establishing a delicate equilibrium at times dominated by abstraction while at others leaning toward an elemental approach to the figure. This tension, in turn, is responsible for written and visual manifestations that were unique in their unabashed embrace of against-the-grain individualism as the basis for artistic creation. In the artist's words: ". . . despite the importance of discovery in art, of the new theory, of the invention, something more important makes the work: that which is really ours and unique to us. That which is really *l'inédit* [the unprecedented] or nonexistent before us."[4]

At the level of visual production, these tensions could only translate into an uncodified eclecticism; one that vacillated between an archaic classicizing approach to naturalism and a cutting-edge, grid-based abstraction. This approach, which sharply contrasted with the formal purity and rigor embedded in the work of leading representatives of international Constructivism such as Piet Mondrian or Theo van

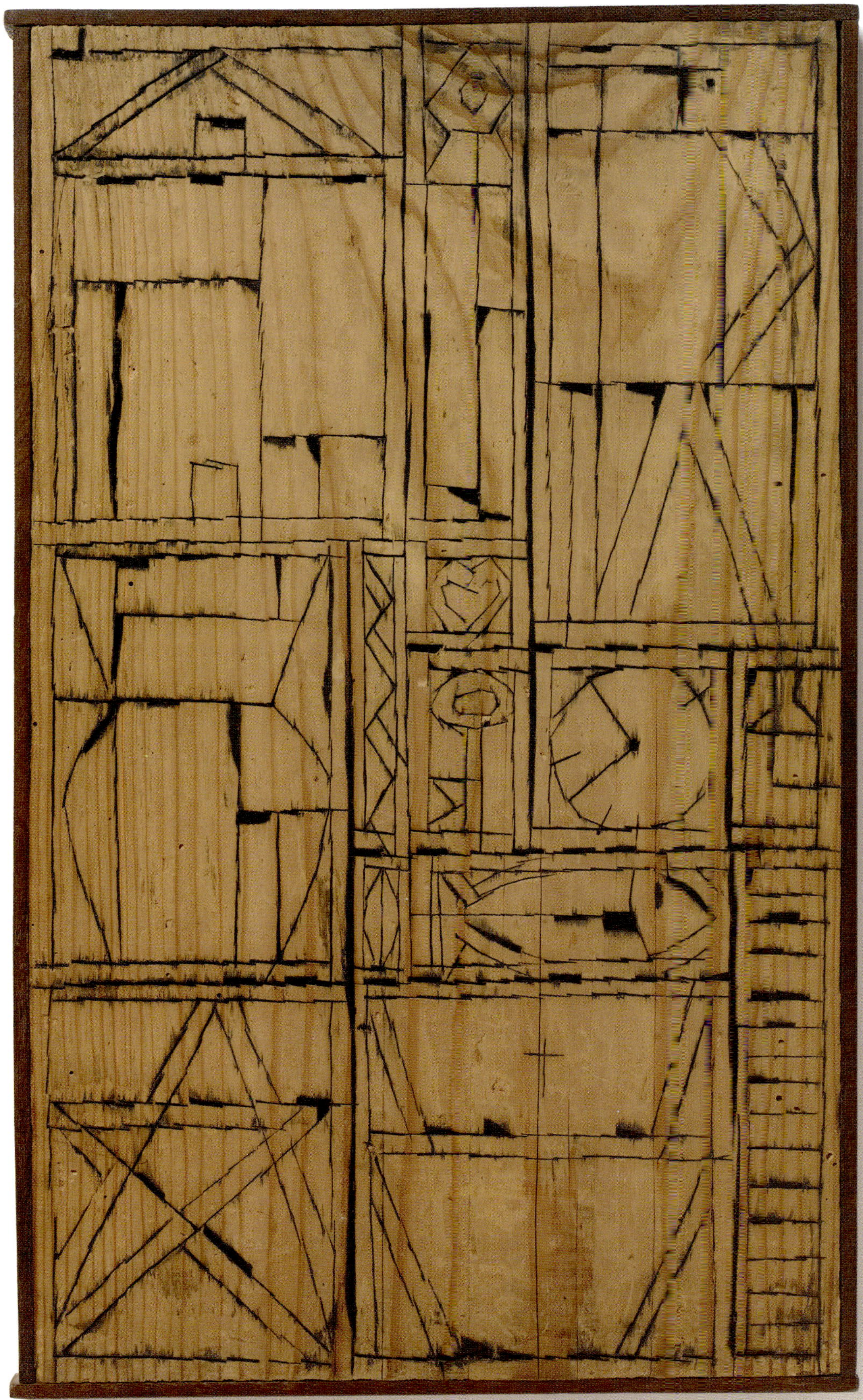

PLATE 13

Joaquín Torres-García • *Constructif en bois incise* [Constructive Composition on Incised Wood], 1932

Doesburg, has often been considered a limitation of the Uruguayan artist's Modernist practice. Yet, as I have argued elsewhere, Torres-García's tenacious attempts to reconcile both theoretical (idea/matter; reason/intuition) and stylistic (naturalism/abstraction) opposites in his conception of an artwork are firmly grounded in the notion of l'inedit that served to guide his artistic path from the very beginning.[5] In Torres-García's view, individuals in general and artists in particular should strive to avoid classification because "moulds [only] lead men to classify themselves and to imitate others. To follow an ART movement, a tendency, or even to paint or sculpt like everyone else is triple nonsense." In his teachings, Torres-García thus called for artists to construct "unclassifiable" objects and things.[6] And his lifelong habit of working simultaneously in different media—painting, drawing, wood—while shifting between a range of stylistic and sometimes opposed vocabularies, from naturalism to abstraction, and so on and on, can be traced to this unswerving resistance to categorization.

The seven works in the Brillembourg Capriles Collection of Latin American Art—produced between 1932 and 1945—illustrate the different stages in Torres-García's singular path *to* and *from* abstraction. The earliest pieces in the ensemble (two *maderas* and one painting) executed in 1932—which was a key year for his transformation—exemplify the high point in the consolidation of the Constructive-universal language. By contrast, the last three oil paintings belong to the late period of the artist's career: one marked by a return to the essential aspects of figures and objects. Considered together, they offer clues for a more comprehensive assessment of his work that takes into account the different and often contradictory series that make up the sum total of his production. Such an examination is long overdue and fills a scholarly lacuna because the majority of studies of Torres-García's oeuvre to date focus almost exclusively on his European period, his role as harbinger of the avant-garde in Latin America, or his pedagogic activities as founder and intellectual leader of the Taller Torres-García [Torres-García Workshop]. As a result, hardly any attention has been paid to his late work. I will argue, however, that only by considering his production as a whole will the profound insights and even the contradictions that characterized his theory and practice from the outset come fully to light.

Toward Abstraction

The synthesis of the pure grid with pictographic symbols that constitutes the core of Constructive Universalism was the result of Torres-García's rejection of the pure, nonobjective parameters of Mondrian's Neo-Plasticism on behalf of a form of abstraction that did not exclude the metaphysical or spiritual dimension of art.[7] The basic elements of this language appeared as early as 1926 but were not fully articulated as a visual proposal until 1929–30. Up until then, Torres-García's work had been straddling the conflict between a reductive—almost primitive—mode of figuration and a referential mode of abstraction. The large number of paintings and drawings produced during the course of 1928 and the beginning of 1929 reveals the increased schematization of figurative and natural elements in which the extremely flat, frontal view dominates. By 1929, striving to resolve the seemingly irreconcilable conflict between *reason* (abstraction) and *emotion* (the natural world), the artist reached an unheard-of solution whereby he reduced the composition to: "the least possible seemingly real element: such as a sign." In his words, "as if unconsciously obeying an internal vision [I put] . . . in their respective niches a House (like those drawn by children), a ship, an anchor, the letter B, a man, a fish . . . ."[8] In my view, rather than opt for one approach or the other, Torres-García combined both into a synthesis of form and subject matter contained inside the Neo-Plasticist grid. In fact, this new synthesis was formally expressed through a pared-down, schematic, and geometric type of drawing—very much akin to children's drawings. Like these, Torres-García's drawings reflected his new approach, which also emphasized flatness and frontality, so as to not disturb the two-dimensional plane of the support.

The basis for his Constructive-universal articulation was the "sign"—i.e., the conflation of visual symbol (form) and idea (content)—that by virtue of its concrete quality was able to convey meaning in a direct, immediate way.[9] Torres-García produced the first drawings with these signs in 1926,[10] and by 1930 he had developed a full inventory of signs. In several drawings made that year he patiently recorded the signs, classifying them in three levels: *intellectual* (geometric figures, numbers, letters, ruler, clock); *spiritual* (man, woman, cross, temple, zodiac signs, scale [of justice], key, ladder, bell); *physical* (snail, fish, plants, flowers, water). By articulating this basic vocabulary, the artist drew from the vast array of heterogeneous sources that constituted his cultural and intellectual universe: Christianity, Theosophy, Freemasonry, ancient art, as well as the art of children and primitive peoples. After his final return to Montevideo in 1934, Torres-García incorporated references to the art of Pre-Columbian civilizations. Grounded in the universal experience of mankind, the Constructive-universal signs, nevertheless, suggest a metaphysical dimension. For this reason, it is tempting to want to *read* specific meanings into his Constructive paintings. A symbol such as the *clock* can be seen as standing for the idea of time; the *ladder* for ascension to the heavens; the *fish* for its association with the origins of Christianity, and so on. However, the purpose of these signs was to tap into archetypal meanings that cut across cultures and, as such, are buried in mankind's collective memory. In this way, he created an innovative abstract language that was both *concrete* and *universal* in its communicative reach.

Constructif en bois incise [Constructive Composition on Incised Wood] (1932) (plate 13) and *Constructivo con dibujo inciso* [Constructive Composition with Incised Drawing] (1932) (plate 14) illustrate this initial stage of the artist's Constructive Universalism. Both works are a pivotal part of an extensive and rather original series of wood constructions—the *maderas*—that Torres-García produced from the mid-1920s to the end of his long career.[11] Created hand in hand with the paintings, this unprecedented series—as I have argued elsewhere—served to test l'inédit and to clarify key components of both Torres-García's path toward abstraction as well as the evolution of his Constructive-universal system.[12] More importantly, such deceivingly simple painted or incised wood panels—with grids and symbols made of natural wood—stood apart from prevailing modes of Constructivism and other avant-garde trends that dominated the international arts scene in the 1920s and 1930s.

From a formal point of view, the already mentioned works—*Constructif en bois incise* and *Constructivo con dibujo inciso*—serve to illustrate how the new sign-based language also allowed Torres-García to abolish the figure/ground dichotomy that had dominated painting since its inception and thus involved a very problematic issue for Constructive artists. In both works the use of wood to convey the new vocabulary is not arbitrary. On the contrary, one could argue that wood played a key role in these two *maderas* as a means to explore flatness, which Torres-García considered an essential condition of the Constructive-universal work. Operating with what amounted to a self-imposed economy of means, the artist assembled slats of wood upon which he painted or even grooved the contours of both the grid and the signs with either a brush or a pointed instrument. Thus, there is no noticeable difference between the grid compartment and the signs it contains. The result is that the grid evolves from mere scaffolding to function simultaneously as the Constructive principle of the work. In the artist's words: "There will no longer be duality between background and images where structure replaces the superimposed images and the painting will have recovered its original identity: *unity*."[13]

As previously stated, both *Constructif en bois incise* and *Constructivo con dibujo inciso* exhibit a similar ensemble of signs re/arranged in their own grid compartments: mask, man, vase, anchor, fish, clock, and ladder. These signs closely correspond with those used by Torres-García in other works made during the same period. The presence of this pictographic vocabulary in constructions and paintings made between 1930 and 1932 is, indeed, pervasive, suggesting that, once he codified it, the theoretician set out to explore its practical potential by means of different formal (that is to say, aesthetic) solutions. By contrast, the oil on canvas painting titled *Pez* [Fish] (1932) (plate 16), one of the most reproduced of the Brillembourg Capriles Collection—is a highly synthetic and extremely refined painting that brings Torres-García's new pictorial language across in a forceful manner. The painting—one of only two the artist made in this format[14]—stands out from all others of the period because the Constructive-universal signs associated with the spiritual realm are organized inside the

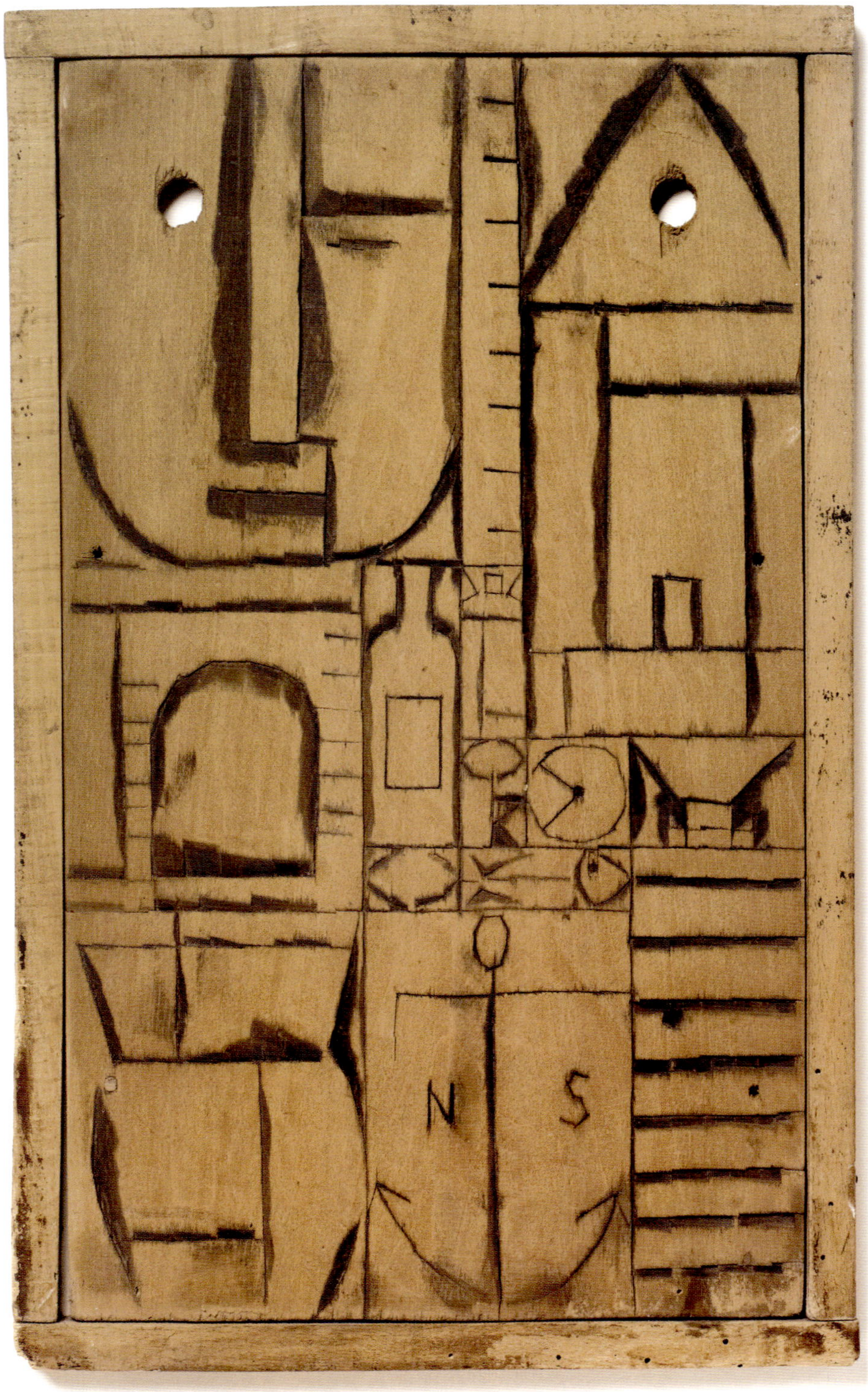

PLATE 14

Joaquín Torres-García • *Constructivo con dibujo inciso* [Constructive Composition with Incised Drawing], 1932 highly connotative shape of the fish. Like the other elements of the Constructive-universal proposal, the pictographic sign of the fish only appears in Torres-García's work in 1929–30. Despite the fact that it has been frequently interpreted as a Christian reference, in Torres-García's inventory of signs, the fish stands for the physical realm comprising the vegetable, animal, and mineral kingdoms. Encapsulating the spiritual inside the physical—as the artist did in this work and in its innermost construct—is a powerful statement that underscores the nexus between *the abstract* and *the concrete* at the core of Torres-García's Constructive Universalism.

From Abstraction

The importance of the year 1932 in Torres-García's life and artistic trajectory is an issue to which we need to return. It not only marked the end of the artist's extremely productive six-year Parisian sojourn but also the beginning of the transition that would take him back to his country via Madrid.[15] Once in Montevideo (1934), the artist would spend the next fifteen years teaching, lecturing, establishing artists' organizations—including the Taller Torres-García—and, above all, further developing the elements of Constructive Universalism. All this activity would become incorporated into an extensive body of mature work. By 1939, however, his painting started to undergo a formal and conceptual transformation that would mark the last stage of his production. As in the past, this shift represented yet another tilting of the delicate balance between abstraction and representation; in this case, the emphasis was clearly on the representational aspects of the equation. This process was introduced in a series of lectures held in 1948–49—a few months before he died—at Montevideo's Facultad de Humanidades y Ciencias [Faculty of Humanities and Sciences], where the artist and professor laid out his last theoretical position: the *recovery of the object*.[16] It could be argued, however, that the progression that led to this last pronouncement most likely began in 1939 with a group of under-recognized paintings depicting urban personages executed almost at the same time as another well-known late series: the Portraits of Remarkable Men.

Of the works in the Brillembourg Capriles Collection, *Muchedumbre* [Crowd] (1940) (plate 17), perfectly embodies this final transition in Torres-García's œuvre while shedding light on the process leading to the reincorporation of recognizable objects and figures into his late paintings. The work is the largest and most complex of a series comprised of a small group of paintings depicting urban personages that he made between 1939 and 1940. In this particular case, at least seven figures, including a woman and five men from the waist up, are compressed into a flat and frontal composition with some of the bodies and portions of the faces cropped out of the scene as if in a snapshot. The subject matter is not new: it harks back to the urban scenes that appeared in the artist's paintings and journal sketches more than a decade earlier in Paris. As in these earlier works, the crowd in *Muchedumbre* is frontal, highly stylized, flat, and obviously anonymous. The difference, however, resides in the fact that the faces and the figures in this work are no longer loosely sketched out or reduced to ideograms. Instead, they are rendered in a more-or-less recognizable manner.

In many ways, it is not surprising that Torres-García would turn to the urban crowd motif in order to explore the direction the last phase of his production would take. This motif, indeed, seems to appear in his work in periods of transition such as 1917 in Barcelona or 1926–28 in Paris, suggesting that the artist relied on this "factual" resource to test new directions in his conceptual and artistic journey. From this point of view, going back to the subject of figures in urban settings could be seen as a way to reimmerse himself in "what is real" in order to determine the next step in his relentless dialectical oscillation between *the abstract* and *the concrete*. In this case, a plausible hypothesis could be that after a number of years of production circumscribed to the Constructive-universal system, Torres-García was ready to move in a slightly different direction. In such a context, works like *Muchedumbre* as well as the Portraits of Remarkable Men (1939–46) gave him the opportunity to practically test the new possibilities that would allow him to arrive at the essential quality of a scene, an object, or a person.[17]

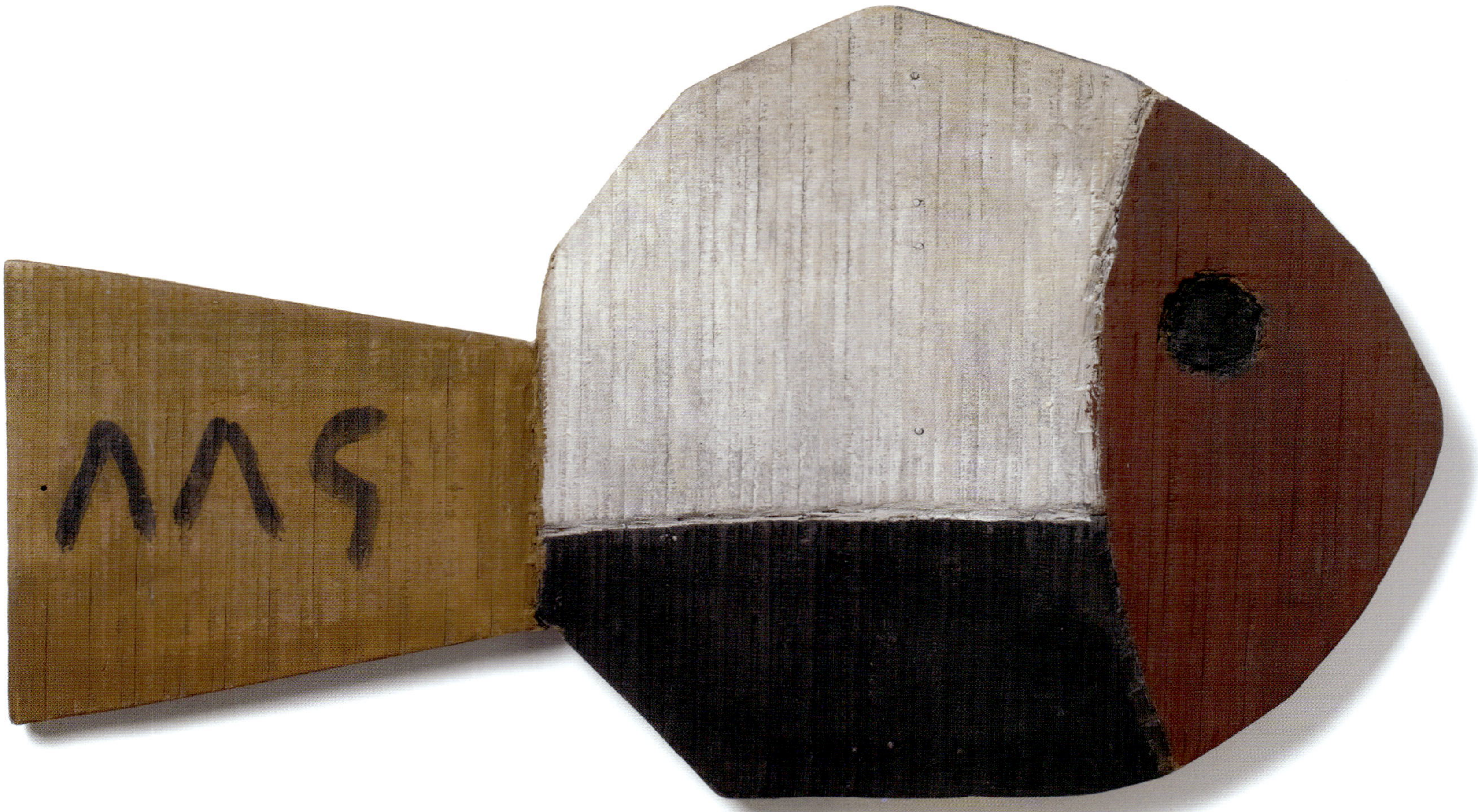

PLATE 15

Joaquín Torres-García • *Pez AAC* [Fish A.A.C.], 1939

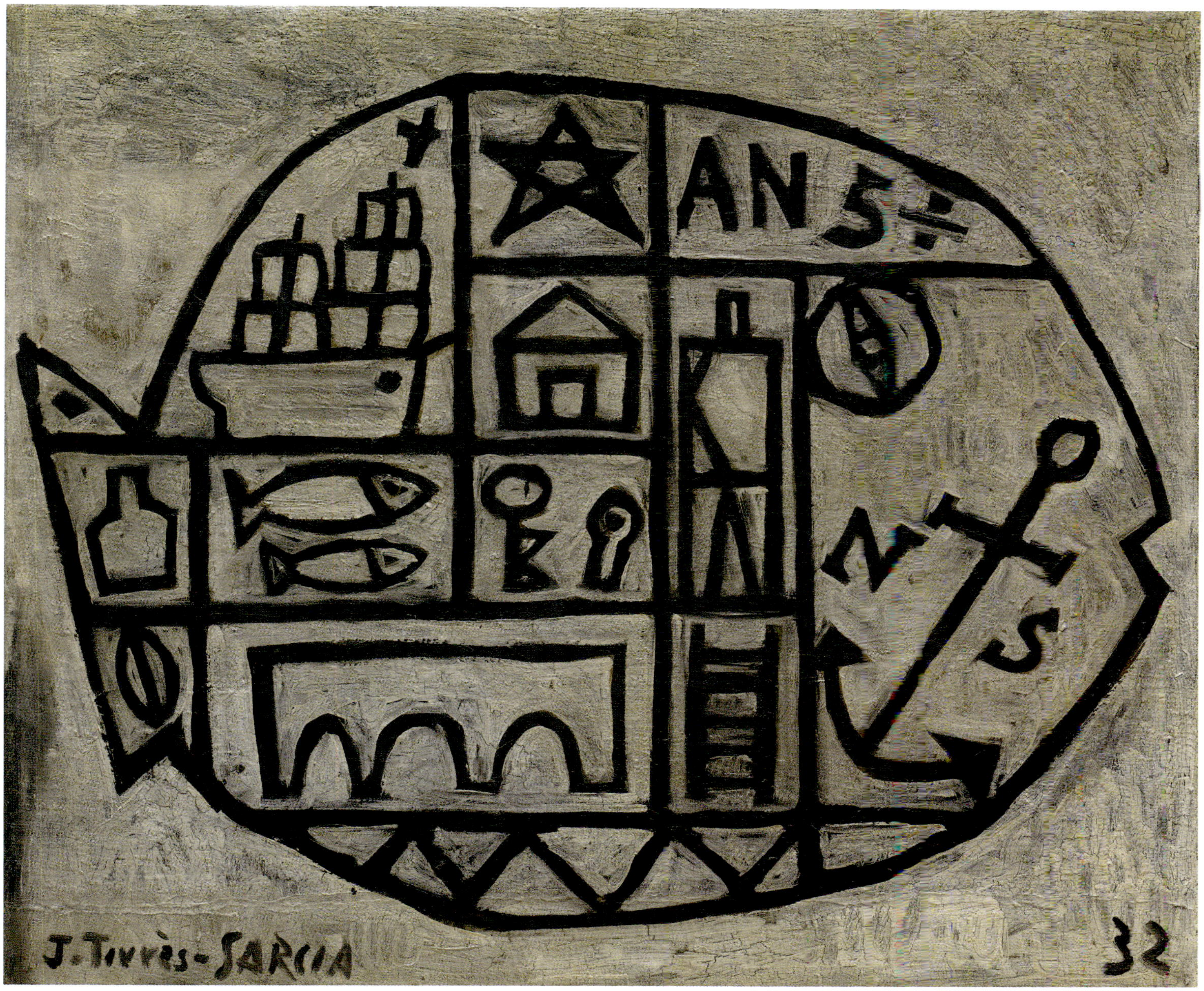

PLATE 16

Joaquín Torres-García • *Pez* [Fish], 1932

© 2013 Alejandra, Aurelio and Claudio Torres

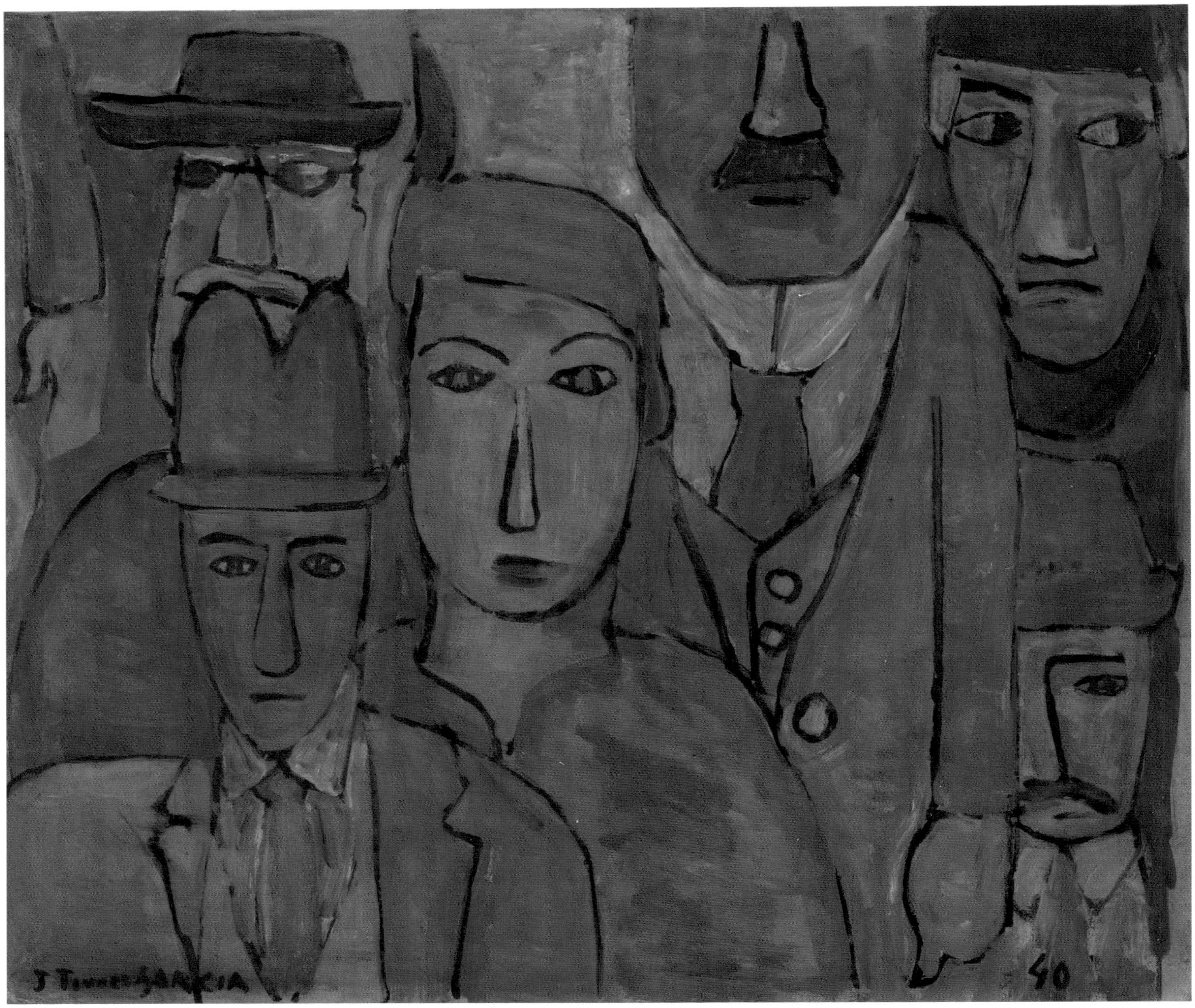

PLATE 17

Joaquín Torres-García • *Muchedumbre* [Crowd], 1940

Indeed, a few years later, while reflecting on the process encompassed by the recovery of the object, he wrote about the need to return to "... a normal, hence human sense: an equilibrium."[18] In so doing, he stressed how necessary it was to reestablish this balance, no matter the cost; and how such a move implied finding the universal dimension in the transient nature of the everyday things that surround the artist. However, Torres-García clarified that doing so did not necessarily imply completely abandoning the rules of Constructivism but rather applying them to representational subject matter. As paradoxical as it may seem, the figures and objects of these new works—exemplified by both the crowd paintings and portraits of remarkable men—would be filtered through the Constructive rules. In this sense, they did not imply a direct mimesis of the external world, as in traditional painting, but an outright reconstruction of the figurative by means of the rules of Constructivism. Hence, while there is no visible grid at all in *Muchedumbre*, its articulating presence is clearly felt in the manner in which the figures appear compressed inside invisible compositional compartments. Similarly, in the case of the portraits, the potential for resemblance was mitigated by the use of the golden section that significantly deformed the represented subjects, turning them into almost caricatures. In this sense, despite the presence of recognizable elements from the natural world, the works associated with these series operate indeed as abstract paintings. Torres-García thus believed that only in this way could the artist pretend to arrive at the timeless essence of "universal" painting. Yet, insofar as it was contained within a new structure, this type of "construction" did not owe anything to the past.[19]

As expected, however, the transition toward the recovery of the object (and figure) embodied in *Muchedumbre* would not remain fixed in Torres-García's production. Having achieved and assimilated a new approach to representational work, the artist dialectically moved back to a new phase of Constructive Universalism that brazenly incorporated the representational element. The last two works in the Brillembourg Capriles Collection— *Construcción universal con gran sol* [Universal Construction with Large Sun] (1945) (plate 18) and *Composición constructiva de estructura coloreada* [Constructive

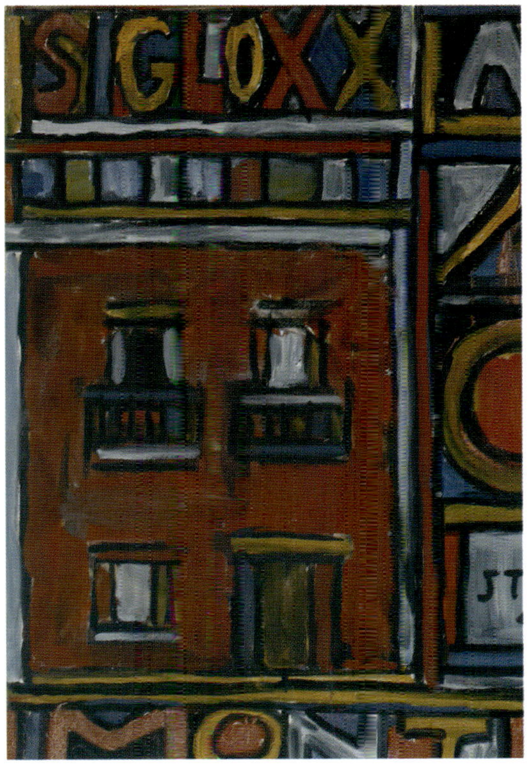

FIG. 1

Composition with Colored Structure] (1943) (plate 19)—exemplify this last iteration of Torres-García's move to and *from* abstraction. Both works recall the classical Constructive-universal paintings of 1930–32. They consist of grid-based structures with the schematic language of signs that the artist assembled in Paris: train, ship, anchor, vessel, abstract man, fish, key, ladder, and so on. Yet, in both cases, the signs have taken on a far more representational or expressive character that was absent in the early 1930s works. In *Composición constructiva de estructura coloreada*, for example, the sign of the house is no longer a schematic rendering but a simplified image of Torres-García's own studio house on Abayubá Street (fig. 1). Additionally, the artist incorporated the actual street address of his studio (Abayubá 2768) into one of the compartments on the top central part of the composition. And, in the middle section, toward the left, the artist's signature appears together with the place (Montevideo) and Torres-García's birth date (28 julio [July] 1943), thereby suggesting that the painting was made to commemorate the artist's sixty-ninth birthday.[20] Although he had often incorporated letters and symbols in his Constructive works, this is probably the first time that full words and dates appear in his paintings. Similarly, almost all

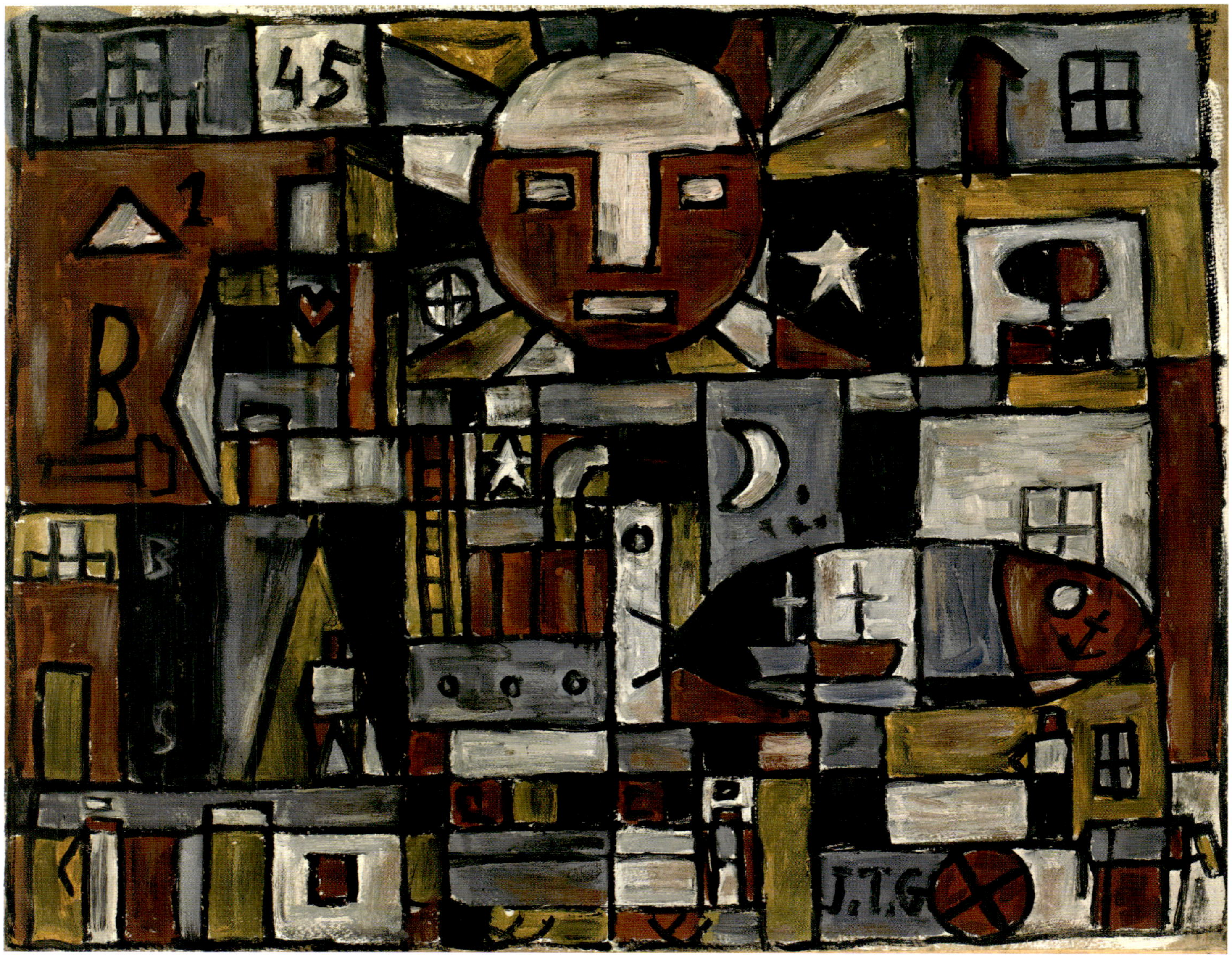

PLATE 18

Joaquín Torres-García • *Construcción universal con gran sol* [Universal Construction with Large Sun], 1945

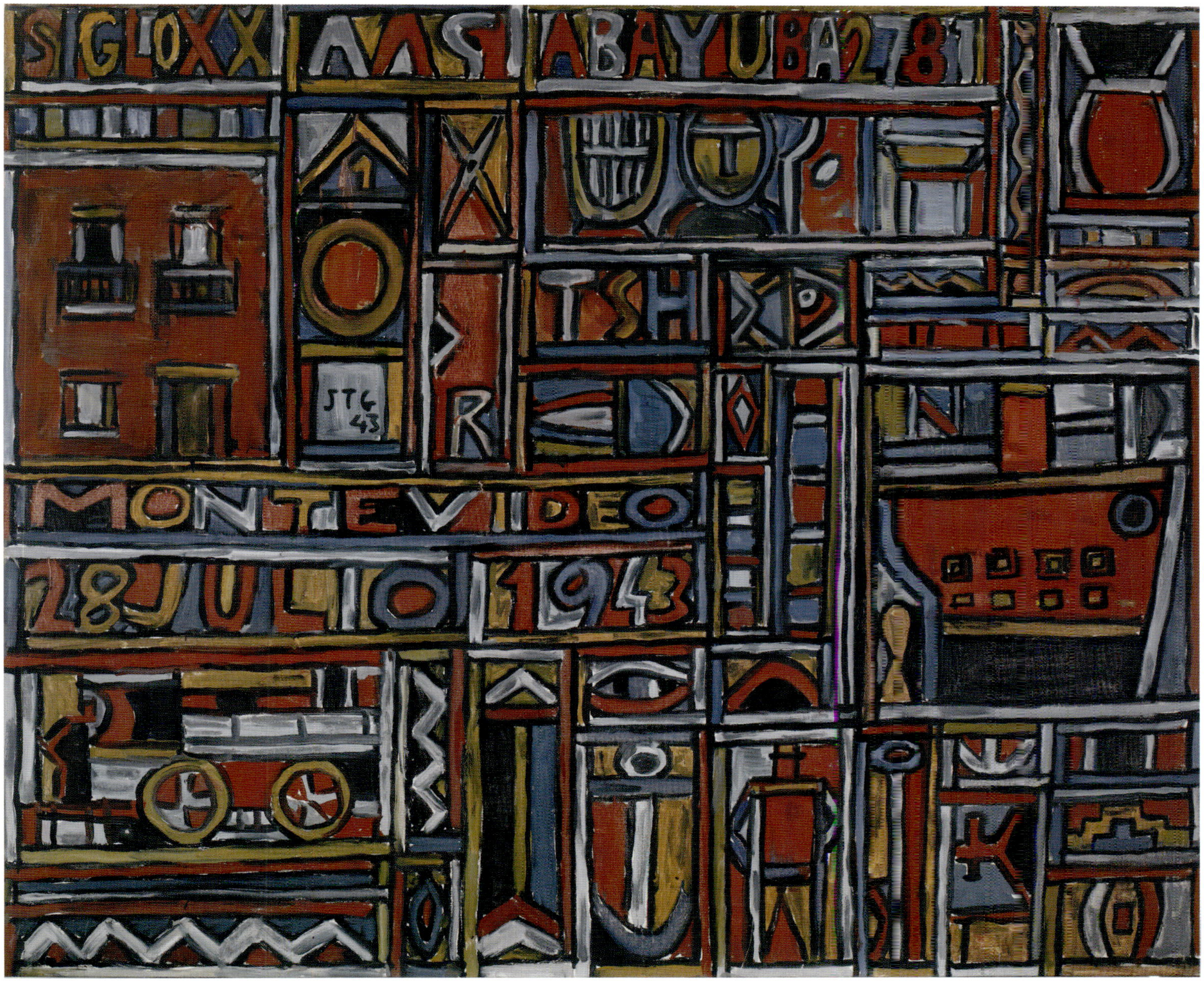

PLATE 19

Joaquín Torres-García • *Composición constructiva de estructura coloreada* [Constructive Composition with Colored Structure], 1943 of the other symbols have taken on a more "representational" quality: the ship appears as a modern-day steamship, and even the ideogram of Constructive man has taken on a more "human" aspect. In all, it seems clear that through this new approach to both the language and motifs characterizing his everyday life, Torres-García aimed to synthesize—i.e., "universalize"—the factual experience of living in Montevideo—the temporal everyday—through the language of Constructive Universalism. The evolution of this process appears in *Construcción universal con gran sol*, where the rhythmic structure of the grid is broken by oversized signs such as the sun and the fish, both of which also have taken on more naturalistic connotations.

Conclusion

As discussed at the beginning of this essay, the act of superimposing symbolic motifs on a purely abstract grid either directly or indirectly led to Torres-García's philosophical split with Neo-Plasticism and other Constructivist artists of his period, for whom any form of representation contradicted abstract art's avowed purism being in overt opposition to its spiritual dimension. Despite his self-conscious iconoclasm, it should be noted that Torres-García was not the only artist to traverse the path *to* and *from* abstraction—a sort of non-codified parameter close to eclecticism that I stressed in the title of this essay. Picasso, Malevich, as well as other paradigmatic figures of twentieth-century abstraction—operating in response to and within different contexts and under pressure from differing circumstances—underwent a similar transformation. What made Torres-García's case different, in my view, was that the path *to* and *from* abstraction did not imply an *either/or* proposition, but achieving a fragile equilibrium between the two.

ILLUSTRATIONS IN TEXT

FIGURE 1
Joaquín Torres-García
Composición constructiva de estructura coloreada [Constructive Composition with Colored Structure] (detail), 1943

NOTES

My appreciation goes to Marcela Guerrero, research coordinator at the International Center for the Arts of the Americas, The Museum of Fine Arts, Houston, for her assistance in researching key aspects of this essay.

1
Joaquín Torres-García, *Historia de mi vida* (completed 1934; first published in Montevideo, Asociación Arte Constructivo, April 20, 1939; repr. [Montevideo: ARCA, 2000], 82–83).

2
Ibid.

3
See, among other sources: Margit Rowell, *Torres-García: Grid, Pattern, Sign: Paris-Montevideo, 1924–1944* (London: Arts Council of Great Britain for Hayward Gallery, 1985); Tomás Llorens, *Torres-García* (Madrid: Museo Nacional Centro de Arte Reina Sofía, 1991); Mario Gradowzyck, *Torres García: Utopía y transgresión* (Montevideo: Museo Torres-García, 2007); Emmanuel Guigon, *Joaquín Torres-García: Un monde construit* (Paris: Fernand Hazan, 2002); *Torres-García darrere la mascara constructive* (Girona, Spain: Fundació Caixa Girona, 2008).

4
Joaquín Torres-García, "L'inedit," n.d. [c.1928], unpublished manuscript, Museo Torres-García Archives, Montevideo.

5
See Mari Carmen Ramírez, "Against the Grain," in *Constructing Abstraction with Wood*, ed. Ramírez (Houston: The Menil Collection, in association with the Museum of Fine Arts, Houston, 2009), 9–12.

6
Joaquín Torres-García, "L'inédit."

7
For the relationship between Torres-García and Mondrian, see Pedro da Cruz, *Torres-García and Cercle et Carré: The Creation of Universal Constructivism, Paris 1927–1932*, PhD diss., University of Lund (Sweden: Hanson and Kotte, 1994), and Ramírez et al., *Constructing Abstraction with Wood*.

8
Joaquín Torres-García, *Historia de mi vida*, 149.

9
See Joaquín Torres-García, *Estructura* (193[illegible]), reproduced in Joaquín Torres-García, *Escritos*, analytical selection and prologue by Juan Fló (Montevideo: Arca Editorial, 1974), 38–39.

10
Joaquín Torres-García: Una vida en papel. Texts by Marianne Elrick-Manley and Cecilia de Torres (Valencia: Museu Valencià de la Illustració i de la Modernitat; Madrid: Museo de Arte Contemporáneo, 2008).

11
Torres-García probably produced 170 *maderas* throughout his lifetime. This number does not include those lost through time. These numbers are based on the research performed to date by Cecilia de Torres for the ongoing catalogue raisonné of Torres-García's *maderas*. See Cecilia de Torres, "Joaquín Torres-García: Works in Wood: 1923–1946," a checklist in progress. For an in-depth discussion of this fascinating genre within Torres-García's production, see Ramírez et al., *Constructing Abstraction with Wood*.

12
See Ramírez, "A Constructed Precariousness: Abstraction Against the Grain," in Ramírez, *Constructing Abstraction with Wood*, 32–49.

13
Joaquín Torres-García, "Vouloir construire," *Cercle et Carré* (Paris), no. 1 (March 15): 3–4.

14
Period photographs suggest that Torres-García painted two versions of the fish with Constructive-universal symbols inside. In one version (in the Brillembourg Capriles Collection), the fish has an open mouth, while in the other it appears closed. The whereabouts of this second version are unknown.

15
After leaving Paris in December 1932, Torres-García and his family spent approximately fifteen months in Madrid before returning to Montevideo in April 1914. There he lectured and continued to exhibit his work. The experience in the Spanish capital also served to deepen his knowledge of Iberian and Pre-Columbian art through visits to the Museo Arqueológico Nacional in Madrid.

16
The lectures were published posthumously in 1952. See Joaquín Torres-García, "La recuperación del objeto," *Revista de la Facultad de Humanidades y Ciencias* (Montevideo), no. 8 (July 1952); reprint edition, Colección de Clásicos Uruguayos, vols. 75 and 76 (Montevideo: Biblioteca Artigas, 1965).

17
For more on this series, see Gradowzyck, *Torres-García: Utopía y transgression*, 294–301.

18
Joaquín Torres-García, *Mística de la pintura*, 194[illegible], reproduced in Joaquín Torres-García, *Escritos*, analytical selection and prologue by Juan Fló, 115.

19
Joaquín Torres-García, *The Recovery of the Object* (1949; 1952), reproduced in Fló, ibid., 117.

20
For a semiotic interpretation of the words and symbols that appear in this work, see Miguel A. Battegazzore, *J. Torres-García: La trama y los signos* (Montevideo: Impresora Gordon, 1999), 182–88.

Rachel Mohl

FRANCISCO MATTO'S MAGICAL MODERNISM

FOR THE URUGUAYAN ARTIST Francisco Matto, the act of creating a work of art assumed magical possibilities because he believed that artistic expression originated in the ritualistic cave drawings of early civilization. Matto's mentor and teacher, Joaquín Torres-García, introduced him to the concept that many ancient cultures shared a similar aesthetic, in which elements from nature were reduced to their fundamental essence. The symbolic characters constituted a collective visual language that was originally used for ceremonial and religious purposes. Therefore, these pictographic symbols were understood to be connected with the universal human spirit and possessed communicative powers with the divine.[1] Striving to engage this universal human spirit, Matto consistently reworked and refined a repertoire of symbols in numerous paintings and wooden reliefs during the 1960s and 1970s, and finally liberated them from the pictorial plane with the creation of his totems (fig. 1), which are considered his most original contribution to the legacy of Uruguayan art. The work *Construcción* [Construction] (1967; plate 20) in the Brillembourg Capriles Collection of Latin American Art represents an important step in Matto's artistic development of the Totems series by establishing a dialogue with international currents of the post-World War II era and solidifying his belief in the magical properties of each individual symbol.

Among the most outstanding artists to have emerged from the Taller Torres-García (TTG), Matto extended the applicability of Torres-García's neo-platonic ideas of Constructive Universalism. In doing so, Matto asserted the magical origins of the symbol and freed it from the Constructivist grid. At the same time, he initiated a unique aesthetic investigation of the "planar dimension," rejecting modeling as a necessary part of sculpture and disregarding the differences between media.[2] Indeed, Matto's deftness as an artist is exemplified by his nontraditional sculptures in which he explored flat planes as volumes within three-dimensional space. These works, which fall in between painting, sculpture, and relief, distinguish Matto from the other artists associated with the TTG, such as Gonzalo Fonseca, who focused on architectonic stone structures, and Julio Alpuy, who in his wood reliefs explored organic symbols related to nature. Although *Construcción* adheres to a compositional grid, the work simplifies Torres-García's lexicon of symbols and investigates the physical depth of the two-dimensional surface, thus heralding a shift in Matto's trajectory.

During the early 1960s, as the TTG disbanded, Matto continued the established modality of creating large works densely populated with a plethora of signs. Toward the latter part of that decade, however, the artist began to focus on a few key symbols to which he would consistently return. *Construcción* demonstrates Matto's process of reducing his imagery to create a more legible, and thus universal, pictorial surface, which he would then transform into singular, freestanding objects. *Constructivo con cinco formas* [Construction in Five Forms] (fig. 2), painted the same year as *Construcción*, reveals a similar process of compositional simplification; however, the work in the Brillembourg Capriles Collection presents clearer and more developed symbols. Indeed, the well-defined images featured in this

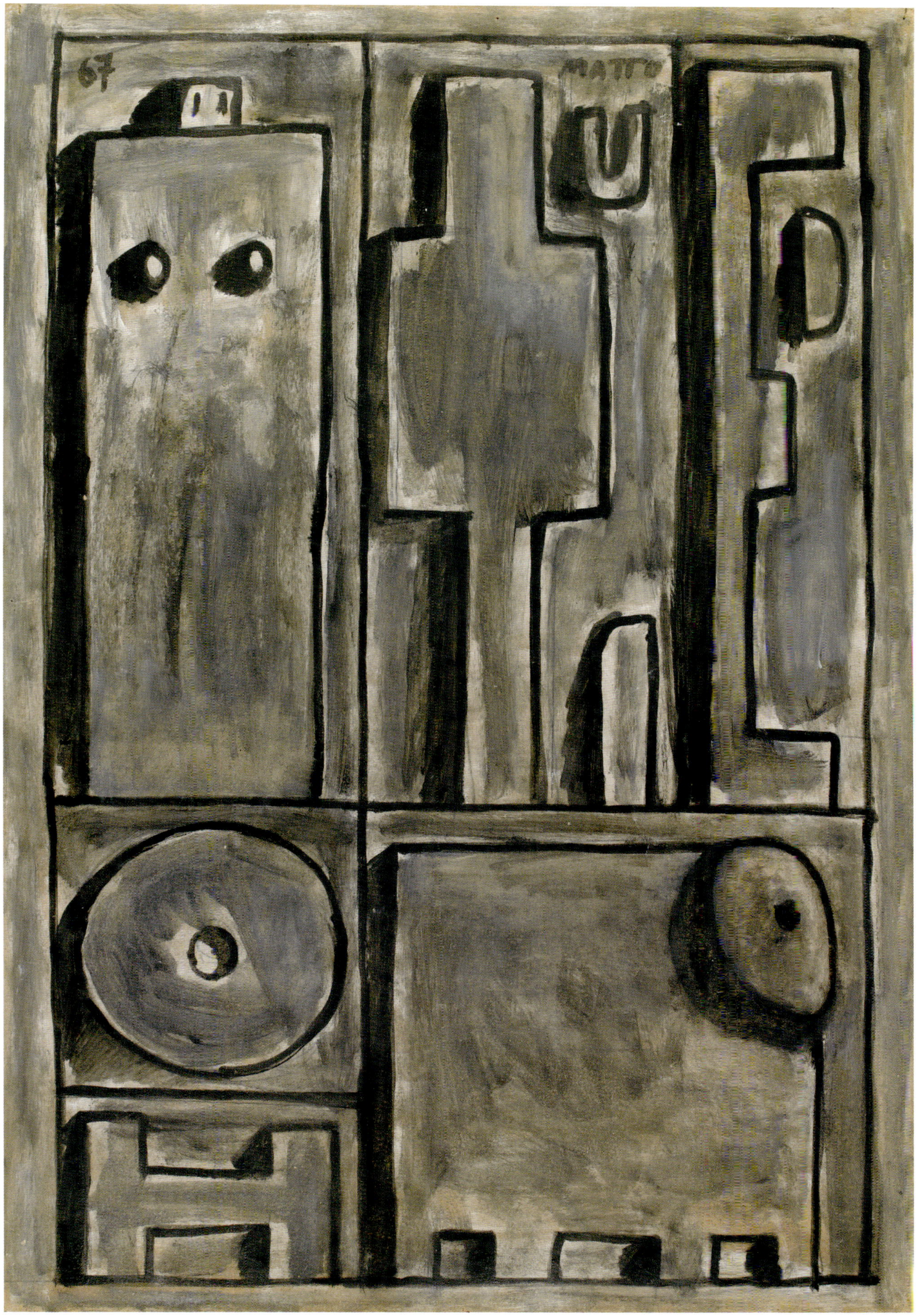

PLATE 20

Francisco Matto • *Construcción* [Construction], 1967

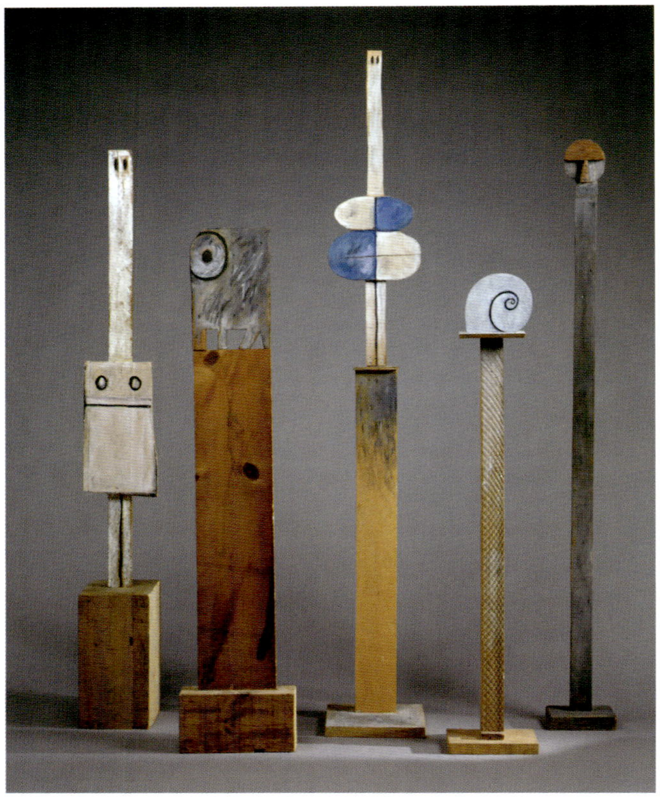

FIG. 1

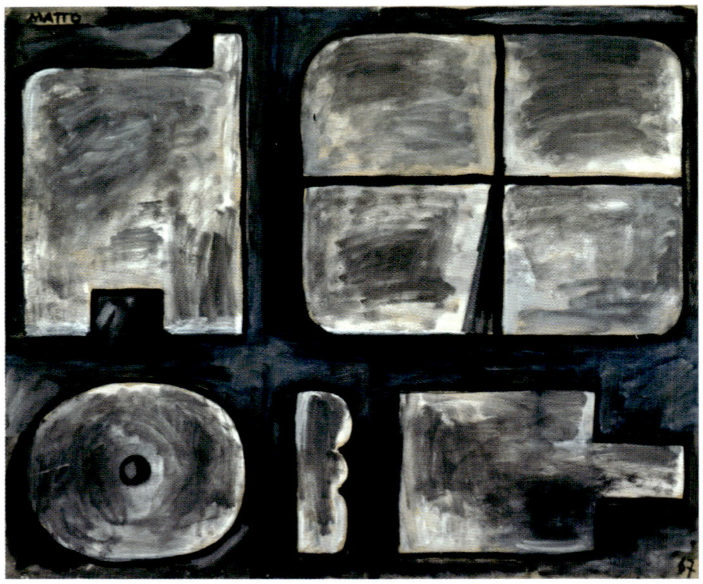

FIG. 2

work—a woman, a lamb, a "U," and a circular structure—become the basis of Matto's later totems of the late 1970s.

Construcción also presents a unique relationship with Matto's reliefs produced during this decade (fig. 3). Although these wooden works were intended to hang on a wall, the artist imbued them with a sculptural quality by rhythmically and proportionally arranging flat, volumetric planes on the pictorial surface. In *Construcción*, Matto instilled the painting with a similar, planar three-dimensionality. The artist diluted the oil paints with water so that the pigments seeped into the artist's board, causing the support to be visible. On one hand, this technique allowed the artist to embrace the intrinsic nature of his support, a technique that he learned from Torres-García and is exemplified by the *maderas* in the Brillembourg Capriles Collection. On the other hand, the texture of the board gives the painting its three-dimensional, stonelike quality, which is enhanced by Matto's strong use of shadows. With this work, the artist tried to create in painting the similar visual effect that he had achieved in his reliefs, thereby obscuring the traditional categories of painting and sculpture. His disregard for convention was part of a larger twentieth-century movement of questioning the standard hierarchies of art history. Specifically, in the case of sculpture, artists such as Louise Nevelson (fig. 4) and David Smith eliminated the necessity to model and sculpt by assembling flat forms to produce planar sculptures. Matto's attempt to give *Construcción* a sculptural quality directly relates to these broader modern practices.

With the creation of his totems, Matto injected an intensely ritualistic aspect into the key symbols identified in *Construcción*. These freestanding objects remain as flat as the wooden board that the artist used, eloquently fusing his focus on the mystical properties of signs with his modern tendencies in planar sculpture. Indeed, the works present Matto's most innovative play with flat volumes in space, and the painting in the Brillembourg Capriles Collection provides an early experiment in the development of this magical modernism.

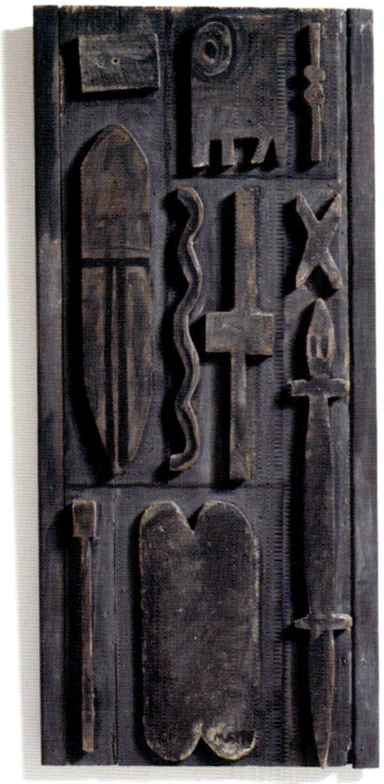

FIG. 3

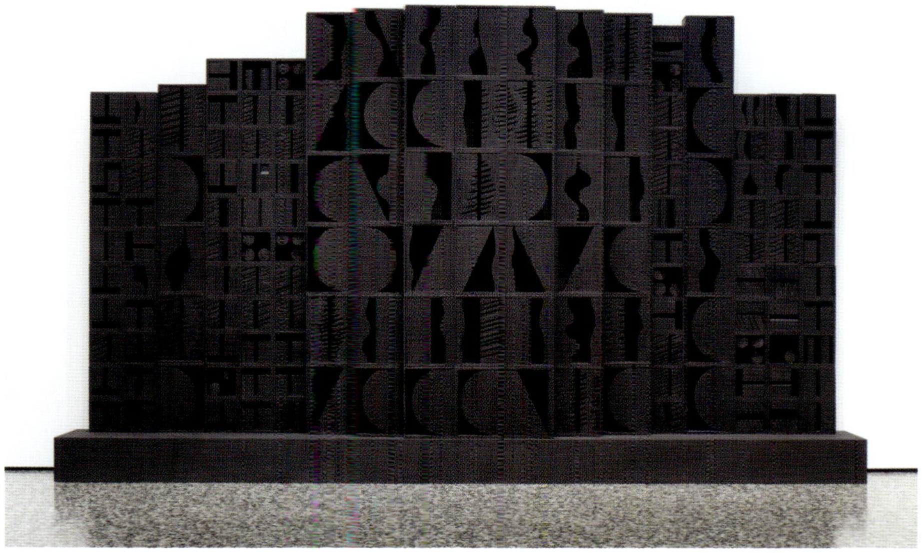

FIG. 4

ILLUSTRATIONS IN TEXT

FIGURE 1
Francisco Matto
Totems (Venus, Cordero, Venus blanquiazúl, Caracol grande, Máscara), 1979–85
Oil on wood
Various dimensions
The Museum of Fine Arts, Houston, gift of Alfred C. Glassell, III and Marli Andrade, Mary and Roy Cullen, Marjorie H. Wortham, Joanna and Richard W. Wortham III, the Wortham Foundation, and the Caroline Wiess Law Foundation, and gift of Ada Antuña de Matto

FIGURE 2
Francisco Matto
Constructivo con cinco formas
[Construction with Five Forms], 1967
Oil on canvas
Private collection, New York

FIGURE 3
Francisco Matto
Ten Forms, 1966
Oil on wood
28 x 12 3/8 inches
Cecilia de Torres, Ltd.

FIGURE 4
Louise Nevelson
Mirror Image I, 1969
Painted wood
117 3/4 x 210 1/2 x 21 inches
The Museum of Fine Arts, Houston, Gift of The Brown Foundation, Inc.

NOTES

1
Joaquín Torres-García, who established Constructive Universalism, posited the belief that artists should reclaim the non-naturalistic aesthetic of a distant past. Matto absorbed this idea of the myth of origins and made it the foundation of his later work.

2
This approach to sculpture was first investigated by Margit Rowell in her 1979 publication *The Planar Dimension: Europe, 1912–1932* (New York: Solomon R. Guggenheim Foundation, 1979).

María C. Gaztambide

THE IMAGE IS NOT A THING

FORM AND DYNAMIC PERCEPTION IN MATTA

The essential principles of human consciousness cannot be grasped until we abandon the psychological attitude of conceiving the image as a petrified thing or object. . . . The image is not a thing. It is an act which must be completed by the spectator. In order to be fully conscious of the phenomenon which the image describes, we ourselves must first of all fulfill the act of dynamic perception.

—KATHERINE S. DREIER AND MATTA, *DUCHAMP'S GLASS*, 1944[1]

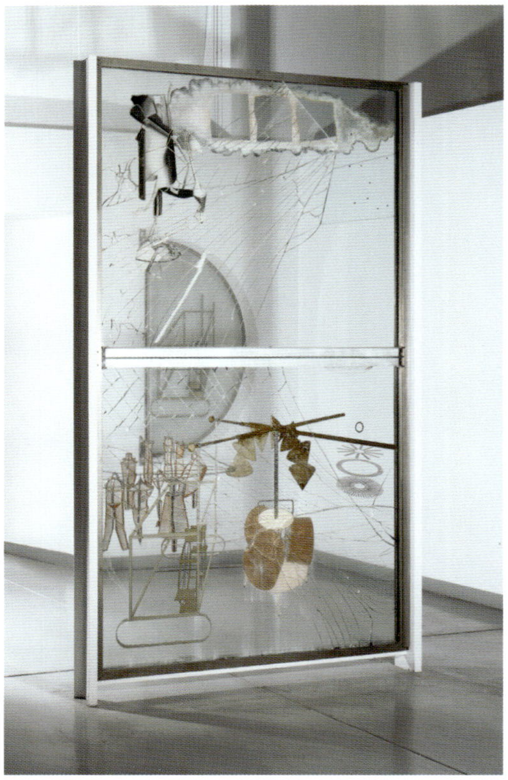

FIG. 1

WHEN IN 1944 MATTA (1911–2002) and the artist and collector Katherine S. Dreier (1877–1952) wrote their watershed treatise on Marcel Duchamp's *La mariée mise à nu par ses célibataires, même* [The Large Glass: The Bride Stripped Bare by Her Bachelors, Even] (1915–23) (fig. 1), they were, in a sense, outlining the main precepts that they followed in their own artistic paths. In their analytical reflection on *The Large Glass*, the authors proclaimed, "reality is created by the artist himself, for the use of the spirit."[2] Moreover, the expectation was that the experience of a certain work of art—in this case *The Large Glass*, which Dreier owned at the time—, would become complete when the spectator entered into a dialogue with the artist. Eschewing representation—indeed the "exploitation of the object or image" that Matta and Dreier denounced in their text—, the outcome of such a two-way relationship would be the realization of a true knowledge of one's self through the active experience of the work. In this way, they envisioned that art could become, "dynamic action, causing a direct shock through which to free the spirit."[3]

This very tension between liberating art from the vestiges of two-dimensionality while at the same time uncovering the psychological aspects of man's physical environment—which Matta recognized as the driving force in Duchamp's work from the 1920s—was in itself at play during much of the Chilean artist's long career. Spanning the period from his New York exile (1939–1948) to the early 1950s, the eight pieces in the Brillembourg Capriles Collection of Latin American Art offer the possibility of rereading Matta's work in light of this tension at a pivotal moment in his career. These works not only

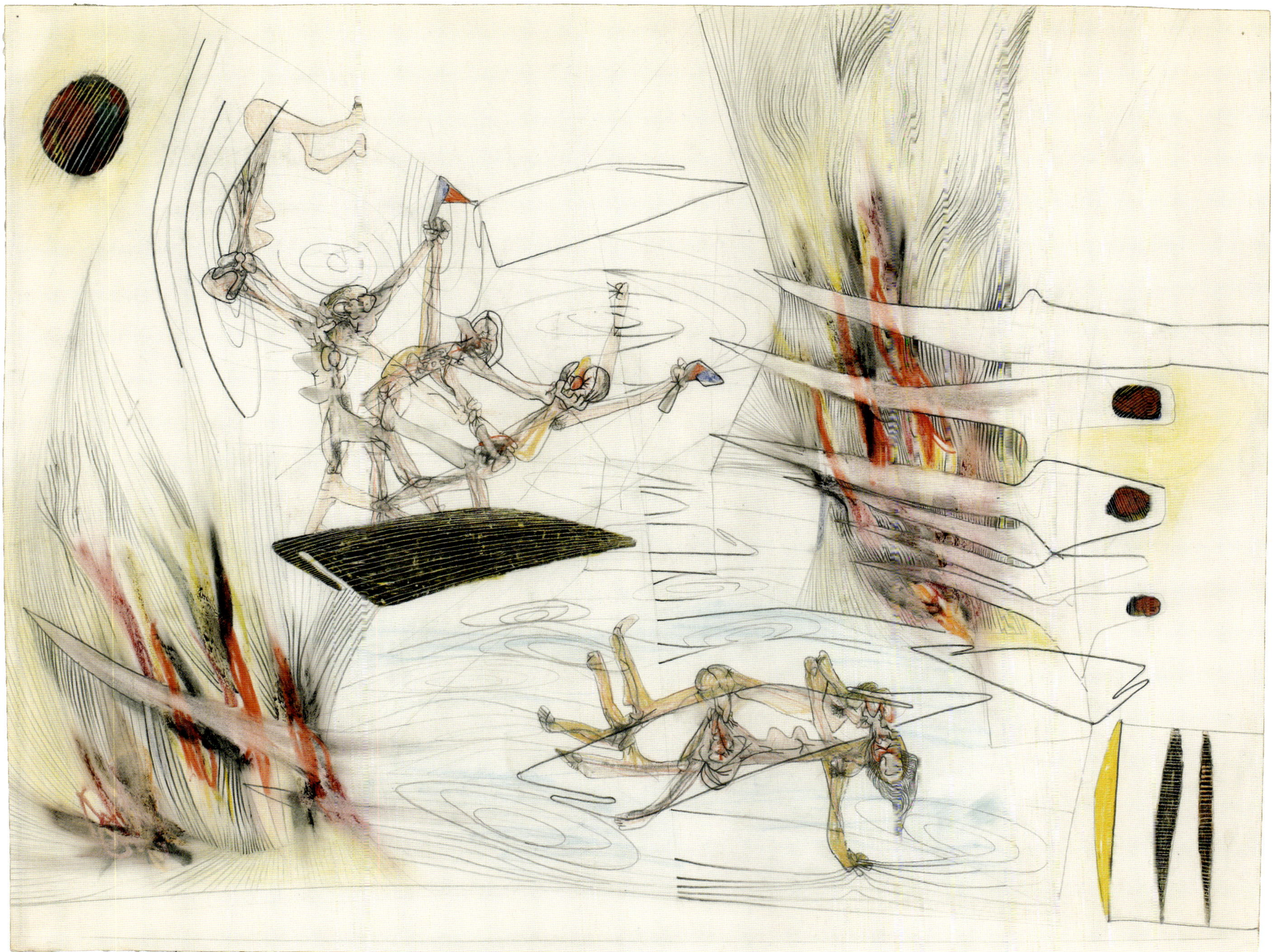

PLATE 21

Matta • *Sin título* [Untitled], 1943–44

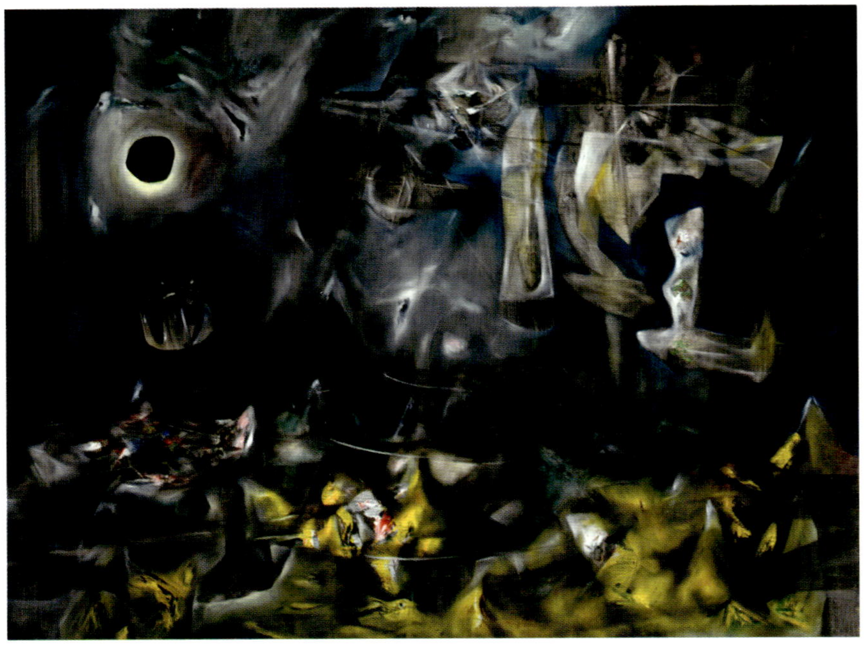

FIG. 2

chronicle the artist's stylistic adherence to and eventual theoretical break with the Surrealists but also showcase the varying stages of his transition to, and departure from, form as he struggled to define an alternate concept of perception that transcended the traditional interpretations of the three-dimensional plane.

Mutatis Mutandis *(Form)*

Figural references appeared often in Matta's early drawings from the 1930s. However, by the early 1940s, Matta had refocused his energy on experimenting with the Surrealist techniques of automatic writing and the principle of chance. These concerns, along with the influence of Freudian psychology, had shifted his attention to the realm of the subconscious. His initial painted series—the Psychological Morphologies of the late 1930s and the Inscapes from the early 1940s, including *Untitled* (fig. 2) of 1942 in the collection of the Museum of Fine Arts, Houston,—traversed the waters of pure abstraction.[4] By the mid-1940s, however, as news trickled into New York regarding the atrocities of World War II, Matta's work began to take another turn toward figuration. The works that emerged beginning in 1943—his Social Morphologies series and related drawings—reflected a growing concern with the human condition in the external world.[5]

Figurative drawings from the mid-1940s including *Untitled* of 1943–44 (plate 21), *Untitled* of 1944–45 (plate 22), and *Naturaleza muerta* [Still Life] (c. 1945) (plate 23),[6] all in the Brillembourg Capriles Collection, offer improbable juxtapositions of geometric shapes and humanoids. They evoke the postwar context in which they were created; however, unlike the work of many of the Surrealists, there is no narrative at play here. "Objects are but the instruments the artist selects to use, in search of the Spirit,"[7] Matta and Dreier wrote in *Duchamp's Glass* of 1944. To afford Matta's figures more weight vis-à-vis the other elements of his compositions would be to fall into the trap of representation. *Objectified*, they are clearly one of the many rungs on a ladder leading up to some sort of greater truth.

The tormented figures that one confronts in *Untitled* (1944–45), for example, are engaged in sexual union, in the midst of a physical transformation, or in restless, dynamic action. The gridlike structures anchoring them are reminiscent of comic-book panels; however, Matta did not intend for this spatial disposition to indicate a specific sequence for "reading" the work in narrative terms. What Matta rehearses through these vignettes are possibilities for mutation: tongues become phalluses, two bodies merge into one, bodily orifices become form, and geometries lead to a horizon devoid of any specificity. Likewise, the placements of the figures are not meant to suggest continuity between the vignettes. The viewer relates to them on a visceral level, identifying with their anguish, yet it is never obvious what has transpired or the degree to which they indicate any sort of contextual tension.

Splitting of the Ego (1945) (plate 24) differs from the previously mentioned examples to the extent that Matta seeks to transfer specific meaning throughout the composition. Formally, his vocabulary has not changed much from other drawings of the period—the vortices, the concentric structures (now both positive and negative) of Matta's curvilinear perspective,[8] the orbs and cubes are all here—; however, there is a narrative element at play in *Splitting of the Ego* that has no precedent among the artist's contemporaneous works on paper. Here, he depicts a group of figures agonizing as they toss and catch

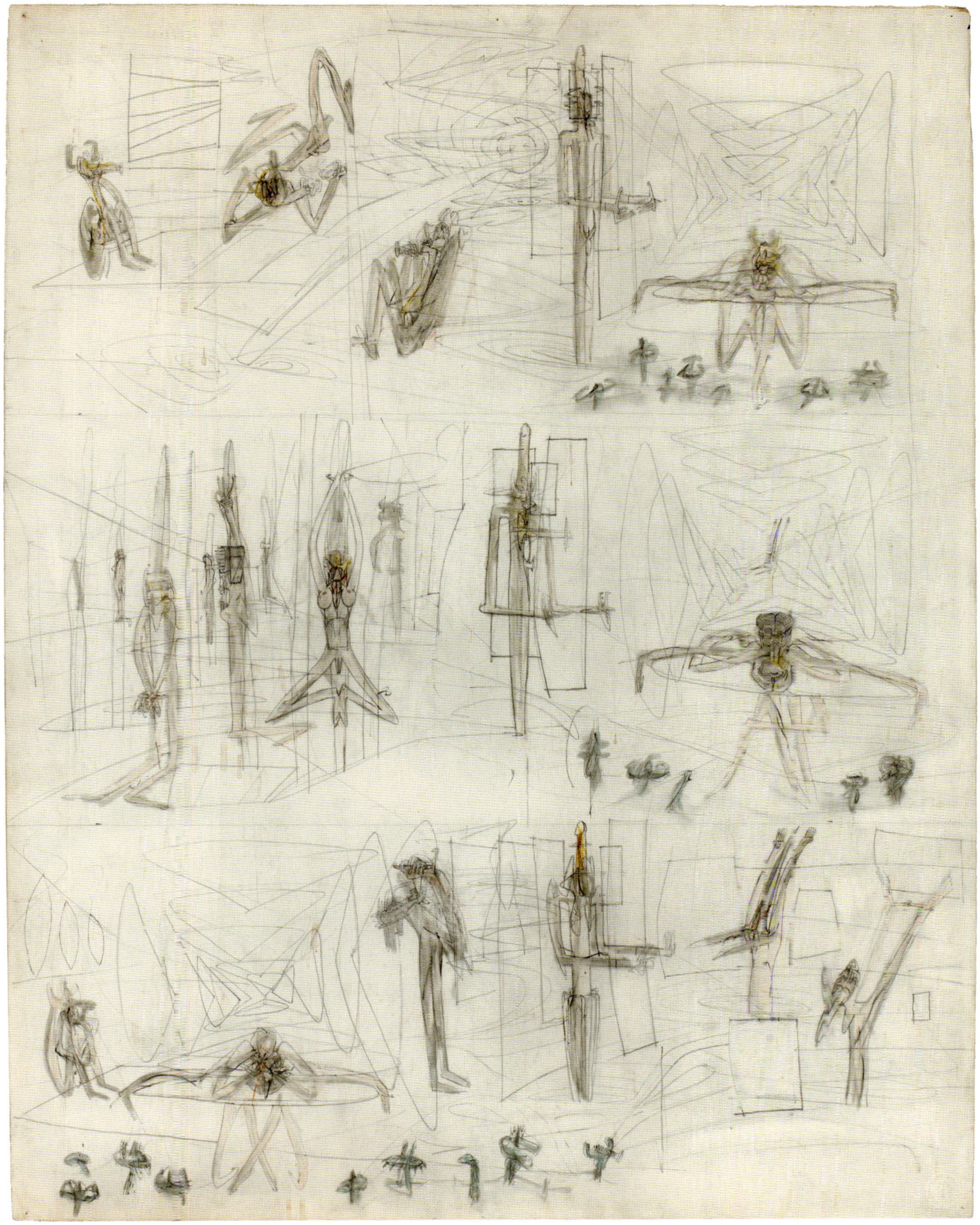

PLATE 22

Matta • *Sin título* [Untitled], 1944–45

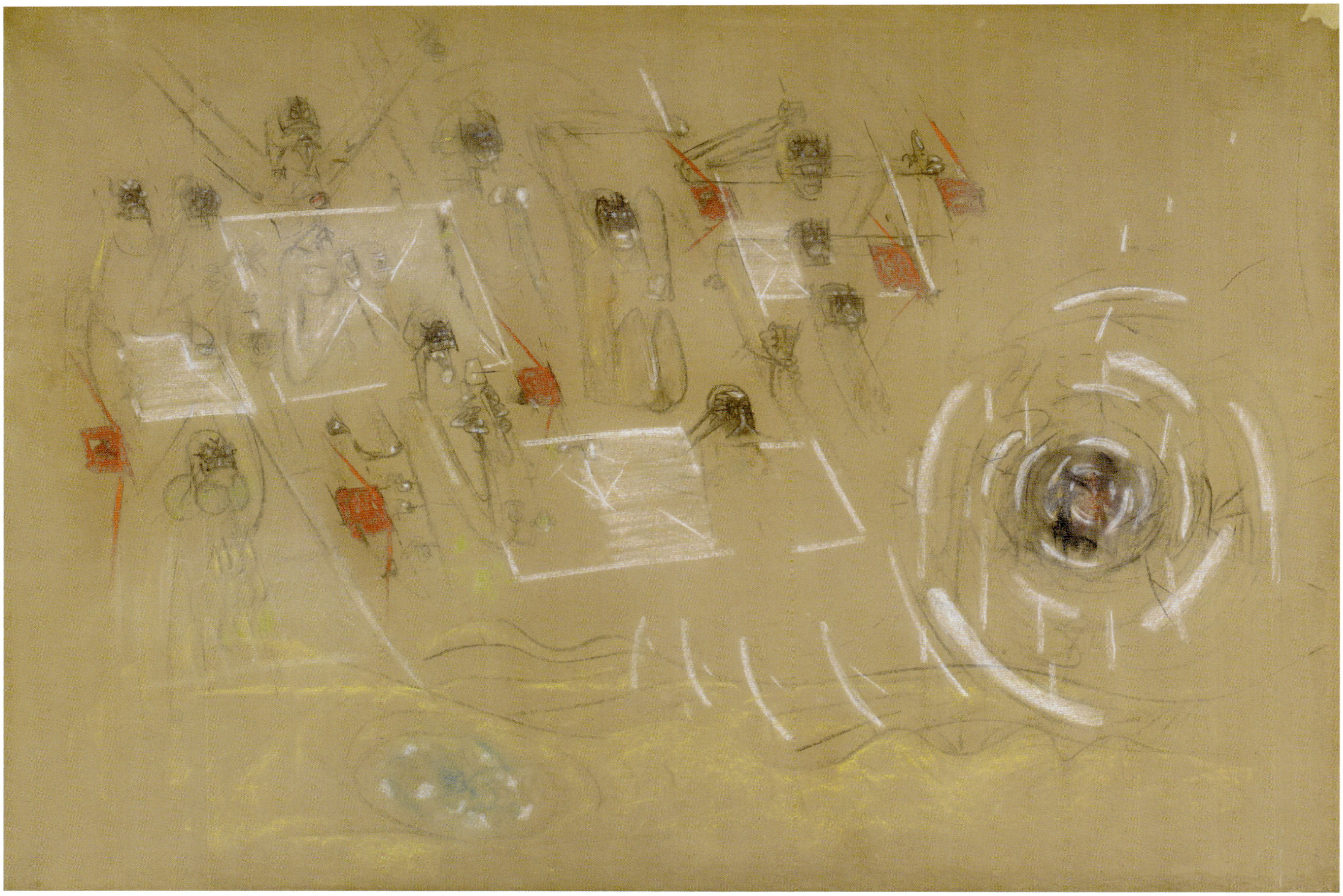

PLATE 23

Matta • *Naturaleza muerta* [Still Life], c. 1945

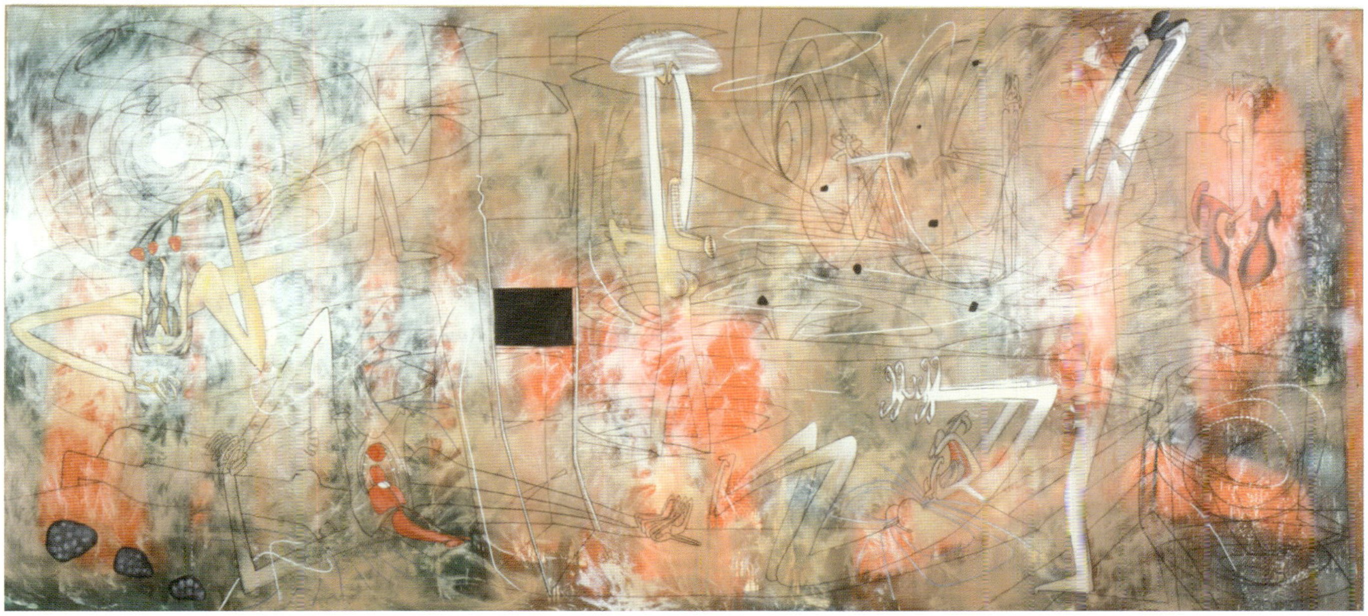

FIG. 3

a number of white semitransparent orbs.[9] Matta is trying to tell us something through the figures' gnarled faces and exaggerated hand gestures. Like *X Space and the Ego* at the Centre Georges Pompidou, Paris (fig. 3), or *Être avec* [Being With] (The Metropolitan Museum of Art, New York), both also from 1945, Matta locates *Splitting of the Ego* "in a situation which [is] more historical: the tortured chambers and so on."[10] He evokes a generalized feeling of despair not unlike what Picasso communicated through *Guernica* (1937). Like *Guernica*, *Splitting of the Ego* or the related painting *X Space and the Ego* does not recount a specific set of events but rather conveys the desolation of man in times of war.[12] Indeed, these works capture "the essence of a spiritual experience" that Matta and Dreier had discussed in light of Duchamp's *The Large Glass* just a year earlier.[13] In contrast to the majority of brown drawings on wove paper, the support for the monumental work *Splitting of the Ego* is ribbed kraft paper, a choice that was surely deliberate. By seaming two already large panels of kraft paper together, Matta was able to create something monumental in scale (measuring close to 6 feet by 7 ½ feet)—and thus groundbreaking for a work on paper.[14] Moreover, the ribbing of the kraft paper may have offered Matta's typically spontaneous trace some slight resistance through which to better suggest the emotional state of the figures.

Matta's interest in motion and mutating forms is heightened by his choice of brown paper for a number of his works on paper. Although the artist used this support infrequently, it prevails among the works in the Brillembourg Capriles Collection, including *Naturaleza muerta*, *Splitting of the Ego*, *Abstract Composition* (1949) (plate 25), *Autómata* [Automaton] (1942) (plate 26), and *Composition et Étude* [Composition and Study] (1952) (plate 27). In all but one of these drawings from the late 1940s and early 1950s—*Splitting of the Ego*, which is on kraft paper—Matta used a commercially available wove paper.[15] It not only allowed him to use a support that far exceeded the dimensions of sheet paper—consistent with his preference for large-scale work—but also provided an extremely smooth surface, similar in many ways to a gessoed wall, which he seemed to have preferred for many of his works on paper.[16] In these drawings, the artist is able to achieve a greater degree of simultaneity and movement in his gestures since the unribbed surface offers no friction nor is it weighed down by paint. Matta's very deliberate range of color also facilitated the articulation of his conceptual and theoretical ideas. The versatility in the artist's use of white, for instance, indicates that he may have been cognizant of how the paper would darken over time with light exposure and perhaps even welcomed this effect.[17] More than a half-century after these drawings were created, the distinction between figures and support has become so imperceptible that they appear to be actively metamorphosing *into* the brown paper.

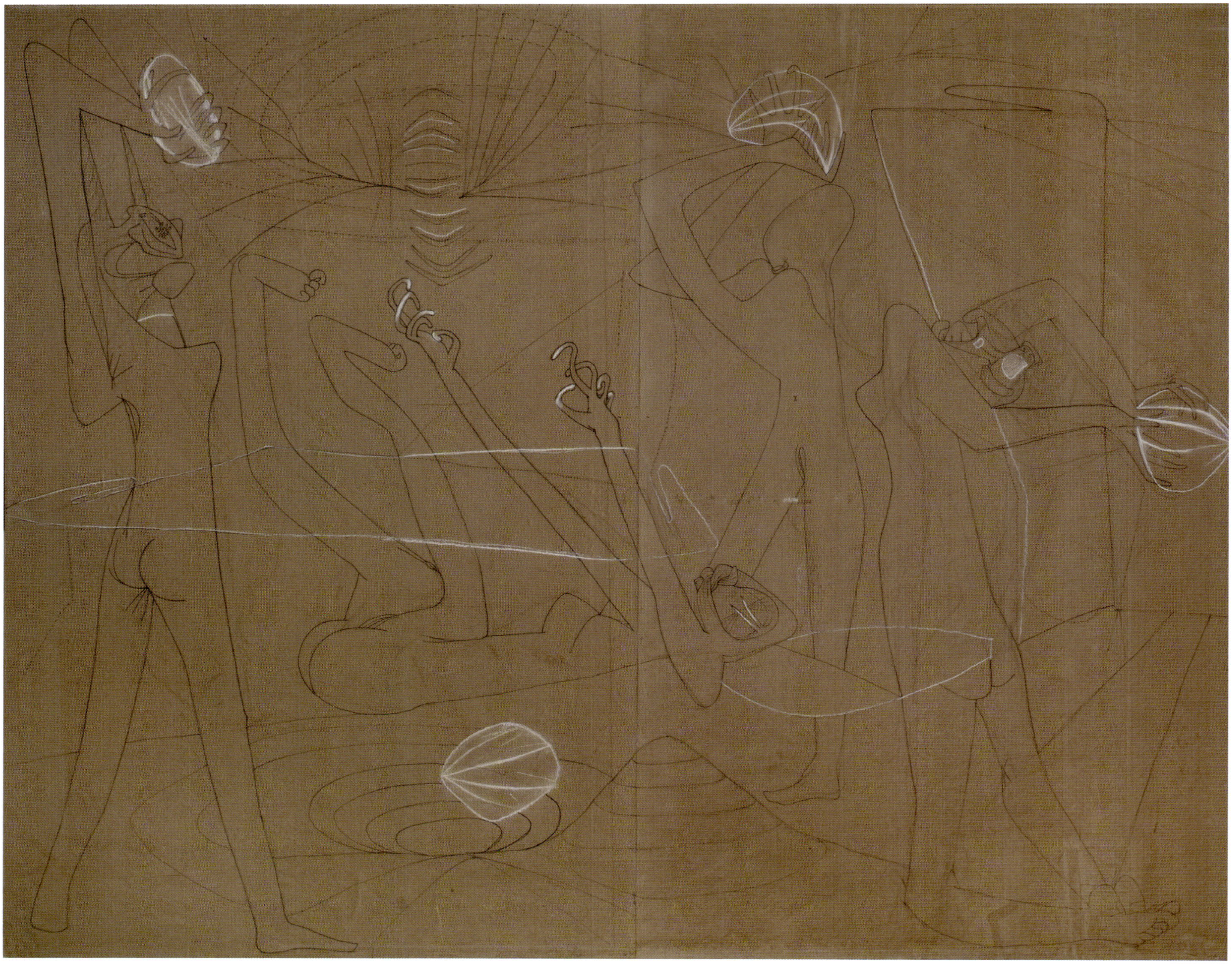

PLATE 24

Matta • *Splitting of the Ego,* 1945

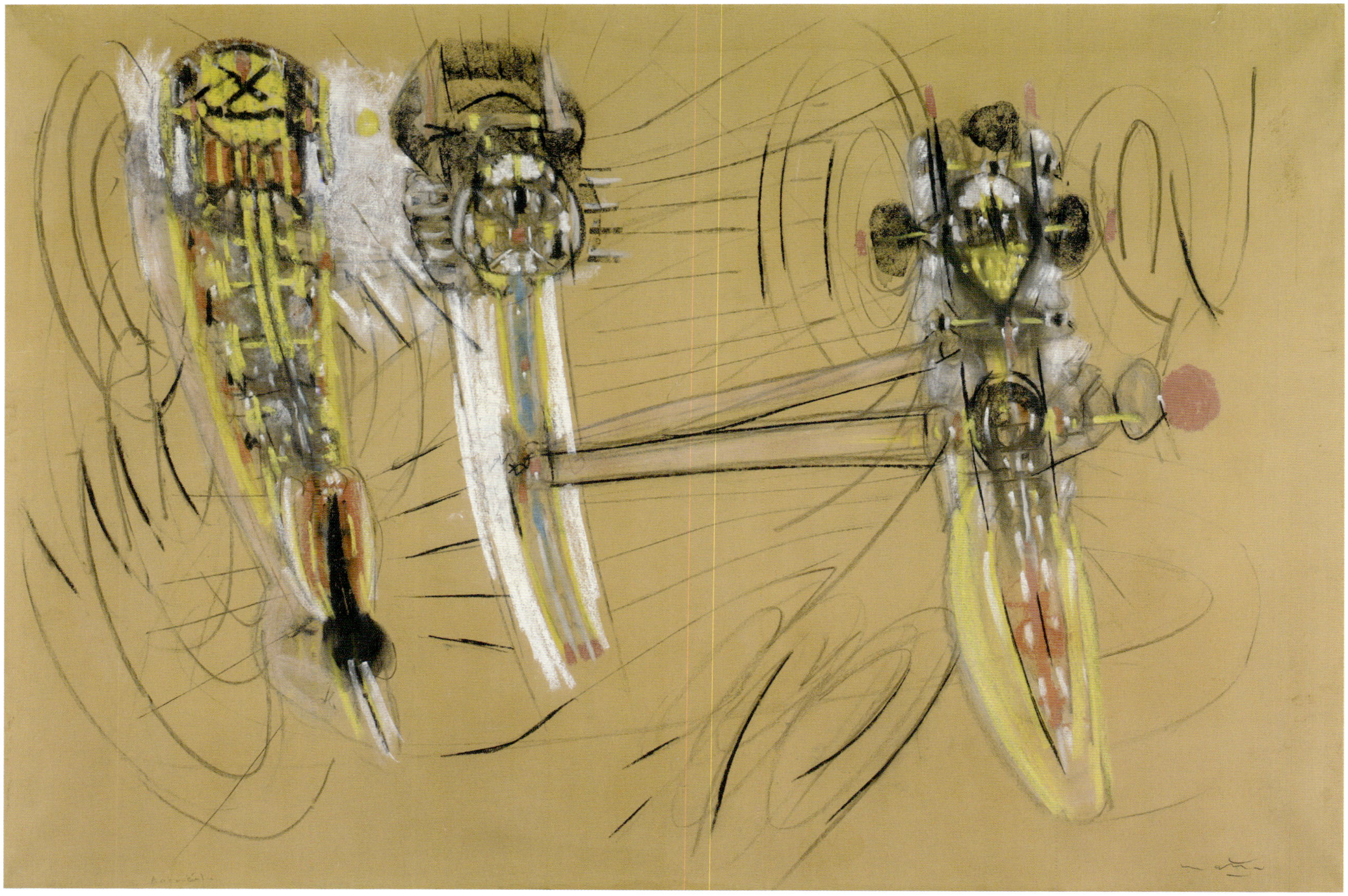

PLATE 25

Matta • *Abstract Composition*, 1949

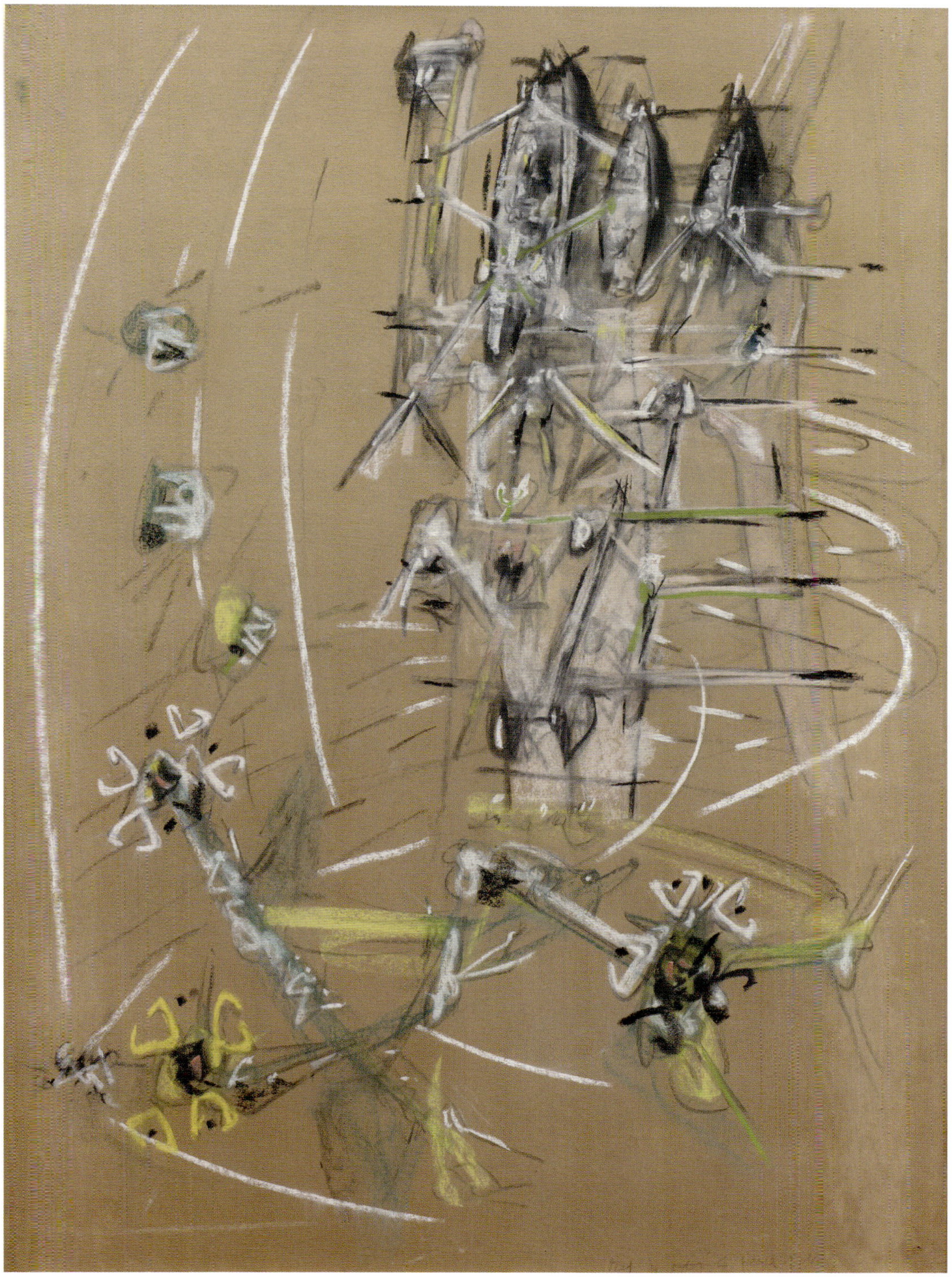

PLATE 26
Matta • *Autómata* [Automaton], 1942

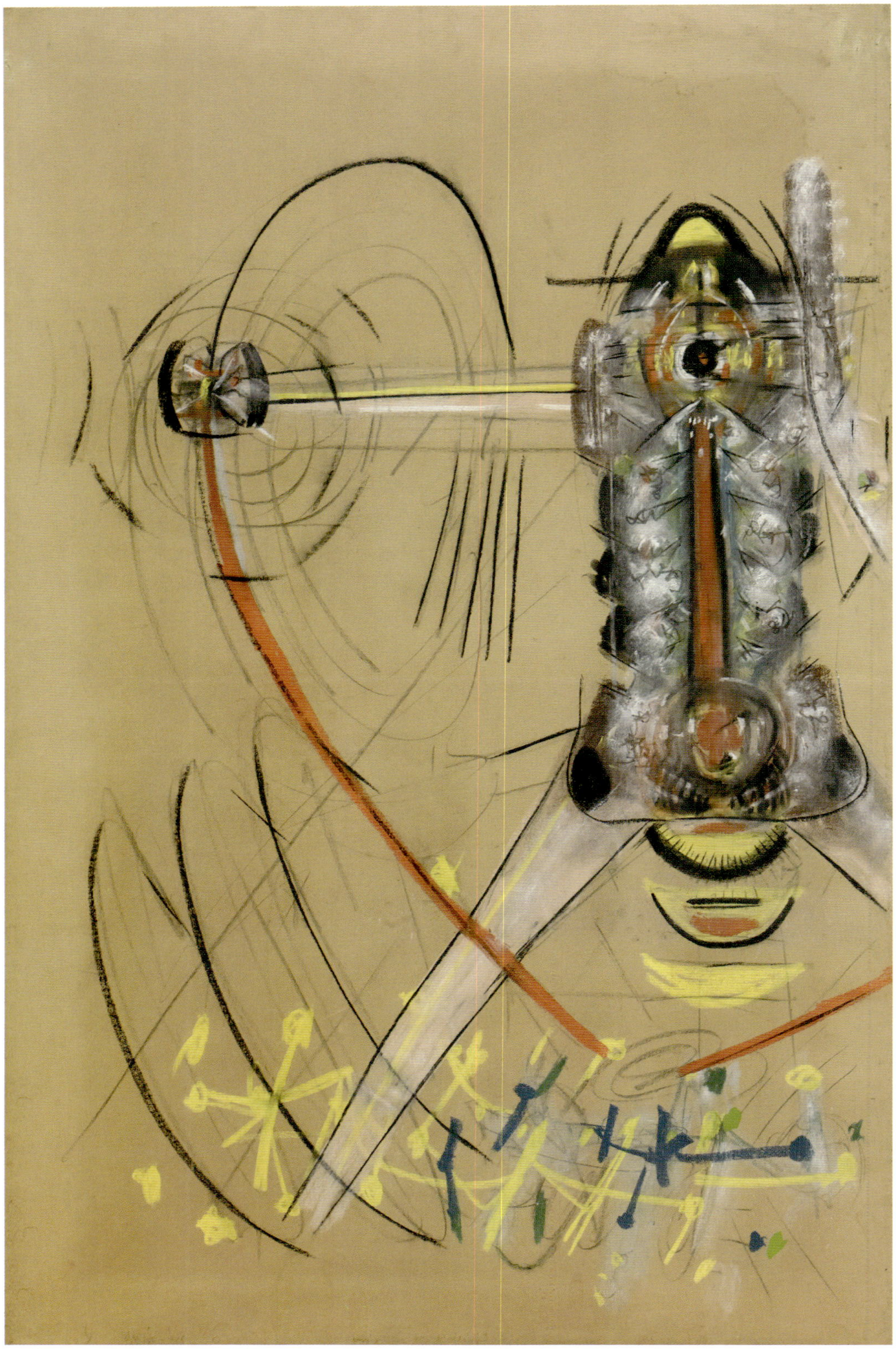

PLATE 27

Matta • *Composition et Étude* [Composition and Study], 1952

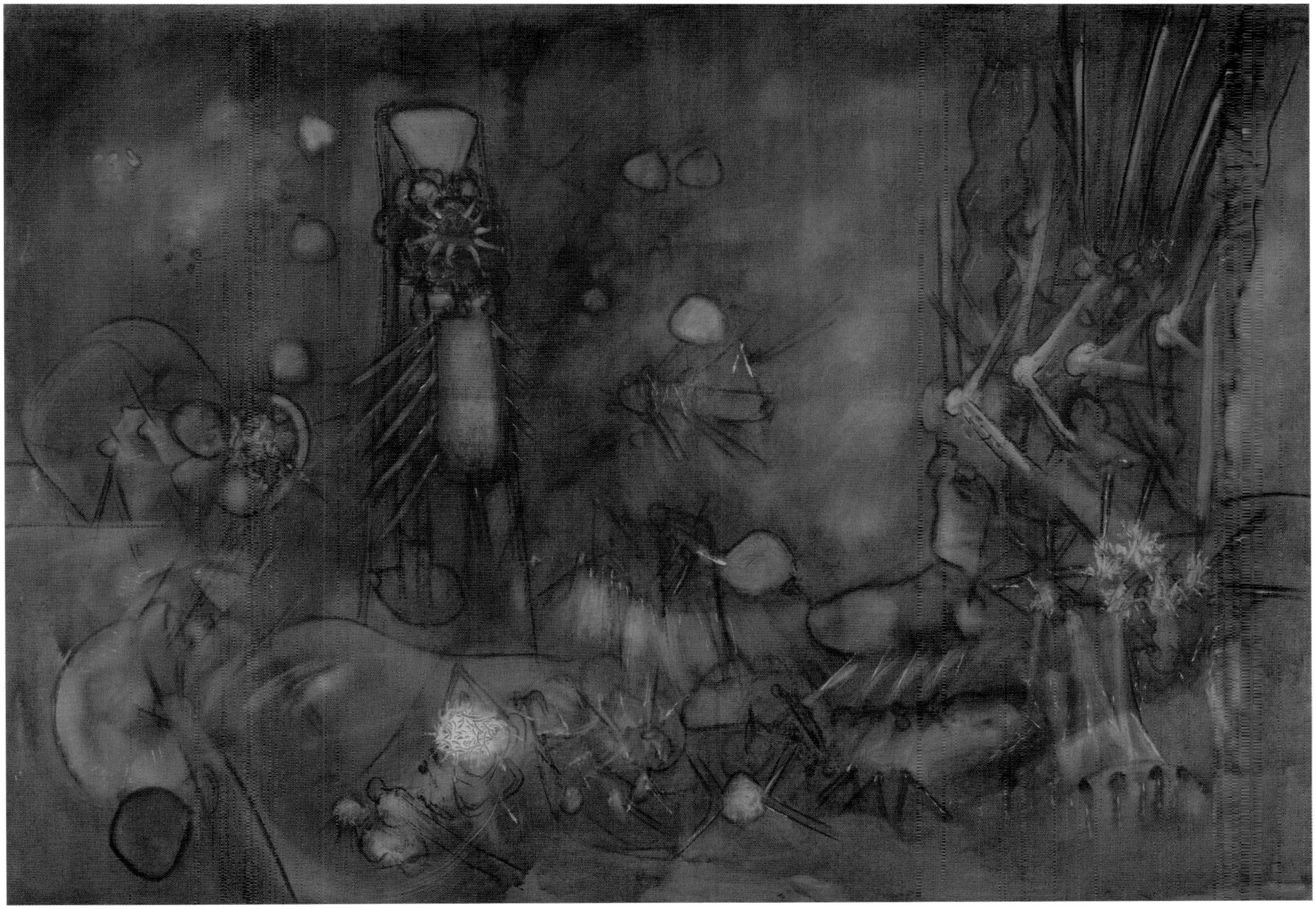

PLATE 28

Matta • *Soul without Terror,* 1953

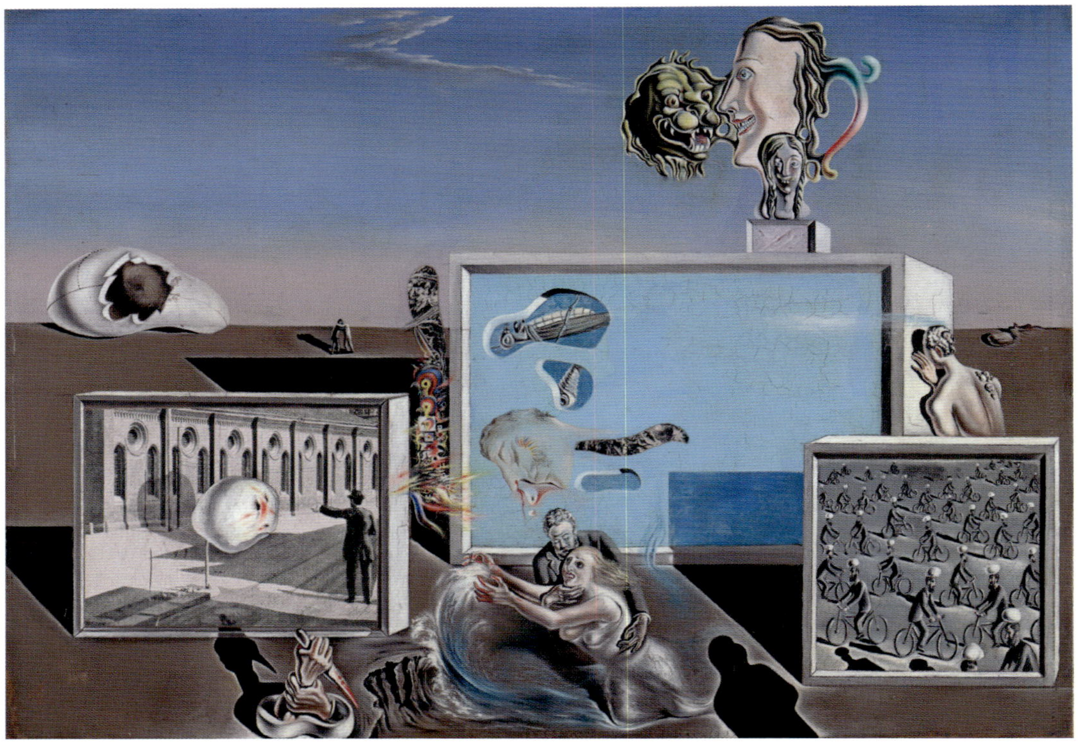

FIG. 4

Around 1950, Matta once again moved away from the figure. *Soul without Terror* (1953) (plate 28), which the artist painted in Italy five years after returning to Europe, marks a transitional moment as he loosened up figures and fleshed out his version of sidereal landscapes of the 1950s (the El espacio de la especie series).[18] It is certainly much darker in overall tonality than paintings from Matta's earlier painted series and is, in fact, closer to later works from El espacio de la especie [The Space of the Species] in the billowy treatment of the background. Moreover, the figures here—the vertebraic motif to the right of the canvas and the central insectoid—are far less defined than in the works on paper from the 1940s. *Soul without Terror* sharply contrasts with the sparse backgrounds in which Matta locates the activated scenes of his works on paper. However, it is equally masterful in his use of materials, particularly in the illusion of dense color achieved with a minimum amount of pigment.[19] The background is applied first and becomes the road map for what Matta draws over it. "I don't paint," Matta once said of his process. "I see a cosmos in the [stained canvas]. My point of departure is the stains."[20] In *Soul without Terror*, the process is not linear: the stained background suggests the shapes that he delineates with dry media; color is filled in and rubbed back; the distance between foreground and background is blurred. The result is a remarkable ambiguity of form reminiscent of how his figures often merge with the muted backdrops in his works on paper.

'Kill the Optical' (Perception)

In addition to reflecting Matta's shifting relationship with figuration, the works in the Brillembourg Capriles Collection reveal an artist struggling to transcend the traditional limitations of the three-dimensional plane. Gordon Onslow Ford (1912–2003), the British Surrealist who introduced him to the group, recalls that in their early collaborations Matta often remarked on the need to "kill the optical" in expanding consciousness beyond sense perception.[21] For Matta, Onslow Ford noted, the problem stemmed from a belief that "the eye saw only a cross section of reality" and that much sensory information was lost in this skewed perception.[22] In 1938, Matta described reality as "the sequence of the explosive convulsions modeled in a pulsatory and rotatory medium subjected to rhythms."[23] Within that dynamic framework, the eye functioned as "the agent of memory" and as a "means of simplifying" awareness. Matta's proposition for a new art required that the eye and consciousness construct the "immediate and impulsive graphics" through which to trace a more complete rendering of the totality of reality.[24]

Matta's concern for the liminal had much to do with a deep-rooted interest in both the scientific and the mystical side of the fourth dimension.[25] Matta was not the only Surrealist to have portrayed multiple dimensions of time and space in his work. Other Surrealists, including Salvador Dalí (1904–1981) and Yves Tanguy (1900–1951), often sought to depict notions of alternate realities and simultaneity through a reliance on the trompe-l'oeil technique. *Illumined Pleasures* of 1929 by Dalí (fig. 4), for example, is suggestive of an interconnectedness between the three disjointed shadow boxes, yet there is no indication that they are related in a transcendental way to a fourth dimension. Matta, on the other hand, consistently went beyond merely hinting at simultaneous realities; instead, he obsessed over how to graphically represent a fourth dimension that is hidden from plain sight, yet deeply felt emotionally.

Duchamp's work was an important referent for Matta. In 1944, Matta praised *The Large Glass* for its breakthrough in establishing a revolutionary model of interaction between the work of art and the viewer. Executed on two panes of glass with materials such as lead foil, fuse wire, and dust, the work requires the "conscious participation of the on-looker" in order for it to be fully completed. "While we gaze upon the bride," wrote Dreier and Matta, "there appears through the glass the image of the room wherein we stand and on the radiation of the mirror design lives the image of our own body."[26] *The Large Glass* called for the incorporation of the spectator and his environment into the experience of the work through reflection, play of light, and the visual information that filtered through the glass panes.

Much in the same way, Matta established a different subject/object relationship that was based on viewer perception and, to a large degree, on the spatial dynamics between the two. He asked his viewers to locate themselves at a nontraditional vantage point. Matta's intention was for viewers' eyes to fall not in front of the piece—the customary position for considering a work of art—but rather in the center of colliding and multidirectional perspectives. Matta called this 360-degree viewpoint the *central knot of perception*.[27] *Abstract Composition*, *Autómata*, and *Composition et Study* all play on this novel idea. *Abstract Composition*, in particular, records a "take off" moment. Here, and to a lesser degree also in the other two drawings, the figure is no longer floating but in the process of being rapidly propelled. Spectators are charged with the impossible task of contemplating its blastoff from a variety of angles. Matta plays on the tension resulting from the figure's (perceived) violent movement versus its (actual) immobility on the picture plane at the very moment of its ascendance into another (unseen) plane.

"A painter is a man who reveals to the eye things that man has as yet been unable to see properly," Matta once said about the dynamic relationship between mankind and the space we inhabit. "I want to express reality and what contradicts it in ourselves, inner life and its conflicts with the external world, the distance that separates the id hidden deep down with [what] is on the surface."[28] Despite its many contradictions, a consideration of Matta's continual experimentation with form and perception in the postwar period reveals one of those rare moments when theory and praxis almost seamlessly converged.

ILLUSTRATIONS IN TEXT

FIGURE 1
Marcel Duchamp
The Bride Stripped Bare by Her Bachelors, Even (The Large Glass), 1915–23
Oil, varnish, lead foil, lead wire, and dust on two glass panels
109 1/4 x 70 x 3 3/8 inches
(277.5 x 177.8 x 8.6 cm)
Philadelphia Museum of Art, Bequest of Katherine S. Dreier, 1952

FIGURE 2
Matta
Untitled, 1942
Oil on canvas
38 1/4 x 51 1/4 inches (97.2 x 130.2 cm)
The Museum of Fine Arts, Houston, The Joseph and Sylvia Slifka Collection, 2004.144

FIGURE 3
Matta
Xpace and the Ego, 1945
Oil on canvas
79 5/8 x 180 inches (202.2 x 457.2 cm)
Musée Nacional d'Art Moderne, Centre Georges Pompidou, Paris, France

FIGURE 4
Salvador Dalí
Illumined Pleasures, 1929
Oil and collage on composition board
9 3/8 x 13 3/4 inches (23.8 x 34.7 cm)
The Museum of Modern Art, New York, The Sidney and Harriet Janis Collection

NOTES

1
Katherine S. Dreier and Matta Echaurren, *Duchamp's Glass. La mariée mise à nu par ses célibataires, meme. An Analytical Reflection*. (New York: Société Anonyme, Inc./The Museum of Modern Art, 1944), n/p.

2
Ibid.

3
Ibid.

4
In his *Psychological Morphologies*, Matta devised a morphology of the cosmos, of the human experience or its internal aspects. "When I started painting," he wrote of these early paintings, "it was through necessity, of trying to find an expression which I call a morphology, of the functioning of one's thinking, or one's feeling." Matta, quoted in Andrew Crispo Gallery, *Matta: A Totemic World*, exh. cat. (New York: Andrew Crispo Gallery, 1975), n/p. Following the morphologies, Matta incorporated planar, geometric shapes, and swirling lines; he applied these elements over the softer, biomorphic shapes characteristic of his earlier pictures. He called these works from the early 1940s *Inscapes* because the intent was to transpose the mind's otherwise abstract inner workings into what seem to be actual, three-dimensional spaces. For an analysis of the series, see Álvaro Medina, "The Mobile Matter of Sebastián Matta," *Art Nexus* 17 (September 1995): 68–85.

5
"What interested me at this time," Matta recalled about the later part of his New York period, "was to find some reference in my mental space to the human being, to society." Matta in Sidney Simon, "Concerning the Beginnings of the New York School, 1939–1943: An Interview with Peter Busa and Matta," *Art International* 11, no. 6 (Summer 1967): 19.

6
Originally undated, it is my opinion that *Naturaleza Muerta* was executed contemporaneously with *Untitled*, 1944–45. Here, too, Matta is working out the anatomy of his imaginary figures that share characteristics, in semblance and posturing, with those of *Untitled*. Also, in *Naturaleza Muerta*, Matta is working through the same compositional problems that he addresses in several of the vignettes of *Untitled* of 1944–45: figural groups that interact with cubes and air currents, the presence of black holes and vortexes, and so forth. Moreover, as in *Untitled*, *Naturaleza Muerta* echoes Giacometti's *Invisible Object (Hands Holding a Void)* of 1934.

7
Dreier and Matta, *Duchamp's Glass*, n/p.

8
See Matta's entry for SPACE in "Redefinitions Towards a New Dimension for Painting," where he illustrates the concept with a horizon of precisely these same forms while claiming that "perspective is nothing but a rumor of grandiose prenatal processions." Matta in Germana Ferrari [Matta], *Entretiens Morphologiques: Notebook No. 1, 1936–1944* (London: Sistan Ltd., 1987), 92–97, 92.

9
Matta uses a very similar compositional device in the related drawing *Hand Holding Transparent Seashell*, also of 1945.

10
Matta, in Andrew Crispo Gallery, *Matta: A Totemic World*, n/p. The bulk of these works were painted in 1945, the year that the Russian Red Army liberated the Auschwitz and Birkenau death camps (January), Hitler committed suicide (April), Berlin fell, and victory in Europe was celebrated (May), and, poignantly, the atomic bomb was dropped on Hiroshima and Nagasaki, Japan (August 6 and 9, respectively), killing more than 250,000 people.

11
Matta may have gained firsthand knowledge of the work through Picasso himself, as they met in Paris in 1937 while the Spaniard was working on the monumental homage to the victims of the bombing at Guernica. That same year, Matta took a job with the architects of the Spanish Republican Pavilion at the Paris International Exhibition, where he had prolonged access to *Guernica*. Matta must have viewed the work again while in New York during the exhibition *Picasso: 40 Years of His Art*, organized by the Museum of Modern Art in 1939, or sometime during its prolonged stay in the United States. See Ferrari [Matta], *Entretiens Morphologiques*, 14.

12
Works such as *Splitting of the Ego* and *X Space and the Ego* also herald Matta's lifelong involvement with political action and social-justice causes. He was active during the Parisian May of 1968, traveled often to Cuba after the revolution, participated in the Chilean political milieu after the election of Salvador Allende, and condemned the former's ousting (and "suicide") in 1973. Moreover, throughout the span of his long career, Matta incorporated his political thought in other works including the 1937 drawing *La guerra en civil*; *La tierra es un hombre*; the script that he wrote in condemnation of the assassination of Federico García Lorca, a family friend, in 1936; *Les roses sont belles*, a 1951 painting that alludes to the trial against Julius and Ethel Rosenberg—two communist Jewish Americans who in 1953 were convicted and executed for conspiracy to commit espionage during a time of war; *La Pregun-tortura* (1957), on the torture of French-Algerian journalist Henri Alleg during the Algerian War (1954–1962); *Burn, Baby, Burn* (1967), Matta's defense of the Vietnamese people at the height of the conflict with the Viet Cong; *Les Juges partent en guerre* (1967) about the Nuremberg Trials (1945–46); and *La vida Allende la muerte* (1973) on the 1973 Chilean coup d'état that ousted Allende and led to his suicide.

13
Dreier and Matta, *Duchamp's Glass*, n/p.

14
Following a 1941 trip to Mexico with Robert Motherwell and their spouses during which he gained hands-on knowledge of the large-scale mural work that Rivera, Siqueiros, and Orozco had been engaged in creating since the 1920s, Matta presented some of his oversized canvases—most notably, *The Earth Is a Man* (1941–42), the first of these large-scale works exhibited during his first one-man exhibition in the United States in March 1942 at the Pierre Matisse Gallery in New York. By the time of his second solo show at the Pierre Matisse Gallery in 1946, Matta had already achieved a monumental scale in his

work that spoke of his earlier exposure to the Mexican muralists' work. And, in 1947, Matta was included in the exhibition *Large-Scale Modern Paintings*, organized by the Museum of Modern Art in New York. See Pierre Matisse Gallery, *Matta Echaurren*, exh. cat. (New York: Pierre Matisse Gallery, March 31–April [illegible], 1942); and Pierre Matisse Gallery, *Matta Echaurren*, exh. cat. (New York: Pierre Matisse Gallery, Apr. 11–May 4, 1946).

Indeed, as William S. Rubin notes in *Dada, Surrealism, and Their Heritage* (1968), Matta preceded by several years the New York–based Abstract Expressionists in adopting oversized supports. See William S. Rubin, *Dada, Surrealism, and Their Heritage*, exh. cat. (New York: The Museum of Modern Art, 1968), 168.

These early large-format works on both paper and canvas foreshadow Matta's forays into the mural technique. Examples of this line of work include a fresco for the EUR district in Rome (1952), now destroyed; the mural *Les doutes des trios mondes* for UNESCO in Paris (1956); the twelve-meter mural *Vivir enfrentado las flechas* that he painted for Santiago's Universidad Técnica in 1961 (now destroyed); two collaborative murals that he developed with students at the Museo Nacional de Bellas Artes and Casa de las Américas, both in Havana, in 1963; and *The First Goal of the Chilean People*, painted in 1971 at an old municipal swimming pool in La Granja, Santiago, in commemoration of the election of Salvador Allende.

15
I am grateful to Wynne Phelan, former conservation director, and Maite M. Leal, paintings conservator, at the Museum of Fine Arts, Houston, for their insights and observations regarding Matta's process and choice of materials.

16
Wove paper is characterized by a uniform surface that lacks the ribbing or watermarks that are typical of laid paper. Matta seemed to have preferred this and other smooth papers for his works on paper. He often also opted for calendered sheet paper, as in *Untitled* (1943), which was produced with a paper-making process that includes various types of calenders or hard-pressure rollers used to form or smooth sheets. The calendered sheet paper, too, is far smoother and glossier than other types of paper and, like wove paper, provides a surface upon which color can glide more easily.

17
Matta employs a consistent palette of white and black accents, orange to pink reds, and different tones of green. For black accents, charcoal is often used to establish form as more of a vector that suggests movement and velocity. The only value differentiation occurs in his whites, which he uses for a variety of purposes: to sharply accentuate and define structural elements (as in *Naturaleza Muerta* and *Splitting of the Ego*), to fill the bodies of his beings (*Composition et Study*, *Abstract Composition*, and *Autómata*), to diffuse color (*Naturaleza Muerta*), as well as to suggest both movement (*Autómata*) and a certain "vapor trail" of ephemeral color (*Naturaleza Muerta*).

18
In a 1978 interview with the French philosopher Félix Guattari, he described the several breakthroughs in his career and recalled how at this time, "[I] threw [myself] into something that I called 'The space [of the] species' ['El espacio de la especie'] and I established several locations that could be compared to non-Euclidean geometries." See [Matta], "Entrevista con Félix Guattari," c. 1978, in IVAM, *Matta 1911–2011*, (Valencia: Institut Valencià d'Art Modern, 2011), 132–39, 137, trans. 193. The interview first appeared in the French journal *Chimère*.

19
It is well documented that Matta began his works on canvas by rubbing pigment directly over the surface, without subjecting it to a preparatory process—a technique he may have borrowed from the British Surrealist Gordon Onslow Ford, who gave him his first canvases and encouraged him to paint—and that he often drew shapes with a brush or applied more paint directly from the tube. Onslow Ford perfected the *coulage* technique later championed by the Abstract Expressionists. In *coulages*, paint and other pigments are poured directly on a canvas, resulting in an involuntary composition. See Gordon Onslow Ford, "Notes on Matta and Painting (1937–1941)," in Ferrari [Matta], *Entretiens Morphologiques*, 23–25, 24.

20
"Yo no pinto, yo veo en las manchas un cosmos. Yo parto de las manchas. Como la gente ve vacas en las nubes, yo veo mundos en las manchas." Matta, in Eduardo Carrasco, *Conversaciones con Matta* (Santiago de Chile: Ediciones Universidad Diego Portales, 2011), 65.

21
Onslow Ford, "Notes on Matta and Painting (1937–1941)," 24.

22
Ibid.

23
Matta, "Psychological Morphology," 1938. Translated by Gordon Onslow Ford in Ferrari [Matta], *Entretiens Morphologiques*, 218.

24
Ibid.

25
Onslow Ford, "Notes on Matta and Painting (1937–1941)," 24. Onslow Ford recalls that in the summer of 1938, they were equally impressed with Ouspensky's *Tertium Organum* (1912), a systematic treatise on epistemology, and his theories of the fourth dimension.

In "The Fourth Dimension and Non-Euclidian Geometry in Modern Art: Conclusion," Linda Dalrymple Henderson discusses the dual definition of the fourth dimension accepted by many of the Surrealists. On one hand, Breton and his circle were acutely interested in Ouspensky's thesis of a spatial fourth dimension possessing mystical and even irrational associations that went against the temporal fourth dimension of the relativity theory. On the other hand, Breton actively quoted the Spanish artist Oscar Dominguez's (1906–1957) 1942 text "La Pétrification du temps," in which he introduced the concept of a "lithochronic surface" and upheld *time* as the primary definition of the fourth dimension (in the tradition of Einstein's Theory of Relativity). Essentially, Dominguez—who rehearsed many of the precepts of a "lithochronic surface" in his own sculptural work and Surrealist objects—proposed that this surface graphically connected two or more objects (moving or still) and served as a receptacle for their formal difference across time. See Linda Dalrymple Henderson, "The Fourth Dimension and Non-Euclidean Geometry in Modern Art: Conclusion," *Leonardo*, vol. 17, no. 3 (1984), 205–10, 208.

26
Dreier and Matta, *Duchamp's Glass*, n/p.

27
Thomas R. Monahan, Matta's Chicago dealer and friend, understood this shifting perspective as an eye that "senses what is above, below and behind it..."; capturing the frame or movement in "*furious* motion." Thomas R. Monahan, "Introduction: Following the Footsteps of a Giant," in Carter and Monahan, *Matta: Surrealism and Beyond*, 9–19. Emphasis mine.

28
[Matta], "Entrevista con Alain Jouffroy," in IVAM, *Matta 1911–2011* (Valencia: Institut Valencià d'Art Modern, 2011), 127–31, 127.

Michael Wellen

WIFREDO LAM CIRCA 1942

METAMORPHOSIS AND THE FEMALE FORM

BETWEEN 1938 AND 1941, Wifredo Lam produced approximately 190 paintings. The majority of them—at least 150—feature women as their subject. They are mysterious figures; their faces either featureless, like those of wooden mannequins, or masklike, as in *Femme Violet* [Woman in Violet] (1938) (plate 29). Each has straight dark hair falling behind her shoulders. Many of them appear in vibrant interior settings. Some stand alone, some sit, others recline, a few carry children, and others intimately embrace men. Lam's focus on women is not surprising given the importance of the female figure (particularly the nude) as an archetype in art history. His paintings convey his appreciation for the work of Henri Matisse and Pablo Picasso, artists whom he befriended upon moving to Paris in 1938 and for whom the female figure was the primary vehicle for avant-garde explorations of form. Through his depictions of women, Lam rehearsed and synthesized aspects of early Modernism and African sculpture.

However, in 1942 a dramatic transition occurred in his work: his figures began morphing into mystical hybrids of human, animal, and vegetal life. The Cuban artist took greater interest in creating unique kinds of visual space—spaces marked by a mysterious depth, where figural elements emerge from mists or appear juxtaposed amid layers of leaves and vines. This shift in subject matter corresponds with the changing circumstances of Lam's life. In 1940, he and his partner Helena Holzer were forced to flee Paris because of World War II. They went to the port city of Marseilles, waiting for months before they found passage to Havana, a city Lam had not seen since his youth. In her memoirs, Holzer recalls 1942—their first full year in Cuba—as one marked by reclusiveness, a period in which the artist devoted his time and energy to his work. He produced approximately 126 paintings in that year alone and started two of his most famous works, *The Jungle* (1942–43) and *The Chair* (1943). In these and his other large-format paintings, the women that characterized his French period were no longer visible. Eventually, by about 1947, his pictorial language changed again: his color palette darkened; his figures became more angular and ominous; and his compositions became less concerned with conveying foliage and transparency. But, circa 1942, Lam developed the motifs and figures, particularly the *femme-cheval* (horse-headed woman), that came to define his artistic career.

The nineteen works in the Brillembourg Capriles Collection of Latin American Art, the majority of which date from 1938 to 1942, provide a focused view of Lam's experimentations with the female figure, as they relate to formal considerations such as space, color, and composition, but also to his construction of mystical characters that embody the hybridity of the Afro-Atlantic world. These works reveal a hitherto "unknown" Wifredo Lam, providing a more nuanced understanding of his artistic path, the achievements he transposed to larger works, as well as the dead ends he encountered and overcame.[1] Like many of his monumental paintings such as *The Jungle*, these lesser-known works were often done on paper (and later adhered to board). It was a decision prompted partly by economic necessity, but it was also Lam's aesthetic preference. He preferred the smoothness of the paper's surface; its dryness allowed for sharp and expressive lines

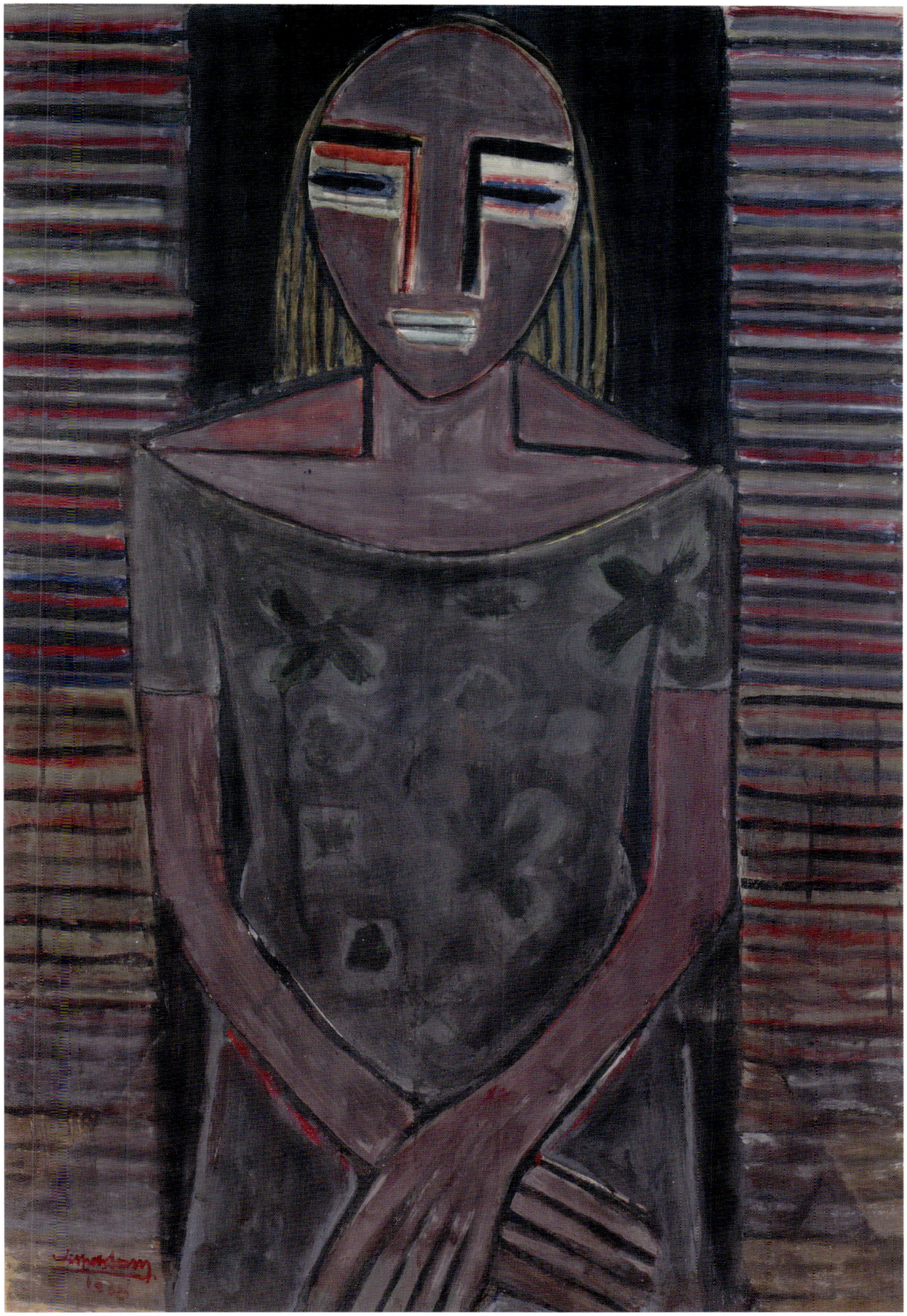

PLATE 29

Wifredo Lam • *Femme violette* [Woman in Violet], 1938

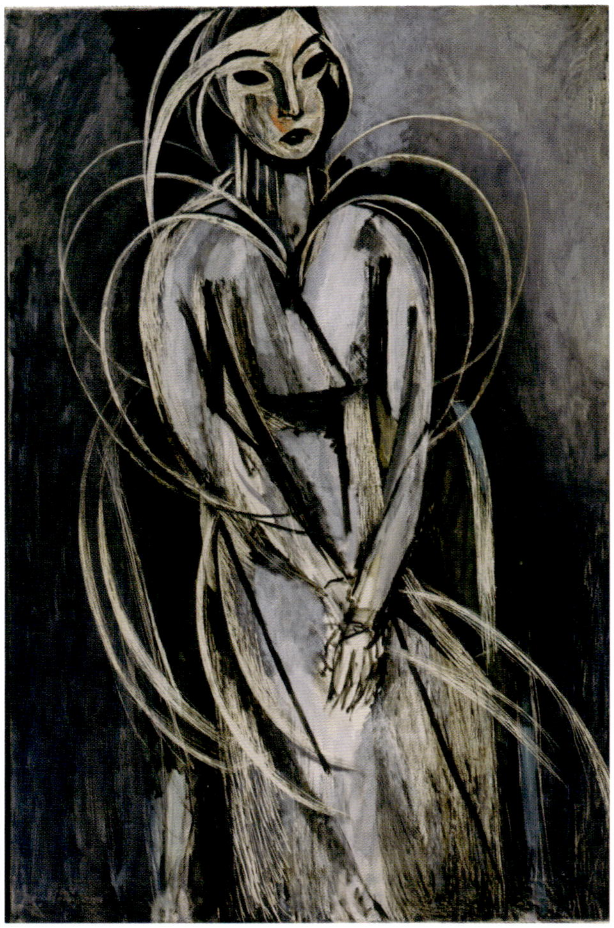

FIG. 1

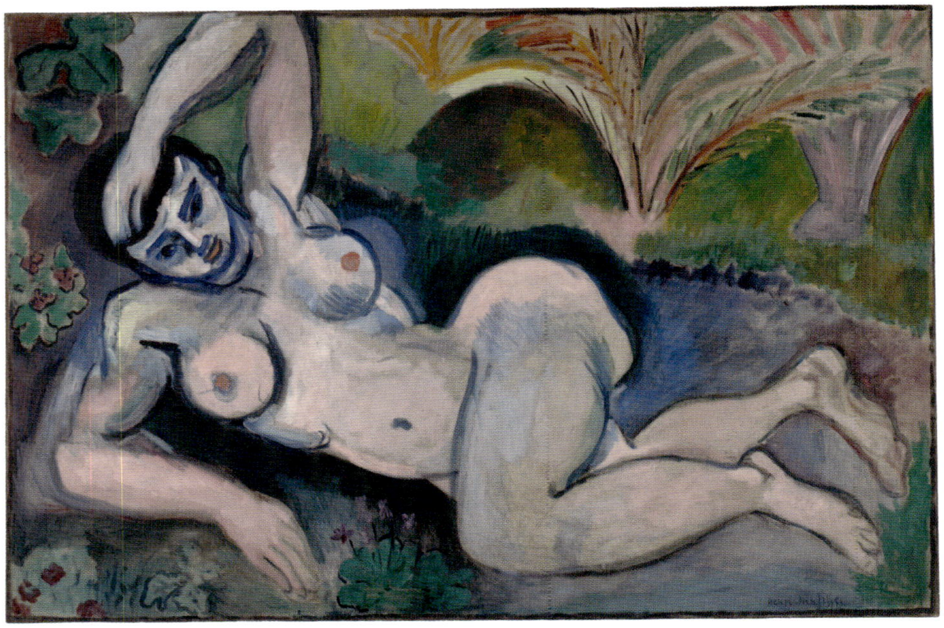

FIG. 2

and textural versatility. Certain paper stock showed resistance to the application of paint, leading to the magnificent appearance of marble-like veins in works such as *Femme aux cheveux longs, III* [Woman with Long Hair, III] (1942) (plate 34). Like an alchemist changing base metals into gold, Lam possessed the ability to transform cheap and fragile paper into the appearance of enduring stone. The period of 1938 to 1942, then, marked a stage in his career when his experiments with portraying the female figure ran parallel with his experiments in artistic media.

The Brillembourg Capriles Collection provides a representative sampling of Lam's work as he transitioned from Paris to Havana, showing the importance of his early contact with Matisse and Picasso as well as how he gradually shed their influences. For instance, the composition and subdued color palette of *Femme aux bras croisés* [Woman with Crossed Arms] (1938) (plate 30) can be associated with one of Matisse's most experimental works, *Portrait of Yvonne Landsberg* (1914) (fig. 1). For that painting, Matisse innovatively used the back of his brush to carve winglike forms, what he called "lines of construction," around the central figure, lines that impart texture to the canvas and dynamism to a simplified figure.[2] While Matisse is best known for his bold colors, in this portrait the Fauve painter restricts himself to only a few streaks of red and green, highlighting aspects of the sitter's face and the edges of her chair. These colors reveal themselves gradually to viewers. By comparison, Lam used color more consistently to outline his figures. In *Femme aux bras croisés*, one sees ochre highlighting the nose, forearms, breasts, and belly of the sitter. Arching lines of black and iridescent blue along the woman's shoulders and arms fall in a heart-shape, Lam's very own "lines of construction." These fluorescent highlights suggest that he was also experimenting with the techniques Matisse employed in his historic *Blue Nude (Memory of Biskra)* (1907), where swathes of blue paint surround the shoulders and breasts of the woman, creating a sense of the nude's radiance and intoxicating beauty (fig. 2). That stated, Lam's

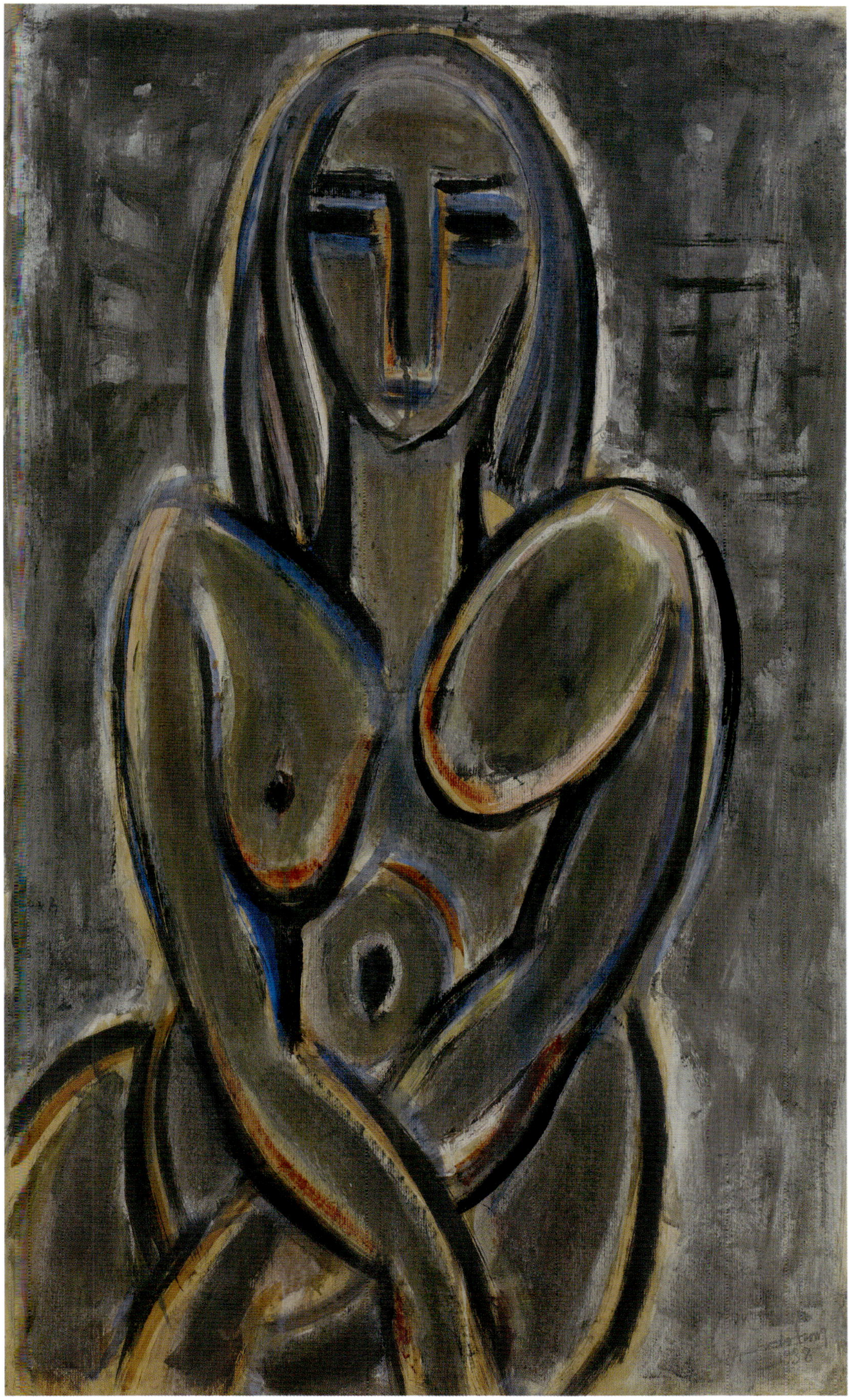

PLATE 30
Wifredo Lam • *Femme aux bras croisés* [Woman with Crossed Arms], 1938

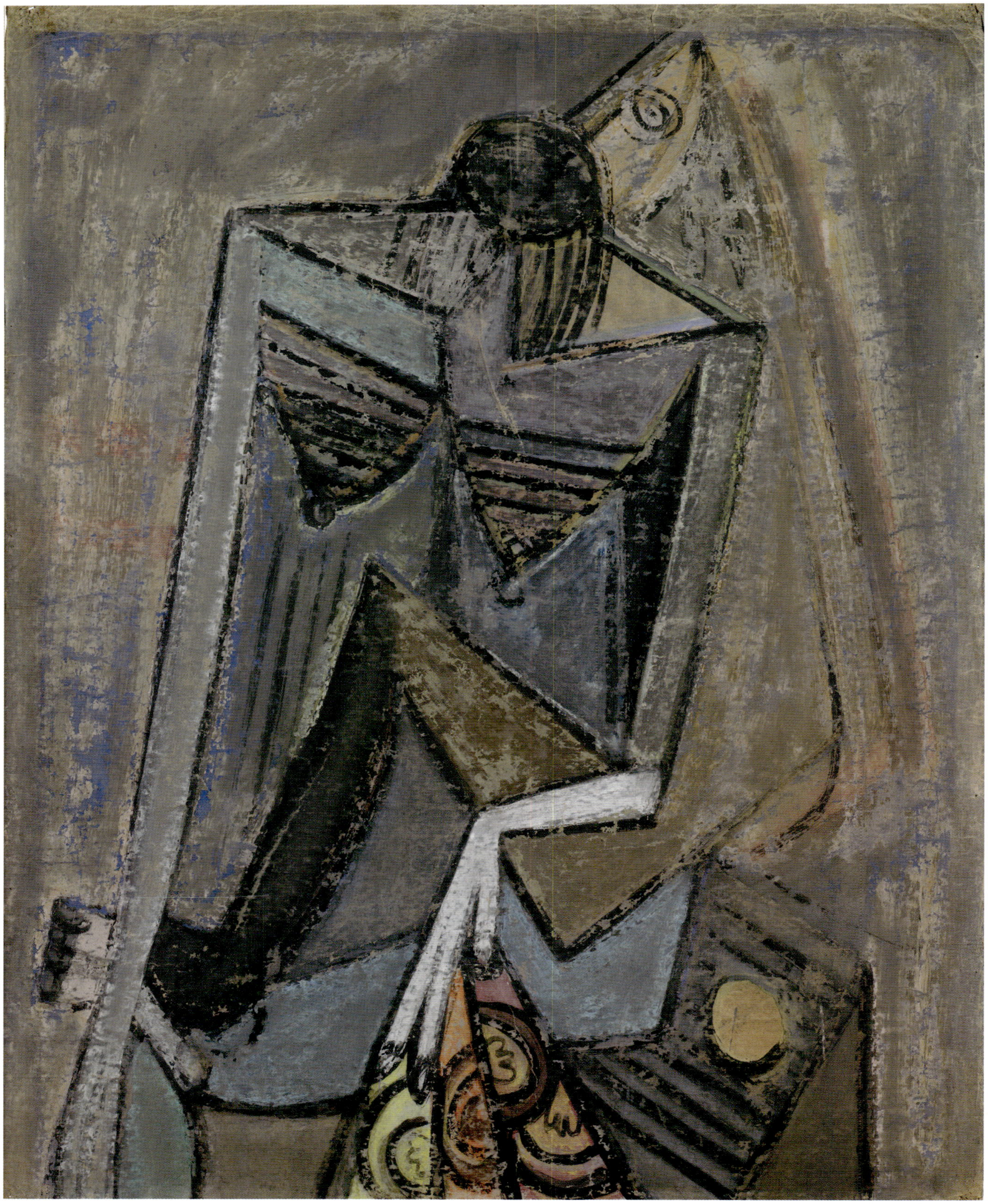

PLATE 31

Wifredo Lam • *Femme à l'éventail, II* [Woman with Fan, II], 1942 color palette is decidedly his own. He masterfully creates a mysterious night scene using an austere grayish background that sets off the glowing figure.

Like Matisse, Lam preferred to depict his figures in shallow spaces, using patterns and color to convey depth rather than traditional one-point perspective. For *Femme Violet*, he initially painted the figure standing on a yellow and blue checkered floor, still visible at the bottom left and right of the painting. But he decided to add alternating bands of color (green, blue, black, and red) to tightly frame the figure. Perhaps these bands represent light pouring through wooden shutters—the kind prominent in many Matisse portraits of women—or they may be textiles. Nonetheless, they are vital to the composition, deliberately flattening and enlivening what was originally a more traditional representation of architectural depth.

Lam played with this compositional structure later in his career, accentuating his figures by placing them between bands of color, as in *Femme-Oiseau* [Woman-Bird] (1950), where a central band of blue highlights the head and torso of a woman with thin horns (plate 33). In place of the woman's face is a horned dove, likely a symbol of intelligence and an allusion to Santería, a syncretic Cuban religious tradition influenced by West African, Caribbean, and Roman Catholic practices.[3] Two grey bands of color run alongside the figure. His *Mujer con pájaro* [Woman with Bird] (1957) uses the tripartite color structure even more subtly to re-create a sense of transformation (plate 32). On a background of black and brown, the artist creates what initially looks like two birds, one white and one light blue. But the image fluctuates with extended viewing. The white bird doubles as the simplified head of a woman, and blue tail feathers represent the woman's hand and forearm. The central figure holds the blue bird as an offering or a purification rite as she herself transforms into a bird. The fluctuation between bird and woman may even drift into a third visualization: the woman's head and neck also appear like a cup, her dark hair doubling as the vessel's overflowing contents; this cup/woman ambiguity appears in many of Lam's other paintings of the period. This painting exemplifies the sophistication

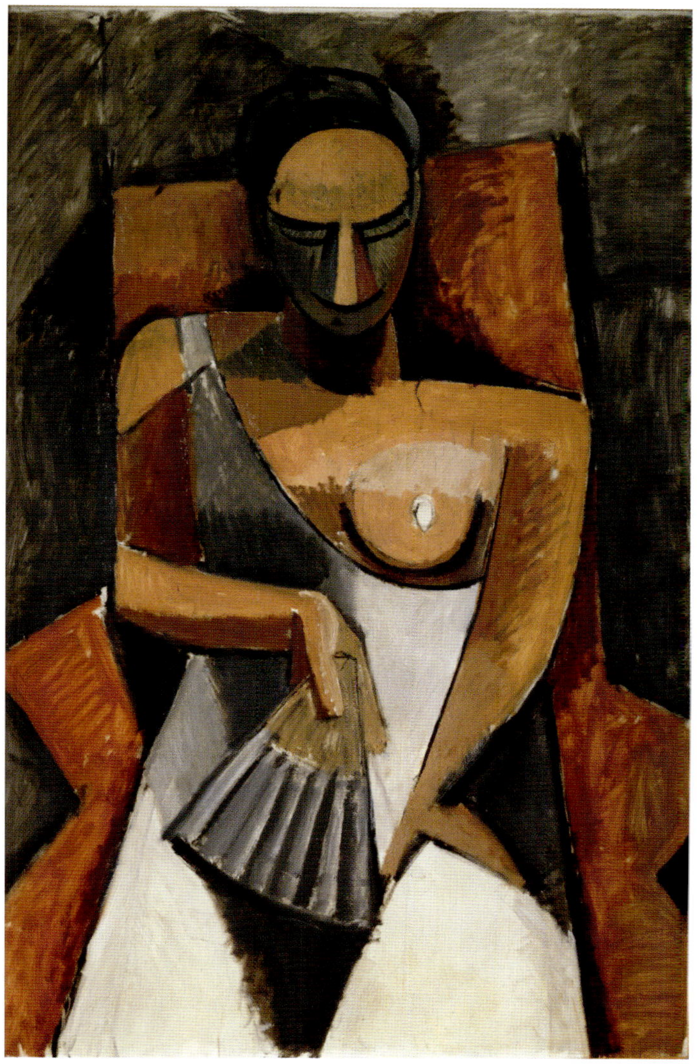

FIG. 3

of Lam's mature style, in which his early interest in Matissean colors, patterns, and the seated/reclining female nude are conspicuously absent. Instead, Lam summons a mystical figure from delicate lines and washes of earthen tones.

Several works in the Brillembourg Capriles Collection also show Lam's idiosyncratic engagement with Cubism while living in Havana. The composition of *Femme à l'éventail, II* [Woman with Fan, II] (1942) (plate 31) pays homage to Picasso's *Woman with Fan* (1908) (fig. 3), one of the touchstones of early Cubism, which presents a composite view (both overhead and frontal) of a seated woman. Whereas Picasso uses shading to create volumetric forms, Lam instead draws shapes that appear as flat as possible, producing a fresco-like surface texture. He simplifies the woman's head into an

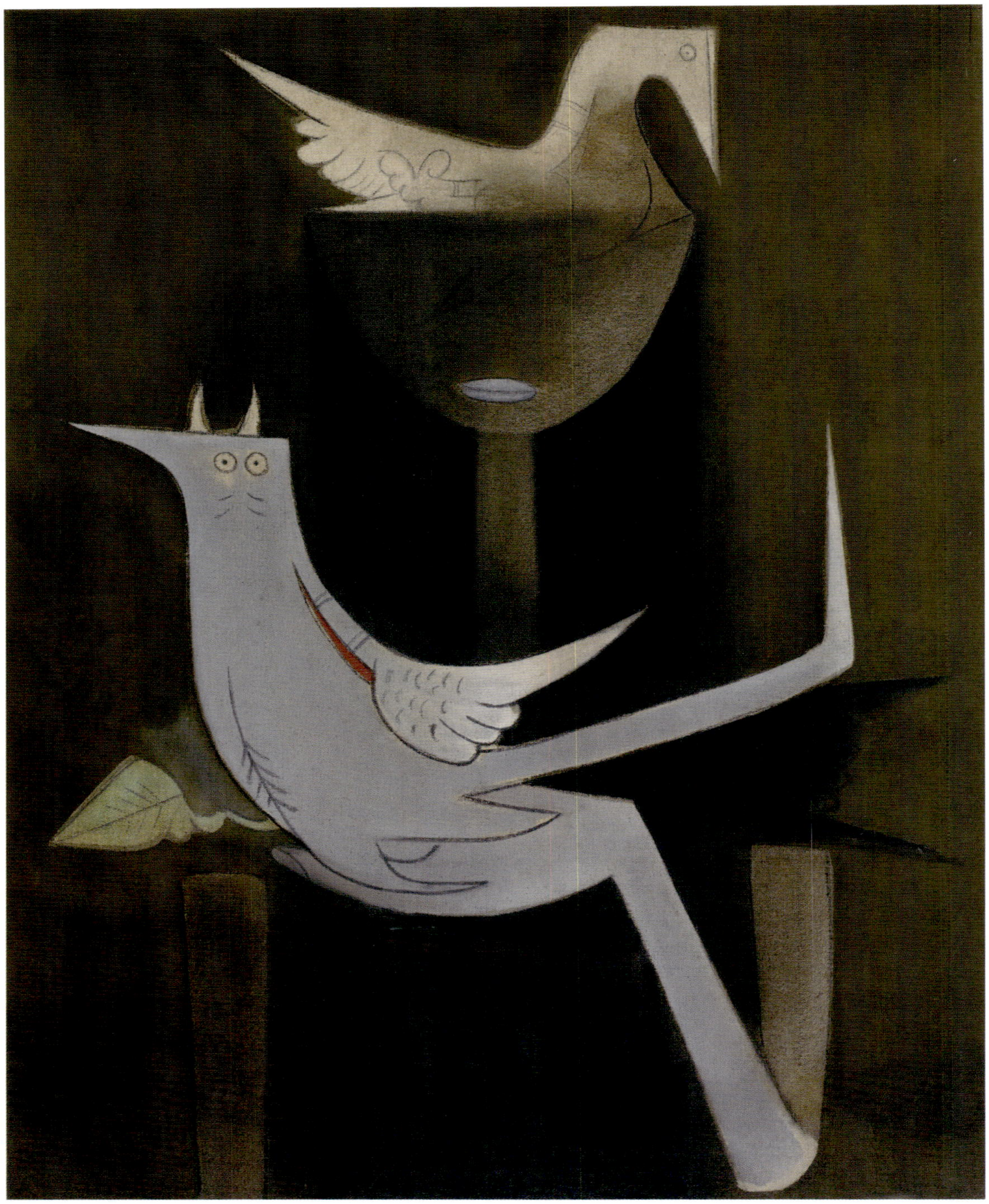

PLATE 32
Wifredo Lam • *Mujer con pájaro* [Woman with Bird], 1955

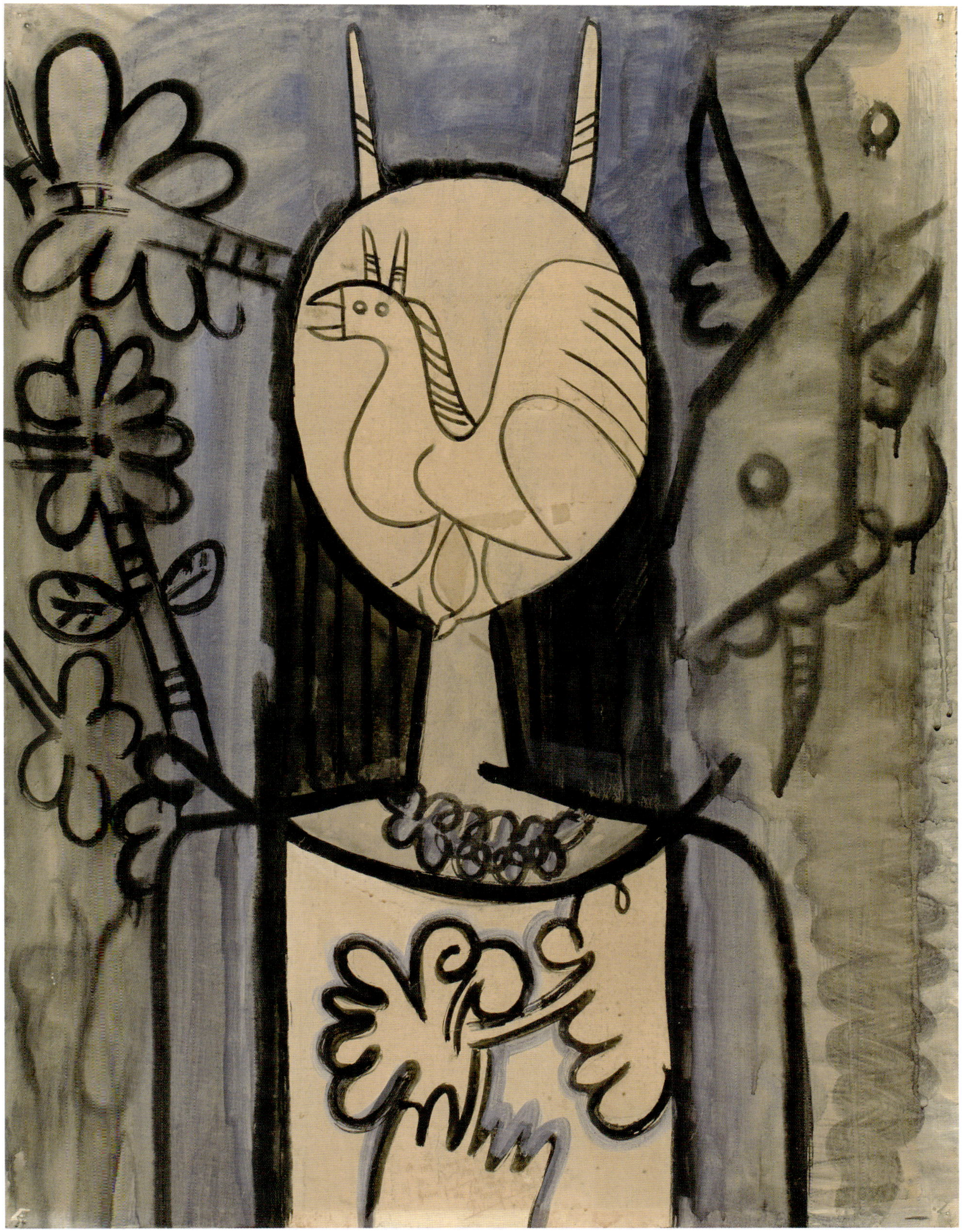

PLATE 33
Wifredo Lam • *Femme-Oiseau* [Woman-Bird], 1950

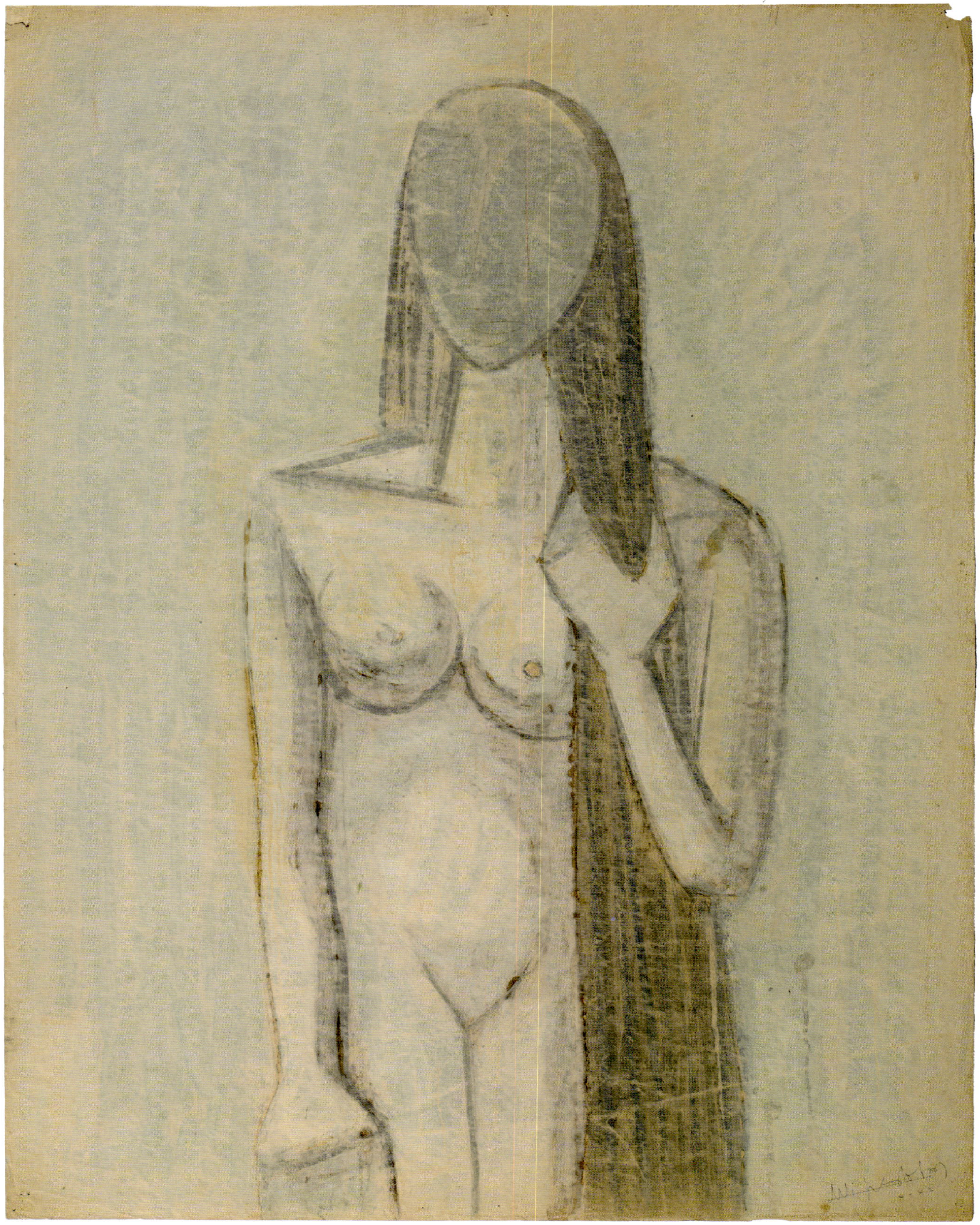

PLATE 34
Wifredo Lam • *Femme aux cheveux longs, III*
[Woman with Long Hair, III], double-sided painting (*Homme* on reverse), 1942

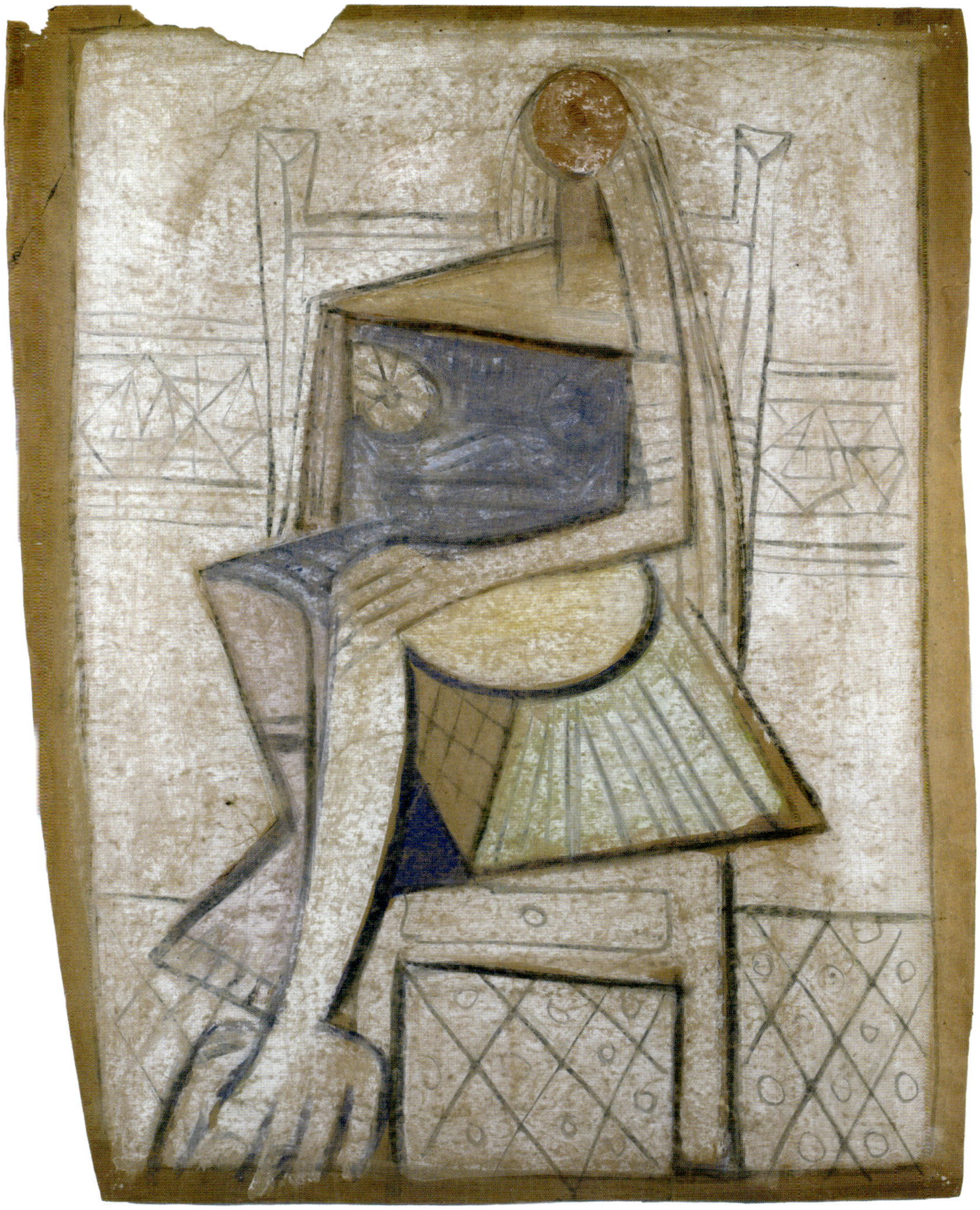

PLATE 35

Wifredo Lam • *Femme* [Woman], double-sided painting (*Cheval* on reverse), c. 1942 oval with streaks of black hair. He reverses Picasso's composition, and, instead of a white fan, Lam paints a colorfully patterned one. The triangular fan echoes his other studies of the period, such as *Femme* [Woman] (c. 1942) (plate 35), where a woman's dress rigidly fans out below her exposed legs. In *Woman with Fan, II*, Lam adds a ghostly second figure: a horse-like or half-moon face that peers out from behind the woman's head. This figure likely represents Ogun, a major deity in Yoruba and African-Caribbean religions, who ceremonially possesses a devotee by what is commonly referred to as "mounting" or "riding" that person like a horse—a metaphor laden with sexual innuendo.[4] We see a brown leg with bare feet sweeping across the woman's torso, seemingly belonging to both the nude and to the horse figure riding on her back.

Lam's experimentations with Cubism led him to one of his most stunning achievements of the 1940s: his creation of complex forested settings that convey indeterminate spatial depth. *The Jungle* perhaps best epitomizes this accomplishment, but other lesser-known works in the Brillembourg Capriles Collection also demonstrate the range of the painter's experiments with space. In *Maternité Yoruba* [Yoruba Maternity] (1942) we see a figure, her head bifurcated by a half-moon shape out of which three leaves appear (plate 37). The title of the work suggests that Lam drew inspiration from Yoruba sculpture, examples of which could be found in the small collection of African art he formed while living in Havana.[5] With *Maternité Yoruba*, he effectively transposed the notion of carving to paper, using sharp pencil lines and dashes of paint to hew a central figure. But Lam also creates the remarkable appearance of transparency, as if layers of gauze shroud the central figure. Inspired by the distinctiveness of Caribbean light that he found in Cuba, he made paintings that increasingly show a concern with values of density rather than color. He later remarked, "Our light is so transparent that the leaves on some trees give the impression of being lighted from within. . . . Actually, I can't talk about how I see colors, only about their transparency, which suggests a new relation between their values."[6] In works such as *Maternité Yoruba*, one can see how such impressions translated into painting. Using minimal accents of color, Lam creates a scene where the figure and plant life seem to possess their own inner light.

Two works in the Brillembourg Capriles Collection, *Homme* [Man] (1942) and *Sin título* [Untitled] (1942), show Lam laying the groundwork for what he achieves more masterfully in *Maternité Yoruba*. In *Homme*, a faceless male figure dominates the full length of the painting (plate 38). Despite his large size, the figure is not the center of attention here, but rather the focus is on the interaction between figure and ground. Blue sheets with yellow-patterned trim form a complex backdrop of folds. The man holds similarly colored sheets in his hands. Lam uses several shades of blue to distinguish one sheet of fabric from another. Still, their location in space is uncertain. The faint edges of drapery reappear in *Maternité Yoruba*, a compositional element that helps establish the pliable appearance of the setting. *Sin título* [Untitled] shows a decidedly more Cubist approach to figure and ground (plate 39). As in *Homme*, Lam depicts a figure before a blue-curtained backdrop. This time the woman is seated, her body fractured into triangular and rectangular planes in shades of blue, yellow, and grey. Their sharp edges cause her body to dematerialize. While there is a suggestion of a hand supporting her head, the torso and legs of the figure are impossible to decipher. The sitter is probably Helena Holzer, who accompanied the artist most nights as he worked late into the evening. Of this period, she writes, "While he was painting or drawing we talked or I read to him, mostly from books about the lores and idiosyncrasies of primitive civilizations. The radio was always on very softly. We never retired before three or four in the morning."[7] Perhaps this painting shows Holzer's movements over the course of these late-night sittings. We see a blue rectangular shape, possibly a book, which appears in multiple places at once: below the head of the sitter, at reading distance, and on her lap, as though she has temporarily put the book down. As with *Homme*, some of the lines created by the backdrop reappear in *Maternité Yoruba*, where he invents planes that are decidedly soft and organic compared to the hard edges of this Cubist study.

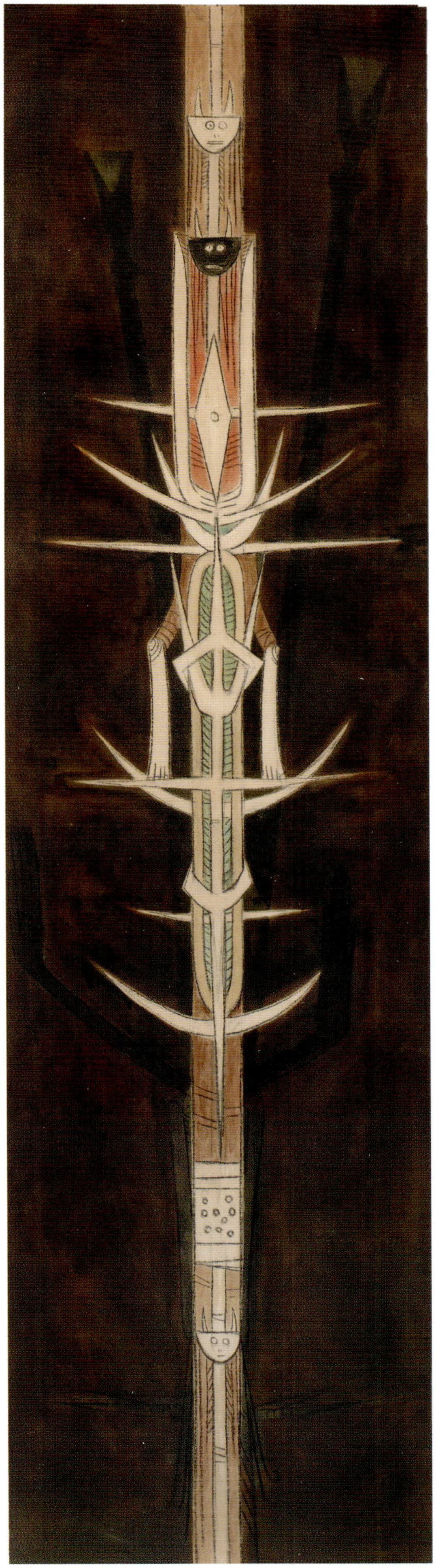

PLATE 36

Wifredo Lam • *Reflets d'eau*

[Water Reflections], 1957

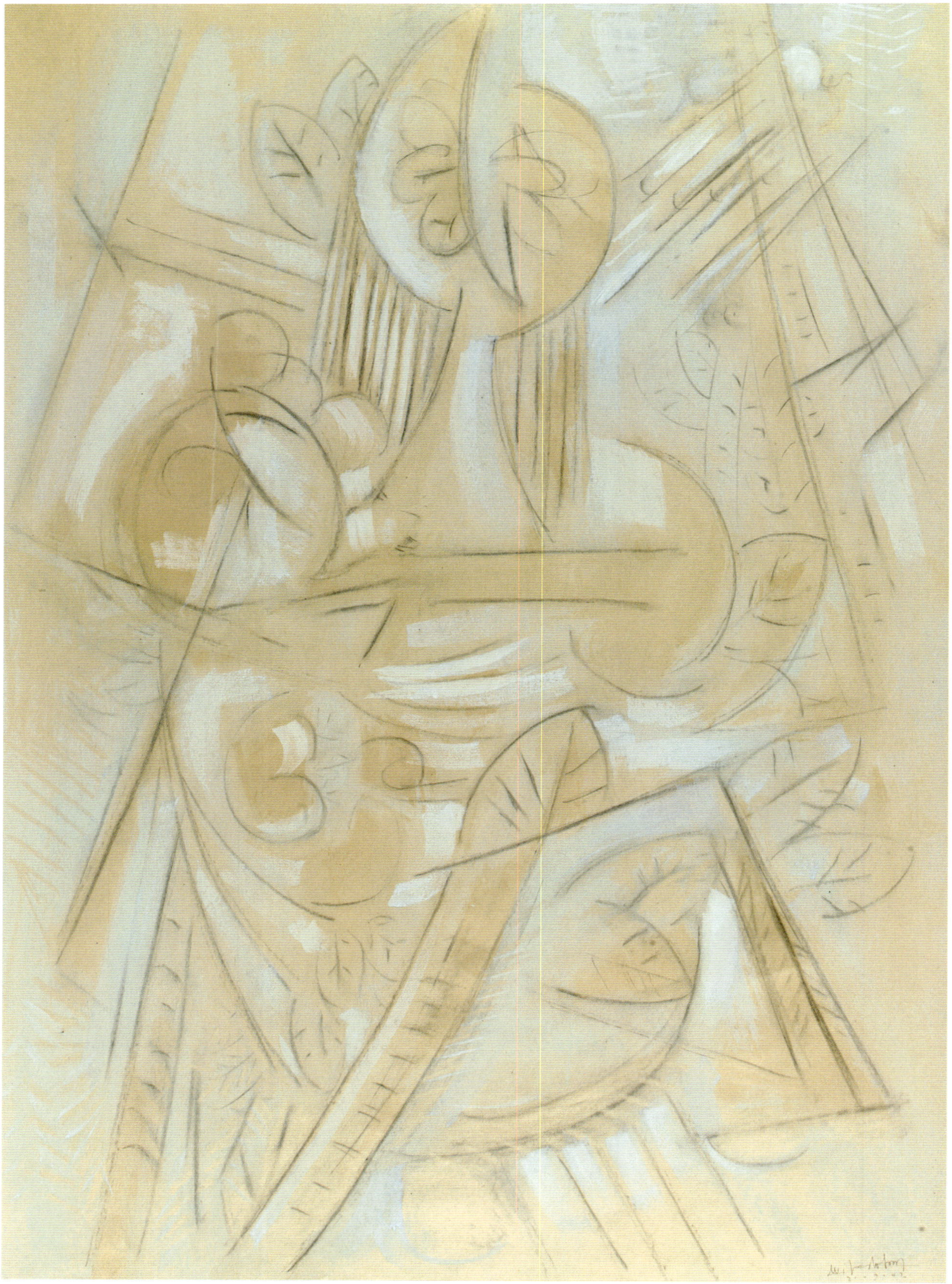

PLATE 37

Wifredo Lam • *Maternité Yoruba* [Yoruba Maternity], 1942

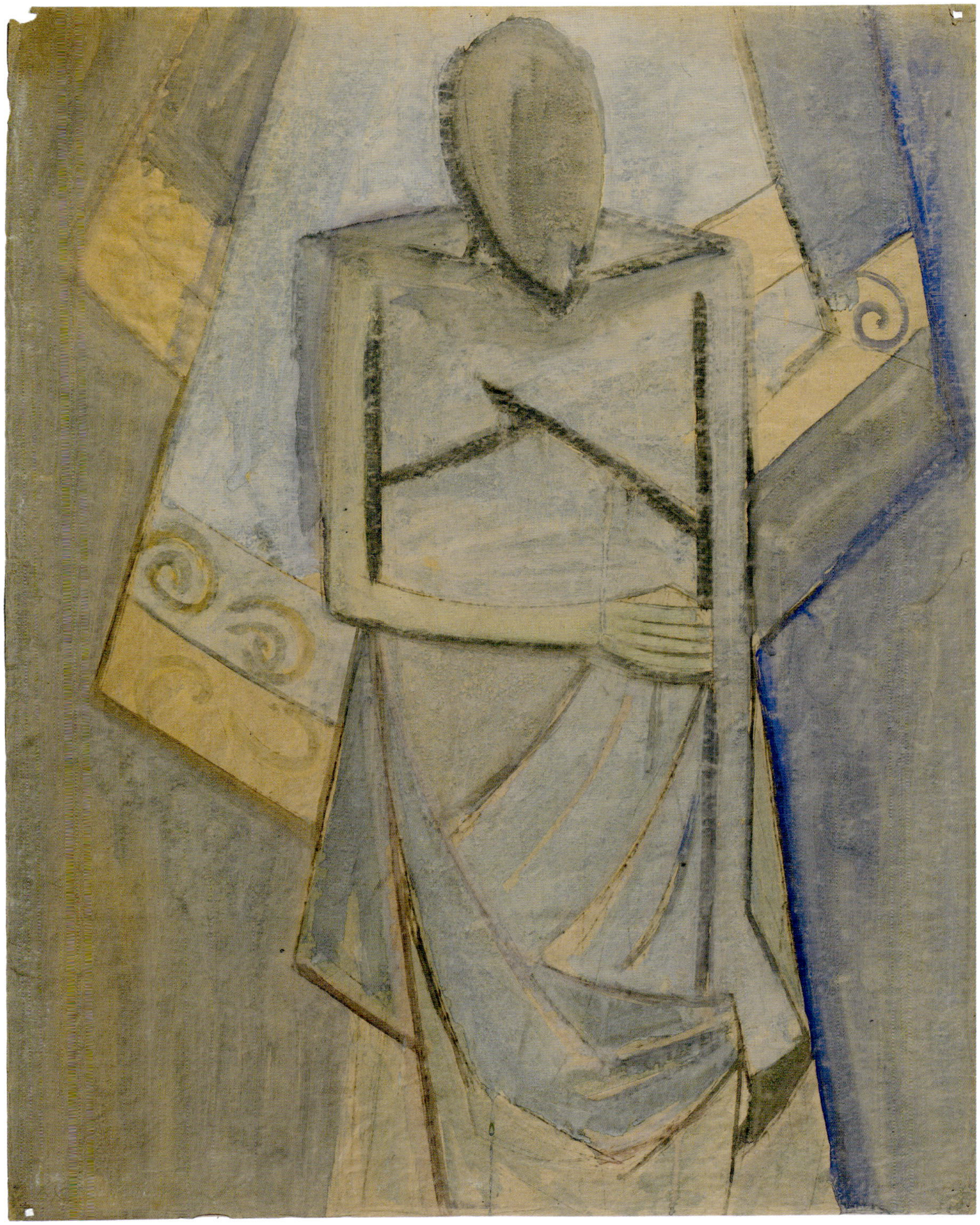

PLATE 38
Wifredo Lam • *Homme* [Man] double-sided painting (*Femme aux cheveux longs, III,* on reverse), 1942

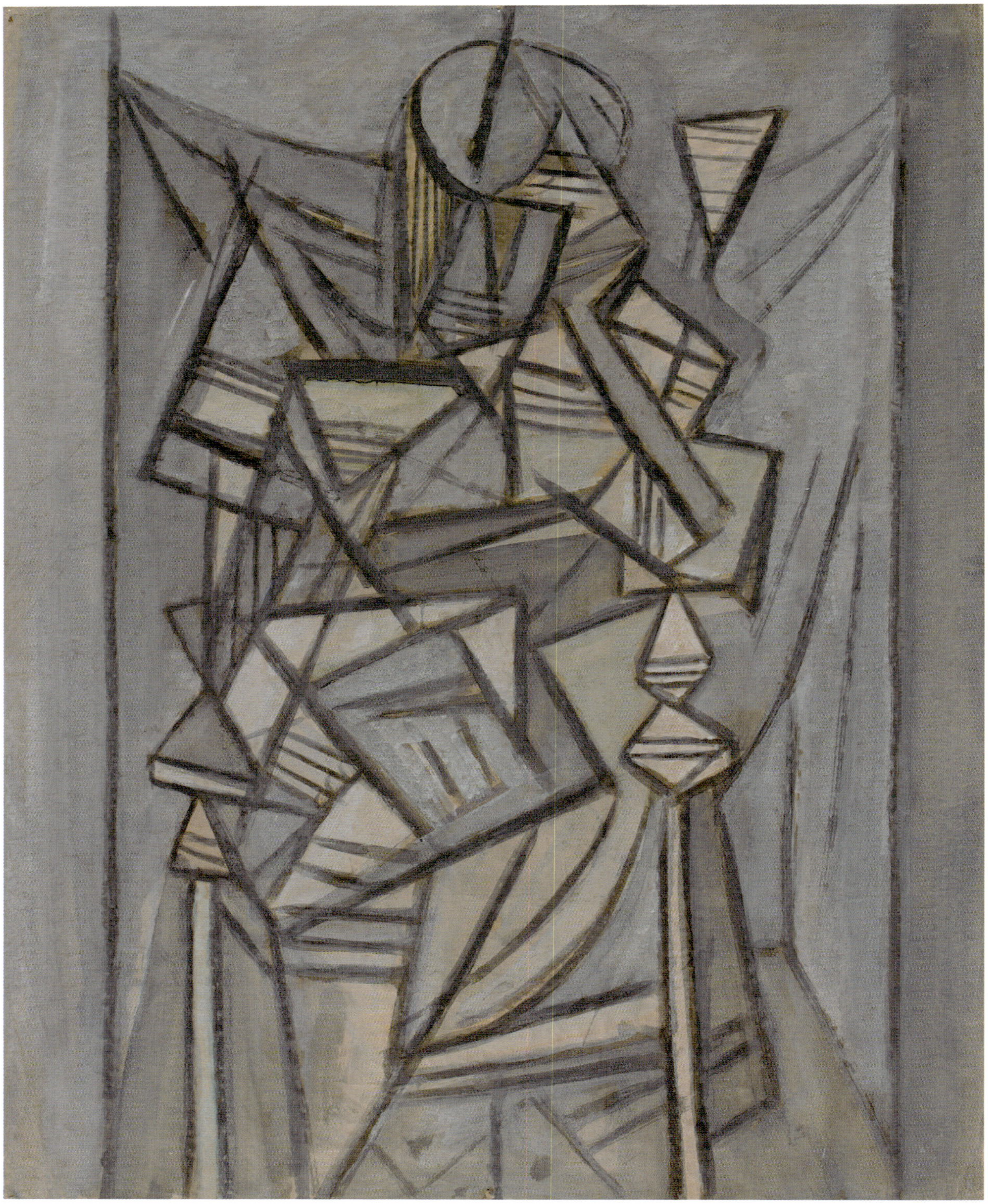

PLATE 39
Wifredo Lam • *Sin título* [Untitled], c. 1942

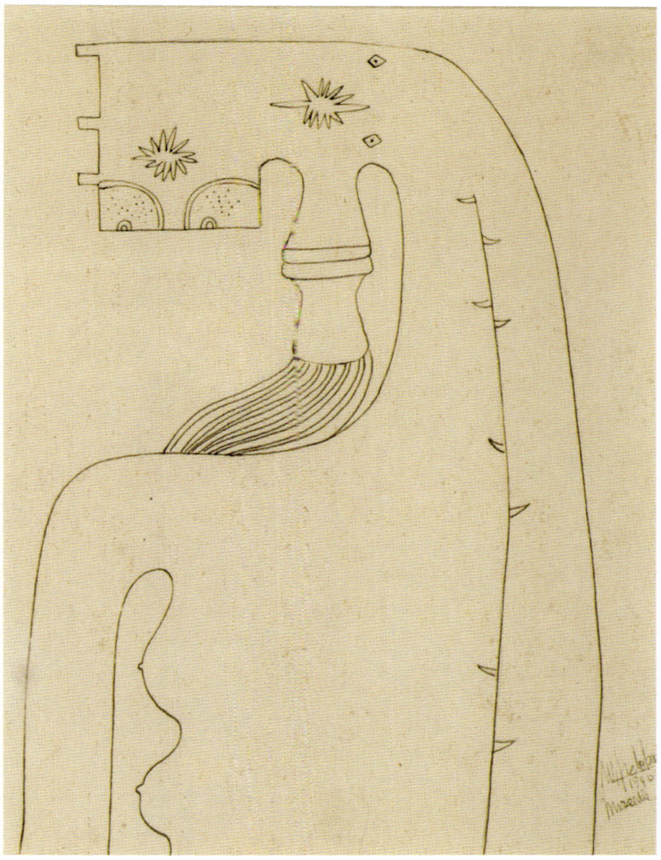

FIG. 4

Leafy-faced fertility goddesses, horse-headed spirits, horned birds, and ladies—these are but a few of the mystical figures that populate Lam's paintings beginning in the 1940s. His innovations in form, space, and color cannot be separated from the social, cultural, and spiritual concepts at the heart of his work. He was an artist defined by his movement through the Afro-Atlantic diaspora, establishing roots not in one place, but in many. His transnational identity informs his oeuvre. Even a minor work, such as *Sin título (La gallina)* [Untitled (The Hen)] (1958), remains open to transnational interpretations; it may be considered one of his *Coqs des Caraïbes* [Caribbean Cocks] for which Lam proudly borrowed the colors of the Cuban flag, but it also may relate to the rooster as a French symbol of liberty, a pictorial tradition famously employed by Picasso during World War II. Art historians have long read Lam as the artistic intermediary between Europe, Africa, and the Americas, positing that his art could speak to both colonizer and colonized. It was a position the artist himself appreciated; in 1980, he described his art as "an act of decolonization."[8]

The *femme-cheval*—one of his most iconic and culturally syncretic figures—became a recurring subject of his work from circa 1942 onward.[9] The character first appears in the pen-and-ink drawings he made in 1940–41 while waiting in Marseilles with André Breton and others seeking to escape the war. During this period, Lam drew "exquisite corpses" and designed playing cards to occupy himself and his friends. Contained in his sketchbooks, one of which is referred to as the "Interlude Marseilles," one finds a coterie of characters, each drawn sharply in black and white (fig. 4). In Havana, he used those drawings as the basis for larger paintings.[10] *Untitled (Cheval)* [Horse] (c. 1942) is one such work, where he experiments with color, painting the figure in rich shades of blue (plate 40).[11] In this early period, the woman has simple, circular eyes and thick lips attached to a protruding chin. Lam depicts the figure frontally, the snout jutting from the side of her head. Other variations on the *femme-cheval* from that same year include *Los Amantes* [The Lovers] (1942), one of his most romantic paintings of the 1940s, which shows two figures conjoined to form a single horse-headed entity (plate 41). His depiction of two semiabstract and stony-white figures recalls the quiet drama of Constantin Brancusi's *The Kiss* (1907–8) and its reiterations. A rather unusual *femme-cheval* appears in *Personage con sombrero* [Personage with Hat] (1942), which contains the similar eyes, nose, and testicular chin seen in the Marseilles notebooks (plate 42). By comparison, the body is more radically abstracted into colored planes that recall the Cubist sculptures of Picasso, where entirely abstract elements combine to suggest objects or figures. These variations show Lam intently playing with form and representations of gender that break from the more static female forms of his Paris period.

In the works in the Brillembourg Capriles Collection, there is an indication that Lam's process—his experimentation and revisions—was a visible component of the finished image. In *Homme-cheval* [Horse-Headed Man] (1942) (plate 43), one sees a blue-green figure with a combined half-moon face and horse head set on a grey background. His bottom lip and chin together suggest a phallus; the figure's arms are placed casually behind his head. Lam reworked the composition several times to get the proportions to his exact liking: just below the

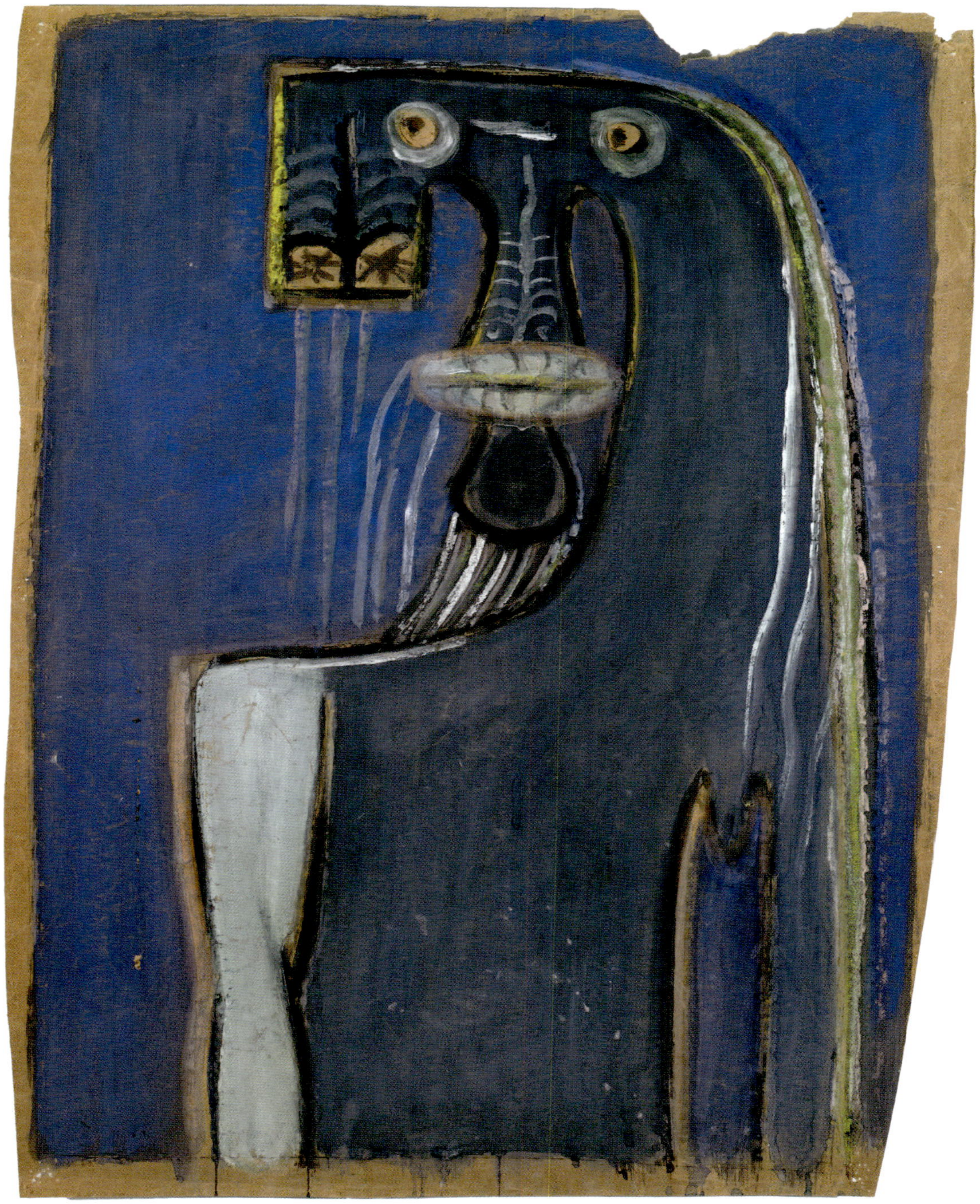

PLATE 40

Wifredo Lam • *Cheval* [Horse], double-sided painting (*Femme* on reverse) , c. 1942

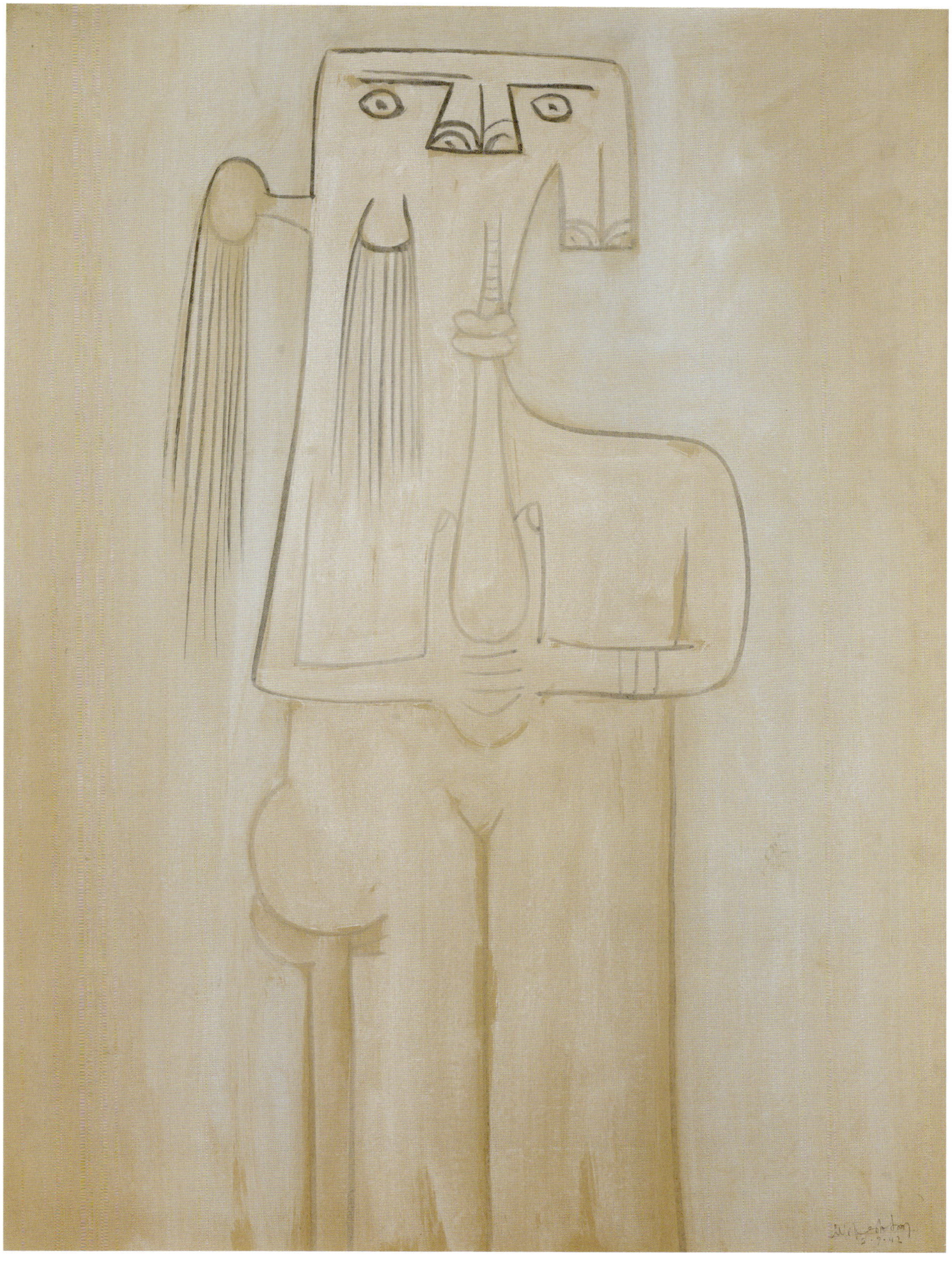

PLATE 41
Wifredo Lam • *Los Amantes* [The Lovers], 1942

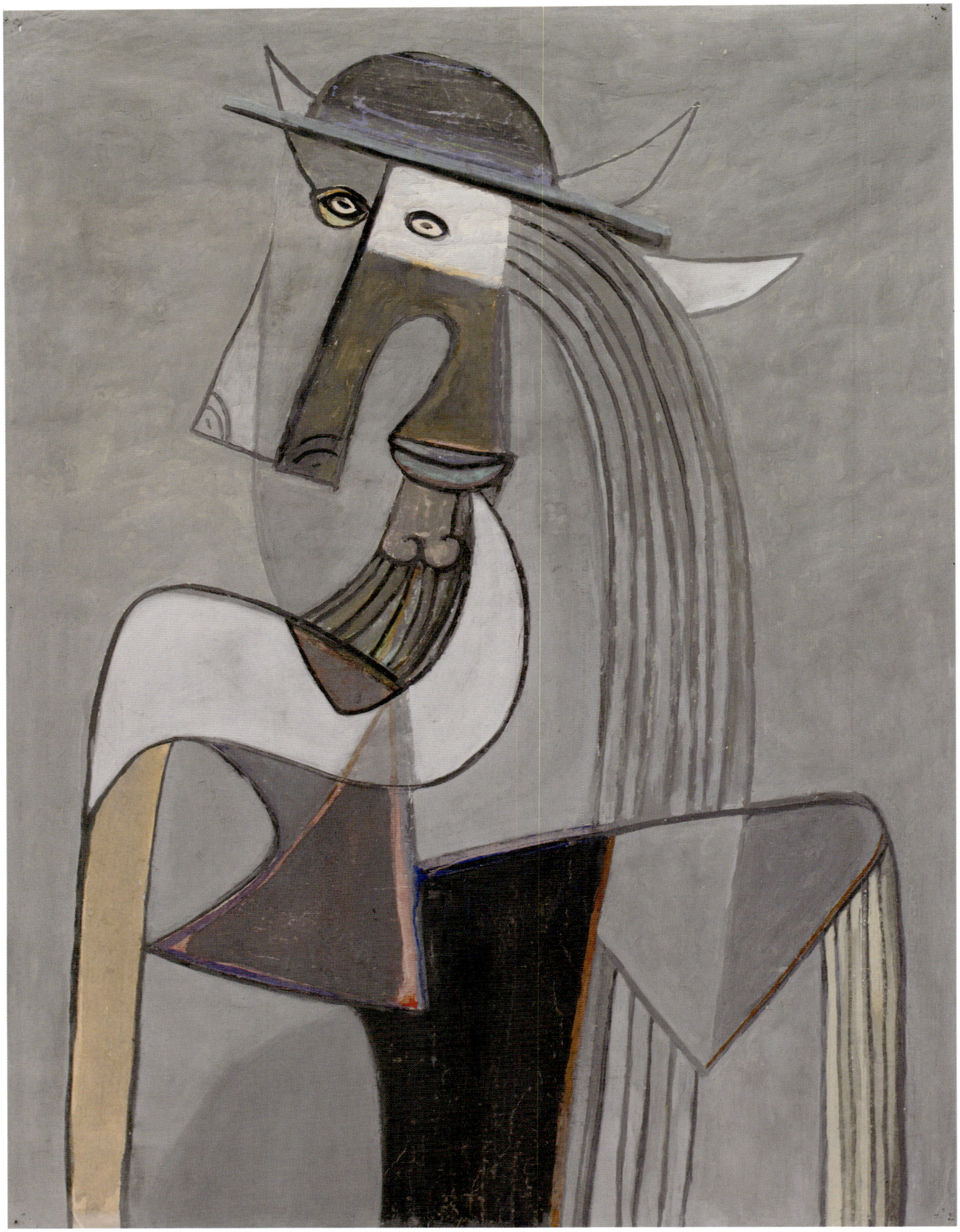

PLATE 42

Wifredo Lam • *Personaje con sombrero* [Personage with Hat], c. 1942

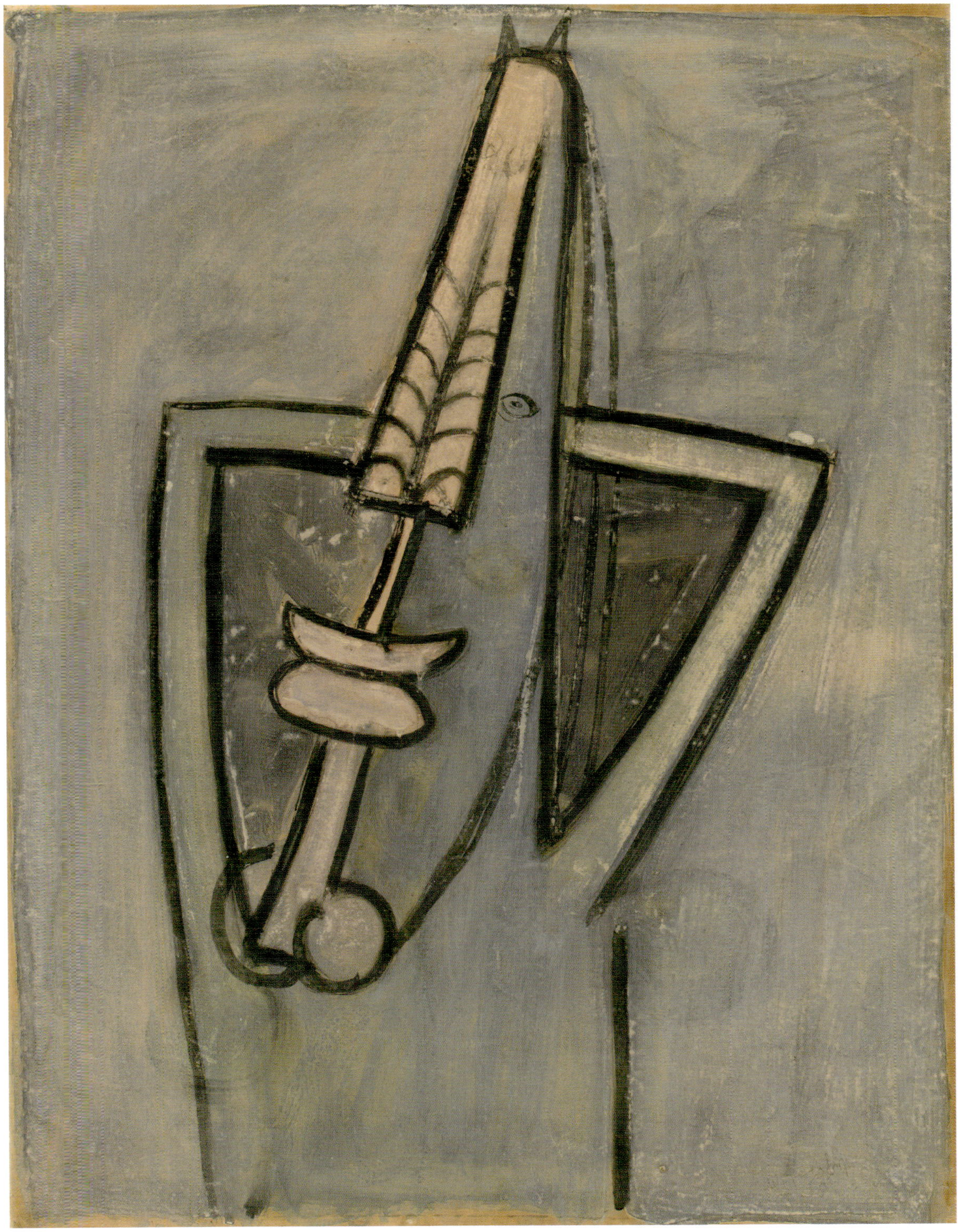

PLATE 43

Wifredo Lam • *Homme-Cheval* [Horse-headed Man], 1942

chin are circular forms suggesting he resized the head; likewise, a second, larger eye appears on the cheek of the figure; and at the upper right, at least two versions of the figure's bent arm are painted over in grey. This is not pentimenti, but instead a deliberate decision by the artist to leave the construction of his painting visible.[12] Art historian and curator Lowery Stokes Sims notes that Lam usually drew his compositions with charcoal before adding paint: "At times the more densely applied surfaces of the paintings . . . open up, and Lam allows the underdrawing to show through or exist on its own as part of the final composition."[13] One sees this technique in *Homme-cheval* and in later works, such as *Sur la main droite* [On the Right Hand] (1962), where the underdrawing provides a ghostly sense of depth. A six-fingered *femme-cheval* at center seems to float in and out of a cloudy backdrop, as does the outline of a horned woman with a Spanish-style comb in her hair. Emerging from behind the horse is an arm holding up an image of an Elegua head, an orisha in the Yoruba religion who inhabits stones and often serves as a protector against evil.

Lam continued to experiment with the morphology of the horse-headed woman in the late 1940s and 1950s, giving her a more ominous and birdlike appearance, extending the snout into a sharp hatchet and often adding spikes and horns. His *Femmes-Cheval* [Horse-headed Women] (1953) shows multiple versions of this figure on a single sheet of paper. Her poses are charted as though they form an alphabet (plate 44). By this point in time, Lam felt a personal connection with this motif. A photographic portrait of him taken in 1957 by Cuban photographer Jesse Fernández shows the shadow of the *femme-cheval* looming over him like a protective spirit (fig. 5). Lam continued to make adaptations to the *femme-cheval* until his death in 1982. These changes were partly inspired by the different objects he collected from the Caribbean, Africa, Indonesia, and the Native American Northwest.

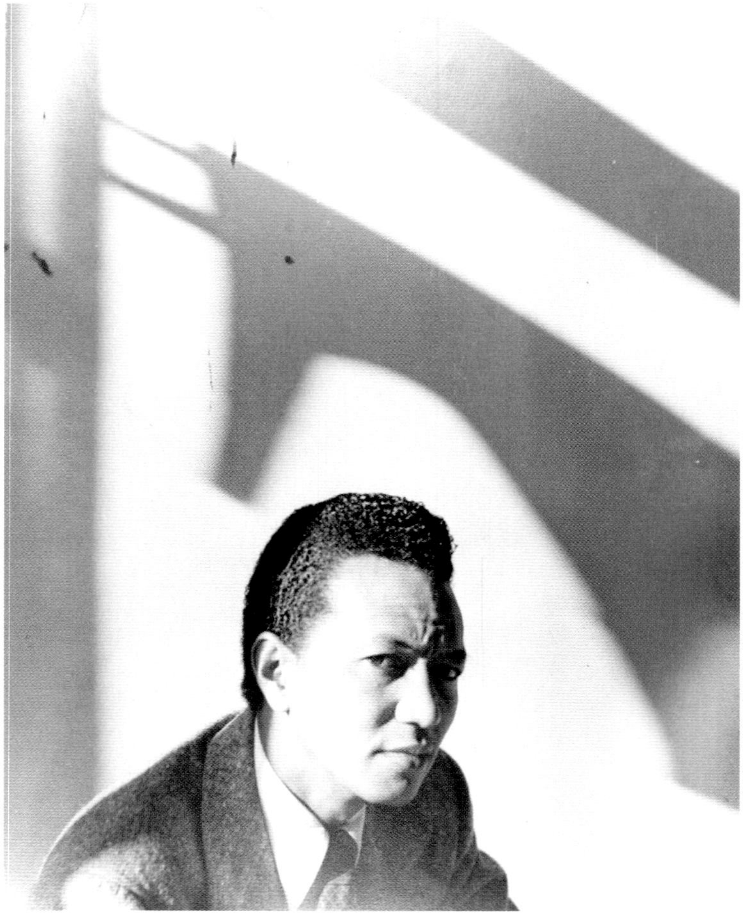

FIG. 5

The Brillembourg Capriles Collection contains *Reflets d'eau* [Water Reflections] (1955), one of his monumental totem paintings of which Lam made only four (plate 36), as well as an untitled pen-and-ink study that shows an earlier interest in creating elongated totemic designs (plate 45).[14] In his totem paintings, one sees a central spiky stalk of sugar cane, populated with Elegua heads and mystical symbols, like the lozenge shape representing fertility. However, this work is the only one of the totems that contains a *femme-cheval* hidden in its midst: within the brown washes of the background, one finds black hooves and arms of a diving horse-headed figure.

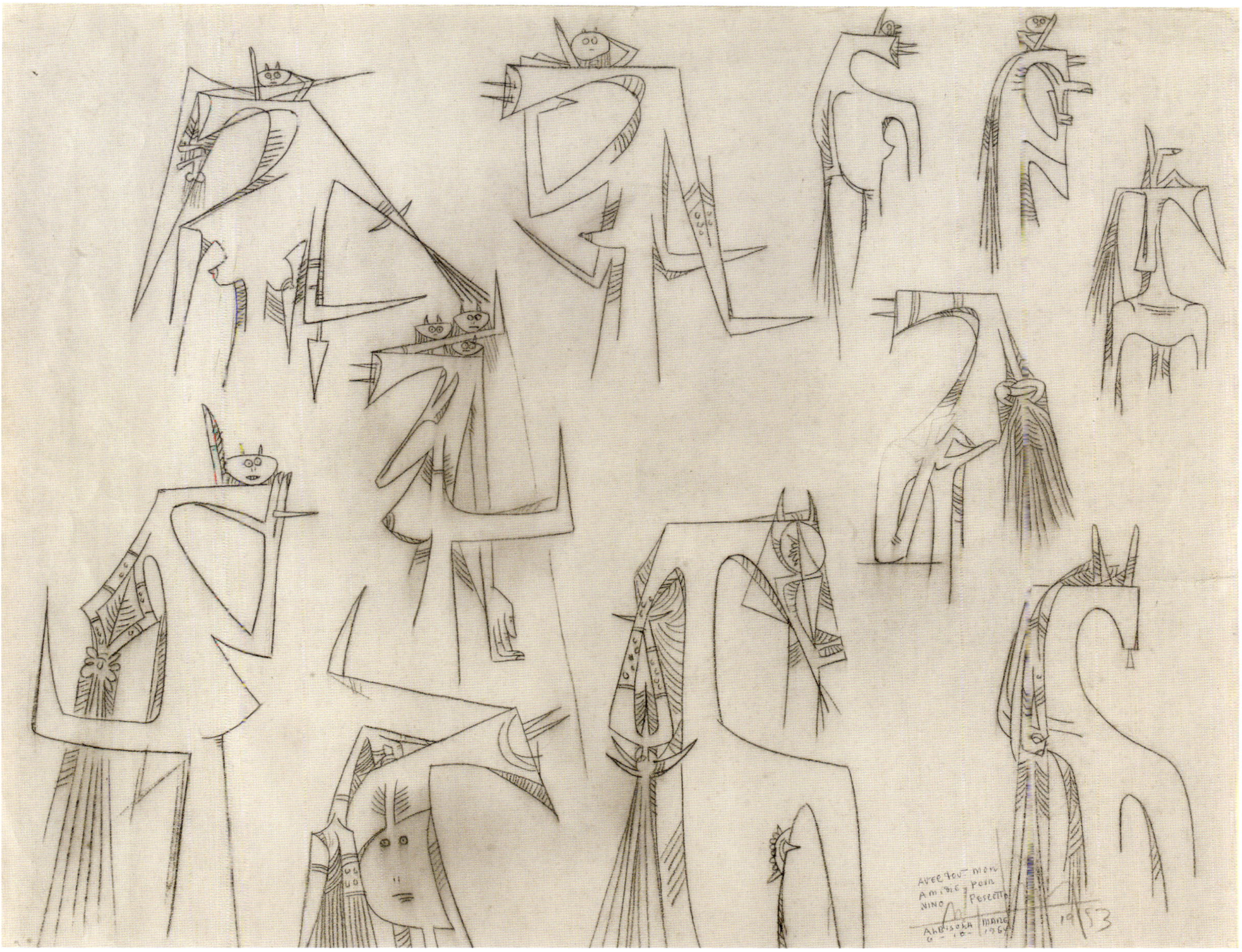

PLATE 44

Wifredo Lam • *Femmes-Cheval* [Horse-Headed Women], 1953

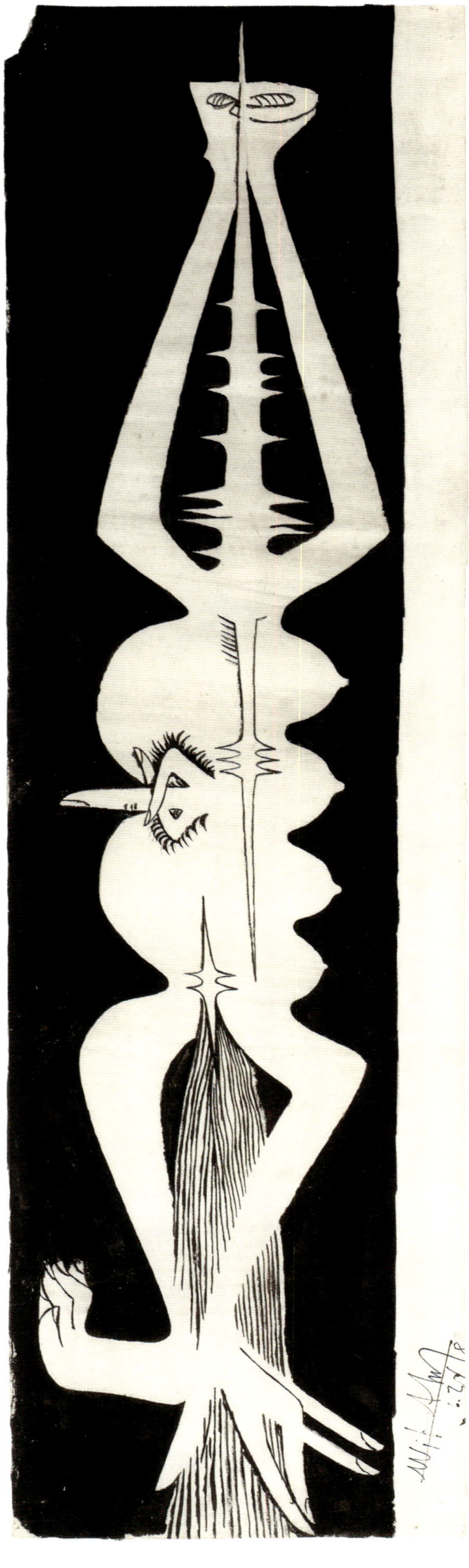

PLATE 45

Wifredo Lam • *Sin título* [Untitled], 1948

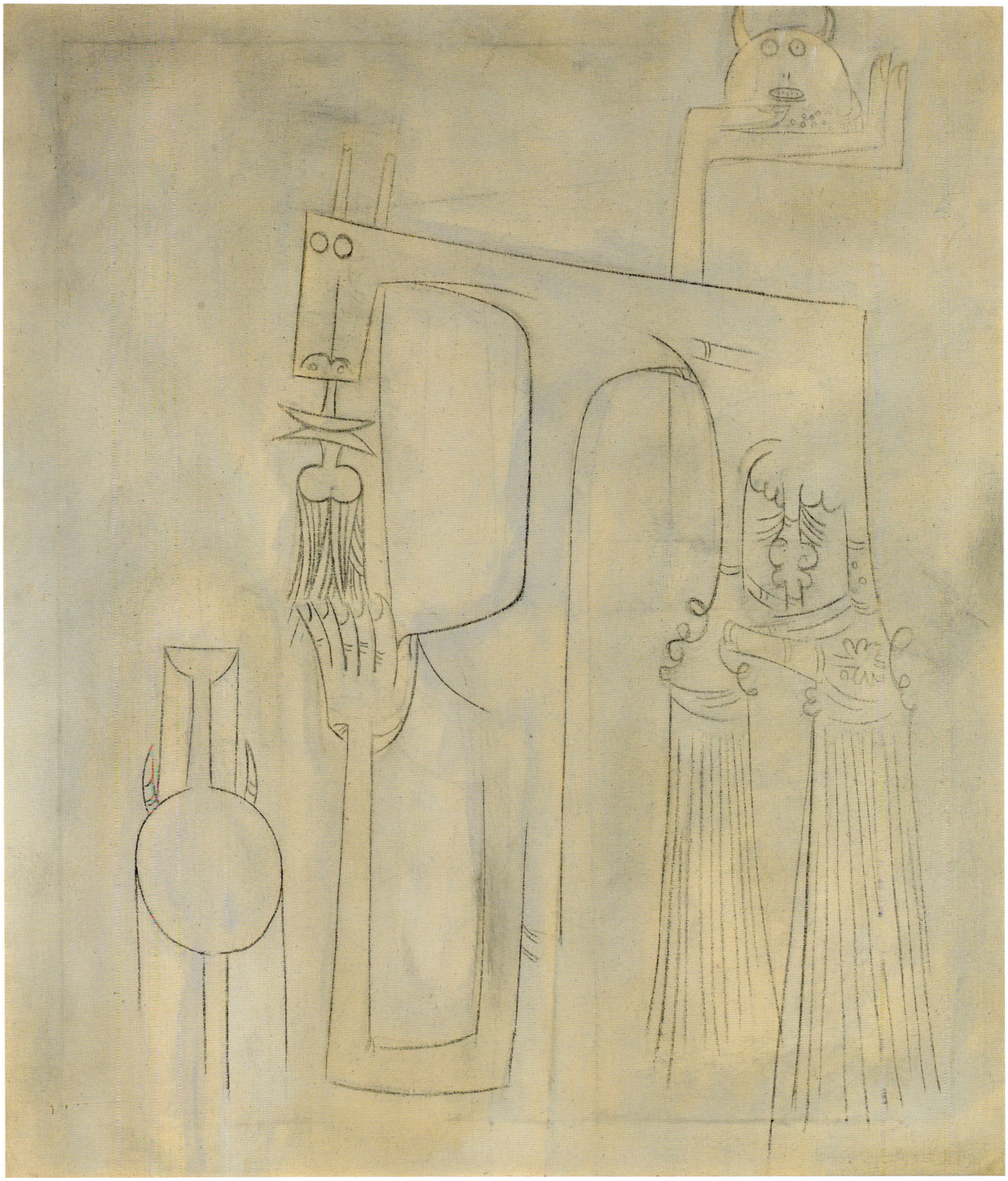

PLATE 46

Wifredo Lam • *Sur la main droite* [On the Right Hand], 1962

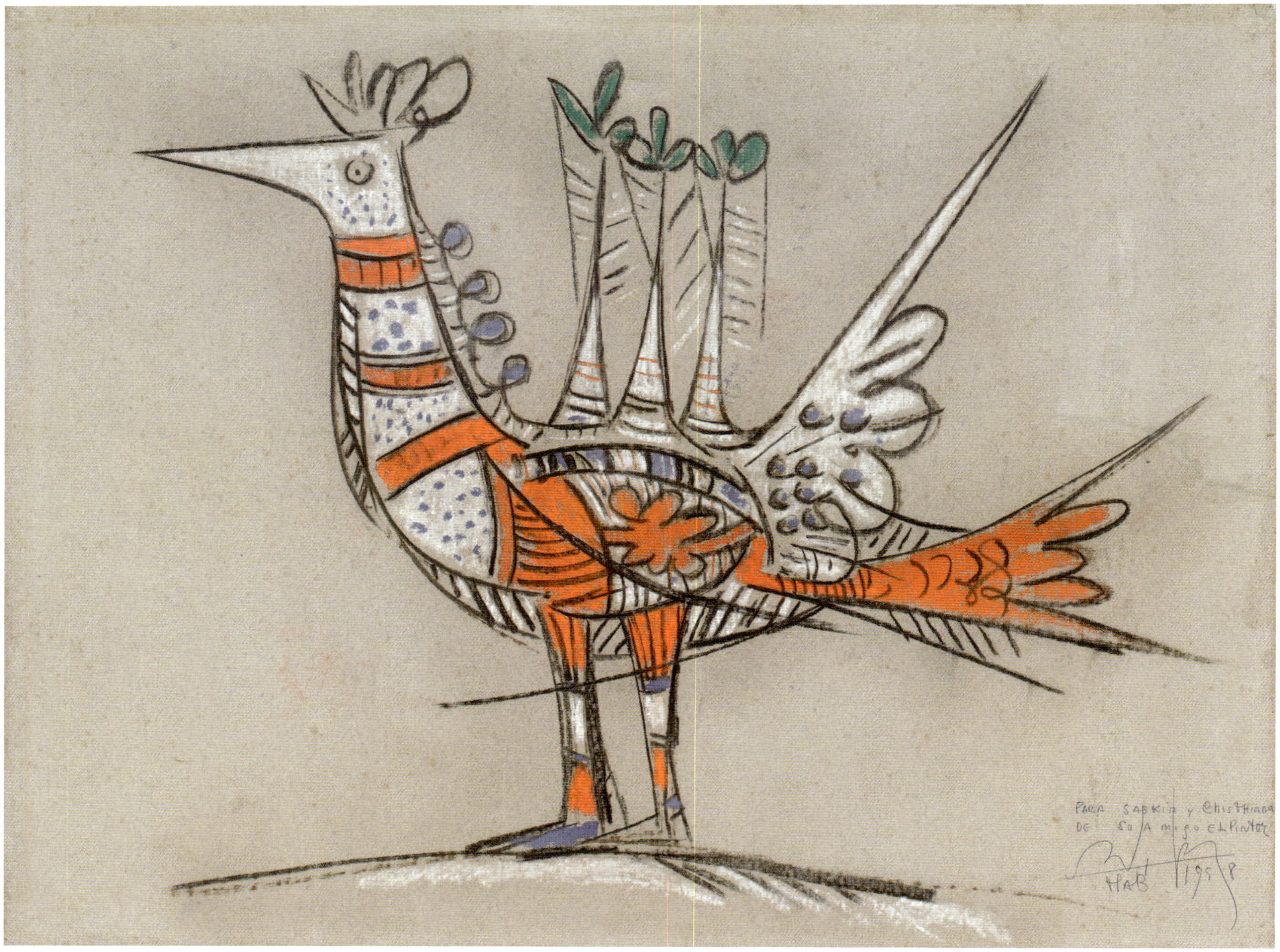

PLATE 47

Wifredo Lam • *Sin título (La gallina)* [Untitled (The Hen)], 1958

Lam spent the majority of his professional life creating a world of nimble and attenuated figures; their specific attributes change and evolve, yet these mystical characters consistently appear in his work from the late 1940s to the 1980s. Lam's career could be read as a long investigation into how these figures inhabited and adapted themselves to different aspects of art-making, to changes in color, size, format, and media, but also to changes in reception and cultural environment. These figures have their roots in the transitions Lam made between 1938 and 1942, particularly as he altered his approach to depicting the female form. The Brillembourg Capriles Collection offers a rare opportunity to see the artist, his inspirations, and his techniques together in the process of metamorphosis through which he created the most powerful and defining images of his career.

ILLUSTRATIONS IN TEXT

FIGURE 1
Henri Matisse
Portrait of Yvonne Landsberg, 1914
Oil on canvas
58 x 38 3/8 inches (147.3 x 97.5 cm)
Philadelphia Museum of Art, The Louise and Walter Arensberg Collection, 1950

FIGURE 2
Henri Matisse
Blue Nude (Souvenir de Biskra), 1907
Oil on canvas
36 1/4 x 55 1/4 inches (92.1 x 140.4 cm)
The Baltimore Museum of Art, The Cone Collection, formed by Dr. Claribel Cone and Miss Etta Cone of Baltimore, Maryland, BMA 1950.228

FIGURE 3
Pablo Picasso
Woman with a Fan, 1908
Oil on canvas
59 7/8 x 39 7/8 inches (152 x 101 cm)
Hermitage, St. Petersburg, Russia

FIGURE 4
Wifredo Lam
Interlude Marseilles, 1940–41
Ink and pencil on paper
8 3/4 x 6 3/4 inches (22.23 x 17.15 cm)
Los Angeles County Museum of Art, Gift of Dr. and Mrs. James Luhn Sheehy

FIGURE 5
Jesse A. Fernández
Portrait of Wifredo Lam, c. 1957
Estate Jesse A. Fernández, Collection France Mazin Fernández

NOTES

1
For a more thorough discussion of the "unknown" Wifredo Lam, see José Manuel Noceda and Roberto Cobas Amate, "Wifredo Lam desconocido," in *Cuarto Bienal de La Habana 1991* (Havana, Cuba: Centro Wifredo Lam and Editorial Letras Cubanas), 155–60.

2
Matisse first spoke of these "lines of construction" in an interview with Alfred H. Barr, Jr., in 1951. See John Klein, *Matisse Portraits* (New Haven: Yale University Press, 2001), 169. For a more recent analysis of Matisse's *Portrait of Yvonne Landsberg*, see Stephanie D'Alessandro and John Elderfield, *Matisse: Radical Invention, 1913–1917* (New Haven: Yale University Press, 2011), 210–14.

3
I am indebted to conversations with Lowery Stokes Sims, who pointed out the symbolism of these birds. She writes that the supreme deity and creator of the world, Olofi or Olodumare, is commonly represented as a vulture that lives in the heads of devotees. See Lowery Stokes Sims, *Wifredo Lam and the International Avant-Garde, 1923–1982* (Austin: University of Texas Press, 2002), 124.

4
See Sims, *Wifredo Lam and the International Avant-Garde*, 1923–1982, 117. David Craven also discusses this tradition in relation to Lam's work in his book *Art and Revolution in Latin America, 1900–1990* (New Haven: Yale University Press, 2006), 109. These rituals of possession are commonly described in highly sexualized terms, usually to convey the sense of union between orisha and devotee. See Margaret Thompson Drewal, "Dancing for Ogun in Yorubaland and in Brazil," in *Blackness in Latin America and the Caribbean, Volume 2: Social Dynamics and Cultural Transformations*, edited by Norman E. Whitten, Jr., and Arlene Torres (Bloomington: Indiana University Press, 1998), 256–84.

5
Lam did not always title works himself. In the 1940s, he sometimes looked to André Breton for poetic titles or to Cuban anthropologist Lydia Cabrera, one of the first to take an interest in Lam's work on the island; Cabrera suggested titles based on correspondences between the work and African and Afro-Caribbean ceremonial traditions. Nonetheless, Lam was certainly familiar with Yoruba carving as exemplified by works in Picasso's studio and at Paris's natural history museum, Musée de l'Homme, which he visited regularly with anthropologist Michel Leiris, a supporter of the Surrealist movement.

6
Lam's statements originally appeared in Antonio Núñez Jiménez, *Wifredo Lam* (Havana: Editorial Letras Cubanas, 1982), 232. This translation comes from Roberto Cobas Amate, "Lam, A Visual Arts Manifesto for the Third World," in *Cuba: Art and History from 1868 to Today* (Montreal: Montreal Museum of Fine Arts/Prestel Publishing, 2008), 196–203: 198.

7
Helena Benitez, *Wifredo and Helena: My Life with Wifredo Lam*, 1939–1950 (Switzerland: Acatos, 1999), 80.

8
This statement comes from an interview conducted by art historian Gerardo Mosquera. For a version of the interview in English, see David Craven, "'My Painting is an Act of Decolonization': An Interview with Wifredo Lam by Gerardo Mosquera (1980)," *Journal of Surrealism and the Americas* [online], 3, no. 1 (March 20, 2010).

9
Lowery Stokes Sims has written extensively on the significance of the femme-cheval in Lam's work, identifying her as a politically potent figure. For an analysis of the *femme-cheval*'s links to European Surrealism, African and Caribbean religions, and classically Western notions of beauty, see Sims, "Lam's Femme Cheval: Avatar of Beauty," in *Wifredo Lam in North America* (Milwaukee: Haggerty Museum of Art, 2008), 27–36.

10
See Cobas Amate, 196.

11
This work is on the reverse side of *Femme* and may indicate that both of these were studies.

12
Art historians Stephanie D'Alessandro and John Elderfield describe a similar phenomenon characterizing the most radical work of Matisse and argue for a reinterpretation of the term "pentimenti." See their essay "Matisse, 1914–1917, and the Methods of Modern Construction," in *Matisse: Radical Invention, 1913–1917*, 18–30.

13
Lowery Stokes Sims, "Myths and Primitivism: The Work of Wifredo Lam in the Context of the New York School and the School of Paris, 1942–1952," in *Wifredo Lam and His Contemporaries, 1938–1952* (New York: Studio Museum in Harlem and Harry N. Abrams, Inc., 1992), 49.

14
In the 1950s Lam became interested in totemic sculptures from Papua New Guinea, objects he began collecting at that time. See Cobas Amate, 202.

María C. Gaztambide

THE ELUSIVE MYSTICISM OF RENÉ PORTOCARRERO

Art for the creative artist should be a deep and mysterious call from the unknown. The artist should be far from any dialectic which will enable him to preserve the purity of observation. . . .

—RENÉ PORTOCARRERO, C. 1943[1]

IN 1944, ALFRED H. BARR, JR., famously dismissed modern Cuban art for its ". . . reckless exuberance, gayety, candor and love of life. . . ."[2] Since Barr, Cuba's national art project at mid-century has been reduced to a binary model focused on the adherence to one of two mutually exclusive thematic routes: either *Afrocubanismo*, which responded to an interest in Afro-Cuba,[3] or *Criollismo*, a conflictive tendency that exalted the "white" Hispanic or European root in its two main manifestations [the rural peasantry (*guajiros*)[4] and the culture of Creole urbanites].[5] This reductive historiography belies the actual complexity of a school of painting that coalesced in Havana from the 1920s through the 1940s as well as the significance of its most notable practitioners, including René Portocarrero (1911–1985). His *Brujo* [Sorcerer] (plate 48) and *Sin título* [Untitled] (plate 49), both in the Brillembourg Capriles Collection of Latin American Art, present a rare opportunity to challenge some of the narratives that have enveloped him and many of his contemporaries since Barr's early assessment. These works reveal an artist embarking on an esoteric direction that reconciled, at least fleetingly, the seemingly opposing poles of African and white Cuban culture.

Brujo is part of a short-lived series on sorcerers that Portocarrero executed wholly during 1945. The series is in itself unusual since the artist did not revisit the theme over time, as he often did with other series throughout his career. It thus constitutes a nucleus of works that has received little critical attention relative to more prolific series such as Interiores de El Cerro [El Cerro Interiors] (begun in 1943) (fig. 1).[6] In Brujos, the artist explores a sorcerer's interrelated roles (religious, curative, and divinatory) in order to offer a commentary on the pervasiveness of Afro-Cuban traditions on the island.[7] Portocarrero reconciles the plural worldview of the African religions that were preserved in the Americas—featuring the coexistence of the vital and the destructive, the terrible and the beautiful, the fruitful and the evil—with Christianity's good/evil polarity.[8] Indeed, the belief in the spirits of the Santería pantheon was so widely held in Cuba and so deeply merged with Christianity that even Jesus was thought to have been a *yerbero* [sacred man], as the social anthropologist Lydia Cabrera notes in *El Monte* (1954), her watershed study of Cuban religiosity, magic, superstitions, and folklore.[9]

The Brillembourg Capriles painting stands out vis-à-vis other works in the series—including *Brujo de Carnaval* [Carnival Sorcerer] in a private collection in New York (1945) (fig. 2)—in that it channels a geometric quality that sharply contrasts with their more literal representation of the sorcerer and his accoutrements. Here, Portocarrero foreshadows the muted geometric abstraction that he introduced in 1946 in series such as Gestáltica (fig. 3) and turned to again from 1949

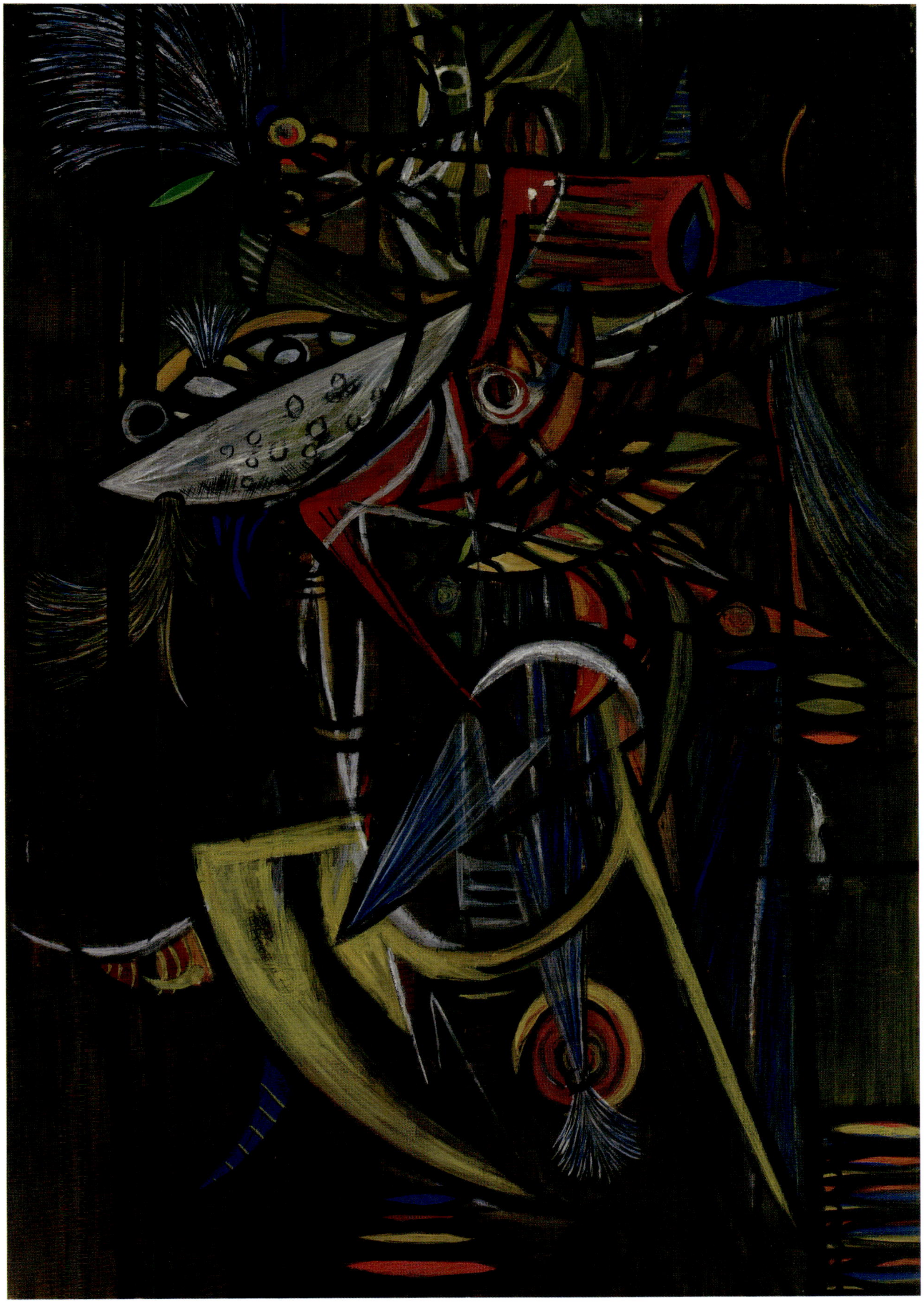

PLATE 48

René Portocarrero • *Brujo* [Sorcerer], 1945

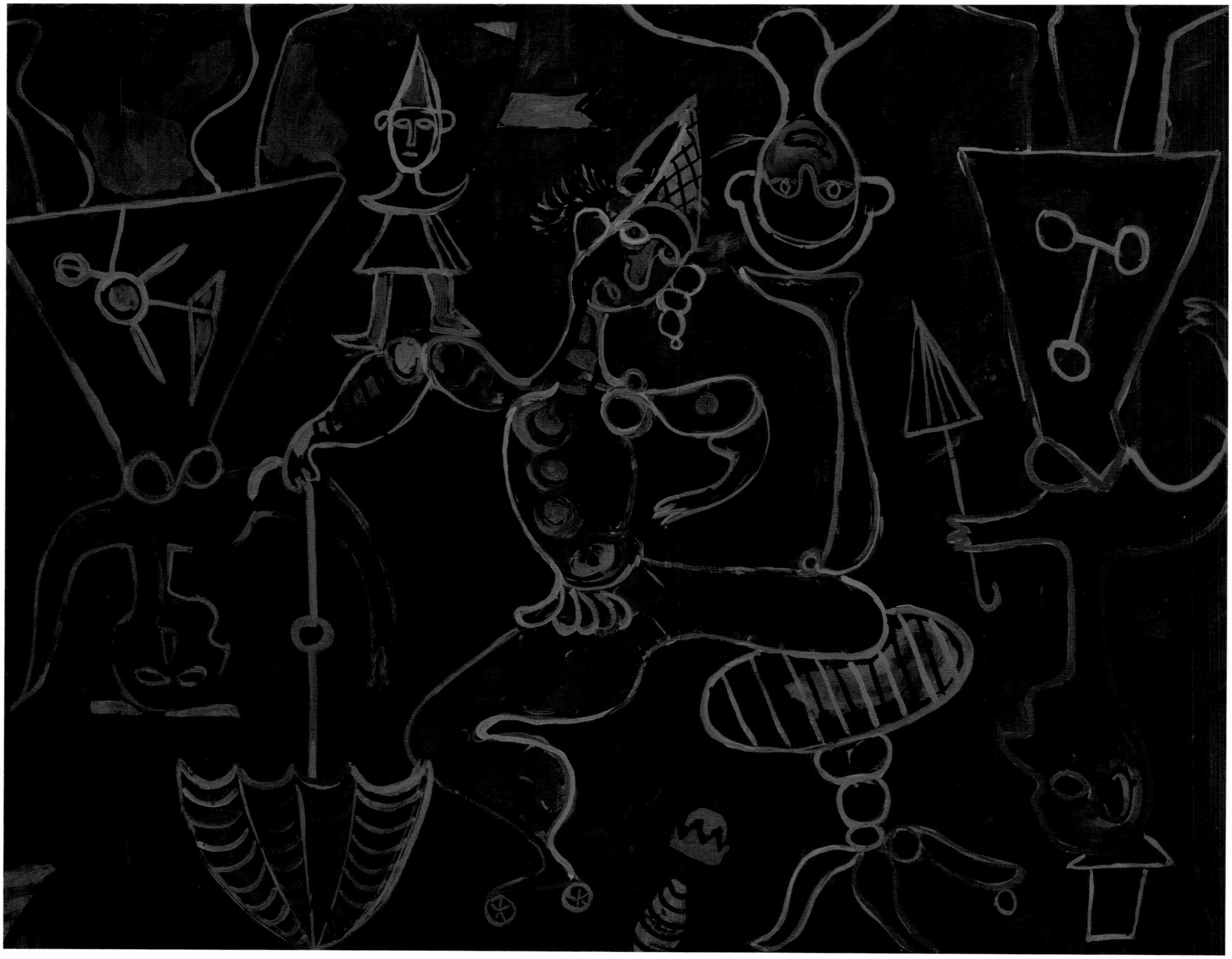

PLATE 49
René Portocarrero • *Sin título* [Untitled], 1945

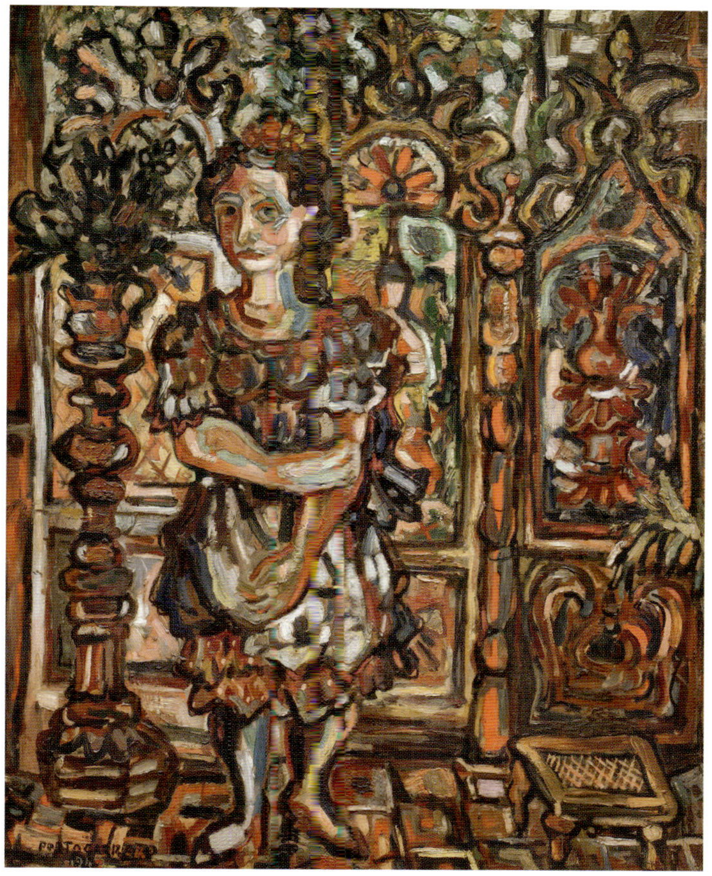

FIG. 1

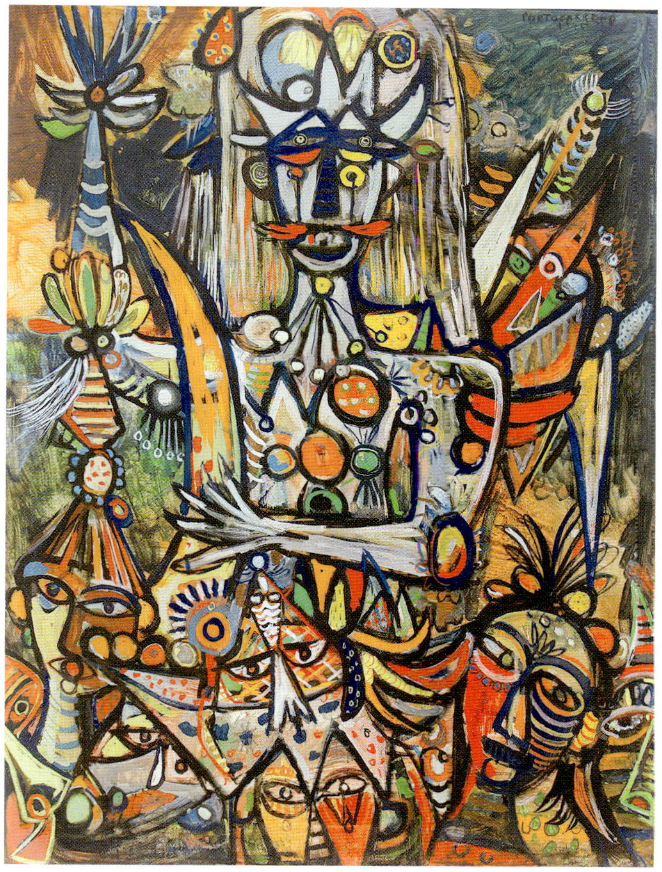

FIG. 2

to 1953.[10] In the Brillembourg Capriles *Brujo*, the rectilinear elements of the grid in the background are deconstructed and simultaneously transformed into the organic and enlivened components of the central figure. Much in the same way that the figure is formally merged with the background, the sorcerer is shown already metamorphosed into a deity in the Afro-Cuban pantheon. Furthermore, contrasting with the *Brujo de Carnaval*'s more literal representation (particularly of the sorcerer's staff and headdress), in *Brujo* meaning is conveyed through the symbols associated with the religious ritual preceding the transformation. In this version, ritualistic elements including the plumed headdress, the offerings and devotional receptacle, the talismans, as well as the sorcerer's blue necklaces—which may be a reference to Portocarrero's devotion to the syncretic figure of the Virgin of Regla/Yemanyá[11]—are highly schematized and decomposed. Brujos is nonetheless a revelatory series from an important moment in the artist's oeuvre where we see him synthesizing seemingly opposing polarities within Cuban culture.

Untitled of 1945 explores similar syncretic aspects of Cuban culture and is equally indicative of the breath of Portocarrero's mystical interests at this critical juncture. The focus here is his understanding of Carnival, which the artist would reclaim as a thematic source in the 1960s with his series Color de Cuba [Cuban Color].[12] In this work from 1945 he offers his take on the masquerade and purification rites associated with the Roman Catholic festivity, to which the Afro-Cuban tradition transferred much meaning. In *Untitled* a central jester is flanked by several figures with costumes and accessories that would be seen during the Christian revelries: mountebanks, old-time cavaliers, masks, umbrellas, the (phallic) staff of command. The Brillembourg Capriles Collection example constitutes a departure

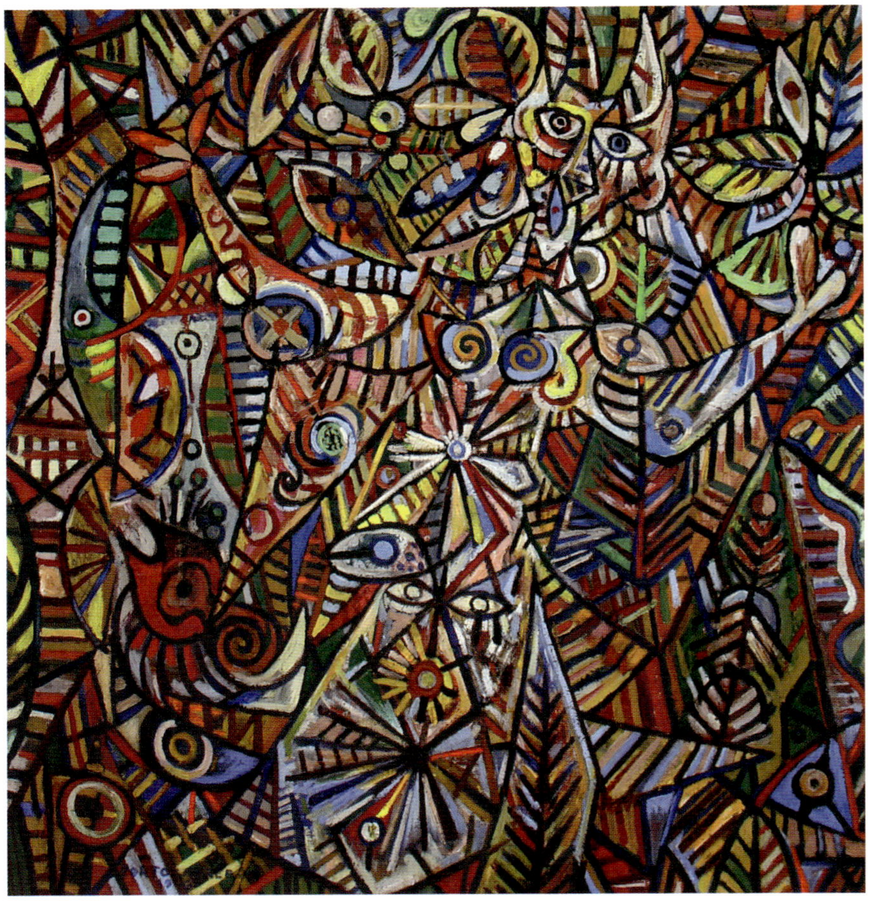

FIG. 3

from Portocarrero's signature style, however, in its subdued application of paint and neutral palette; perhaps a deliberate break through which to call attention to the purification and redemptive aspects of the festivity.[13]

Portocarrero mentioned in a 1961 interview that "... all national art is an artist's transformation of the world that engulfs him."[14] Paintings such as *Brujo* and *Untitled* are obvious nods to the key esoteric concepts of metamorphosis and transfigurations in the supernatural order.[15] More importantly, on the national front, they also demonstrate the little-acknowledged racial fluidity of the Cuban social fabric at midcentury.

ILLUSTRATIONS IN TEXT

FIGURE 1
René Portocarrero
Interior de El Cerro [Interior of El Cerro], 1943
Oil on Wood
28 x 22 5/8 inches (71 x 57.5 cm)
Museo Nacional de Bellas Artes,
Havana, Cuba

FIGURE 2
René Portocarrero
Brujo de Carnaval [Carnival Sorcerer], 1945
Mixed media on board laid down on canvas
36 1/4 x 27 3/4 inches (92.7 x 70.5 cm)
Private collection, New York

FIGURE 3
René Portocarrero
Gestaltica, 1946
Oil on wood
27 x 26 inches (68.6 x 66 cm)
Private Collection

NOTES

1
René Portocarrero, "Notas para el Museum of Modern Art, de Nueva York por René Portocarrero," c. 1943, unpublished typescript (New York: The Museum of Modern Art, René Portocarrero artist's file, various dates), 1–3, 1.

2
Alfred H. Barr, Jr., "Modern Cuban Painters," *The Bulletin of the Museum of Modern Art*, vol. 11, no. 5, *Modern Cuban Painters* (April 1944), 2–14, 5.

3
Afro-Cubanismo responded to the interest in primitivism and African art among the European artistic mainstream as well as to the work of other members of the Cuban avant-garde, including ethnomusicologist Lydia Cabrera, essayist Fernando Ortiz, poet Nicolás Guillén, and writer Alejo Carpentier.

Juan A. Martínez warns that some of the *vanguardia* artists—including Eduardo Abela, Carlos Enríquez, Lorenzo Romero Arciaga, and Antonio Gattorno—may have naively emphasized the exotic and obvious aspects of Afro-Cuban religion and myth, and in doing so furthered the stereotype of blacks as "energetic and rhythmic." See Juan A. Martínez, *Cuban Art and National Identity: The Vanguardia Painters, 1927–1950* (Gainesville: University of Florida Press, 1994), 74, 87–90.

4
The concern for the Cuban peasant and the countryside stemmed from a romanticized view of the *guajiros'* importance to past revolutionary processes. The presence of the rural peasantry was particularly felt during the Cuban War of Independence, which was waged in the countryside and where many guajiros enlisted as *mambises*, or freedom fighters. Ibid., 51.

5
For the reigning periodization approach toward the Cuban avant-garde, see Giulio V. Blanc, "Cuban artists of the twentieth century = Artistas cubanos del siglo XX," *Cuban Artists of the Twentieth Century: October 22, 1993–January 2, 1994*, exh. cat. (Fort Lauderdale: Museum of Art, Fort Lauderdale, 1993), 7–34; and Ricardo Pau-Llosa, "Identity and variations: Cuban visual thinking in exile since 1959," in *Outside Cuba: Contemporary Cuban Visual Artists = Fuera de Cuba: Artistas Cubanos Contemporáneos*, exh. cat. (New Brunswick: Office of Hispanic Arts, Mason Gross School of the Arts, Rutgers, the State University of New Jersey; Coral Gables: Research Institute for Cuban Studies, Graduate School of International Studies, University of Miami, 1988).

6
This may be due in part to the fact that many of the works from the series were first shown and bought outside of Cuba, where they remain. Many entered U.S. collections following his shows at the San Francisco Museum of Modern Art [*Cuban Painting Today: Girona, Mariano, Portocarrero* (October 9–November 4, 1945)] and his first solo exhibition at Julien Levy's East 57th Street gallery in New York later in November 1945. See SFMoMA, *Finding Aid to the San Francisco Museum of Modern Art Exhibition Records, 1934–ongoing [bulk 1935–1975]* (San Francisco: SFMoMA, April 1998), 53; Julien Levy, *Memoir of an Art Gallery* (New York: G.P. Putnam's Sons, 1977), 310; Ingrid Schaffner and Lisa Jacobs, *Julien Levy: Portrait of an Art Gallery* (Cambridge, MA, and London: The MIT Press, 1998), 186.

7
For a detailed description of the multiple hats that Cuban sorcerers wear, see Fernando Ortiz, *Los negros brujos* [1906] (Havana: Editorial de Ciencias Sociales, 2007), 71.

8
The Cuban art critic Gerardo Mosquera has rightfully argued that it is no longer possible to continue to discuss the cultural effect of Africans on America by using terms such as "influence" or "impact." Rather, he writes, African culture was a "constitutive ingredient" that cannot be masked by a discriminatory hierarchy that ostracizes the black root. Indeed, as he has noted, Wifredo Lam was the first artist to become conscious of this fact and to offer a vision *from* the African presence in America. The work that emerged during his return to Cuba (1941–52), including *Maternité Yoruba* [Yoruba Maternity] (1942) in the Brillembourg Capriles Collection (plate 37), suggested the possibility of "communicating, more than strictly representing, a modern mythology of the Caribbean." Moreover, Lam also validated for the members of the Havana School the use of a European lexicon to convey an integral vision of the syncretic religions that emerged in America. Gerardo Mosquera, "Elegguá at the (Post?) Modern Crossroads: The Presence of Africa in the Visual Art of Cuba," in Arturo Lindsay, ed., *Santería Aesthetics in Contemporary Latin American Art* (Washington, D.C., and London: Smithsonian Institution Press, 1996), 225–58, 225, 230–31.

9
"¿Jesús no hace en el monte sobre un montón de yerba", dice C "y para irse al cielo a ser Dios no muere en un monte, el Monte Calvario? Siempre andaba metido por los montes. ¡Era yerbero!" Lydia Cabrera, *El Monte. Igbo. Finda. Ewe Orisha. Vititi Nfinda (Notas sobre las religiones, la magia, las supersticiones y el folklore de los negros criollos y el pueblo de Cuba)* [1954] (Miami: Colección del Chicherekú, 1986), 17.

10
During this later period he painted a number of geometric figures not unlike the sorcerer in the Brillembourg Capriles Collection, including *The Idol* (1949) and *Woman with Arrows* (1953). *Brujo*'s stylistic proximity to these works may be indicative, in fact, of its relative terminal position within the series.

11
In *Los negros brujos* (1906), Fernando Ortiz writes extensively on the significance of these and other ritual elements in Afro-Cuban devotional practices. See Ortiz, *Los negros brujos*, 96–98.

12
The exhibition was initially staged at the Galería La Habana from May 20 to June 25, 1963. It traveled or was "reincarnated" as seven other shows, each of the same title, from 1964 through 1980, including Panama and Bulgaria. For a complete list of these exhibitions, see René Portocarrero, *René Portocarrero: exposición antológica, Museo Español de Arte Contemporáneo de Madrid, diciembre 1984–enero 1985* (Madrid: Ministerio de Cultura, Dirección General de Bellas Artes y Archivos, 1984), 74. Alejo Carpentier wrote the presentation for the 1963 catalogue, and Roberto Fernández Retamar published at least one reflection on the significance of that body of work. See Carpentier [Más que un estilo, es lo barroco] [1963], reprinted in *René Portocarrero: exposición antológica* (citation above), 25–26; and Roberto Fernández Retamar, "Portocarrero: Color de Cuba." *Cuba. Revista mensual* (Havana), year II, no. 16 (1963), reprinted in René Portocarrero, *25 años de color de Cuba: René Portocarrero* ([Havana] Ministerio de Cultura, 1988), n/p. The text may also have been reprinted in *Islas* (Havana), no. 2 (1966). For a reappraisal of the exhibition's historical importance, see the previously cited *25 años de color de Cuba: René Portocarrero*.

13
Lezama Lima notes, in the context of Portocarrero's work, that the Carnival series has to do with transcendence and transformation into the spiritual realm. In Christian lore Carnival is the period when the faithful must partake of the purification exercises through which to welcome [Christ's] death: "riddance and purification, the first outfit for a visit from the deceased." Lezama Lima, "Homenaje a René Portocarrero," *La cantidad hechizada* (Madrid: Ediciones Júcar, 1974), 249–98, 270–71.

14
Portocarrero, in J. Rodríguez Feo, "Entrevista. Portocarrero," *Bohemia*, May 28, 1961. Reprinted in René Portocarrero. *René Portocarrero: exposición retrospectiva* ([Havana]: Museo Nacional, 1967), n/p.

15
Lezama Lima, "Homenaje a René Portocarrero," 261, 282.

James Oles

RUFINO TAMAYO

ESCAPE AND ECSTASY

SINGLE FIGURES, ISOLATED WITHIN THE FRAME, their forms abstracted yet never losing their essential humanity, are featured in all five works by Rufino Tamayo in the Brillembourg Capriles Collection of Latin American Art. Ranging in date from 1950 to 1973, they represent different facets of the artist's prolific postwar career, during which he sought to forge a path between the "descriptive realism" of the so-called Mexican School (best emblematized in this catalogue by Diego Rivera's *Portrait of Columba Domínguez* [plate 8] and David Alfaro Siqueiros's *The Challenge* [plate 9], both from the 1950s) and the non-figurative abstraction of the New York School and its European counterparts, like Art Informel.[1] In fact, with the possible exception of a 1961 portrait, the works discussed here do not refer overtly to Mexico, though Tamayo always insisted that "Mexicanness" emerged spontaneously in his work. Rather, they focus our attention on human experience in general, as well as the artist's capacity for continuing formal experimentation. As the painter himself said in 1950: "My struggle consists of helping to place Mexico at the level of universal art."[2]

Free from the Cage

The postwar decades were a time of tremendous critical and commercial success for Tamayo: in 1948, he was given his first major retrospective, held at the Museo Nacional de Artes Plásticas in Mexico City; his work was sold by such prestigious New York galleries as Pierre Matisse and Knoedler's; and, in 1950, his paintings were included alongside those of the consecrated Rivera, Siqueiros, and José Clemente Orozco at the XXV Venice Biennale. *Woman with Birds* [plate 50] and *Liberated Birds* [plate 51], the two earliest Tamayos in the Brillembourg Capriles Collection, reveal Tamayo's rapid stylistic evolution in the 1950s, when he worked through post-Cubism and other pictorial devices typical of the School of Paris, as well as explored the fascination with "primitive art" (in Tamayo's case, from ancient America more than from Africa) that so many of his Mexican and European contemporaries shared.

The first of these is a large pencil drawing of the bust of a woman whose gender is indicated by her long hair. She seems aloof from, or perhaps startled by, the bird perched on what appears to be her shoulder; another stands in front of her on what may be a tabletop. Like several other polished drawings from the late 1940s, this is more likely a finished work rather than a preparatory sketch.[3] It directly correlates with no known painting, and, as Diana du Pont has noted, Tamayo emphasized intuition in his process, often beginning directly with the canvas.[4]

The woman's features show clear debts to Pablo Picasso, whose work Tamayo had first studied up close at *Picasso: Forty Years of His Art*, held at the Museum of Modern Art in New York in the winter of 1938–40, and which he used as a touchstone—along with that of Georges Braque and Henri Matisse—for the rest of his life.[5] The flattened nostrils and lips and glaring eyes with energetic lashes—one seen in profile, the other straight-on—are loosely derived from Picasso's portraits of his mistress, Dora Maar (fig. 1), though the

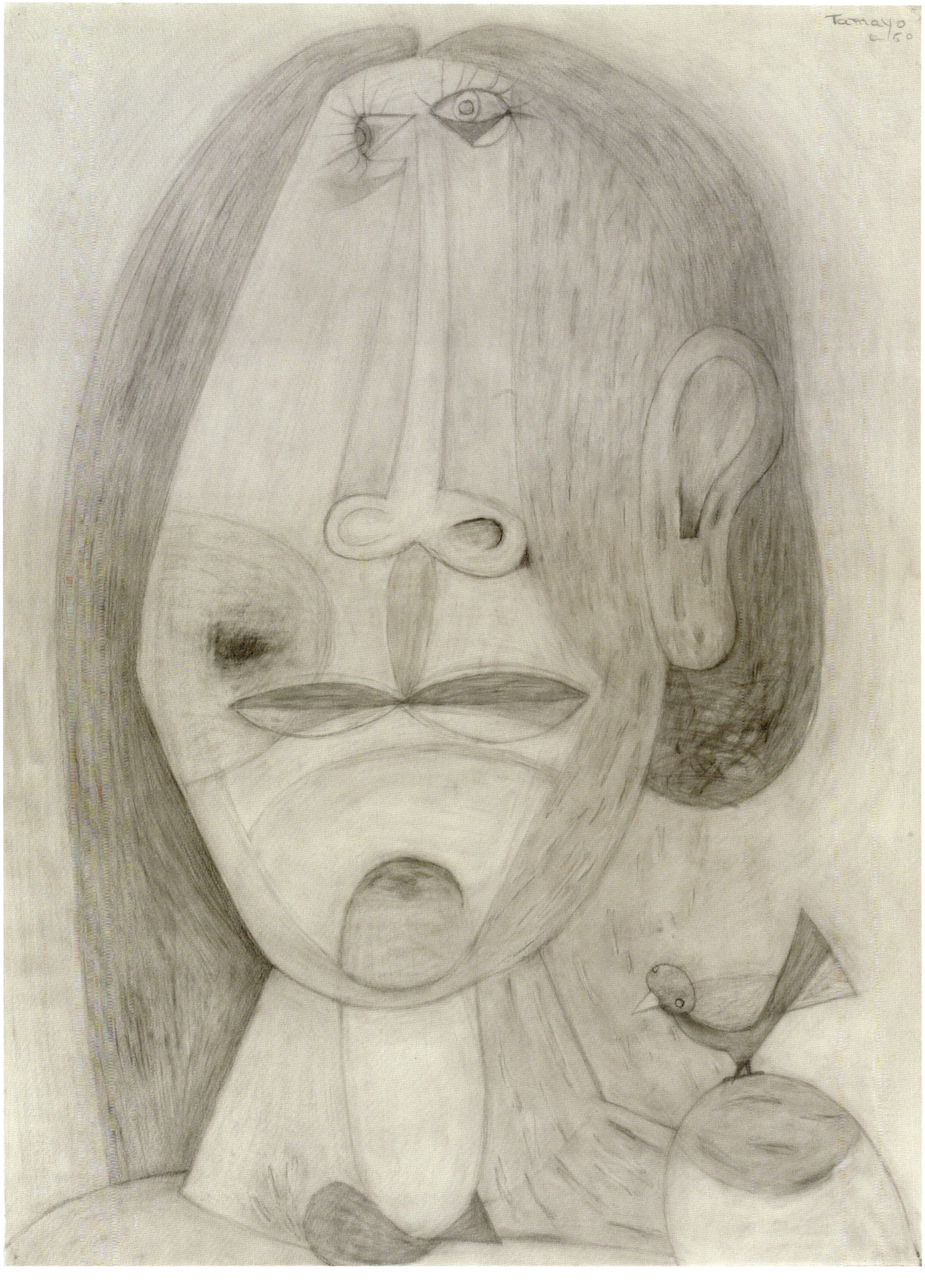

PLATE 50

Rufino Tamayo • *Mujer con pájaros* [Woman with Birds], 1950

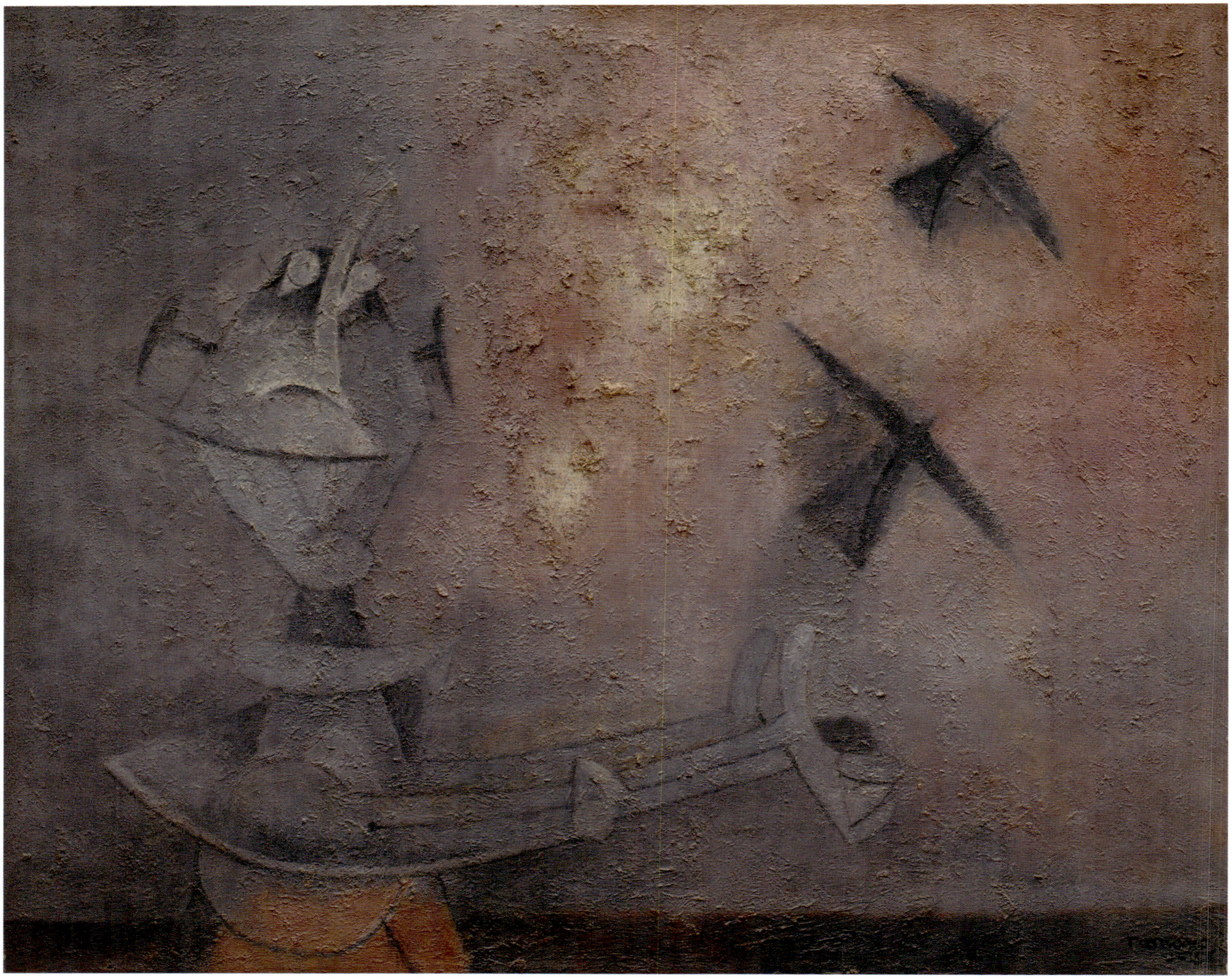

PLATE 51

Rufino Tamayo • *Pájaros liberados* [Liberated Birds], 1956

surface here is far more extensively, even cautiously, elaborated. It may be that the model—despite the generic title—was the artist's wife, Olga. Although many of Tamayo's images of the immediate postwar years seem informed by nuclear-age anxieties, here the overtly Surrealist distortions and lopsided features underscore the painter's sense of humor.

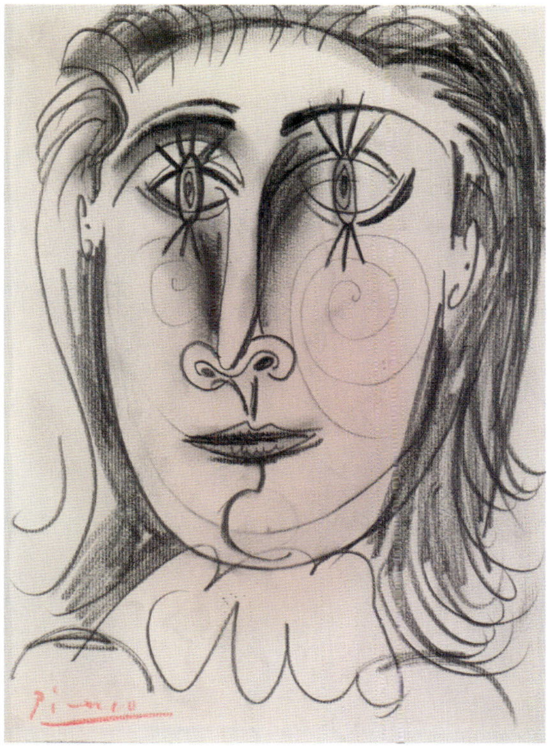

FIG. 1

Liberated Birds was painted just six years later.[6] The work reveals Tamayo's rapid shift to a more elaborate and idiosyncratic representation of the figure in space: body parts are increasingly stretched, abbreviated, and exaggerated, almost becoming caricaturesque and leaving gender ambiguous. The figure reaches forward to release two dark birds: curving forms, which often extend beyond the contours of the head or body, express a sense of motion (this formal device was taken from Cubo-Futurism, perhaps filtered through the 1930s work of Siqueiros). As is common in Tamayo's paintings of this period, the surrounding space is minimally represented, here by a low horizon line and a smudgy light at the center, apparently the sun emerging from the haze. The rough surface, rendered in complementary pinks and grays, was created by mixing oil paint with sand or marble dust: this technique, which Tamayo began using in the 1940s, was partly inspired by the contemporary paintings of Jean Dubuffet. In fact, Tamayo was hoping here to create a similarly direct, "authentic," even Primitivist effect.

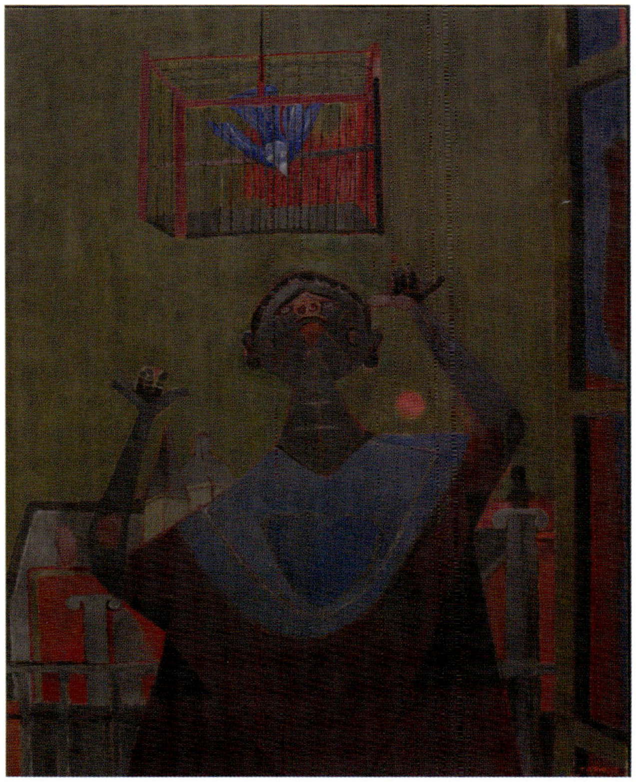

FIG. 2

Images of birds are common in Tamayo's work. He and his wife kept caged songbirds in their home, and birds are a recurring theme in both ancient Mesoamerican art and Mexican folk art, though they had far broader symbolic import for the artist. The birds in Tamayo's paintings have been variously interpreted as messengers, symbols of sacrifice, harbingers of war, existential threats, or ambassadors of peace.[7] In some paintings, like the 1944 *Woman and Bird* (fig. 2), the creatures are trapped in a cage; in others, they appear as aggressors (*Girl Attacked by a Strange Bird*, 1947; Museum of Modern Art, New York); in yet others, such as *Figures Contemplating Birds* (fig. 3) and *Homage to the Mexican Race*, a portable mural of 1952,

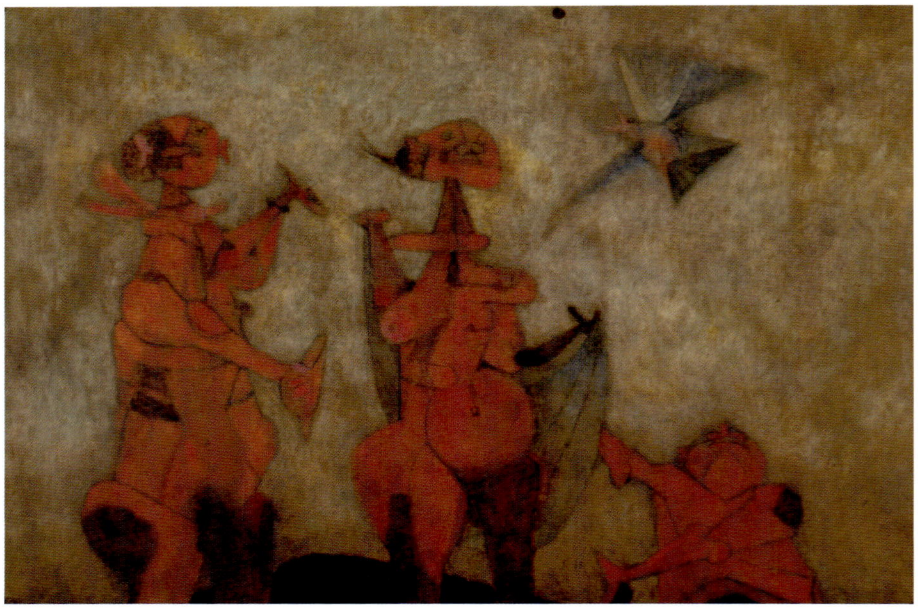

FIG. 3

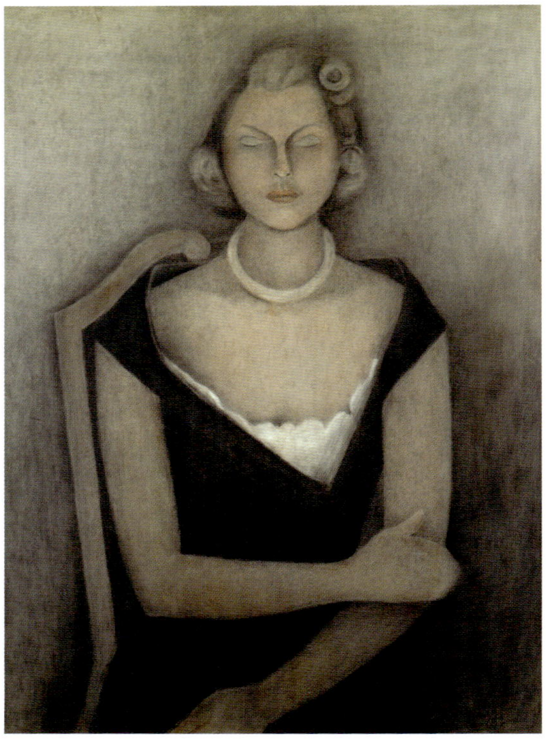

FIG. 4

they simply fly around, with no obvious purpose other than enlivening the composition. But the gesture in *Liberated Birds* is explicit and may subtly refer to Tamayo's own desire for aesthetic "liberation," for freedom to pursue his personal path rather than to be "caged" in by the legacy of the Mexican School. Perhaps this is partly why *Liberated Birds* was illustrated in the important monographs by Paul Westheim (1957) and Octavio Paz (1959), books that further cemented Tamayo's reputation.

Women in White

Tamayo also worked as an accomplished portraitist, though apart from an ongoing series of images of his wife, he created far fewer portraits than Rivera, partly because Olga—who functioned as Tamayo's agent—notoriously charged high fees for commissions.[8] Whatever the case, Alfonso de Antuñano was able to afford a portrait of his wife, Mercedes Ballesteros (plate 52). She appears from the waist up, with a white *rebozo* pulled rather tightly over her torso, accentuating the reddish tint of her skin. She is seated in a traditional wooden ladder-back chair of a type common in Mexican markets: similar chairs, often painted, appear in contemporary photographs showing Tamayo in his studio, as well as in portraits by Rivera and Frida Kahlo. Both the rebozo and the chair are explicit markers of Mexican identity; Tamayo shows Olga draped in a rebozo in several earlier portraits (and, indeed, Olga wears them in period photographs as well). By comparison, Tamayo's portraits of Natasha Gelman (fig. 4) and Rosalyn Richards (1948) show the sitters in urban dresses and somewhat elegant chairs.[9] The Antuñano portrait was created for a woman as cosmopolitan as Tamayo sought to be in his paintings, but one who was also confidently Mexican, even if she was unwilling to go so far as to dress up as a *tehuana*.

The pale, fresco-like quality of this picture is common in Tamayo's portraits beginning in the late 1940s, including that of Gelman. In the case of Mercedes de Antuñano's portrait, the effect was partly the result of his technique, in which pastels were applied to a gessoed wood panel. But all of these portraits also may consciously cite Picasso's similarly pale Neoclassical *Woman in White* (1923; The Museum of Modern Art, New York). In fact, the faces, arms, and torsos in Tamayo's portraits are far more solid and conservatively represented than in the allegorical paintings he was doing at the same time. Tamayo, of course, was concerned with representing individuals rather than archetypes, but surely his sitters had little interest in being converted into fragmented, whirling, or even archaic forms.

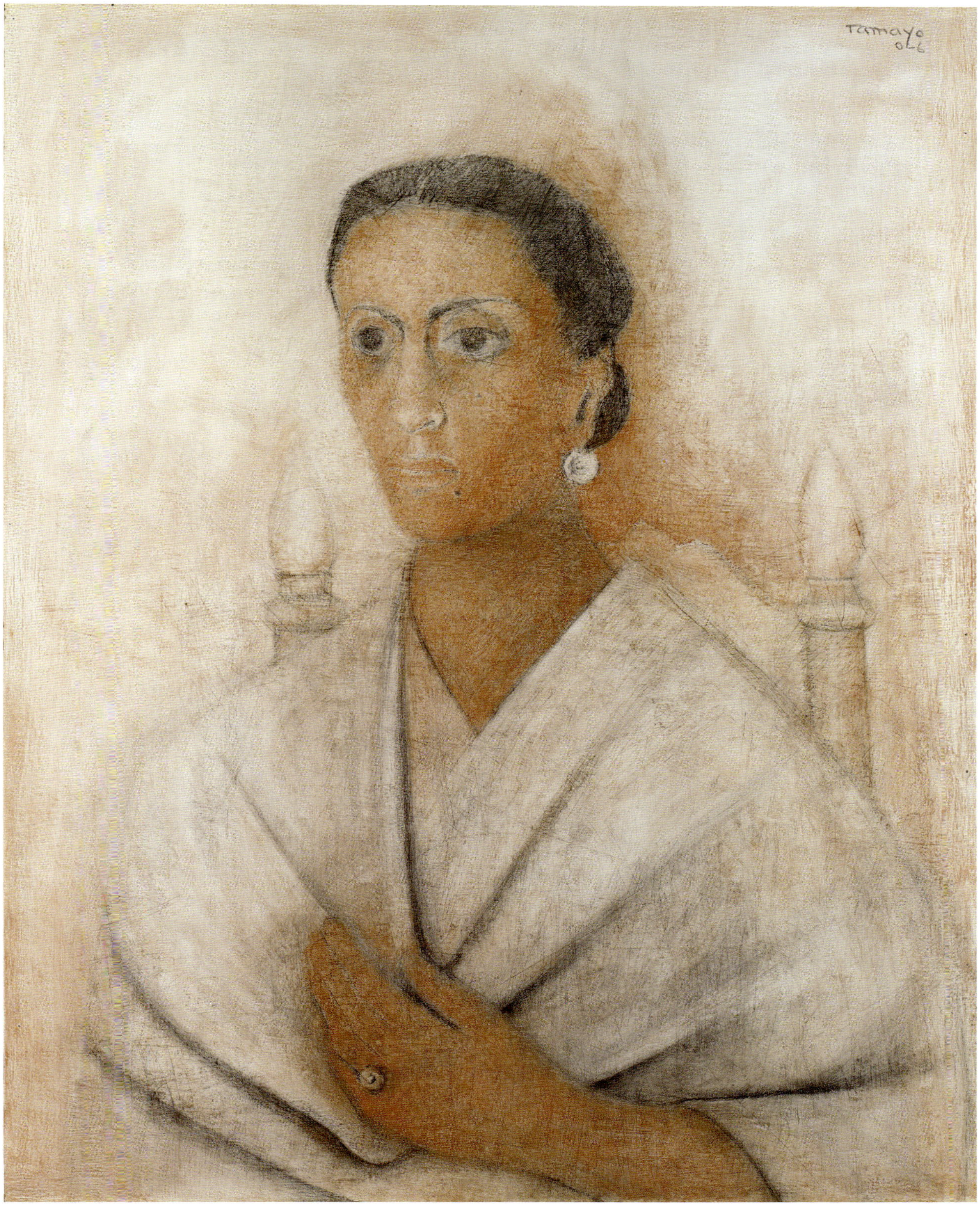

PLATE 52
Rufino Tamayo • *Retrato de la señora Mercedes Ballesteros de Antuñano*
[Portrait of Mrs. Mercedes Ballesteros de Antuñano], 1961

Essence in Color

As early as 1950, Tamayo had foretold his push toward greater simplicity: "My figures should become a mere nucleus. I will eliminate more and more. Perhaps in my next paintings there will be neither eyes nor mouths."[10] Throughout the ensuing decades, one can indeed detect an increasing refining of forms as part of his ongoing search for this essence of the human condition. The strange Cubo-Futurist elements gradually drop away, and heads become circles, arms become curves or angles, legs become posts: man becomes geometry. Tamayo's work is commonly connected to that of Dubuffet or Francis Bacon (though the parallels to Wifredo Lam are even more powerful), yet we might compare this ongoing refinement of forms while maintaining figuration to that of the Guatemalan-born artist Carlos Mérida, a close associate of Tamayo who was pursuing his own path beyond post-Cubism in those same years (fig. 5).

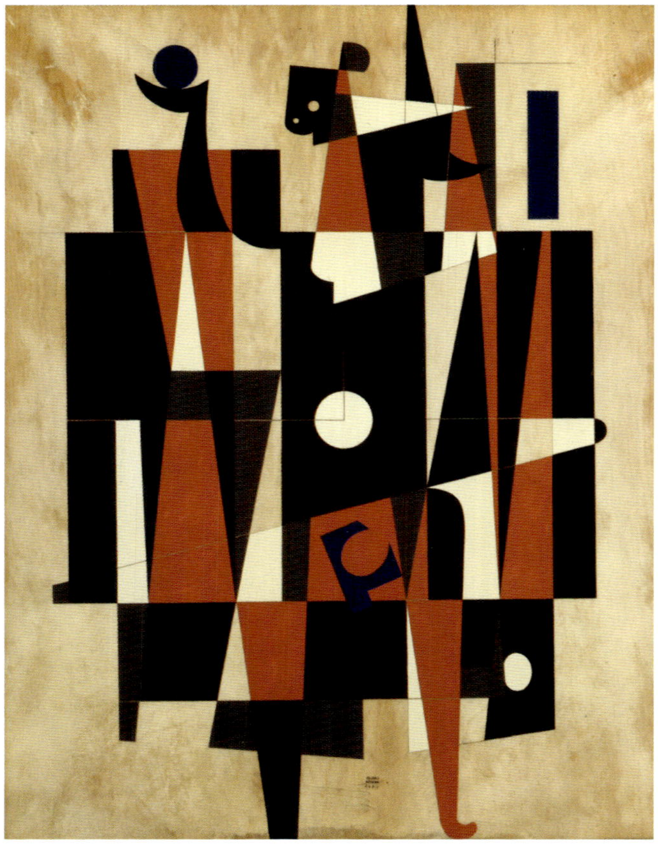

FIG. 5

Both *Figure in Red and Black* [plate 53] and *Personage in Green* [plate 54] show an isolated human figure in an ambiguous space, arms fully extended in a frontal pose that directly confronts the viewer. The titles are now purely descriptive rather than allusive or poetic. In the former, the more evanescent of the two, the robot-like figure stands before what might be a doorway: partly transparent, the head looks like a glass dome of the sort used to cover precious treasures. Crossed lines suggest where the eyes and nose should be placed. Although the outstretched arms might indicate an expression of joy or a call for an embrace, the dark spidery fingers—which appear in works from the 1940s onward—seem slightly sinister. The strongest visual elements in the painting are the blood-red lines, repeated in several works of the 1970s. They emphasize the basic armature of the figure, but also indicate the life force or even "sexual axes."[11]

Though more subtle, a similar red line runs vertically through the figure in *Personage in Green*, from the nose down to the base of the torso. (The gender of this figure is also unclear, though the swollen hips might indicate a female form.) Here, the head is also rounded, though placed within a rectangle, with a more elaborated face. The white triangles to the left and right of the red lines suggest that the figure is swaying against this axis, and, indeed, the arms—with their blunt, bud-like hands—appear to swing on pivots. The figure is set against a strange radiant yellow form—a portal? an aura?—that may have no meaning beyond energizing the background. As in *Figure in Red and Black*, the principal colors repeat across the surface, varying in intensity but never fully confined to any one area. In fact, the surfaces of Tamayo's paintings never become slick or simplified: instead, they are scraped and scumbled to create rich textures, often marked by an energized use of color, loosely echoing Pierre Bonnard and the Fauves, but also reflective of bright Color Field paintings and—in the case of *Personage in Green*—psychedelic art.

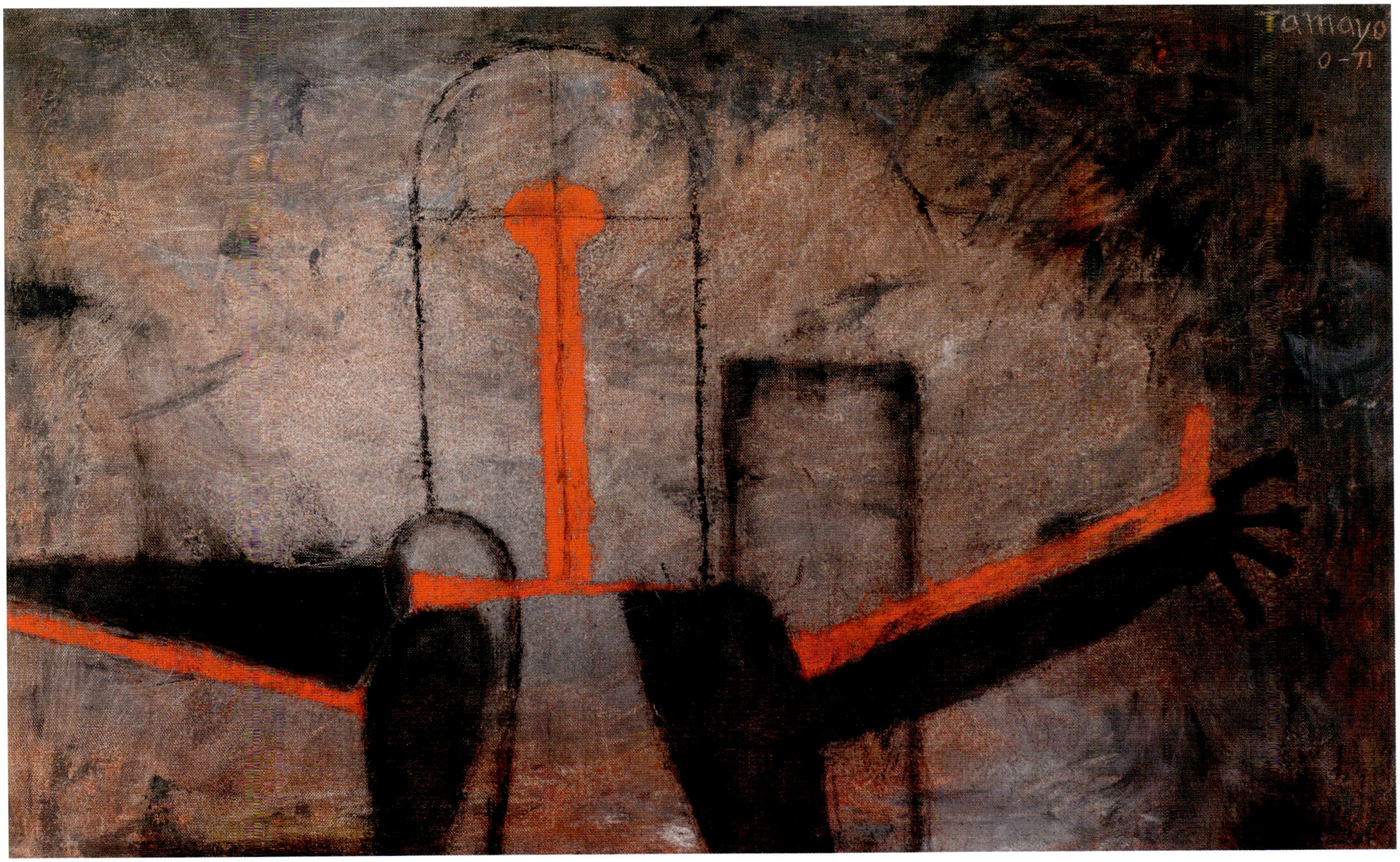

PLATE 53

Rufino Tamayo • *Figura en rojo y negro* [Figure in Red and Black], 1971

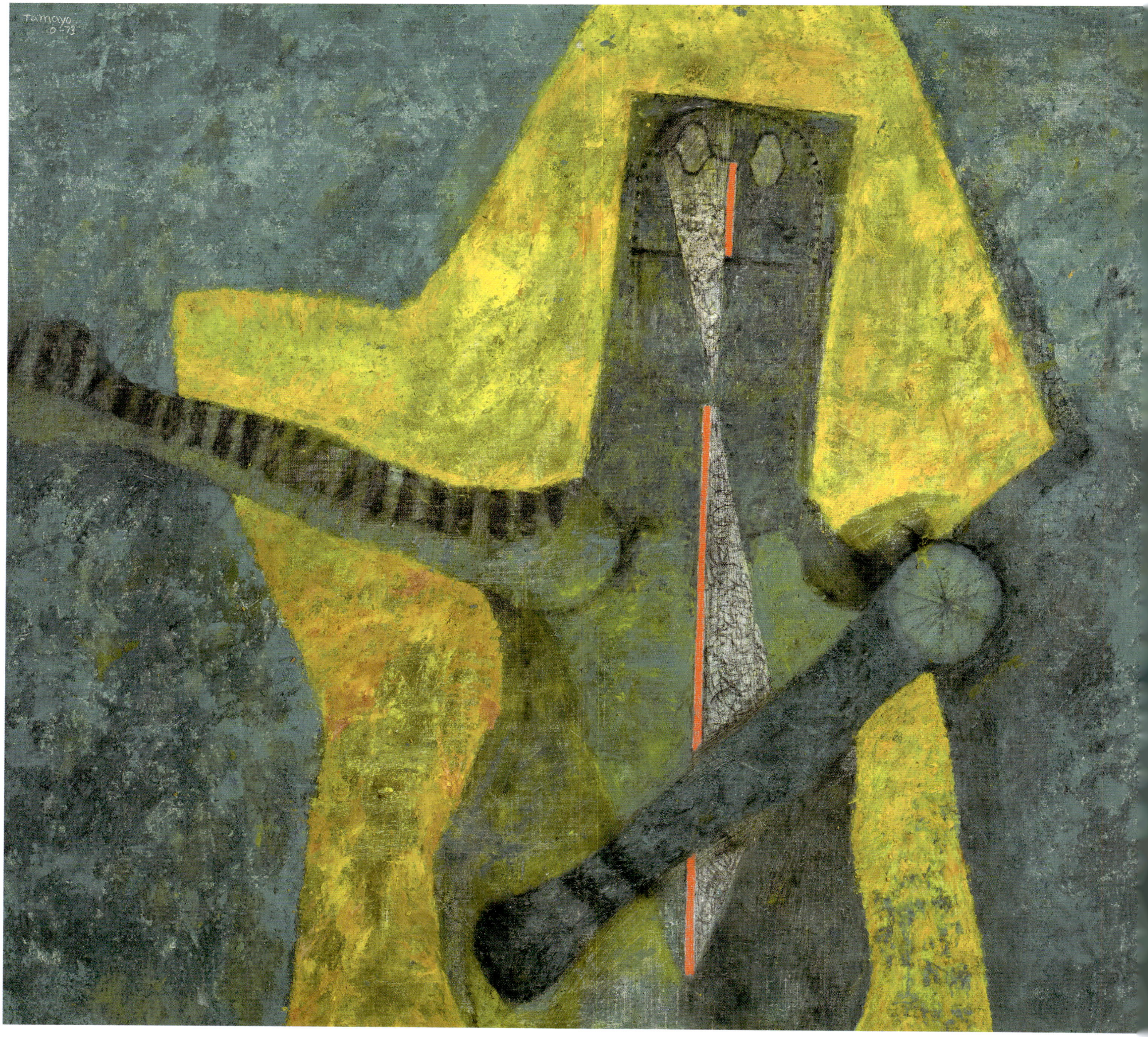
Tamayo

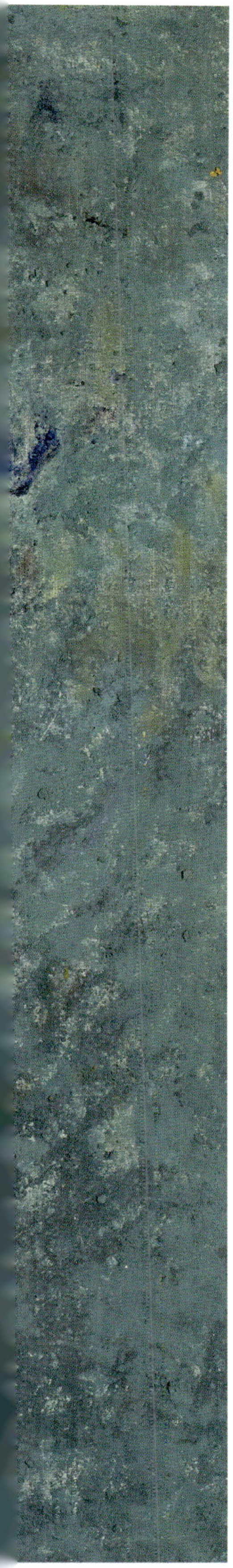

PLATE 54

Rufino Tamayo • *Personaje en verde*

[Personage in Green], 1973

These two works, albeit rather simple in terms of iconography, reveal that "sentimental humanism" that distinguished Tamayo's late work and that never acknowledged the growing political and economic tensions that wracked Mexico in the late 1960s and 1970s.[12] The battle he had fought since the 1920s was over form, over the purpose of art, but he was on the losing end: political meanings remained crucial, even if now increasingly shaped by conceptual practice. Thus, of the myriad sources that might have informed these abstracted bodies, from ancient Mezcala stone carvings to clay dolls from Juchitán,[13] perhaps we might consider the papier-mâché Judas figures that are one of the iconic folk art forms of traditional Mexico, works that Tamayo—and more famously Rivera and Kahlo—collected (fig. 6). Symbols of evil, of betrayal, they are deployed on the Saturday before Easter, swaying above the street, before being detonated to the delight of the crowd. Tamayo's formal innovations were similarly explosive in their time, bobbing before an enraptured audience, but then vanishing into thin air.

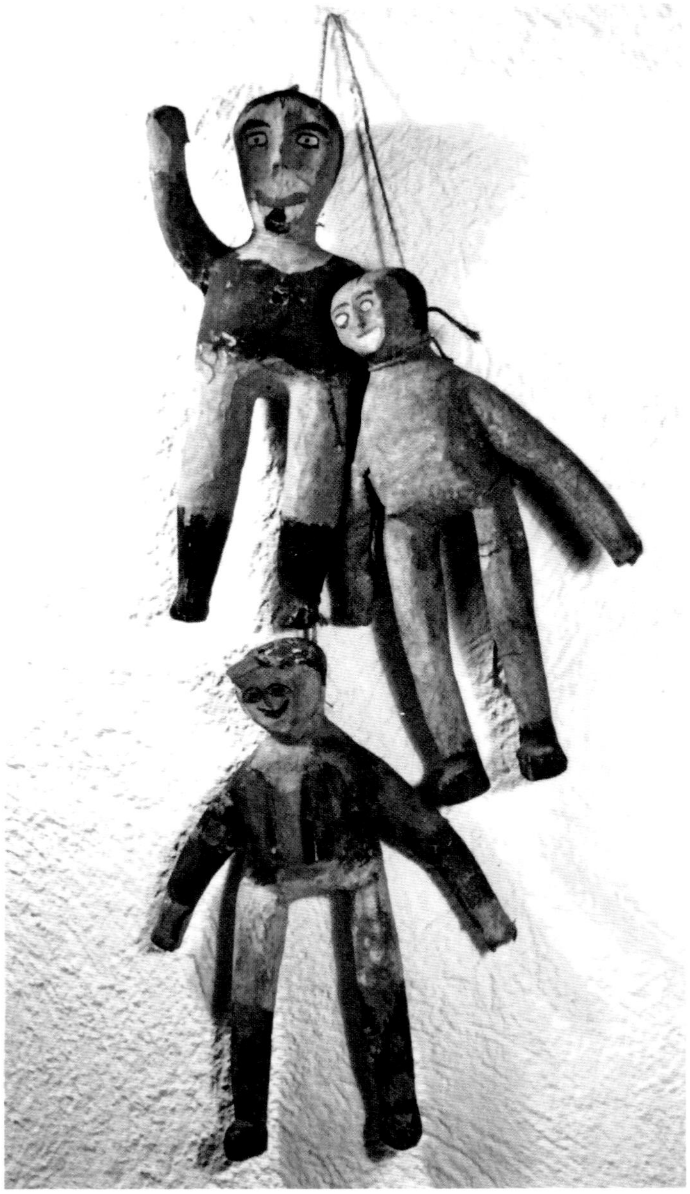

FIG. 6

ILLUSTRATIONS IN TEXT

FIGURE 1
Pablo Picasso
Head of a Woman (Dora Maar), 1941
Pencil on paper
12 x 9 1/4 inches (30.5 x 23.5 cm)
Private Collection

FIGURE 2
Rufino Tamayo
Woman and Bird, 1944
Oil on canvas
42 x 33 7/8 inches (106.5 x 86 cm)
The Cleveland Museum of Art,
Gift of Leonard C. Hanna, Jr. 1950.583

FIGURE 3
Rufino Tamayo
Personages Contemplating Birds, 1950
Oil on canvas
51 3/4 x 79 inches (131.5 x 200 cm)
Krannert Art Museum,
University of Illinois, Champaign-Urbana

FIGURE 4
Rufino Tamayo
Retrato de la señora Natasha Gelman
[Portrait of Mrs. Natasha Gelman], 1948
Oil and charcoal on Masonite
47 1/4 x 35 13/16 inches (120 x 91 cm)
The Jacques and Natasha
Gelman Collection, Mexico.

FIGURE 5
Carlos Merida
Poma Azul [The Blue Apple], 1962
Parchment and plastic
29 7/8 x 23 1/2 inches (75.9 x 59.7 cm)
Phoenix Art Museum, Gift of the
Friends of Mexican Art 1964.206

FIGURE 6
Three Judas figures, formerly in the collection of Olga and Rufino Tamayo. photographer unknown.

NOTES

1
This position stimulated rather virulent debates with the muralists, especially Siqueiros. For key statements from this polemic, which actually extended tensions between political and "pure" art options that had been brewing in Mexico since the 1920s, see Judith Alanís and Sofía Urrutia, *Rufino Tamayo: Una cronología/1899–1987* (Mexico City: Museo de Arte Contemporáneo Internacional Rufino Tamayo, 1987), 44ff. See also Mary K. Coffey, *How a Revolutionary Art Became Official Culture: Murals, Museums, and the Mexican State* (Durham: Duke University Press, 2012), 62–63.

2
Víctor Alba, "¡Tamayo habla a *Hoy* desde Paris!," *Hoy* , no. 723 (December 30, 1950): 24–25 [DIGITAL ARCHIVE 758996].

3
See Teresa del Conde, ed., *Tamayo* (Boston: Bulfinch Press, 2000), 240–45.

4
Diana C. du Pont, "'Realistic, Never Descriptive': Tamayo and the Art of Abstract Figuration," in Diana C. du Pont, ed., *Tamayo: A Modern Icon Reinterpreted* (Santa Barbara: Santa Barbara Museum of Art, 2007), 58.

5
Tamayo's debts to Picasso have been extensively discussed, but here I would like to point out that the title of his 1948 retrospective directly copied the title of Picasso's MoMA show.

6
Beginning in 1943, Tamayo dated his paintings using the letter "O" as a prefix (as, here, "O-56") to honor Olga.

7
Among other scholars' discussions of birds, see my own "The Howl and the Flame: Tamayo's Wartime Allegories," in *Tamayo: A Modern Icon Reinterpreted*, 302–8.

8
Notes from a conversation with Juan Carlos Pereda, Mexico City (September 21, 2012). I am grateful to Arden Decker for interviewing Pereda and doing preliminary research on this and other works by Tamayo in the Brillembourg Capriles Collection.

9
I have not been able to find information on Richards, but it is likely she was from the United States.

10
Rosamond Bernier, "Tamayo at Home and Abroad," *Look* (February 2, 1951), cited in Alanís and Urrutia, 60.

11
Teresa del Conde, "Consideraciones sobre la iconografía de Rufino Tamayo," in Raquel Tibol, ed., *Rufino Tamayo: 70 años de creación* (Mexico City: Museo de Arte Contemporáneo Internacional Rufino Tamayo/Museo del Palacio de Bellas Artes, 1987), 48.

12
See du Pont, 92.

13
These small sculptures (or *tang-yu*), which do resemble the figures in many of Tamayo's paintings, including *Personage in Green*, are discussed in Juan Coronel Rivera, "A Modern Prometheus," in *Tamayo* (2000), 152–53.

Rachel Mohl

THE PAINTER AS CRAFTSMAN

ARMANDO MORALES'S INNOVATIVE APPROACH TO TRADITION

WHEN NICARAGUAN ARTIST Armando Morales burst onto the international art scene, winning first prize in the 1957 *Gulf-Caribbean Art Exhibition* at the Museum of Fine Arts, Houston, art critic José Gómez Sicre noted that Morales "applies himself devotedly to the production of an object [. . .] which we can call painting."[1] Morales asserted in various interviews that he was not an artist, but rather a painter concerned with painting-as-craft. For him, "the goal of painting is to paint. . . . The artist, I believe, thinks about expressing an idea; however I'm not interested in that. To be a painter and artisan gives me a lot of freedom, and that is the key to everything. . . ."[2] With this conviction, Morales responded to the events occurring within the international art world. Beginning in the 1960s, numerous artists and critics questioned the validity of painting and sought to undermine the traditional values attached to the medium. Other forms of expression, such as Minimalism and Conceptualism, superseded what some artists claimed to be the limited, two-dimensional canvas. In the face of an art world questioning the effectiveness of painting, Morales strove to validate the medium by referencing its past while developing an innovative painterly technique based on craftsmanship. By using a superficial painting method to create imaginary worlds, which revised traditional motifs, he sought to demonstrate that painting can encompass both pictorial artifice and illusionistic depth.

Morales's focus on the past is connected to a particular tendency among Latin American artists, including Fernando Botero, José Luis Cuevas, and Luis Caballero, who sought to update classical techniques and motifs through an emphasis on the human figure. Their explorations were couched within the larger, international discourse on painting. Amid this debate, those who upheld the two-dimensional medium proposed various strategies for painting to maintain its relevancy within contemporary art. Revered art critic and formalist Clement Greenberg promoted artists who embraced the intrinsic nature of the medium, using characteristics exclusive to painting—the flat surface, the shape of the support, and the properties of the pigment. By calling attention to painting-as-painting, artists could establish an area of competence unique to the medium.[3] Dore Ashton proposed a more intuitive approach than Greenberg's, in which she embraced the artist's ability to conceive the impossible and to acknowledge the mystery of human existence.[4] Using psychological studies as evidence that the imagination is a key faculty of the mind, she posited that art, whether figurative, abstract, or nonobjective, intrinsically activates the brain, causing it to create an image that goes beyond the materiality of the artwork. Illusion is characteristic of imaginative activity, and, therefore, is part of the experience of art, for both the artist and the viewer.[5]

Although both critics' strategies seem divergent, specifically in what they contend are the qualities inherent in painting, Morales weaves elements of their arguments together to produce a distinct approach. He works on the painting's surface in a physical, craftsmanlike manner, upholding the two-dimensionality of the canvas while simultaneously shaping the surfaces into imaginative mise-en-scènes that reuse themes culled from art history. This approach to meld the intrinsic flatness of the medium with classical illusionistic

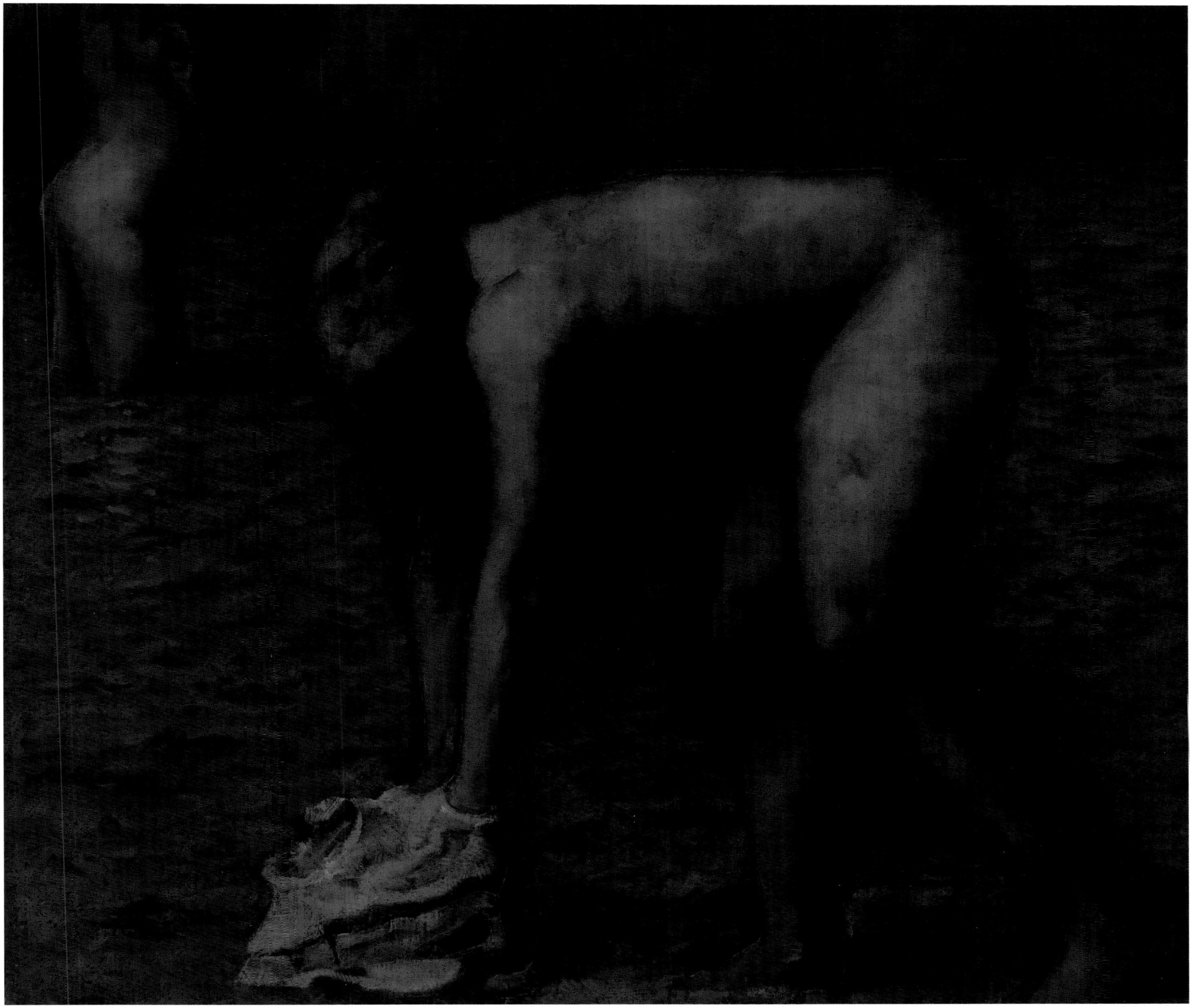

PLATE 55

Armando Morales • *Escena lacustre I, Granada Harbor* [Lakeside Scene I, Granada Harbor], 1978

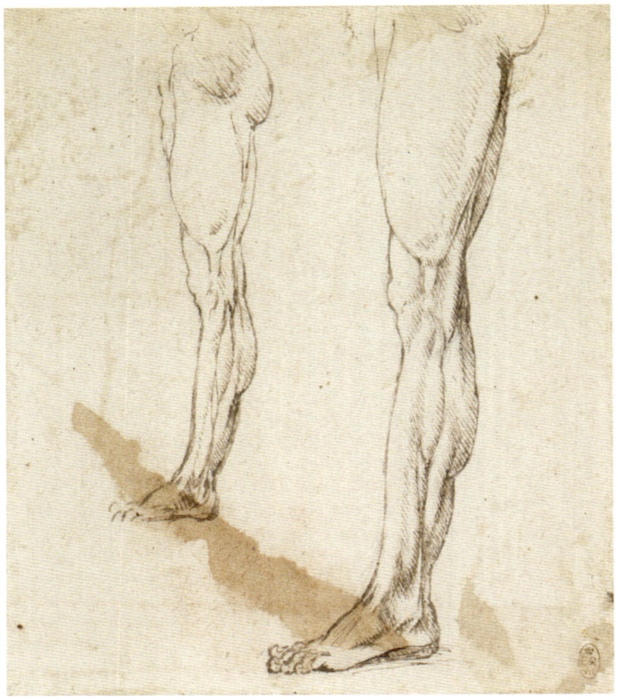

FIG. 1

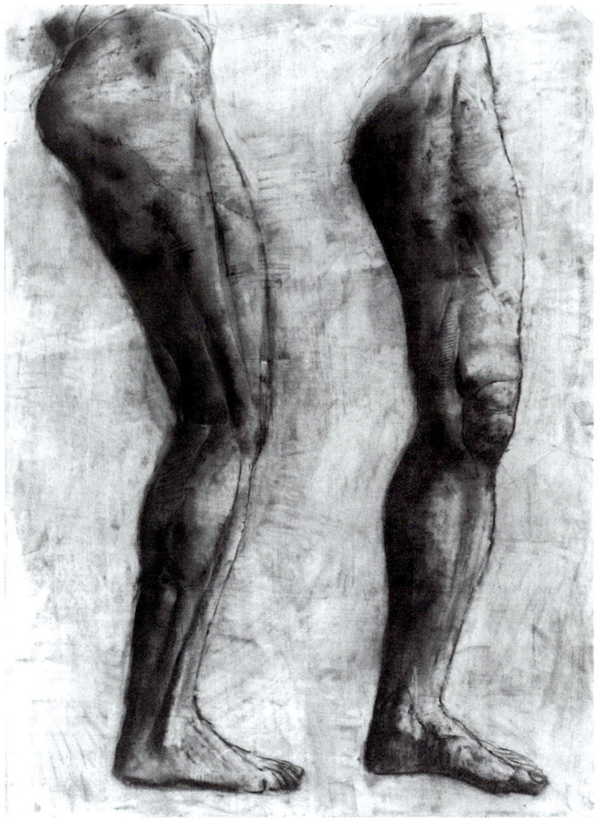

FIG. 2

representation makes him unique within the international artistic milieu. Unlike other figurative painters of the period, Morales's paintings present no symbolic meaning; nor do they offer an entryway into the subconscious, like the Surrealists' works. Moreover, they also eschew the critical and deconstructive approach to Western tradition taken by artists like Willem de Kooning and Robert Rauschenberg, as well as avoid any reference to material culture and consumerism, as exhibited by Pop art. Morales, rather, focused on crafting artificiality both in form and content, thereby connecting his own notion of painting, grounded in the classical past, to contemporary debates. Indeed, the idea of painter-as-artisan dates back to the Medieval and early Renaissance guild structure, in which artists were trained in a particular niche and spent their careers perfecting that skill.

Morales began his career in the vein of abstraction; however, in 1966, after returning to New York from a trip to Europe where he had visited Spain, England, Germany, and Italy, he abruptly decided that nonobjective art was a dead-end street. Influenced by the classical art and architecture he experienced during his journey, the artist began to explore ways to rejuvenate painting and cultivate his own manual dexterity while focusing mainly on the human figure. *Escena lacustre I, Granada Harbour* [Lakeside Scene I, Grand Harbor] (1978) (plate 55) in the Brillembourg Capriles Collection of Latin American Art provides the most successful example of Morales employing his refined technique to create an oneiric scene that reuses classical motifs.

As seen in this work, the first part of Morales's painting method required a physical reworking of the canvas. To hide the weave of the canvas, Morales scraped the surface smooth with a razor blade, rubbed it with a tack cloth, and applied a thick coat of white underpaint, all of which resulted in an effect resembling a freshly plastered wall.[7] Then, Morales divided his canvas into squares, helping him to achieve precision when transferring his preparatory sketches onto the canvas.[8] This process of painting in small sections onto a completely leveled surface mimics Renaissance fresco painting, whereby artists partitioned plastered walls into small areas using a ruler and chalk[9] before creating cartoons on heavy sheets of paper or cardboard. In a process called pouncing, the design was then pressed through the paper onto the wall with a stylus, leaving a faint outline of the figures engraved in the plaster.[10] In *Escena lacustre I*, as with most of his works, Morales scratched the outline of the main figure onto the finished work, mimicking the lines left by the pouncing process, and concurrently calling the viewer's attention to the extremely smooth and flat surface of the work. In this way, he revises the Renaissance practices, relating them to the discourse on the media's intrinsic qualities.

His numerous preparatory sketches and drawings for *Escena lacustre I*, in which he explored various poses and details, further demonstrate Morales's attempt to rejuvenate historical Western art practices. Many scholars attribute his studies of the body to an interest in the works of Flemish anatomist Andreas Vesalius. Morales studied Vesalius's fundamental work and anatomical treatise, *De corporis humani fabrica*,[11] a publication that was part of a broad interest in the human body during the Renaissance. In fact, during this time period, artists played a crucial role in advancing the field of anatomy with their detailed drawings based on dissection. Many of Leonardo da Vinci's sketches were used to illustrate Vesalius's treatise.[12] Indeed, some of Morales's drawings closely resemble those of Leonardo's, specifically his studies of legs in preparation for *Escena lacustre I* (figs. 1 and 2). Morales employed Renaissance methods of representing the human form by painting realistic figures that he re-imagined through an exploration of colors

After creating the sketches and priming the canvas, Morales then applied numerous layers of paint onto the work, each coat a shade lighter than the previous one. Using a variety of blues, Morales scratched off parts of one shade with a razor and thinly painted over it in another tone. As he approached the final layer of the painting, he finely crosshatched his brushstrokes so that the previous layers could be visible. Within any part of the painting, the transparency created by the brushstrokes and scraping allows a number of tones to be visible at once (fig. 3). Morales then contrasted the undulating blue

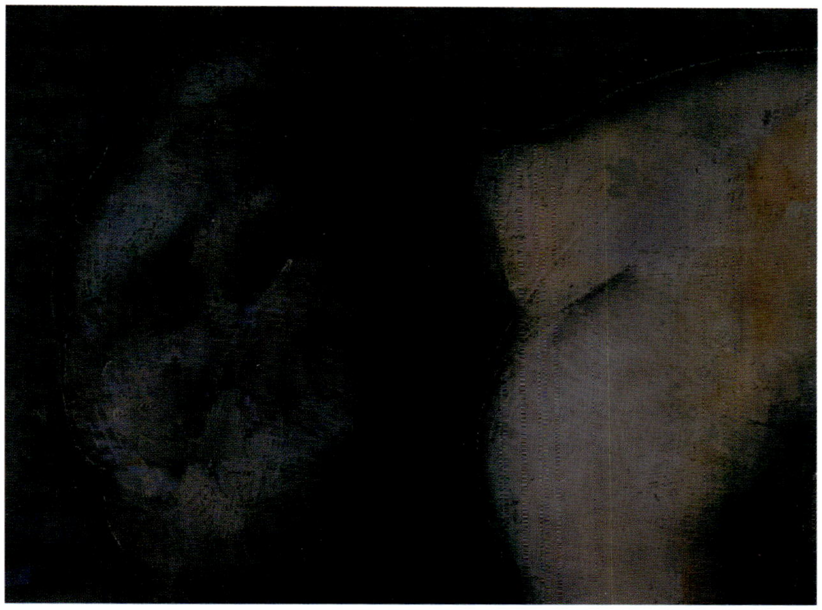

FIG. 3

atmosphere with patches of pink and dark orange on the women's skin, imbuing this mundane scene with an unnatural, dreamlike appearance. He leaves the scene mysterious and open-ended, allowing infinite possibilities of interpretation. His unparalleled technique gives the work an illusionistic, three-dimensional depth while simultaneously emphasizing painting as merely a flat, two-dimensional surface that has been physically manipulated and carved by the painter-craftsman.

With this dual approach to painting, Morales reworks the classical bather. Although this theme dates to Greco-Roman works of art, in *Escena lacustre I*, Morales looks to the recent history of art, as the figure alludes to Edgar Degas's many works of crouching female nudes at the bath (fig. 4). Both Degas's figures and Morales's bather bend to reach for a washcloth and are unaware of the viewer's presence, thereby facilitating entry into the painting. Unlike the fin-de-siècle artist, however, Morales does not represent the task as an everyday occurrence within the home, but rather transforms the act of bathing into an imaginary scene, which carries the viewer into another world beyond reality.

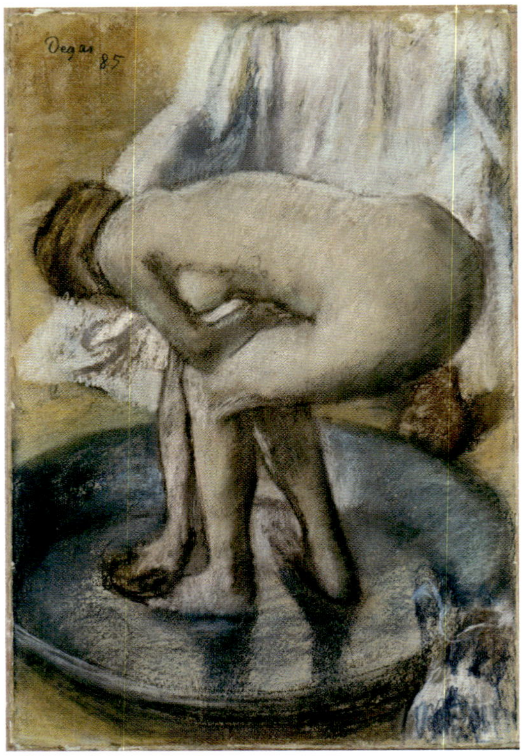

FIG. 4

The particular reevaluation of traditional painting practices and classic poses in *Escena lacustre I* proved to be so successful that the artist reused this process continuously throughout his career, as seen in *Mujer ante un espejo* [Woman before a Mirror] (1979) (plate 56) and *At the Circus, V* (1981) (plate 57), both in the Brillembourg Capriles Collection of Latin American Art. The 1979 work reassesses the art-historical theme of a woman looking at her reflection. Morales, however, diverges from his crosshatched, translucent colors in favor of loose, broad brushstrokes. This painting, done on paper rather than canvas, is in fact the first that Morales executed using this subject, indicating that this may have been a preparatory oil sketch for future paintings. Indeed, this work lacks the depth of his previous paintings, and it presents a less developed scene than in *Escena lacustre I* and *At the Circus, V.* After completing the sketch, Morales returned a number of times to the theme of a nude in front of a mirror, as he had with many of his other themes in order to hone his technique and execution. This repetition relates to the high degree of specialization within a narrow skill set required to be a master-craftsman.

Morales's other figurative works in the Brillembourg Capriles Collection that predate *Escena lacustre*, including *Desnudo* [Nude] (1960) (plate 58), *Sin título* [Untitled] (1971) (plate 59), and *Mujer al punto de regresar* [Woman at the Point of Return] (1973) (plate 60), demonstrate steps in the development of Morales's unique painting method and artificial worlds. In fact, the 1960 nude is indeed a surprising painting, considering he had spent nearly the previous decade committed to abstraction and would not return to the figure for another six years. While Morales had made other works that included a human presence, such as the Tauromaquia series, *Desnudo* stands out for its static focus on the classical notion of feminine beauty. Standing in a slight contraposto, the female figure is idealized in her symmetric proportion and distracted gaze, which make her unassuming and unthreatening.[13] *Desnudo*, the first full-figured nude by Morales, thus provides an important precursor of the figurative painting that marks the majority of the artist's career.

Like *Escena lacustre*, this work references Renaissance techniques as evidenced by Morales's *sui generis* use of chiaroscuro. Traditionally, artists used darker colors to give realistic depth to figures and forms. In the case of *Desnudo*, however, Morales reversed the process by first painting the canvas black and then adding layers of paint one or two shades lighter than the previous. Light, not shadow, becomes the key to modeling in Morales's works, allowing the figures to emerge out of the darkness, rather than being formed from it. This painting evidences the beginning of Morales's use of layering paint to create innovative atmospheric effects, which enhance the work's dreamlike quality.

Morales concurrently draws attention to the materiality of the painting by dragging a dry brush across the previous layers of the canvas. This method, a predecessor to the more developed crosshatching in *Escena lacustre*, leaves open spaces that reveal the initial layers of paint, making his reverse chiaroscuro visible to the viewer. Broad, expressive brushstrokes incorporating large drops of dry paint demonstrate his engagement with Informalist methods of drawing the viewer's focus to the surface of a work of art. In this way, Morales re-created the classic female figure through a modern sensibility—acknowledging the past while making use of a superficial pictorial language, which he continued to develop.

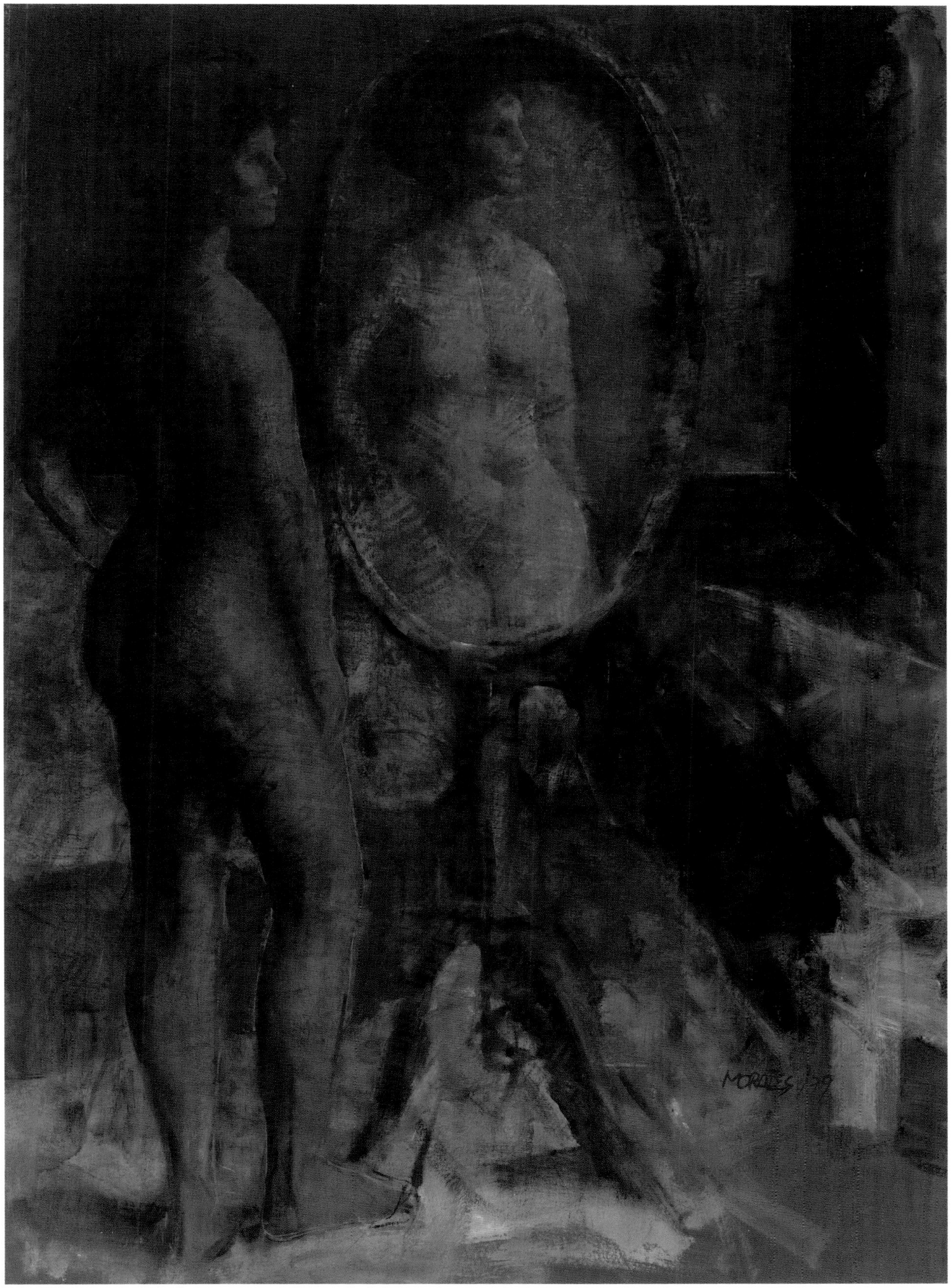

PLATE 56

Armando Morales • *Mujer ante un espejo* [Woman before a Mirror], 1979

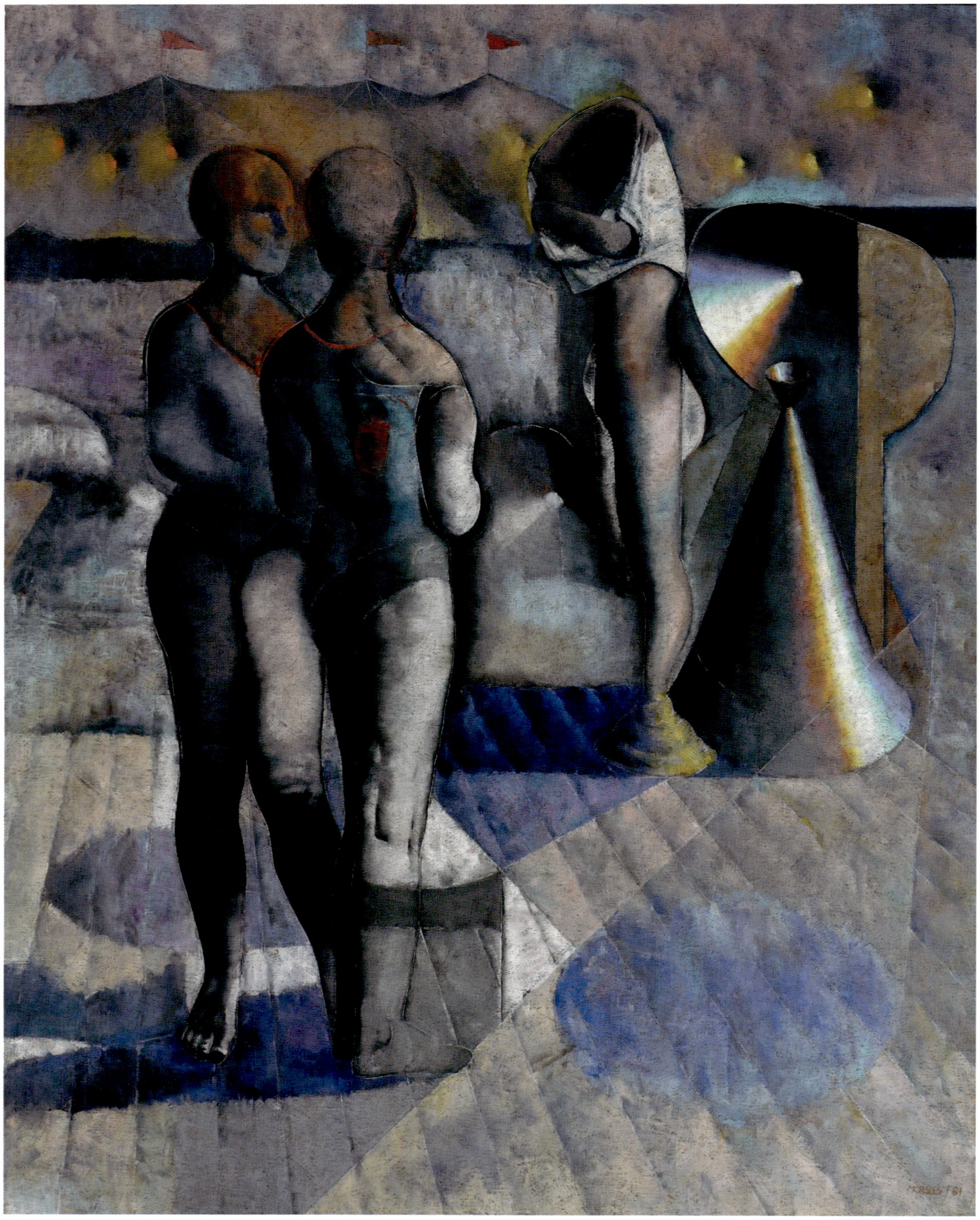

PLATE 57

Armando Morales • *At the Circus, V,* 1981

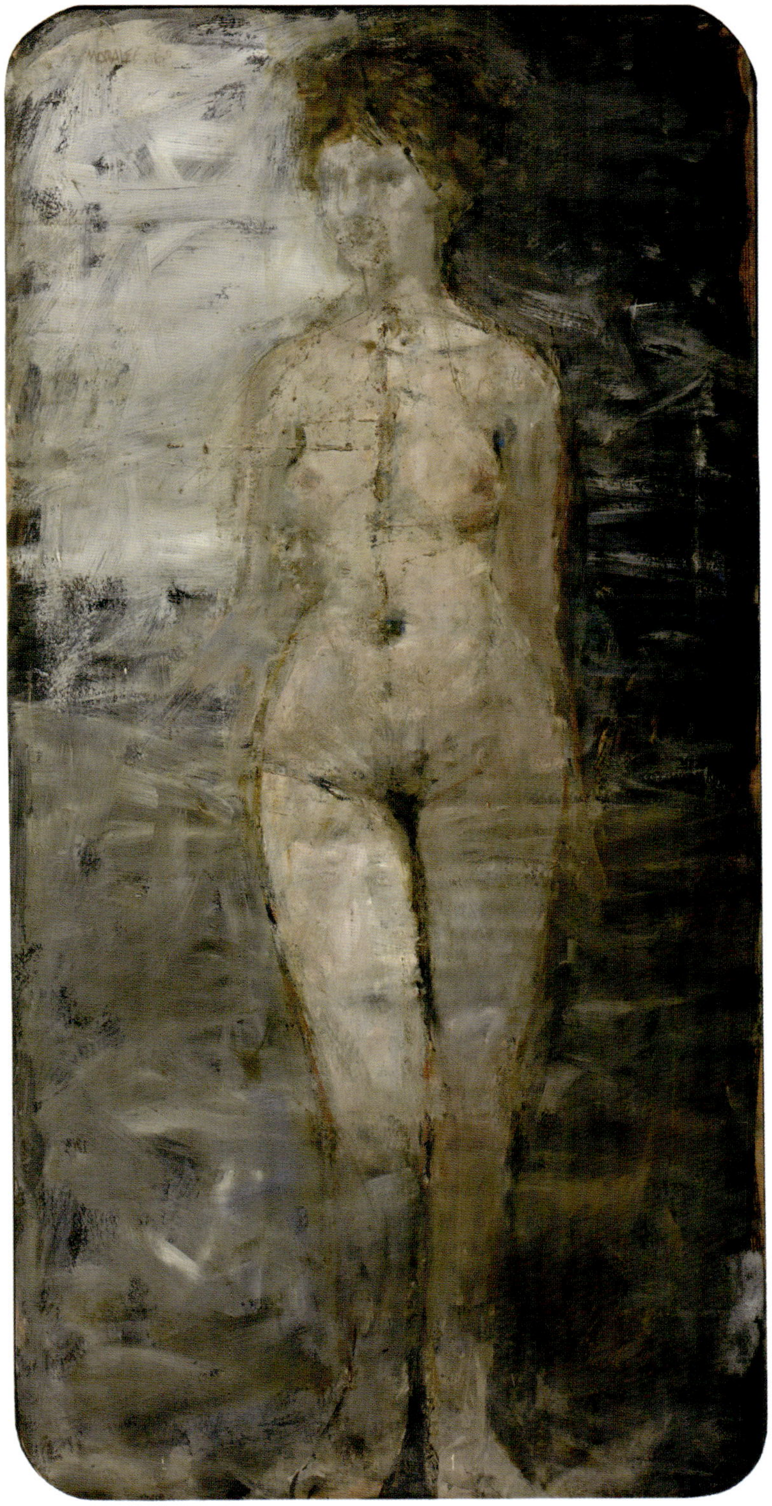

PLATE 58
Armando Morales • *Desnudo* [Nude], 1960

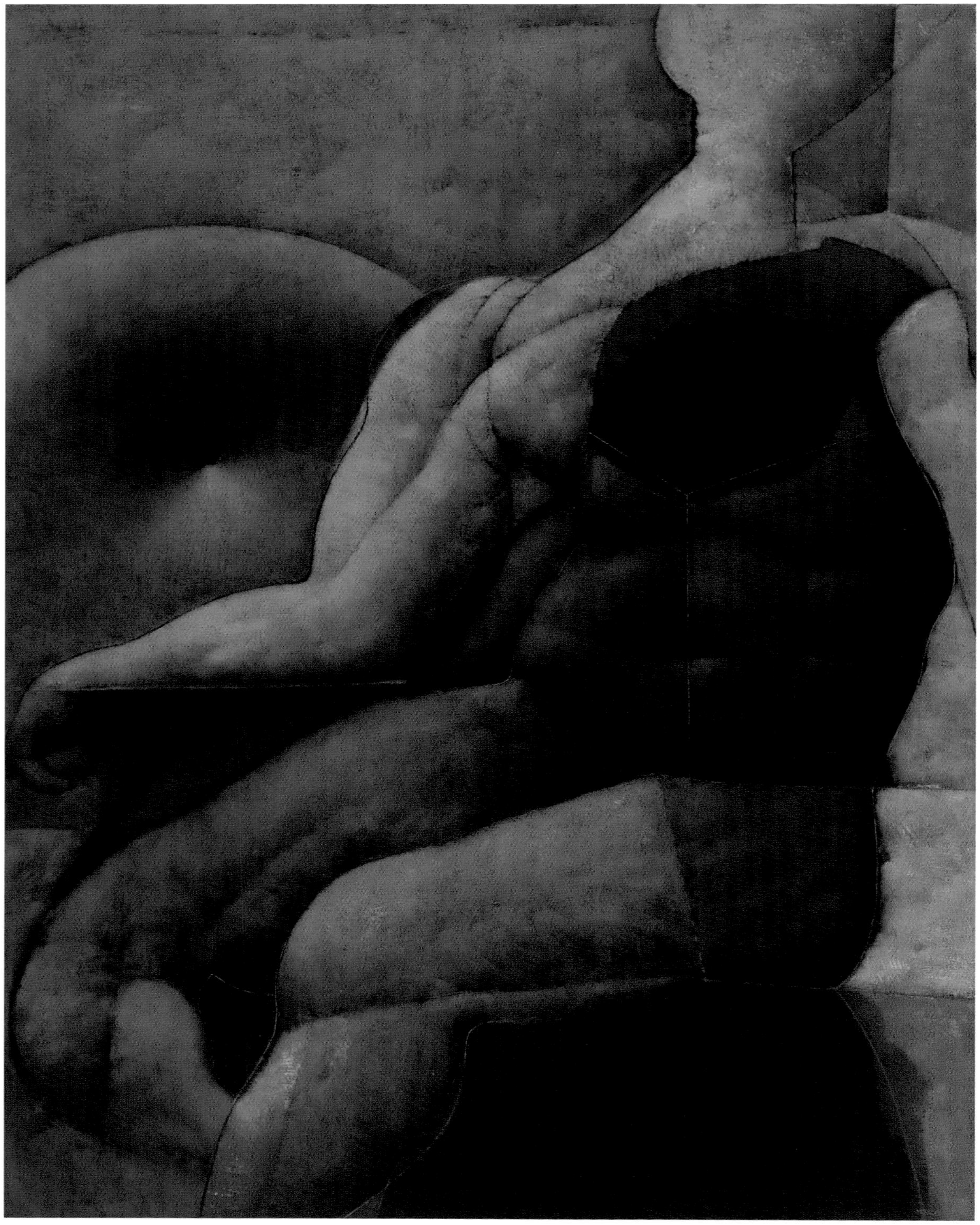

PLATE 59

Armando Morales • *Sin título* [Untitled], 1971

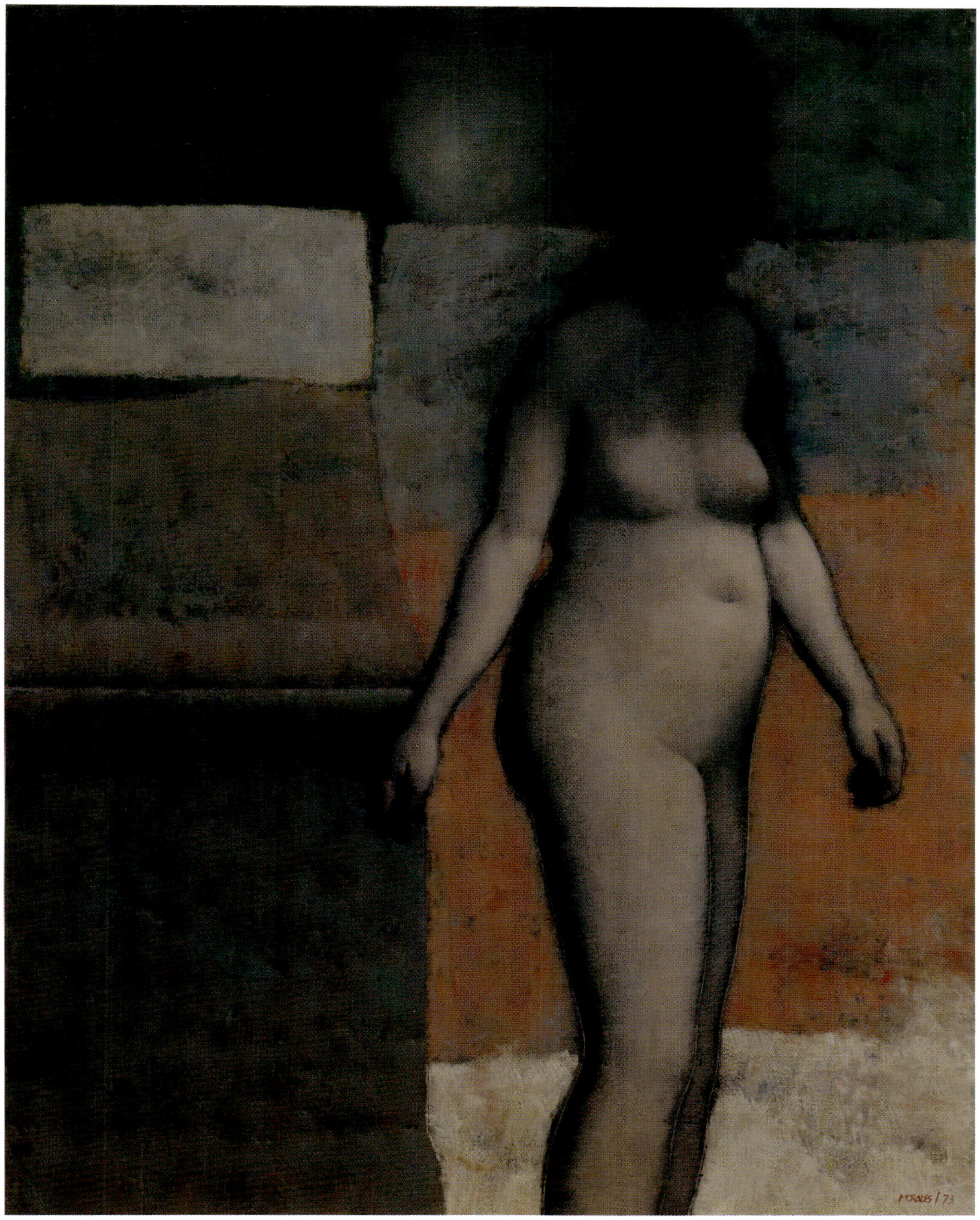

PLATE 60

Armando Morales • *Mujer a punto de regresar* [Woman at the Point of Return], 1973

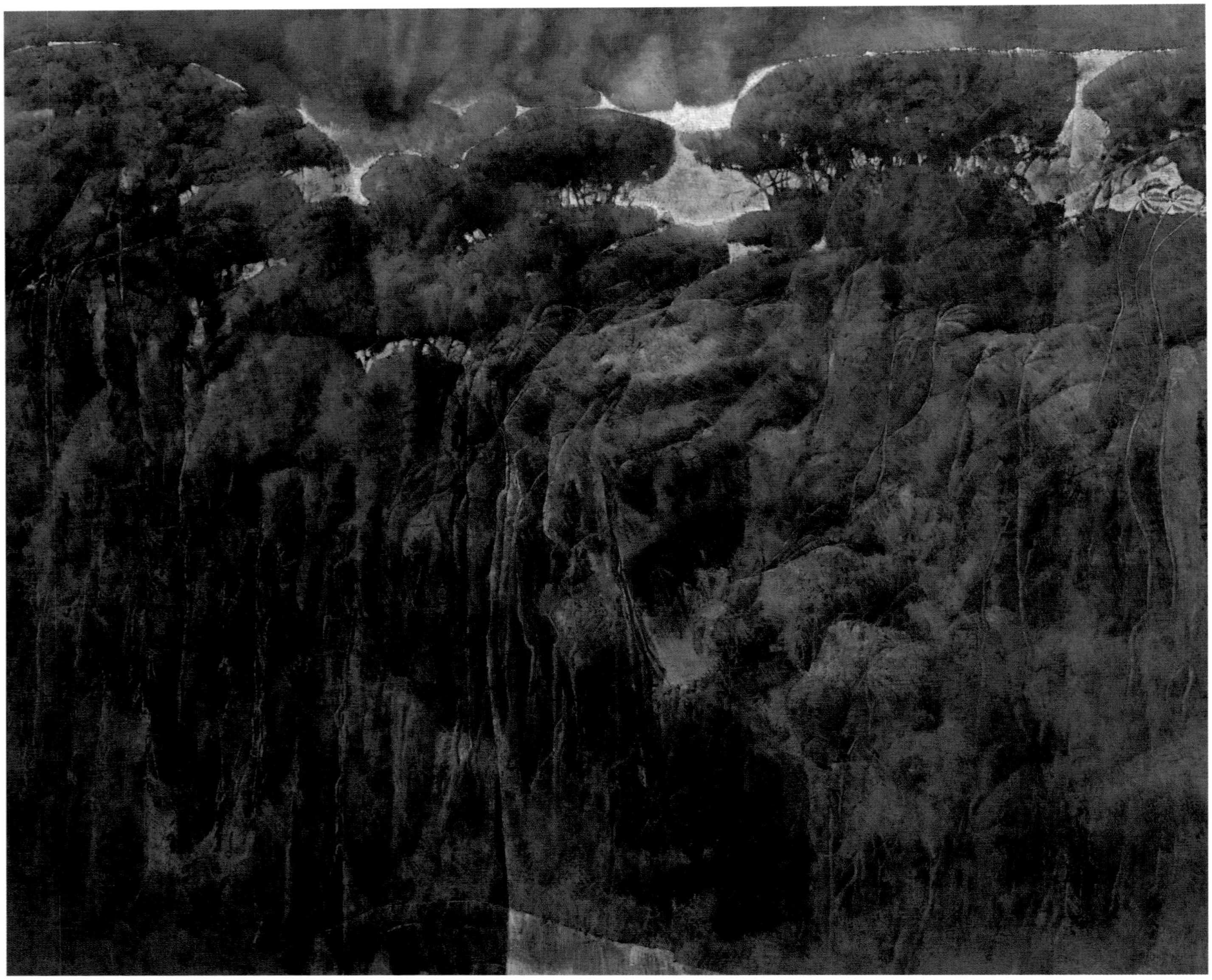

PLATE 61

Armando Morales • *Forêt tropicale dans une orage* [Tropical Forest in a Storm], 1991

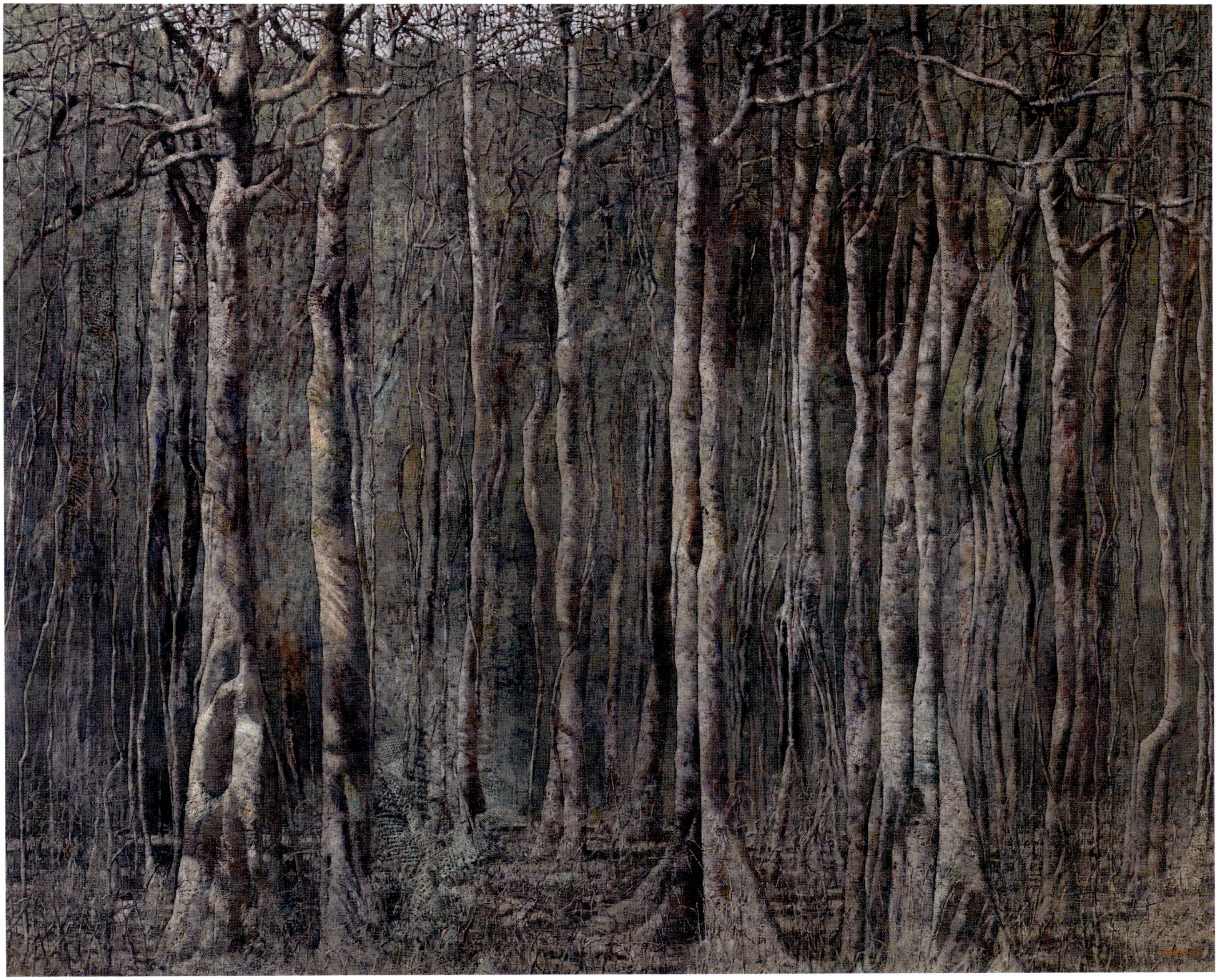

PLATE 62
Armando Morales • *Forêt tropicale* [Tropical Forest], 1992

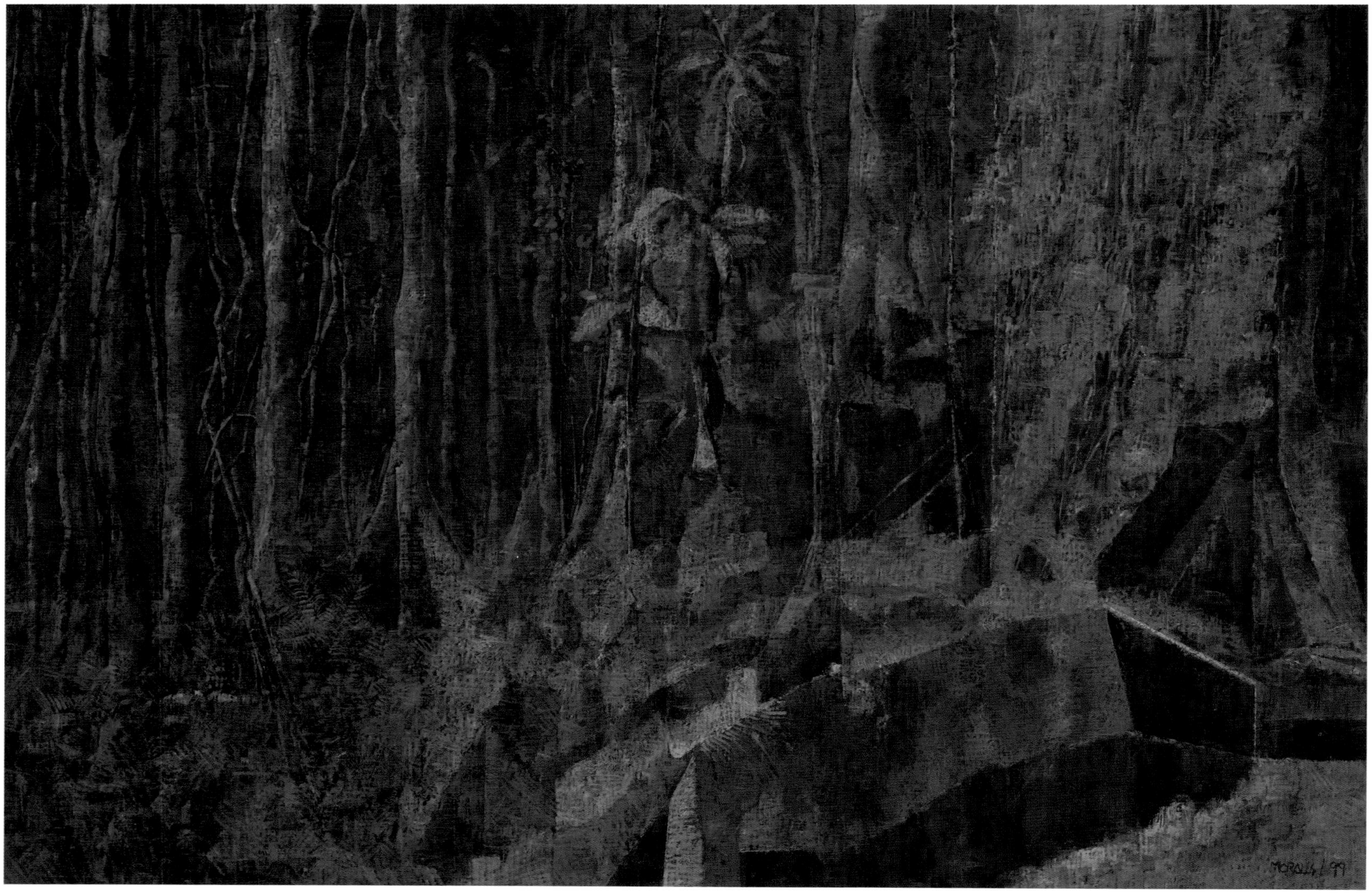

PLATE 63
Armando Morales • *Forêt tropicale: ruines d'une plantation d'indigo*
[Tropical Forest: Ruins of an Indigo Plantation], 1999

At the same time that Morales reevaluated the classical figure in his works, he applied the same craftsman-like method to various paintings of tropical forests, three of which belong to the Brillembourg Capriles Collection: *Forêt tropicale dans une orage* [Tropical Forest in a Storm] (1991) (plate 61), *Forêt tropicale* [Tropical Forest] (1992) (plate 62), and *Forêt tropicale: ruines d'une plantation d'indigo* [Tropical Forest: Ruins of an Indigo Plantation](1999) (plate 63). He began to seriously explore this subject once he had established a permanent studio in Paris in 1982. The artist stated that these works combined his memories of the Nicaraguan jungles with his imagination.[14] Although Morales gave these paintings titles that indicate place, the visual experience of his forests does not necessarily provide an identifiable location, and the landscape could, in fact, be anywhere, thereby producing a mysterious, open-ended fantasy.

Broaching abstraction, Morales's paintings of forests, specifically *Forêt tropicale dans une orage*, rework notions of "realistic" or three-dimensional space, both figuratively and literally. As he applies the paint, Morales builds layers onto the canvas, resulting in a surface that is no longer physically flat; yet each layer adds to the visual illusion of a dense jungle. The painting can be read as an exploration of discordant and concordant patches of colors, as well as a recession into the depths of an imaginary setting. The modulation of transparency and opacity of colors create a rippling effect on the surface of the painting, which is heightened by the lack of a defined foreground and background. Simultaneously, Morales pulls the depictions of trees from the shadows, using his reverse chiaroscuro and scratching lines onto the surface of the canvas to delineate tree trunks. These techniques are successful in producing an innovative reevaluation of the sublime landscape by embracing the painting as both an artificial craft and a gateway to another world. Thus, while the traditional appearance of his paintings have caused them to be largely dismissed as retrograde within current scholarship, Morales's focus on the past provided him with materials, methods, and ideas to reinvigorate painting, uniting the debates between artifice and image, abstraction and figuration, and art and craft.

ILLUSTRATIONS IN TEXT

FIGURE 1
Leonardo da Vinci
Two Studies of a Man's Left Leg from a Ledger from Milan Cathedral, c. 1488–90
Pen and ink over traces of black chalk
7 3/4 x 12 3/8 inches (19.6 x 31.3 cm)
Royal Collection, England

FIGURE 2
Armando Morales
Deux jambes [Two Legs], c. 1977
Black chalk on newspaper
31 7/8 x 23 5/8 inches (81 x 60 cm)
Private collection

FIGURE 3
Armando Morales
Escena lacustre I, Granada Harbor [Lakeside Scene I, Granada Harbor] (detail), 1978
Oil and beeswax on canvas
18 15/16 x 22 9/16 inches (48.1 x 57.3 cm)
The Brillembourg Capriles Collection of Latin American Art

FIGURE 4
Edgar Degas
Woman Bathing in a Shallow Tub, 1885
Charcoal and pastel on light green wove paper, now discolored to warm gray, laid down on silk bolting
32 x 22 1/8 inches (81.3 x 56.2 cm)
The Metropolitan Museum of Art, New York, H. O. Havemeyer Collection, Bequest of Mrs. H. O. Havemeyer, 1929, 29.100.41

NOTES

1
José Gómez Sicre, in Armando J. Florez, "Morales exhibe en Nuesta York," *Miami Herald*, 1981; reprinted in *Armando Morales: Catalogue Raisonné Volume 1* (Vaumarcus: ArtAcatos Sàrl, 2010), 294.

2
Armando Morales, *Paula*, 1986, in *Armando Morales: Catalogue Raisonné Volume 1*, (Vaumarcus: ArtAcatos Sàrl, 2010), 405.

3
Clement Greenberg, "Modernist Painting," 1961, reprinted in *Art Theory and Criticism: An Anthology of Formalist Avant-Garde, Contextualist and Post-Modernist Thought* (North Carolina: McFarland & Company, Inc., Publishers, 1991), 110–18.

4
Dore Ashton, "Science, Art and Intuition," *The Unknown Shore: A View of Contemporary Art* (Boston: Little, Brown & Company, 1962), 228–38.

5
Dore Ashton, "In Praise of Illusion," 1965, reprinted in *Art Theory and Criticism*, 125–31. Ashton specifically geared this article toward critics, encouraging them to understand the imagination and to take a more intuitive approach to art criticism.

6
Armando Morales, *Armando Morales*, exh.cat. (México: Museo Rufino Tamayo, 1990), 23.

7
Edward Sullivan, "Armando Morales: Southern Visions of the Mind," *Arts Magazine* 61 (November 1987): 62–65.

8
Ibid.

9
H.W. Janson and Anthony Janson, *History of Art: The Western Tradition*, 6th ed. (Upper Saddle River, New Jersey: Pearson Education, 2004), 355.

10
Ibid.

11
Xuriguera, Gerard. "Un scenographie crepusculaire," *Armando Morales: Catalogue Raisonné Volume 1* (Vaumarcus: ArtAcatos Sàrl, 2010), 13-29.

12
Carmen Bambach, "Anatomy in the Renaissance," in *Heilbrunn Timeline of Art History* (New York: The Metropolitan Museum of Art, 2000). http://www.metmuseum.org/toah/hd/anat/hd_anat.htm (October 2002).

13
Patricia Simmons, "Women in Frames," reprinted in *The Expanding Discourse: Feminism and Art History* (New York: Icon Editions, 1992), 40.

14
Armando Morales, *Armando Morales*, exh. cat., 30.

James Oles

FRANCISCO TOLEDO

FEAR AT THE CIRCUS

FRANCISCO TOLEDO IS RENOWNED TODAY for fantastical paintings, prints, and sculptures featuring humans, skeletal figures, and an often eroticized bestiary, inspired by—but never fully dependent on—traditional Zapotec myths, as well as social anthropology, natural history, and Surrealist theory (fig. 1). Influenced by artists as disparate as Rufino Tamayo, Jean Dubuffet, Paul Klee, and Marc Chagall, Toledo developed his earthy figurative style in the mid-1960s, in part in reaction to slick internationalist tendencies such as Pop and Minimalism, then dominating the art world. Less familiar to scholars, however, are Toledo's more abstract paintings from earlier in the decade, of which *El circo* [The Circus] (1961) [plate 64] in the Brillembourg Capriles Collection of Latin American Art is a prime example. These works contain hints of his later figurative practice, but they also represent a path toward non-representational painting that he quickly rejected. In fact, many major catalogues and monographs on Toledo—probably reflecting the artist's own opinion—marginalize paintings from this early period.[1]

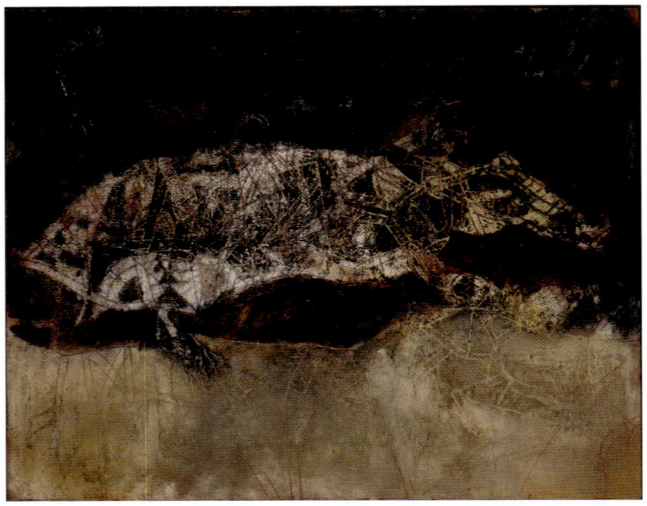

FIG. 1

Like a thickly piled red carpet, *The Circus* is dense and richly textured, practically inviting the viewer to stroke its surface. Although almost monochromatic, brown and mustard yellow highlights, as well as lines roughly incised into the impasto (a somewhat lumpy mixture of fine sand and oil paint), allow some tentative observations as to iconography, even if the painter holds us at bay, denying an easy reading. Three discrete objects are sketched out in the center: to the left, below an undefined form, is an inverted human skull; also at the left, its identity facilitated by the title of the picture, is a large circular form atop a base: a Ferris wheel. The sandy surface might thus echo the sawdust-strewn arena beneath the tent, but it also iterates a sense of the handmade and ephemeral, as if we are looking at a primitive carving. Although the forms are barely legible, *The Circus* has more figurative elements than Toledo's work of just a year before (fig. 2), indicating a directional shift away from non-representational painting.

Like the carnival, the modern circus as a space of fantasy and escape and as liminal world located between reality and theater, was a

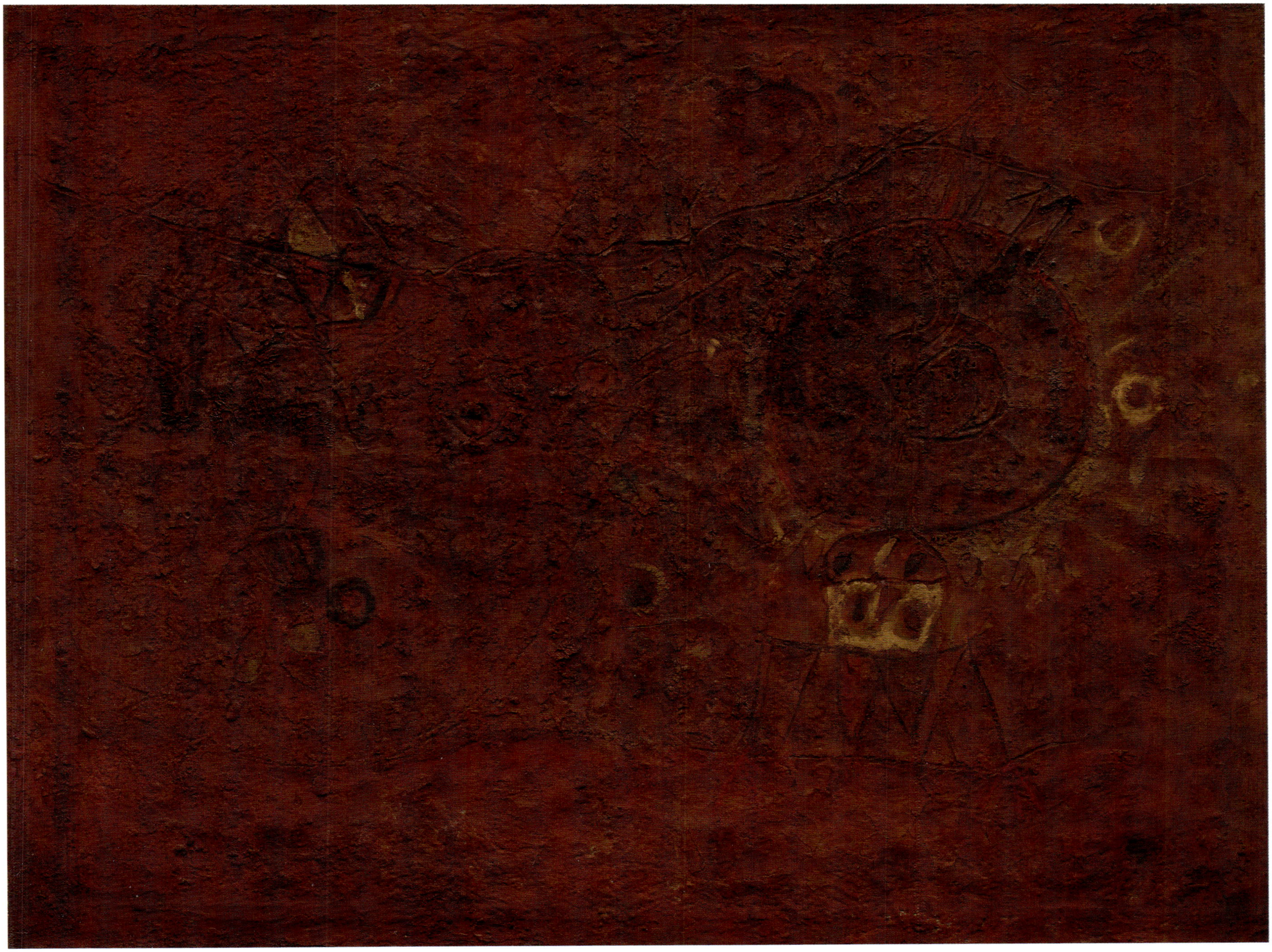

PLATE 64

Francisco Toledo • *El circo* [The Circus], 1961

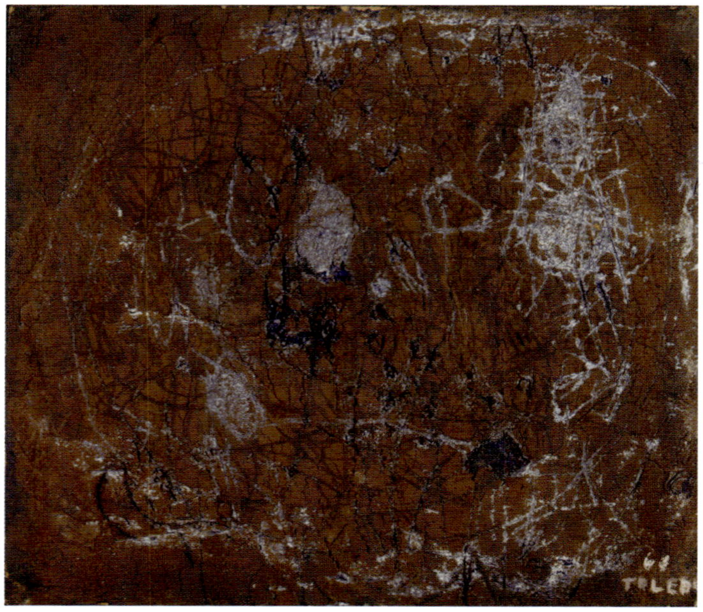

FIG. 2

common subject for many artists, from Seurat to Chagall, from Calder to Weegee, and, in Mexico, from María Izquierdo to Alfonso Michel.[2] Some of these pictures express the joy of circus life, while others comment on its bleaker aspects, from the hard life of the circus hand to the dangers faced by lion tamers and acrobats. In a recent interview, the characteristically taciturn artist spoke little of the picture, only recalling a childhood memory: once, while on a Ferris wheel (known in Mexico as a "rueda de la fortuna," or wheel of fortune), he became deathly frightened because it stopped when he was at the top. According to Toledo, this led to a subsequent fear that "planes might stop when they are at their highest point, that they will be caught hanging on a cloud."[3] Serpent-like forms around and inside Toledo's Ferris wheel may indicate motion, though they too could have a sinister aspect. The painting thus hints at the darker emotions unleashed at the circus, even making reference to death—the blood-red ground, the skull—rendered as if drawn into the sand by a child.

Toledo never considered himself affiliated with any group, whether in Mexico or Europe, though his debts to Tamayo, another painter from Oaxaca who had already made his way in Paris, are clear. Nevertheless, Toledo's work of the early 1960s formed part of a dense web of local and international influences that—in terms of Mexican historiography—are just now being disentangled. Indeed, a painting such as *The Circus* must be understood within the complex history of Surrealism, as it evolved in Europe as well as the Americas, and also with regard to the networks of postwar abstraction, particularly what in Paris became known as Art Informel and, in Mexico, as the Generación de la Ruptura.[4] For example, if we only consider Toledo's use of sand, we would have to explore a genealogy that goes back at least to André Masson in the 1920s and that would include not only Jean Fautrier and Jean Dubuffet, but also Tamayo and Gunther Gerzso, to name just two other painters closer to home.

Among artists connected to the Surrealist movement, one might find echoes of Paul Klee, as art historian Teresa del Conde has observed,[5] but even more direct antecedents in Mexico are to be found in the equally sandy surfaces of Alice Rahon (1904–1987), a French émigré and former wife of the Austrian painter Wolfgang Paalen, resident in Mexico since 1939 and, like Toledo, an artist represented by Galeria Antonio Souza. Although far more representational, Rahon's *Music Box* (1944) (fig. 3), shows a similar neo-primitive technique of

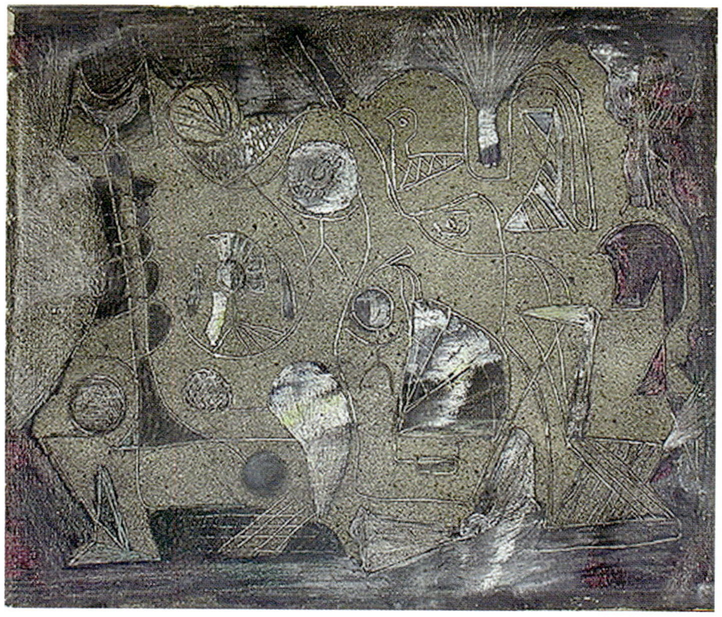

FIG. 3

incising lines into a sandy surface that Toledo later employed. Rahon's *The Ballad of Frida Kahlo* (1956) (fig. 4), though far larger and more elaborate, includes the image of a Ferris wheel, executed in a linear fashion that resonates with Toledo's 1961 painting.[6]

Toledo's greater deployment of abstraction, however, resonates more with European contemporaries such as Dubuffet and Antoni Tàpies, who also created works distinguished by rough surfaces; as part of that elusive search to bring authentic and emotional forces back into modern art, these artists turned for inspiration to graffiti and the drawings of children and the insane.[7] Toledo's early abstractions, including *The Circus*, engage with this broader context, though his precise connections to these and other artists have yet to be fully explored. At the same time, however, iconographic devices—like the crudely drawn skull in this painting—foreshadow what was to come, as Toledo set forth to construct a modern Primitivism with deep and sophisticated roots in both local culture and international Modernism.

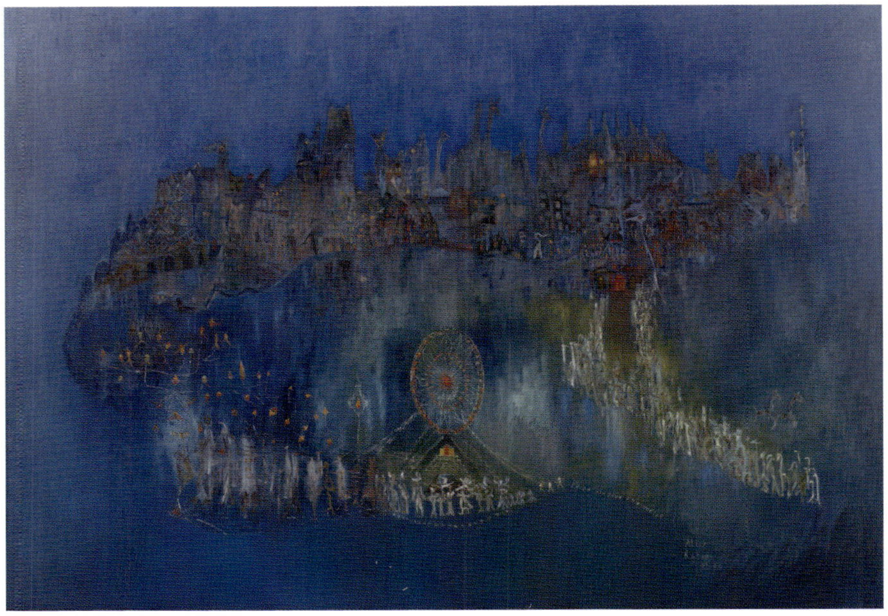

FIG. 4

ILLUSTRATIONS IN TEXT

FIGURE 1
Francisco Toledo
Lagarto, 1973
Oil on canvas
47 1/4 x 62 1/4 inches (120 x 158 cm)
Museo de Arte Moderno, Mexico City

FIGURE 2
Francisco Toledo
Abstract Blue Forms, 1960
Oil and sand on panel
laid down on wood
13 x 15 inches (33 x 38 cm)
Private Collection

FIGURE 3
Alice Rahon
Boite à musique [Music Box], 1944
Oil on sand and canvas
13 5/8 x 15 1/2 inches (34.5 x 39.5 cm)
Collection Mariana Pérez Amor.
Galería de Arte Mexicano, Mexico City

FIGURE 4
Alice Rahon
Balada para Frida Kahlo
[Ballad for Frida Kahlo], 1956–66
Oil on canvas
47 1/4 x 70 1/8 inches (120 x 178 cm)
Museo de Arte Moderno, Mexico City

NOTES

1
See, for example, Elena Horz de Sotomayor, ed., *Francisco Toledo* (Mexico City: Smurfit Cartón y Papel de México, 2002), which includes no work made prior to 1970.

2
On images by U.S. artists, see Donna Gustafson et al., *Images from the World Between: The Circus in 20th-Century American Art* (Cambridge, MA: The MIT Press, 2001); several Mexican circus scenes are discussed in James Oles, ed., *Arte Moderno en México: Colección Andrés Blaisten* (Mexico City: UNAM, 2007).

3
I am grateful to the artist's daughter, Laureana Toledo, for asking her father about this painting and for sending me a loose transcription of their conversation (summer 2012).

4
Toledo never considered himself to be part of this generation. Many of the artists of the so-called Ruptura—Lilia Carrillo, Manuel Felguérez, Vicente Rojo—showed at the Galería Juan Marin in Mexico City, but Toledo did not join the gallery until 1968, despite having been back in Mexico since 1965. His conceptual and formal links to these artists will have to await future study.

5
Teresa del Conde, *Francisco Toledo* (Mexico City: Secretaría de Educación Pública, 1981), 24.

6
The Great Wheel, erected in Paris for the 1900 world's fair, was a symbol of triumphant modernity for many artists, including Diego Rivera. Both Toledo and Rahon, however, surely depict more modest structures in popular fairs or circuses.

7
Children's art had deeply inspired Tamayo and many other Mexican artists as early as the 1920s.

Marcela Guerrero

THE SKINNY ON FERNANDO BOTERO

WHEN I WAS YOUNG, and whenever I would visit my family in Ecuador, I was confronted by a range of conflicting emotions. On one hand, I felt elated, because I was able to be with my father's family; on the other hand, I dreaded spending time with my male cousins, who would tease me (affectionately) by calling me "Fernando Botero's model." This reference is not reserved exclusively for describing a once-chubby Puerto Rican girl. Nor does the reference resonate only with Ecuadorians. As Edward Sullivan has pointed out, it is possible that even a group of presumably low-income Hispanics riding on a New York City public bus would understand the reference if, when spotting a person who resembles one of the artist's figures, someone were to exclaim: "Look at that Botero!"[1]

For the past fifty years, the round and voluptuous forms that dominate Fernando Botero's paintings, drawings, and sculptures either have been praised or criticized, and not only by Latin Americans. As if paying homage to Alfred H. Barr—the first director of the Museum of Modern Art (MoMA)—, who in 1961 questioned, "Who can look at this disturbing work without taking sides?"[2] opinions of, as well as the literature on, Botero's work have been, at worst, polarizing and reduced to a discussion of the artistic value of his so-called fat figures or, at best, formally analyzed, with special attention paid to the important role that volume plays in his works. The seven examples by Fernando Botero in the Brillembourg Capriles Collection of Latin American Art were carefully selected by the collector, as they highlight the developing aspects of Botero's style instead of the formulaic expression that has characterized his work of the last three decades.

Art critic Marta Traba, an early advocate of Botero's art, laid the foundation for understanding the work of this Colombian artist when she commented about *La camera degli sposi, Homenaje a Mantegna* [The Couple's Chamber, Homage to Mantegna] (1958) (fig. 1): "The curiosity to see how contemporary art resolves a pictorial fact of another time under new conventions, adds to the painting a sense of adventure out of which are not excluded neither risk nor, therefore, heroism."[3] In contrast, art historians such as Rosalind Krauss consider Botero's work to be of "absolutely no consequence to twentieth-century fine arts."[4] However pervasive these opinions may be in the art world, Botero's early works challenge Traba's and Krauss's perspectives. The works elucidate the varied strategies Botero employed during the first two decades of his career—roughly between 1960 and 1980—when he was one of the key figurative artists working in New York who would soon become the quintessential exponent of the revival of the figure in art. As I will explain in this essay, the four paintings and the three works on paper in the Brillembourg Capriles Collection exemplify the pursuits of an artist struggling to create a figurative vocabulary that would be of consequence, both to him and to the history of art. Hence, the two sections into which this essay is divided will tackle, first, Botero's early formal experiments that went beyond his concern with volume, and, second, how along with these investigations, the development of a proto-Colombian Pop art language sought to analyze the popular dimensions of well-known paradigms of universal and Colombian art history.

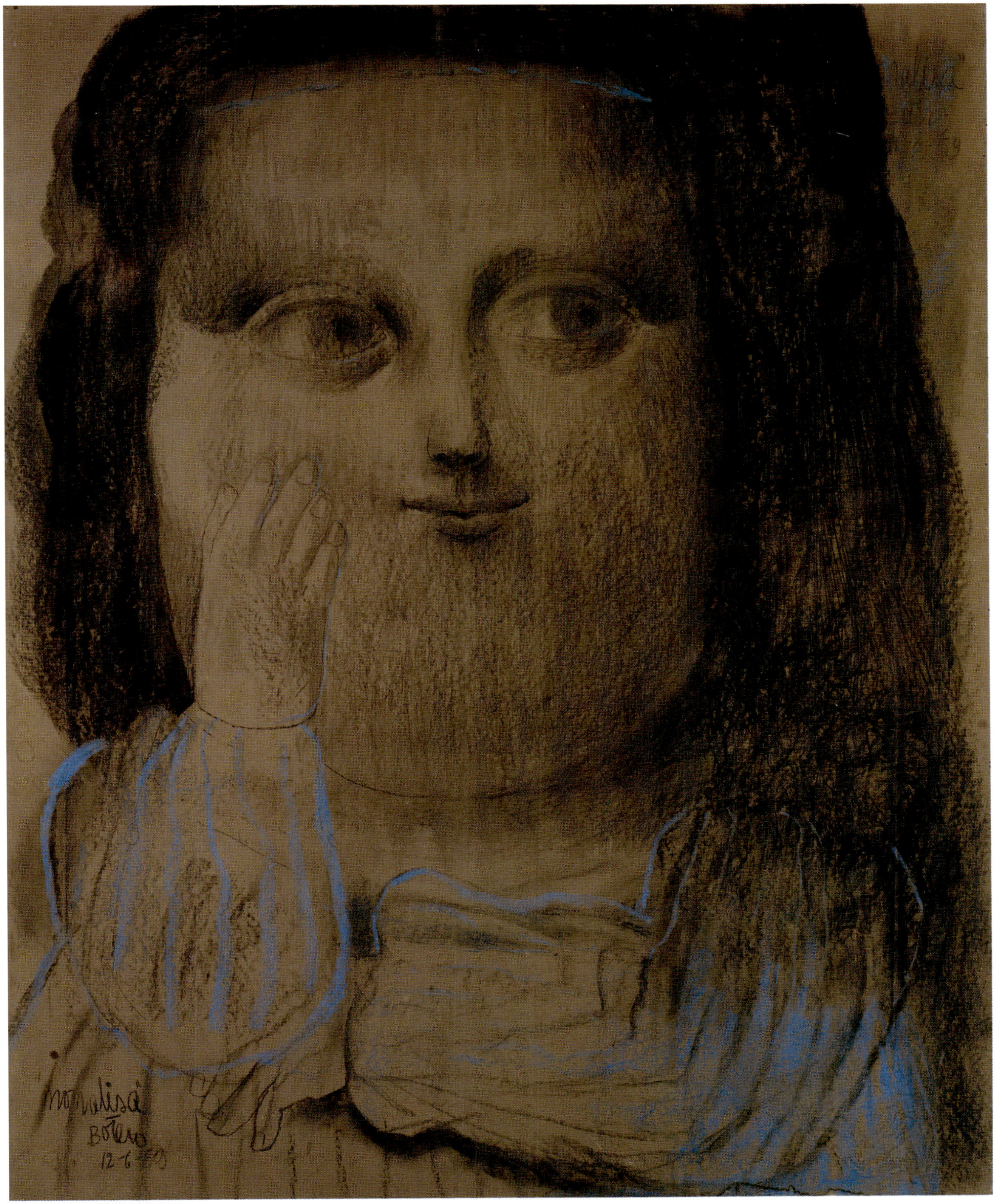

PLATE 65

Fernando Botero • *Mona Lisa,* 1959

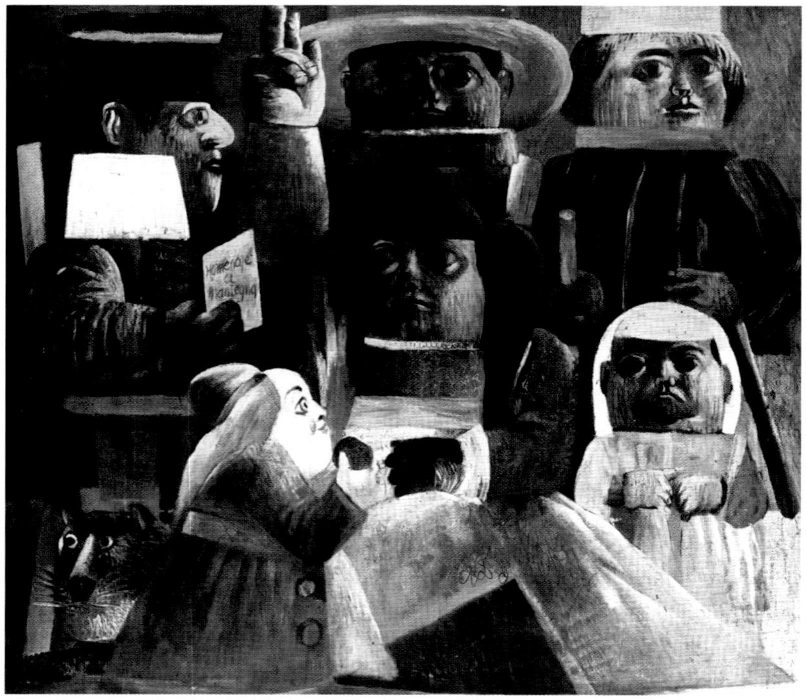

FIG. 1

Volume Is Clichéd

As alluded to previously with the reference to *La camera degli sposi,* Botero's means of revising and, therefore, making an original contribution to the history of painting was achieved by taking Renaissance art (and subsequent art-historical periods) as his point of departure. Marta Traba observed how, as was the case with any emerging Latin American artist, Botero was free to select his own ancestors. In choosing Italian Renaissance painting, Botero tapped this art-historical reservoir as a means to an end; that is, as a "springboard" that would help him to "propel forward."[5] Traba understood that, by quoting from Renaissance painting, Botero was simply setting the gold standard against which he could weigh the potential success of his formal experiments. More precisely, Traba noted Botero's courageous distancing from the idealism of Renaissance painting, his consistent move toward deforming the figure, and his earnest attempt to become a great colorist.[6]

Both elements—the deformation of the figure and the heightened colors—can be appreciated in Botero's earliest work in the Brillembourg Capriles Collection, a drawing contemporaneous with *La camera degli sposi.* In *Mona Lisa* (1959) (plate 65), Botero applies cerulean blues to highlight the striations of the woman's sleeves as well as her veil, hands, and eyes. The clean lines colored in blue contrast with the busier hatched lines used to depict hair, shadows, or a combination of both. In addition to the gestural lines—an immediate way of distorting the clean and crisp surface of the original Mona Lisa painted by Leonardo in the fifteenth century—, Botero has further deformed the referent by enlarging the head and disproportionately drawing the hands and facial features. And, although it is true that Botero was by no means the only artist in the late 1950s pushing the naturalist limits of the figure, he was nonetheless the only one, perhaps excepting Francis Bacon, interested in using famous personages from the canon of art history to elaborate a formal language of his own.

Through his use of formal resources, such as the inflation and the minimization of the proportions in Leonardo's *Mona Lisa,* as well as in his own *El niño de Vallecas* [The Boy from Vallecas] (1959) (fig. 2), another work plucked from the vault of art history, Botero explores a psychological dimension, even if the artist himself discourages such readings. Although he has stated that "there is no message," and that his work "is not a commentary on reality,"[7] it would be a disservice to his paintings, as art critic Ricardo Pau-Llosa has noted, to bank "too heavily on Botero's declared intentions."[8] In fact, Pau-Llosa, in his book review of Carter Ratcliff's *Botero*, argues, "If indeed Botero obscures [the] psychological dimensions of [the] human Being in order to reveal a pristine physicality, this need not mean that the images lack a profound social dimension or symbolism."[9] Moreover, the psychological extent of a figurative work is, certainly, not only the province of art that depicts human beings. In his still life titled *Variaciones sobre Cézanne* [Variations on Cézanne] (1963) (plate 66), Botero uses rich reds and pinks symbolically. Hence, when we question the presence of the white robe under the bowl of fruit, and the tinges of red on the knife, *Variaciones* becomes an intriguing work. What gives the knife its color? Was the knife tinged with blood, or was it used to cut a grapefruit, for example? The red and pink backdrop helps to flatten the surface of the painting, thereby pushing the elements of suspense closer to the viewer's eye.

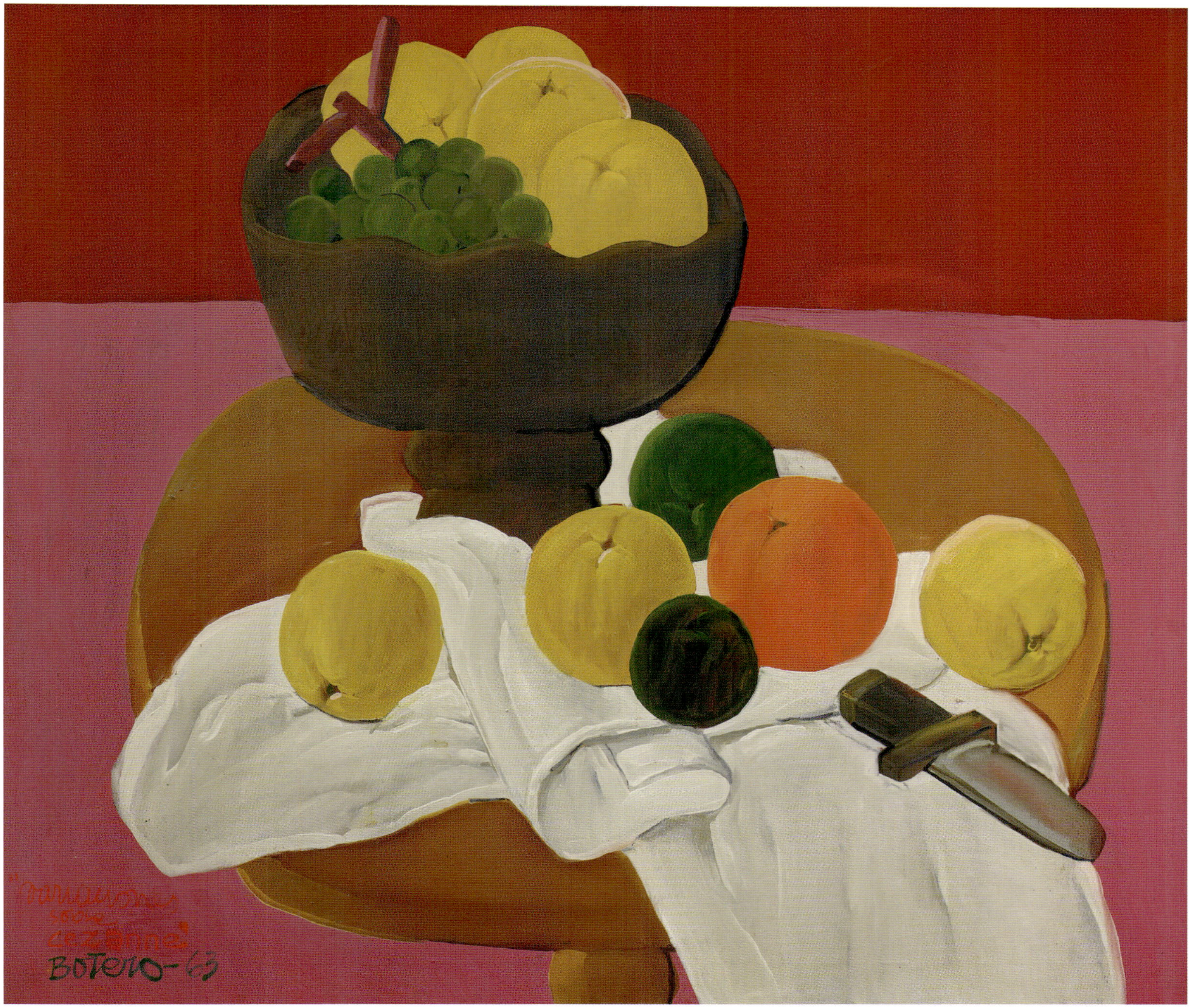

PLATE 66

Fernando Botero • *Variaciones sobre Cézanne* [Variations on Cézanne], 1963

It is all too easy to succumb to the oft-cited inaccuracies and the reductive discourse that surround Botero's early work, which, in fact, deserves to be accurately assessed according to the milieu in which the artist worked. His early phase of experimentation, and the rendering of a psychological dimension, did not occur in a vacuum. For instance, the rapid handwork, looser application of line and color, and conspicuous impasto evident in the works discussed thus far can probably be understood best in a historical context. In 1957, after having his first solo exhibition in Washington, D.C., Botero went to New York, where he became acquainted with the Abstract Expressionist style of Jackson Pollock and Willem de Kooning.[10] Yet no matter the prominence of these stylistic elements, writers insist on celebrating Botero's daring decision to continue to employ an incorruptible figurative vocabulary while the art world was rejecting all that did not champion abstraction.

Erroneous information also has shrouded Botero's preference for depicting the human figure. In 1960, after showing *Mona Lisa, Age Twelve* (1959) (fig. 3)—a painting for which the drawing on paper in the Brillembourg Capriles Collection could have been a study—at the 5th São Paulo Bienal, Botero moved to New York, where he would live for more than a decade. One year after he arrived, a fortuitous though unplanned meeting[11] with Dorothy Miller, one of MoMA's most influential curators, led to the purchase of *Mona Lisa, Age Twelve* for the museum's collection.[12] It has been incorrectly stated that this painting was the only figurative one the museum purchased that year. In fact, a press release for MoMA's recent acquisitions exhibition of December 1961 explicitly affirms that the show "offers a dissenting comment on the familiar claim that today's art is so dominated by a single international style," and adds that "twenty-six of these very recent paintings and sculptures can be classified as abstract, 16 as semi-abstract, 20 clearly representational."[13] Thus, contrary to Botero's comment that, in the early 1960s, "if you weren't Abstract Expressionist, you were not a painter, you didn't exist," the truth was that the tastemakers of the art world had already realized that Abstract Expressionism was becoming an academic style. Museums were intent on acquiring representational works, as witnessed in the flourishing of Pop art.[14]

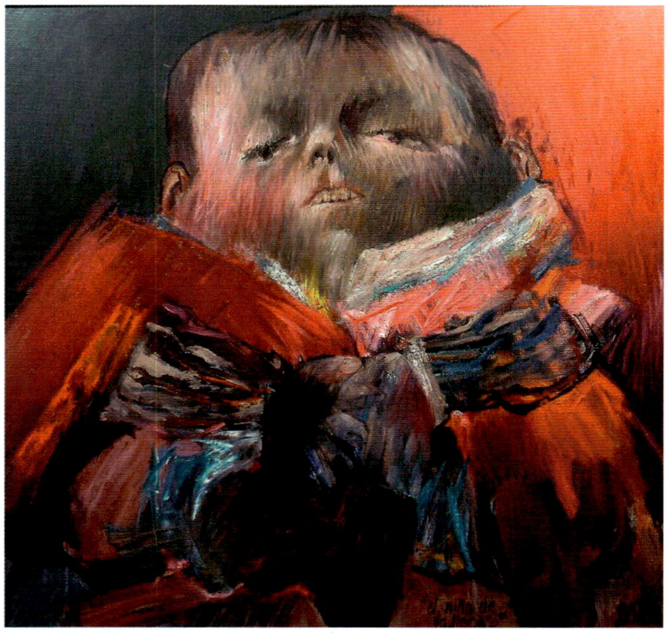

FIG. 2

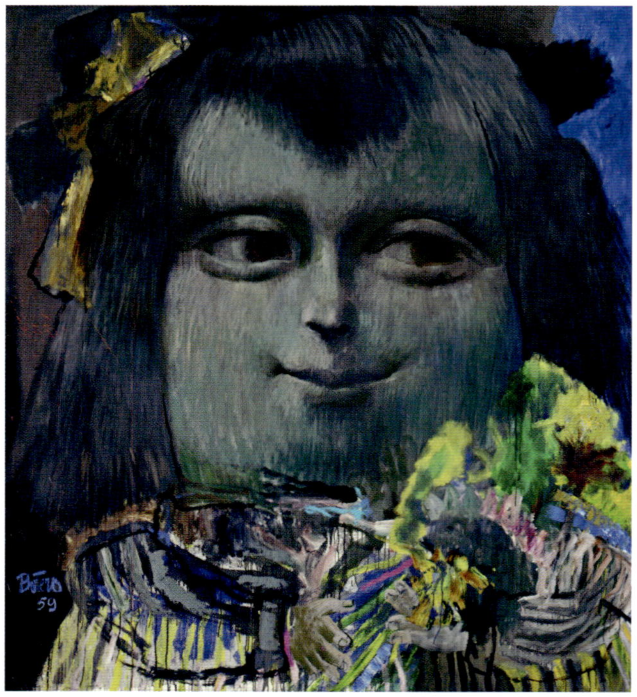

FIG. 3

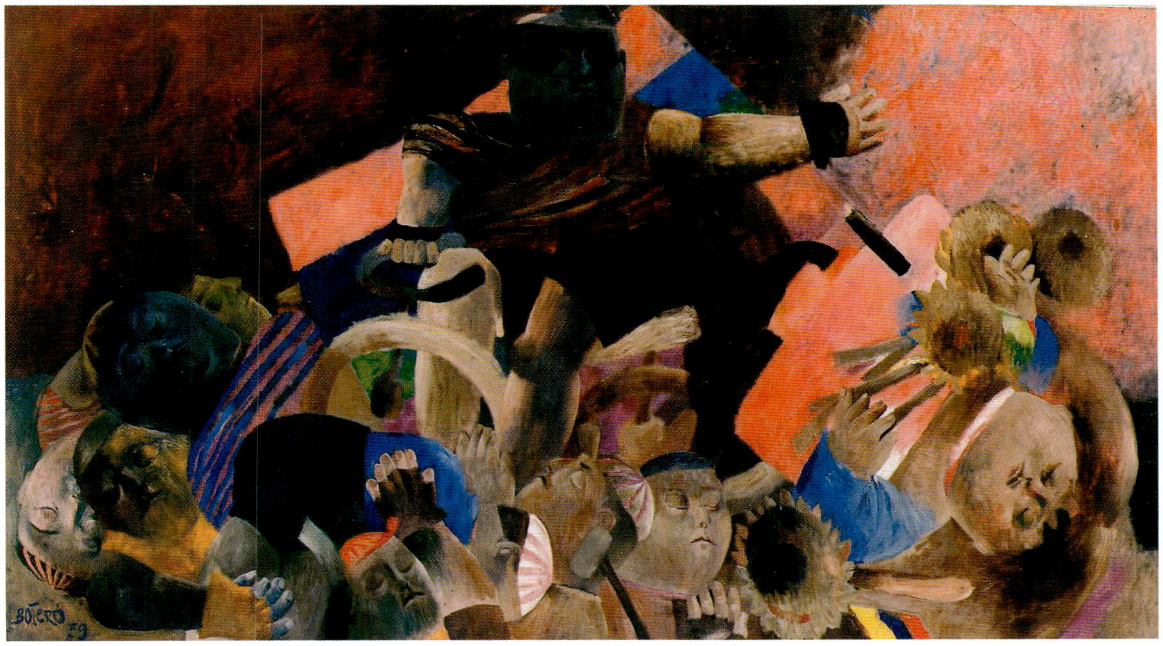

FIG. 4

As a matter of fact, the late 1950s and the early 1960s were critical years during which artists reintroduced the human form. To name a few examples, the *New Images of Man* exhibition of 1959 was received with lukewarm enthusiasm, only because critics were expecting artists to take a fresher, bolder look at the emotions then afflicting modern man. This new appraisal occurred in 1960, when Andy Warhol and Roy Lichtenstein began using cartoons and advertisements as sources for their paintings, a moment in time now recognized as heralding the birth of Pop art. A year later, Claes Oldenburg, whose gargantuan sculptures of deflated objects have been compared to Botero's works, arrived on the scene with *The Store*. In an overview of this two-year period, from 1959 to 1960, we can see how Botero's work not only was conversant with contemporary events in the art world, but also aimed to offer an original reading on how to translate images from everyday life into art. This is the case with *La apoteosis de Ramón Hoyos* [The Apotheosis of Ramon Hoyos] (1959) (fig. 4), whose subject matter tapped into Colombian culture.[15]

Proto-Colombian Pop Art

Botero has often been labeled Latin America's answer to Pop art, even though he has never been concerned with celebrating or satirizing consumer culture, nor with adopting modern technological methods, which distinguish him markedly from the Pop movement. Nevertheless, there are several similarities worth noting, especially because in many ways he was using Pop art elements *avant la lettre*. Responding to a questionnaire sent by MoMA after the museum had purchased *Mona Lisa, Age Twelve* and had publicized its acquisition in a press release, Botero commented: "Leonardo's *Mona Lisa* is so popular that perhaps it is no longer art. It is like a movie star or a football player. Hence an obvious satirical element in my painting. . . ."[16] With this in mind, it not only would be a more-accurate account of history but also would depict Botero in a more-positive light if we assumed he knew that the heyday of Abstract Expressionism was over, and that he was knowingly proposing an original way of rendering in paint the figure of an iconic superstar, one who might justifiably be called the Marilyn Monroe of the cinquecento.

Words of caution about proceeding along this path have been expressed by more than one scholar of Latin American Pop art. Jacqueline Barnitz reminds us that, in Latin America, Pop art was not a manifestation of industrialism or consumerism, as it was in the United States and England, but rather an object-based style accessible to the masses.[17] Art historian Mercedes Trelles Hernández concurs with Barnitz but goes one step further by highlighting that, in Latin American Pop art, the connection between popular art and national culture became evident, thus bypassing the social and economic hierarchies referenced by and alluded to in Anglo-Saxon Pop art.[18] About 1964, at the same time that Pop art first became part of the working vocabulary in Colombia, Traba was beginning to develop her idea of a

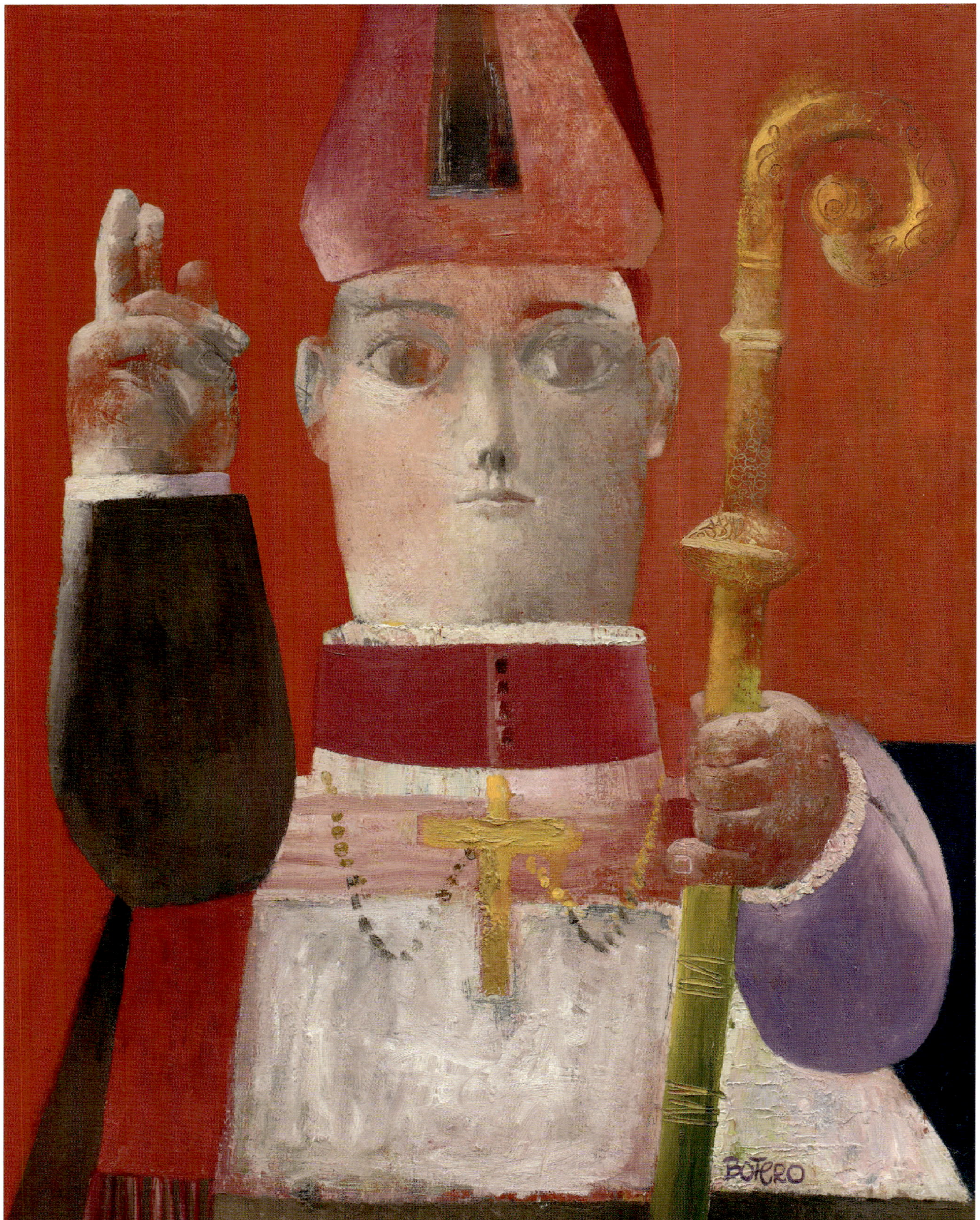

PLATE 67

Fernando Botero • *El nuncio* [The Nuncio], 1962

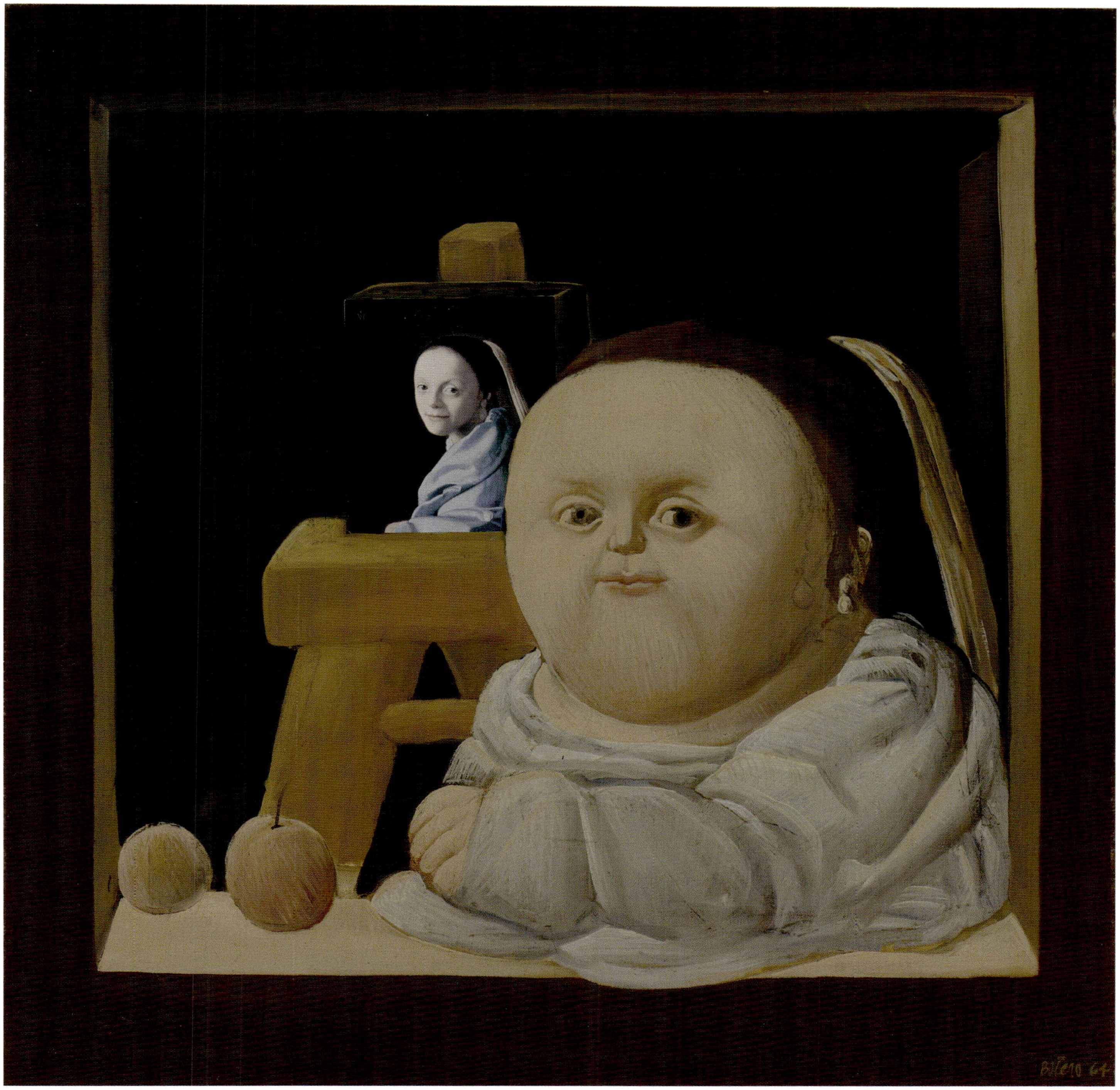

PLATE 68

Fernando Botero • *El taller de Vermeer* [Vermeer's Atelier], 1964

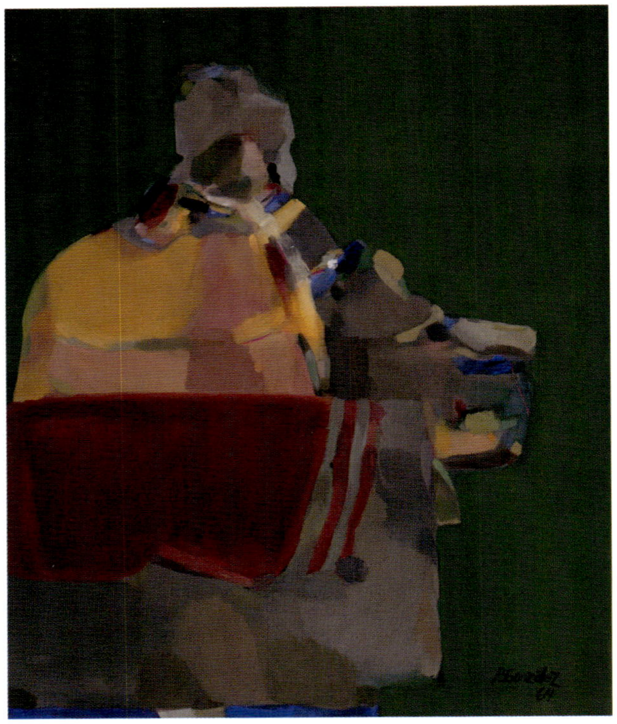

FIG. 5

"culture of resistance" that was predicated on rejecting influences foreign to Latin America and instead on accepting an art deemed authentic, according to the conditions of the continent.[19] Thus, similar to Botero's refusal to adopt Abstract Expressionism, Traba not only argued against acquiescing to North American styles but also warned that if Pop references were to appear in Colombian art, they had to be used in an ironic way.[20] For Pop art that developed in Colombia in the late 1960s and 1970s, some of the principal tendencies observed are the questioning of the medium of painting and the use of elements drawn from popular culture.[21] Botero, who practiced what perhaps could be called a proto-Colombian Pop art—because his art was never about fully referencing/incorporating everyday materials—, deployed some of the commonly known characteristics of American Pop art and also other more culturally specific references.

Writing in *The Baroque World of Fernando Botero*, David Elliot observes how "Botero has repeated certain images throughout his career in an almost serial way, and cuts in on his figures and objects using close-ups like a photographer with a zoom lens. Most significantly, the reception of his images across the world has achieved an almost iconic status."[22] These three characteristics are as applicable to Botero's *Mona Lisa* as they are to his oil-on-canvas painting *El nuncio* [The Nuncio] (1962) (plate 67). In *El nuncio*, we understand the nuance of the term "Pop art" in a country such as Colombia, a stronghold of Catholicism, where its church-going citizens are surrounded by polychrome statues of religious figures or clergymen. These hollow sculptures, often made of wood, *are* a part of popular culture because religion is so pervasive. Similarly, the staff or crosier carried by the nuncio appears to be made from *guadua*, a type of bamboo widely used in construction in Colombia.

Quoting from or using reproductions of artworks by the Old Masters as a way of expanding the possibilities of painting was another popular practice in Colombian Pop art.[23] In fact, in *El taller de Vermeer* [Vermeer's Studio] (1964) (plate 68), Botero includes a reproduction of Johannes Vermeer's *Study of a Young Woman*, c. 1665–67, effectively making the reproduction part of a collage. In several interviews, Botero has recalled that his first encounter with modern art was through reproductions. In her television show, Traba herself used reproductions of famous artworks as illustrations and decorated the walls of her studio with color plates framed in construction paper.[24] Likewise, fellow Colombian artist Beatriz González painted, also in 1964, a series titled *Encajera*, referencing Vermeer's *The Lacemaker* (1669–70). Yet González and Botero differ. In *Encajera Almanaque Pielroja* [Lacemaker Pielroja Almanac] (1965) (fig. 5), González transforms the classic Dutch genre scene into a resolutely Colombian space painted with the same commercial colors used by the tobacco company Pielroja for its giveaway calendars.[25] Botero does not combine the lofty world of art with the sphere in which popular objects reside; instead, he is more interested in using a reproduction as a source for exploring the surface of the canvas.

Further implying a connection with Pop art's vocabulary, Botero has painted the sitter in *El taller de Vermeer* from a copy, not from nature. Many of the formal decisions Botero makes in *El taller* seem to be informed by his observation of Vermeer's *Study*, a companion to Vermeer's *Girl with a Pearl Earring* (c. 1665). For instance, art historians have noted the oversized pearl earring as a contemporary costume

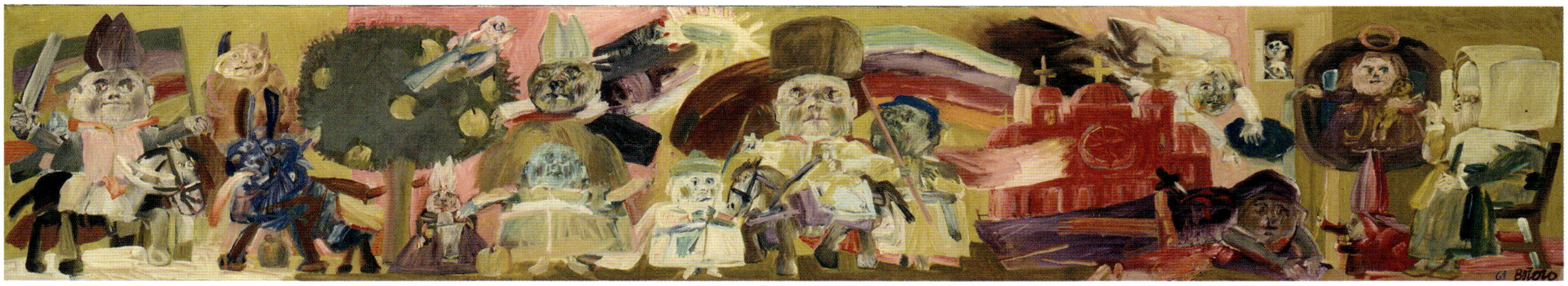

FIG. 6

accessory. Its disproportionate size must have appealed to Botero, who decided instead to minimize the earring in his depiction of the young woman while also enlarging her head. Another feature that Botero reinterprets is the noted awkward left hand of Vermeer's sitter. In what must have been a tongue-in-cheek reference to the Dutch artist, Botero has painted the arm exactly as Vermeer had and then repainted it in a more anatomically correct way, leaving slight traces of both renderings still visible on the canvas. Here, it is refreshing to see this and other types of imperfections, such as the outline of an ear that was first painted and then moved to the right, or the thick creases of impasto near the dress worn by Botero's model. These imperfections make us wonder: Did Botero purposely make them visible in order to give his painting the sense of a preparatory study instead of a final product, as suggested by Vermeer's title? If so, it is an interesting experiment, making a study of a study that is ultimately a finished painting.

About the same time that Botero painted his series on artists' studios, he was also using a different format for his paintings: the lengthened canvas. The stretched-out, rectangular format and the religious subject matter of works from the 1960s, such as *The Life of Honorius III* (1961) (fig. 6), call to mind the predellas he must have seen in Florence. Botero, now drawing on the more-secular source of yellow journalism, depicts in *El secuestro* [The Kidnapping] (1966) (plate 69) two men harassing a girl who tries to flee only to be captured by her abductors. Heightening the theatrical aspect of this work is its arrangement; divided into three sections and two flanking wings, *El secuestro* reads as a sort of scene or tableau from a play.[26] However, *El secuestro* finds as a referent two actual, violent events in mid-twentieth-century Colombian history. The first one involves the crimes committed in the late 1930s and 1940s by Nepomuceno Matallana (aka "Doctor Mata"), a psychopath who, posing as a lawyer, abducted and killed his clients in order to steal their money.[27] Botero immortalized the gruesome murders in works such as *Teresita la descuartizada* [Teresita, the Woman Cut into Pieces] (1963) and *El asesinato de Ana Rosa Calderón* [The Murder of Ana Rosa Calderón] (1969) (fig. 7). In *El asesinato*, Botero also includes the presence of black birds, identified as a symbol of the government's hired assassins during the period known as *La violencia* [The Violence, 1946–1966]. *La violencia* concluded the same year that Botero painted *El secuestro*.[28] Less explicit in terms of the atrocities committed by either "Doctor Mata" or the *pájaros* [stand-ins for the government], *El secuestro* nonetheless captures a national feeling: the fear of an imminent loss of innocence and the ensuing surge of violence.

After 1965, Botero began perfecting and consolidating his style: He reduced his palette to five colors, which he no longer applied directly to the canvas, mixing them instead before applying them in layers to the surface.[29] An example of these changes is *El secuestro*, which fashions a smoother finish and a simpler color scheme. Botero's lines

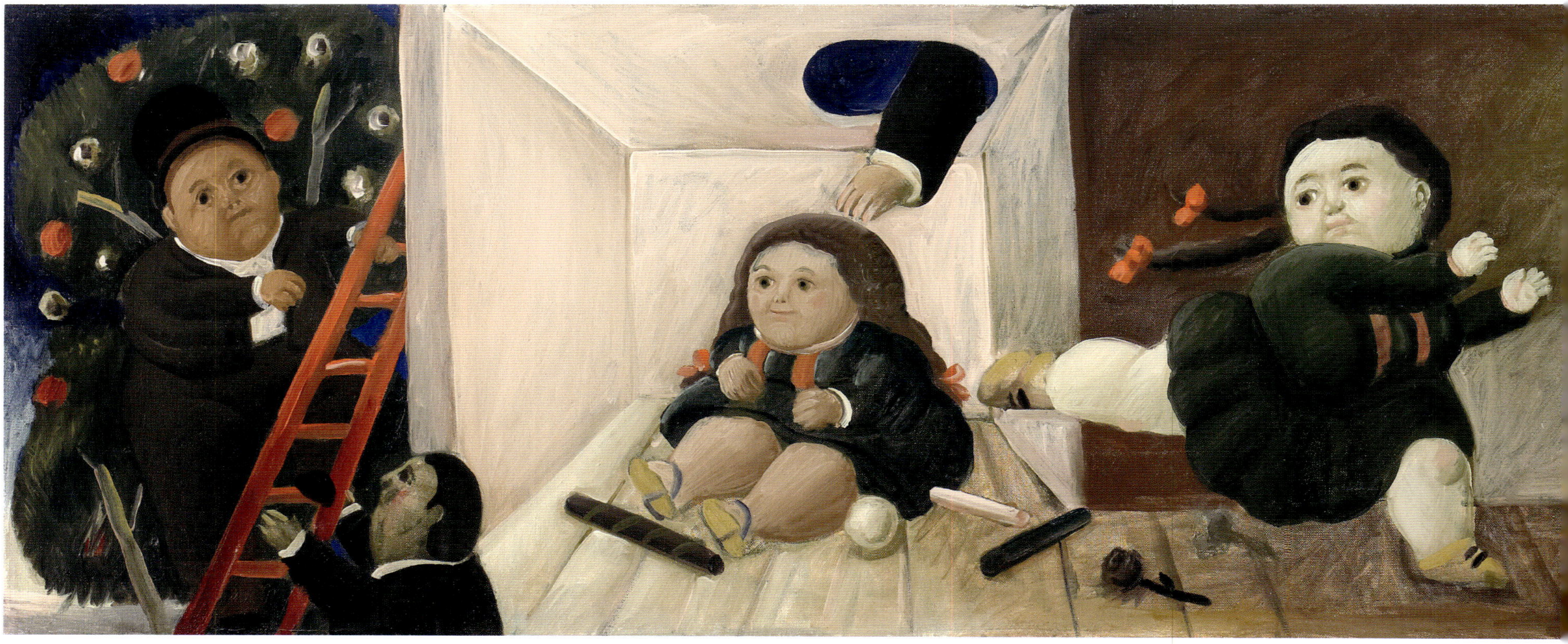

PLATE 69

Fernando Botero • *El secuestro* [The Kidnapping], 1966

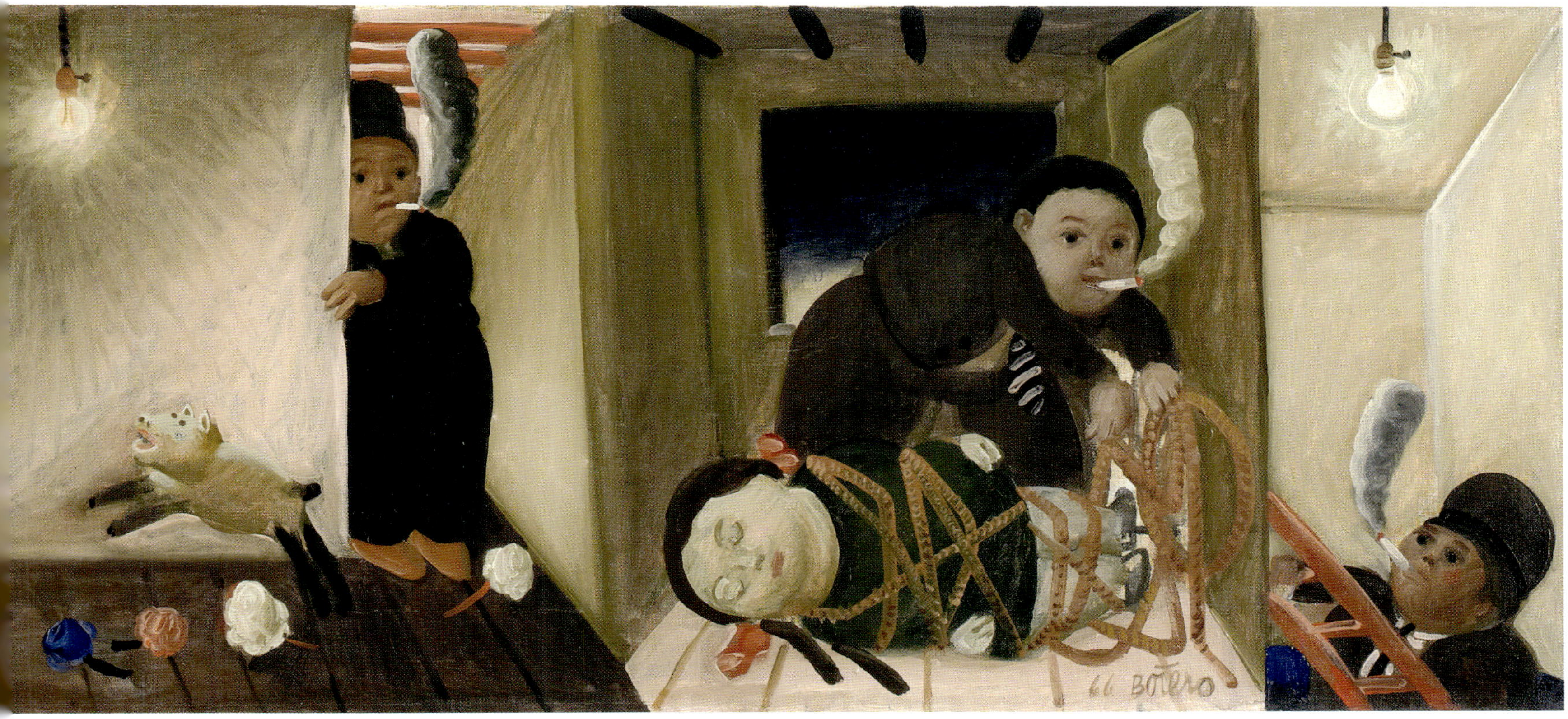
66 BOTERO

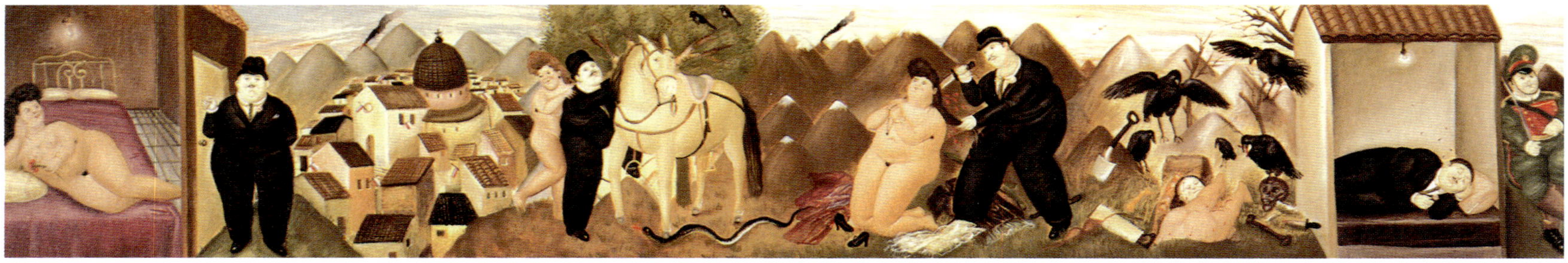

FIG. 7

are also more controlled, as demonstrated in *Bowl of Fruits* (1975) (plate 70). In this drawing, Botero shows his virtuosity as a draftsman. Here, Botero's use of graphite is like metal point, achieving a perfect shadowing and modeling of the fruit, which works in consonance with the oxidation of produce that has been cut and left to stand for only a couple of minutes. Equally, as with the *Bowl of Fruits,* Botero's watercolor titled *Naturaleza muerta* [Still Life] (1980) (plate 71) shows his absolute mastery of a technique other than painting. In this work, there are no traces of Botero's brush, an astonishing feat for such an unforgiving medium. The gradations are so even that it looks as if the work were aided by a mechanical tool, such as an airbrush. All of this is to say that, by this time, any individual touches or traces of the artist's hand had been completely eradicated from his works. In describing Botero in an essay published in 1969, Marta Traba wrote that, "[the artist] who stands out, in such a grading city like New York, is precisely he who remains 'different' and not the one who repeats, like a simian, the stipulated gestures."[30] Even if this phrase rang true once, it proves today to be a sad paradox. A careful study of Botero's catalogue raisonné, which curiously covers only his paintings from 1975 to 1990, does nothing but reiterate that starting in the late 1970s and continuing into the 1980s, Botero's works began to suffer from a malady that still follows him to this day: facile repetition. For instance, the year *Naturaleza muerta* was painted, Botero also made eleven other pictures of fruit or pitchers, which raises eyebrows whether he has developed a cottage industry that panders to the art market. However, and regardless of the direction his work has taken, to see the artwork of Fernando Botero through the lens of the Brillembourg Capriles Collection of Latin American Art is to gain insight into the life of an artist whose early struggles are now, in retrospect, a breath of fresh air. What is regrettable is that, after the mid-1960s, the artist began consolidating his repertoire and utilizing a style that has become too trivial for its own good.

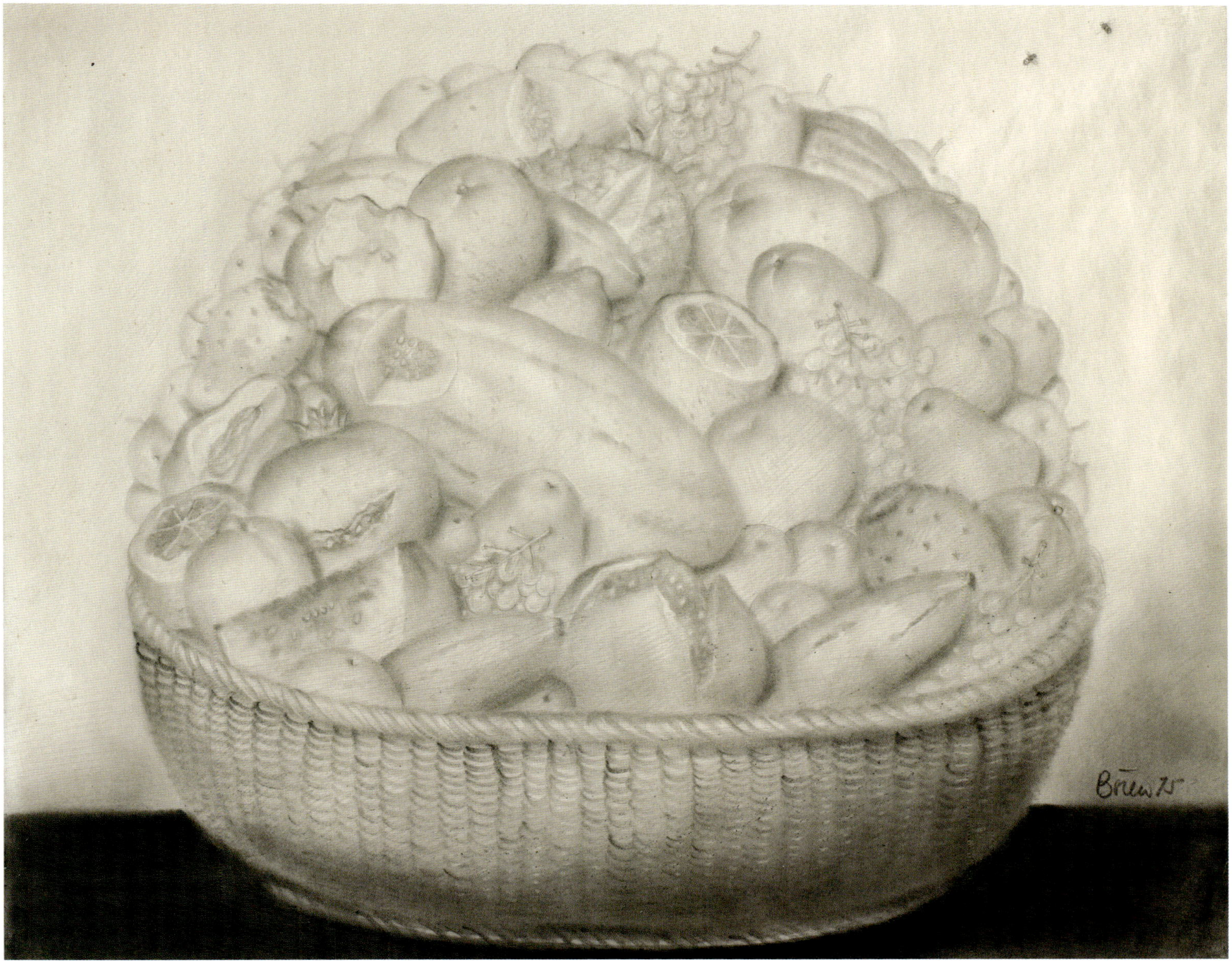

PLATE 70
Fernando Botero • *Bowl of Fruits,* 1975

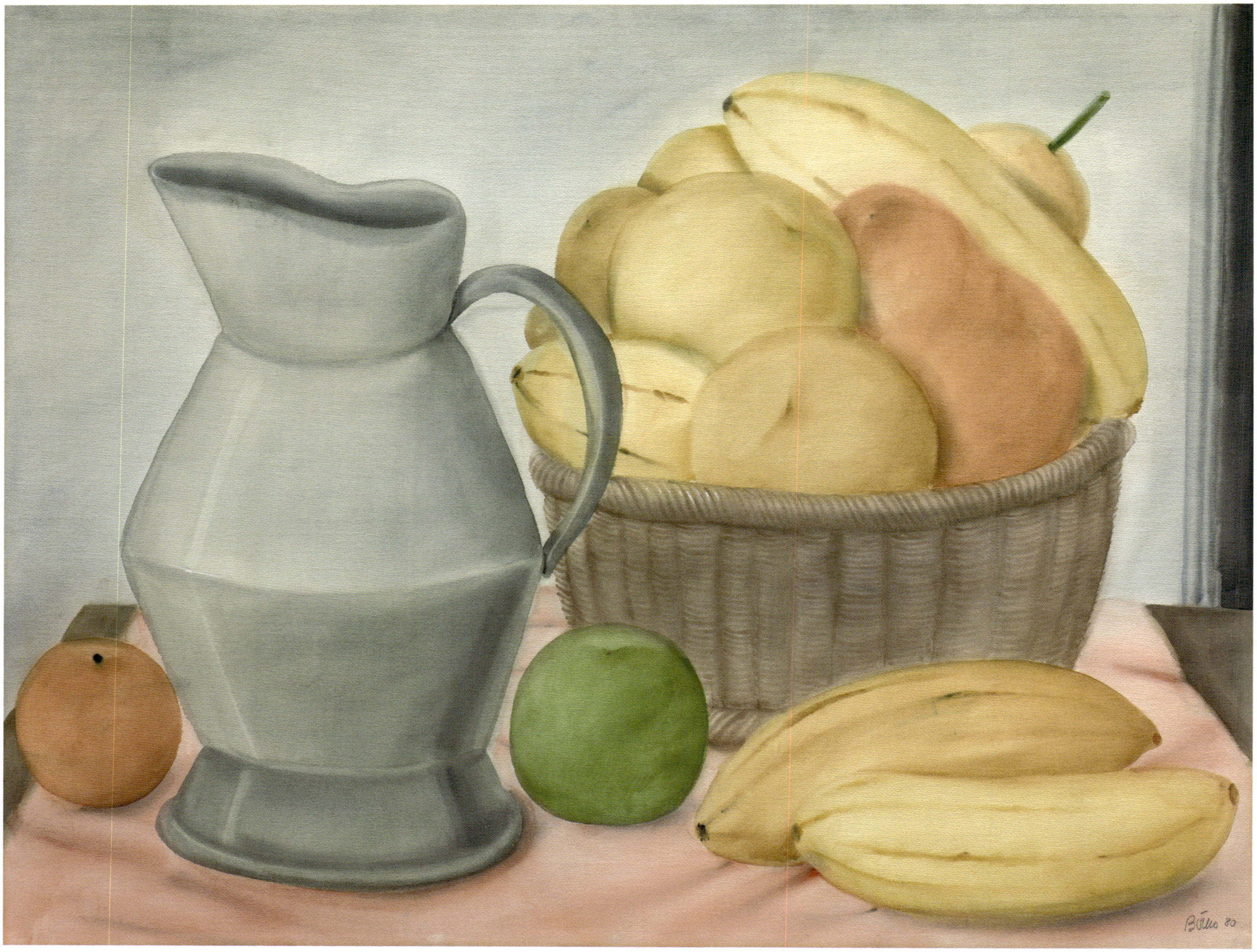

PLATE 71

Fernando Botero • *Naturaleza muerta* [Still Life], 1980

ILLUSTRATIONS IN TEXT

FIGURE 1
Fernando Botero
La camera degli sposi, Homenaje a Mantegna I [The Couple's Chamber, Homage to Mantegna I], 1958
Oil on canvas
67 x 79 inches (170 x 201 cm)
Private collection

FIGURE 2
Fernando Botero
El niño de Vallecas
[The Boy from Vallecas], 1959
Oil on canvas
52 x 55 ½ inches (132 x 141 cm)
From the collection of Fernando Botero

FIGURE 3
Fernando Botero
Mona Lisa, Age Twelve, 1959
Oil and tempera on canvas
83 ⅛ x 77 inches (211 x 195.5 cm)
The Museum of Modern Art, New York, Inter-American Fund

FIGURE 4
Fernando Botero
La apoteosis de Ramón Hoyos
[The Apotheosis of Ramón Hoyos], 1959
Oil on canvas
67 ¾ x 123 ½ inches (172 x 314 cm)
From the collection of Fernando Botero

FIGURE 5
Beatriz González
Encajera Almanaque Pielroja
[Lacemaker Pielroja Almanac], 1964
Oil on canvas
39 x 33 ½ inches (100 x 85 cm)
From the collection of Beatriz González, Bogotá, Colombia

FIGURE 6
Fernando Botero
The Life of Honorius III, 1961
Oil on canvas
21 x 107 ½ inches (53 x 273 cm)
Hirshhorn Museum and Sculpture Garden, Smithsonian Institution, Washington, DC, Gift of Joseph H. Hirshhorn, 1966

FIGURE 7
Fernando Botero
El asesinato de Ana Rosa Calderón
[The Murder of Ana Rosa Calderón], 1969
Oil on canvas
111 ½ x 18 ½ inches (283 x 47 cm)
Private collection

NOTES

1
Edward Sullivan, "Fernando Botero: Critical Strategies," in *The Baroque World of Fernando Botero* (Alexandria, VA, and New Haven, CT: Art Services International and Yale University Press, 2007), 49.

2
The Museum of Modern Art, "Recent Acquisitions of Paintings and Sculptures on View at the Museum of Modern Art," news release, December 20, 1961, http://www.moma.org/docs/press_archives/2938/releases/MOMA_1961_0153_151.pdf?2010.

3
Marta Traba, "Un gran cuadro en el Salón Nacional," *El Tiempo*, September 14, 1958, 12.

4
"Botero," *60 Minutes*, CBS Broadcasting Inc., November 8, 1998, quoted in Monique Roelofs, "Theorizing the Aesthetic Homeland: Racialized Aesthetic Nationalism in Daily Life and the Art World," in *Constructing the Nation: A Race and Nationalism Reader*, eds. Mariana Ortega and Linda Martin Alcoff (New York: State University of New York Press, 2009), 212.

5
Marta Traba, "Las dos líneas extremas de la pintura colombiana: Botero y Ramírez Villamizar," *Eco* (Bogotá: Colombia, 1969); repr., *Marta Traba* (Bogotá: Planeta, 1984), 51.

6
Ibid.

7
Fernando Botero and Peter Stepan, "Interview with Fernando Botero," in *Fernando Botero: Paintings and Drawings*, ed. Werner Spies (Munich: Prestel-Verlag, 1992), 154.

8
Ricardo Pau-Llosa, "Botero and the New Folklore," *Art International* 26 (1983): 60.

9
Ibid.

10
In 1962, thanks to his friendship with Marina Ospina, Botero met Willem de Kooning, Franz Kline, and Mark Rothko.

11
Miller was looking for another artist's studio.

12
Nubia Janeth González Ruiz, "Colombia en la pintura de Fernando Botero: El realismo mágico en el imaginario Boteriano" (Ph.D. diss., Universitat Politècnica de Catalunya, 2006), 77.

13
The Museum of Modern Art, "Recent Acquisitions," news release, December 20, 1961.

14
Cynthia Jaffee McCabe, *Fernando Botero* (Washington, DC: Hirshhorn Museum and Sculpture Garden, 1979), 15. Comments such as this one are not infrequent in interviews with Botero and in the literature about his work. However, this is a distortion of history, probably due to the scathing reviews he received for his solo show at The Contemporaries gallery in New York in 1962. For instance, Jack Kroll wrote in *Artnews*: "This is his first show in New York but last year one of these specialties disfigured a whole wall in a Museum of Modern Art 'New Acquisitions' show. The specialty is a monstrously glandiose [sic] Lolita cramming a large canvas, like the secret spawn of Mussolini and an idiot peasant girl." "Reviews and Previews: New Names this Month," *Artnews* 61 (1962): 20.

15
Ramón Hoyos was a famous Colombian cyclist born in 1932 in Antioquia, the same province as Botero.

16
The Museum of Modern Art, "Recent Acquisitions," news release, December 20, 1961.

17
Jacquline Barnitz, *Twentieth-Century Art of Latin America* (Austin, TX: University of Texas Press, 2001), 251–52.

18
For a more-substantive argument regarding the definitions of and differences between Latin American and American and English Pop art, see Mercedes Trelles Hernández, "The Contested Object: Pop Art in Latin America, 1964–1974" (Ph.D. diss., Harvard University, 2001–2), 1–32.

19
In her dissertation, Trelles Hernández explains that, "according to investigator Maria Iovino, the first time the word 'Pop' was used in Colombia was in relation to Bernardo Salcedo's work in an article that appeared on November 1, 1964, in the newspaper *El Tiempo*." Ibid., 81.

20
Ibid., 29–30.

21
Ibid., 84.

22
David Elliot, "A Painter of Lost and Angry Pictures," in *The Baroque World of Fernando Botero*, 40–41.

23
This was also an international trend: In the United States, Larry Rivers made this practice popular; in Mexico, Alfredo Gironella, Alejandro Colunga, and other artists; in Peru, Hermán Braun. For more information, see Oriana Baddeley, *Drawing the Line: Art and Cultural Identity in Contemporary Latin America, Critical Studies in Latin American Culture* (New York, New York: Verso, 1989); repr., Verso, 1992, 43–67.

24
In Colombia, galleries and bookstores organized exhibitions of reproductions. See Trelles Hernández, "The Contested Object," 92–93.

25
Ibid., 96–97.

26
One of Botero's first jobs in Colombia was that of set designer—a job he obtained because of his friendship with the writers Carlos Jiménez, Jaime Piedrahita, and Gonzalo Arango. Walter Engel, *Botero* (Bogotá: Casa Editorial Eddy Torres, 1952), 6.

27
Santiago Londoño Vélez, *Botero in the Museo Nacional de Colombia, New Donation 2004* (Bogotá: Villegas Editores, 2004), 9.

28
Ana María Reyes, "Fernando Botero's Pictorial Language of *La Violencia* (1946–1996) in Colombia" (MA diss., University of Chicago, 1996, revisions 2000), 20.

29
González Ruiz, "Colombia en la pintura de Fernando Botero," 82 and 89.

30
Traba, "Las dos líneas extremas de la pintura colombiana," 54.

Marcela Guerrero

ANTONIO SEGUÍ

"THE CHORUS OF *ACTIVE* FOOTSTEPS"[1]

CAUGHT WALKING IN MIDAIR, as if he is exiting the canvas on which he has lived his solitary life, the man whom Antonio Seguí depicts in his works has been forever present. For the past fifty years, Seguí has captured—from his studio house in France—the tension of a man surrounded by an air of innocent humor but who, after closer inspection, reveals an uneasy attitude toward the city. In three paintings by Seguí from the Brillembourg Capriles Collection of Latin American Art, the artist enlivens his primarily static figure with a sense of movement that calls to mind a passage from French theorist Michel de Certeau's *The Practices of Everyday Life*:

> The ordinary practitioners of the city live "down below," below the thresholds at which visibility begins. They walk—an elementary form of this experience of the city; they are walkers, *Wandersmänner*, whose bodies follow the thicks and thins of an urban "text" they write without being able to read it. The practitioners make use of spaces that cannot be seen; their knowledge of them is as blind as that of lovers in each other's arms.[2]

Certeau's essay, a semiotic analysis of the rhetoric of urban life, contrasts the vantage point of looking down from a building from where one can "read" the "text" with the actual practices of "writing" it. According to Certeau, to stand atop the 110th floor of one of the most iconic buildings in New York City is to admire the elevation that transforms the viewer into a voyeur. Standing before Seguí's paintings creates a similarly healthy distance that permits one to read the ways in which his ubiquitous wanderer weaves the diverse, conflicting languages of a city into the fibers of his being. Seguí invites us as viewers to play the role of voyeur as a way of gaining insight into his vocabulary as a painter of postwar art.

Central to both Certeau's and Seguí's work is the representation of the human figure as a protagonist struggling to make sense out of the complexities of urban life. Consider that, in the case of Seguí, he began working in the 1950s, when figuration fell out of favor and echoes of Clement Greenberg's statement that, "any painter not working abstractly is working in a minor mode," resounded loudly. Yet certain groups of artists in both Europe and the Americas weathered the nonobjective storm and revived, in the 1950s and 1960s, the appreciation for the human figure in art. Their desire to restore the figure's historically prominent place in painting provided a means of countering the existential anxiety engendered by the postwar years. Moreover, the reintroduction of the figure symbolized the need for a greater humanity in the world of contemporary economics, politics, and culture. In *El que piensa demasiado* [The One Who Thinks Too Much] (1986) (plate 72), *Una ciudad, una historia, un tormento* [A City, A History, A Torment] (1990) (plate 73), and *Gente rodeando el monumento a Humphrey Bogart* [People Surrounding the Monument of Humphrey Bogart] (1993) (plate 74), Seguí focuses on the figure of a peripatetic man whose erratic movements speak to his conflictive relationship with his immediate surroundings. Seguí projects onto his provincial *flâneur* an identity that he constructed from his childhood memories of Córdoba in the 1930s and 1940s, as well as from his later experiences in Paris, which informed his mature style of painting. This identity reflects his own philosophy: "I'd rather be a

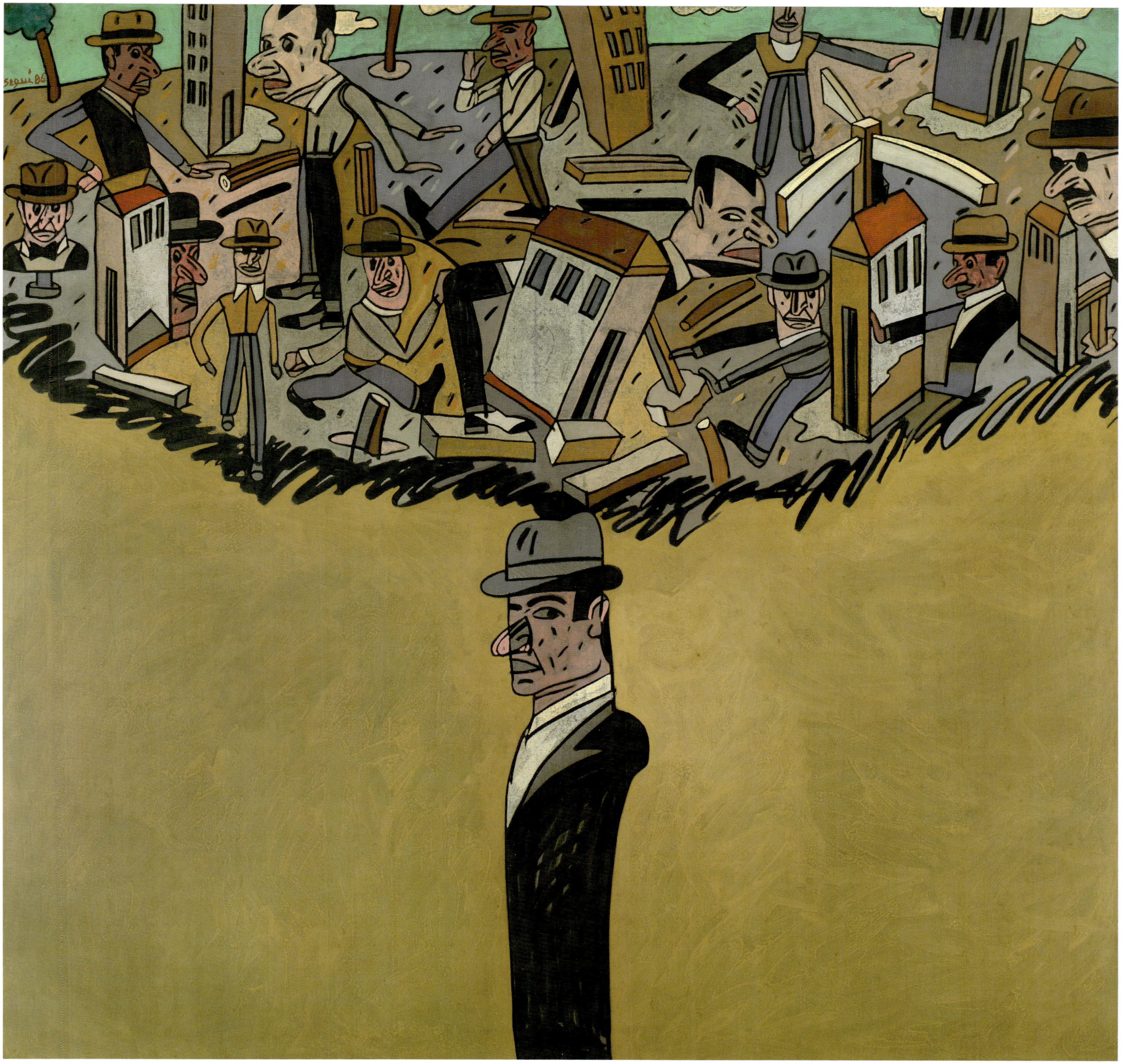

PLATE 72

Antonio Seguí • *El que piensa demasiado* [The One Who Thinks Too Much], 1986

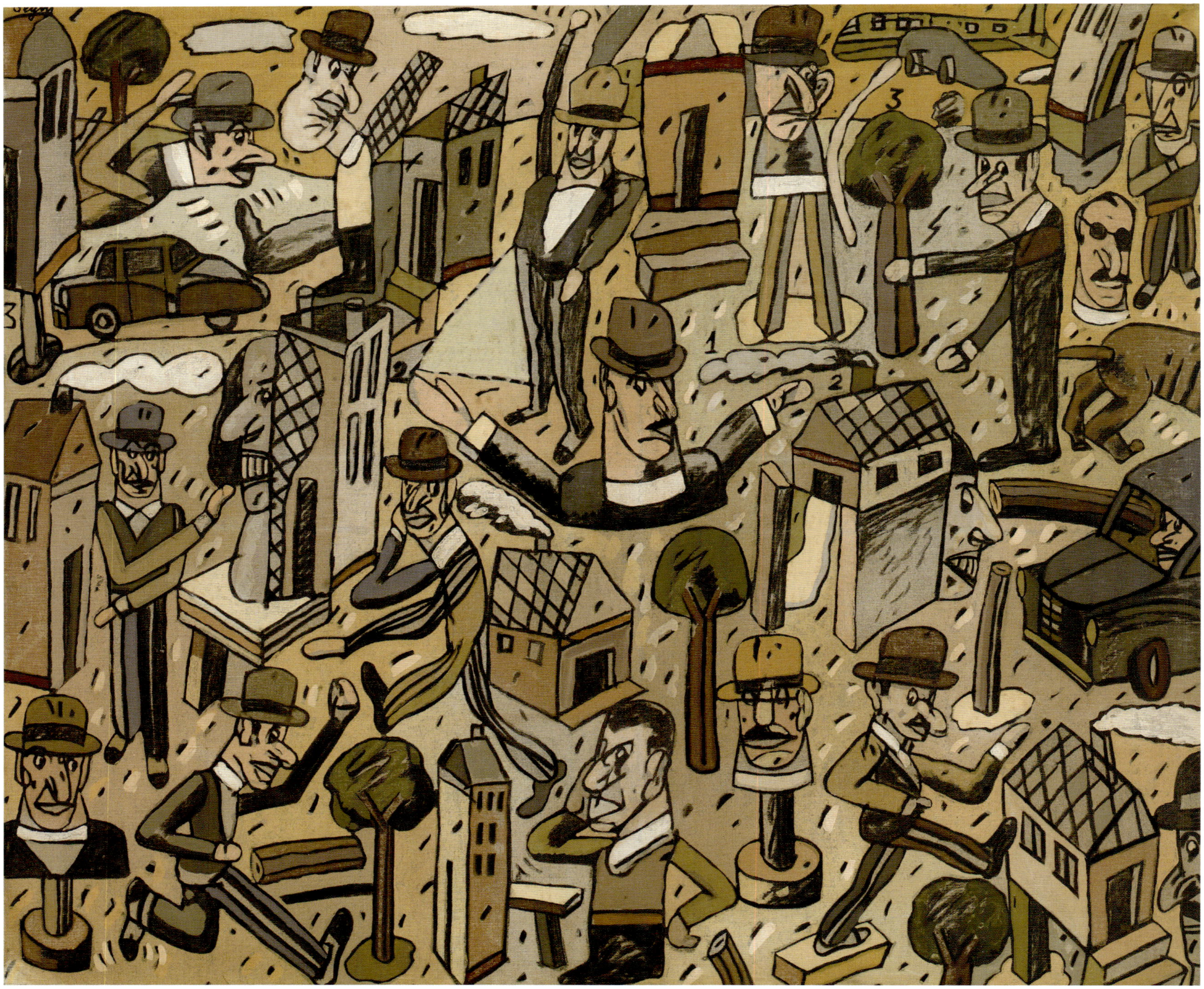

PLATE 73

Antonio Seguí • *Una ciudad, una historia, un tormento* [A City, A History, A Torment], 1990

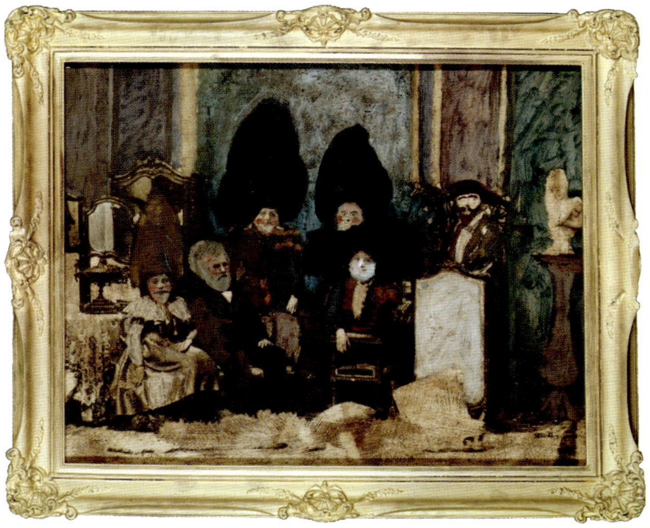

FIG. 1

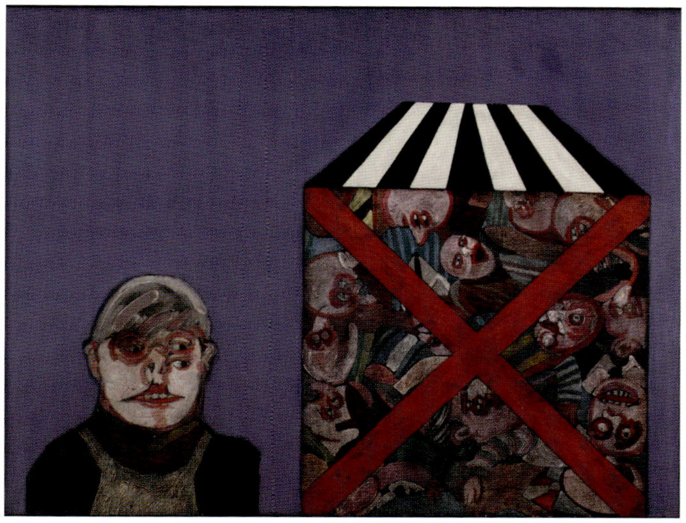

FIG. 2

Latin American in Paris than a *cordobés* in Buenos Aires."[3] To convey this feeling of cultural marginality, Seguí employs the vocabularies of French Figuration narrative [Narrative Figuration] and transatlantic Pop art without feeling a need to profess an allegiance to or join either artistic group or movement.

Seguí first brought his wanderer to life on canvas between 1963 and 1965. Before he moved to France in 1963, and after a prolonged sojourn in Latin America, Seguí returned to his native Argentina, where he exhibited with the Otra figuración [Another Figuration] artists.[4] During this period, Seguí experimented artistically, seeking to eliminate any trace of academicism in Argentine art. Shortly after participating in the group show *Arte destructivo* [Destructive Art] in 1961, Seguí brought back the human figure to his work and also introduced numbers, letters, and other graphic elements reminiscent of comics.[5] Leading up to his departure for France, Seguí worked on a series of garishly framed collages titled *Metamorfosis de Doña Felicitas Naón* [The Metamorphosis of Doña Felicitas Naon] (fig. 1) that were intended as mordant commentaries on the bourgeois families of contemporary Buenos Aires.

The Felicitas Naón series heralded a transitional moment, not only because Seguí decided to stay in France after exhibiting his series there, but also because his technique and content would undergo transformative changes. Having benefited from absorbing artistic sensibilities on both sides of the Atlantic, Seguí began to tone down his palette: He flattened the thickness of the impasto and rendered the figure of a man (as opposed to the woman seen in the Felicitas Naón series) more prominently and through systematic repetition.[6] Seguí's grappling with contemporary society took an introspective turn with the focus on a single figure: Señor Gustavo [Mr. Gustavo][7] is based on Segui's childhood memories of the way his father, grandfather, and male tango dancers, or *compadritos*, used to dress when he was growing up in Córdoba. Donning a fedora, a double-breasted jacket, and a pair of two-tone wingtip shoes (a style that Seguí embraces to this day), the man in paintings such as *Una ciudad, una historia, un tormento* also dates back to Seguí's memories of playing with lead soldiers modeling sharp gestures and stiff stances.[8] In *Gente rodeando el monumento a Humphrey Bogart*, he transcends the *horror vacui* of his canvases by not staying inside the lines, and the numbers all around the canvas are, according to him, a playful reference to connect-the-dots drawings.

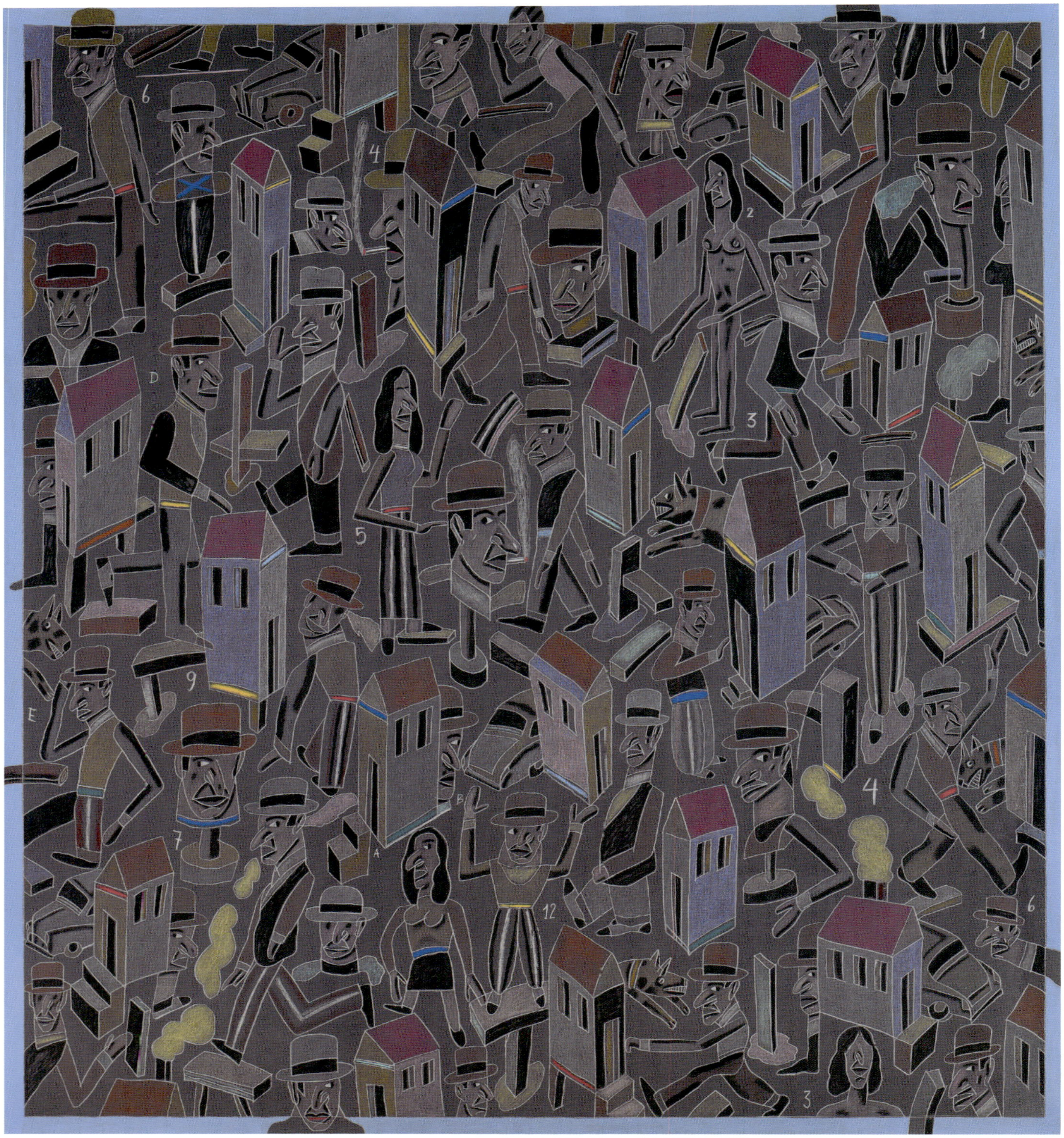

PLATE 74

Antonio Seguí • *Gente rodeando el monumento de Humphrey Bogart*
[People Surrounding the Monument of Humphrey Bogart], 1993

The character development one begins to see in an untitled work from 1963 (fig. 2), for example, was not the result of happenstance. Among the many artistic novelties occurring in France during those first years of Seguí's arrival was the recent creation by Argentine artist Antonio Berni of the fictional character Ramona Montiel (fig. 3), which he unveiled at the *Berni: Gravures récentes* [Berni: Recent Prints] exhibition held at the Galerie du Passeur in May 1963.[9] A year later, French critic Gérald Gassiot-Talabot organized the exhibition *Mythologies quotidiennes* [Everyday Mythologies], in which Berni and a host of other Figuration narrative artists participated. What motivated this group of artists to exhibit together, according to Gassiot-Talabot, was not only a desire to distance themselves from the flood of American Pop and Neo-Dada works then arriving in France, but also the realization that it was time to critically evaluate the daily societal influences that "traumatize modern man."[10] While not artistically involved with this group, Seguí took stock of the situation by tapping into his own biography and portraying the unrelenting tension between a man and a city that is not his own. Works such as *La visita* [The Visit] (1982) (fig. 4) invite a reading of Seguí's everyman who, whether in Buenos Aires or Paris, cannot escape the push-pull forces that ultimately cause him to feel perpetually displaced. However, the throwback to 1930s and 1940s Argentine compadritos—coupled with the frenetic, almost paranoid figure shown in constant movement—point to a popular vocabulary that transcended the art scene in France.

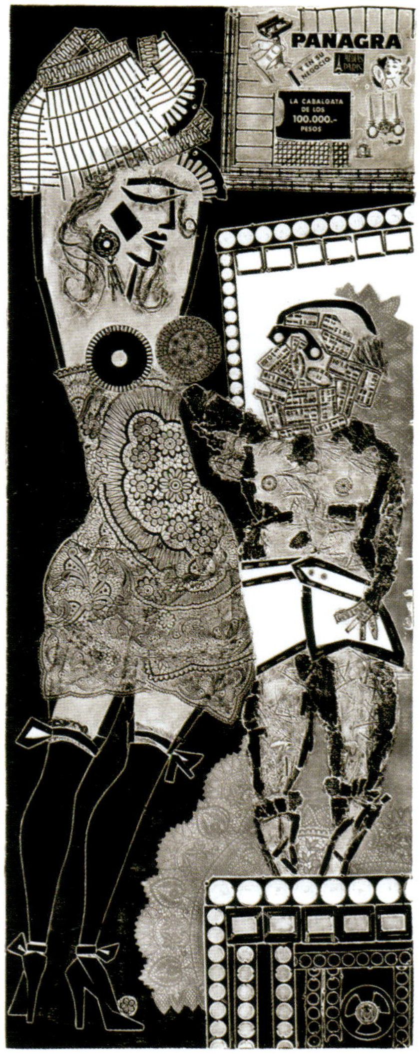

FIG. 3

The Figuration narrative movement in France was not the only one that had an impact on Seguí's artistic development. Seguí believes that the dose of humor he injects into his works is informed by his native Córdoba—a city noted for its unmistakable wit—and by his appreciation of British Pop art, which he most likely had the opportunity to examine at the Troisième Biennale de Paris [Third Paris Biennial] in 1963, where he, too, exhibited his work.[11] And while the mass-produced effect of Pop and the impersonality of the characters portrayed are at odds with his paintings, Seguí still borrows from the legacy of transatlantic Pop art the telegraphic language of comic strips, specifically the use of the comic-strip balloon in *El que piensa*

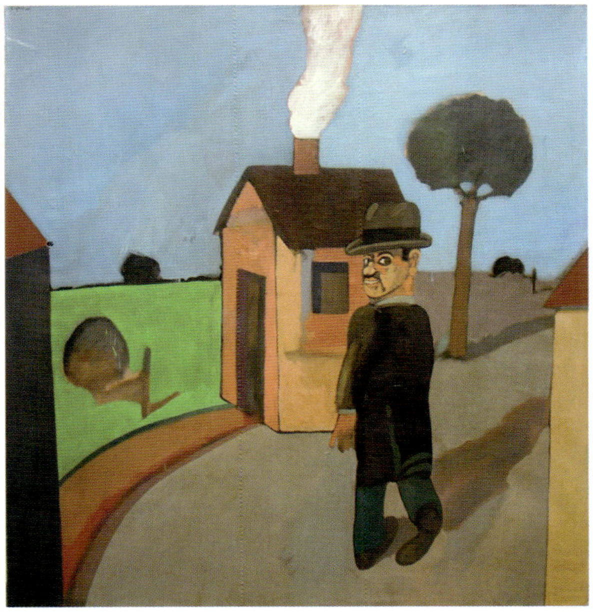

FIG. 4

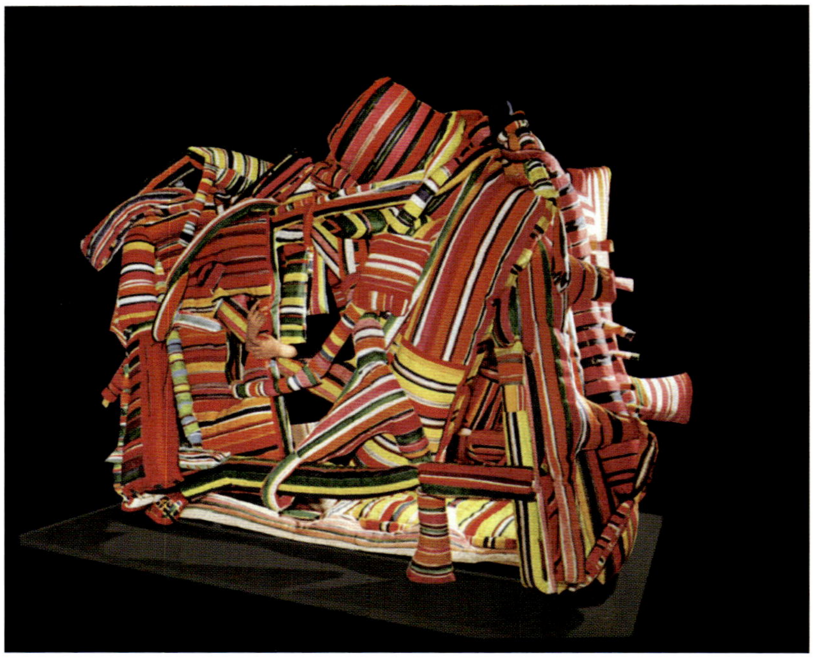

FIG. 5

demasiado and the interspersed short lines one associates with rain or rapid movements.[12] He further highlights the vocabulary of Pop art by painting the upper register of *El que piensa demasiado* to resemble a newspaper: grayish ink matter so characteristic of daily journals seeps through the background. This is in part because Seguí never begins with a white canvas; instead, after applying acrylic, he removes part of it with blotting paper.[13] In *Una ciudad, una historia, un tormento* and *Gente rodeando el monumento a Humphrey Bogart*, we also see the playful presence of numbers (and a few letters) that have been scattered throughout the paintings, repeated, and even skipped.[14]

Pop art at that time was not only an Anglo-Saxon phenomenon; in 1964 and 1965, the presence of French critic Pierre Restany in Latin America was quite important to the development of Pop art on the continent.[15] As the titular head of the 1960 movement Nouveau Réalisme [New Realism], the French response to American and British Pop art, Restany had published "Buenos Aires y el nuevo humanismo" [Buenos Aires and the New Humanism] in the Argentine journal *Planeta* in 1965. Restany championed Argentine artists' awareness of the folklore found in the streets of Buenos Aires and the incorporation of this cosmopolitan vocabulary into what he called "Pop *lunfardo*" (Argentine slang Pop art).[16] According to Restany, Pop lunfardo captures the physical and psychological dimensions of Buenos Aires cosmopolitism,[17] an essence that Seguí illustrates when, in his urban scenes, he paints a man who goes everywhere yet never arrives at a particular destination. Nevertheless, this is where the similarities between Seguí's work and Pop art in Argentina end. As exemplified by the quintessential Pop artist Marta Minujín (fig. 5), Pop art in this country was about producing an "art of things" that embraced the ephemeral: transient objects, installations, and happenings.[18]

Ultimately, what distinguishes Seguí's work from that of the Figuration narrative and Pop artists is the shift in the content and tone of his works. While seemingly naïve, his paintings soon take a turn into chronicling darker and more mischievous behaviors that are often the consequence of living in an urban city and coping with its rapid pace. Beyond Seguí's stated intentions, the scholarship on Seguí has overlooked other unaccounted-for elements. For instance, the figure of a man protruding limb by limb from a constrictive structure that stands on shaky grounds in *El que piensa demasiado* (fig. 6) illustrates the tension between the private space of a house and the public acts performed in open spaces. This marks the most confounding realization about Seguí's work; for all of its childlike qualities, there is no escaping the more provocative and transgressive acts carried out by the figure traversing space. Tree trunks, structural columns, dog tails, and smoke-blowing cigarettes often create the phallic imagery seen in each of the three canvases. The shape and angle of the noses could also be read as stand-ins for phalli. In *Gente rodeando el monumento a Humphrey Bogart*, one of the women that Seguí depicts is rendered naked and with masculine features that are emphasized by the diagonal log depicted directly in front of her; a small puddle that is suggestive of semen runs down the canvas.

To circle back to the beginning of this essay: the *Wandersmänner* whom Certeau describes and whom Seguí brings to life in the figure of Señor Gustavo attempts with each step to secure his footing in a

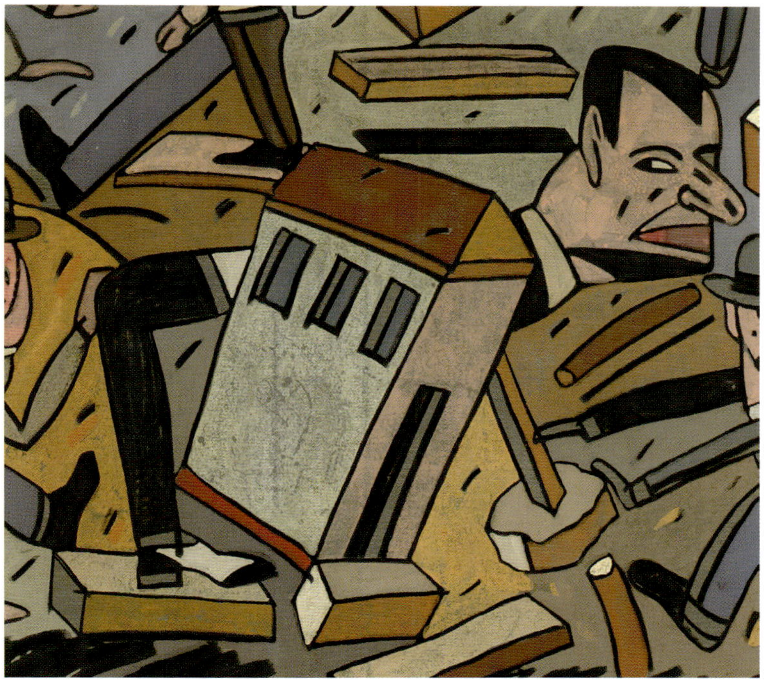

FIG. 6

world that is not home. By conjuring a fragmented space created from his childhood memories of Argentina in the 1930s and 1940s, Seguí has denounced the physical and moral alienation that he experienced as a Latin American artist from Córdoba working in France. As readers of these complex paintings, we realize that with our critical proximity to this wanderer, we help him break his solitary confinement. In the end, Seguí has summoned us from our voyeuristic perch and placed us closer, more intimately, to the urban dweller caught between the light and the dark sides of the city.

ILLUSTRATIONS IN TEXT

FIGURE 1
Antonio Seguí
Familia de Felicitas, Estado Final
[Felicita's Family, Final State]
From the series *Metamorfosis de Doña Felicitas Naón* [The Metamorphosis of Doña Felicitas Naon], 1962
Oil on photograph mounted on wood
31 ½ x 39 ⅜ inches (80 x 100 cm)
Private collection, Zürich, Switzerland

FIGURE 2
Antonio Seguí
Sin título [Untitled], 1963
Oil on canvas
38 x 51 inches (96.3 x 130 cm)
Museo de Arte Moderno de Buenos Aires

FIGURE 3
Antonio Berni
Ramona y el viejo [Ramona and the Old Man]
From the series *Los amigos de Ramona* [Ramona's Friends], 1962
Xilo-collage relief
55 ¾ x 21 ½ inches (142 x 55 cm)
The Museum of Fine Arts, Houston, Gift of Eduardo and Eugenia Grüneisen, 2003.258

FIGURE 4
Antonio Seguí
La visita [The Visit], 1982
Oil on canvas
59 x 59 inches (150 x 150 cm)
Nohra Haime Gallery

FIGURE 5
Marta Minujín
Revuélquese y viva
[Wallow Around and Live], 1964
Installation with polychrome mattresses and wood
8 x 7 x 6 ft. (2.40 x 2.20 x 2 m)

FIGURE 6
Antonio Seguí
Detail of *El que piensa demasiado*
[The One Who Thinks Too Much], 1986
Acrylic on canvas
59 ⅛ x 63 ⅛ inches (150.2 x 160.3 cm)
The Brillembourg Capriles Collection of Latin American Art

NOTES

1
"The Chorus of Idle Footsteps" is the name of the second section in Chapter Seven, "Walking in the City," of Michel de Certeau's *The Practices of Everyday Life* (Berkeley: University of California Press, 1984), 97. I want to make clear that by changing the word "idle" to "active," I am not challenging Certeau's argument. "Idle footsteps," or better "*des pas perdu*," is his expression for the trace of fleeting footsteps within the city. Because of how swiftly passersby experience the city, it is impossible for urban planners and architects to prescribe or to predict the infinite possibilities for the ways in which pedestrians move around their urban environments, and this movement is for Certeau akin to the construction of language. I have used the word "active" to emphasize the actions performed by the figures in Seguí's paintings—a point I develop further in this essay.

2
Ibid., 93.

3
"Yo preferí ser un latinoamericano en París que un cordobés en Buenos Aires." Horacio Bilbao, "Entrevista con Antonio Seguí en París (Horacio Bilbao)," October 22, 2011. http://www.youtube.com/watch?v=4xokZZqz8xg

4
The Otra figuración artists were Rómulo Macció (b. 1931), Ernesto Deira (1928–1986), Jorge de la Vega (1930–1971), and Luis Felipe Noé (b. 1933).

5
Miriam Mabel Martínez, "Cronología," *Antonio Seguí: Hombre de ciudades* (Ciudad de México, DF: Museo Rufino Tamayo, 1997), 64.

6
Antonio Segui: Exposición retrospectiva 1958–1990 Premio Instituto Torcuato di Tella 1989 (Buenos Aires: Museo Nacional de Bellas Artes, 1991), 44.

7
Sr. Gustavo is the name given by art critic Caleb Bach, not by Seguí, as is often attributed.

8
"Reconstructing Childhood," Bleecker Street, 2004. http://www.antonio-segui.com/html-as-english/bleecker-en.html

9
Prior to this, in 1959 Antonio Berni (1905–1981) had created the character of Juanito Laguna, a boy from the slums of Argentina, which Seguí most likely saw in the artwork exhibited in November 1961 at the Galería Whitcomb (Whitcomb Gallery), where he also exhibited frequently.

10
Gérald Gassiot-Talabot, *Mythologies Quotidiennes* (Paris: Musée d'Art Moderne de la Ville de Paris, 1964), n.p.

11
In 1963, Seguí was invited to participate in the *Troisième Biennale de Paris: Manifestation biennal et international des jeunes artists* held at the Musée d'Art Moderne de la Ville de Paris, from September to November 1963. Daniel Abadié, *Antonio Seguí* (Paris: Editions Hazan, 2010), 281. Also showing works in this exhibition was a group of British Pop artists, namely Joe Tilson, Gerald Laing, Francis Morland, Peter Phillips, Peter Blake, Derek Boshier, Allen Jones, and David Hockney. David E. Brauer, *Pop Art: U.S./U.K. Connections, 1956–1966* (Ostfildern-Ruit, Germany: Hatje Kantz Verlag, 2001), 73.

12
In previous interviews, Seguí has talked about some of the political cartoons that served as a source of inspiration and that were published in magazines such as *Billikén*, *Leoplán*, *Caras y Caretas*, and in the famous almanacs named *Alpargatas*, which Molina Campos illustrated. However, I think these examples summarize the sources of inspiration for his graphic and early works. I would like to suggest that comic strips such as "Mutt and Jeff" (published in Argentina as "Mutt y Jeff" despite the fact that in other parts of Latin America, the comic strip was known as "Benitín y Eneas") could have been part of the comic milieu from which Seguí's work emerged. According to Siulnas (born Oscar Vázquez Lucio), author of *Historia del humor gráfico y escrito en la Argentina, Volumes I & II* (Buenos Aires: Eudeba, 1985 and 1987), "Mutt y Jeff" was published for the first time in Argentina in the magazine *Atlántida* in 1923 under the title "Paragüita y Miquelino" and, after 1936, under its official name, in the newspaper *Crítica*. In 1944 the comic strip was picked up by the comic magazine *Pandilla* and by the newspaper *Clarín*, in which it was published until 1979. Siulnas, email message to author, July 24, 2012.

13
Telephone conversation with the artist, July 19, 2012.

14
Although the use of numbers in art has a long history, it was the Neo-Dada and Pop artists in the late 1950s and 1960s who analyzed them for their semiotic value in contemporary culture. For example, when Jasper Johns initiated the Figures series, in 1955, he left the sequence 0 to 9 incomplete (he made paintings only for the numbers 1, 2, 5, and 7) and painted them without a particular order in mind as a way of denying the possibility of sequential counting. In Seguí's case, the deliberate disorderly arrangement of the numbers both disavows the premise of the eye focusing on a single element at once and reinforces the allover quality of the work.

15
In 1964, Restany was invited to participate as a juror in that year's edition of the Premio del Instituto Torcuato di Tella, whose national prize was awarded to Marta Minujín.

16
This is a paradigmatic text in the historiography of Argentine art of the 1960s because in it, Restany also foretells the imminent entry of Buenos Aires into the art market: "No está lejano el día en que Buenos Aires se cubrirá de una nube de coleccionistas, galerías, críticos y analistas, y sobre todo de creadores 'de un arte 100% o.'" (The day is not far when Buenos Aires will be covered by a cloud of collectors, galleries, critics, and analysts and, above all, creators of 'an art that is 100% Argentine.') Pierre Restany, "Buenos Aires y el nuevo humanismo," *Planeta*, no. 5 (May–June 1965), 119–29.

17
Ibid., 120.

18
Mercedes Trelles Hernández, "The Contested Object: Pop Art in Latin America, 1964–1974" (Ph.D. diss., Harvard University, 2002), 60. Subsequently, the "art of things" was displaced by an art of mass media in which the immateriality of the art object and the emphasis on communicating meaning took center stage.

María C. Gaztambide

THE DIALECTIC OF JACOBO BORGES

RECONCILING AESTHETICS AND POLITICS IN THE EARLY 1970s

IN THE MID-1960s, the Venezuelan painter Jacobo Borges (b. 1931) experienced a seismic rift in his trajectory when he faced the dilemma of whether to continue painting in the expressionistic style that had brought him much acclaim or to pursue an alternative route. At the crux of his theoretical reflection, which led him to abandon painting from 1965 to 1970, was the problem of reconciling his seemingly unrelated political activism in defense of Venezuela's nascent democracy with an aesthetic practice that had little to do with his political raison d'être. In the early 1970s, Borges picked himself up from the proverbial ashes and confronted technology and mass media—indeed, some of the main mechanisms that the dominant circles of power employed in exerting their control—head on. *Llegando de...* [Arriving from...] (1973) (plate 75) in the Brillembourg Capriles Collection of Latin American Art is part of a group of pictures executed following Borges's return to painting that offers an initial response to the artist's existential crisis. On the surface, works from this period incorporate photomechanical techniques borrowed from mass communication with which the artist experimented during his sabbatical from painting. On a deeper level, however, they also offer a lasting reflection on the communicative potential of painting that enabled Borges to merge his various interests at this point in time.

The breakthrough that heralded Borges's revived interest in painting was the realization that this medium could serve effectively to help disseminate his personal creed. The multidisciplinary event *Imagen de Caracas* that he had helped to organize in 1967[1] crystallized the idea

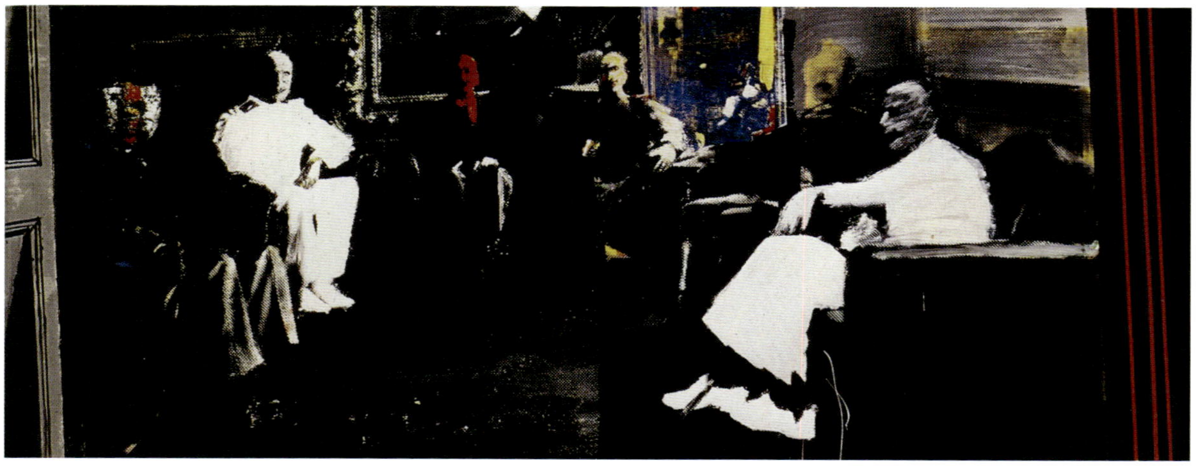

FIG. 1

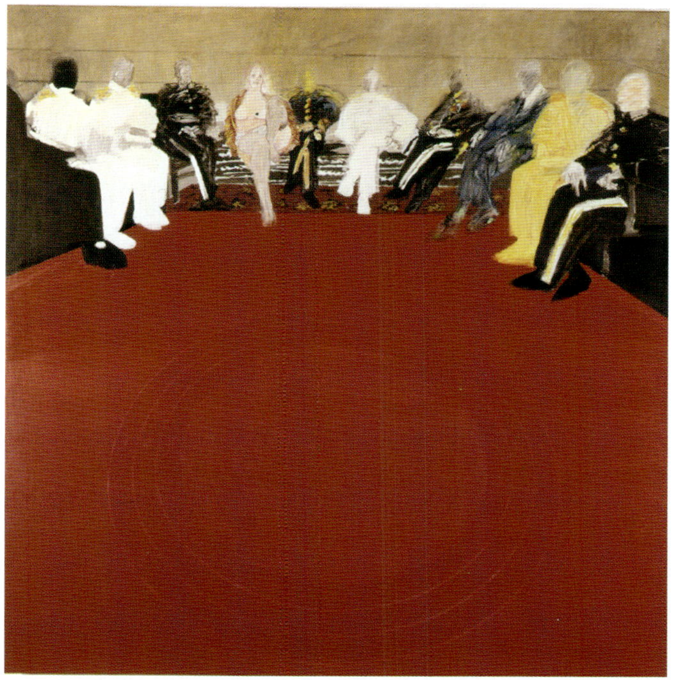

FIG. 2

that he could ostensibly subvert the barrage of mass-media images through his art. With this realization, Borges went on to create paintings that could establish a dialectical relationship with the spectator. What emerged in the early 1970s was a completely different type of nonliteral, *political* work that also reflected his interest in a heightened collective consciousness.

Llegando de. . . is one in a series of at least three works that includes its sister piece, *Esperando a. . .* [Waiting for. . .] (1973) (fig. 1), in the collection of Clara Diament Sujo and a monumental variant, *Reunión con círculo rojo* [Meeting with a Red Circle] (1973) (fig. 2), in the collection of the Museo de Arte Moderno in Mexico City.[2] In these works, Borges forgoes the violent brushstrokes and brutal color, the dislocation of figures, the aggressive metaphors, the illusion of spontaneity, and the fragmentary time characteristic of his expressionistic work from the 1960s, epitomized by *Humilde ciudadano* [Humble Citizen] (1964) (fig. 3). Instead, Borges's proposal shifts to using photographic source material—often an instrument for perpetuating stereotypes in mass media—in unique juxtapositions that drastically alter the weighted meaning that viewers assign to them.[3] Borges may have been exposed to the suggestive possibilities of the transfer of photographic images onto canvas through an exhibition of Robert Rauschenberg's series titled *Dante's Inferno* (1958–60) at Clara Diament Sujo's Estudio Actual in Caracas in 1969.[4] In Rauschenberg's work, including *Canto II: The Descent* from the series *Thirty-Four Illustrations for Dante's Inferno* (1958) (fig. 4) in the collection of The Museum of Modern Art in New York, the physicality of the photographic object remains largely intact, and in many cases the trace of the actual transfer is visible as a gesture that reminds us of his additive source.[5]

Despite his insufficient experimentation with the photographic medium at this time, Borges arrives at an innovative solution that is as effective at suggesting surface tension as the shattered picture planes of *Humilde ciudadano*: he counterweights the singularity and two-dimensionality of the photographic image with a number of technical experiments that further position the source and the art object at odds with one another. In *Llegando de. . .* the artist erases the evidence of his hand in the majority of the figures rendered—with the exception of the painterly figure in the foreground at the far right of the picture—imbuing them with a photomechanical quality that

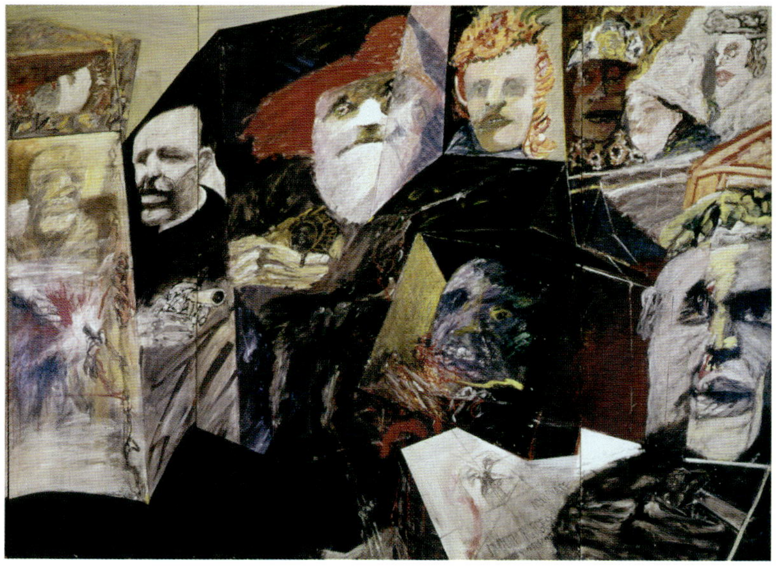

FIG. 3

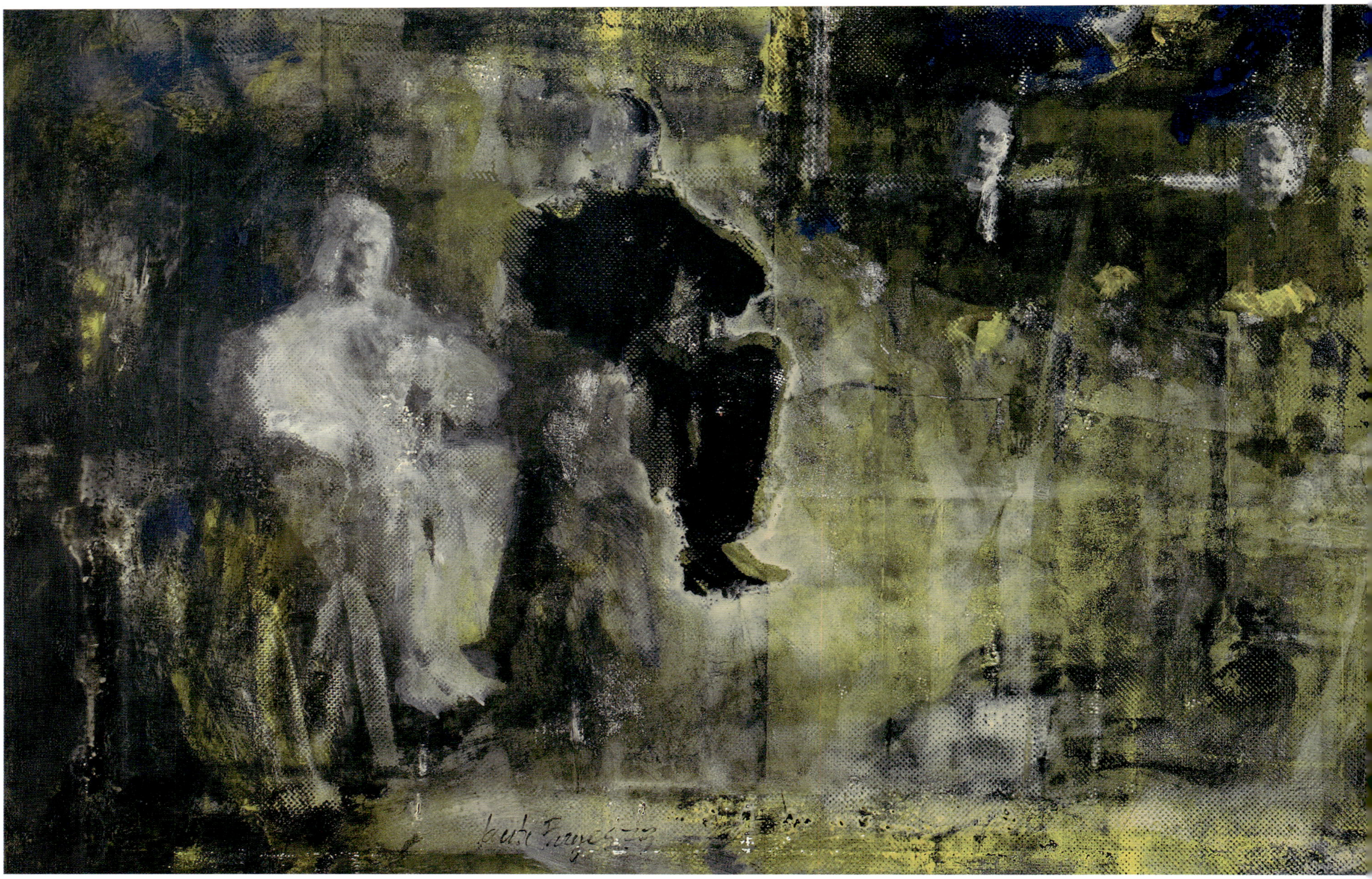

PLATE 75

Jacobo Borges • *Llegando de…* [Arriving from…], 1973

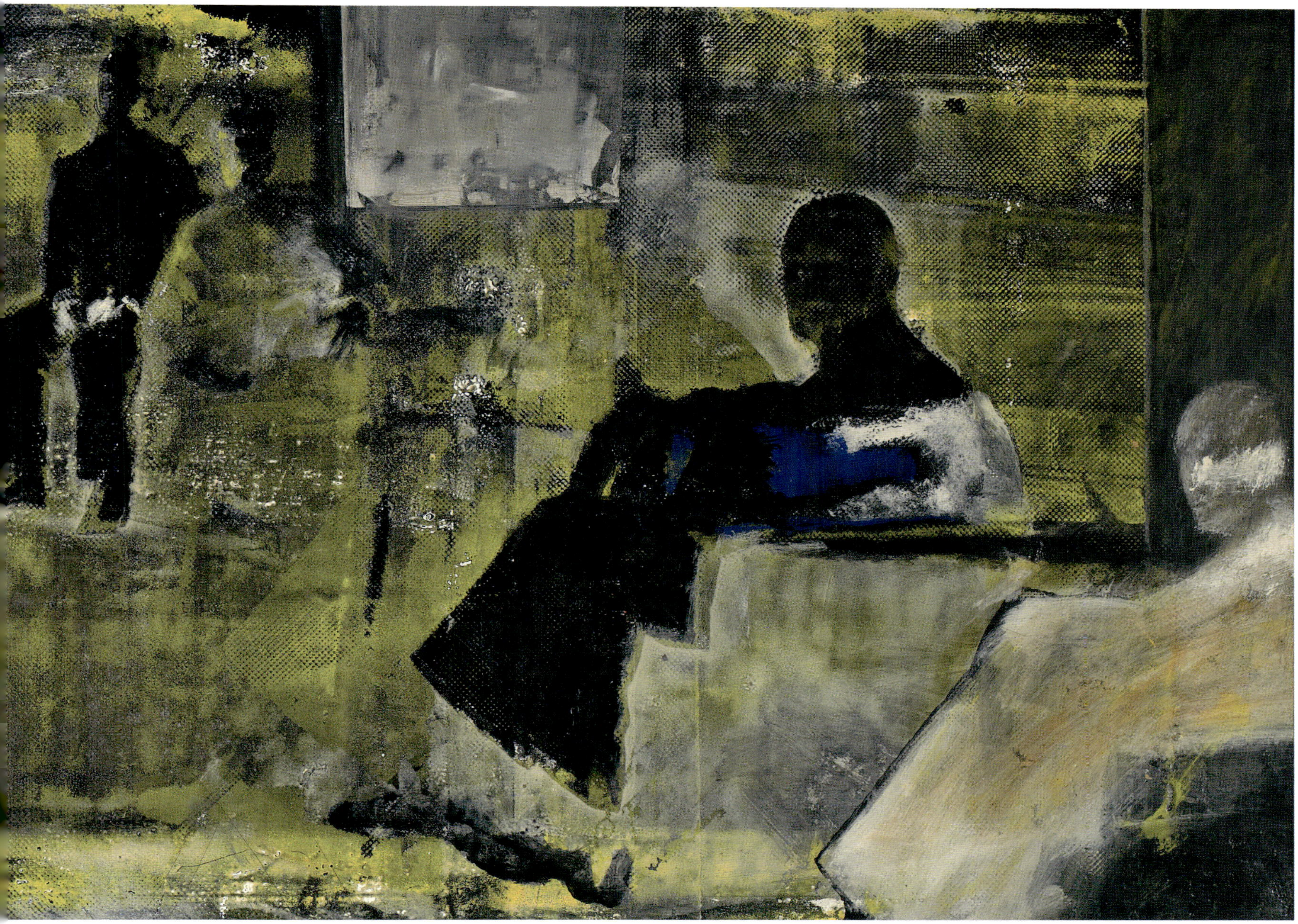

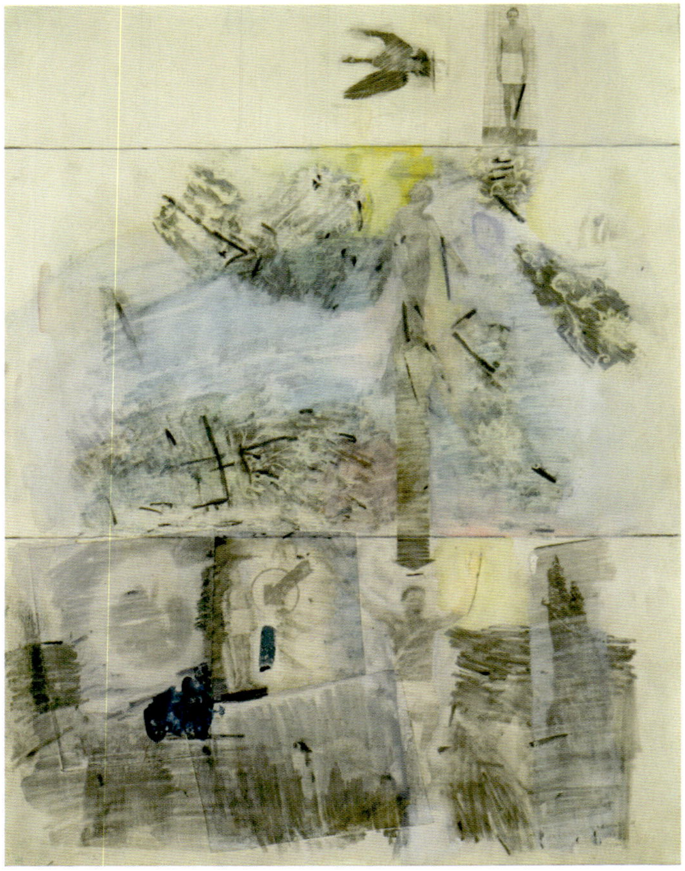

FIG. 4

is a literal nod to his source material. At the same time, however, these static photomechanical figures sharply clash with a dynamically built-up texture[6] and with a material that casts a disconcerting sheen: the overall effect is akin to the finish of a glossy photograph, yet the subjects have been so thoroughly distorted that only a hint of their original semblances remains.[7] Through Borges's hand, the participants in the gathering become stand-ins for the institutions of power that they represent.

What is most significant about Borges's work from the early to mid-1970s is that it represents a short-lived moment in his long trajectory when he questioned the relevance of painting and successfully utilized both mass-media techniques and source materials as sounding boards for his unyielding opposition to the Venezuelan sociopolitical system.[8] By the late 1970s, Borges had refocused his energies to create a portfolio of drawings, engravings, and paintings that revolved around the disenfranchisement that such a system perpetuated and its chaotic consequences in Caracas.[9] In the mid-1980s, the artist abandoned the photographic transfer technique altogether, and his style evolved further into a more placid version of his expressionistic work of the 1960s, a variant of which he still practices to this day. Borges's purposeful return to painting in the early 1970s and his experimentations with the communicative role of the medium (strengthened by his incursions into the photographic transfer technique), however, compel us to wonder what would have happened had the artist continued to develop his work along this elusive path. Certainly, it would have further affirmed how it is indeed possible for an artist to conceptually align his artistic and political selves.

ILLUSTRATIONS IN TEXT

Jacobo Borges
Esperando a... [Waiting for...], 1973
Oil on canvas
19 7/8 x 59 1/2 inches (50.5 x 151 cm)
Collection of Clara Diament Sujo

Jacobo Borges
Reunión con círculo rojo
[Meeting with Red Circle], 1973
Oil on canvas
63 x 59 inches (160 x 150 cm)
Colección Museo de Arte Moderno, México

Jacobo Borges
Humilde ciudadano [Humble Citizen], 1964
Oil on wood
78 7/8 x 110 inches (200 x 280 cm)
Colección Museo de Arte Contemporáneo, Caracas

Robert Rauschenberg
Canto II: The Descent, from the series *Thirty-Four Illustrations for Dante's Inferno*, 1959–60
Transfer drawing, colored pencil, gouache, and pencil on paper
14 1/2 x 11 1/2 inches (36.7 x 29.2 cm)
The Museum of Modern Art, New York, given anonymously

NOTES

1
Imagen de Caracas was Venezuela's most ambitious effort to integrate the arts, "combining image, colors, forms, various stages and kinds of architecture, movement, music, sound, light, the spoken and written word: everything available in the new world of audio-visual expression." See Inocente Palacios, Adriano González León, and César Rennert, "Imagen de Caracas," *The Drama Review: TDR*, vol. 14, no. 2, *Latin American Theater* (Winter 1970), 130–37, 137.

2
This last piece is important for having served as the inspiration for the Argentinean writer Julio Cortázar's (1914–1984) short story of the same title, included in the volume *Alguien que anda por ahí y otros relatos* of 1977 (Madrid: Ediciones Alfaguara, D.L.).

3
The point of departure for these three canvases is photographs of official state ceremonies taken by the Venezuelan photographer Luis Felipe Toro (also known as Torito, c. 1881–1955). Over the years, Borges has assembled an extensive collection of this material, which the artist typically rearranged to fit the specific demands of his own work. Email to the author from Jacobo Borges, October 19, 2012.

4
Rauschenberg's transfer drawings—shown in Caracas as *El infierno en versión de Rauschenberg* [Rauschenberg's Version of the Inferno]—employ the solvent transfer technique that the American artist pioneered, beginning with the Combines mixed-media works of the 1950s. Rauschenberg began with a photographic print into which he intervened graphically with pencil and, after saturating the sheet with solvent, transferred the reworked image onto a sheet of paper or canvas. See Julia Blaut, "Transfer Drawings, Prints, and Silkscreened Paintings," *Robert Rauschenberg: A Retrospective* (New York: The Solomon R. Guggenheim Museum, 1997), 154–56.

5
Conversely, Borges opts to rework the photographic surface to the point of disintegration. Employing the technique toward vastly different objectives, he manipulates his source image to such an extreme that only a hint of its photomechanical origin remains.

6
Borges uses a screen or mesh to apply texture: paint appears almost kneaded, forcefully rubbed in through the screen, wiped off, only to be reapplied. The resulting positive and negative dotted patterning is reminiscent of the halftone dots used in the printing process to simulate continuous or smooth tones, which sharply contrast with the rich impasto of paint in the work's texture. Even black-and-white film, when observed at a microscopic level, consists of a two-color halftone arrangement and not the infinite range of continuous tone suggested by the developed print.

7
Close examination by the MFAH conservation staff has revealed that the gloss and compactness of Borges's material of choice is consistent with any number of commercially available paints—including enamels, alkyd-based paints, and nitrocellulose paint—that may have been available to Borges and many of his Latin American contemporaries. At mid-century, alkyd paints were the rage among artists in Rio de Janeiro, and some, including Hélio Oiticica and Lygia Clark, habitually used the material in their work. I thank Wynne Phelan, former conservation director , and Maite M. Leal, paintings conservator, at the Museum of Fine Arts, Houston, for alerting me to the subtle differences between these paints and acrylics.

8
Borges used the same technique in other works from this period, including *La novia I* [The Bride I] and *La novia II* [The Bride II], both from 1975. Mirroring this strategy of incorporating external source material, Borges inserts himself through his own work, into the halls of his imaginary Nymphenburg Palace in the masterful *Nymphenburg* of 1974. Here, versions of earlier paintings, including *Ha comenzado el espectáculo* [The Show Has Begun] (1964) and a canvas from his Cardplayers series, c. mid-1960s, line the walls of the antechamber to a tortuous act perpetrated by uniformed men.

9
This work culminated in 1979 with the publication of the richly illustrated artist's book *La montaña y su tiempo*, inspired by the Ávila Mountain that separates the city from the Caribbean Sea. See Jacobo Borges, *La montaña y su tiempo,o* (Caracas: Armitano Editores, 1979).

Abigail McEwen

LOLÓ SOLDEVILLA, CUBAN *CONCRETA*

A LATE-BLOOMING ARTIST, Dolores (Loló) Soldevilla remains little known in histories of Constructivist Abstraction, both within Cuba and internationally. Yet much like Carmen Herrera, whom she knew in Paris and whose minimalist works have won critical recognition only in the past decade, Soldevilla has gained new visibility in recent years amid growing scholarly interest in Cuban art of the 1950s. Soldevilla embarked on a perspicacious path within abstraction beginning in 1949, when she left Havana for Paris after being appointed to a diplomatic post at the Cuban Embassy in France. Stationed as a cultural attaché, she immersed herself in the milieu of postwar painting as a collector and enthusiast and, with the encouragement of Wifredo Lam, as an emerging artist in her own right. Soldevilla's work soon came to circulate within an international nexus of Constructivist activity and experimentation, and her return to Havana in 1956 would appreciably raise the cosmopolitan horizons of Havana's emergent avant-garde.

The trajectory of Soldevilla's work and the breadth of her contacts from Paris to Havana during the 1950s have not been adequately chronicled. Yet starting with her foray into abstraction, the visual evolution of her work in different media—collage, wood, tempera—suggests multiple intersections in the contemporary field of postwar geometric abstraction. An assiduous student and proponent of abstraction, she catalyzed activity around Concrete art at Havana's Galería Color-Luz, which she founded in 1957, and through her involvement with the group Diez Pintores Concretos (1958–61). Soldevilla developed a distinctive practice within the Constructivist paradigm, and the Brillembourg Capriles Collection of Latin American Art includes significant and representative examples of her work.

Paris, 1949–56

Soldevilla numbers among the earliest arrivals in a generational wave of Latin American artists who migrated to Paris following the Second World War and pursued directions in geometric abstraction. She was friends with the Venezuelan "Disidentes" Jesús Rafael Soto, Omar Carreño, and Víctor Valera and traveled, as they did, within the orbit of postwar Constructivism articulated between the Salon des Réalités Nouvelles and the Galerie Denise René.[1] Moving beyond the gridded spaces and building blocks of Neo-Plasticism, these artists explored perceptual problems of abstraction (i.e., illusionism, movement, color, geometry) through innovations in Op and Kinetic art. It is unlikely that Soldevilla had encountered nonfigurative art before her arrival in Paris, given the ascendancy of the Havana School in Cuban art during the 1940s and its figurative, tropical vernacular. Her proclivity for geometric abstraction has no obvious source in Cuban Modernism, and her beginnings in Constructivist aesthetics can be traced instead to a telling range of historical and contemporary sources that she sought out in Paris.

Inasmuch as Soldevilla kept close personal company with Latin American artists in Paris, as recounted in her memoir *Ir, venir, volver a ir: crónicas (1952–1957)*, she studied and later exhibited within

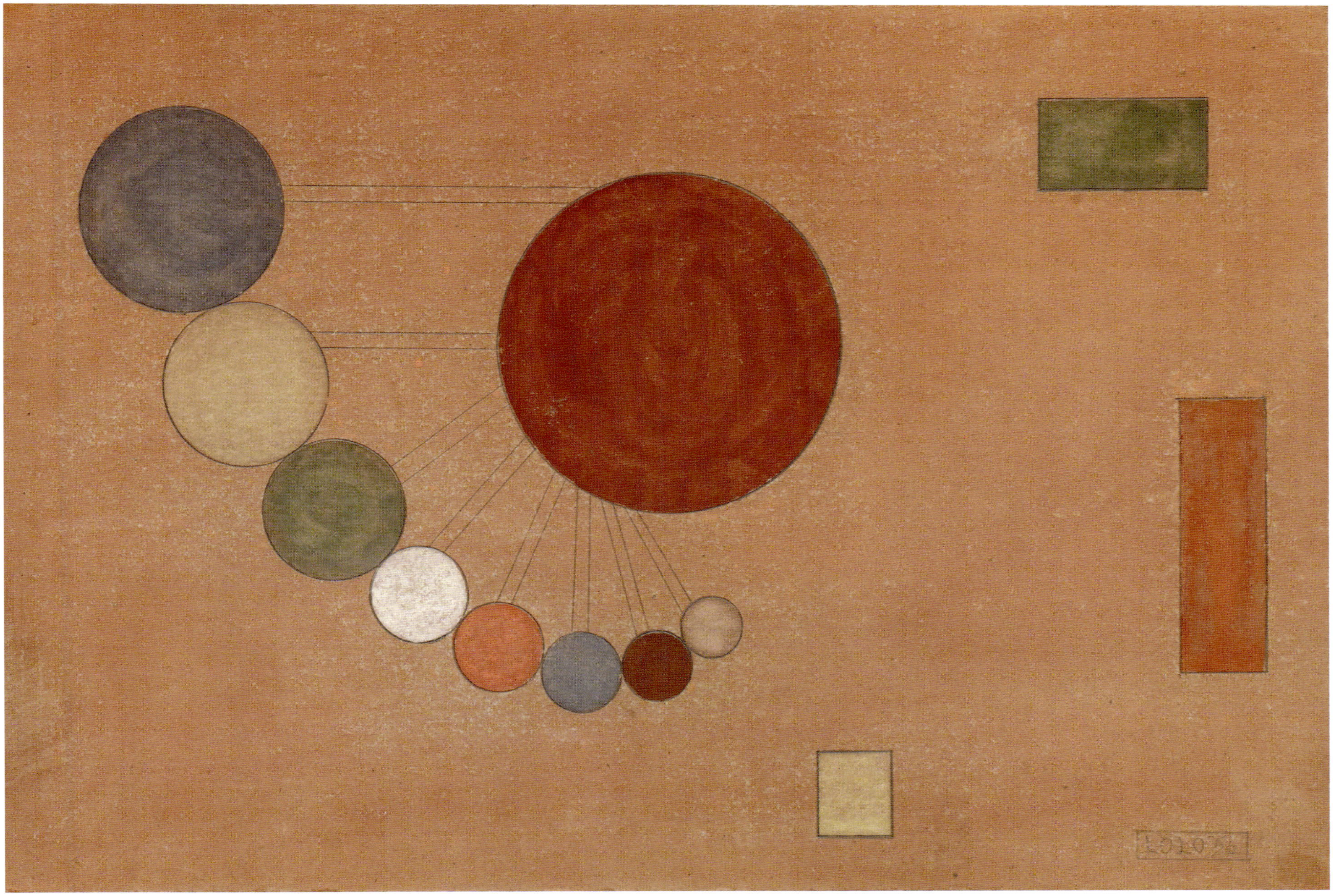

PLATE 76

Loló Soldevilla • *Sin título* [Untitled], 1956

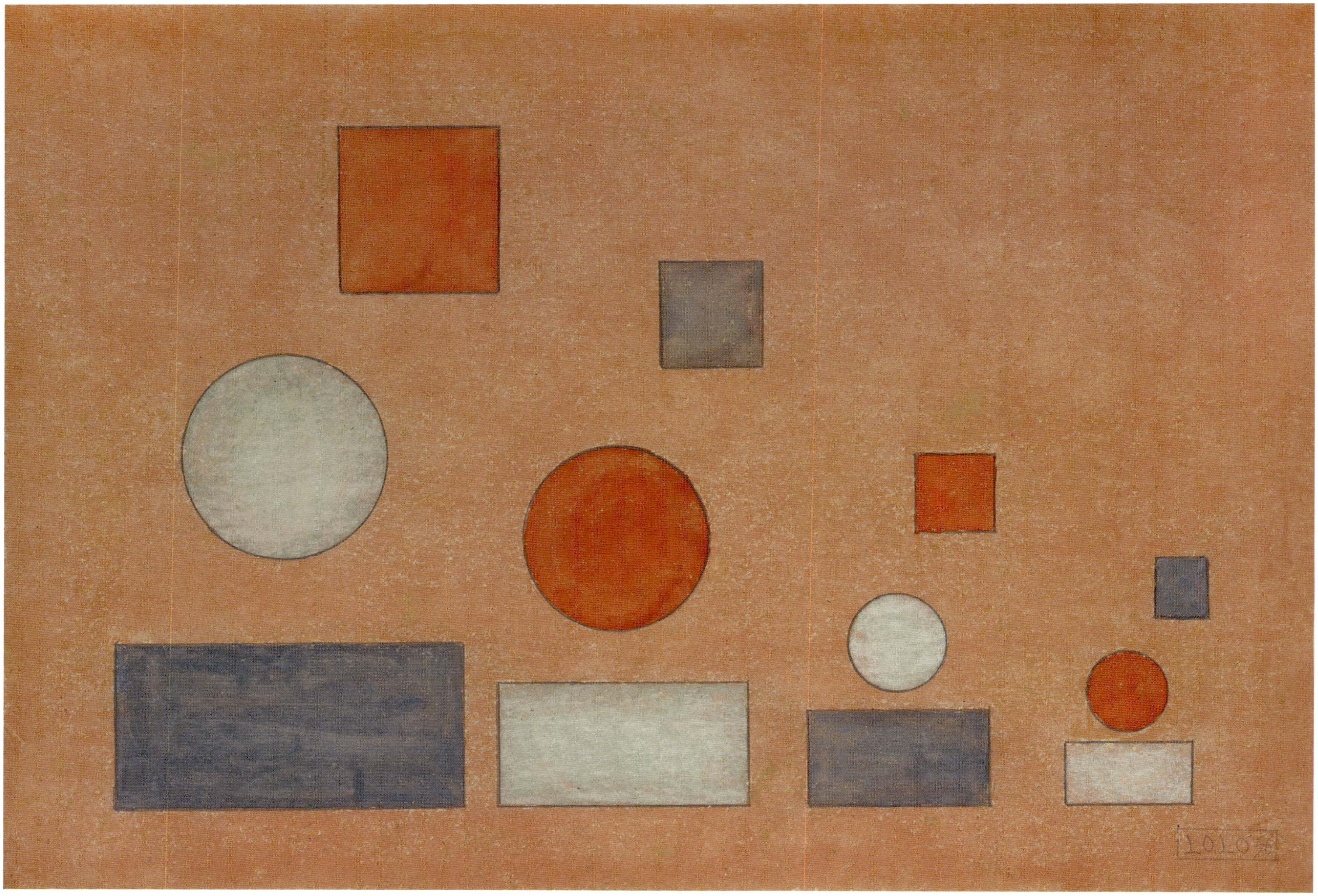

PLATE 77
Loló Soldevilla • *Sin título* [Untitled], 1956

an international community of artists spanning different generations. Soldevilla took classes in 1949 at the Académie de la Grande Chaumière under the Russian-born artist Ossip Zadkine, a principal of the School of Paris and early adept of sculpture drawn on Cubist geometries. She also worked between 1951 and 1953 at the Atelier d'art abstrait, founded by Jean Dewasne and Edgard Pillet in 1950 near the Grande Chaumière. Oriented around a collective approach to aesthetic research, the Atelier organized both "*visites-dialogues*" with elder-generation artists such as Auguste Herbin, Alberto Magnelli, and Victor Vasarely and focused discussions around the work of the Atelier's younger students, among them Wifredo Arcay, Yaacov Agam, and Pascual Navarro.[2] She received informal guidance from others, including Vasarely, Robert Jacobsen, and Jean Arp, likely facilitated through her association with the Atelier.[3] Through Pillet, Soldevilla would also have come into contact with the Groupe Espace, founded by André Bloc and Félix Del Marle in 1951 around the promotion of collaborative and social values within geometric abstraction. The group's advocacy of a synthesis between art and architecture and its public orientation may suggest a precedent for the group Espacio, which Soldevilla founded in Havana in 1964.

Soldevilla's very early work in still life and portraiture expressed what Zadkine, her first teacher, described at the time as "wild poetry," but by 1952–53 she was working capably within the rationalist restraints of Constructivism.[4] Her collages from this period analyze the geometries of circles, triangles, and rectangles in primary colors, suggesting visual rhythms through the repetition and variation of shapes and colors. Soldevilla dedicated a number of collages made between 1954 and 1956 to luminaries of Modernism—Arthur Rimbaud, Kazimir Malevich, Jean Arp, Franz Kafka, even Sandú Darié—and her pieces in this medium might be specially understood as working exercises within historical abstraction. The Brillembourg Capriles Collection contains several examples of collages, although none are illustrated here. One work, in which red and yellow forms are dynamically offset over a central blue rectangle, appears to pay homage to Malevich. In another collage from 1954, she distills and geometricizes the flatly contoured compaction of forms seen, for example, in the work

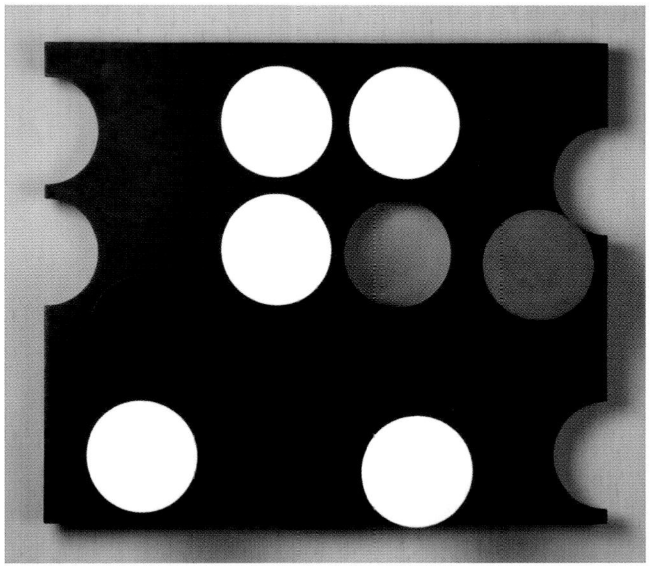

FIG. 1

of contemporaries such as Eduardo Ramírez Villamizar, in Paris between 1950 and 1952 and similarly moving in the realm of Fernand Léger and the School of Paris. Working as almost always on an intimate scale, Soldevilla here describes the interrelationship between shapes, both breaking them apart and combining them to suggest composite forms (e.g., two triangles that form a lozenge). A third collage in the Brillembourg Capriles Collection introduces a greater number of visual elements and a more strongly reiterated linearity. Made following her return to Havana, it bears a formal relationship to the work of the young Cuban *Concreto* José Mijares.

The additive aspect of Soldevilla's collages relates closely to her constructions in wood and metal. Occupying a space between painting and sculpture, the wood reliefs are built upon the repetition of circular and rectangular forms in black and white. They have a precedent in Sophie Taeuber-Arp's polychrome *Rectangular Reliefs* (fig. 1), which articulate positive and negative space through serial geometric forms. Soldevilla almost certainly knew of Taeuber-Arp through her acquaintance with Arp, but her wood reliefs lack the bright colors and game-like whimsy—Jean Arp called them "chessboards of the night"—that characterize Taeuber-Arp's constructions.[5] The two white-on-white reliefs in the Brillembourg Capriles Collection (plates 78 and 79) convey a more austere rationalism, balancing clusters of circular discs (divided and whole) and horizontal bars between the four quadrants of a rectangle. The underlying grid here is only

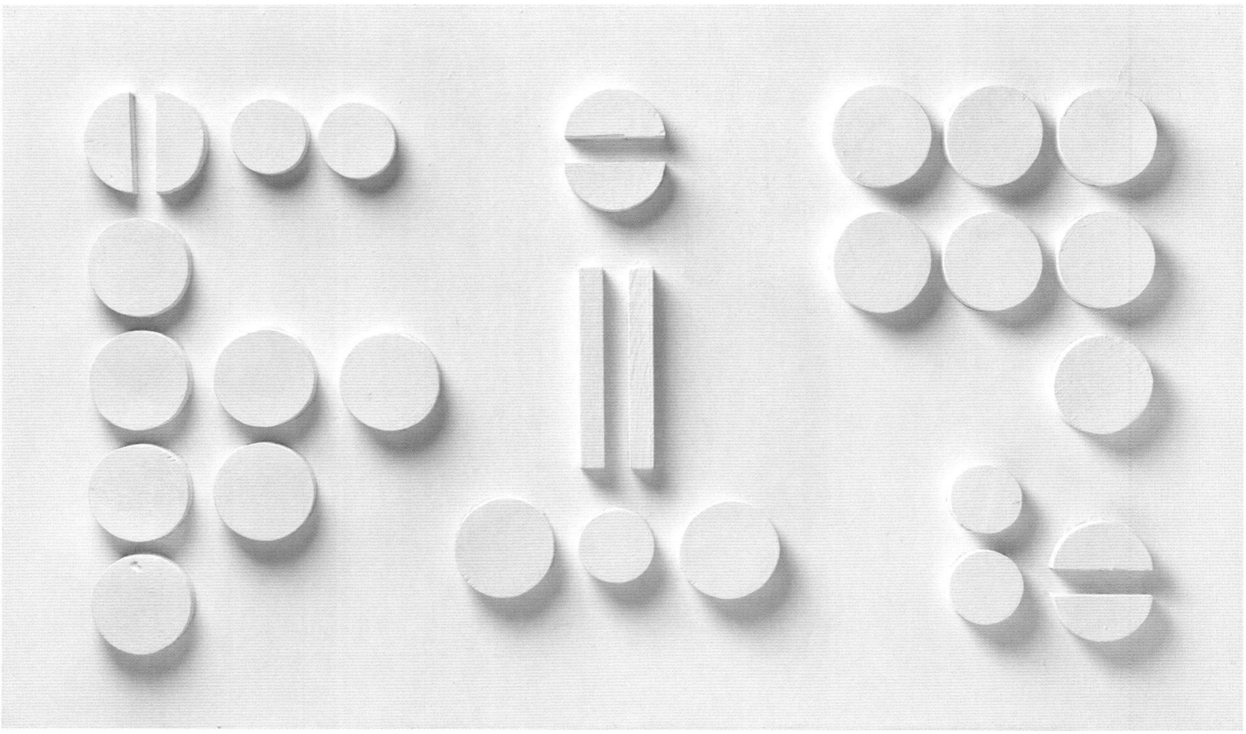

PLATE 78
Loló Soldevilla • *Sin título (abstracción)* [Untitled (Abstraction)], 1956

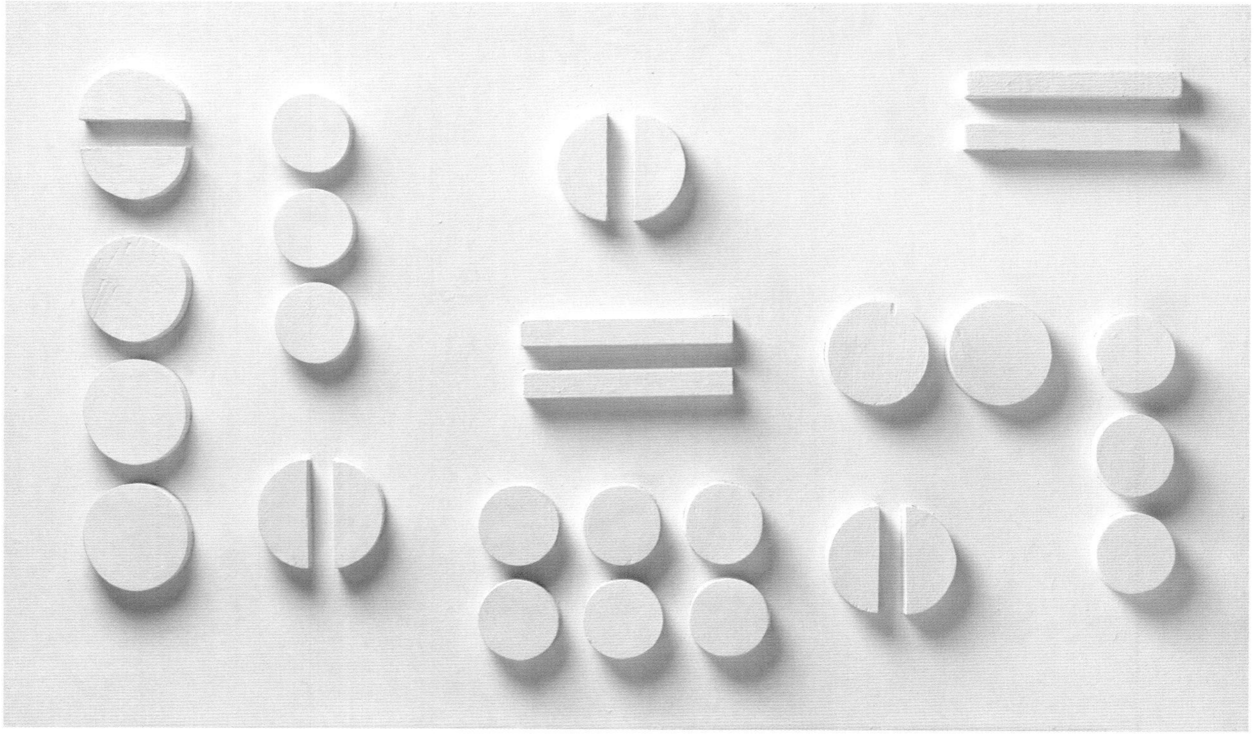

PLATE 79
Loló Soldevilla • *Sin título (abstracción)* [Untitled (Abstraction)], 1956

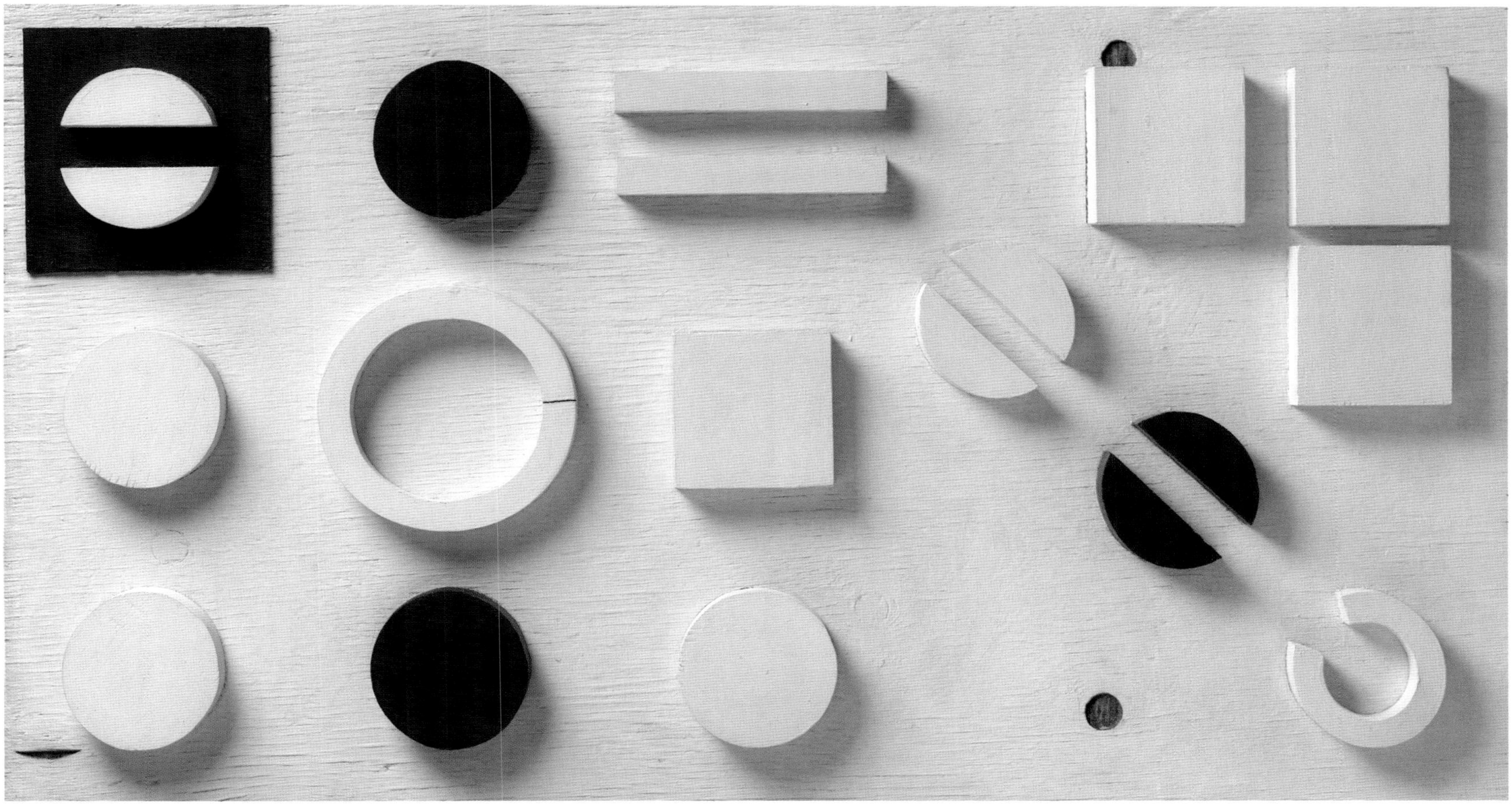

PLATE 80

Loló Soldevilla • *Construcción* [Construction], 1955

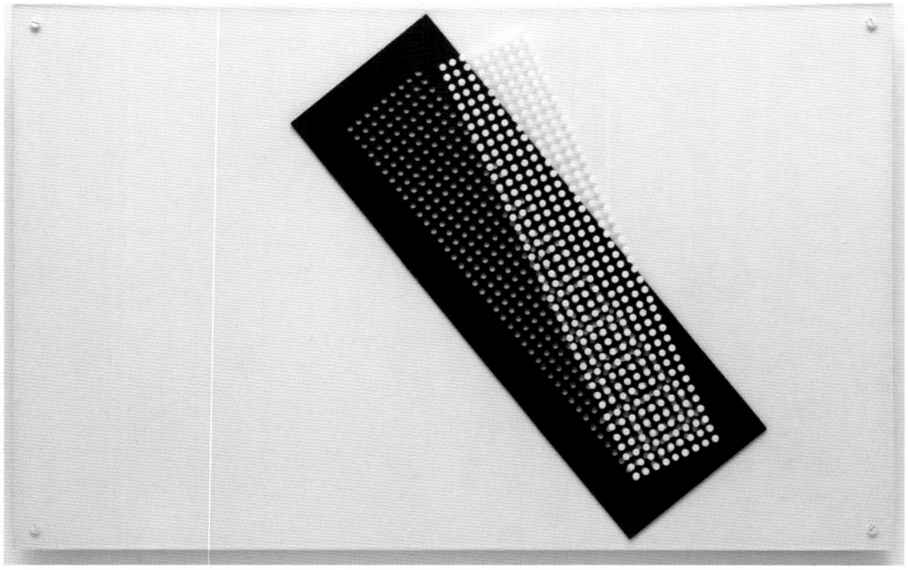

FIG. 2

implied, but its structure regulates the spatial passages in and around the raised elements. In a way akin to the iconic white reliefs of the Brazilian Neo-Concretist Sérgio de Camargo, active in Paris beginning in 1948, the fixed volumes of Soldevilla's constructions invite the dematerializing play of light and shadow across the surface, introducing a subtle opticality and movement into geometric space.

In some instances, Soldevilla punctuated the white monochrome with contrasting black modules or inverted the color relations altogether. The black elements—circles, semicircles, and square—amplify the depth of the construction in one example (plate 80), highlighting in a dramatic way the energized space around each element. In the striking *Composición abstracción* [Abstract Composition] (plate 81), the color relations are reversed: against a black background, white discs radiate along diagonal and horizontal axes that intersect at the center of the composition. An analysis of the circle, *Composición abstracción* describes its rotation and division, magnifying the contrast between positive and negative space along the wooden dowel that describes a centerline across the composition. The shallow projection of the image into the space animated by the wooden discs—i.e., the space between the black ground and the outermost edge of the white cylinders—defines an expanded image field that extends the space of the object outward into the space of the viewer. This rejection of linear perspective and its suggestion of recessive space are also seen in Soldevilla's wood-and-metal constructions, which more explicitly literalize, as it were, the virtual space of the relief.

The Brillembourg Capriles Collection includes two outstanding examples of Soldevilla's mixed wood-and-metal pieces. In both works, only one of which is reproduced here, the underlying grid becomes a relief element, given material form in the metal or wood grating positioned in front of the black or white ground. The grid establishes the space of the object between the ground and the wood relief elements both affixed to, and suspended within, the metal screen. Here, color is virtualized in space: the metal grid is painted around each of the three wooden cubes in *Sin título* [Untitled] (plate 82), creating three, three-by-three squares in yellow, green, and black. The painted metal squares present a perceptual challenge; from a distance, the black square all but disappears against the black ground, releasing into the space behind the grid even as the wooden cubes and the two curvilinear shapes demarcate the outward projection of space toward the viewer. In each work, the layering of the curved shapes, white-on-white or green-on-white, introduces a dynamic, lateral energy across the surface that counters the back-to-front projection established by the grid. The primary colors and gridded structure of course nod to the early precedent of Piet Mondrian, but they also relate to the contemporary work of Soto, whom Soldevilla knew and whose early Plexi-overlays were included in the landmark exhibition *Le Mouvement* (1955), held at Denise René's gallery. In *Desplazamiento de un elemento luminoso* (fig. 2), Soto "fixed a Masonite radio grill with a regular pattern of black dots between a wooden support and a clear Plexiglas sheet painted with an identical pattern of white dots."[6] The use of the readymade metal object (in Soto's case, purchased at a Paris department store) and the layering of optical surfaces also characterize Soldevilla's reliefs, although her works retain a stronger sculptural orientation.

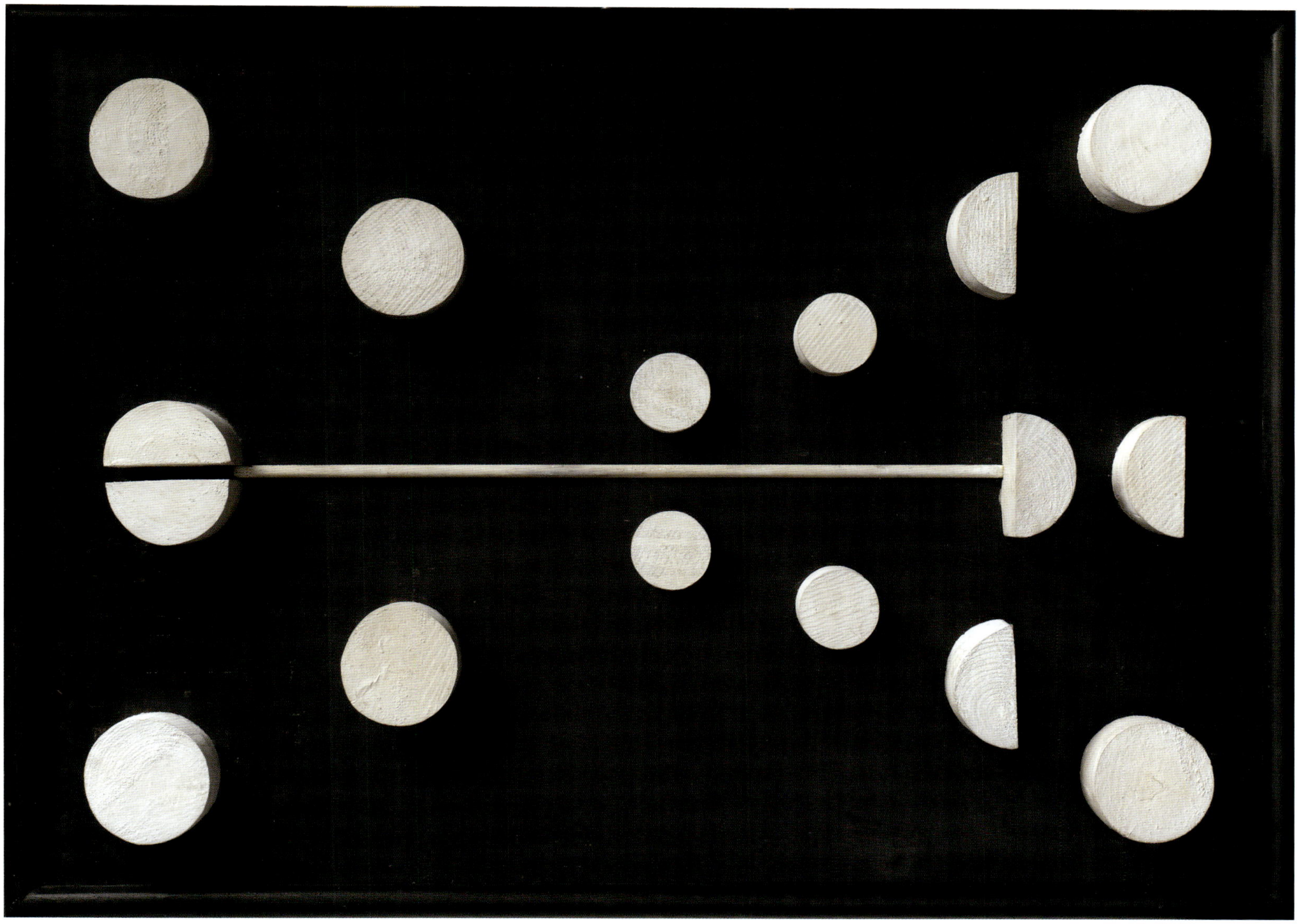

PLATE 81
Loló Soldevilla • *Composición abstracción* [Abstract composition], c. 1954

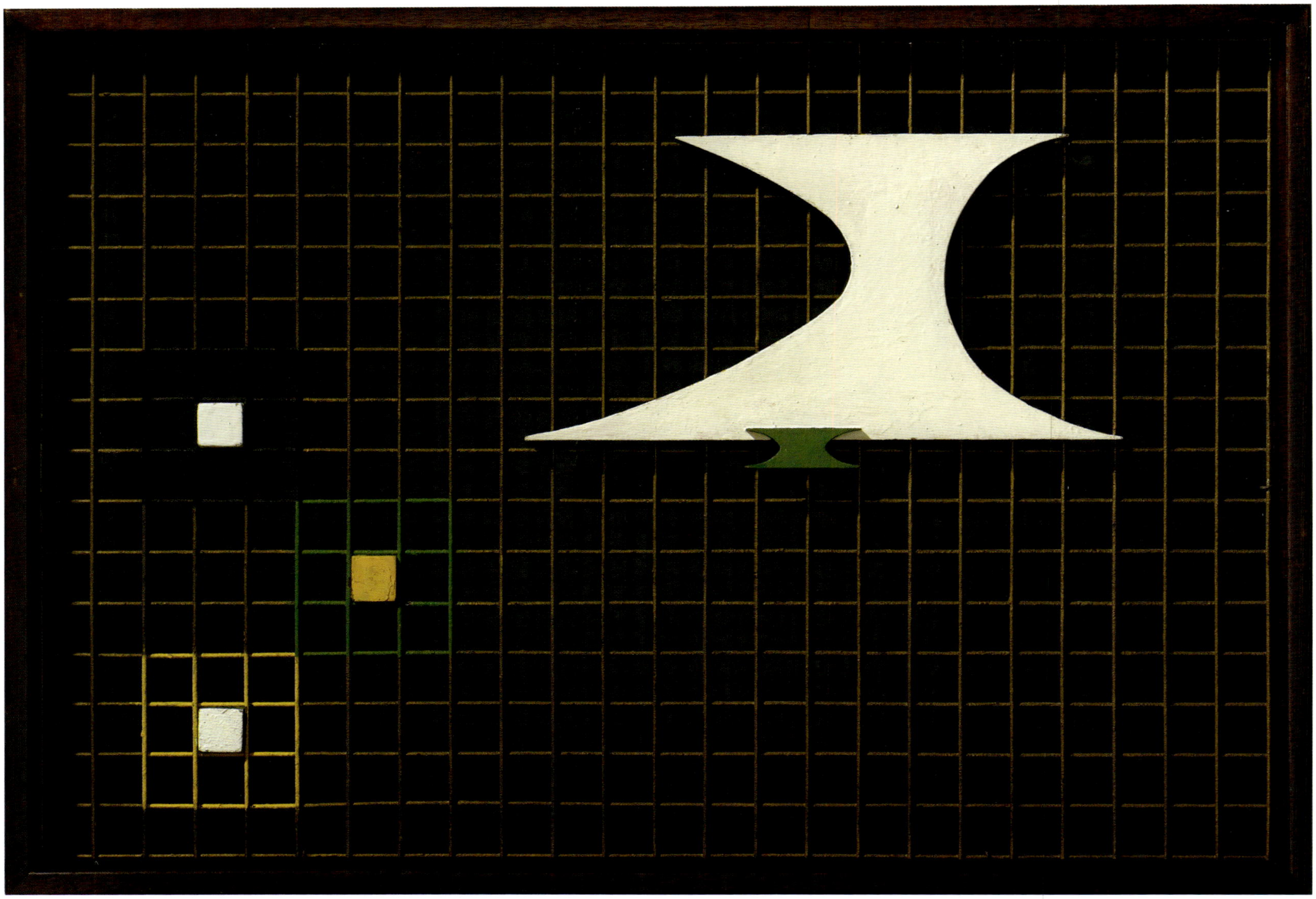

PLATE 82

Loló Soldevilla • *Sin título (abstracción)* [Untitled (Abstraction)], 1956

More spatially complex than the wood reliefs, the gridded constructions constitute an intermediary position between her reliefs and the small series of metal stabiles that she made in Paris. As in the reliefs and mixed-media objects, the metal sculptures (plate 84) engage spatial relationships through basic geometries set in two and three dimensions: lines and planes, circles and cubes. In a way like the wooden cubes that Soto suspended in front of painted backgrounds, the black cube projecting upward at the center of Soldevilla's stabile introduces a kinetic energy that responds dynamically with the environment into which it is placed. Against the typical white wall of a gallery or museum, the black cube functions like the black relief elements in the wood relief (plate 80), galvanizing the space and channeling paths of movement. Here, fully three-dimensional, the black cube stabilizes the centrifugal tendency suggested by the rotation of both the six circular forms and the angular wires that connect them. Like many of Soldevilla's stabiles, this piece is meant to be manipulated by its observer; the metal parts move, inviting different incursions into the surrounding space.

Among Soldevilla's most intriguing works from these years are the *Relieves luminosos*, which she developed with the Spanish Kineticist Eusebio Sempere, a student at Arcay's atelier and an assistant at the Galerie Denise René, and exhibited in the Salon des Réalités Nouvelles in 1955. Based on the geometries of the circle and square and produced in black and white, the boxes projected light through reiterated grids, making mechanical the optical play of light and shadow.[7] In 1955, Soldevilla and Sempere published a "Manifesto," in which they drew an evolutionary history of light from Leonardo da Vinci through Caravaggio and laid out the material parameters and poetics of changing light and transparency effects.[8] They understood light as a means of "expanding the horizons of nonfigurative art," and Soldevilla's light reliefs suggest a logical progression beyond her earlier constructions in wood and metal.[9] None of these works is believed to survive, unfortunately, and Soldevilla did not pursue further experiments in this direction following her return to Cuba.

Havana, 1956–61

Although artists such as Sandú Darié had introduced Concrete art to Cuba at the beginning of the 1950s, the subsequent rise of abstraction hewed more closely to the gestural painting advanced by the New York School over the course of the decade. Lacking the existential physicality of Abstract Expressionism, Concretism evolved as an intellectual pursuit and remained largely apart from the aggravated social politics that characterized the latter years of the Fulgencio Batista regime (1952–59). Soldevilla's return to Cuba at the start of 1956 marked a turning point in the trajectory of geometric abstraction in Havana, and she played a critical role in disseminating Concrete aesthetics to a younger generation of artists through various exhibition projects and the Galería Color-Luz, which she founded with the poet and artist Pedro de Oraá in 1957.[10]

Soldevilla produced a significant number of small works in mixed media in 1956 that show her continuing engagement with School of Paris aesthetics. The familiar geometries of circle, square, and rectangle are typically ordered in clear relation to a grid, as in the wood reliefs and constructions, but often they describe curvilinear patterns that soften the straight lines seen to characterize her work in other media. Variations within close harmonies of tone and similarly scaled (plates 85 and 86), these works suggest an excursus on geometric relationships, distilled through fine gradations of color and shape against a dark ground. Other examples (plates 76, 77, 83, 87, and 88) experiment with a brighter tonal range, positing dynamic sequences of color and form within a consistently used rectangular frame.

Some of the most cogent examples in the Brillembourg Capriles Collection focus solely on the form of the circle, which invokes metaphysical as well as purely visual interests. In one work, the composition is perfectly symmetrical; in another, Soldevilla describes rhythmic, but irregular serpentine patterns. Her analysis of the circle, probed through differences of scale, material, and color, bears familial resemblances to works by Wassily Kandinsky, František

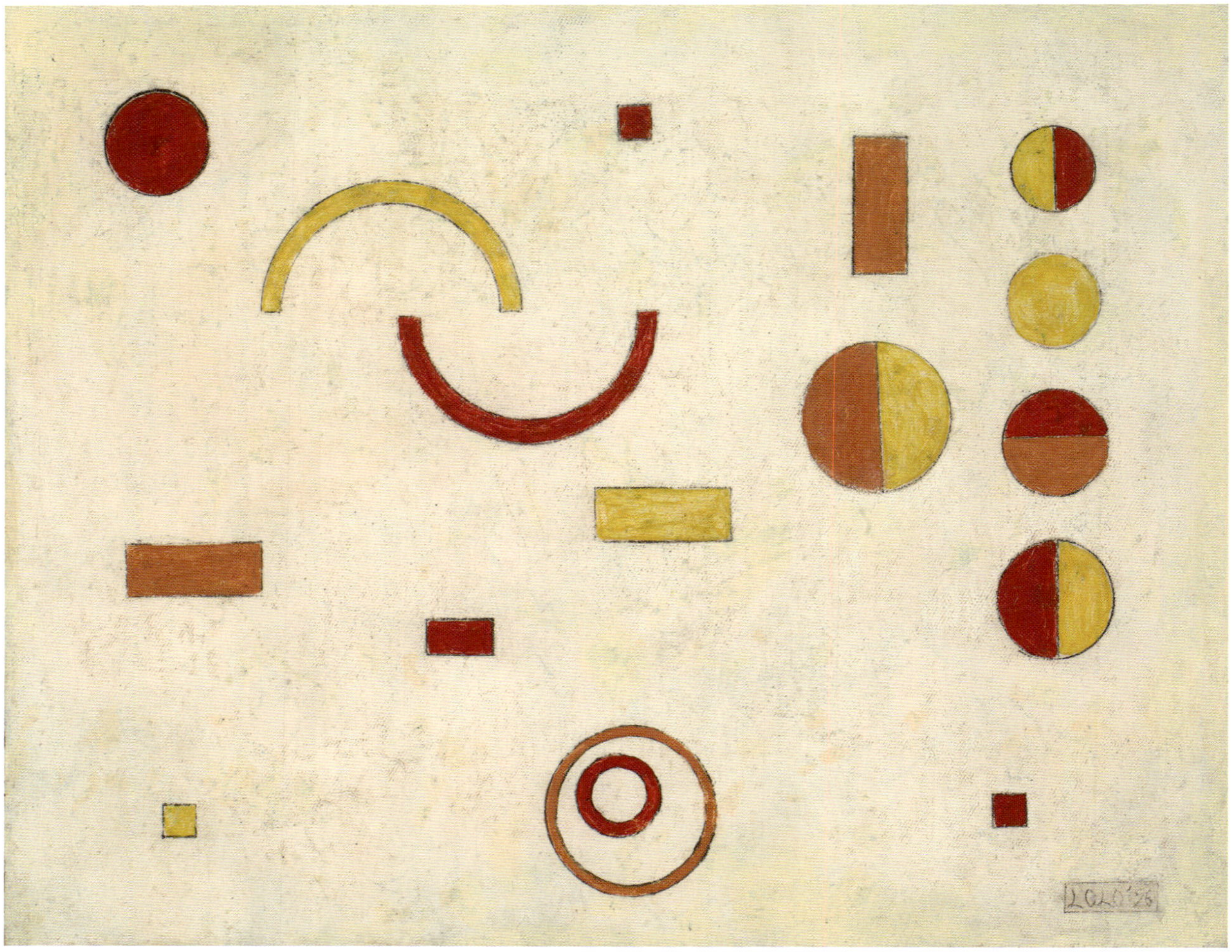

PLATE 83
Loló Soldevilla • *Sin título* [Untitled], 1956

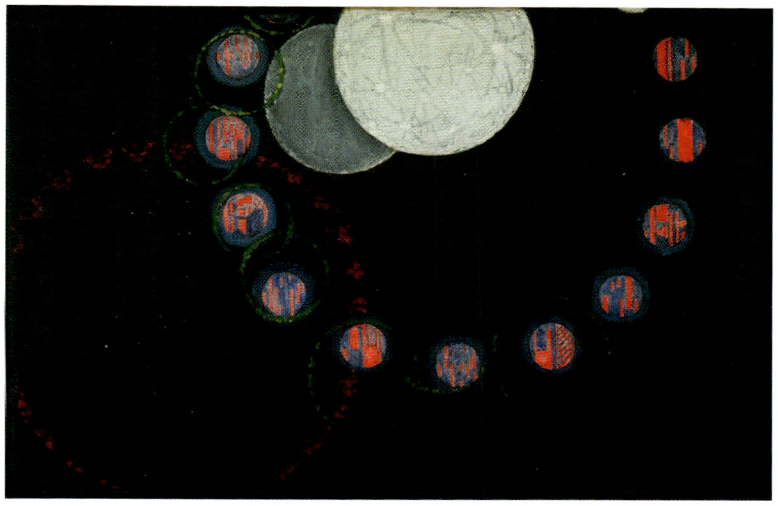

FIG. 3

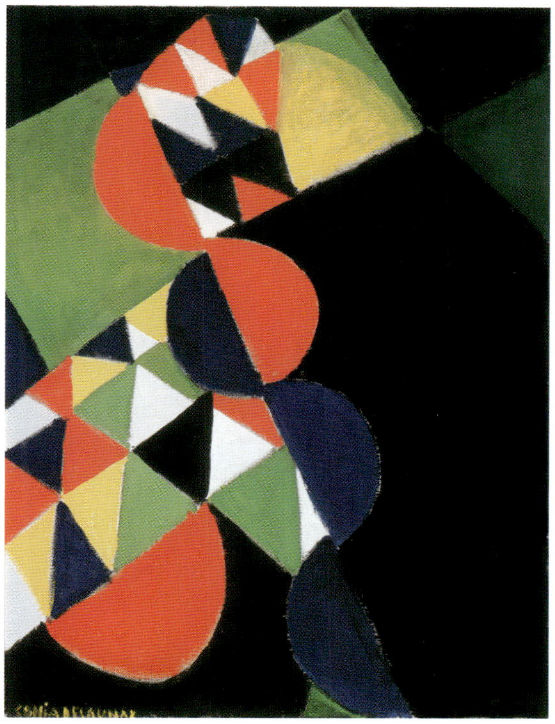

FIG. 4

Kupka (fig. 3), and Sonia Delaunay (fig. 4), all historically affiliated with the School of Paris. Delaunay was a founder-member of Réalités Nouvelles and an artist whose work, from its Simultanist origins through her later design practice and public artworks, Soldevilla surely knew in Paris. Delaunay's graphic geometries constitute a visual point of reference, but the cosmological preoccupations of Kandinsky and Kupka may suggest affinities at a metaphysical level as well. Soldevilla visited Nina Kandinsky's collection of her husband's paintings while in Paris, and she may well have been familiar with Kandinsky's classic treatise, *Concerning the Spiritual in Art* (1911), and his Bauhaus-period abstractions.[11] For Kandinsky the most elementary form, the circle embodied ultimate states of equilibrium and transcendence; for him and also for Kupka, his contemporary and another pioneer of European abstraction, the circle's universality and cosmological metaphor also related to ideas of synthesis and integration within the arts. Analogies between art and music—and indeed, between art and technology—similarly informed the cohort of Concrete artists who gathered in Havana in the later 1950s, and Soldevilla's reprise of the circle may speak to the utopian projections of Cuba's Concretos.

Soldevilla's return to Havana facilitated the convergence of contemporary School of Paris aesthetics and South American Concretismo, first proposed by the Romanian-born Madí artist Sandú Darié at the beginning of the decade. The integrative, interdisciplinary initiatives of both the Madí movement and the Groupe Espace, whose collectivist approach to Constructivism Soldevilla knew in Paris, informed the values of the group Diez Pintores Concretos, to which Soldevilla and Darié both belonged.[12] "The humanist dream of the integration of the arts appeared to find in this nascent moment its possibility of realization," de Oraá later explained of the group's early ambition to radicalize the formal and the social spaces of art.[13] Soldevilla's *Relieves luminosos* provided both the name and the insignia of the Galería Color-Luz, and for four years she presided over exhibitions drawn from her personal collection (e.g., *Homenaje al pequeño cuadrado*, a nod to Joseph Albers's iconic series Homage to the Square, and *El arte abstracto en Europa*, which presented examples of both geometric and *informel* tendencies).[14] "Los Diez" sought to insinuate themselves within Havana's political landscape through exhibitions that expressed the participatory ideals to which they aspired: anonymity,

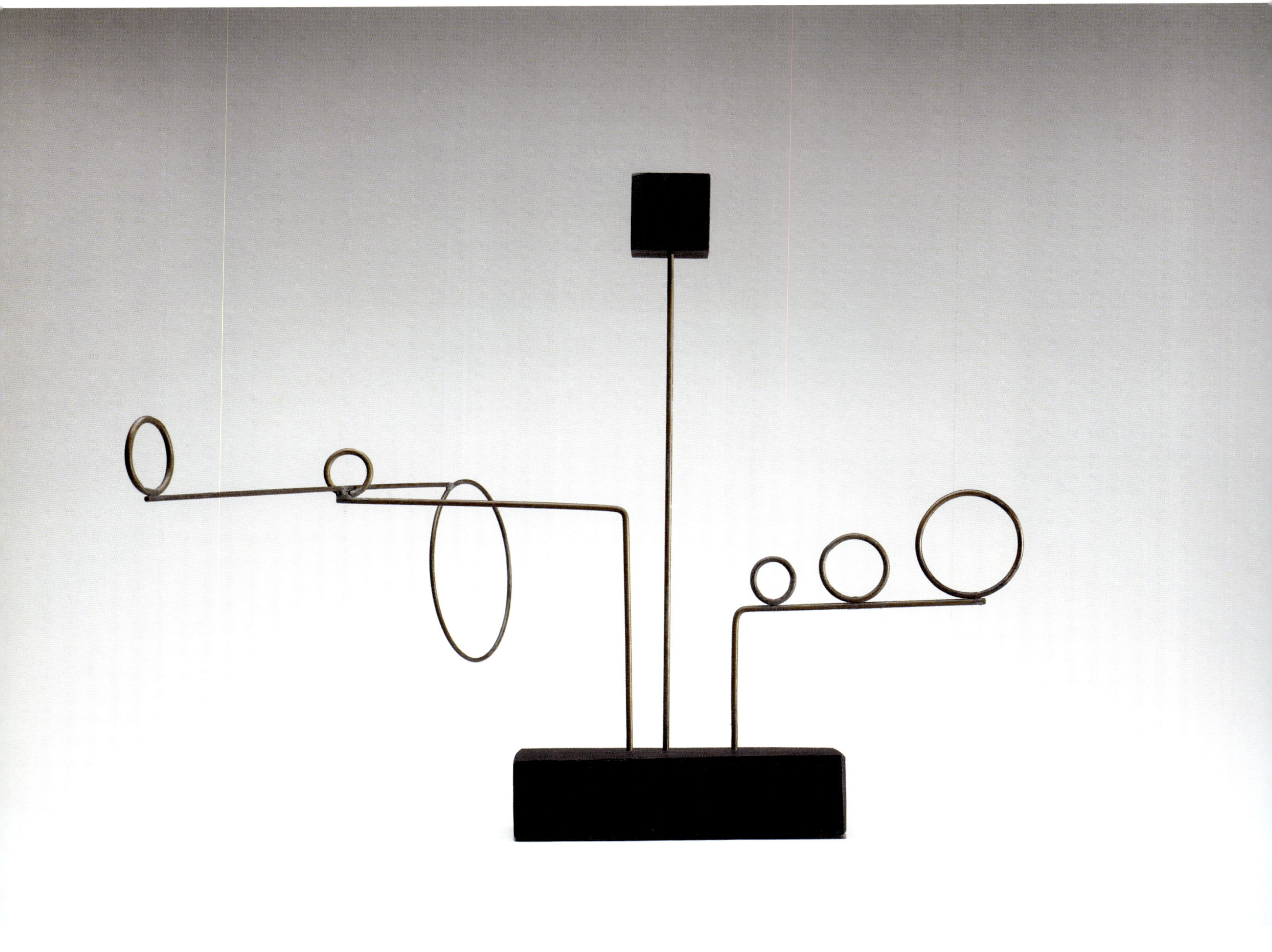

PLATE 84

Loló Soldevilla • *Stabile*, 1954

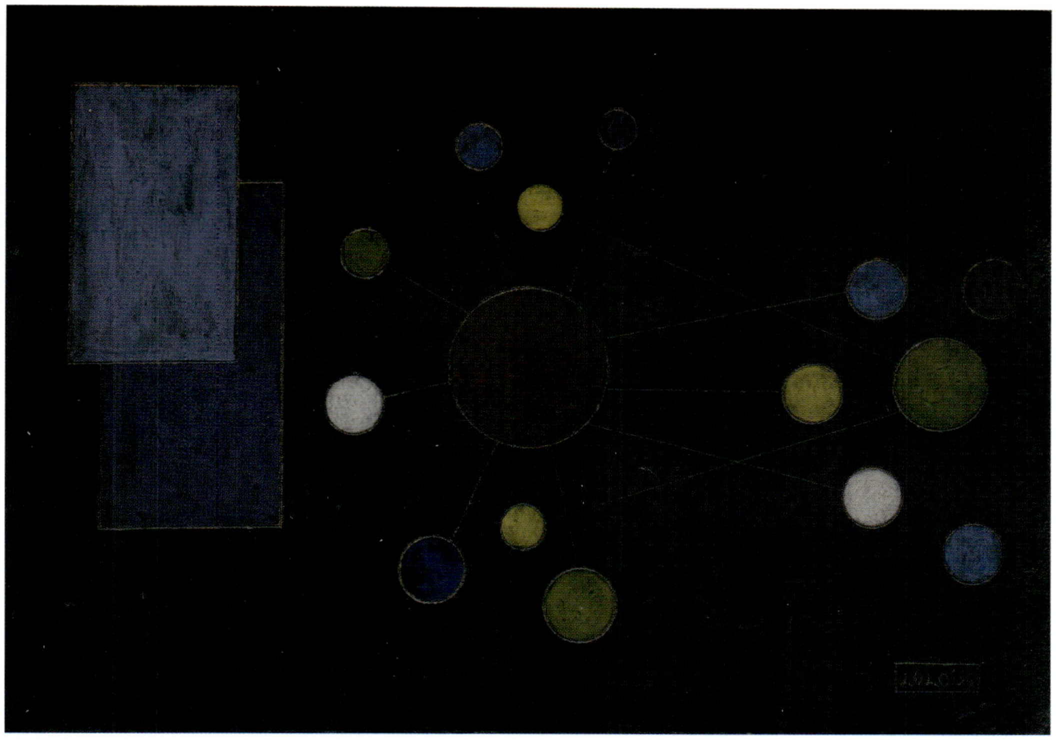

PLATE 85

Loló Soldevilla • *Sin título* [Untitled], 1956

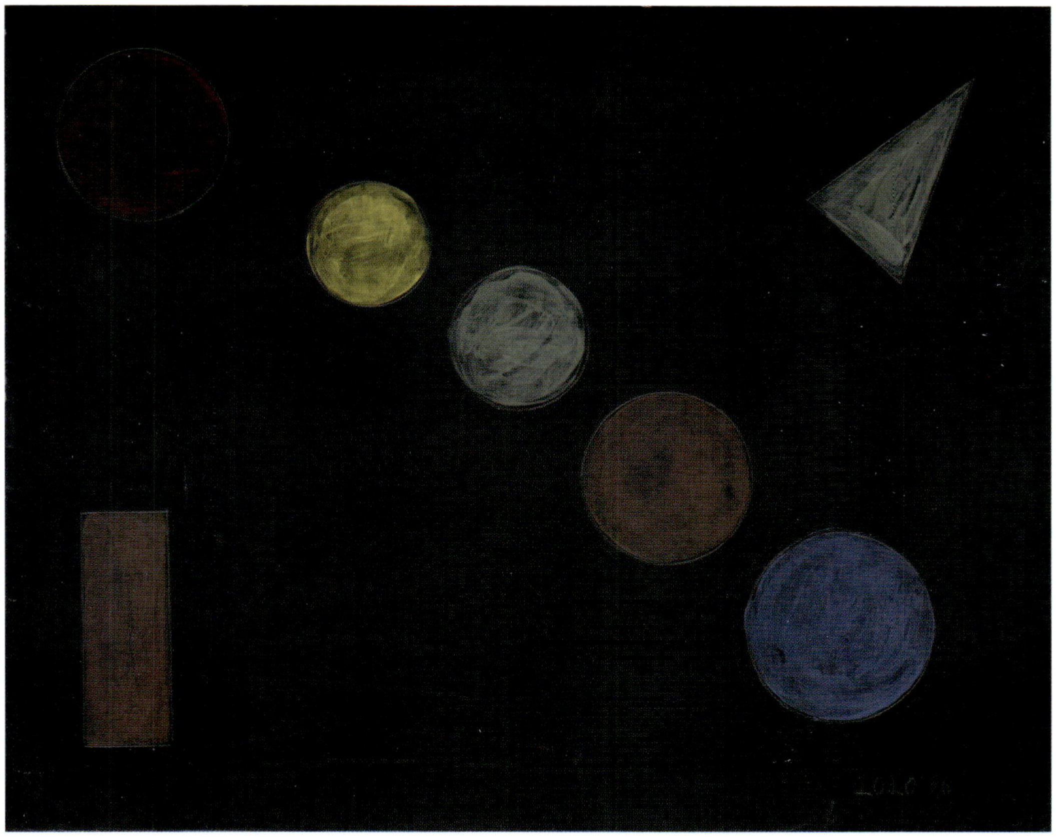

PLATE 86

Loló Soldevilla • *Sin título* [Untitled], 1956

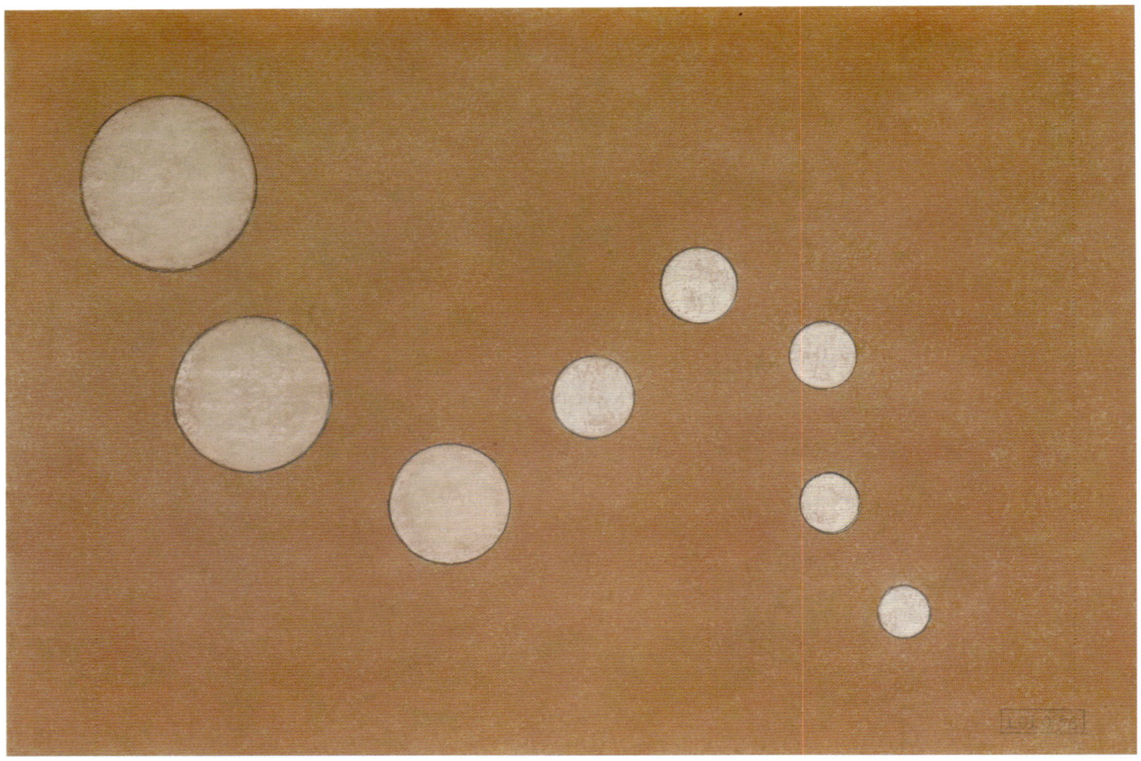

PLATE 87
Loló Soldevilla • *Sin título* [Untitled], 1956

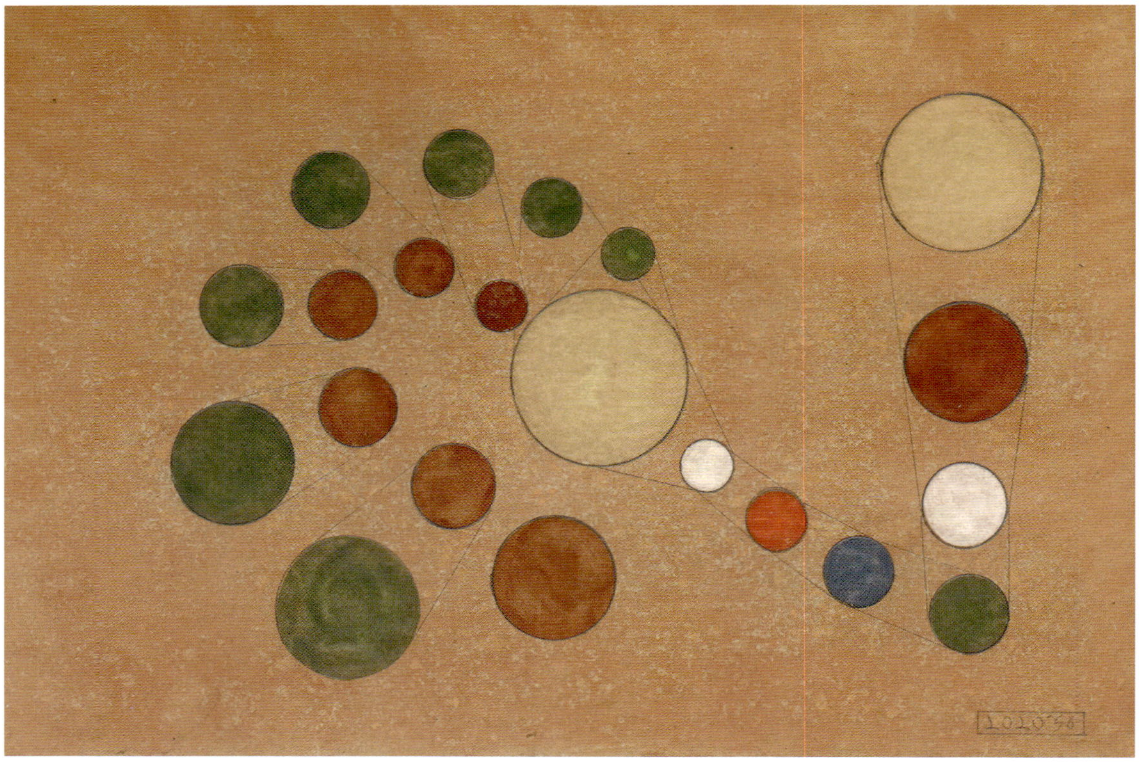

PLATE 88
Loló Soldevilla • *Sin título* [Untitled], 1956

collaboration, universalism. Although the group's social manifesto was quickly overshadowed by the Revolution and its transformational vision ultimately left unrealized, "Los Diez" nevertheless embodied an unprecedented moment of utopian possibility and aesthetic innovation within Cuba's *vanguardia* tradition.

Soldevilla exhibited infrequently after 1959, and following the closure of the Galería Color-Luz in 1961 she dedicated herself as much to literary as to artistic pursuits.[15] Although her career in abstract art spanned little more than a decade, the sophistication of her pathways into Concrete art constitutes a remarkable contribution to the movement's international history. An artistic latecomer but a perceptive student and participant, Soldevilla bridged historical and contemporary Constructivist practices from Paris to Havana. The principal facilitator of School of Paris aesthetics into Cuba's cultural milieu, she must also be credited with expanding the cosmopolitan purview of the Caribbean and with inculcating an aesthetic radicalism on par with the contemporary politics of dissent and revolution. Although her work and that of "Los Diez" remain little known, their recent recuperation within histories of Cuban art holds promise for new research into her work and cultural influence for Havana's avant-garde generations of the 1950s and 1960s.

ILLUSTRATIONS IN TEXT

FIGURE 1
Sophie Taeuber-Arp
Relief rectangulaire, cercles découpés, cônes surgissants [Rectangular Relief, Cutout Circles, and Rising Cones], 1936
Oil on wood
21.7 x 25.6 inches (55 x 65 cm)
Emanuel-Hoffmann Foundation, permanent loan to the Offentliche Kunstmuseum Basel

FIGURE 2
Jesús Rafael Soto
Desplazamiento de un elemento luminoso [Displacement of a Luminous Element], 1954
Mixed media on wood
39.4 x 39.4 x 15 inches (100 x 100 x 38 cm)
Patricia Phelps de Cisneros Collection

FIGURE 3
František Kupka
The First Step, 1910–13 (dated 1909 on painting)
Oil on canvas
32 3/4 x 51 inches (83.2 x 129.6 cm)
The Museum of Modern Art, New York, Hillman Periodicals Fund

FIGURE 4
Sonia Delaunay
Colored Rhythm, 1958
Oil on canvas
45 x 34 inches (114.3 x 86.4 cm)
Albright-Knox Gallery, Buffalo, New York, gift of Seymour H. Knox, Jr., 1964 (K1964:23)

NOTES

1
Pedro de Oraá, "Una experiencia plástica: los Diez Pintores Concretos," *Visible e invisible* (Havana: Editorial Letras Cubanas, 2006), 114.

2
Marc Ducourant, "L'art d'Edgard Pillet," *Edgard Pillet* (Grenoble: Musée de Grenoble, 2001), 12.

3
De Oráa, "Una experiencia plástica," 114.

4
Ossip Zadkine, quoted in *Loló Soldevilla* (Havana: Galería Edificio MINSAP, 1971).

5
Jean Arp, quoted in Carolyn Lancher, *Sophie Taeuber-Arp* (New York: The Museum of Modern Art, 1981), 16.

6
Estrellita B. Brodsky, "Relocating the Dislocated: Collage, Décollage, and Assemblage in the Work of Jesús Soto," *Soto: Paris and Beyond, 1950–1970* (New York: Grey Art Gallery, New York University, 2012), 27.

7
María Vicenta Pastor Ibáñez, *Eusebio Sempere* (Alicante: Instituto de Estudios Alicantinos de la Excma. Diputación Provincial, 1978), 7, 10.

8
Loló Soldevilla (Havana: Galería Edificio MINSAP, 1971). The biographical chronology included in Soldevilla's 1971 retrospective exhibition names her as an author of a "Manifesto" published to accompany the *Relieves luminosos*. Later publications of Sempere's work do not credit her as a coauthor, though it seems likely that Soldevilla contributed to the text in light of their collaboration on the reliefs.

9
Eusebio Sempere, "Manifeste," *Eusebio Sempere* (Alicante: Instituto de Estudios Alicantinos de la Excma. Diputación Provincial, 1978).

10
In March 1956, Soldevilla organized the exhibition *Pintura de hoy: vanguardia de la escuela de París* for the Palacio de Bellas Artes in Havana, exhibiting a selection of works by forty-six artists at the forefront of hard-edge, Op, and Kinetic art, among them Wifredo Arcay, Serge Poliakoff, Jesús Soto, Jean Arp, André Bloc, Victor Vasarely, Sonia Delaunay, Nicholas Schoeffer, and Michel Seuphor. Elder-generation Cuban artists Mario Carreño and Sandú Darié contributed related pedagogical programming, and Cuban Concretismo began to develop in the wake of the exhibition.

11
De Oráa, "Una experiencia plástica," 114.

12
"Los Diez" originally included the following artists: Pedro Alvarez, Wifredo Arcay, Salvador Corratgé, Sandú Darié, Luis Martínez Pedro, Alberto Menocal, José Mijares, Pedro de Oraá, Loló Soldevilla, and Rafael Soriano. José Rosabal later replaced Alvarez.

13
De Oráa, "Una experiencia plástica," 119.

14
Ibid., 108.

15
In 1963, Soldevilla published a book of vignettes from her years in Paris, *Ir, venir, volver a ir: crónicas (1952–1957)*. Her novel *El Farol* (1964) describes Cuba's literacy campaign of 1961; Raúl Martínez, a young artist whose work spanned gesture painting and Pop art, designed the cover as a work of Concrete poetry. Other works from this period include the ballet *Filo diez mil* (1965) and the plays *Bombardeo* (1965) and *Samuel dos veces* (1965).

Abigail McEwen

CUBA'S MADISTA

SANDÚ DARIÉ IN THE 1950s

"THE EXISTENCE OF MADINEMSOR IS BRILLIANT," Sandú Darié wrote to Gyula Kosice in early 1950 upon receipt of the second issue of the journal *Arte Madí Universal*. "It is the concern of a group of men who arrive at the same conclusions in the plastic arts, amid the divided aesthetic of our times."[1] The sole Cuban member of the Madí movement, based in Buenos Aires and led by Kosice, Carmelo Arden Quin, and Rhod Rothfuss, Darié established Havana as a satellite of Madí activity in the 1950s. Since his arrival from Paris in 1941, he had introduced a new visual sophistication and transatlantic mentality to the Cuban art world through his early advocacy of geometric abstraction and wide-ranging international contacts. Darié pioneered Concrete and Kinetic art in Havana, and his commitment to the Constructivist precepts of the Madí group and others radiating from the School of Paris constitutes a remarkable, if still virtually unknown, episode in the history of Latin American abstraction.

Darié's work underwent a critical transformation between 1949 and 1951, shedding the lyrical poetics of earlier drawings as his orbit expanded to New York and Buenos Aires. His first solo exhibition, which traveled from Havana's Lyceum to New York's Carlebach Gallery, in 1949, consisted of what Stuart Preston, writing for *The New York Times*, described as "mists of rainbow color. . .seen through zig-zag bars of black" and applied through scratches and spatterings of paint.[2] *Composición abstracta* [Abstract Composition] (plate 91) marks a half-step between the intuited subjectivity of his earliest drawings and the non-objective works that emerged the following year. Bright patches of yellow highlight an all-over pattern of red, black, and gray shapes that float in space, their forms rotating just off-axis and freed from their former, descriptive role. *Composición abstracta* likely dates from this transitional period, during which time Darié encountered works by artists such as Piet Mondrian, Joseph Albers, and Georges Vantongerloo and probed the formal (and spiritual) values of abstract art.[3]

Darié's close engagement with the aesthetic precepts of the Madí movement steered the evolution of his mature work over the next decade, as he embraced its radical rejection of representational form and affirmation of pure, plastic invention. Darié first became aware of the Madí movement at the time of the Carlebach exhibition through his acquaintance with the Greek-American artist Jean Xceron, a transatlantic figure associated with the group Abstraction-Création in Paris and later, in New York, with the American Abstract Artists. Writing from Havana on November 26, 1949, Darié introduced himself to Kosice, explaining the connection through Xceron and inquiring about Madí publications and other activities.[4] Their frequent correspondence during the 1950s touched upon subjects ranging from aesthetic theory to mundane matters of publishable photography and printing fees, and the letters shed light on the early nexus of activity around geometric abstraction in Havana and on Darié's advancing aesthetic sensibility.

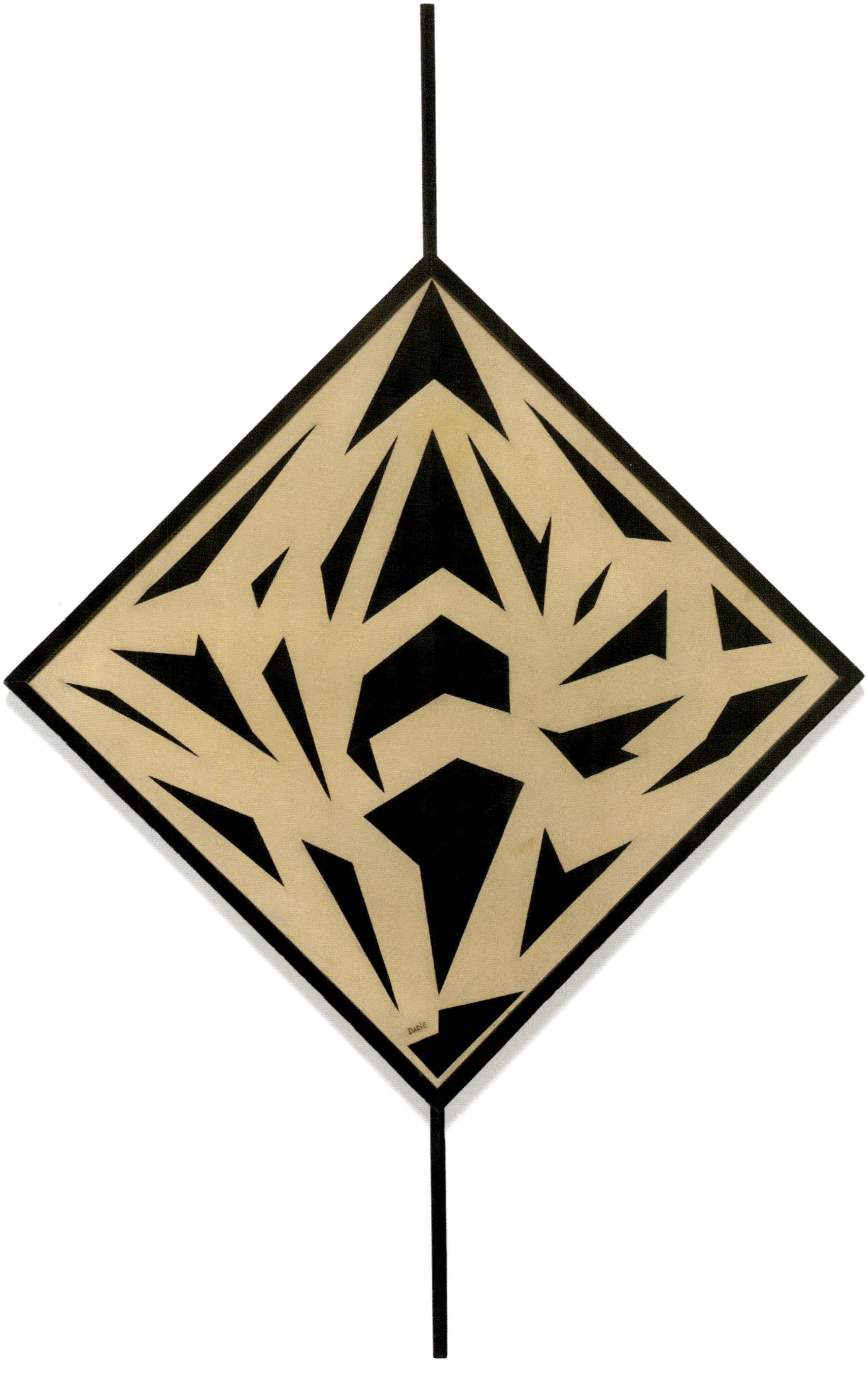

PLATE 89

Sandú Darié • *Sin título* [Untitled], c. 1950

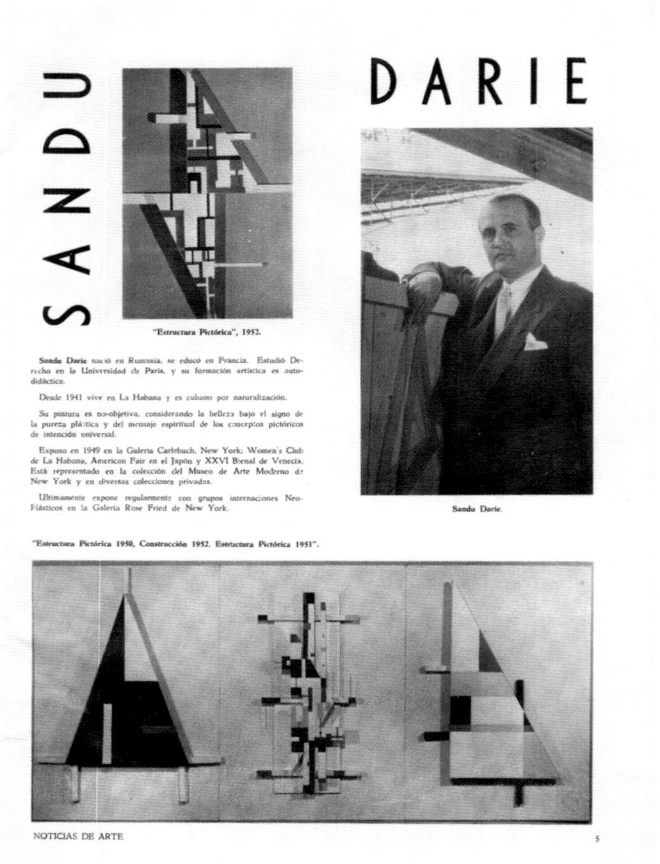

SANDU DARIE

"Estructura Pictórica", 1952.

Sandu Darie nació en Rumania, se educó en Francia. Estudió Derecho en la Universidad de Paris, y su formación artística es autodidáctica.

Desde 1941 vive en La Habana y es cubano por naturalización.

Su pintura es no-objetiva, considerando la belleza bajo el signo de la pureza plástica y del mensaje espiritual de los conceptos pictóricos de intención universal.

Expuso en 1949 en la Galeria Carlrbach, New York; Women's Club de La Habana, American Fair en el Japón y XXVI Bienal de Venecia. Está representado en la colección del Museo de Arte Moderno de New York y en diversas colecciones privadas.

Ultimamente expone regularmente con grupos internaciones Neo-Plásticos en la Galeria Rose Fried de New York.

Sandu Darie.

"Estructura Pictórica 1950, Construcción 1952, Estructura Pictórica 1951".

NOTICIAS DE ARTE 5

FIG. 1

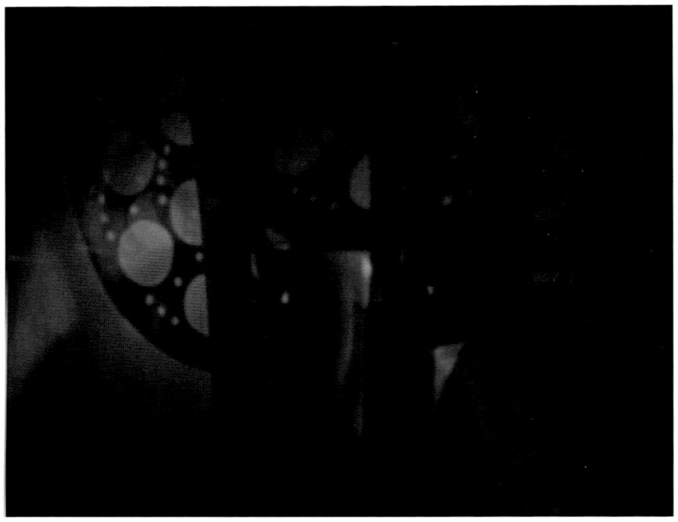

FIG. 2

Darié's wood reliefs, such as *Sin título* [Untitled] (plate 90), number among his first works made in clear accordance with Madí ideas. A spatialization of the underlying grid that informs earlier works such as *Composición abstracción*, *Sin título* presses the image field outward through the open structure of overlapping geometric shapes. Painted in primary colors that nod to Mondrian and early Constructivist practice, the relief dispenses with the traditional "frame" of painting in a classic Madí gesture, instead orienting its composition through relationships of shape and color that take on Constructive, three-dimensional form. Darié introduced movement to some of these early wood reliefs, examples of which he sent both to Kosice and to the second São Paulo Bienal in 1953 (fig. 1).[5]

Madist influence persisted in Darié's work throughout the decade and informed his contributions to the group Diez Pintores Concretos ("Los Diez"), active in Havana between 1958 and 1961.[6] "This is concrete painting because each painting is a new reality," Darié explained at the time, affirming the artwork's direct relationship with the world and its utopian integration into the social landscape.[7] Since 1950, his wood reliefs had interrogated the structural properties of painting, extending the grid beyond the edges of the frame and into three dimensions. Like the contemporary work of Kosice and other Madí artists, Darié's dynamic geometries affirmed the participatory, social role of art—no less, around the time of the Cuban Revolution (1959)—and the integration of different media. Many of his sculptures have articulated parts, inviting the viewer's interaction; his film *Cosmorama: electro-pintura en movimiento* [Cosmorama: Electro-Painting in Motion] (fig. 2) introduced Concrete music and mechanical movement to nonobjective forms. A catalyst of abstract art in Havana, Darié engaged avant-garde movements in Paris, New York, and Buenos Aires, and his work from the 1950s speaks to his role in advancing Constructivist aesthetics across the Americas.

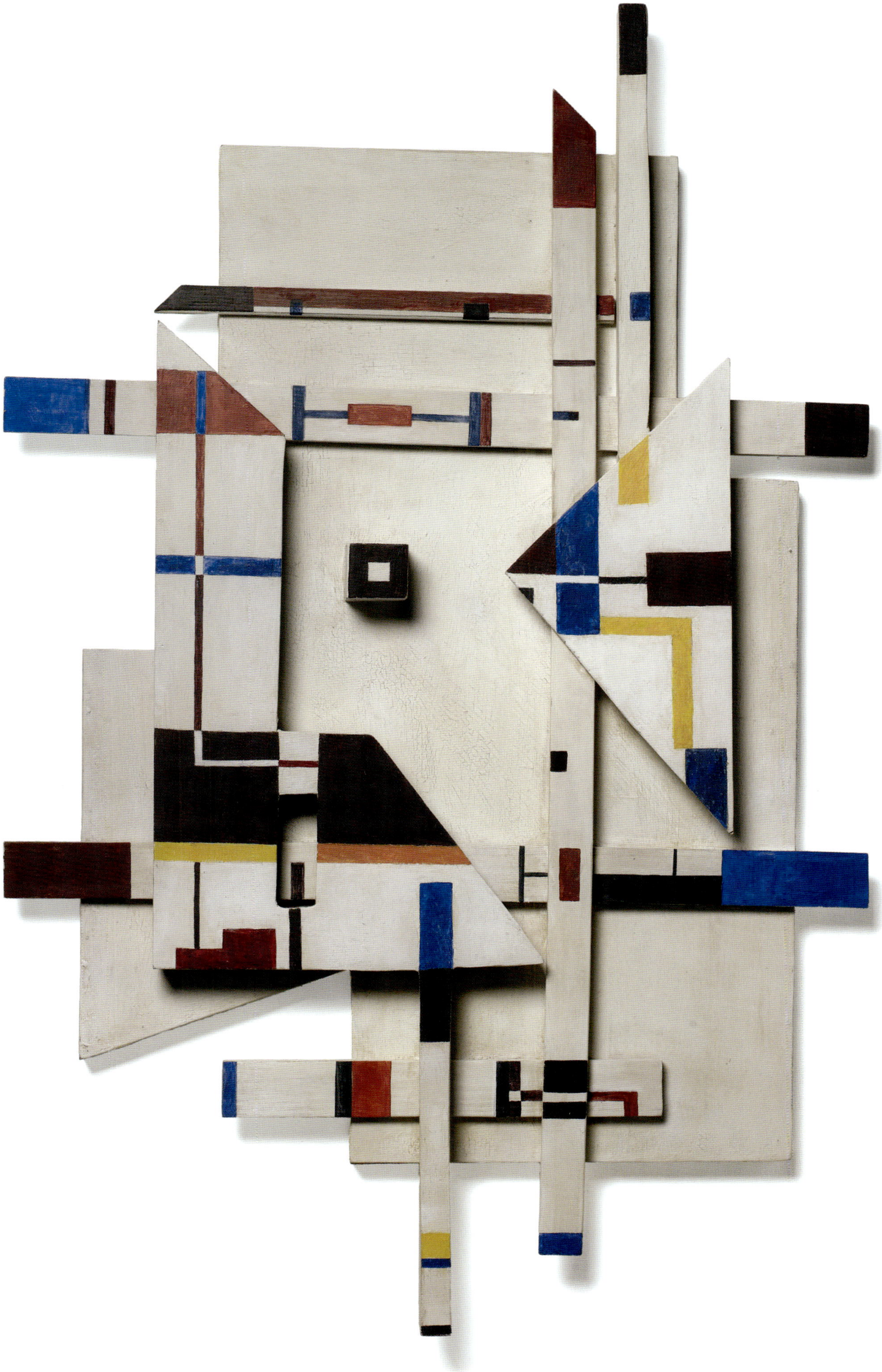

PLATE 90

Sandú Darié • *Sin título*

[Untitled], c. 1950

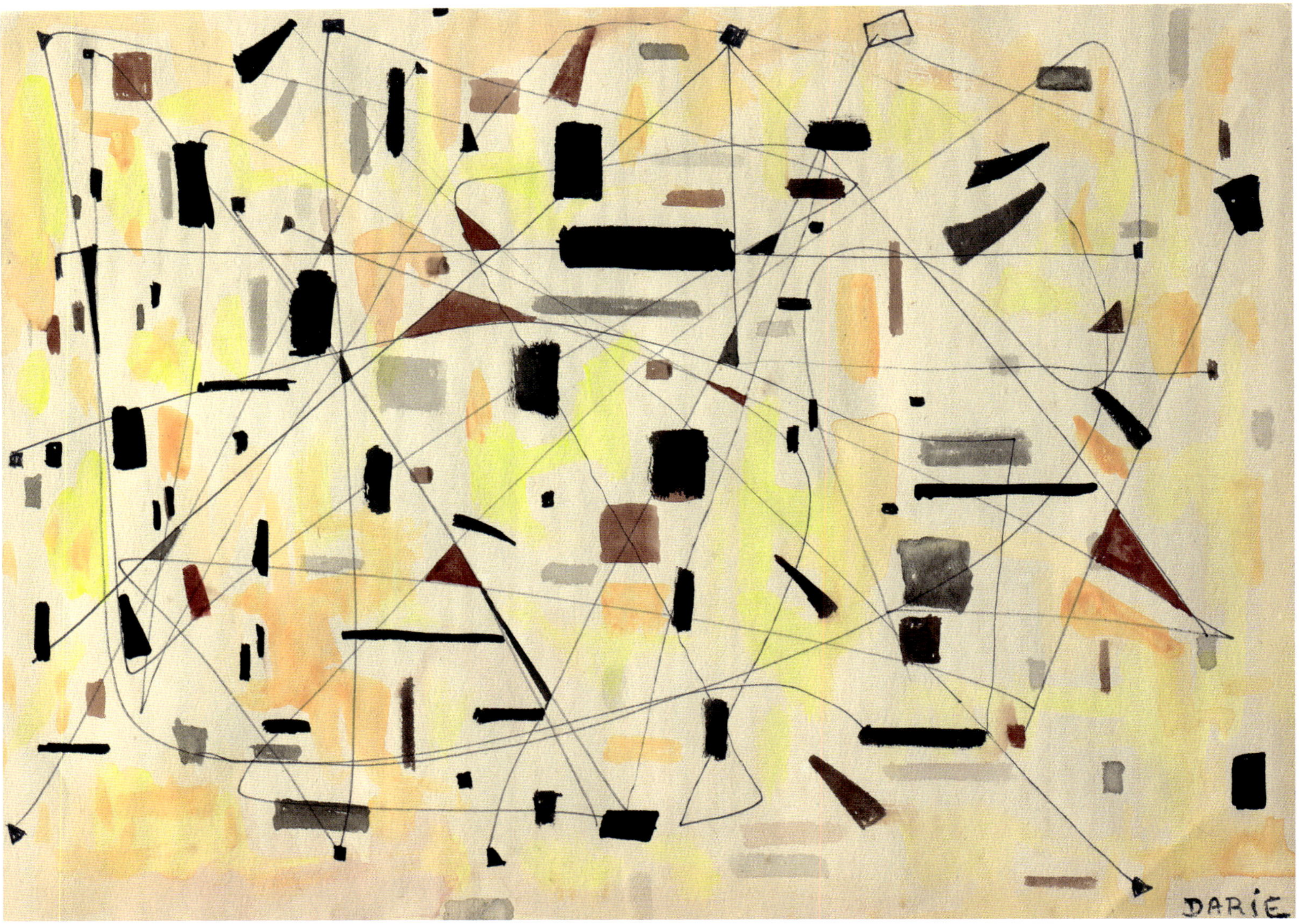

PLATE 91

Sandú Darié • *Composición abstracta* [Abstract Composition], no date

ILLUSTRATIONS IN TEXT

FIGURE 1
"Cuba en la Bienal de Brasil"
Special Issue, *Noticias de Arte* 1, no. 11
October/November 1953:5

FIGURE 2
Sandú Darié
Cosmorama: electro-pintura en movimiento
[Cosmorama: Electro-Painting in Motion]
Film still, 1964

NOTES

1
Sandú Darié to Gyula Kosice, January 30, 1950, trans. Michael Agnew, in *Cold America: Geometric Abstraction in Latin America (1934–1973)*, ed. Osbel Súarez (Madrid: Fundación Juan March, 2011), 466.

2
Stuart Preston, "Currently on View," *The New York Times*, October 30, 1949.

3
In 1951, Darié participated in a group show at Rose Fried Gallery, *Some Areas of Search—1913–1951*, which also included work by Piet Mondrian, Robert Delaunay, Georges Vantongerloo, Joseph Albers, and Fritz Glarner. These metaphysical inclinations were quickly discouraged by Kosice, who tellingly changed the title of Darié's 1951 essay "Madist Spirituality" to "Madist Thought" before publishing it in the fifth issue of *Arte Madí Universal* (October 1951). Although Darié mostly relinquished this earlier spiritual ground during the 1950s, he later returned to metaphysical themes—notably, with regard to Jewish cosmology—in his work from the 1960s and 1970s.

4
Darié to Kosice, November 26, 1949, trans. Michael Agnew, in *Cold America*, 465.

5
Darié founded *Noticias de Arte* in Havana with the artists Mario Carreño and Luis Martínez Pedro and contributed its "International Art" leader, reporting on art from Mexico, Argentina, Chile, and Brazil.

6
The group originally included the following artists: Pedro Alvarez, Wifredo Arcay, Salvador Corratgé, Sandú Darié, Luis Martínez Pedro, Alberto Menocal, José Mijares, Pedro de Oraá, Loló Soldevilla, and Rafael Soriano. José Rosabal later replaced Alvarez.

7
Darié, quoted in Edmundo Desnoes, "1952–1962 en la pintura cubana," in *Pintores Cubanos*, eds. Oscar Hurtado and Edmundo Desnoes (Havana: Ediciones Revolución, 1962), 47.

Rachel Mohl

CARLOS ROJAS'S SUBJECTIVE LANDSCAPES

AS COLOMBIAN ARTIST CARLOS ROJAS traversed the North American continent in 1960, traveling from Alaska through Canada and the United States, and stopping in Mexico before returning home, he focused on the various distinct landscapes that he encountered. Rojas noted in his later writings that through this journey, he discovered that the lines of the Amazon are different from those of New York.[1] For him, the experience of landscape encompassed more than the mere physical nature of a place; it included everything in a particular environment—physically, emotionally, culturally, and historically.[2] Influenced by Constructive art, Rojas acknowledged the existence of a geometric order within this surrounding landscape; yet he also suggested that individuals perceived and interpreted this order through their own perspectives. Truth and reality constantly mutated, and this cultural, social, political, and historical relativity defined both how people viewed their environment and how they formed part of it. In this way, Rojas differentiated the Latin American landscape from other areas, and he focused on the Latin American's experience of landscape as distinct from others. In his works, Rojas thus used Constructivism to convey his personal perception of the Latin American landscape, both concretely and metaphorically, thereby humanizing the language of abstraction.

Rojas's interest in nature appears early in his career, as evidenced by his illusionistic drawings of Colombian flora and fauna, which he created while studying architecture at the Universidad Javeriana in the early 1950s. When he left this faculty and joined the avant-garde artistic circles in Bogotá, he started to emphasize in his works the structural and formal elements of painting, while maintaining a focus on nature. In an undated drawing from this time period (fig. 1), Rojas investigated the underlying structure of a papaya leaf by using its outer points to inscribe it inside of a hexagon. The artist continued to connect various points within the leaf, thereby extrapolating the various structural and geometric principles implicit in it. He did this specifically for the purpose of "discovering the abstract reason and concrete values of line" as they related to nature.[3]

This interest in form and structure was a direct result of Rojas's contact with the pioneers of Constructive art in Colombia, Edgar Negret (1920–2012) and Eduardo Ramírez Villamizar (1923–2004). The ideas promoted by these two artists can actually be traced to the forerunner of Constructivism in Latin America, Uruguayan Joaquín Torres-García (plates 13–19), who was the first to assert that abstraction was indigenous to the region, dating back to Pre-Columbian art. Such a form of expression placed Latin America on the same level as all the cultures of antiquity (Egyptian, Mesopotamian, and so forth), thereby establishing the foundation for a universal form of expression that was called Constructive Universalism. This language combined ancient references with the latest developments in European abstraction. Taking their cue from Torres-García,[4] Ramírez Villamizar and Negret engaged the idea that form could transcend time as well as maintain a universal and spiritual connection with nature through its relationship with Pre-Columbian culture.

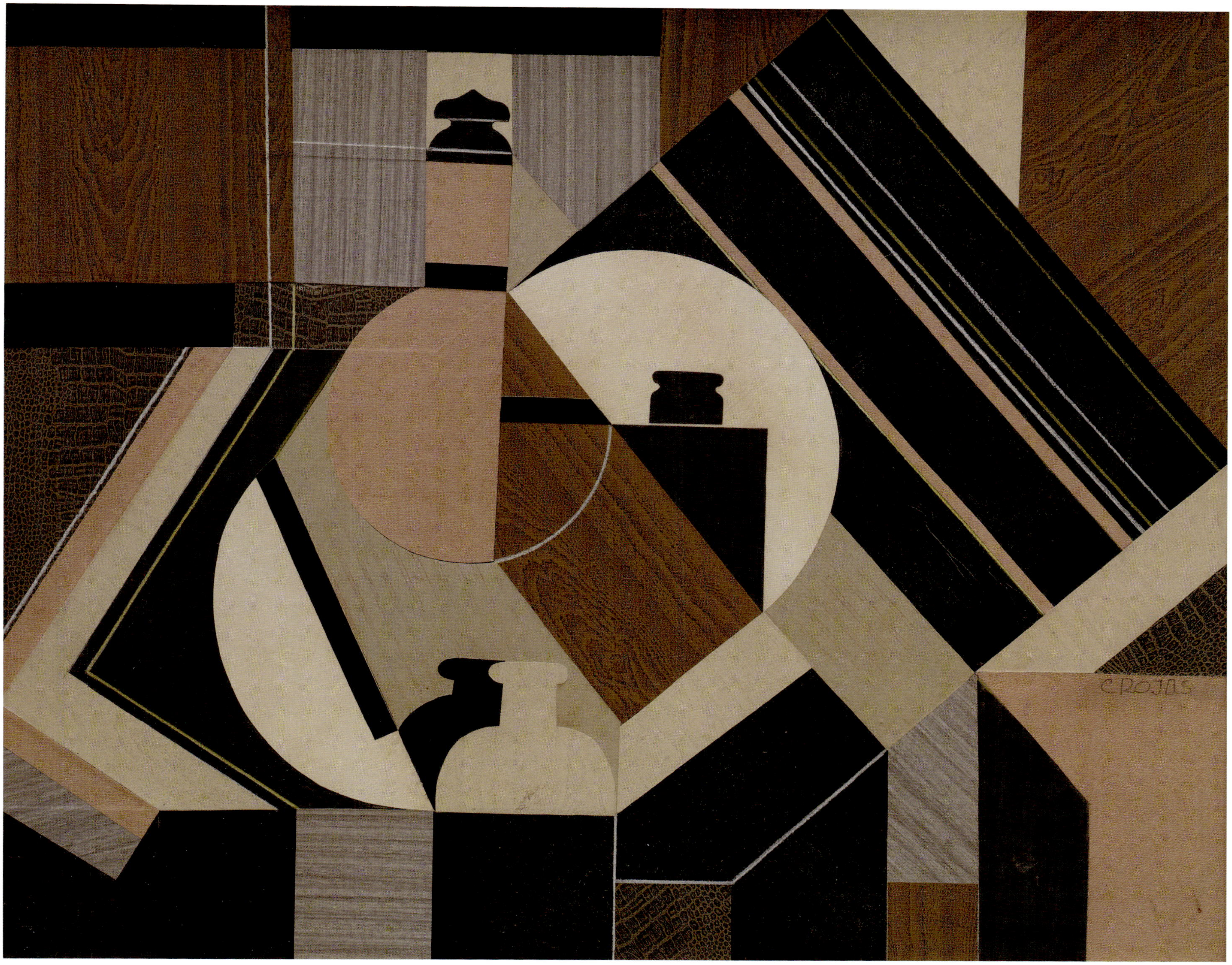

PLATE 92

Carlos Rojas • *Sin título,* de la serie *Papeles pegados* [Untitled, from the Pasted Papers series], c. 1959

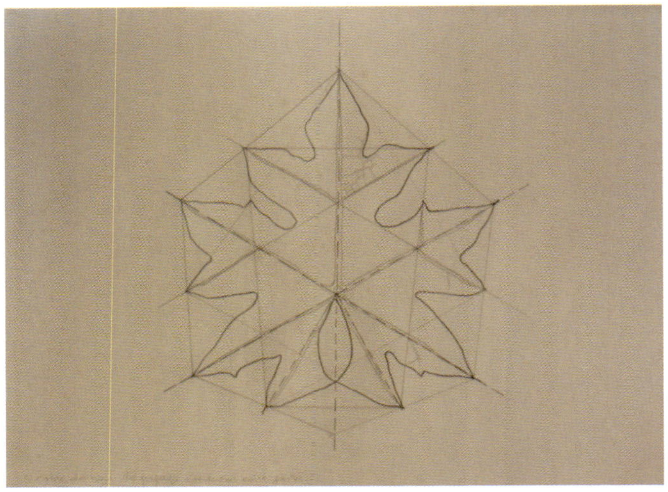

FIG. 1

Although Rojas was influenced by linearity and structure as they related to Pre-Columbian art, he did not apply these principles universally. Thus, the artist differed from Torres-García, Ramírez Villamizar, and Negret, in that he did not believe in one underlying, immutable truth but rather in a reality that was in a constant process of transformation. As he stated in a conversation with the scholar Carmen Jaramillo, "What is called sunset is not the same in all parts of the world; [hence] there is an individuality to all concepts."[5] Indeed, Rojas's idea of fluctuating realities meant that the Latin American landscape was continuously changing. In order to capture his shifting environment, Rojas created various series, each focusing on different aspects of this landscape, such as horizons, towns, and urban cities. Within a particular series, each work represents Rojas's experience of his surroundings at a moment in time. By applying the Constructivist language to his subjective perspective, he transmitted the essence and sensation of his experience through his works. The five works by Rojas in the Brillembourg Capriles Collection of Latin American Art represent three distinct series, which demonstrate the development of this artistic proposal.

Rojas completed his first series, Papeles pegados [Pasted Papers] (plate 92), while studying in Europe in 1958–59. Comprised of an assemblage of materials, including wallpaper, rubber, and colored paper, the works in this series subtly suggest still lifes, taking the Cubist collages by Georges Braque and Pablo Picasso as their starting point. They present an important exploration of the concept of *simultaneity of vision* that became a key element in later series such as América: horizontes, Pueblos, and América: cruzadas. Furthermore, in Papeles pegados, Rojas investigated the construction of space in a physical, tactile manner: He built these works by hand, pasting pieces of paper to the support in a craftsman-like manner. By doing so, he developed a deeper understanding of the structure of space, an important Constructivist concept, which he then applied to the Latin American landscape.

In 1960, shortly after Rojas returned from his travels in Europe and the United States, where he spent time in New York City and Washington, D.C., he began his series Ingeniería de la visión (plates 93 and 94), in which he combined Constructivist principles with Minimalist elements that he had encountered abroad. The artist considered this series the most rational of his work,[6] with form taking precedence and the square becoming the guiding principle. This shape represented the ideal proportion between the horizontal and the vertical, and by formatting his canvases as perfect squares, he imbued his works with a natural equilibrium. Understanding that he was not the first artist to find importance in this shape, Rojas many times titled works in this series as an homage to others like him, such as Josef Albers, Kazimir Malevich, and Piet Mondrian, all of whom emphasized the square as a unifying geometric principle.

The primarily black-and-white works in Ingeniería de la visión also constitute an abstract exploration of the structure of space, specifically notions of interior and exterior, as well as limited and infinite space. The two paintings from this series in the Brillembourg Capriles Collection present a number of squares inscribed within squares. While the outer square frames and limits the smaller one, it also extends the inner square's presence, because the two become spatially integrated. Thus, the smaller shape is at once surrounded, while also becoming part of its larger surroundings.

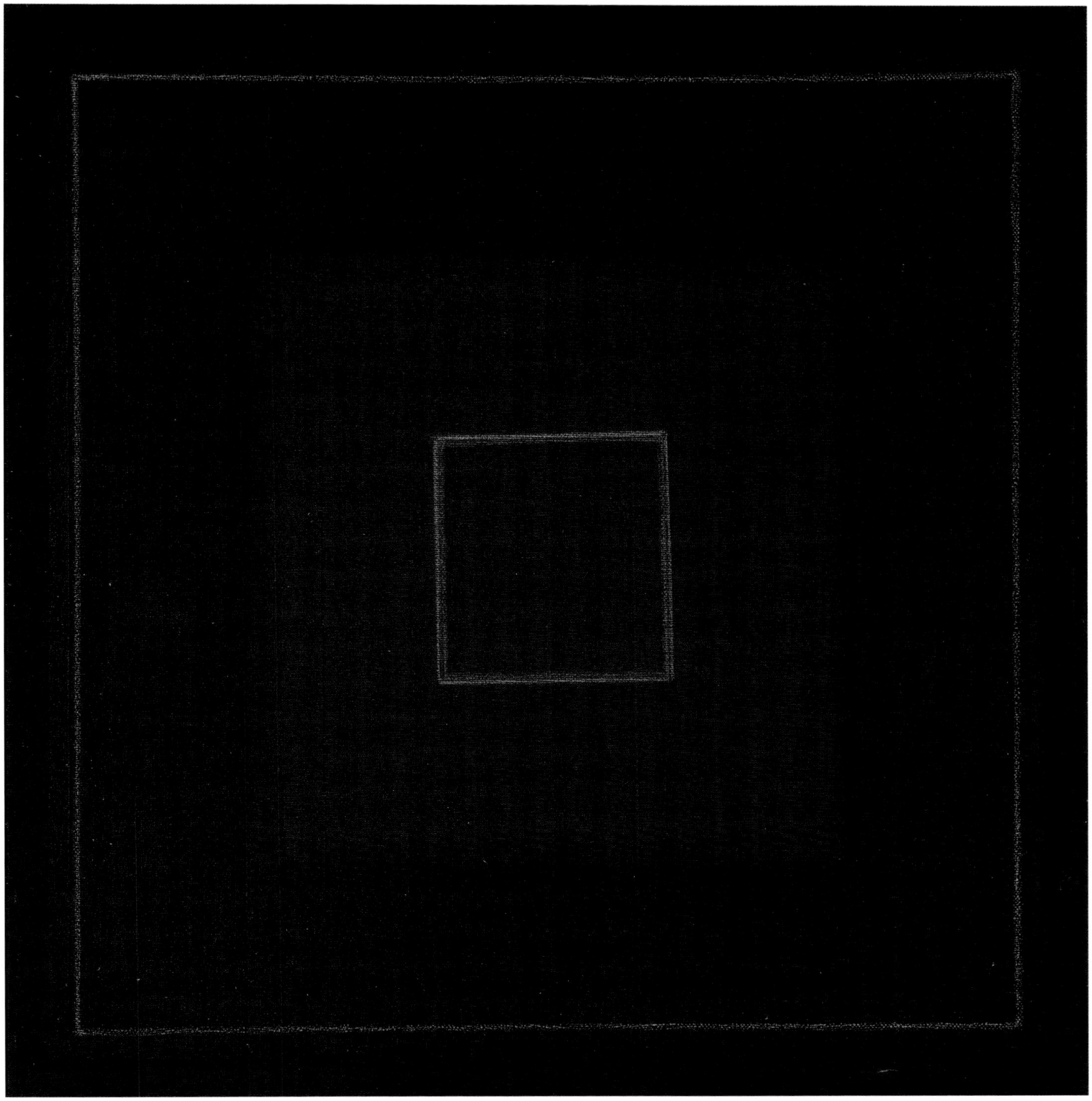

PLATE 93

Carlos Rojas • *Sin título,* de la serie *Ingeniería de la visión* [Untitled, from the Engineering of Vision series], c. 1960

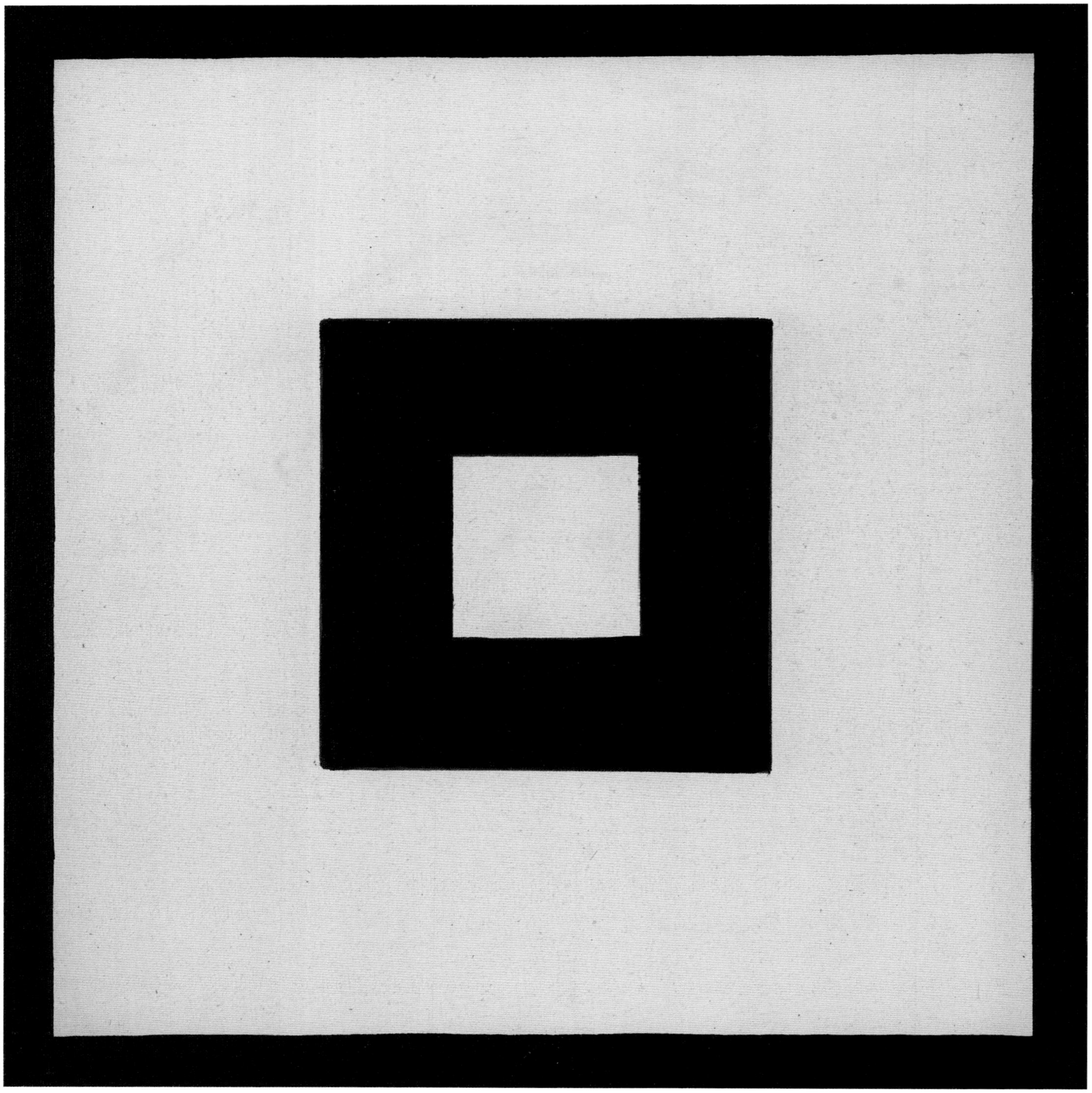

PLATE 94

Carlos Rojas • *Sin título,* de la serie *Ingeniería de la visión* [Untitled from the Engineering of Vision series], c. 1960

FIG. 2

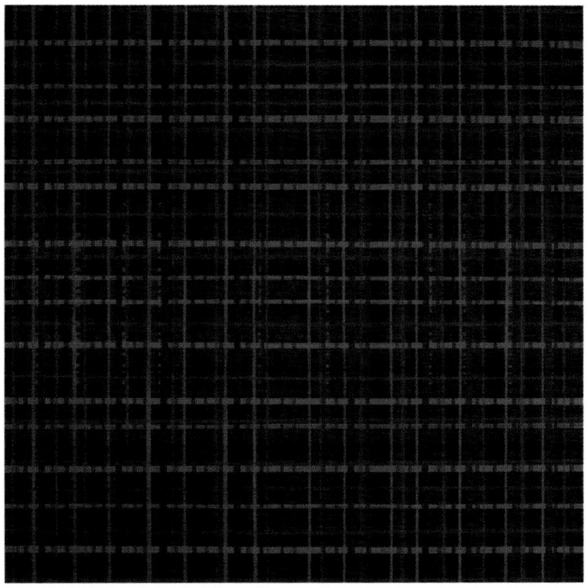

FIG. 3

Rojas's structural investigation of space led to the creation of the Pueblos series, beginning in 1962, a group of works that constitutes a subset of the Ingeniería de la visión series (fig. 2). Although the Brillembourg Capriles Collection does not contain a work from the Pueblos series, it is important to cite these paintings because they were the first in which Rojas directly and concretely tied Constructive tendencies to the Latin American landscape, in this case the rural towns in Colombia. He applied the idea of surrounded and surrounding space, first explored in Ingeniería de la visión, to elements, objects, and people within the landscape of these villages. Rojas rarely denoted the specific place, but rather allowed the combination of form and color to transmit the physical, emotional, and cultural experience of these environments.

The artist continued using this subjective approach to abstraction to portray the Latin American landscape in his series América, which exemplifies his fully developed artistic proposal. Composed of two related, but distinct, types of landscape, the series depicts the rural, natural environment of the region in *Horizontes* [Horizons], begun in 1962 (plates 95 and 96), and its urban cityscapes in *Cruzados* [Crossed], begun in 1965 (fig. 3). The two *Horizontes* of 1988 in the Brillembourg Capriles Collection are both square canvases comprised of colored, horizontal lines surrounded by a painted, black frame. Each strip represents a stratum of the horizon, such as the foreground, the background, and every parallel band in between. In this way, Rojas captured the structural essence of the natural landscape and compressed its topographic depth into one flat plane on the surface of the canvas. In one of the *Horizontes* from the Brillembourg Capriles Collection, the bands break through the limits of the black outline, implying the infinite quality of the horizon, and the false, painted frame seems to cast a faint shadow onto horizontal lines, which gives the painting the slightest suggestion of depth.

This series provides the viewer with the sensation of seeing various parts of an environment simultaneously, an idea that Rojas explored in the earlier Papeles pegados series. The horizontal lines induce rhythmic vibrations, which are meant to express the intimate experience of a place beyond its material nature. The artist's interest in the sensations produced by the interaction of line and color relate to a post-World War II artistic exploration of the subjective experience. Mark Rothko, with whom Rojas most likely came into contact during his stay in New York, used large patches of color to evoke certain

PLATE 95

Carlos Rojas • *Sin título,* de la serie *América Horizontes* [Untitled, from the America Horizons series], 1988

PLATE 96

Carlos Rojas • *Sin título,* de la serie *América Horizontes* [Untitled from the America Horizons series], 1988

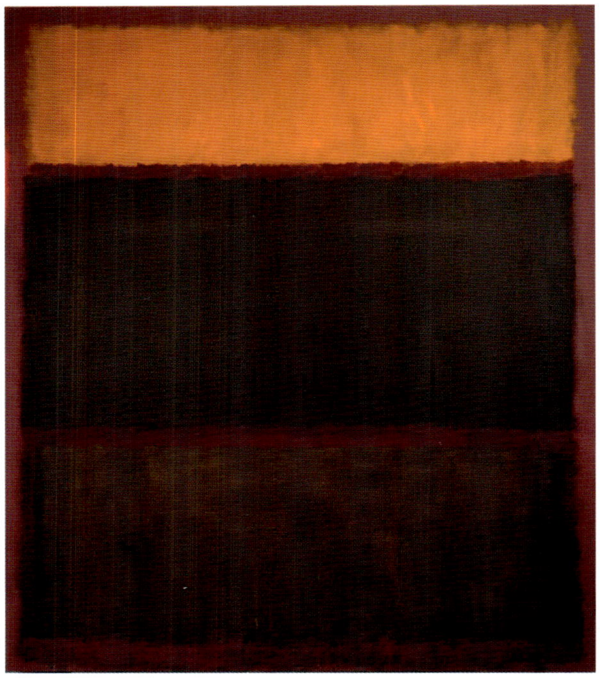

FIG. 4

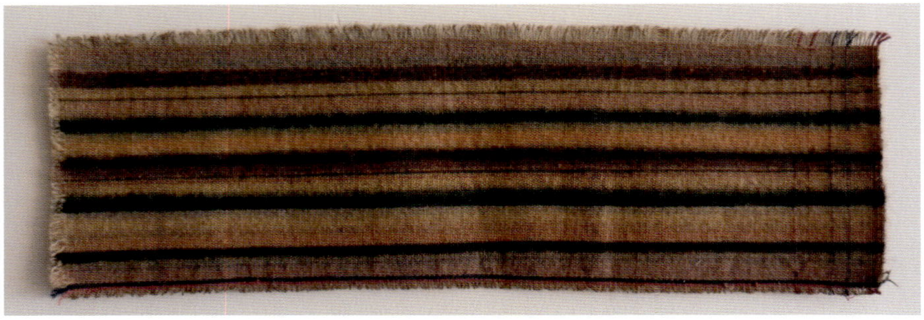

FIG. 5

moods and emotions (fig. 4). Unlike Rothko, Rojas used the Constructive language to create the physical, cultural, and historical experience of actual environments. For instance, the use of gold in both paintings from the *Horizontes* series in the Brillembourg Capriles Collection not only evokes the hues seen in the physical landscape, but also relates to the historic Spanish quest for this mineral, which resulted in the mix of societies and traditions that makes up the contemporary Latin American cultural landscape.

Furthermore, Rojas deviated from the hard-edge geometry seen in previous paintings by allowing each horizontal band of color to subtly seep into the next one. This conforms to the eye's tendency to view the surrounding environment as a whole, rather than as distinct, separate parts, and thereby humanizes the Constructive language. Such a technique also mimics the dyed textiles created by Colombian folk artists, who drew on the long tradition of Pre-Columbian weavings. Indeed, using natural dyes made from indigenous plants, Rojas created a number of *Horizontes* on woven fabric to imitate this process (fig. 5). According to Rojas, these cultures perceived their environment in linear terms, and this perception is reflected in their textiles.[7] Similarly, the artist employed Constructive tendencies to convey the experience and sensation of his present-day Latin American surroundings in his works.

Rojas's unique integration of color and form with aspects of his environment, including cultural customs and historical implications, individualized the Constructivist tendencies in order to communicate a subjective experience of landscape. Throughout his later career, the artist continued to produce innovative iterations of this artistic proposal, including *América: cruzados, El dorado* [Gold], and *Mutantes* [Mutants]. All are meant to assert, in various ways, the specificity of Latin America vis-à-vis the rest of the world.

ILLUSTRATIONS IN TEXT

FIGURE 1
Carlos Rojas
Calco de hoja de papayo. Relación entre partes
[Papaya Leaf Tracing. Relationship between Parts], c. 1950s
Graphite on paper
$19\ ^{11}/_{16}$ x $27\ ^{1}/_{2}$ inches (50 x 70 cm)
Private Collection

FIGURE 2
Carlos Rojas
Sin título, de la serie *Ingeniería de la visión: Pueblos* [Untitled, from the series Engineering of Vision: Towns], 1969–70
Acrylic on canvas
$47\ ^{3}/_{4}$ x $47\ ^{3}/_{4}$ inches (120 x 120 cm)
Colección Casa Carlos Rojas

FIGURE 3
Carlos Rojas
Segunda avenida, de la serie *América: Cruzados*
[Second Avenue, from the series America: Crossed],1972
Oil on canvas
$66\ ^{15}/_{16}$ x $66\ ^{15}/_{16}$ inches (170 x 170 cm)
Colección Casa Carlos Rojas

FIGURE 4
Mark Rothko
Untitled (Orange, Dark Ruby, Brown on Maroon), 1961
Oil on canvas
$104\ ^{3}/_{4}$ x $92\ ^{1}/_{2}$ inches (266.1 x 235 cm)
Collection of Christopher Rothko

FIGURE 5
Carlos Rojas
Sin título, de la serie *América: Horizontes*
[Untitled, from the series America: Horizons], c. 1970s
Mixed media on indigenous-made textile
$5\ ^{5}/_{16}$ x $16\ ^{1}/_{8}$ inches (13.5 x 41 cm)
Private Collection

NOTES

1
Carlos Rojas, "Testimonio de una obra," *Carlos Rojas* (Bogotá: Ediciones El Museo, 1995), 132.

2
Galaor Carbonell, "Conversación con Carlos Rojas: dieciocho apartes," *Carlos Rojas: telas de la serie América* (Bogotá: Museo de Arte Moderno, 1977), 10.

3
"... descubrir la razón abstracta y los valores concretos de esa línea," Rojas, "Testimonio," 131.

4
While this topic merits further research, César Paternosto mentions the connection between the two Colombian artists and Torres-García in a footnote in his book *The Stone and the Thread: Andean Roots of Abstract Art* (Austin: The University of Texas Press, 1996), 250.

5
"que lo que se llama atardecer no es en todas partes igual; que hay una individualidad de los conceptos..." Rojas, "Testimonio," 133.

6
Rojas, "Testimonios," 132.

7
Carbonell, "Carlos Rojas," 12.

Cecilia Fajardo-Hill

ELIAS CRESPIN

THE INTERPLAY BETWEEN THE MATERIAL AND THE IMMATERIAL[1]

ELIAS CRESPIN is one of the leading abstract artists practicing today in Latin America. His work reflects dual, parallel influences: both of his parents were mathematicians, and his grandparents, Gego (Gertrud Goldschmidt) and Gerd Leufert, were outstanding abstract artists. Crespin graduated with a degree in computer science from the Universidad Central de Venezuela and worked for seventeen years in computer programming and software development before undertaking a personal experiment in 2002. This experiment led him to produce (from 2004 on) increasingly complex and sophisticated abstract kinetic structures, the motorized movements of which are determined by computer programs. Crespin creates a "geometric choreography,"[2] in which he explores movement, light and shadow, form, dynamic formal relations, and gravity.

Crespin was close to Gego during her lifetime and aware of the Abstract-Geometric tradition in Venezuela and also of the broader development of Kinetic art internationally. Nevertheless, in the same way that Gego did not believe that she belonged to any specific art movement, Crespin does not want his work to be pigeonholed. Still, he has considered the work of many Kinetic artists to be important references on the subject of motorized movement in art, and he may be seen as a new protagonist in a long line of abstract and Kinetic artists—particularly in Venezuela. And, it is inevitable that one would connect Crespin's work to Gego's, because both artists' oeuvres are informed by a unique sense of improbability and an organic quality that transform the grid and the geometric structure.

Crespin's encounter with Jesús Soto's *Cubo virtual* [Virtual Cube], in 2000, would have great impact on his work. He imagined the lines of *Cubo virtual* as tridimensional pixels to which the dimension of time could be added by introducing movement to the lines. Crespin started to experiment with aesthetic forms once he realized that he could control the independent and synchronized movement of objects.

From his early experiments at the end of the 1970s with programming algorithms in Apple II, the artist knew that it would be possible to realize this idea; nevertheless, it took another four years before Crespin made his first work, *Malla electrocinética 1* [Electrokinetic Net 1] (2004), in which he applied the Cartesian plane in an articulated, interconnected grid of flexible squares hanging from nylons, which were tensed and moved by hidden pulleys commanded by a computer program.

The infinite variability of form via movement in Crespin's works is given by computer software programmed with mathematical formulas and elements of calculus and geometry. Once the programming concludes, Crespin uses these formulas to freely create the work's form and to determine its curve, speed, vibration, and so on. He has asserted that this software allows for a high degree of abstraction in order to define easily the configurations he is seeking. Ultimately, the software program enables him to synchronize with exacting precision the timing and type of movement of each element. Crespin's creative visual process undergoes two stages: first, the selection of

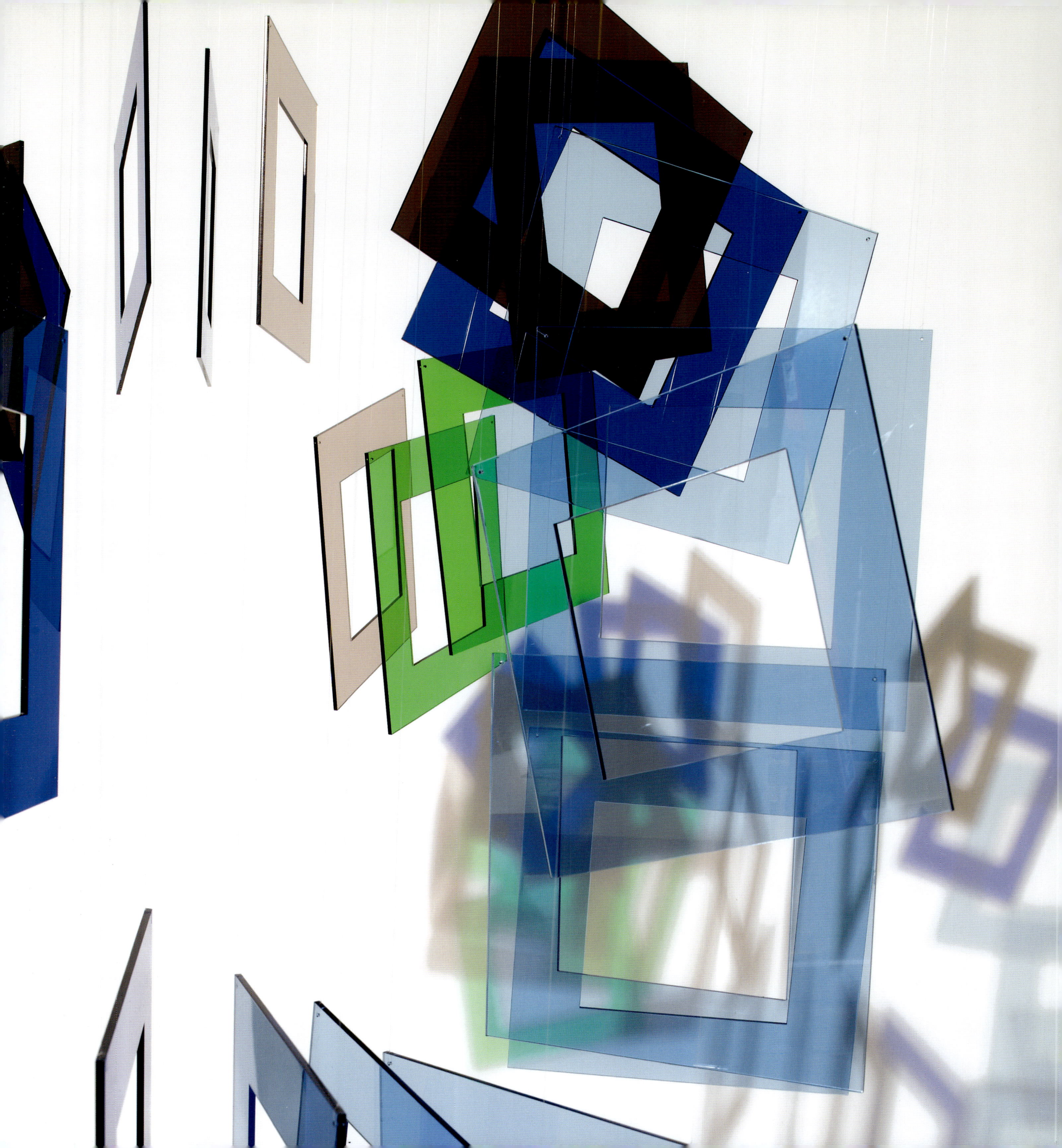

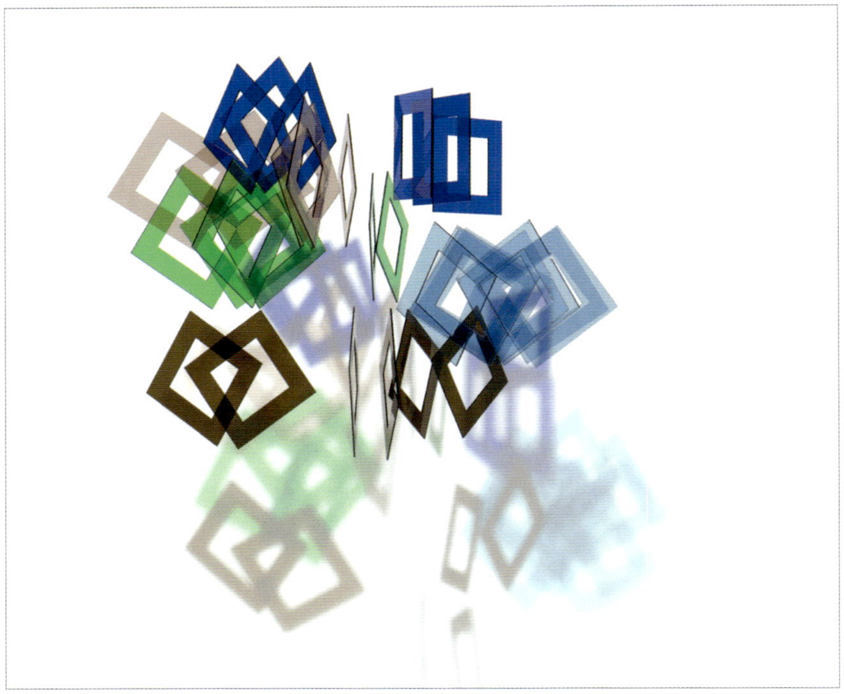

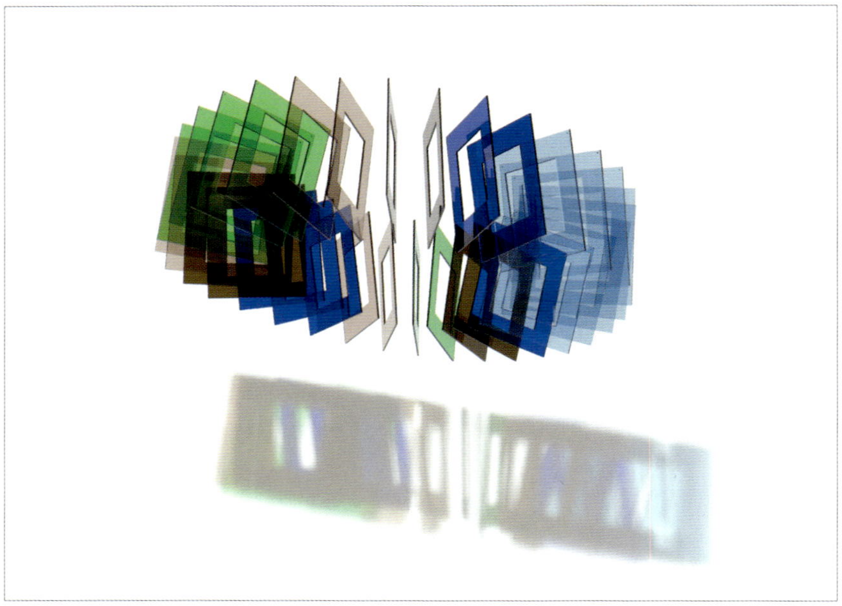

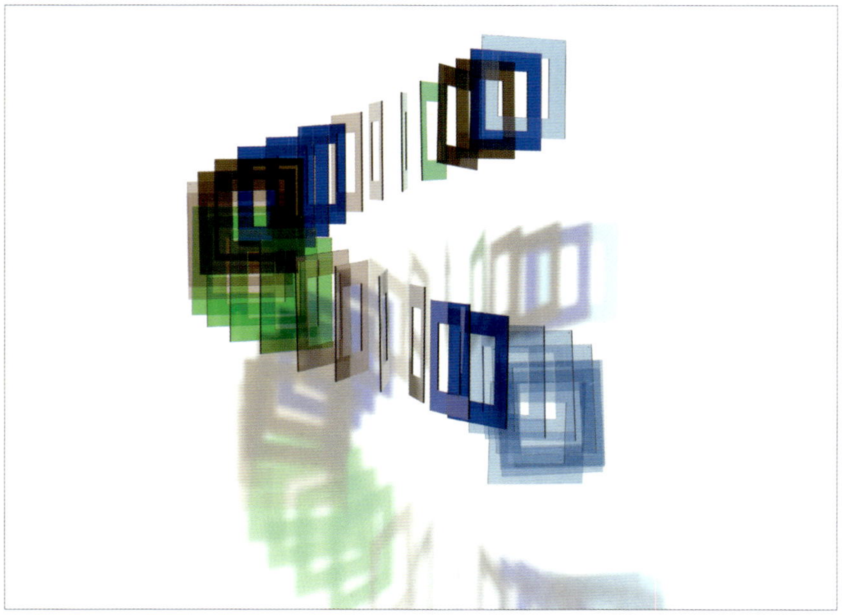

PLATE 97
(PREVIOUS PAGE, RIGHT)
Elias Crespin
Tetralineados Circular Policromático
[Circular Polychromatic Tetralines], 2009

visual elements for the piece, for which he makes sketches, both on paper and in 3D simulations—the scale, forms, thickness of the line, number of elements, and proportions are determined in this way—and, second, the creation of forms and movements from a general predetermined idea of a type of movement. During an intuitive and delicate process of elaboration, new and unexpected configurations appear that may shape a completely different piece. His sculptures are suspended structures motorized by engines connected to a computer, which are hidden in an unobtrusive platform/box. The metallic elements of Crespin's pieces rest on leads that accomplish a double role: they guarantee the tension in the nylon threads during the modulation of movement, and they are an important element of the visual vocabulary of the piece.

Crespin develops his work primarily using the geometric shapes of squares, triangles, prisms, circles, and hexagons. Most recently, he has begun working with the pentagon. Structurally he uses these shapes in two different ways: either the shapes such as the square or the circle are rigid, a continuous line of metal or an acrylic cut frame; or the square is flexible, as is structured within a malleable mesh/grid with interlocking "*Geguian* unions,"[3] which allow for the flexibility of movement of the organic structure.

Crespin's background in math and computer science and art is in constant dialectical interplay in his work. A paradoxical sense of pragmatism and skepticism coexists in Crespin, who is keenly aware that there is an order in the universe that may be explained, apprehended,

FIG. 1

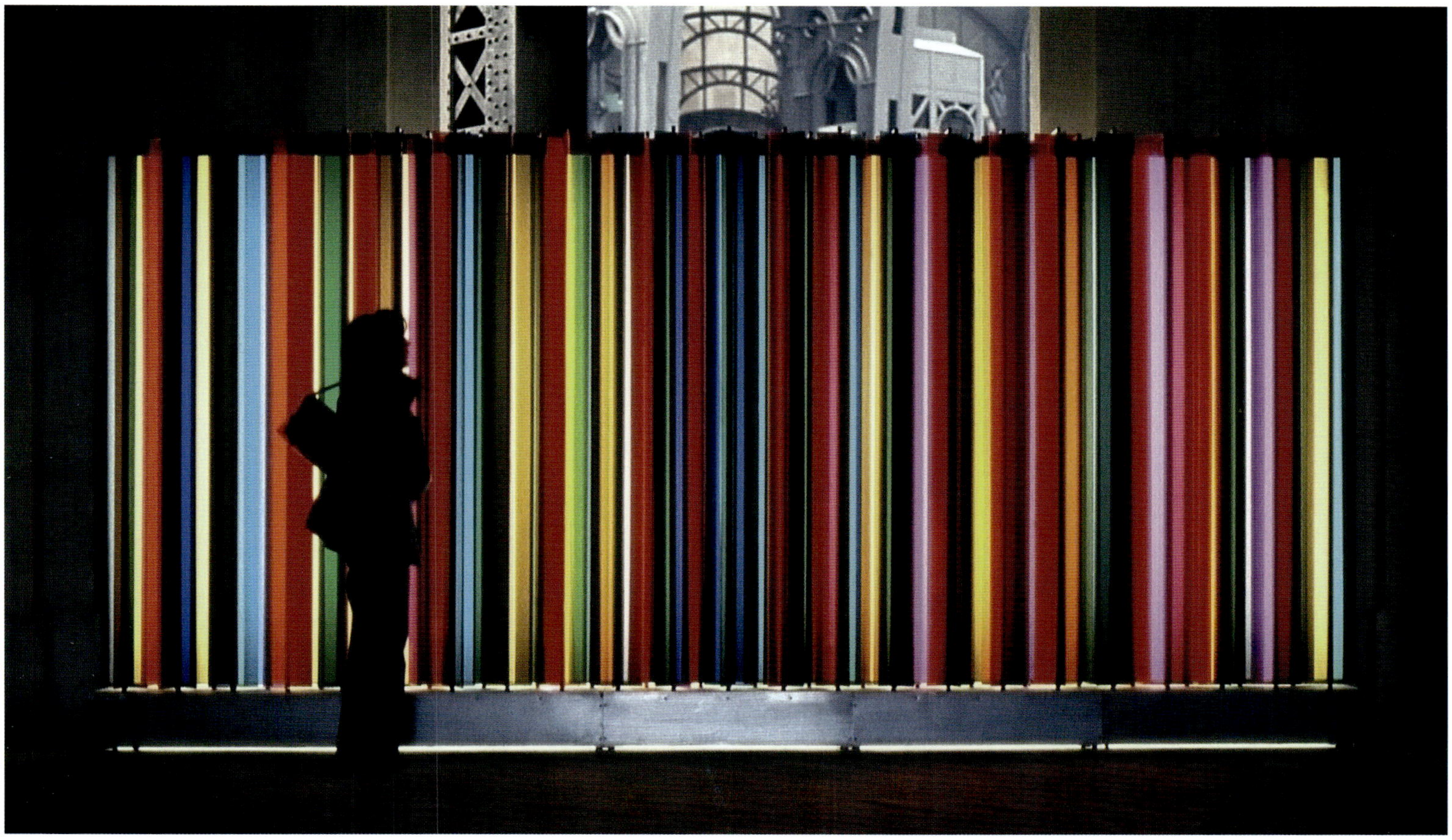

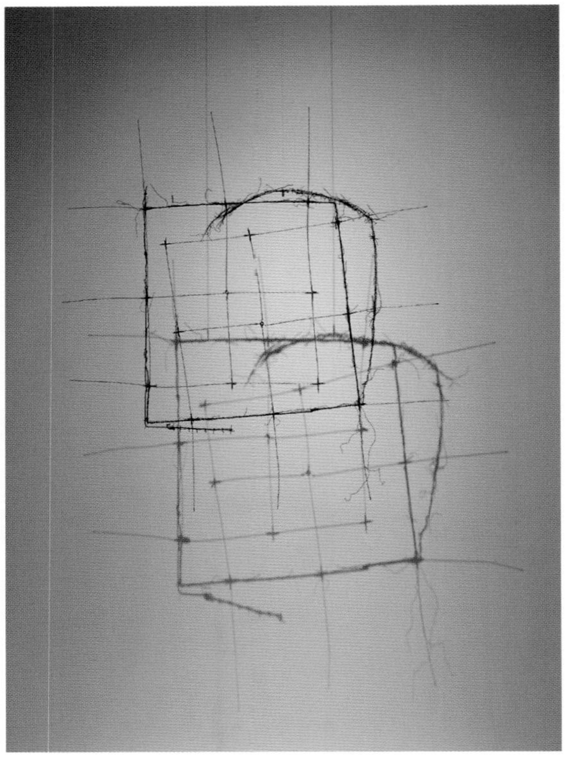

FIG. 2

and comprehended. These pieces may be seen as a reflection and part of the phenomenology of the universe. They may suggest the patterns, laws (here meaning law of gravity, the computer programming, logic, conversion of circular movement of the pulleys into rectilinear, electricity, and so on), and variables that allow ultimately the balance for everything to work. The multiplicity and complexity of the forces and physical laws that govern the universe are simultaneously wonderful and wondrous—even for today's science still a conundrum—and a "plain," unquestionable reality. Crespin's pieces function within a comparable dialectic: the intuitive and the pragmatic, the infinite and the finite, the mechanical and the aesthetic.

Crespin developed his computer skills during more than twenty years in the abstract and removed realm of the screen. Since 2004, the structures he has created implode the abstractedness and impersonality of the computer program in favor of the more intuitive and expanded life of the material objects. Intuition plays an important role here, for once the physical structures are ready and installed in his studio, the artist focuses on the movement of the pieces. Doing so requires that he typically spends two to three days interacting directly with the engineered structure, programming the permutations in a slow process wherein careful planning, predetermined ideas, elements of surprise, improvisation, editing, and trial and error come together in sequences of fifteen to thirty minutes of modulations. The result of this careful process is that the work has an additional plastic quality.

Beginning in 2009, and for the next two years, Crespin began experimenting with color, after having thought for some time about the possibility of integrating this element into his motorized works. Crespin's breakthrough occurred after the artist visited the studio of Carlos Cruz-Diez in Paris, where he saw *Transchromie* (1965–2007) (fig. 1), a Plexiglas multicolored structure for which Cruz-Diez had superimposed screens of colors onto each other; these colors optically combine and change through the movement of the spectator. Crespin announced to Cruz-Diez that he would produce work inspired by this piece and started creating *Tetralineados* [Tetralines], structures he had already been making in metal, by cutting square frames in colored Plexiglas—red, orange, green, and blue, and sometimes in polychrome combinations. By placing many acrylic squares of the same color together, the color becomes denser, and depending on the position of the squares in the modulation of the movements, segments of each square appear more transparent, more luminous. Because of the refraction of the surface, it becomes a sort of mirror that reflects the surroundings, and the edges of the squares become delineated in contrast to the rest of the solid surface. A variation on this concept is shown in *Tetralineados Circular Policromático* [Circular Polychromatic Tetralines] (2009) (plate 97) in the Brillembourg Capriles Collection of Latin American Art. This work is composed as a consecutive arrangement of blue, black, and green Plexiglas, thus creating further structural and visual complexity. Crespin made a colorless Plexiglas *Tetralineados transparente* (2010), and when either light or shadow is projected onto the work, a net of lines emerges on the wall. This effect creates an intricate changing drawing, one that takes on a sort of parallel life or a multiple reality to the delicate and organized tridimensional structure moving in space. Crespin's work reminds us of Gego's *Dibujos sin papel* [Drawings without Paper] (fig. 2), only here it is the insubstantial transparency of the acrylic, not the solid elements, that creates the lines, and it is the small piercing of holes for the nylon

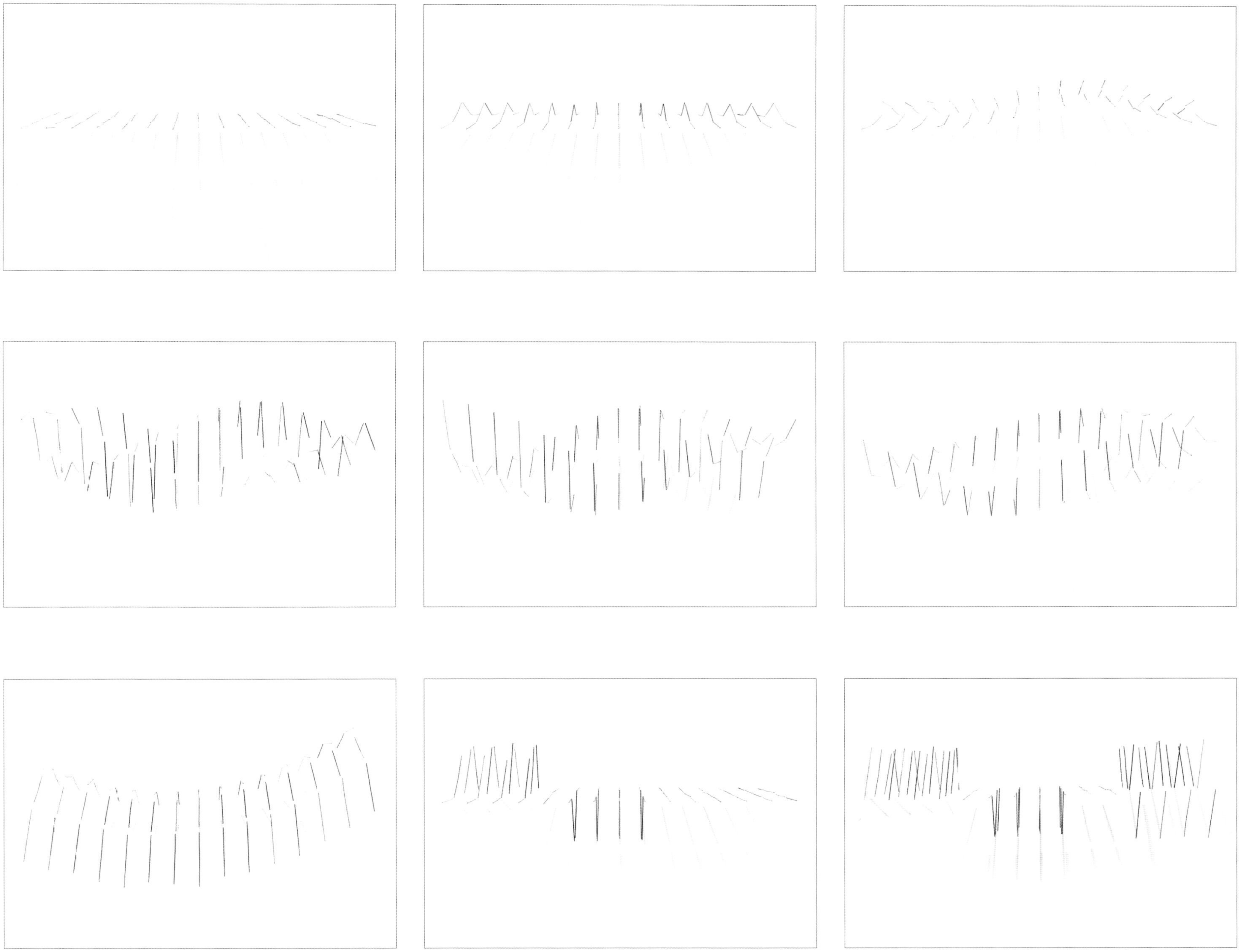

PLATE 98

Elias Crespin • *Hiperficie,* 2010

(sequence of movements appears left to right, top to bottom)

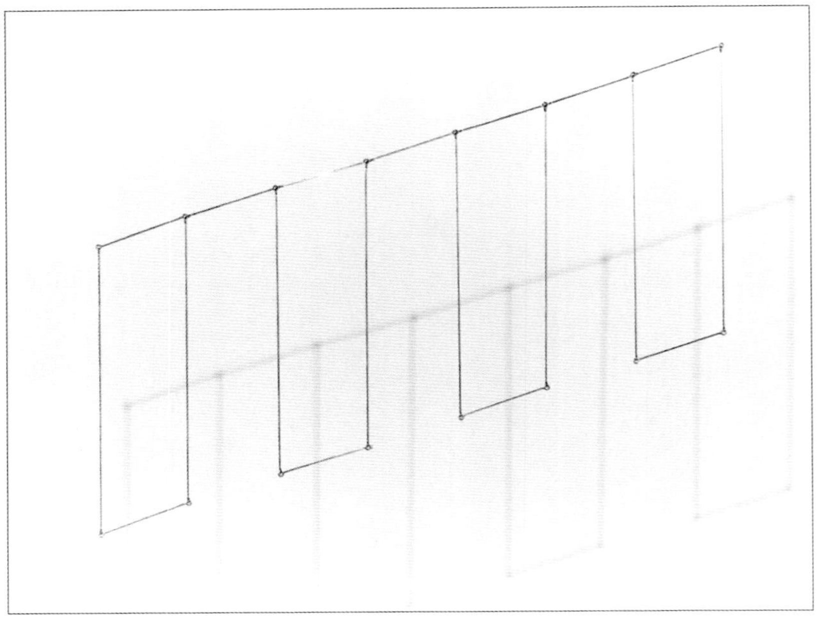
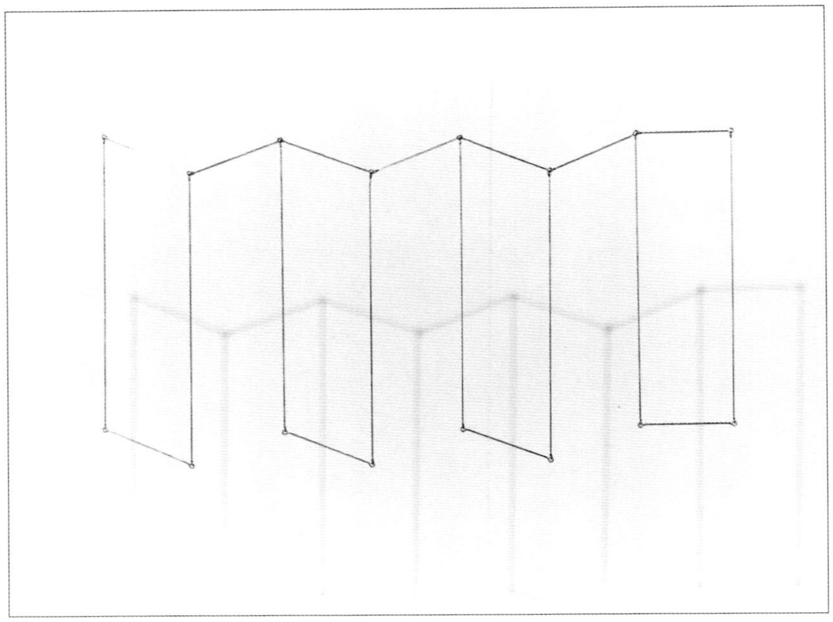
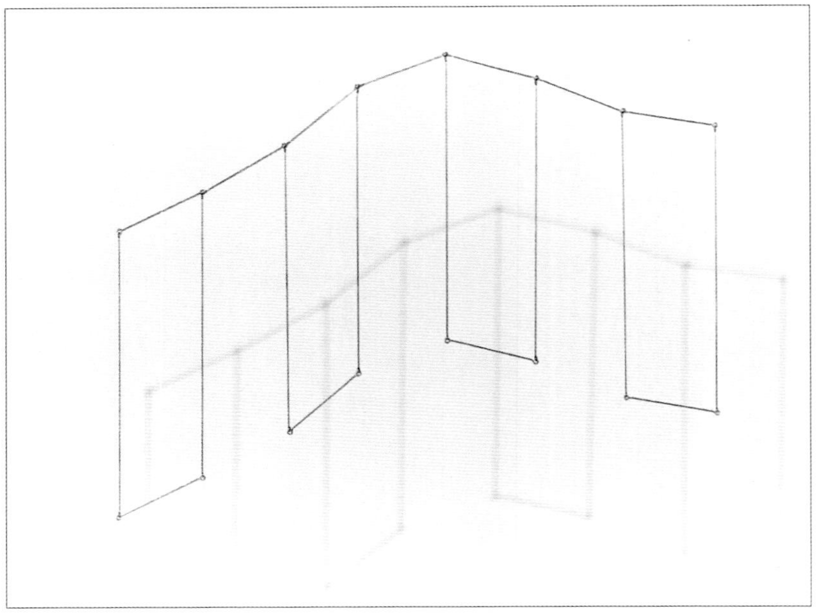
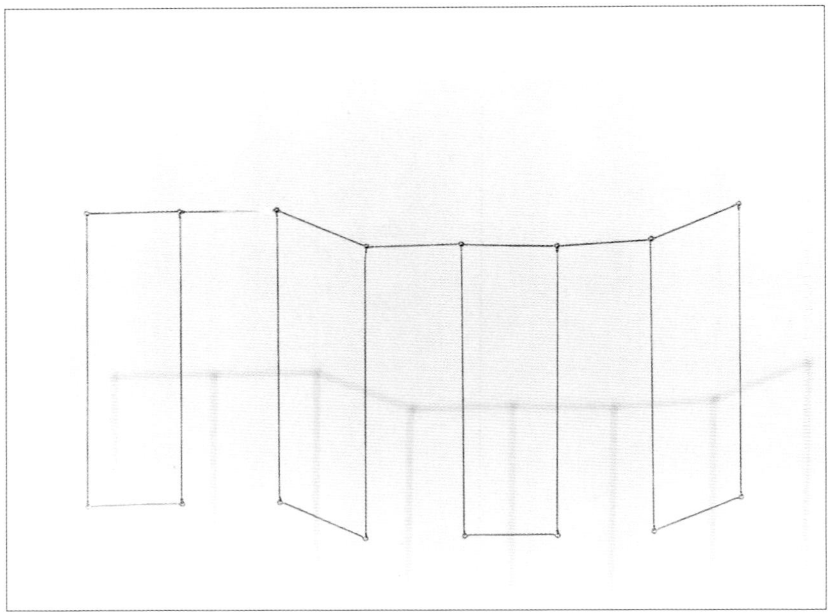
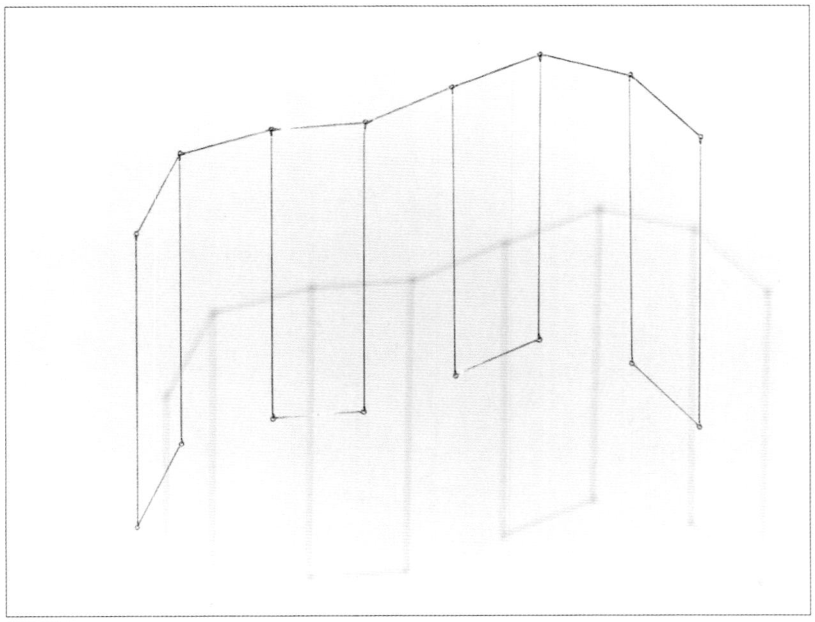
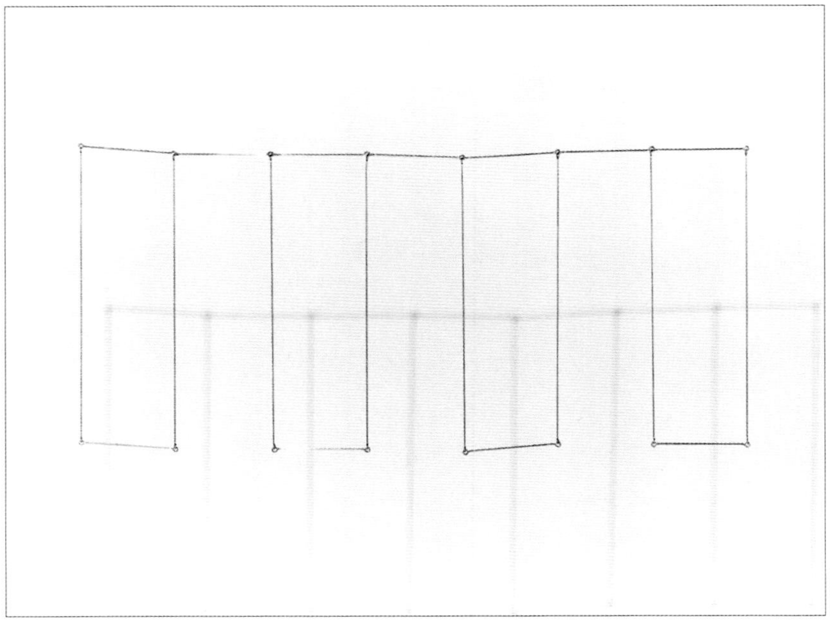

holding the squares that produces the dots in the walls. Finally, it is the refraction of the light on the moving acrylic surface and edges that multiplies and "reorganizes" the lines on the wall in seemingly impossible ways.

Since Crespin produced *Triada* [Triad] in 2006, when he began to create separate groups for one structure, his work has become increasingly complex. In *4Net* (2012), his most monumental work to date (247 x 247 cm, and 224 engines), the structure was created by an intricate and very large net of lines within a square, no longer united in a mesh, but nevertheless functioning as a grid: the intersection of the lines is established by the perception of the spectator through movement. By eliminating the interlocking unions, the freedom of movement becomes much greater. The lines can go up and down independently from the neighboring lines. In this work, Crespin uses lines of two colors, metallic gold and silver, which are distributed in a random manner, both to break with the uniformity and perfection of the work and also to demonstrate that despite the difference introduced in the piece, the difference is abstracted in the whole and works harmoniously.

Guy Brett, in "The Century of Kinesthesia," writes that "artists no less than scientists, make 'models of the universe.' Their models are arrived at intuitively but are no less valid, no less a form of knowledge. A thread of 'cosmic speculation' (...), the structures that artists have arrived at combine an investigation of reality with an investigation of the aesthetic."[4] This quote is relevant to Crespin's oeuvre, as the artist's work emerges at the intersection of his fascination, knowledge, and intuition with the order of the universe. His pieces speak to the interplay between science and art, between the material and the immaterial.

PLATE 99
Elias Crespin • *Tapiz Electrocinético 4*
[Electro-kinetic Tapestry 4], 2011
(sequence of movements appears left to right, top to bottom)

ILLUSTRATIONS IN TEXT

FIGURE 1
Transchromie at the exhibition *60/72. Douze ans d'art contemporain en France* [60/72. Twelve Years of Contemporary Art in France] presented at the Grand Palais, Paris, France, 1972.

FIGURE 2
Gego (Gertrud Goldschmidt)
Dibujo sin papel 85/12
[Drawing without Paper 85/12], 1985
Stainless steel wires, thread, and metal junctures
41 x 39 ¾ inches (104 x 101 cm)
The Museum of Fine Arts, Houston, Gift of the Fundación Gego, 2005.355

NOTES

1
An extended and slightly different version of "Elias Crespin: The Interplay between the Material and the Immaterial" was published in *Elias Crespin: Parallels* (New York: Cecilia de Torres Gallery, April 2012). The text is the result of several conversations and exchanges with the artist between 2008 and 2012.

2
Personal correspondence with the artist between October 2008 and January 2009. All references to comments and assertions by the artist in this text stem from these exchanges.

3
In my conversation with the artist on March 3, 2012, he called the connections "uniones Gegianas," referring not only to their direct relation to Gego's unions but also to the faultless and ideal flexibility that these interlocking unions give to the structure.

4
Guy Brett, "The Century of Kinesthesia," in *Force Fields: Phases of the Kinetic* (Barcelona: Museu d'Art Contemporani de Barcelona (MACBA), 2000), 10.

CHECKLIST OF THE EXHIBITION

ALL WORKS LISTED ARE FROM
THE BRILLEMBOURG CAPRILES COLLECTION OF LATIN AMERICAN ART

JACOBO BORGES (Venezuelan, b. 1931)
Llegando de... [Arriving from...], 1973
Photo transfer and mixed media on canvas
19 $^{15}/_{16}$ x 59 $^{5}/_{16}$ inches (50.6 x 150.7 cm)
PLATE 75

EXHIBITIONS: *Jacobo Borges*, Estudio Actual, Caracas, 1973.

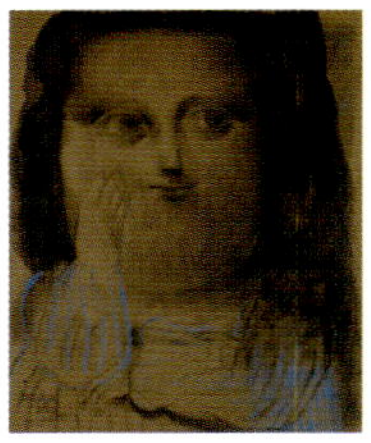

FERNANDO BOTERO (Colombian, b. 1932)
Mona Lisa, 1959
Pastel and charcoal on paper
52 $^{15}/_{16}$ x 43 $^{1}/_{2}$ inches (134.5 x 110.5 cm)
PLATE 65

PROVENANCE: Mrs. Alba Lucía Ruiz, Colombia, 1959; Marta Gutiérrez Fine Arts, Miami; acquired in 1985 by Tanya Capriles de Brillembourg.

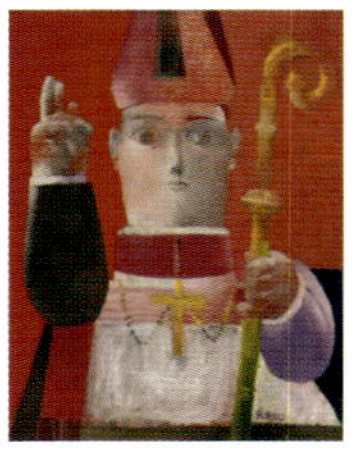

FERNANDO BOTERO (Colombian, b. 1932)
El nuncio [The Nuncio], 1962
Oil on canvas
47 $^{1}/_{8}$ x 36 $^{3}/_{16}$ inches (119.7 x 94.5 cm)
PLATE 67

PROVENANCE: CDS Gallery, New York; acquired by Tanya Capriles de Brillembourg in 1992.

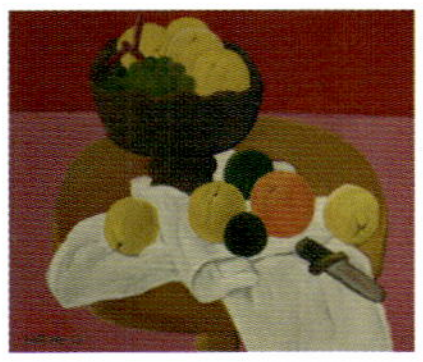

FERNANDO BOTERO (Colombian, b. 1932)
Variaciones sobre Cézanne
[Variations on Cézanne], 1963
Oil on canvas
49 $^{3}/_{4}$ x 58 $^{3}/_{4}$ inches (126.4 x 149.2)
PLATE 66

PROVENANCE: Brickell Gallery, Miami; private collection, c. 1970; Marta Gutiérrez Fine Arts, Miami; acquired in 1992 by Tanya Capriles de Brillembourg.

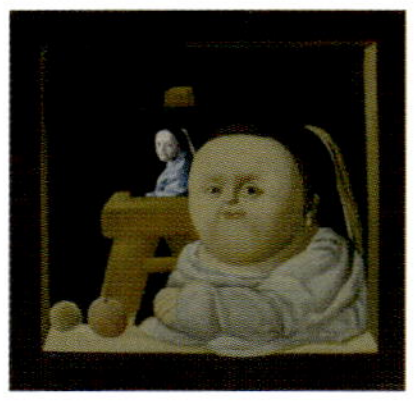

FERNANDO BOTERO (Colombian, b. 1932)
El taller de Vermeer
[Vermeer's Atelier], 1964
Oil on canvas
41 $^{1}/_{8}$ x 42 $^{1}/_{8}$ inches (104.5 x 107 cm)
PLATE 68

PROVENANCE: CDS Gallery, New York; acquired in 1983 by Tanya Capriles de Brillembourg.

EXHIBITIONS: *Homage to Botero*, Estudio Actual, Caracas, 1976.

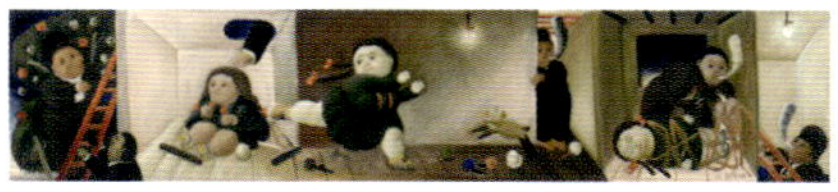

FERNANDO BOTERO (Colombian, b. 1932)
El secuestro [The Kidnapping], 1966
Oil on canvas
16 $^{3}/_{8}$ x 77 $^{3}/_{4}$ inches (41.6 x 197.5 cm)
PLATE 69

PROVENANCE: Galería Conkright, Caracas; acquired by CDS Gallery, New York, 1992, at Christie's New York, *Important Latin American Paintings, Drawings and Sculpture*, November 24 and 25, 1992, lot 61 (illustrated, p. 112); acquired in 1992 by Tanya Capriles de Brillembourg.

EXHIBITIONS: *Fernando Botero: Recent Works*, Milwaukee Art Center, 1966–67.

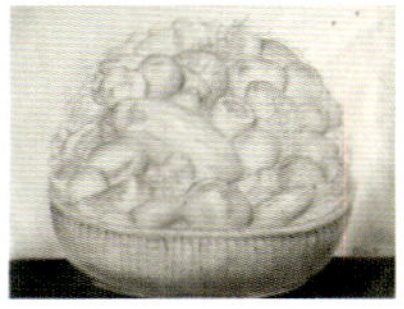

FERNANDO BOTERO (Colombian, b. 1932)
Bowl of Fruits, 1975
Graphite on paper
13 $^{3}/_{8}$ x 16 $^{15}/_{16}$ inches (34 x 43 cm)
PLATE 70

PROVENANCE: Sold at Sotheby's New York, *Important Latin American Paintings, Drawings and Sculpture*, May 29 and 30, 1984, lot 33 (illustrated, n.p.); sold at Sotheby's New York, *Latin American Art*, November 20 and 21, 1989, lot 142 (illustrated, n.p.); Gary Nader Fine Arts, Miami; acquired in 1992 by Tanya Capriles de Brillembourg.

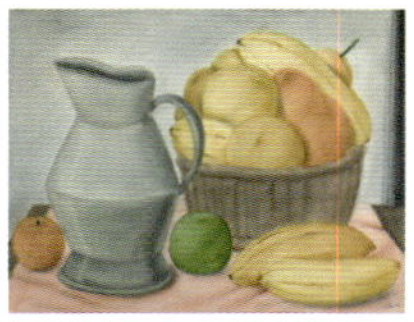

FERNANDO BOTERO (Colombian, b. 1932)
Naturaleza muerta [Still Life], 1980
Watercolor on paper
44 $^{3}/_{16}$ x 58 $^{15}/_{16}$ inches (112.2 x 149.7 cm)
PLATE 71

PROVENANCE: Marta Gutiérrez Fine Arts, Miami; acquired in 1985 by Tanya Capriles de Brillembourg.

EXHIBITIONS: Foire Internationale d'Art Contemporain (FIAC), Paris, 1980.

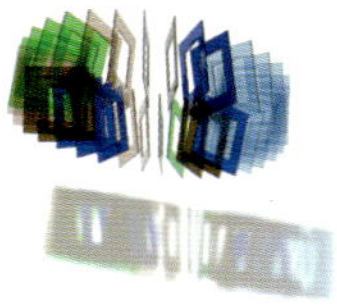

ELIAS CRESPIN (Venezuelan, b. 1965)
Tetralineados Circular Policromático
[Circular Polychromatic Tetralines], 2009
Plexiglas, nylon, motors, computer and electronic circuits
7 $^{7}/_{8}$ x 31 $^{1}/_{2}$ x 31 $^{1}/_{2}$ inches (20 x 80 x 80 cm)
PLATE 97

PROVENANCE: Acquired in 2010 from Cecilia de Torres, Ltd., by Tanya Capriles de Brillembourg.

EXHIBITIONS: *Art Basel Miami Beach 2009*, Cecilia de Torres, Ltd., December 2009; *The Armory Show—Modern 2010*, New York, Cecilia de Torres, Ltd., March 2010; Muestra Electrocinética, Ideobox Artspace, Miami, 2010.

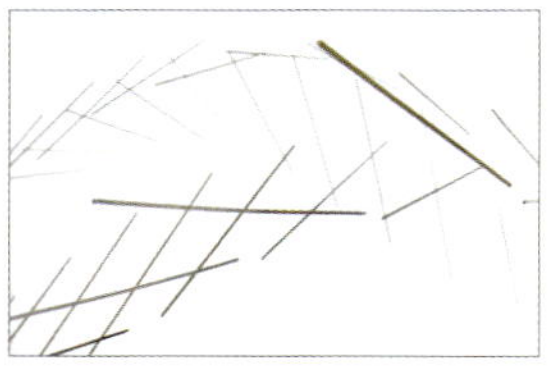

ELIAS CRESPIN (Venezuelan, b. 1965)
Hiperficie, 2010
Brass, steel, nylon, motors, computer and electronic circuits
82 $^{5}/_{8}$ x 76 $^{3}/_{4}$ inches (210 x 195 cm)
PLATE 98

PROVENANCE: Acquired in 2010 from Cecilia de Torres, Ltd., New York, by Tanya Capriles de Brillembourg.

EXHIBITIONS: *Hiperficies: Elias Crespin*, Ars Longa, Paris, April–March 2010; *Muestra Electrocinética*, Ideobox

Artspace, Miami, 2010; *Visionary Collection Vol. 14: Elias Crespin—Electrokinetics*, Haus Konstruktiv, Zurich, February 24–May 1, 2011.

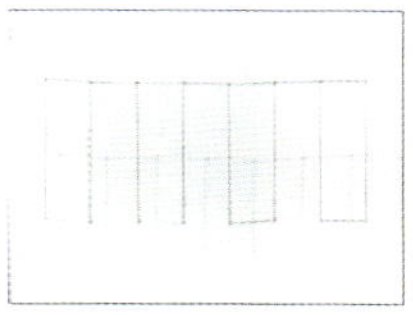

ELIAS CRESPIN (Venezuelan, b. 1965)
Tapiz Electrocinético 4
[Electro-kinetic Tapestry 4], 2011
Aluminum, nylon, motors, computer and electronic circuits
55 1/8 x 23 5/8 inches (140 x 60 cm)
PLATE 99

PROVENANCE: Acquired in 2011 from Cecilia de Torres, Ltd., New York, by Tanya Capriles de Brillembourg.

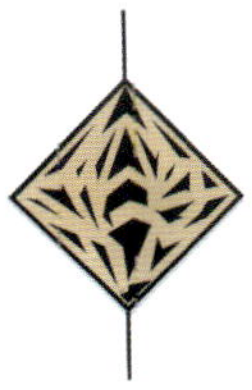

SANDÚ DARIÉ (Cuban, 1908–1991)
Sin título [Untitled], c. 1950
Oil on linen collage on canvas and wood
62 5/16 x 39 9/16 inches (159.9 x 100.5 cm)
PLATE 89

PROVENANCE: Acquired from Artens, Inc., Miami, by Tanya Capriles de Brillembourg.

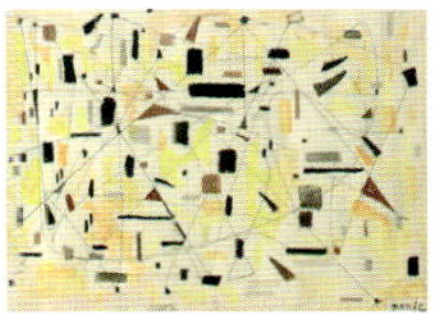

SANDÚ DARIÉ (Cuban, 1908–1991)
Composición abstracta
[Abstract Composition], No date
Watercolor and ink on paper
8 1/2 x 11 9/16 inches (21.6 x 29.4 cm)
PLATE 91

PROVENANCE: Acquired from Artens, Inc., Miami, by Tanya Capriles de Brillembourg.

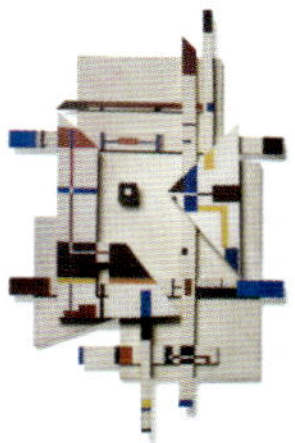

SANDÚ DARIÉ (Cuban, 1908–1991)
Sin título [Untitled], c. 1950
Tempera and gouache paints on wood and Masonite construction
36 1/16 x 23 15/16 inches (91.6 x 60.8 cm)
PLATE 90

PROVENANCE: Acquired from Artens, Inc., Miami, by Tanya Capriles de Brillembourg.

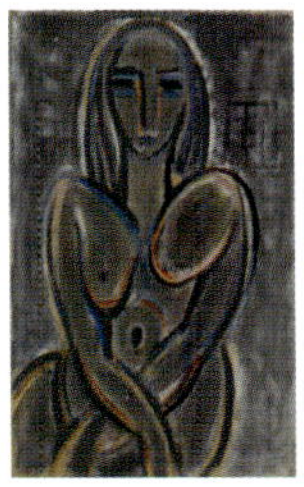

WIFREDO LAM (Cuban, 1902–1982)
Femme aux bras croisés
[Woman with Crossed Arms], 1938
Gouache on paper
36 1/16 x 22 1/16 inches (91.6 x 56 cm)
PLATE 30

PROVENANCE: Perls Galleries, New York; D. Cantor, Indianapolis; CDS Gallery, New York; acquired in 1984 by Tanya Capriles de Brillembourg.

EXHIBITIONS: *Wifredo Lam. A Retrospective of Works on Paper*, Americas Society, New York, September 18–December 20, 1992; *Wifredo Lam: Obra sobre papel*, Fundació "la Caixa," Barcelona, January 21–March 21, 1993 (illustrated, no.17, p. 94).

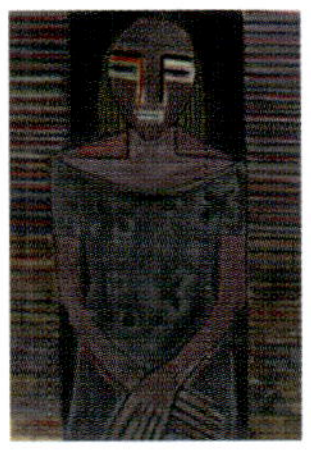

WIFREDO LAM (Cuban, 1902–1982)
Femme violette [Woman in Violet], 1938
Gouache on paper
38 1/16 x 26 1/4 inches (96.7 x 66.7 cm)
PLATE 29

PROVENANCE: Perls Galleries, New York; D. Cantor, Indianapolis; CDS Gallery, New York; acquired by Tanya Capriles de Brillembourg.

EXHIBITIONS: *Crosscurrents of Modernism, Four Latin American Pioneers: Diego Rivera, Joaquín Torres-García, Wifredo Lam, Matta*, Hirshhorn Museum and Sculpture Garden, Washington, D.C., June 11–September 7, 1992 (illustrated, no. 52, p. 194).

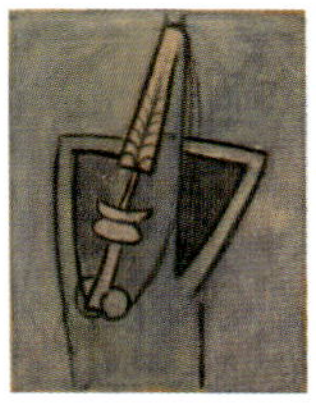

WIFREDO LAM (Cuban, 1902–1982)
Homme-Cheval [Horse-Headed Man], 1942
Oil and wax on paper mounted on canvas
36 1/16 x 27 7/8 inches (91.6 x 70.8 cm)
PLATE 43

PROVENANCE: Private collection, Havana; Pierre Matisse Gallery, New York; Dr. J. Salazar Meneses, Caracas; Estudio Actual, Caracas; CDS Gallery, New York; acquired by Tanya Capriles de Brillembourg.

EXHIBITIONS: *Lam Paintings*, Pierre Matisse Gallery, New York, 1942; *Inaugural Exhibition*, CDS Gallery, 1981 (illustrated, no. 29); *Wifredo Lam in North America*, Haggerty Museum of Art, Milwaukee, October 11, 2007–January 21, 2008; Miami Art Museum, February 8–May 18, 2008; Museum of Latin American Art, Long Beach, June 12–August 31, 2008; Salvador Dalí Museum, St. Petersburg, Florida (illustrated, no. 20, p. 93).

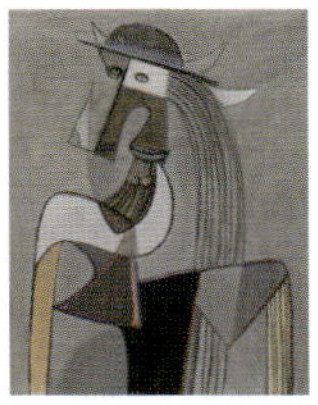

WIFREDO LAM (Cuban, 1902–1982)
Personaje con sombrero
[Personage with Hat], c. 1942
Gouache on paper
37 1/16 x 28 15/16 inches (94.1 x 73.5 cm)
PLATE 42

PROVENANCE: Marta Gutiérrez Fine Arts, Miami; acquired in 1986 by Tanya Capriles de Brillembourg.

EXHIBITIONS: *Wifredo Lam in North America*, Haggerty Museum of Art, Milwaukee, October 11, 2007–January 21, 2008; Miami Art Museum, February 8–May 18, 2008; Museum of Latin American Art, Long Beach, June 12–August 31, 2008; Salvador Dalí Museum, St. Petersburg, Florida (illustrated, no. 18, p. 91); *North Looks South: Building the Latin American Art Collection*, Museum of Fine Arts, Houston, June 7–September 27, 2009.

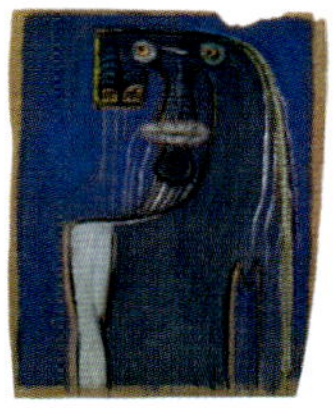

WIFREDO LAM (Cuban, 1902–1982)
Cheval [Horse], c. 1942
Gouache on paper, double-sided painting (*Femme* on reverse)
36 x 29 1/8 inches (91.4 x 74 cm)
PLATE 40

PROVENANCE: Marta Gutiérrez Fine Arts, Miami; acquired in 1986 by Tanya Capriles de Brillembourg.

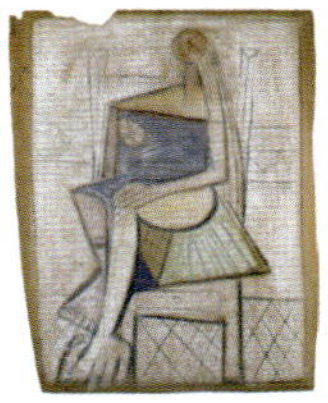

WIFREDO LAM (Cuban, 1902–1982)
Femme [Woman], c. 1942
Gouache on paper, double-sided painting (*Cheval* on reverse)
36 x 29 1/8 inches (91.4 x 74 cm)
PLATE 35

PROVENANCE: Marta Gutiérrez Fine Arts, Miami; acquired in 1986 by Tanya Capriles de Brillembourg.

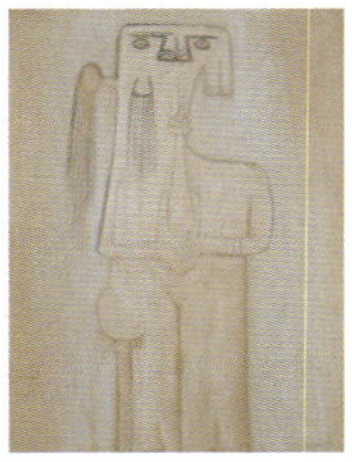

WIFREDO LAM (Cuban, 1902–1982)
Los Amantes [The Lovers], 1942
Gouache on paper mounted on canvas
40 3/16 x 30 7/16 inches (102.1 x 77.3 cm)
PLATE 41

PROVENANCE: Helena Holzer Benítez (formerly Mrs. Wifredo Lam), Saarbrücken, Germany; Galerie Albert Loeb, Paris; Marta Gutiérrez Fine Arts, Miami; acquired by Tanya Capriles de Brillembourg in 1984.

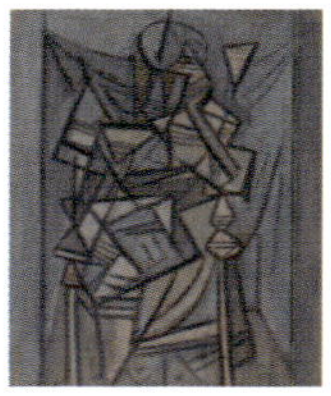

WIFREDO LAM (Cuban, 1902–1982)
Sin título [Untitled], c. 1942
Gouache on paper
41 3/8 x 33 7/8 inches (105.1 x 86 cm)
PLATE 39

PROVENANCE: Marta Gutiérrez Fine Arts, Miami; acquired in 1986 by Tanya Capriles de Brillembourg.

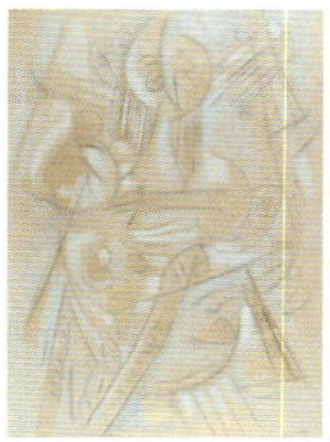

WIFREDO LAM (Cuban, 1902–1982)
Maternité Yoruba [Yoruba Maternity], 1942
Gouache and charcoal on paper
41 7/16 x 35 inches (105.3 x 88.9 cm)
PLATE 37

PROVENANCE: Helena Holzer Benítez (formerly Mrs. Wifredo Lam), Saarbrücken, Germany; Dr. Federico Dumenigo, Miami; Marta Gutiérrez Fine Arts, Miami; acquired by Tanya Capriles de Brillembourg in 1984.

EXHIBITIONS: *Wifredo Lam. A Retrospective of Works on Paper*, Americas Society, New York, 18 September–December 20, 1992; *Wifredo Lam Obra sobre papel*, Fundació "la Caixa," Barcelona, January 21–March 21, 1993 (illustrated, no.49, p. 121).

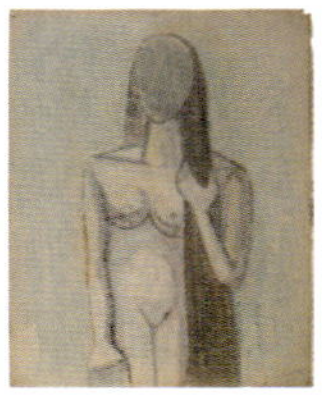

WIFREDO LAM (Cuban, 1902–1982)
Femme aux cheveux longs, III [Woman with Long Hair, III], 1942
Gouache on paper, double-sided painting (*Homme* on reverse)
41 7/8 x 33 9/16 inches (106.4 x 85.2 cm)
PLATE 34

PROVENANCE: Helena Holzer Benítez (formerly Mrs. Wifredo Lam), Saarbrücken, Germany; Galerie Albert Loeb, Paris; Marta Gutiérrez Fine Arts, Miami; acquired by Tanya Capriles de Brillembourg in 1986.

EXHIBITIONS: *Wifredo Lam. A Retrospective of Works on Paper,* Americas Society, New York, 18 September–December 20, 1992; *Wifredo Lam Obra sobre papel,* Fundació "la Caixa," Barcelona, January 21–March 21, 1993 (illustrated, no. 29, p 102).

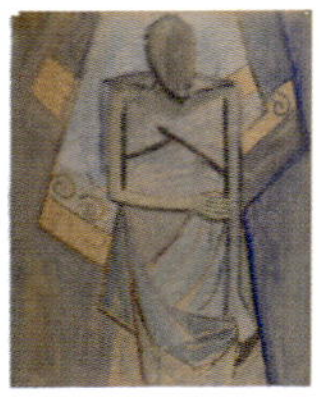

WIFREDO LAM (Cuban, 1902–1982)
Homme [Man], 1942
Gouache on paper, double-sided painting (*Femme aux cheveux longs, III* on reverse)
41 7/8 x 33 9/16 inches (106.4 x 85.2 cm)
PLATE 38

PROVENANCE: Helena Holzer Benítez (formerly Mrs. Wifredo Lam), Saarbrücken, Germany; Galerie Albert Loeb, Paris; Marta Gutiérrez Fine Arts, Miami; acquired by Tanya Capriles de Brillembourg in 1986.

EXHIBITIONS: *Wifredo Lam: A Retrospective of Works on Paper*, Americas Society, New York, 18 September–December 20, 1992; *Wifredo Lam. Obra sobre papel*, Fundació "la Caixa," Barcelona, January 21–March 21, 1993 (illustrated, no. 29, p. 103).

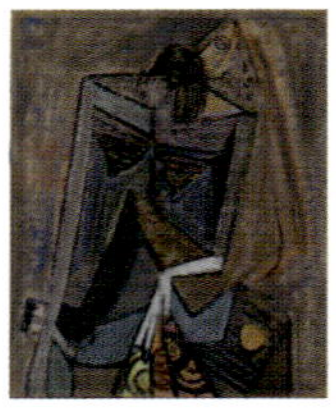

WIFREDO LAM (Cuban, 1902–1982)
Femme à l'éventail, II [Woman with Fan, II], 1942
Gouache on paper
41 13/16 x 33 15/16 inches (106.2 x 86.2 cm)
PLATE 31

PROVENANCE: Marta Gutiérrez Fine Arts, Miami; acquired by Tanya Capriles de Brillembourg in 1985.

EXHIBITIONS: *North Looks South: Building the Latin American Art Collection,* Museum of Fine Arts, Houston, June 7–September 27, 2009; *Cosmopolitian Routes: Houston Collects Latin American Art,* Museum of Fine Arts, Houston, October 24, 2010–February 6, 2011.

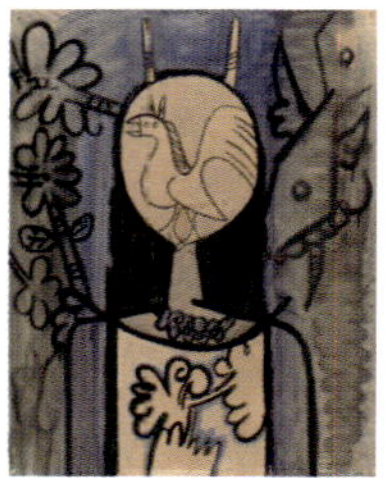

WIFREDO LAM (Cuban, 1902–1982)
Femme-Oiseau [Woman-Bird], 1950
Gouache on paper
37 1/16 x 29 1/8 inches (94.1 x 74 cm)
PLATE 33

PROVENANCE: Galerie Nathalie Seroussi, Paris; private collection (possibly Manuel Mato); Marta Gutiérrez Fine Arts, Miami; acquired by Tanya Capriles de Brillembourg in 1984.

EXHIBITIONS: *Wifredo Lam: A Retrospective of Works on Paper,* Americas Society, New York, September 18–December 20, 1992 (illustrated, no. 59, p. 33). *Wifredo Lam. Obra sobre papel,* Fundació "la Caixa," Barcelona, January 21–March 21, 1993 (illustrated, no. 84, p. 46 and 155).

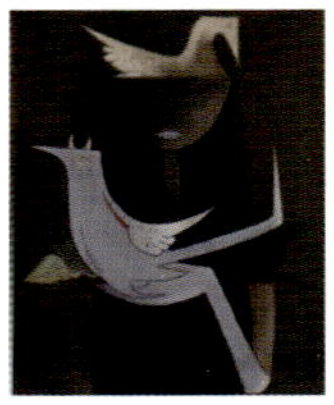

WIFREDO LAM (Cuban, 1902–1982)
Mujer con pájaro [Woman with Bird], 1955
Oil on canvas
29 x 23 11/16 inches (73.7 x 60.2 cm)
PLATE 32

PROVENANCE: Private collection, Paris; collection of Clara Diament Sujo, Caracas, 1976; CDS Gallery, New York, 1980; acquired by Tanya Capriles de Brillembourg in 1982.

EXHIBITIONS: *Lam*, Museo de Bellas Artes, Caracas, 1955; *Masters of the Americas,* CDS Gallery, Caracas, May 3–July 3, 1981; *South American Masters*, CDS Gallery, November 18–January 15, 1983; *Wifredo Lam,* Museo Nacional Centro de Arte Reina Sofía, Madrid, September 29–December 14, 1992; Fundación Joan Miró, Barcelona, January 21–March 28, 1993 (illustrated, p. 109); *Wifredo Lam in North America*, Haggerty Museum of Art, Milwaukee, October 11, 2007–January 21, 2008; Miami Art Museum, February 8–May 18, 2008; Museum of Latin American Art, Long Beach, June 12–August 31, 2008; Salvador Dalí Museum, St. Petersburg, Florida (illustrated, no. 54, p. 128).

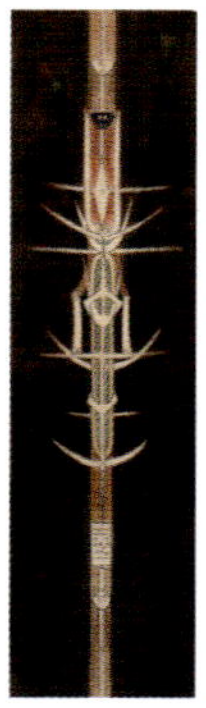

WIFREDO LAM (Cuban, 1902–1982)
Reflets d'eau [Water Reflections], 1957
Oil on canvas
99 15/16 x 27 3/8 inches (253.8 x 69.5 cm)
PLATE 36

PROVENANCE: Galerie Albert Loeb, Paris; Mr. and Mrs. Rafael Lorie, Washington, D.C.; Marta Gutiérrez Fine Arts, Miami; acquired by Tanya Capriles de Brillembourg in 1983.

EXHIBITIONS: *XIV Salon de Mai*, Paris, 1958–1959; *The 1958 Pittsburgh Bicentennial International Exhibition of Contemporary Paintings and Sculpture*, Carnegie Institute, Pittsburgh, PA; *Lam, Paintings from 1938 to 1962*, Albert Loeb Gallery, New York, 1962; *Wifredo Lam and His Contemporaries 1938–1952*, The Studio Museum in Harlem, New York, December 6, 1992–April 11, 1993 (illustrated, no. 54, p. 147).

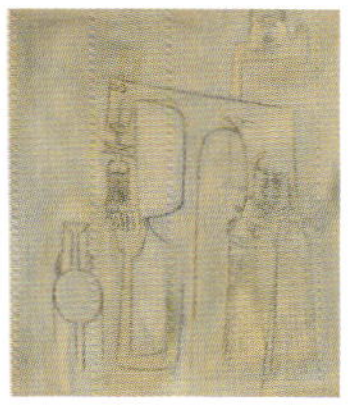

WIFREDO LAM (Cuban, 1902–1982)
Sur la main droite [On the Right Hand], 1962
Oil on canvas
41 7/16 x 35 inches (105.3 x 88.9 cm)
PLATE 46

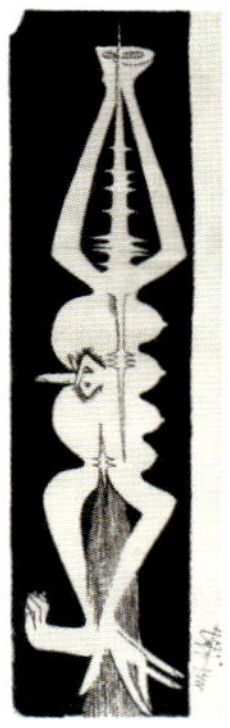

WIFREDO LAM (Cuban, 1902–1982)
Sin título [Untitled], 1948
Ink on paper
9 7/16 x 31 1/8 inches (24 x 79.1 cm)
PLATE 45

PROVENANCE: Private collection; Gimpel Weitzenhoffer Gallery, New York; private collection, New York; Marta Gutiérrez Fine Arts, Miami; acquired by Tanya Capriles de Brillembourg in 1987.

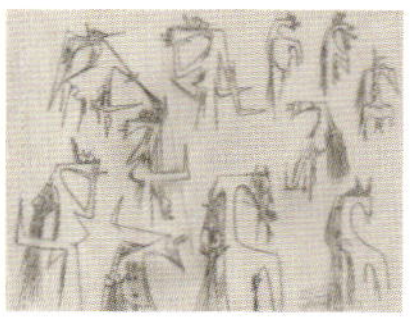

WIFREDO LAM (Cuban, 1902–1982)
Femmes-Cheval [Horse-Headed Women], 1953
Black chalk on paper
19 1/4 x 25 1/4 inches (48.9 x 64.1 cm)
PLATE 44

PROVENANCE: Dedicated to Nino Pescetto (the artist's gardener), Albisola Marina, Italy, 1964; Antonello di Meo, Paris; Marta Gutiérrez Fine Arts, Miami; acquired in 1986 by Tanya Capriles de Brillembourg.

EXHIBITIONS: *Wifredo Lam: A Retrospective of Works on Paper,* Americas Society, New York, September 18–December 20, 1992 (illustrated, no. 60, p. 54); *Wifredo Lam. Obra sobre papel,* Fundació "la Caixa," Barcelona, January 21–March 21, 1993 (illustrated, no. 85, p. 145).

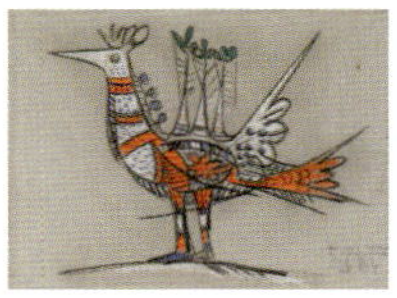

WIFREDO LAM (Cuban, 1902–1982)
Sin título (La gallina) [Untitled (The Hen)], 1958
Pastel and crayon on paper
19 3/8 x 25 9/16 inches (49.2 x 64.9 cm)
PLATE 47

PROVENANCE: Dedicated to Saskia and Christhiana (surname unknown), Havana, 1958; Manuel Mato; Marta Gutiérrez Fine Arts, Miami; acquired by Tanya Capriles de Brillembourg in 1984.

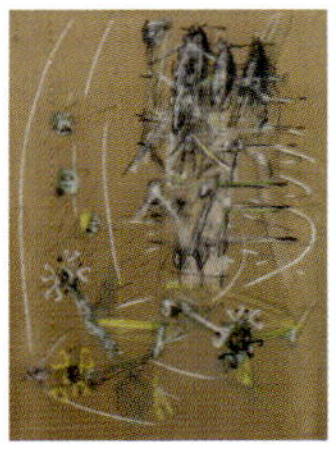

MATTA (Chilean, 1911–2002)
Autómata [Automaton], 1942
Charcoal and pastel on brown paper
29 x 39 inches (73.7 x 99.1 cm)
PLATE 26

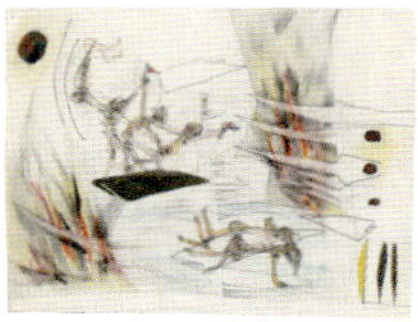

MATTA (Chilean, 1911–2002)
Sin título [Untitled], 1943–44
Pastel and pencil on paper
15 11/16 x 20 3/4 inches (39.4 x 52.7 cm)
PLATE 21

PROVENANCE: Pierre Matisse Gallery, New York, c. 1985; Nicolás Acquavella Gallery, New York; acquired by Tanya Capriles de Brillembourg.

EXHIBITIONS: *Matta*, Centre Georges Pompidou/Musée national d'art modern, 1985, (illustrated, no.54, p. 132); *Matta in America: Paintings and Drawings of the 1940s*, Museum of Contemporary Art Chicago, September 2001–January 2002 (illustrated, p. 61).

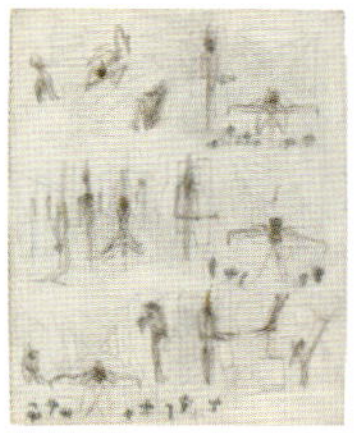

MATTA (Chilean, 1911–2002)
Sin título [Untitled], 1944–45
Graphite and crayon on paper
29 1/16 x 23 3/16 inches (73.8 x 58.9 cm)
PLATE 22

PROVENANCE: Pierre Matisse Gallery, New York, c. 1985; Nicolás Acquavella Gallery, New York; acquired by Tanya Capriles de Brillembourg.

EXHIBITIONS: *Matta*, Centre Georges Pompidou/Musée national d'art modern, 1985 (illustrated, no. 60, p. 136).

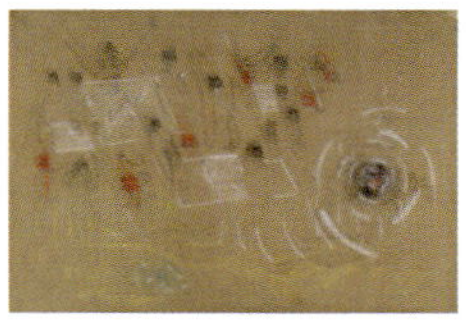

MATTA (Chilean, 1911–2002)
Naturaleza muerta [Still Life], c. 1945
Pastel and charcoal on brown paper mounted to canvas
39 3/4 x 59 5/16 inches (101 x 150.7 cm)
PLATE 23

MATTA (Chilean, 1911–2002)
Splitting of the Ego, 1945
Pencil and pastel on brown paper mounted on canvas
70 3/4 x 91 3/4 inches (179.7 x 233 cm)
PLATE 24

PROVENANCE: Possibly Andrew Crispo Gallery, New York, c. 1975; Mr. Schneyder, New York; Marta Gutiérrez Fine Arts, Miami; acquired in 1986 by Tanya Capriles de Brillembourg.

EXHIBITIONS: *Matta: A Totemic World*, Andrew Crispo Gallery, New York, 1975, no. 44, listed as "Study for Splitting the Ergo [sic]."

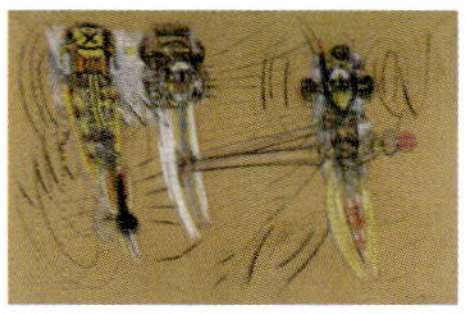

MATTA (Chilean, 1911–2002)
Abstract Composition, 1949
Oil and pastel on paper mounted on canvas
39 7/8 x 60 inches (101.3 x 152.4 cm)
PLATE 25

PROVENANCE: One in a series of eight works on brown paper acquired directly from the artist by Alexander Iolas Gallery, New York; Badley Gallery, New York, acquired 1955; private collection, New York; Dannenberg Collection, New York; private collection, New York; Lerner-Heller Gallery, New York; acquired in 1986 by Tanya Capriles de Brillembourg.

EXHIBITIONS: *The Interpretative Link: Abstract Surrealism into Abstract Expressionism: Works on Paper 1938–1948*, Newport Harbor Art Museum, California, 1986; *North Looks South: Building the Latin American Art Collection*, Museum of Fine Arts, Houston, June–September, 2009.

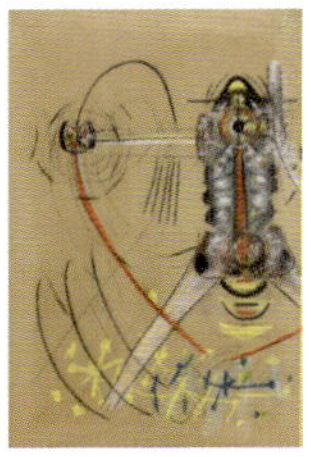

MATTA (Chilean, 1911–2002)
Composition et Étude [Composition and Study], 1952
Pastel, graphite, and charcoal on brown paper mounted on canvas
59 7/8 x 39 1/4 inches (150.2 x 99.7 cm)
PLATE 27

PROVENANCE: Gallery Daniel Malingue, Paris; Thomas Levy, Hamburg; Mary-Anne Martin/Fine Art, New York; acquired by Tanya Capriles de Brillembourg in 1983.

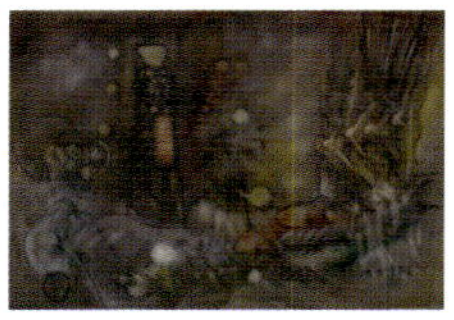

MATTA (Chilean, 1911–2002)
Soul without Terror, 1953
Oil on canvas
47 1/4 x 68 5/16 inches (120 x 173.5 cm)
PLATE 28

PROVENANCE: Mr. and Mrs. Randall Shapiro, Chicago; Joseph R. and Jory Shapiro, Oak Park, IL; Museum of Contemporary Art, Chicago; Sotheby's New York, Latin American Art Sale, June 3, 1999, lot 00056; Gary Nader Fine Art, Miami, VII Latin American Auction, January 23, 2000, lot 025; acquired by Tanya Capriles de Brillembourg.

EXHIBITIONS: *Mr. and Mrs. Randall Shapiro Collection*, Art Institute of Chicago, February–April, 1985.

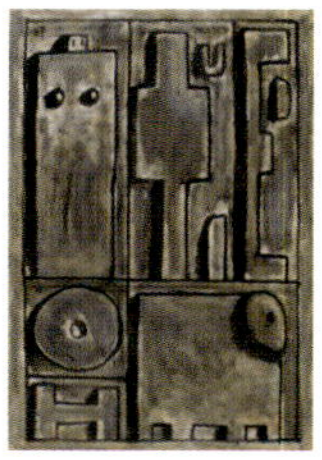

FRANCISCO MATTO (Uruguayan, 1911–1995)
Construcción [Construction], 1967
Oil on artist board
39 15/16 x 27 1/2 inches (101.4 x 69.9 cm)
PLATE 20

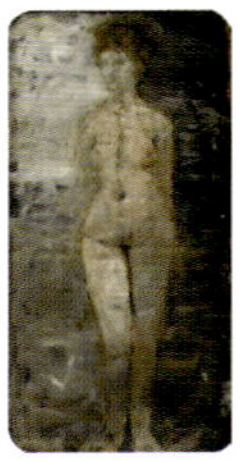

ARMANDO MORALES
(Nicaraguan, 1927–2011)
Desnudo [Nude], 1960
Oil and mixed media on paper mounted on particle board
58 15/16 x 29 15/16 inches (149.7 x 76 cm)
PLATE 58

PROVENANCE: Gary Nader Fine Arts, Miami; acquired by Tanya Capriles de Brillembourg in 1992.

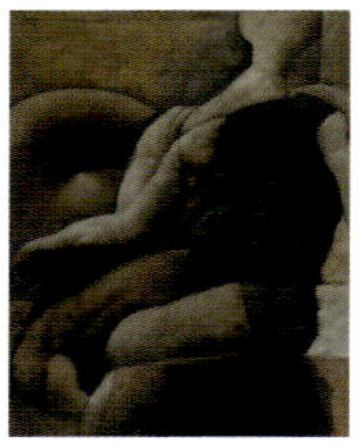

ARMANDO MORALES
(Nicaraguan, 1927–2011)
Sin título [Untitled], 1971
Oil and beeswax on canvas
63 15/16 x 51 7/16 inches (162.4 x 130.7 cm)
PLATE 59

PROVENANCE: CDS Gallery, New York; acquired by Tanya Capriles de Brillembourg in 1989.

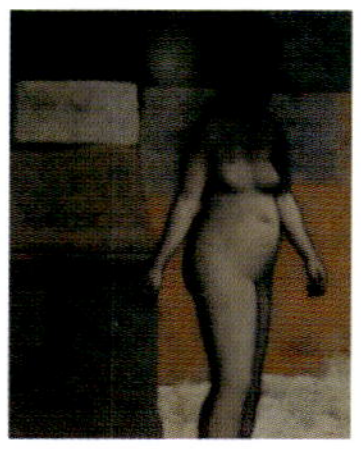

ARMANDO MORALES
(Nicaraguan, 1927–2011)
Mujer a punto de regresar [Woman at the Point of Return], 1973
Oil and beeswax on canvas
50 3/16 x 40 1/8 inches (127.5 x 101.9 cm)
PLATE 60

PROVENANCE: Collection of the artist; acquired directly from the artist by Mrs. Sandra González Chou; Marta Gutiérrez Fine Arts; acquired by Tanya Capriles de Brillembourg in 1985.

EXHIBITIONS: *Tribute to Picasso*, Art Museum of the Americas, Organization of American States (OAS), Washington, D.C., 1973.

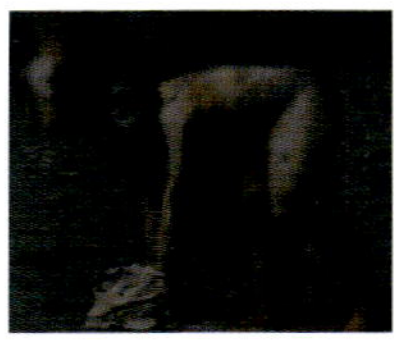

ARMANDO MORALES
(Nicaraguan, 1927–2011)
Escena lacustre I, Granada Harbor [Lakeside Scene I, Granada Harbor], 1978
Oil and beeswax on canvas
18 15/16 x 22 9/16 inches (48.1 x 57.3 cm)
PLATE 55

PROVENANCE: Estudio Actual, Caracas, 1978; Christie's New York, Latin American Paintings, Drawings, & Sculpture, November 21, 1989, lot 24; acquired by Tanya Capriles de Brillembourg in 1989.

EXHIBITIONS: *Morales: Pinturas, dibujos*, Estudio Actual, Caracas, 1978; *Armando Morales*, Gary Nader Fine Arts, Miami, 1997.

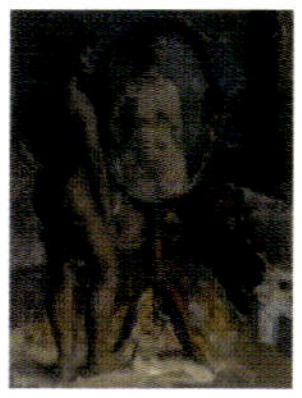

ARMANDO MORALES
(Nicaraguan, 1927–2011)
Mujer ante un espejo [Woman before a Mirror], 1979
Oil and mixed media on laminated board mounted on wood
30 1/4 x 22 1/4 inches (76.8 x 56.5 cm)
PLATE 53

PROVENANCE: Marta Gutiérrez Fine Arts, Miami; acquired by Tanya Capriles de Brillembourg in 1984.

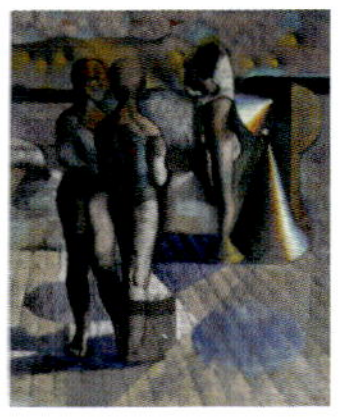

ARMANDO MORALES
(Nicaraguan, 1927–2011)
At the Circus, V, 1981
Oil and beeswax on canvas
64 3/16 x 51 11/16 inches (163 x 131.3 cm)
PLATE 57

PROVENANCE: CDS Gallery, New York, 1981; acquired by Tanya Capriles de Brillembourg, 1983.

EXHIBITIONS: *Morales: Paintings*, CDS Gallery, New York, November 12–December 31, 1981; *Armando Morales*, CDS Gallery, November 1983.

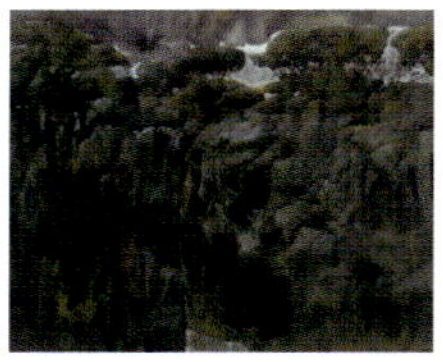

ARMANDO MORALES
(Nicaraguan, 1927–2011)
Forêt tropicale dans une orage [Tropical Forest in a Storm], 1991
Oil and beeswax on canvas
51 3/8 x 64 inches (130.5 x 162.6 cm)
PLATE 61

PROVENANCE: Galerie Claude Bernard, Paris, 1992; acquired by Tanya Capriles de Brillembourg in 1992.

EXHIBITIONS: Galerie Claude Bernard, Paris, 1992; *Armando Morales: peintures*, Foire Internationale d'Art Contemporain (FIAC), Paris, October 24–November 1, 1992; *Armando Morales*, Gary Nader Fine Arts, Miami, 1997.

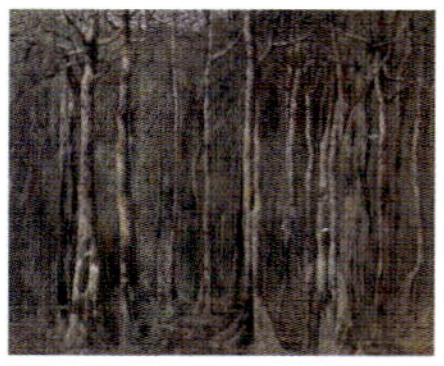

ARMANDO MORALES
(Nicaraguan, 1927–2011)
Forêt tropicale [Tropical Forest], 1992
Oil and beeswax on canvas
70 7/8 x 88 3/4 inches (180 x 225.4 cm)
PLATE 62

PROVENANCE: Private collection, Texas; Marta Gutiérrez Fine Arts, Miami; acquired by Tanya Capriles de Brillembourg in 1992.

EXHIBITIONS: Galerie Claude Bernard, Paris, 1992; *Armando Morales: peintures*, Foire Internationale d'Art Contemporain (FIAC), Paris, October 24–November 1, 1992; *Armando Morales*, Gary Nader Fine Arts, Miami, 1997.

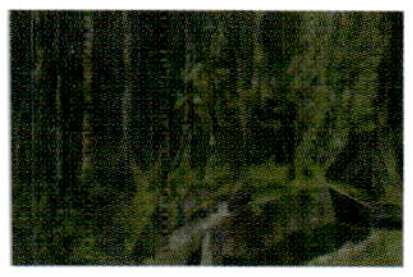

ARMANDO MORALES
(Nicaraguan, 1927–2011)
Forêt tropicale: ruines d'une plantation d'inaigo [Tropical Forest: Ruins of an Indigo Plantation], 1999
Oil and beeswax on canvas
$26\frac{3}{4}$ x $40\frac{9}{16}$ inches (67.9 x 103 cm)
PLATE 63

PROVENANCE: Galerie Claude Bernard, Paris, 2000; acquired by Tanya Capriles de Brillembourg in 2000

EXHIBITIONS: *Armando Morales: Peintures récentes*, presented by Galerie Claude Bernard at Foire Internationale d'Art Contemporain (FIAC), Paris, October 25–30, 2000.

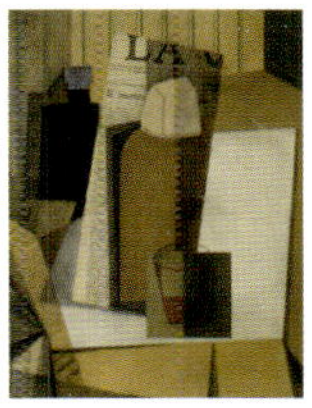

EMILIO PETTORUTI
(Argentinean, 1892–1971)
La Voce [The Voice], 1916
Pastel, charcoal, and collage on paper board
$19\frac{1}{4}$ x $14\frac{3}{4}$ inches (48.9 x 37.5 cm)
PLATE 1

PROVENANCE: CDS Gallery; acquired by Tanya Capriles de Brillembourg.

EXHIBITIONS: *Emilio Pettoruti: Paintings 1914–1959*, Molton Gallery, London, April 27–May 15, 1960.

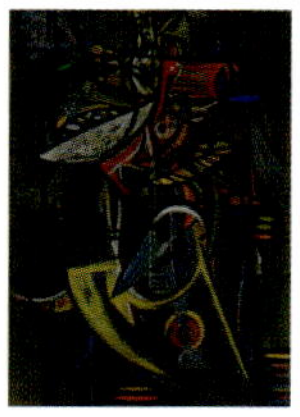

RENÉ PORTOCARRERO (Cuban, 1911–1985)
Brujo [Sorcerer], 1945
Oil on paper mounted on Masonite
$39\frac{1}{4}$ x $27\frac{3}{4}$ inches (99.7 x 70.5 cm)
PLATE 48

PROVENANCE: Gary Nader Fine Arts, Miami, V Latin American Art Auction: Important Paintings, Sculpture & Drawings, January 11, 1998, lot 00106; acquired by Tanya Capriles de Brillembourg.

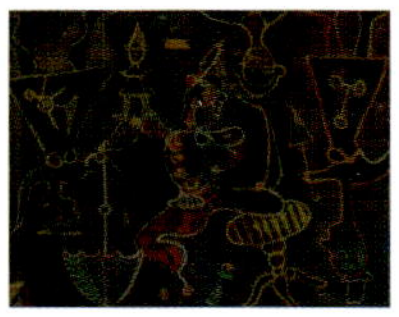

RENÉ PORTOCARRERO (Cuban, 1911–1985)
Sin título [Untitled], 1945
Oil on laminated paper card mounted on aluminum honeycomb panel
$28\frac{5}{16}$ x $36\frac{5}{16}$ inches (71.9 x 92.2 cm)
PLATE 49

PROVENANCE: Gary Nader Fine Arts, Miami; acquired in 1992 by Tanya Capriles de Brillembourg

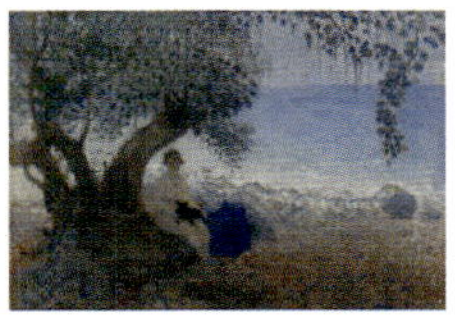

ARMANDO REVERÓN
(Venezuelan, 1889–1954)
Figura bajo un uvero [Figure under a Sea-Grape Tree], 1920
Oil on burlap
$27\frac{1}{2}$ x $39\frac{1}{2}$ inches (69.9 x 100.3 cm)
PLATE 10

PROVENANCE: Commissioned by Luis Enrique Yanes, Caracas, 1920; Sotheby's New York, *Important Latin American Paintings, Drawings, and Sculpture*, May 29 and 30, 1984, lot 15 (illustrated, n.p.); transferred to CDS Gallery, New York, 1984; acquired in 1984 by Tanya Capriles de Brillembourg

EXHIBITIONS: *Armando Reverón: Pinturas*, Centro Venezolano Americano, Caracas, 1951; *Exposición retrospectiva de Armando Reverón*, Museo de Bellas Artes, Caracas, July 1955; *Armando Reverón*, Institute of Contemporary Art, Boston, January 6–February 12, 1956; Isaac Delgado Museum of Art, New Orleans, February 16–March 12, 1956; Museum of Fine Arts, Houston, April 9–May 12, 1956; National Academy, New York, June 6–June 29, 1956; San Francisco Museum of Modern Art, August 20–September 23, 1956; Corcoran Gallery of Art, Washington, D.C., October 6–November 11, 1956; *Obras Maestras de Armando Reverón*, Museo de Arte Contemporáneo de Caracas, Caracas, 1979; *Art of the Fantastic: Latin America, 1920–1987*, Indianapolis Museum of Art, Indianapolis, June 28–December 6,1987; Queens Museum, New York, October 10–December 6, 1987; The Center for Fine Arts, Miami, January 15–March 4, 1988; Centro Cultural/Arte Contemporáneo, Mexico City, March 25–May 22, 1988; *Armando Reverón (1889–1954). Exposición antológica*, Museo Nacional Centro de Arte Reina Sofía, Palacio de Velázquez, Madrid, 1992.

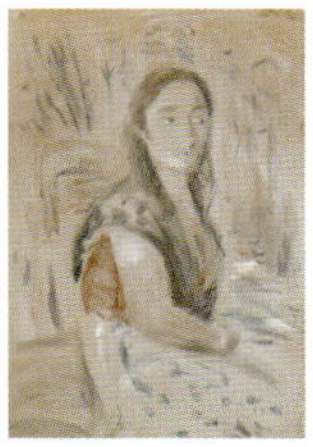

ARMANDO REVERÓN
(Venezuelan, 1889–1954)
Retrato de Mujer [Portrait of a Woman], c. 1934
Gouache on paper mounted on cardboard
$33\frac{1}{8}$ x $23\frac{9}{16}$ inches (84.1 x 59.8 cm)
PLATE 11

PROVENANCE: Naná Corao de Moles, Caracas; Zina Vaisberg, Caracas; acquired by CDS Gallery, New York, at Christie's New York, *Important Latin American Paintings, Drawings, and Sculpture*, November 24 and 25, 1992, lot 129 (illustrated, p. 185); acquired in 1992 by Tanya Capriles de Brillembourg

EXHIBITIONS: *Exposición retrospectiva de Armando Reverón*, Museo de Bellas Artes, Caracas, 1955.

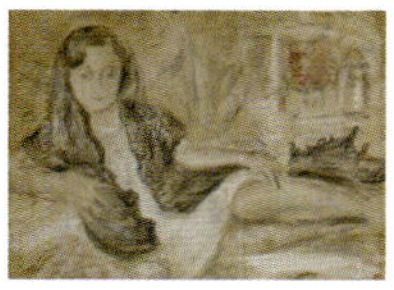

ARMANDO REVERÓN
(Venezuelan, 1889–1954)
Figura reclinada, o Mujer con mantilla acostada [Reclining Figure or Reclining Woman with Mantilla], c. 1934
Gouache on paper mounted on Masonite board
$29\frac{5}{8}$ x $41\frac{1}{4}$ inches (75.2 x 104.8 cm)
PLATE 12

PROVENANCE: William H. Phelps, Caracas; private collection; Stambul Rojas, Caracas; Eduardo Rojas (heir of Stambul Rojas), Caracas; Galería Acquavella, Caracas; acquired by Tanya Capriles de Brillembourg in 1999.

EXHIBITIONS: *Exposición retrospectiva de Armando Reverón*, Museo de Bellas Artes, Caracas, 1955; *Armando Reverón*, Instituto Venezolano Italiano de Cultura, Caracas, 1961.

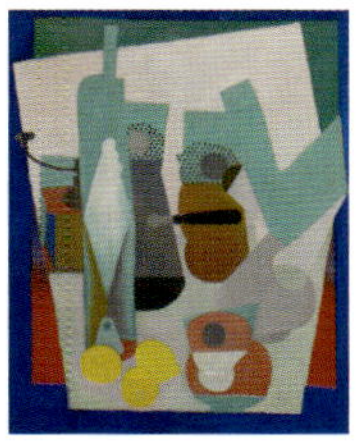

DIEGO RIVERA (Mexican, 1886–1957)
Naturaleza muerta con limones [Still Life with Lemons], 1916
Oil on canvas
$31\frac{13}{16}$ x $25\frac{11}{16}$ inches (80.8 x 65.2 cm)
PLATE 2

PROVENANCE: Acquired directly from the artist by Enrique Freyman; private collection (heir of Freyman); sold at Parke-Bernet Galleries, New York, *Diego Rivera: Twenty-Seven Paintings of the Period 1909–1917*, October 28, 1959, lot 16 (illustrated, n.p); Otto Preminger; Marlborough Gallery, London and New York; Richard L. Feigen Gallery, New York; probably entered private collection; CDS Gallery, New York; acquired in 1988 by Tanya Capriles de Brillembourg.

EXHIBITIONS: *Diego Rivera: The Cubist Years*, Phoenix Museum of Art, March 10–April 29, 1984; IBM Gallery of Science and Art, New York, June 13–August 8, 1984; San Francisco Museum of Modern

Art, September 27–November 11, 1984; Museo de Arte Moderno, Mexico City, December 6, 1984–February 11, 1985, (cat. no. 50); *Renacimiento en el Arte Mexicano: Orozco, Rivera y Siqueiros,* Nagoya City Art Museum, Japan, May 27–June 16, 1989; Seibu Museum of Art, Japan, July 22–August 20, 1989; Fukuoka City Art Museum, Japan, September 5–October 1, 1989 (illustrated no. 45, p. 93).

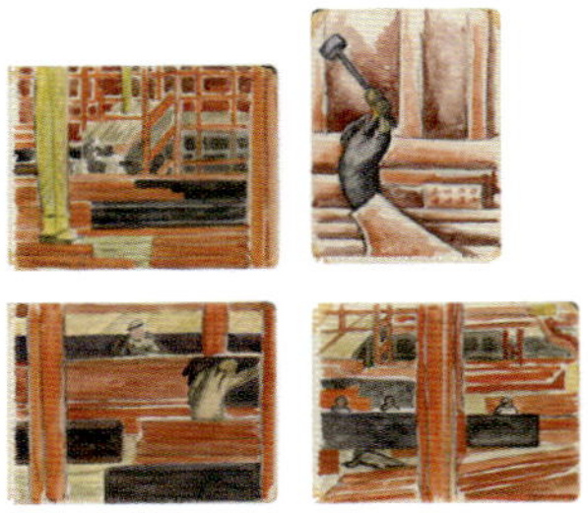

DIEGO RIVERA (Mexican, 1886–1957)
Construction of Rockefeller Center: Four Notebook Sketches, 1931–32
Watercolor and chalk on paper
5 5/16 x 7 1/16 inches each (13.5 x 17.9 cm each)
PLATES 3–6

PROVENANCE: Galería de Arte Mexicano, Mexico City; Lester Wolfe, New York; Estate of Lester Wolfe, New York; Sotheby's, New York, *Important Latin American Paintings, Drawings and Sculpture,* May 29, 1984, lot 26 (illustrated, n.p.); CDS Gallery, New York; acquired in 1984 by Tanya Capriles de Brillembourg.

EXHIBITIONS: *Contemporary Mexican Art,* Rockefeller University, New York, 1965–66, cat. 23.

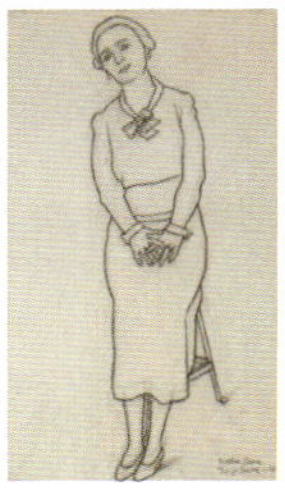

DIEGO RIVERA (Mexican, 1886–1957)
Retrato de Alice-Leone Moats [Portrait of Alice-Leone Moats], 1938
Chalk on paper
24 1/2 x 18 1/2 inches (62.2 x 47 cm)
PLATE 7

PROVENANCE: Alice-Leone Moats; sold at Sotheby's New York, Latin American Art, May 16, 1989, lot 99; transferred to CDS Gallery, New York; acquired in 1989 by Tanya Capriles de Brillembourg

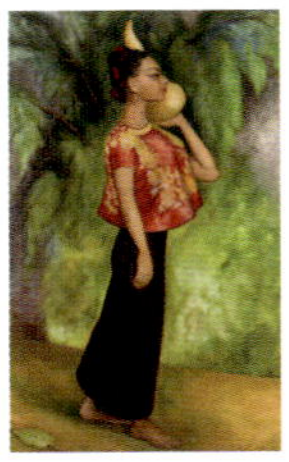

DIEGO RIVERA (Mexican, 1886–1957)
Retrato de Columba Domínguez o Tehuana [Portrait of Columba Domínguez or Woman from Tehuantepec], 1950
Oil on cotton duck canvas
76 x 47 5/16 inches (193 x 120.2 cm)
PLATE 8

PROVENANCE: Columba Domínguez; Galería Arvil, Mexico City; CDS Gallery; acquired in 1988 by Tanya Capriles de Brillembourg.

EXHIBITIONS: *Imagen de México,* Schirn Kunsthalle, Frankfurt, December 5, 1987–February 28, 1988; Messepalast, Vienna, May 17–July 31, 1988; Dallas Museum of Art, August 28–October 30, 1988, cat. 76.

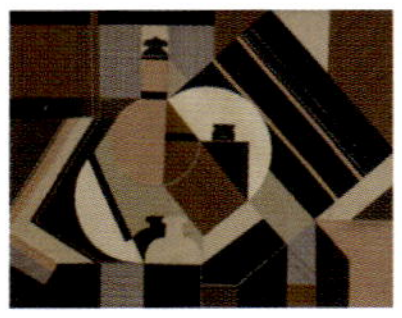

CARLOS ROJAS (Colombian, 1933–1997)
Sin título de la serie *Papeles pegados* [Untitled from the Pasted Papers series], c. 1959
Paper or vinyl sheeting on prepared plywood, mixed media and textured surface coating
24 1/16 x 30 7/8 inches (61.1 x 78.4 cm)
PLATE 92

PROVENANCE: Acquired directly from artist by a private collection; Galería Casas Reigner, Bogotá, 2008; acquired in 2012 by Tanya Brillembourg.

CARLOS ROJAS (Colombian, 1933–1997)
Sin título de la serie *Ingeniera de la visión* [Untitled from the Engineering of Vision series], c. 1960
Acrylic on canvas
15 13/16 x 15 1/4 inches (40.1 x 40.1 cm)
PLATE 93

PROVENANCE: Estate of the artist, Bogotá; acquired by Tanya Brillembourg.

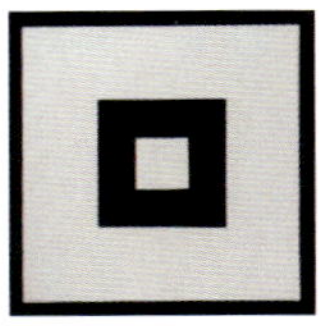

CARLOS ROJAS (Colombian, 1933–1997)
Sin título de la serie *Ingeniera de la visión* [Untitled from the Engineering of Vision series], c. 1960
Acrylic on canvas
15 11/16 x 15 1/4 inches (39.8 x 40 cm)
PLATE 94

PROVENANCE: Estate of the artist, Bogotá; acquired by Tanya Brillembourg.

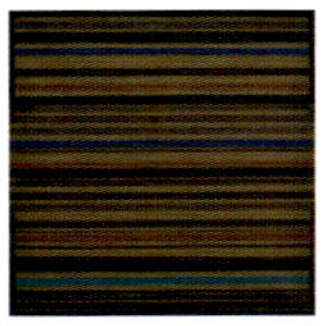

CARLOS ROJAS (Colombian, 1933–1997)
Sin título de la serie *América Horizontes* [Untitled from the American Horizons series], 1988
Oil an metallic paint on canvas
31 1/2 x 31 7/16 inches (80 x 79.9 cm)
PLATE 96

PROVENANCE: Estate of the artist, Bogotá; Galería Casas Reigner, Bogotá, 2008; acquired in 2012 by Tanya Brillembourg.

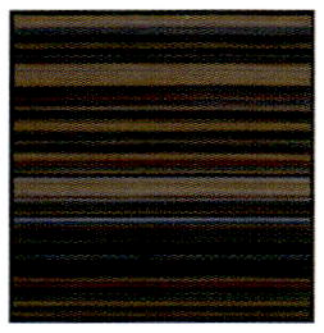

CARLOS ROJAS (Colombian, 1933–1997)
Sin título de la serie *América Horizontes* [Untitled from the American Horizons series], 1988
Oil an metallic paint on canvas
39 3/8 x 39 3/8 inches (100.1 x 100.1 cm)
PLATE 95

PROVENANCE: Estate of the artist, Bogotá; colección Luis Fonseca, Bogotá; acquired in 2012 by Tanya Brillembourg.

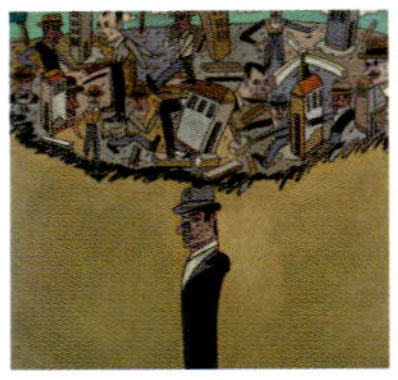

ANTONIO SEGUÍ (Argentinean, b. 1934)
El que piensa demasiado [The One Who Thinks Too Much], 1986
Acrylic on canvas
59 1/8 x 63 1/8 inches (150.2 x 160.3 cm)
PLATE 72

PROVENANCE: Acquired directly from artist by Tanya Capriles de Brillembourg in 1993.

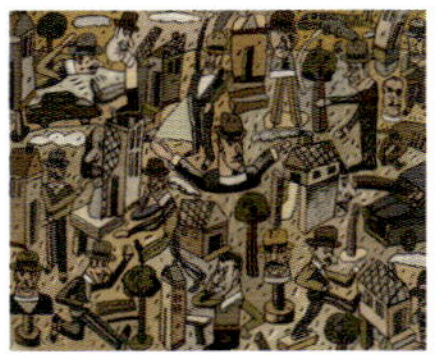

ANTONIO SEGUÍ (Argentinean, b. 1934)
Una ciudad, una historia, un tormento [A City, A History, A Torment], 1990
Acrylic on canvas
32 x 39 3/8 inches (81.3 x 100 cm)
PLATE 73

PROVENANCE: Acquired directly from artist by Tanya Capriles de Brillembourg in 1993.

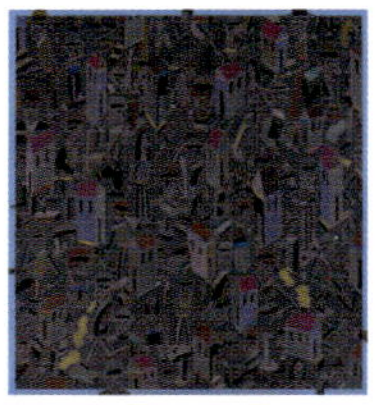

ANTONIO SEGUÍ (Argentinean, b. 1934)
Gente rodeando el monumento de Humphrey Bogart [People Surrounding the Monument of Humphrey Bogart], 1993
Acrylic on canvas
63 1/8 x 59 1/8 inches (160.3 x 150.2 x cm)
PLATE 74

PROVENANCE: Acquired directly from artist by Tanya Capriles de Brillembourg in 1993.

EXHIBITIONS: Group show, Pavillon Joséphine, Strasbourg, France, 1996; *Antonio Seguí. Peintures, sculptures, rétrospective de dessins,* Théâtre/Scène Nationale, Saint-Quentin-en-Yvelines, France, September 24–November 15, 1997.

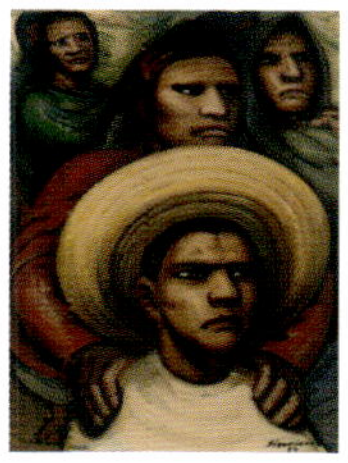

DAVID ALFARO SIQUEIROS
(Mexican, 1896–1974)
El reto [The Challenge], 1954
Pyroxylin on Masonite
39 3/8 x 29 1/2 inches (100 x 74.9 cm)
PLATE 9

PROVENANCE: Galería de Arte Mexicano, Mexico City; Paul Sanders, Hartsdale, New York; Martin Sanders, North Tarrytown, New York; by descent to private collector, New York; Sotheby's, New York, Latin American Art, May 19, 1987, lot 13; CDS Gallery, New York; acquired in 1987 by Tanya Capriles de Brillembourg.

EXHIBITIONS: *Imagen de México,* Schirn Kunsthalle, Frankfurt, December 5, 1987–February 28, 1988; Messepalast, Vienna, May 17–July 31, 1988; Dallas Museum of Art, August 28–October 30, 1988; cat. 85; *The Latin American Spirit: Art and Artists in the United States, 1920–1970,* The Bronx Museum of the Arts, New York, September 29, 1988–January 29, 1989; El Paso Museum of Art, February 27–April 23, 1989; San Diego Museum of Art, May 22–July 16, 1989; Instituto de Cultura Puertorriqueña, San Juan, August 14–October 8, 1989; Center for the Arts, Vero Beach, Florida, January 28–March 31, 1990 (illustrated, p. 190).

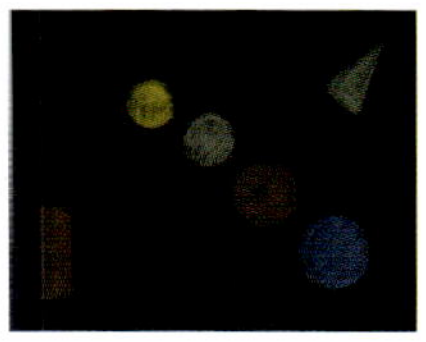

LOLÓ SOLDEVILLA (Cuban, 1901–1971)
Sin título [Untitled], 1956
Tempera and incised graphite lines on cardboard
14 x 11 inches (35.6 x 27.9 cm)
PLATE 86

PROVENANCE: Acquired from Artens, Inc., Miami, by Tanya Capriles de Brillembourg.

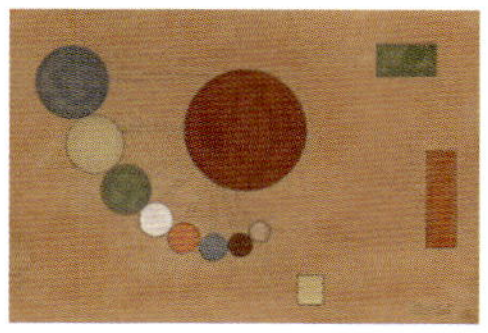

LOLÓ SOLDEVILLA (Cuban, 1901–1971)
Sin título [Untitled], 1956
Tempera and incised graphite lines on cardboard
11 1/4 x 16 3/4 inches (28.6 x 42.5 cm)
PLATE 76

PROVENANCE: Acquired from Artens, Inc., Miami, by Tanya Capriles de Brillembourg.

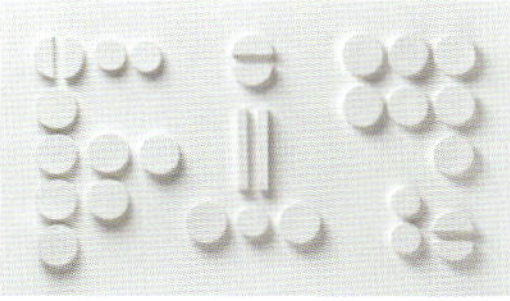

LOLÓ SOLDEVILLA (Cuban, 1901–1971)
Sin título (abstracción) [Untitled (abstraction)], 1956
Oil on plywood with wood blocks
24 1/8 x 41 1/8 x 1 11/16 inches (61.3 x 104.5 x 4.3 cm)
PLATE 78

PROVENANCE: Acquired from Tresart Gallery, Miami, in 2011 by Tanya Capriles de Brillembourg.

EXHIBITIONS: *Loló Soldevilla,* Tresart Gallery, Miami, November 29, 2011–January 6, 2012.

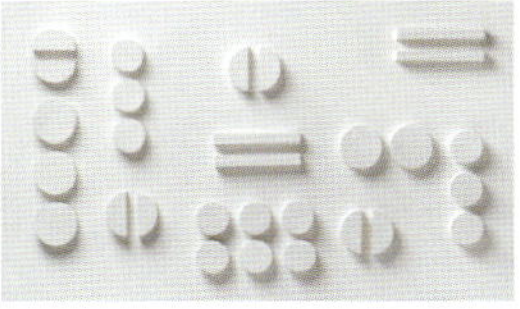

LOLÓ SOLDEVILLA (Cuban, 1901–1971)
Sin título (abstracción) [Untitled (abstraction)], 1956
Oil on plywood with wood blocks
22 3/4 x 38 7/8 x 1 11/16 inches (57.9 x 98.8 x 4.3 cm)
PLATE 79

PROVENANCE: Acquired from Tresart Gallery, Miami, in 2011 by Tanya Capriles de Brillembourg.

EXHIBITIONS: *Loló Soldevilla,* Tresart Gallery, Miami, November 29, 2011–January 6, 2012.

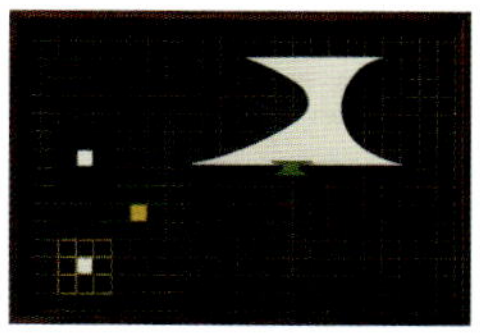

LOLÓ SOLDEVILLA (Cuban, 1901–1971)
Sin título [Untitled], 1956
Wood and steel grid with acrylic and oil paint
25 3/4 x 37 11/16 x 2 1/2 inches (65.4 x 95.8 x 6.4 cm)
PLATE 82

PROVENANCE: Acquired from Artens, Inc., Miami, by Tanya Capriles de Brillembourg.

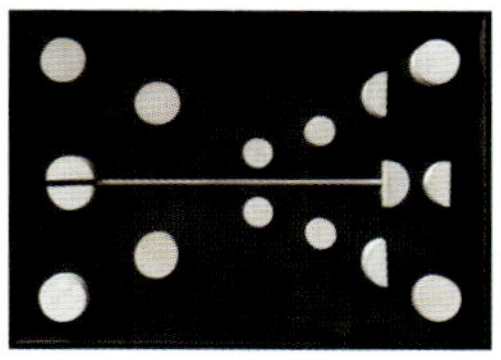

LOLÓ SOLDEVILLA (Cuban, 1901–1971)
Composición abstracción [Abstract Composition], c. 1954
Oil paint on plywood with casein-painted blocks
23 1/2 x 33 x 2 1/2 inches (59.6 x 83.8 x 6.4 cm)
PLATE 81

PROVENANCE: Acquired from Artens, Inc., Miami, by Tanya Capriles de Brillembourg.

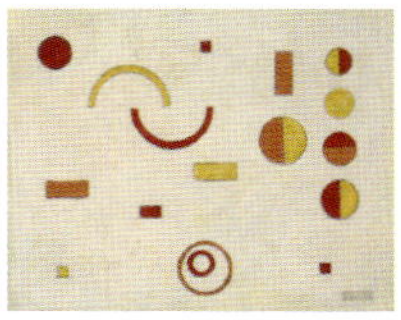

LOLÓ SOLDEVILLA (Cuban, 1901–1971)
Sin título [Untitled], 1956
Oil and tempera-type paint on canvas mounted on Masonite
10 5/16 x 14 1/16 inches (27.8 x 35.7 cm)
PLATE 83

PROVENANCE: Acquired from Artens, Inc., Miami, by Tanya Capriles de Brillembourg.

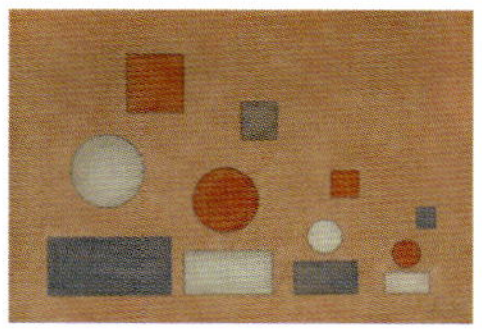

LOLÓ SOLDEVILLA (Cuban, 1901–1971)
Sin título [Untitled], 1956
Tempera and incised graphite lines on cardboard
11 1/4 x 16 5/8 inches (28.6 x 42.2 cm)
PLATE 77

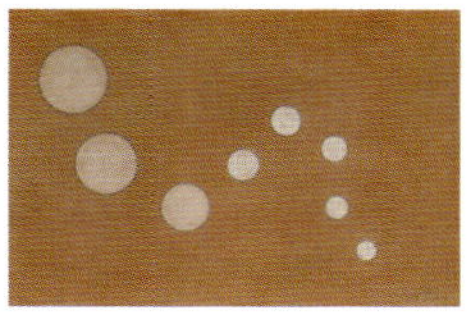

LOLÓ SOLDEVILLA (Cuban, 1901–1971)
Sin título [Untitled], 1956
Tempera and incised graphite lines on cardboard
11 1/4 x 16 7/8 inches (28.6 x 42.9 cm)
PLATE 87

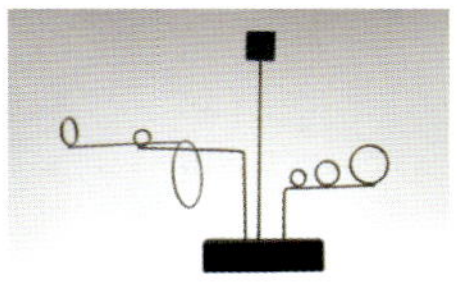

LOLÓ SOLDEVILLA (Cuban, 1901–1971)
Stabile, 1954
Wood and bronze
16 3/4 x 20 1/16 x 8 13/16 inches (42.6 x 51 x 22.5 cm)
PLATE 84

PROVENANCE: Acquired from Tresart Gallery, Miami, in 2011 by Tanya Capriles de Brillembourg.

EXHIBITIONS: *Loló Soldevilla,* Tresart Gallery, Miami, November 29, 2011–January 6, 2012.

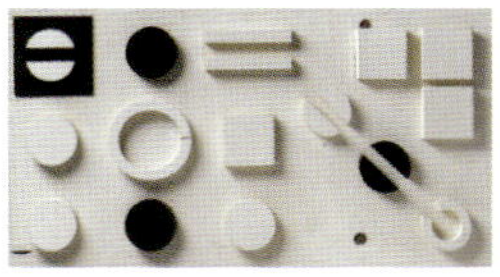

LOLÓ SOLDEVILLA (Cuban, 1901–1971)
Construcción [Construction], 1955
Acrylic on plywood with wood blocks
21 1/2 x 39 inches (54.6 x 99.1 cm)
PLATE 80

PROVENANCE: Acquired from Tresart Gallery, Miami, in 2011 by Tanya Capriles de Brillembourg.

EXHIBITIONS: *Loló Soldevilla*, Tresart Gallery, Miami, November 29, 2011–January 6, 2012.

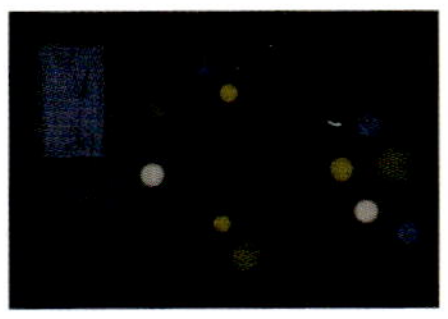

LOLÓ SOLDEVILLA (Cuban, 1901–1971)
Sin título [Untitled], 1956
Tempera on cardboard
$13\frac{1}{2}$ x $19\frac{1}{2}$ inches (34.3 x 49.5 cm)
PLATE 85

PROVENANCE: Acquired from Artens, Inc., Miami, by Tanya Capriles de Brillembourg.

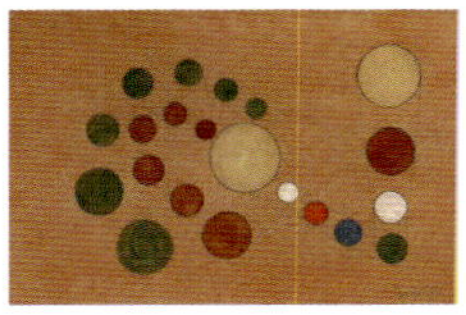

LOLÓ SOLDEVILLA (Cuban, 1901–1971)
Sin título [Untitled], 1956
Tempera and incised graphite lines on cardboard
$11\frac{1}{4}$ x $16\frac{13}{16}$ inches (28.6 x 42.7 cm)
PLATE 88

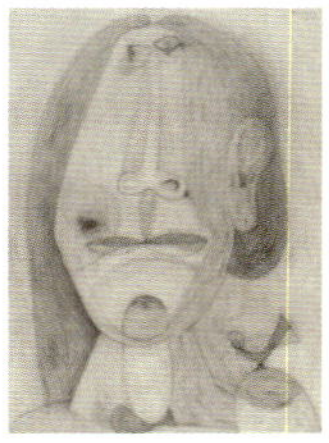

RUFINO TAMAYO (Mexican, 1899–1991)
Mujer con pájaros
[Woman with Birds], 1950
Graphite on paper
$30\frac{7}{8}$ x $22\frac{5}{8}$ inches (78.4 x 57.5 cm)
PLATE 50

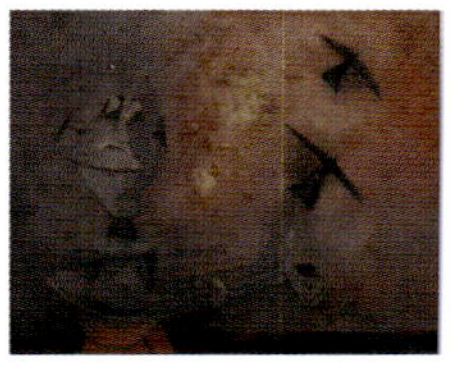

RUFINO TAMAYO (Mexican, 1899–1991)
Pájaros liberados [Liberated Birds], 1956
Oil and sand on canvas
$31\frac{3}{4}$ x $39\frac{5}{8}$ inches (80.6 x 100.6 cm)
PLATE 51

PROVENANCE: M. Knoedler & Co., New York, 1956; Marcel Roche, Caracas, 1960; M. Knoedler & Co., New York, 1965; private collection; Sotheby's, New York, 19th- and 20th-Century Latin American Paintings, Drawings, Sculpture, and Prints, May 7, 1981, lot 51; CDS Gallery, New York; acquired in 1982 by Tanya Capriles de Brillembourg.

EXHIBITIONS: *Recent Works by Rufino Tamayo*, M. Knoedler & Co., New York (1956), no. 8; *9th Exhibition of Modern Art*, Mary Washington College of the University of Virginia, Fredericksburg, 1964, cat. no. 43; *Mexican Masters*, Hooks-Epstein Galleries, Houston, 1980.

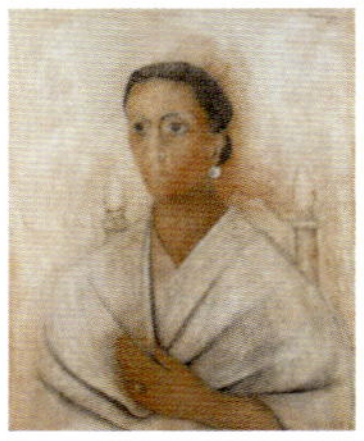

RUFINO TAMAYO (Mexican, 1899–1991)
Retrato de la señora Mercedes Ballesteros de Antuñano [Portrait of Mrs. Mercedes Ballesteros de Antuñano], 1961
Charcoal and red chalk on gessoed Masonite
$39\frac{1}{4}$ x $31\frac{7}{8}$ inches (99.7 x 81 cm)
PLATE 52

PROVENANCE: Alfonso de Antuñano, Mexico; private collection, Mexico; Sotheby's, New York, Latin American Art, May 19, 1987, lot 11; The Window South Collection, Menlo Park, California; CDS Gallery; acquired in 1989 by Mr. and Mrs. David Brillembourg.

EXHIBITIONS: *El retrato contemporáneo mexicano*, Palace of Fine Arts, Mexico City (1961), cat. 51; *Imagen de México*, Schirn Kunsthalle, Frankfurt, December 5, 1987–February 28, 1988; Messepalast, Vienna, May 17–July 31, 1988; Dallas Museum of Art, August 28–October 30, 1988 (illustrated, no. 193, p. 323); *Un Panorama del Arte México*, Mexican Cultural Institute, Washington, D.C., 1990.

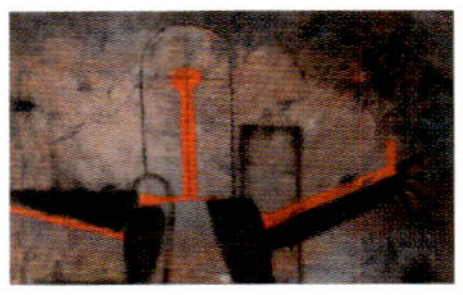

RUFINO TAMAYO (Mexican, 1899–1991)
Figura en rojo y negro [Figure in Red and Black], 1971
Oil on canvas
16 x $25\frac{11}{16}$ inches (40.6 x 65.2 cm)
PLATE 53

PROVENANCE: Perls Galleries, New York; Winifred Breuning, Los Angeles; Mary-Anne Martin/Fine Art, New York; acquired in 1983 by Tania Capriles de Brillembourg.

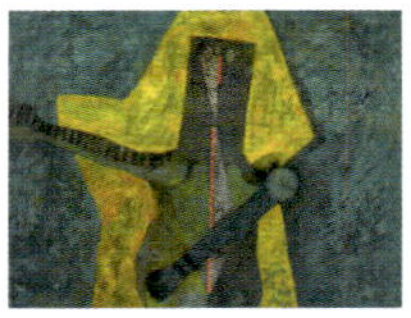

RUFINO TAMAYO (Mexican, 1899–1991)
Personaje en verde [Personage in Green], 1973
Oil and sand and inclusions on canvas
$43\frac{3}{4}$ x $57\frac{1}{2}$ inches (111.1 x 146.1 cm)
PLATE 54

PROVENANCE: Lee Ault and Co., New York; James Maroney, New York; Mary-Anne Martin/Fine Art, New York; acquired in 1985 by Tanya Capriles de Brillembourg.

FRANCISCO TOLEDO (Mexican, b. 1940)
El circo [The Circus], 1961
Oil and sand on canvas
$38\frac{3}{8}$ x $51\frac{5}{16}$ inches (97.5 x 130.3 cm)
PLATE 64

PROVENANCE: Private collection, Mexico City; Christie's, New York, Important Latin American Paintings, Drawings, and Sculpture, May 19, 1992, lot 139; acquired in 1992 by Tanya Capriles de Brillembourg.

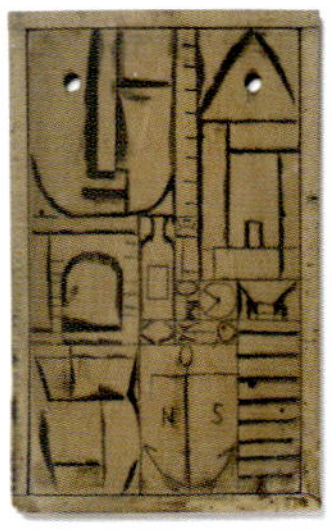

JOAQUÍN TORRES-GARCÍA (Uruguayan, 1874–1949)
Constructivo con dibujo inciso [Constructive Composition with Incised Drawing], 1932
Incised wood
$17\frac{1}{8}$ x $10\frac{1}{2}$ inches (43.5 x 26.7 cm)
PLATE 13

PROVENANCE: Estate of the artist, Montevideo; Royal S. Marks, New York; acquired by CDS Gallery, New York, 1992 at Sotheby's New York, Latin American Paintings, Drawings, Sculpture and Prints, November 23, 1992, lot 7; acquired by Tanya Capriles de Brillembourg in 1992.

EXHIBITIONS: CDS Gallery, New York; *Joaquín Torres-García: Constructing Abstraction with Wood*, The Menil Collection, Houston, September 25, 2009–January 3, 2010 (illustrated, no. 91, p. 172); San Diego Museum of Art, February 20–May 3, 2010.

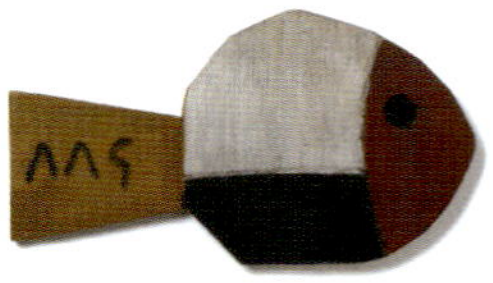

JOAQUÍN TORRES-GARCÍA (Uruguayan, 1874–1949)
Pez AAC [Fish AAC], 1939
Painted wood
$7\frac{7}{8}$ x $14\frac{1}{8}$ x $\frac{1}{2}$ inches (20.1 x 35.8 x 1.3 cm)
PLATE 15

PROVENANCE: Estate of the artist; Horacio Torres, Montevideo; Royal S. Marks, New York, 1983; acquired by CDS Gallery, New York, at Sotheby's New York, November 23, 1992, lot 5; acquired by Tanya Capriles de Brillembourg in 1992.

EXHIBITIONS: *Joaquín Torres-García: Constructing Abstraction with Wood*, The Menil Collection, Houston, September 25, 2009–January 3, 2010 (illustrated no. 91, p. 172); San Diego Museum of Art, February 20–May 3, 2010.

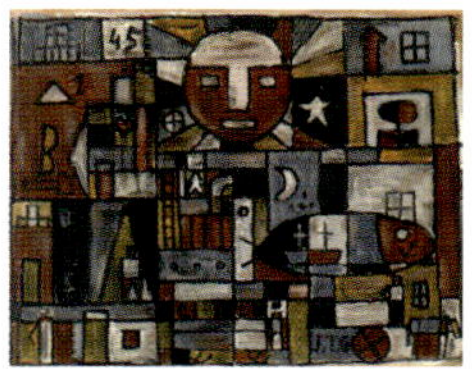

JOAQUÍN TORRES-GARCÍA
(Uruguayan, 1874–1949)
Construcción universal con gran sol [Universal Construction with Large Sun], 1945
Oil on cardboard mounted on canvas
20 1/8 x 25 7/8 inches (51.1 x 65.7 cm)
PLATE 18

PROVENANCE: Estate of the artist; Olimpia Torres; Mr. and Mrs. Perera, Barcelona; CDS Gallery, New York; acquired by Tanya Capriles de Brillembourg.

EXHIBITIONS: CDS Gallery, New York, November 1997; *Joaquín Torres-García: Paintings in Houston Collections,* Museum of Fine Arts, Houston, September 6–January 18, 2010

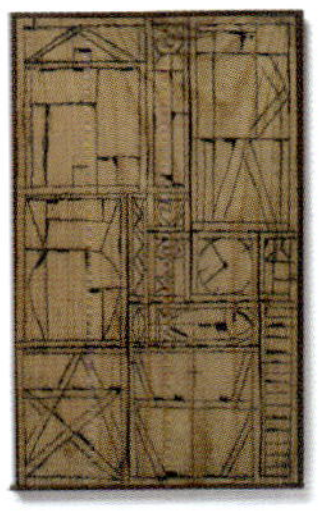

JOAQUÍN TORRES-GARCÍA
(Uruguayan, 1874–1949)
Constructif en bois incise [Constructive Composition on Incised Wood], 1932
Ink on incised wood
19 3/8 x 11 9/16 inches (49.3 x 29.3 cm)
PLATE 14

PROVENANCE: Estate of the artist, Montevideo; Andre Emmerich Gallery, New York; Royal Marks, New York, 1981; acquired by CDS Gallery, New York at Sotheby's New York, Latin American Paintings, Drawings, Sculpture and Prints, November 23, 1992, lot 14; acquired by Tanya Capriles de Brillembourg in 1992.

EXHIBITIONS: *Joaquín Torres-García*, The University of Texas at Austin, December 1, 1971–January 16, 1972 (illustrated, no. 28, n.p.).

JOAQUÍN TORRES-GARCÍA
(Uruguayan, 1874–1949)
Pez [Fish], 1932
Oil on canvas
21 x 25 1/2 inches (53 x 64.8 cm)
PLATE 16

PROVENANCE: Estate of the artist, Montevideo; CDS Gallery, New York; acquired by Tanya Capriles de Brillembourg in 1983.

EXHIBITIONS: *Torres-García: Grid-Pattern-Sign: Paris-Montevideo 1924–1944,* Hayward Gallery, London, November 1985–February 23, 1986 (illustrated, no. 47, p. 49); Fundacio Joan Miro, Barcelona, March 13–May 4, 1986 (illustrated, no. 44, p. 73); Stadtische Kunsthalle Dusseldorf, July–August 1986; Center for the Fine Arts, Miami, September 13–November 9, 1986; Museum of Fine Arts, Houston, February 14–April 6, 1987.

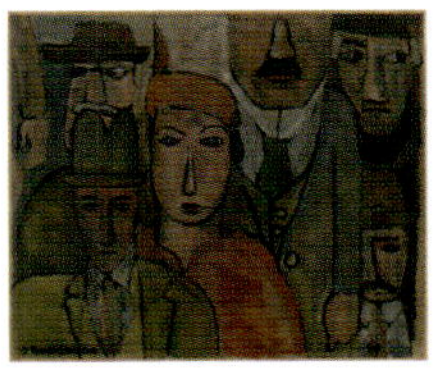

JOAQUÍN TORRES-GARCÍA
(Uruguayan, 1874–1949)
Muchedumbre [Crowd], 1940
Oil on cardboard
19 1/4 x 23 inches (48.9 x 58.4 cm)
PLATE 17

PROVENANCE: Estate of the artist, Montevideo; CDS Gallery, New York; acquired by Tanya Capriles de Brillembourg in 1983.

EXHIBITIONS: *Joaquín Torres-García: Paintings in Houston Collections,* Museum of Fine Arts, Houston, September 6–January 18, 2010.

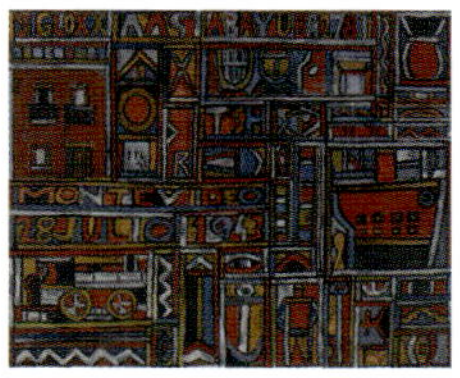

JOAQUÍN TORRES-GARCÍA
(Uruguayan, 1874–1949)
Composición constructiva de estructura coloreada [Constructive Composition with Colored Structure], 1943
Oil on canvas
33 7/8 x 41 5/8 inches (84.5 x 105.7 cm)
PLATE 19

PROVENANCE: Estate of the artist; Rose Fried, New York, November 12, 1961; CDS Gallery New York; acquired by Tanya Capriles de Brillembourg in 1984.

EXHIBITIONS: *Joaquín Torres-García 1874–1949—15th Memorial Exhibition,* Rose Fried Gallery, January 6–February 13, 1964; *Art of the Fantastic: Latin America, 1920–1987,* Indianapolis Museum of Art, Indianapolis, June 28–December 6, 1987 (illustrated, p. 81); The Queens Museum, Flushing, October 10, 1987–December 6, 1987; Center for the Art, Miami, January 15, 1988–March 4, 1988; Centro cultural/Arte contemporáneo, Mexico City, March 25, 1988–May 2, 1988. *Crosscurrents of Modernism, Four Latin American Pioneers, Diego Rivera, Joaquín Torres-García, Wifredo Lam, Matta,* June 11–September 7, 1992 (illustrated, no. 44, p. 143); *Kunst-Welten im Dialog Von Gauguin zur globaler Gegenwart,* November 5, 1999–March 19, 2000 (illustrated, no. 172, p. 225); *Joaquín Torres-García: Paintings in Houston Collections,* Museum of Fine Arts, Houston, September 6–January 18, 2010.

NOTE
The following works in the Brillembourg Capriles Collection of Latin American Art are covered by claims to copyright that, as of the press date of this publication, could not be secured. As a result, these works were not reproduced in the preceding plates:

EMILIO PETTORUTI
(Argentinean, 1892–1971)
Sin título [Untitled], 1917
Graphite on paper
5 1/2 x 3 1/16 inches (14 x 7.7 cm)

EMILIO PETTORUTI
(Argentinean, 1892–1971)
Sin título [Untitled], No date
Conté crayon on paper
4 3/4 x 7 1/2 inches (12.1 x 19.1 cm)

EMILIO PETTORUTI
(Argentinean, 1892–1971)
Naturaleza muerta [Still Life], 1918
Oil on canvas mounted on cardboard laminate
10 1/8 x 13 3/8 inches (25.7 x 34 cm)

PROVENANCE: Galería Bonino, Buenos Aires; Van Riel Galería de Arte, Buenos Aires, 1963; Sotheby's New York, Latin American Paintings, Drawings, Sculpture and Prints, May 19, 1992, lot 17; acquired by Tanya Capriles de Brillembourg in 1992.

EXHIBITIONS: *Fuera del centro: arte argentino en las colecciones venezolanas,* Museo de Bellas Artes de Caracas, Venezuela, 1995.

LOLÓ SOLDEVILLA (Cuban, 1901–1971)
Sin título [Untitled], 1956
Tempera and incised graphite lines on cardboard
11 13/16 x 16 3/4 inches (28.4 x 42.5 cm)

BIOGRAPHIES OF THE ARTISTS

JACOBO BORGES

VENEZUELAN, BORN 1931

Born in Caracas to working-class parents, Jacobo Borges spent his youth and adolescence in the neighborhoods of El Cementerio and Catia. Showing artistic aptitude from an early age, his family enrolled him at the Escuela de Artes Plásticas de Caracas from 1936 to 1944 where he returned as a young adult in 1949. In 1951 Borges worked at the Taller Libre de Arte, a meeting ground for artists and intellectuals such as Alejo Carpentier and Gastón Diehl that sought to renew and modernize the Venezuelan avant-garde. In 1952, a monetary prize for his work allowed him to travel to Paris where he remained for several years. He returned to Venezuela in 1956, exploding onto the artistic scene with powerful figurative work laden with aggressive metaphors, illusionary spontaneity, and fragmentary time. In 1958, Borges designed experimental stage sets for several contemporary Venezuelan playwrights. By the mid-1960s, Borges became increasingly involved in activism and, as his politics radicalized, questioned the pertinence of his aesthetic practice. Ultimately, he abandoned painting from 1965 to 1970, during which time he continued his grassroots, community-focused activism as well as organized the large-scale multidisciplinary event *Imagen de Caracas* [Image of Caracas] (1967). The artworks that emerged in 1970, the same year that he helped to establish the MAS [Movimiento al Socialismo] political party, reflected the artist's heightened collective consciousness. In the mid-1980s, his style further evolved into a more placid version of his expressionistic work of the 1960s, a variant of which he still practices. —MCG

FERNANDO BOTERO

COLOMBIAN, BORN 1932

Born in Medellín, Colombia, Fernando Botero had his first group exhibition in 1948, at age sixteen, when he also began drawing illustrations for the Sunday supplement of *El Colombiano*. After moving to Bogotá in 1952, Botero held his first solo exhibition at the Leo Matiz Gallery, selling most of his works there and at other shows. From 1952–55, he traveled around Europe, where he studied briefly at the Academia de San Fernando, visited museums, and learned about quattrocento artists such as Piero della Francesca and Paolo Uccello. Botero then returned to Bogotá and traveled to Mexico and Washington, D.C., where the Pan-American Union (now the Organization of American States) organized his first solo show in the United States. Back in Colombia, Botero was appointed professor of painting at the Escuela de Bellas Artes de la Universidad Nacional de Colombia in 1958. After achieving success in his native country, he moved to the United States in 1960. While the reception of Botero's work in the States was erratic, his reputation in Europe, especially Germany, was consistently on the rise. In 1973, he left New York and moved to Paris where he began making sculptures. Important retrospectives of his work have been organized by the Hirshhorn Museum and Sculpture Garden in Washington, D.C.; the Museo de Arte Contemporáneo in Caracas; and the Fondation Pierre Gianadda in Martigny, Switzerland. Botero divides his time between Paris, Monte Carlo, Pietrasanta, and New York. —MG

ELIAS CRESPIN

VENEZUELAN, BORN 1965

Born in Caracas, Elias Crespin studied computer science at the Universidad Central de Venezuela and worked as a computer programmer for nineteen years before making his foray into art in 2004. Although Crespin received no formal art training, he gained a thorough knowledge of design and artistic practice from his grandparents, the artists Gego (Gertrud Goldschmidt) and Gerd Leufert, and their contact with other members of the Venezuelan avant-garde, such as Alejandro Otero, Jesús Rafael Soto, and Carlos Cruz-Diez, who explored aspects of Geometric Abstraction and Kineticism in the postwar period. In 2002, Crespin began working on a project inspired by one of Soto's *Cubos virtuales* [Virtual Cubes] and designed a program that animated the lines of the work. Since 2004 he has created more than twenty-five installations in which geometric shapes are suspended by invisible threads and are motorized to create choreographed movements and patterns in space. In 2009 he began experimenting with color acrylic, channeling different effects of light and shadow. Crespin has received growing recognition for his works, which are in museum collections in Latin America, Europe, and the United States. In 2012, he was given his first solo exhibition in the United States at Cecilia de Torres, Ltd., in New York. The artist lives in Paris, where he has resided since 2008. —MW

SANDÚ DARIÉ

CUBAN, 1908–1991

Born in Romania, Sandú Darié moved to Paris in 1926 and worked as an art critic and humorist in the orbit of the Surrealist artists and poets. He immigrated to Cuba in 1941, becoming a citizen in 1947. Darié worked in a lyrical mode of abstraction through the late 1940s, a period that culminated in his first solo exhibition, *Composiciones 1949*, which opened at Havana's Lyceum and traveled to the Carlebach Gallery in New York later that year. At the end of 1949, he began a decade-long correspondence with Gyula Košice, cofounder of the Grupo Madí in Argentina and a leading proponent of Geometric Abstraction in the Southern Cone. By 1950, his work had become purely nonobjective, entering into dialogue with the Madí movement as well as with European developments in Concrete art. In Cuba, Darié promoted Concretism and abstract art in general through his coeditorship (with Luis Martínez Pedro and Mario Carreño) of the magazine

Noticias de Arte [Art News] (1952–53) and through his involvement with the group Diez Pintores Concretos [Ten Concrete Painters] (1958–61). Darié incorporated movement into the early series titled Estructuras transformables [Transformable Structures], first exhibited in 1955, and he later experimented with light and sound effects in such works as the film *Cosmorama: electro-pintura en movimiento* [Cosmorama: Electro-Painting in Motion] (1964) and the ballet *Dinamia* [Dynamics] (1973). His work persistently interrogated the sensorial experience of color, light, and form set in motion, whether by the active participation of the viewer or through multimedia technology. —AM

WIFREDO LAM

CUBAN, 1902–1982

Born in Sagua la Grande, Cuba, Wifredo Lam attended the San Alejandro Academy of Fine Arts in Havana from 1918 to 1920. In 1923, he traveled to Madrid to further his art studies and remained in Spain until 1937. Initially he studied portraiture under Fernando Álvarez de Sotomayor before experimenting with aspects of Art Nouveau and Surrealism. He took part in the Spanish Civil War (1936–39), producing propaganda materials for the Republican cause and participating in the siege of Madrid in 1937. The following year, he relocated to Paris and befriended Pablo Picasso, who introduced him to Fernand Léger, Henri Matisse, Joan Miró, Tristan Tzara, and other artists. While in Marseilles in 1940–41, he became close friends with André Breton, who arranged for Lam to illustrate his Surrealist poem "Fata Morgana." Before returning to Cuba in 1941, he also befriended poet Aimé Césaire in Martinique, tapping into the négritude literary movement. In Havana, Lam painted works infused with references to Afro-Caribbean culture. Visits to Haiti in 1944 and 1946 were influential in furthering his knowledge of Santería. In 1947, he began regularly visiting Paris and New York, where he met Arshile Gorky, Matta, Marcel Duchamp, and others loosely associated with the Surrealism movement. In 1952, he reestablished residence in Paris and associated with the younger generation of artists who had been members of the CoBRa group (1948–51). In 1960, he established a studio in Albissola Marina, Italy, and experimented with printmaking and ceramics. He died in Paris in 1982. —MW

MATTA

CHILEAN, 1911–2002

Matta studied architecture at the Pontificia Universidad Católica (1929–31) and drawing at the Academia de Bellas Artes in his native Chile. In the 1930s, he joined the merchant marines, arriving in Europe where he initially worked in the Parisian studio of Le Corbusier. He also met Federico García Lorca and Salvador Dalí in Madrid and worked briefly with Walter Gropius and Lászlo Moholy-Nagy in London. In 1937, the same year he officially joined the Surrealists, Matta worked for the architects of the Spanish Pavilion of the Republican government at the Paris World Exposition, where he had prolonged access to Picasso's *Guernica*. Matta's initial painted series—including his hallmark Psychological Morphologies of the late 1930s and Inscapes of the early 1940s—are influenced by Freudian psychology and experimentation with the Surrealist notion of automatic writing and the principle of chance. At the outbreak of World War II, Matta traveled to New York with the Surrealists and sought out the artists of the New York School. In the summer of 1941, Matta traveled to Mexico with Robert Motherwell and saw the large-format works of the muralists, a scale that he assimilated into his own production. A significant shift occurred in 1944 when he transitioned from his early interior landscapes to figurative works that reflected a growing concern with mankind. Matta was expelled from the Surrealists in 1947 and he returned to Europe in 1948. Following trips to Cuba in the 1960s, his work took on distinct political and spiritual intentions. —MCG

FRANCISCO MATTO

URUGUAYAN, 1911–1995

Born in Montevideo in 1911, Francisco Matto received his entire education through private lessons at home, which included art classes with the Uruguayan painter Carlos Rúfalo. At age twenty-one, he traveled throughout Tierra del Fuego in Southern Chile and Argentina, acquiring the first objects in what would become an important collection of Pre-Columbian art. After returning to Uruguay, Matto began composing poetry and making paintings, including some on large-size, irregularly shaped wooden panels. In 1939, he met Joaquín Torres-García, who encouraged the younger artist to explore Constructivism. Three years later, with Augusto and Horacio Torres and Alceu and Edgardo Ribeiro, Matto cofounded El Taller Torres-García (TTG), a workshop that provided a space in which Matto and other artists experimented with avant-garde art and became pivotal to the artistic development of Uruguay. Matto made his first trip to Europe in 1950, spending much of his time at the Museé d'Ethnographie du Trocadéro in Paris, studying the museum's collection of Pre-Columbian art. He continued studying and teaching at the TTG until it disbanded in 1962. That same year, Matto opened his own collection of Pre-Columbian art to the public, which unfortunately closed sixteen years later due to the withdrawal of governmental support. While Matto exhibited very little during his lifetime, his dedication to his artistic practice, in which he constantly explored elemental forms as a way to understand the mysteries of the universe, established him as an important innovator in Uruguayan art. —RM

ARMANDO MORALES

NICARAGUAN, 1927–2011

After spending the first three years of his life in the quiet town of Granada, Nicaragua, Armando Morales's family settled in Managua. There, he regularly studied at the National School of Fine Arts under Rodrigo Peñalba, who first introduced the young artist to the works of the European avant-garde, such as Pablo Picasso, Georges Braque, and Paul Cézanne, among others. His abstract painting *Árbol-espanto* won first prize in the Concurso Centroamericano de Pintura, held in 1956 in Guatemala. That same year, José Gómez Sicre invited Morales to participate in the *Gulf-Caribbean Art Exhibition* held at the Museum of Fine Arts, Houston. He traveled to New York City in 1960 to study lithography, etching, and engraving at the Pratt Graphic Art Center, and remained there for the next five years. He spent a year in Europe, but returned to New York and established permanent residency there until 1982. During these years, Morales exhibited his work extensively at international institutions and galleries such as the Biblioteca Luis Ángel Arango del Banco de la República in Bogotá, Colombia (1966); the Museo de Bellas Artes in Caracas, Venezuela (1967); Palacio de Bellas Artes in Mexico City (1968); and Lee Ault Gallery in New York City (1973, 1976, 1978); among many others. In 1982, he moved to Paris, where he established a studio and a close relationship with the Claude Bernard Gallery. In 1991, Morales set up a second studio in London, and amid extensive traveling, worked between there and Paris for the duration of his life. —RM

EMILIO PETTORUTI

ARGENTINEAN, 1892–1971

The son of Italian parents and one of eleven children, Emilio Pettoruti was born in La Plata, Argentina, in 1892. He began his studies at the Academia Provincial de Bellas Artes, and in 1913, after receiving a fellowship from the government, he left for Florence, Italy, to continue his artistic development. Between 1913 and 1924, Pettoruti joined key avant-garde intellectual circles, befriending artists such as Filippo Tommaso Marinetti, Giacomo Balla, Giorgio di Chirico, and Juan Gris, among many others. While absorbing modern artistic tendencies such as Futurism and Cubism, he also studied the quattrocento masters, visiting various cathedrals and palaces in Italy and copying Early Renaissance paintings in the Uffizi Gallery. As his artistic production matured, Pettoruti decided to return to Buenos Aires in 1924, and he mounted an exhibition of his work at the Galería Witcomb, which caused a scandal with a public accustomed to more traditional forms of expression. Determined to advance the development of art in Argentina, Pettoruti joined the intellectual group that edited *Martín Fierro. Periódico de arte y crítica libre*, a bimonthly publication that voiced the views of the avant-garde in Buenos Aires. He actively exhibited internationally, showing at renowned institutions and galleries such as the San Francisco Museum of Art (1942), the National Academy of Design in New York (1943), and Galerie Denise René (1959), among many others. Toward the end of his life, he received the Premio Continental Guggenheim de las Américas (1956) and the Premio Fondo Nacional de las Artes (1967). Pettoruti died in Paris in 1971. —RM

RENÉ PORTOCARRERO

CUBAN, 1911–1985

Born in the suburban Havana neighborhood of El Cerro, René Portocarrero briefly enrolled at the Academia de San Alejandro in 1926. In 1937, he joined the short-lived Ensayo Experimental de Estudio Libre de Pintura y Escultura, which grouped independently minded artists—including Eduardo Abela, Jorge Arche, and Domingo Ravenet—who taught without the constraints of a hermetic academic program. Portocarrero was an active member of Orígenes, the group that coalesced around the writer José Lezama Lima in the 1940s. His first painted series including Festín [Feast] and his landmark Interiores de El Cerro [Interiors of El Cerro] (both begun in 1943) reflect nostalgia for his idyllic childhood and show the influence of the Mexican School. These series extended into Brujos [Sorcerers], based on Afro-Cuban mythology, begun in 1945. Portocarrero spent most of that year in the United States and visited Haiti in 1946 when his work evolved into the muted geometric abstraction that he would pursue again from 1949 to 1953 in series such as Gestáltica [Gestaltic]. In 1950, he made a brief foray into ceramics alongside Wifredo Lam, Mariano, Luis Martínez Pedro, and Amelia Paláez at a workshop in Santiago de las Vegas. What was most notable about his work in the 1950s, however, was the emergence of the architectural themes that would dominate Portocarrero's work for the rest of his life: the urban landscapes inspired by Havana's eclectic architecture (Paisajes de La Habana [Landscapes of Havana] painted from 1961 onward and later in the Ciudades [Cities] series), as well as the recurring theme of the cathedral that had first appeared in his work from the 1940s. —MCG

ARMANDO REVERÓN

VENEZUELAN, 1889–1954

The only child of an affluent family, Armando Reverón studied at the Academia Nacional de Bellas Artes in Caracas from 1908 to 1911. He won a scholarship in 1911 to study in Europe, living in Barcelona, Madrid, and Paris until the dangers of World War I forced him to return home in 1915. In Venezuela, he became a member of the Círculo de Bellas Artes, a group of artists that sought to modernize the country's art academies, and associated with artists interested in Post-Impressionism, Symbolism, and landscape painting, including Russian artist Nikolas Ferdinandov and Venezuelan artists Emilio Boggio and Rafael Monasterio. In 1918, Reverón met Juanita Ríos, who became his lifelong companion and frequently served as the painter's model. The couple settled permanently in Macuto in 1921, where Reverón's work was strongly influenced by the luminosity of the tropics. His mature work is characterized by his subtle portrayals of landscapes, seascapes, reclining nudes, and self-portraits, which he often painted on translucent burlap or brown paper. Beginning in the 1930s, the artist suffered from bouts of depression, nervous breakdowns, and the symptoms of schizophrenia, for which he was later institutionalized. In 1953, he was awarded Venezuela's Premio Nacional de Pintura. He died in Caracas in 1954. —MW

DIEGO RIVERA

MEXICAN, 1886–1957

Born in Guanajuato, Diego Rivera studied at Mexico City's Escuela Nacional de Bellas Artes (Academy of San Carlos) from 1898 to 1905. He left for Madrid in 1907, then Paris, where he became a leading Cubist. Rivera remained in Europe until 1921 (except for a brief return home in 1910–11), missing the major events of the Mexican Revolution. By 1918, Rivera abandoned abstraction for a figurative visual language inspired by the French "return to order," marked by careful draftsmanship, idealized forms, and—in his murals—increasingly dense montages. He was one of several artists commissioned by the postrevolutionary regime as part of a revival of mural painting; for public and private patrons he painted frescoes featuring Mexico's pre-Hispanic past and rural traditions, international political events, and the machine age, for sites in Mexico City, Cuernavaca, San Francisco, Detroit, and New York. His censored mural for the RCA Building at Rockefeller Center (1933) was re-created in the Palace of Fine Arts in Mexico City (1934). Rivera also created hundreds of easel paintings—from landscapes to portraits of socialites—, watercolors, drawings, prints, and book illustrations: his prestige was confirmed by his one-man exhibition at the Museum of Modern Art, New York, in 1930–31. A larger-than-life figure, Rivera had a conflictive relationship with the Communist Party, largely for his association with Leon Trotsky. Beginning in the 1940s, he dedicated attention to Anahuacalli, a neo-Aztec museum housing his vast collection of Pre-Columbian art. He died of cancer in 1957. —JO

CARLOS ROJAS

COLOMBIAN, 1933–1997

One of the most influential abstract artists in Colombia, Carlos Rojas was born in 1933 in the small town of Facatativa, twenty-eight miles northwest of Bogotá. He studied architecture at the Universidad Javeriana and art at the Escuela de Bellas Artes de la Universidad Nacional. In 1958, Rojas received a grant to continue his studies in Italy and traveled throughout Europe. Before returning to Bogotá in 1960, he traveled throughout North America, making stops in Alaska, Canada, the United States, and Mexico. Rojas embraced the structural principles promoted in Constructive art, because, for him, they offered a fundamental understanding of the physical world. Yet his works demonstrate a humanistic approach to geometry in that they soften the rigidity of shapes and lines, and thus contribute a unique perspective to the abstract language. His artistic development advanced through multiple series, including *América: horizontes, América: cruzadas, El dorado, Mater y materia,* and *Mutantes,* in which he rigorously explored a certain set of ideas and aesthetics before moving on to the next. He also completed large-scale, public sculptures based on his explorations of landscape and space. In 1974, Rojas was appointed director of the Museos Nacionales de COLCULTURA and began working with the Organización de Estados Américanos to preserve indigenous customs and traditions. In this capacity, he developed projects to promote folk craft with other countries, including Guatemala, Ecuador, and Costa Rica. In the mid-1970s, Rojas began including geometrically inspired debris in his works, which he continued to do until his death in 1997. —RM

ANTONIO SEGUÍ

ARGENTINEAN, BORN 1934

Antonio Seguí was born in the city of Córdoba, Argentina, on January 11, 1934, where he lived until he was seventeen years old when, financed by his grandmother, he traveled to Europe and North Africa. Back in Córdoba in 1954, Seguí worked briefly for the newspaper *Orientación* and studied for a career in law, which he did not pursue. In 1957, he had his first solo exhibition at the Galería Paideia in Córdoba, followed by a prolonged trip through Latin America. After working for a few years in Mexico, Seguí went back to Argentina in 1960 where he painted with the Otra figuración group until 1963. That same year, he was invited to present his Felicitas Naón [Felicitas Naon] series at the Third Paris Biennial. A year later he was invited to represent Argentina, along with other artists, at the 32nd Venice Biennale. In 1964, he set up his house/studio in Arcueil, France, where he currently resides. With his fame on the rise, Seguí continued showing all over Europe and Latin America. Meanwhile, his interest in collecting Pre-Columbian and African sculptures became more serious and committed. Starting in 1976, after having an accident that left him hospitalized for six months, Seguí suffered from the repercussions of the military dictatorship in Argentina. In France, his house was broken into, his phone tapped, and, in 1982, he survived a shooting at his apartment in Paris. In 1984, after democracy was restored in Argentina, Seguí represented his country at the 41st Venice Biennale. In 1989, he won the Torcuato Di Tella Award for Visual Art and in 1991 had an important retrospective at the Museo Nacional de Bellas Artes in Buenos Aires. Seguí continues working on paintings, prints, murals, and installations. —MG

DAVID ALFARO SIQUEIROS

MEXICAN, 1896–1974

Born José de Jesús Alfaro Siqueiros in Mexico City in 1896, he adopted the name David about 1920. He studied at Mexico City's Escuela Nacional de Bellas Artes (1911–14), then fought with Carrancista forces (1914–17) during the Mexican Revolution. Siqueiros lived in Europe from 1919 to 1922; in Barcelona he published an important Futurist-inspired manifesto (1921). Following his return to Mexico, Siqueiros became a leading figure in both artistic and political spheres; he was a leading organizer of the Mexican Painters' Union. Siqueiros's commitment to an active political life as well as to innovative aesthetic strategies complicated his career. He painted major murals for government buildings and was a prolific painter, but was twice imprisoned (1930–31; 1960–64) by the Mexican government, fought in the Spanish Civil War (1937–39), and, most notoriously, led an unsuccessful assassination attempt on Leon Trotsky in 1940. This activism led to several exiles, imposed or self-imposed: from 1930 to 1945, Siqueiros lived and worked in Los Angeles, Montevideo, Buenos Aires, New York, Chillán (Chile), and Havana, as well as in Mexico City. Through the New York "Experimental Workshop" (1936), lectures, articles, and murals, Siqueiros promoted collective practice and the use of industrial materials (pyroxilin, plywood) and techniques (airbrush, photographic projections). His first major mural, commissioned by the Mexican Electricians' Union (1939–40), and done in collaboration with Josep Renau and others, set the course for most of his subsequent work. Later in life he focused on the grandiose Foro Universal (later Polyforum Siqueiros). He died in 1974. —JO

LOLÓ SOLDEVILLA

CUBAN, 1901–1971

Loló Soldevilla began to paint in the late 1940s while working as a cultural attaché at the Cuban Embassy in France. Encouraged by Wifredo Lam, she worked in the milieu of the School of Paris, enrolling in courses at the Académie de la Grande Chaumière and at the Atelier d'Art Abstrait, founded by Jean

Dewasne and Edgard Pillet. Her practice evolved through dialogue with historical figures, such as Jean Arp and Ossip Zadkine, and the group that emerged around the Galerie Denise René, including Robert Jacobsen and Victor Vasarely. Her work from these years includes metal *Stabiles* and mixed-media reliefs that explore geometric form through light, shape, and movement. Soldevilla exhibited at the Salon des Réalités Nouvelles annually between 1951 and 1955. In 1957, she exhibited the Constructivist *Cajas luminosas* [Light Boxes], made with the assistance of the Spanish Kineticist Eusebio Sempere, at the Galería Sardio in Caracas. Soldevilla's return to Cuba in 1956 generated new enthusiasm around Geometric Abstraction, sparked by an exhibition of School of Paris artists that she organized in Havana. With her partner, the Concrete poet and artist Pedro de Oraá, Soldevilla opened the Galería Color-Luz in Havana's Miramar neighborhood in 1957. Their gallery served as an incubator for a young generation of Concrete artists, and they were founding members of the group Diez Pintores Concretos, which exhibited in Havana (1959), Matanzas (1960), and Camagüey (1960). Soldevilla's work spanned figurative painting, Op Art, and Pop Art by the mid-1960s. In 1964, she founded the group Espacio. —AM

RUFINO TAMAYO

MEXICAN, 1899–1991

Born in Oaxaca, Rufino Tamayo studied at the Escuela Nacional de Bellas Artes (1915–17), experimenting with Post-Impressionism. In the 1920s, he taught drawing in elementary schools using the Best Maugard Method, which inspired his later emphasis on imagination over observation, and the poetic over the political. Tamayo painted murals in Mexico, the United States, and Puerto Rico, but was primarily an easel painter. Accompanied by his wife Olga, whom he married in 1934, he lived and worked for extended periods in New York (1937–49) and Paris (1949–59), seeking to establish an international career. After seeing an exhibition of Picasso's work in New York in 1939, Tamayo adopted post-Cubist strategies, including abstracted figures and flattened forms. Rendered in bright colors and employing gritty surfaces inspired by Jean Dubuffet's Art Brut, Tamayo's mature works feature human protagonists, alone or in groups. Nationalist references common in his paintings, drawings, and prints of the 1920s—often traced by critics to his indigenous heritage—increasingly gave way to allegorical subjects, some informed by Surrealism and existentialism, referencing wartime tensions, atomic-age anxieties, and the art-making process itself. Despite international acclaim, including at the Venice Biennale (1948), Tamayo faced opposition by the leading muralists for his apolitical stance, although mural commissions for Mexico City's Palace of Fine Arts (1952–53) signaled growing acceptance at home. Tamayo founded a museum of pre-Hispanic art in Oaxaca (1972) and another in Mexico City (founded in 1981) that features his collection of international Modern art. He died in 1991 and was acclaimed as Mexico's greatest artist. —JO

FRANCISCO TOLEDO

MEXICAN, BORN 1940

Born Francisco Benjamín López Toledo in Juchitán, Oaxaca, in 1940, the artist dropped his paternal surname beginning in the late 1950s. He studied at the Escuela de Bellas Artes in Oaxaca and the Escuela de Artesanía y Diseño in Mexico City (1952–57). In 1959, Mexico City dealer Antonio Souza gave Toledo his first one-person show, effectively launching his professional career. He moved to Paris, where he lived until 1965: since then, Toledo has been primarily based in his home state of Oaxaca. Toledo's abstractions of the early 1960s are distinguished by a thick application of paint, often mixed with sand, revealing debts to the work of Rufino Tamayo—another "exile" then living in Paris—as well as to Jean Dubuffet, Paul Klee, and perhaps the *art informel* and other forms of abstraction then current in Europe. While in Paris, Toledo began to embrace certain primitivist currents, using natural materials in increasingly fragile works. He eventually tapped into a mythical yet figurative vocabulary tied to his Zapotec roots, usually featuring humans and animals, often with playful or erotic references, and using a variety of techniques, from watercolor to ceramics and photography. Like Diego Rivera and David Alfaro Siqueiros, Toledo has also been a political activist, though this is evident not in his work but in his role as a cultural agent, from the establishment of Casa de la Cultura del Istmo in 1972 to his defense of Oaxaca's patrimony, including support for museums and an art school. Toledo presently lives and works in Oaxaca. —JO

JOAQUÍN TORRES-GARCÍA

URUGUAYAN, 1874–1949

The son of a Catalan father and a Uruguayan mother, Joaquín Torres-García was born in Montevideo in 1874. At age seventeen, Torres-García left Uruguay for Spain along with his parents. While in Barcelona, he made drawings for architect Antoni Gaudí's Sagrada Familia Cathedral, taught art to children at a progressive Mont d'Or school, and pursued his interest in fresco mural painting. In 1909, Torres-García married Manolita Piña; together they had four children. Among his artistic enterprises, he also made a name in the late 1910s as a toymaker, an endeavor he continued in the early 1920s when he and his family moved first to New York, then Italy, followed by France. In 1929, the same year he consolidated his system of symbols known as "Constructive Universalism," he cofounded the group Cercle et Carré with art critic Michel Seuphor in which painters such as Piet Mondrian participated. Feeling the effects of a global economic recession, the Torres-García family left France for Spain where they settled in Madrid in 1932. Encouraged by fellow Uruguayan artists, Torres-García relocated with his family once again; in 1934, after forty-three years of absence, they arrived in Montevideo. In 1935 he founded the Asociación Arte Constructivo, whose magazine *Círculo y Cuadrado* began circulating a year later. His work as a teacher is recorded in the book *500a conferencia de las dadas por J. Torres García en Montevideo entre los años 1934 y 1940*, published in 1940, after he gave his five-hundredth lecture in Uruguay. Inspired by the teachings he imparted to a younger generation of Uruguayan artists, he formed the Taller Torres-García in 1943. Eight months after moving to his new home on the outskirts of Montevideo—an example of Constructivism applied to architecture—Torres-García died in 1949. —MG

CONTRIBUTORS

CECILIA FAJARDO-HILL is a British-Venezuelan art historian and curator of contemporary art. She holds an M.A. in art history from the Courtauld Institute of Art, London, and a Ph.D. in art history from the University of Essex. From 2003 to 2005, she served as Director and Chief Curator for The Cisneros Fontanals Art Foundation and the Ella Fontanals-Cisneros Collection and was Chief Curator at the Museum of Latin American Art in Long Beach from 2009 to 2011.

MARÍA C. GAZTAMBIDE is Director of the Documents of 20th-Century Latin American and Latino Art Project for the International Center for the Arts of the Americas at the Museum of Fine Arts, Houston. She holds an M.A. in arts administration from the University of New Orleans and an M.A. in art history from Tulane University, where she has completed most of the requirements toward a Ph.D. in Latin American studies.

MARCELA C. GUERRERO is Research Coordinator for the International Center for the Arts of the Americas at the Museum of Fine Arts, Houston, and regularly collaborates on exhibition projects and other initiatives of the Latin American Art Department at the Museum. Born in San Juan, Puerto Rico, she is a Ph.D. candidate focusing on Caribbean art in the Department of Art History at the University of Wisconsin, Madison.

ABIGAIL McEWEN is Assistant Professor of Latin American art history at the University of Maryland, College Park. In 2012 she received her Ph.D. from the Institute of Fine Arts, New York University, where she focused on the practices of Latin American avant-gardes during the twentieth century. She is currently working on a book project, *Revolutionary Horizons: Art and Polemics in 1950s Cuba.*

RACHEL MOHL is Curatorial Assistant of Latin American and Latino Art at the Museum of Fine Arts, Houston. Before assuming this position, she worked at the Museo de Arte de Ponce in Puerto Rico as the Exhibitions Coordinator and Curatorial Assistant. Mohl received her M.A. in modern and contemporary Latin American art history from the University of Texas at Austin in 2008.

JAMES OLES divides his time between Mexico City, where he works as an independent curator and art historian, and Wellesley College, Massachusetts, where he teaches in the Art Department and serves as adjunct curator of Latin American art at the Davis Museum. He received his Ph.D. in art history from Yale University.

MARI CARMEN RAMÍREZ is the Wortham Curator of Latin American Art and founding Director of the International Center for the Arts of the Americas at the Museum of Fine Arts, Houston, where she oversees the landmark initiative Documents of 20th-Century Latin American and Latino Art: A Digital Archive and Publications Project. Ramirez received her Ph.D. in art history from the University of Chicago. She has curated numerous exhibitions and has published widely on Latin American art and artists as well as on issues of globalization, identity, and representation.

MICHAEL WELLEN is Assistant Curator of Latin American and Latino Art at the Museum of Fine Arts, Houston. He received his Ph.D. in art history from the University of Texas at Austin, where he specialized in modern and contemporary art, criticism, and Cold War cultural exchanges between Latin America and the United States.

INDEX

Bold page numbers refer to plates and figures.

A

Abbott, Berenice, *Rockefeller Center under Construction*, 47, **47**

Abstract Expressionism, 170, 171, 174

Abstract-Geometric tradition, 230

African art: and Lam, 104, 109, 114, 119, 124, 129n5, 135n8; and Portocarrero, 130, 133

Albers, Joseph, 209, 214, 222

Alemán, Miguel, 54

Arp, Jean, 201

Art Informel, 136, 164

Ashton, Dore, 148

B

Bacon, Francis, 142

Bakhtin, Mikhail, 62

Barnitz, Jacqueline, 171

Barr, Alfred H., Jr., 130, 166

Batista, Fulgencio, 207

Berni, Antonio, *Ramona y el viejo* [Ramona and the Old Man], 187, **187**

Boccioni, Umberto, *States of Mind I: The Farewell*, 40–41, **41**

Bonnard, Pierre, 142

Borges, Jacobo, 192–93, 196, 197nn5–8

Borges, Jacobo, works of: *Esperando a...* [Waiting for...], **192**, 193; *Humilde ciudadano* [Humble Citizen], 193, **193**; *Llegando de...* [Arriving from...] (plate 75), 192, 193, **194–95**, 196; *Reunión con circulo rojo* [Meeting with a Red Circle], 193, **193**

Botero, Fernando, 148, 166, 168, 170–71, 174–75, 178, 181n26

Botero, Fernando, works of: *La apoteosis de Ramón Hoyos* [The Apotheosis of Ramon Hoyos], 171, **171**; *El asesinato de Ana Rosa Calderón* [The Murder of Ana Rosa Calderón], 175, **178**; *Bowl of Fruits* (plate 70), 178, **179**; *La camera degli sposi, Homenaje a Mantegna* [The Couple's Chamber, Homage to Mantegna], 166, 168, **168**; *The Life of Honorius III*, 175, **175**; *Mona Lisa, Age Twelve*, 170, **170**, 171; *Mona Lisa* (plate 65), **167** 168, 174; *Naturaleza muerta* [Still Life] (plate 71), 178, **180**; *El niño de Vallecas* [The Boy from Vallecas], 168, **170**; *El nuncio* [The Nuncio] (plate 67), **172**, 174; *El secuestro* [The Kidnapping] (plate 69), 175, **176–77**; *El taller de Vermeer* [Vermeer's Work] (plate 68), **173**, 174–75; *Teresit la descuartizada* [Teresita, the Woman Cut into Pieces], 175; *Variaciones sobre Cézanne* [Variations on Cézanne] (plate 66), 168, **169**

Boulton, Afredo, 62, **62**, **63**, 69n2

Brancusi, Constantin, *The Kiss*, 119

Braque, Georges, 44, 46, 136, 222

Breton, André, 119, 129n5

Brett, Guy, 237

Brillembourg, David, 9, 15, **16**, 17, 18, 19, 23–24, 25, 27, 31

Brillembourg Capriles, Tanya, **28**

C

Caballero, Luis, 148

Cabrera, Lydia, 129n5, 130

Camargo, Sérgio de, 204

Capriles, Mayra, 15–16, 24

Capriles, Miguel Ángel, 15, 16–18, **16**, 19, 30

Capriles, Perla, 15, 17–18

Capriles de Brillembourg, Tanya, 9 11–12, 15–34, **16**, 28

Capriles López, Miguel Ángel, 16–17

Carpentier, Alejo, 19, 135n12

Carreño, Omar, 198

Certeau, Michel de, 182, 188, 190n1

Cézannisme, 44

Chagall, Marc, 162

Color Field, 142

Conceptualism, 148

Concretism, 207, 209, 213, 213n10, 214, 216

Conde, Teresa del, 164

Constructive art: avant-garde of, 29; and Darié, 214, 216; and Groupe Espace, 209; and Matto, 84, 86; and Rojas, 220, 222, 225, 228; and Soldevilla, 198, 201, 213; and Torres-García, 21, 30, 70, 72–73, 75, 79, 82, 83n14, 84, 87n1, 220, 222

Costantini, Eduardo, 26, 27

Crespin, Elias, 230, 233, 234, 237, 237n3

Crespin, Elias, works of: *4Net*, 237; *Hiperficie* (plate 98), **235**; *Malla electrocinética 1* [Electrokinetic Net 1], 230; *Tapiz Electrocinético 4* [Electro-kinetic Tapestry 4] (plate 99), **236**; *Tetralineados Circular Policromático* [Circular Polychromatic Tetralines] (plate 97), **231–32**, 234; *Tetralineados transparente*, 234; *Triada* [Triad], 237

Cruz-Diez, Carlos, **28**, 29

Cruz-Diez, Carlos, works of: *Physichromie*, 22; *Transchromie*, **233**, 234

"Cuba en la Bienal de Brasil" Special Issue, *Noticias de Arte*, 216, **216**

Cuban Revolution (1959), 216

Cubism: and Lam, 109, 114, 119; and Pettoruti, 38, 40; and Picasso, 44, 109, 119, 222; and Rivera, 23, 44, 47, 50

Cubo-Futurism, 139, 142

Cuevas, José Luis, 148

D

Dalí, Salvador, 101

Dalí, Salvador, works of, *Illumined Pleasures*, **100**, 101

Darié, Sandú, 29, 201, 207, 209, 214, 216, 219n3

Darié, Sandú, works of: *Composición abstracta* [Abstract Composition] (plate 91), 214, 216, **218**; *Cosmorama: electro-pintura en movimiento* [Cosmorama: Electro-Painting in Motion], 216, **216**; *Sin título* [Untitled] 1950 (plate 89), **215**; *Sin título* [Untitled] 1950 (plate 90), 216, **217**

Degas, Edgar, *Woman Bathing in a Shallow Tub*, 151, **152**

de Kooning, Willem, 150, 170

Delaunay, Sonia, *Colored Rhythm*, 209, **209**

Diez Pintores Concretos, 198, 209, 213, 216

Domínguez, Columba, 51, **53**, 54, 55

Dreier, Katherine S., 88, 90, 93, 101

Dubuffet, Jean, 139, 142, 162, 164, 165

Duchamp, Marcel, 88

Duchamp, Marcel, works of, *La mariée mise à nu par se célibataires, même* [The Large Glass: The Bride Stripped Bare by Her Bachelors, Even], 88, **88**, 93, 101

E

Elliot, David, 174

Espacio, 201

F

Fautrier, Jean, 164

Fauvism, 106

Fernández, Jesse, *Portrait of Wifredo Lam*, 124, **124**

Figari, Pedro, 29

Freyman, Enrique, 46–47

Friends of Children with Cancer Foundation, 31

Futurism, 38, 40

G

Gassiot-Talabot, Gérald, 187

Gego (Gertrud Goldschmidt), 29, 230, 237n3

Gego (Gertrud Goldschmidt), works of, *Dibujos sin papel* [Drawings without Paper], 234, **234**

Generación de la Ruptura, 164, 165n4

Geometric art, 23, 29

Gerzso, Gunther, 164

Gómez Sicre, José, 148

González, Beatriz, *Encajera Almanaque Pielroja* [Lacemaker Pielroja Almanac], 174, **174**

Greco-Roman art, 148, 150, 151, 152, 161

Greenberg, Clement, 148, 182

Gris, Juan, *La botella de anís* [The Bottle of Anise], 38, **40**

Group Espace, 201, 209

H

Havana School, 135n8, 198

Henderson, Linda Dalrymple, 103n25

Herrera, Carmen, 198

Holzer, Helena, 104, 114

I

International Center for the Arts of the Americas (ICAA), 20, 21–22, 27

J

Jaramillo, Carmen, 222

Johns, Jasper, 191n14

K

Kafka, Franz, 201

Kahlo, Frida, 47, 50, 54, 140, 146

Kandinsky, Nina, 209

Kandinsky, Wassily, 207, 209

Kinetic art, 198, 207, 213n10, 214, 230

Klee, Paul, 162, 164

Kosice, Gyula, 214, 216

Krauss, Rosalind, 166

Kupka, František *The First Step*, 207, 209, **209**

L

Lam, Wifredo: and African art, 104, 109, 114, 119, 124, 129n5, 135n8; and female form, 104, 106, 109, 114, 119, 124, 129, 129n9; Fernández's portrait of, **124**; and Papua New Guinea, 129n14; and Tamayo, 142

Lam, Wifredo, works of: *Los Amantes* [The Lovers] (plate 41), 119, **121**; *The Chair*, 104; *Cheval* [Horse] (plate 40), 119, **120**; *Femme à l'éventail, II* [Woman with Fan, II] (plate 31), **108**, 109, 114; *Femme aux bras croisés* [Woman with Crossed Arms] (plate 30), 106, **107**; *Femme aux cheveux longs, III* [Woman with Long Hair, III] (plate 34), 106, **112**; *Femme-Oiseau* [Woman-Bird] (plate 33), 109, **111**; *Femmes-Cheval* [Horse-Headed Women] (plate 44), 124, **125**; *Femmes-Cheval* [Horse-Headed Women] (plate 44) (detail), **2**; *Femme violette* [Woman in Violet] (plate 29), 104, **105**, 109; *Femme* [Woman] (plate 35), **113**, 114; *Homme-cheval* [Horse-Headed Man] (plate 43), 119, **123**, 124; *Homme* [Man] (plate 38), 114, **117**; *Interlude Marseilles*, 119, **119**; *The Jungle*, 104, 114; *Maternité Yoruba* [Yoruba Maternity] (plate 37), 114, **116**, 135n8; *Mujer con pájaro* [Woman with Bird] (plate 32), 109, **110**; *Personage con sombrero* [Personage with Hat] (plate 42), 119, **122**; *Reflets d'eau* [Water Reflections] (plate 36), **115**, 124; *Sin título* (La gallina) [Untitled (The Hen)] (plate 47), 119, **128**; *Sin título* [Untitled] 1942 (plate 39), 114, **118**; *Sin título* [Untitled] 1948 (plate 45), 124, **126**; *Sur la main droite* [On the Right Hand] (plate 46), 124, **127**; *Tótem* [Totem], 18

Léger, Fernand, 201

Leirner, Adolpho, 26

Leonardo da Vinci, 151

Leonardo da Vinci, works of: *Mona Lisa*, 168, 171; *Two Studies of a Man's Left Leg from a Ledger from Milan Cathedral*, **150**, 151

Leufert, Gerd, 230

Lichtenstein, Roy, 171

Linati, Claudio, 51

M

Madí movement, 209, 214, 216

Malevich, Kazimir, 82, 201, 222

Martin, Mary-Anne, 21

Martin Fierristas, 42

Marzio, Peter, 27

Masaccio, *Tribute Money*, 41

Masson, André, 164

Matisse, Henri, 46, 58, 104, 106, 109, 136

Matisse, Henri, works of: *Blue Nude (Memory of Biskra)*, 106, **106**; *Portrait of Yvonne Landsberg*, 106, **106**

Matta: historical context of painting, 102n10; monumental scale in work, 102–3n14; and Picasso, 93, 102n11; and Surrealism, 88, 90, 93, 100–101, 102nn4–5; techniques of, 103nn16–19

Matta, works of: *Abstract Composition* (plate 25), 93, **96**, 101, 103n17; *Autómata* [Automaton] (plate 26), 93, **97**, 101, 103n17; *Composition et Étude* [Composition and Study] (plate 27), 93, **98**, 101, 103n17; *Être avec* [Being With], 93; *Naturaleza muerta* [Still Life] (plate 23), 90, **92**, 93, 102n6, 103n17; *Sin título* [Untitled], 1942, 90, **90**; *Sin título* [Untitled], 1943–44 (plate 21), **89**, 90; *Sin título* [Untitled], 1944–45 (plate 22), 90, **91**, 102n6; *Soul without Terror* (plate 28), **99**, 100; *Splitting of the Ego* (plate 24), 90, 93, **94–95**, 102n12, 103n17; *X Space and the Ego*, 93, **93**, 102n12

Matto, Francisco, 84, 86, 87n1

Matto, Francisco, works of: *Construcción* [Construction] (plate 20), 84, **85**, 86; *Constructivo con cinco formas* [Construction in Five Forms], 84, 86, **86**; *Ten Forms*, 86, **87**; *Totems (Venus, Cordero, Venus blanquiazúl, Caracol grande, Máscara)*, 84, **86**

Mérida, Carlos, *Poma Azul* [The Blue Apple], 142, **142**

Mexican School, 54, 136, 140

Mijares, José, 201

Miller, Dorothy, 170

Minimalism, 148, 162

Mionujín, Marta, *Revuélquese y viva* [Wallow Around and Live], 188, **188**

Moats, Alice-Leone, 50–51, **52**

Modernism: and Lam, 104; and Matto, 84, 86; and Rivera, 44, 46, 54; and Soldevilla, 198, 201; and Toledo, 165; and Torres-García, 72

Mondrian, Piet, 21, 70, 72, 204, 214, 222

Moore, Henry, *Head Working Model*, 22, 23

Morales, Armando, 148, 150–52, 161

Morales, Armando, works of: *At the Circus, V* (plate 57), 152, **154**; *Desnudo* [Nude] (plate 58), 152, **155**; *Deux jambes* [Two Legs], **150**, 151; *Escena lacustre I, Granada Harbor* [Lakeside Scene I, Granada Harbor] (plate 55), **149**, 150–52; *Escena lacustre I, Granada Harbor* [Lakeside Scene I, Granada Harbor] (plate 55) (detail), **151**; *Forêt tropicale dans une orage* [Tropical Forest in a Storm] (plate 61), **158**, 161; *Forêt tropicale: ruines d'une plantation d'indigo* [Tropical Forest: Ruins of an Indigo Plantation] (plate 63), **160**, 161; *Forêt tropicale* [Tropical Forest] (plate 62), **159**, 161; *Mujer al punto de regresar* [Woman at the Point of Return] (plate 60), 152, **157**; *Mujer ante un espejo* [Woman before a Mirror] (plate 56), 152, **153**; *Sin título* [Untitled] 1971 (plate 59), 152, **156**

Mosquera, Gerardo, 135n8

N
Narrative Figuration, 185, 187, 188
Negret, Edgar, 220, 222
Neo-Concretism, 204
Neo-Dada, 187, 191n14
Neo-Plasticism, 72, 82, 198
Neo-Realism, 58
Nevelson, Louise, *Mirror Image I*, 86, **87**
New Realism, 188
New York School, 58, 136
Novecento movement, 41
O
Oldenburg, Claes, 171
Onslow Ford, Gordon, 100, 103nn19, 25
Op art, 198, 213n10
Oraá, Pedro de, 207
Orozco, José Clemente, 54, 58, 136
Ortega y Gasset, José, 26
Otero, Alejandro, 29
Otero, Alejandro, works of: *Don Quijote*, 22; *Orbital Sculpture for the Interior of a Building*, 22
P
Parra, Teresa de la, 60, 62, 65, 68, 69n1
Pau-Llosa, Ricardo, 168
Pettoruti, Emilio, 38, 40–42
Pettoruti, Emilio, works of: *Armonia-movimiento-spazio (disegno astratto)* [Harmony-Movement-Space (Abstract Design)], 40, **40**; *Bailarines* [Dancers], 42, **42**; *Un pintor ante el espejo* [A Painter before the Mirror], 41; *Still Life*, 41; *Untitled* (1917), 41; *La Voce* [The Voice] (plate 1), 24, 38, **39**, 40, 41
Phelps, Luisa, 62, **63**
Picasso, Pablo: abstraction, 82; and Cubism, 44, 109, 119, 222; and Lam, 104, 106, 109, 114; and Matta, 93, 102n11; and Tamayo, 136, 139, 140, 147n5
Picasso, Pablo, works of: *Guernica*, 93, 102n11; *Head of a Woman (Dora Maar)*, 136, **139**; *Still Life with Bottle of Rum*, 46; *Woman in White*, 140; *Woman with Fan*, 109, **109**, 114
Pollock, Jackson, 170
Pollock, Jackson, works of, *Psychoanalytic*, 22
Pop art: and Botero, 166, 170–71, 174; and consumerism, 150, 171; and Seguí, 185, 187–88, 191n14; and Toledo, 162
Portocarrero, René, 130, 133–34, 135nn6, 10, 12–13
Portocarrero, René, works of: *Brujo de Carnaval* [Carnival Sorcerer], 130, 133, **133**; *Brujo* [Sorcerer] (plate 48), 130, **131**, 133, 134, 135n10; *Gestáltica*, 130, **134**; *Interior de El Cerro* [Interior of El Cerro], 130, **133**; *Sin título* [Untitled] 1945 (plate 49), 130, **132**, 133–34
Pre-Columbian art, 47, 50, 73, 83n15, 136, 146, 220, 222, 228
Preston, Stuart, 214
Primitivism, 139, 165
proletarian art, 56
Q
Quattrocento masters, 38, 41
Quin, Carmelo Arden, 214
R
Rahon, Alice: *Balada para Frida Kahlo* [Ballad for Frida Kahlo], 165, **165**; *Boite à musique* [Music Box], 164–65, **164**
Ramírez, Mari Carmen, 15–34
Ramírez Villamizar, Eduardo, 201, 220, 222
Rauschenberg, Robert, 150
Rauschenberg, Robert, works of: *Canto II*, 193, **196**; *Dante's Inferno*, 193, 197n4
Réalités Nouvelles, 198, 207, 209
Renaissance art, 38, 41, 150–151, 168
Restany, Pierre, 188, 191nn15–16
Reverón, Armando: painting Luisa Phelps, photographed by Alfredo Boulton, 63, **63**; portraits of women, 60, 62–63, 65, 68; rebellion of, 69n1
Reverón, Armando, works of: *Cruz de Mayo o Dama con mantilla* [May Cross or Lady with Mantilla], 65, **68**; *Desnudo detrás de la mantilla* [Woman behind the Mantilla], 65, **65**; *Fiesta en Caraballeda* [Festival in Carabelleda], 63, 65; *Figura bajo un uvero* [Figure under a Sea-Grape Tree] (plate 10), 24, 60, **61**, 62–63; *Figura bajo un uvero* [Figure under a Sea-Grape Tree] (plate 10) (detail), **8**; *Figura reclinada o Mujer con mantilla acostada* [Reclining Figure or Reclining Woman with Mantilla] (plate 12), 60, 65, **66–67**; *Mujer con mantilla* [Woman with Mantilla], 65, **65**; *Procesión de la Virgen en el Valle* [Procession of the Virgin in the Valley], 63; *Retrato de Mujer* [Portrait of a Woman] (plate 11), 60, 63, **64**
Richards, Rosalyn, 140
Rimbaud, Arthur, 201
Ríos, Juanita, 60, 62
Rivera, Diego: Cubism, 23, 44, 47, 50; folk art forms, 146; Modernism, 44, 46, 54; portraits, 50–51, 54, 140; Venice Biennale, 54, 58, 136
Rivera, Diego, works of: *Bottle of Anis*, 46; *Construction of Rockefeller Center: Four Notebook Sketches* (plates 3–6), 47, **48–49**, 50; *The Embrace of the Peasant and the Worker*, 56; *La mujer de Tehuantepec* [Woman from Tehuantepec], 24; *Naturaleza muerta con limones* [Still Life with Lemons] (plate 2), 23, 44, **45**, 46, 47, 50; *Portrait of Cuca Bustamante*, 54, **54**; *Retrato de Alice-Leone Moats* [Portrait of Alice-Leone Moats] (plate 7), 50, **52**; *Retrato de Columba Domínguez o Tehuana* [Portrait of Columba Domínguez or Woman from Tehuantepec] (plate 8), 51, **53**, 54, 136; *Still Life with Bread Knife*, 46, **46**; *Still Life with Gray Bowl*, 46, **46**
Rojas, Carlos, 220, 222, 225, 228
Rojas, Carlos, works of: *Calco de hoja de papayo. Relación entre partes* [Papaya Leaf Tracing. Relationship between Parts], 220, **222**; *Segunda avenida*, de la serie *América: Cruzados* [Second Avenue, from the series America: Crossed], 225, **225**; *Sin título*, de la serie *América Horizontes* [Untitled, from the America Horizons series] 1970s, 228, **228**; *Sin título*, de la serie *América Horizontes* [Untitled, from the America Horizons series] 1988 (plate 95), 225, **226**, 228; *Sin título*, de la serie *América Horizontes* [Untitled, from the America Horizons series] 1988 (plate 96), 225, **227**, 228; *Sin título*, de la serie *Ingeniería de la visión: Pueblos* [Untitled, from the Engineering of Vision series: Towns], 225, **225**; *Sin título*, de la serie *Ingeniería de la visión* [Untitled, from the Engineering of Vision series] (plate 93), 222, **223**; *Sin título*, de la serie *Ingeniería de la visión* [Untitled, from the Engineering of Vision series] (plate 94), 222, **224**; *Sin título*, de la serie *Papeles pegados* [Untitled, from the Pasted Papers series] (plate 92), **221**, 222, 225
Rothfuss, Rhod, 214
Rothko, Mark, 225, 228
Rothko, Mark, works of, *Untitled (Orange, Dark Ruby, Brown on Maroon)*, 228, **228**
Ruiz Cortines, Adolfo, 56
S
SaludArte Foundation, 31–34, **32**
School of Paris, 58, 136, 201, 207, 209, 213, 214
Seguí, Antonio, 182, 185, 187, 188–89, 191nn12, 14
Seguí, Antonio, works of: *El que piensa demasiado* [The One Who Thinks Too Much] (plate 72), 182, **183**, 187–88, **189**; *Gente rodeando el monumento a Humphrey Bogart* [People Surrounding the Monument of Humphrey Bogart] (plate 74), 182, 185, **186**, 188; *Gente rodeando el monumento a Humphrey Bogart* [People Surrounding the Monument of Humphrey Bogart] (plate 74) (detail), **186**; *Metamorfosis de Doña Felicitas Naón* [The Metamorphosis of Doña Felicitas Naon], 185, **185**; *Sin título* [Untitled] 1963, **185**, 187; *Una ciudad, una historia, un tormento* [A City, A History, A Torment] (plate 72), 182, **184**, 185, 188; *Una ciudad, una historia, un tormento* [A City, A History, A Torment] (plate 72) (detail), **14**; *La visita* [The Visit], 187, **187**
Sempere, Eusebio, 207
Sims, Lowery Stokes, 124, 129nn3, 9
Siqueiros, David Alfaro, 54, 56, 58–59, 136, 139
Siqueiros, David Alfaro, works of: *Echo of a Scream*, 58; *For the Complete Social Security of All Mexicans*, 59, **59**; *La patrona* [The Patroness], 56, **58**; *The People for the University, The University for the People*, 58–59; *El Reto* [The Challenge] (plate 9), 23–24, 56, 57, 58, 136; *The Sob*, 58; *The Yell*, 56
social realism, 58
Soffici, Ardengo, 38, 40
Solar, Xul, 29, 38
Soldevilla, Loló: color relations, 204; Concretism, 207, 209, 213, 213n10; Constructivist art, 198, 201, 213; Cuban art, 29
Soldevilla, Loló, works of: *Composición abstracción* [Abstract Composition] (plate 81), 204, **205**; *Construcción* [Construction] (plate 80), **203**, 204, 207; *Relieves luminosos*, 209; *Sin título (abstracción)* [Untitled (Abstraction)] 1956 (plate 78), 201, **202**; *Sin título (abstracción)* [Untitled (Abstraction)] 1956 (plate 79), 201, **202**; *Sin título (abstracción)* [Untitled (Abstraction)] 1956 (plate 82), 204, **206**; *Sin título* [Untitled] 1956 (plate 76), **199**; *Sin título* [Untitled] 1956 (plate 77), **200**; *Sin título* [Untitled] 1956 (plate 83), 207, **208**; *Sin título* [Untitled] 1956 (plate 85), 207, **211**; *Sin título* [Untitled] 1956 (plate 86), 207, **211**; *Sin título* [Untitled] 1956 (plate 87), 207, **212**; *Sin título* [Untitled] 1956 (plate 88), 207, **212**; *Stabile* (plate 84), 207, **210**
Soto, Jesús Rafael, 29, 198, 207
Soto, Jesús Rafael, works of: *Banda plata*, 22; *Cubo virtual* [Virtual Cube], 230; *Desplazamiento de un elemento luminoso* [Displacement of a Luminous Element], 204, **204**
Studio card for the film "Pueblerina" with portrait of Columba Domínguez by Miguel Covarrubias, 54, **55**
Sujo, Clara Diament, 9, 11, 20–25, 27, 30, 193
Sullivan, Edward, 166
Surrealism: and Matta, 88, 90, 93, 100–101, 102nn4–5; and Onlsow Ford, 100, 103nn19, 25; and subconscious, 150; and Tamayo, 139; and Toledo, 162, 164
Symbolism, 44
T
Taeuber-Arp, Sophie, *Relief rectangulaire, cercles découpés, cônes surgissants* [Rectangular Relief, Cutout Circles, and Rising Cones], 201, **201**
Taller Torres-García [Torres-García Workshop], 72, 84
Tamayo, Olga, 140
Tamayo, Rufino: and color, 142; folk art forms, 146; and images of birds, 139–40; and Picasso, 136, 139, 140, 147n5; portraits, 140; and Toledo, 162, 164; Venice Biennale, 54, 58, 136
Tamayo, Rufino, works of: *Figura en rojo y negro* [Figure in Red and Black] (plate 53), 142, **143**, 146; *Girl Attacked by a Strange Bird*, 139; *Homage to the Mexican Race*, 139–40; *Mujer con pájaros* [Woman with Birds] (plate 50), **137**, 139; *Pájaros liberados* [Liberated Birds] (plate 51), 24, 136, **138**, 139, 140; *Personages Contemplating Birds*, 139–40, **140**; *Personaje en verde* [Personage in Green] (plate 54), 142, **144–45**, 146, 147n13; *Retrato de la señora Mercedes Ballesteros de Antuñano* [Portrait of Mrs. Mercedes Ballesteros de Antuñano] (plate 52), 140, **141**; *Retrato de la señora Natasha Gelman* [Portrait of Mrs. Natasha Gelman], 140, **140**; *Woman and Bird*, 139, **139**
Tanguy, Yves, 101
Tàpies, Antoni, 165
Three Judas figures, 146, **146**
Toledo, Francisco, 162, 164–65, 165n4
Toledo, Francisco, works of: *Abstract Blue Forms*, 162, **164**; *El circo* [The Circus] (plate 64), 162, **163**, 164, 165; *Lagarto*, 162, **162**
Torres-García, Joaquín: Constructive art, 21, 30, 70, 72–73, 75, 79, 82, 83n14, 84, 87n1, 220, 222; *maderas*, 72, 73, 83n11, 86; pre-Columbian art, 73, 83n15; recovery of the object, 70, 75, 79
Torres-García, Joaquín, works of: *Composición constructiva de estructura coloreada* [Constructive Composition with Colored Structure] (plate 19), 25, 79, **81**; *Composición constructiva de estructura coloreada* [Constructive Composition with Colored Structure] (plate 19) (detail), 79, **79**; *Construcción universal con gran sol* [Universal Construction with Large Sun] (plate 18), 79, **80**; *Constructif en bois incise* [Constructive Composition on Incised Wood] (plate 13), **71**, 73; *Constructivo*, 25; *Constructivo con dibujo inciso* [Constructive Composition with Incised Drawing] (plate 14), 25, 73, **74**; *Muchedumbre* [Crowd] (plate 17), 25, 30, 75, **78**, 79; *Pez AAC* [AAC Fish] (plate 15), 25, **76**; *Pez* [Fish] (plate 16), 25, 30, 73, 75, **77**
Traba, Marta, 166, 168, 171, 174, 178
Trelles Hernández, Mercedes, 171
V
Valera, Victor, 198
Vantongerloo, Georges, 214
Venice Biennale (1950), 54, 58, 136
Vermeer, Johannes: *Girl with a Pearl Earring*, 174–75; *The Lacemaker*, 174; *Study of a Young Woman*, 174
Vesalius, Andreas, 151
W
Warhol, Andy, 171
Weston, Edward, *Alice-Leone Moats*, 50–51, **51**
X
Xceron, Jean, 214
Y
Young women posing as Indians at "El Castillete," photographed by Alfredo Boulton, 62, **62**
Z
Zadkine, Ossip, 201

COPYRIGHT AND PHOTOGRAPHIC CREDITS

Copyright Credits

© Berenice Abbott/Commerce Graphics, Ltd. Inc., Courtesy Howard Greenberg Gallery, New York: p. 47

© José Antonio Berni: p. 187 (top)

© Jacobo Borges, Caracas: pp. 192–95, 238

© Fernando Botero: pp. 167–73, 175–80, 238

© María Elena Rico Covarrubias: p. 55

© Elias Crespin: pp. 231-32, 235–36, 238-39

© 2013 Carlos Cruz-Diez/Artists Rights Society (ARS), New York/ADAGP, Paris: p. 233

© 2013 Salvador Dalí, Gala-Salvador Dalí Foundation/ Artists Rights Society (ARS) New York/ADAGP, Paris: p. 100

Artwork by Sonia Delaunay: © 2013 Artists Rights Society (ARS), New York: p. 209 (right)

Artwork by Marcel Duchamp: © 2013 Artists Rights Society (ARS), New York/ADAGP, Paris: p. 88

© Estate Jesse A. Fernández, Collection France Mazin Fernández: p. 124

© Fundación Alberto Vollmer: pp. 62–63

© Fundación Gego: p. 234

© Beatriz González: p. 174

Artwork by František Kupka: © 2013 Artists Rights Society (ARS), New York/ADAGP, Paris: p. 209 (left)

Artwork by Wifredo Lam: © 2013 Artists Rights Society, New York/ADAGP, Paris:

Back cover, frontispiece, and pp. 105, 107–8, 110–13, 115–23, 125–28, 239–40

© 2013 Succession H. Matisse, Paris/Artists Rights Society (ARS), New York /ADAGP, Paris: p. 106

Artwork by Matta: © 2013 Artists Rights Society (ARS), New York /ADAGP, Paris: pp. 89–94, 96–99, 241–42

© Estate of Francisco Matto: pp. 85–87, 242

Artwork by Carlos Merida: © 2013 Artists Rights Society (ARS), New York: p. 142

© Marta Minujín: p. 188

© Alejandra Morales, Sebastián Morales, Nicolás and Andrés Morales Benítez, and Mariana Benítez-Morales: pp. 149, 150 (bottom), 151, 153–60, 242–43

© 2013 Estate of Louise Nevelson/Artists Rights Society (ARS), New York: p. 87

© Estate of Emilio Pettoruti: pp. 39, 40 (right), 42, 243

© 2013 Estate of Pablo Picasso/Artists Rights Society (ARS), New York: pp. 109, 139 (top)

Artwork by Alice Rahon: Courtesy of Galería Oscar Román, México, D.F.: pp. 164 (bottom), 165

© Estate of Robert Rauschenberg/Licensed by VAGA, New York, NY: p. 196

© 2013 Banco de Mexico Diego Rivera & Frida Kahlo Museum Trust, Mexico, D.F /Artists Rights Society (ARS), New York: Cover and pp. 45–46, 48–49, 52–54, 243–44

© Casa Carlos Rojas: pp. 221–27, 228 (right), 244

© 1998 Kate Rothko Prizel & Christpher Rothko/Artists Rights Society (ARS), New York: p. 228 (left)

Artwork by Antonio Segui: © 2013 Artists Rights Society, New York /ADAGP, Paris: pp. 14, 183–86, 187 (bottom), 189, 244

Artwork by David Alfaro Siqueiros: © 2013 Artists Rights Society (ARS), New York: pp. 57–59, 245

Artwork by Loló Soldevilla: Courtesy of Magaly Barba de Soldevilla and Martha Flora Carranza Barba © 2013, All rights reserved: pp. 199-200, 202–3, 205–6, 208, 210–12, 245–46

Artwork by Jesús Rafael Soto: © 2013 Artists Rights Society (ARS), New York /ADAGP, Paris: p. 204

Art © Tamayo Heirs/Mexico/Licensed by VACA, New York, NY: pp. 137–38, 139 (bottom), 140–41, 143–45, 246

Artwork by Sophie Taeuber-Arp: © 2013 Artists Rights Society (ARS), New York/PROLITTERIS: p. 201

Courtesy of Francisco Toledo: pp. 162–63, 164 (top), 246

© 2013 Alejandra, Aurelio and Claudio Torres: pp. 71, 74, 76–81, 246–47

Artwork by Edward Weston: © 2013 Center for Creative Photography, Arizona Board of Regents/Artists Rights Society (ARS), New York: p. 51

Photographic credits

Albright-Knox Gallery/Art Resource, NY: p. 209 (right)

Album/Art Resource, NY: p. 40 (left)

Mariana Perez Amor, GALLERIA DE ARTE MEXICANO: p. 164 (bottom)

Jenny Antill: p. 28 (center, top and bottom)

Archivo Museo Provincial de Bellas Artes Emilio A. Caraffa: p. 42

Baltimore Museum of Art; Photography by: Mitro Hood: p. 106 (right)

Mariana Benitez: p. 150 (bottom)

Jacobo Borges: pp. 192–93

The Bridgeman Art Library: p. 139 (top)

René Brillembourg: p. 16 (top, bottom, and bottom right)

Christopher Burke, New York /Art Resource, NY: p. 228 (top)

Cecilia de Torres, Ltd.: p. 86 (right)

Cernuda Arte, Miami: p. 133 (right); photo by Pablo Lazo: 134

© The Cleveland Museum of Art: p. 139 (bottom)

CNAC/NMAM/Dist. RMN/Grand Palais/Art Resource, NY: p. 93

Colección Pérez Simón, Mexico © Rafael Doniz: p. 65 (left)

Columbus Museum of Art: p. 46 (right)

Carlos Cruz-Diez: p. 232

Davis Museum and Cultural Center, Wellesley College, Wellesley, MA: p. 47

© Fundación Alberto Vollmer: pp. 62–63

The Jacques and Natasha Gelman Collection of 20th-century Mexican Art. Courtesy of The Vergel and Tarpon Foundations: p. 140 (right)

Rosse Mary Morales González: pp. 222, 228 (right)

Hirshhorn Museum and Sculpture Garden, photography by Lee Stalsworth: p. 175

Lyndon Baines Johnson Presidential Library and Museum, Austin, Texas: p. 46 (left)

Krannert Art Museum: p. 140 (left)

Kunstmuseum Basel, Martin P. Bühler: p. 201

© Malba – Fundación Costantini, Buenos Aires: p. 40 (right)

MAMBA: p. 185 (right)

Mary-Anne Martin Fine Art NY: p. 58

Abigail McEwen: p. 216

© The Metropolitan Museum of Art /Image source: Art Resource, NY: p. 152

Marta Minujín: p. 188

Museo de Arte Moderno, Mexico City: pp. 162, 165

Museo Nacional de Bellas Artes, Havana, Cuba: p. 133 (left)

© 2013 Museum Associates /LACMA, Licensed by Art Resource, NY/© Artres: p. 119

© The Museum of Fine Arts, Houston, Thomas R. DuBrock, photographer: pp. 14, 53, 78, 86 (left), 87, 89–91, 94–95, 112–13, 115, 117, 120, 127, 143–45, 153, 155–56, 158–59, 176–77, 179, 183–84, 187 (top), 189, 194–95, 215, 231, 233–36

© The Museum of Fine Arts, Houston, Will Michels, photographer: frontispiece, pp. 8, 39, 45, 48–49, 52, 57, 61, 64, 66–67, 71, 74, 76–77, 79, 80–81, 85, 92, 96–99, 105, 107–8, 110–11, 116, 118, 121–23, 125–26, 130, 128, 131–32, 137–38, 141, 149, 151, 154, 157, 160, 163, 167, 169, 172–73, 180, 186, 199, 201–2, 204–6, 208, 210–11, 225, 217–18, 221, 223–27

© The Museum of Modern Art /Licensed by SCALA/Art Resource, NY: pp. 41, 100, 170 (right), 196, 209 (left)

Nohra Haime Gallery: p. 187 (bottom)

James Oles: p. 55

Gianni Dagli Orti/The Archive at Art Resource, NY: p. 54

Mariano Costa Peuser: p. 28 (left and top right)

Patricia Phelps de Cisneros Collection: p. 204

The Philadelphia Museum of Art/Art Resource: pp. 88, 106 (left)

Phillips www.PHILLIPS.com: p. 164 (left)

Phoenix Art Museum: p. 142

Javier del Real, courtesy of Vicente Galaso at Saludarte Foundation: p. 32

Royal Collection Trust/© HM Queen Elizabeth II 2012: p. 150 (top)

Scala/Art Resource, NY: p. 109

Bob Schalkwijk Photography: p. 59

SDO Wifredo Lam, Paris: p. 124

Antonio Seguí: p. 185 (left)